SNAKE DANCE:
UNRAVELLING THE MYSTERIES OF JONESTOWN

by

Laurie Efrein Kahalas

ISBN 155212207-7

RED ROBIN PRESS
P.O. BOX 1801
NEW YORK, NEW YORK 10156

Author may be written at:
Red Robin Press
P.O. Box 1801
New York, New York 10156

Author's website: www.jonestown.com

COVER DESIGN by the author
Executed by Trafford Publishing
Special artwork by Ana Navarro
Photographs from "A Feeling of Freedom,"
  published by Peoples Temple about the
  community of Jonestown.

This book may be purchased from:

TRAFFORD

This book was published "on-demand" in cooperation with Trafford Publishing.
On-demand publishing is a unique process and service of making a book available for retail sale to the public taking advantage of on-demand manufacturing and Internet web marketing. **On-demand publishing** includes promotions, retail sales, manufacturing, order fulfilment, accounting and collecting royalties on behalf of the author.

Suite 2, 3050 Nanaimo St., Victoria, B.C. V8T 4Z1, CANADA
Phone   250-383-6864   Toll-free   1-888-232-4444 (Canada & US)
Fax   250-383-6804   E-mail   sales@trafford.com
Web site www.trafford.com   TRAFFORD PUBLISHING IS A DIVISION OF TRAFFORD HOLDINGS LTD.
Trafford Catalogue #98-0011   www.trafford.com/robots/98-0011.html
10   9   8   7   6   5   4   3   2

Canadian Cataloguing in Publication Data

Kahalas, Laurie Efrein, date.
  Snake dance

  ISBN 1-55212-207-7

  1. Peoples Temple. 2. Jones, Jim, 1931-1978. I. Title.
BP605.P46K3 1998   289.9   C98-910556-3

Copyright 1998 by Laurie Efrein Kahalas
All rights reserved. No part of this publication may be reproduced, stored in a retrieval system, or transmitted in any form or by any means, electronic, mechanical, photocopying, recording, or otherwise, without the writton prior permission of the author.

For my friends who died at
Jonestown, Guyana, November 18, 1978.
God bless them,
and may they rest in peace.

SNAKE DANCE:
UNRAVELLING THE MYSTERIES OF JONESTOWN

I. OFF TO A FRAGILE START

I.	Touchpoint from Beyond.	2
II.	A Rebel with Many Causes.	8
III.	To Save or Be Saved (Doom or Be Doomed).	20
IV.	A Phoenix Arises from a World Fallen Ashen at My Feet...	33
V.	"Go West, Young Woman!"	41

II. LIFE RAW AND REAL

VI.	My Destiny Point Arrives.	51
VII.	I Set Out on the Rocky Road.	61
VIII.	"And All That Believed Were Together"	67
IX.	My Place, Albeit a Shaky One.	73
X.	A Promise.	80
XI.	"Father is God."	86
XII.	Preludes to Disaster.	92
XIII.	The Long Hot Summer	102
XIV.	"Family" Turns "Enemy" -- the Unthinkable Happens.	109
XV.	We "Protect Ourselves from Ourselves."	115
XVI.	"*Tim* Found Us Guyana."	118
XVII.	I Make the Mistake of Telling the Truth.	124
XVIII.	My Muse Arrives, and Doesn't Get Along with My God.	129
	INSERT: "ALLEGORY"....1-22	
XIX.	Let's Kill the Messenger.	139
XX.	Los Angeles is Not "Angelic" to Me.	147

XXI.	"Heaven Help Anyone Who Opted to be Caught Within the Crunch."	159
XXII.	"Foul Times Require Foul Tests."	163
XXIII.	A Parting Tort, and Jim Jones is Forever Gone.	171

III. WHAT THOU HAST MOST FEARED HAST COME UPON THEE

XXIV.	A New World Arises as My Own Sinks.	186
XXV.	"Let the Games Begin," said Goliath to David.	191
XXVI.	The Pawn that Would Ensnare the King.	202
XXVII.	I Make the Break, or *It* Breaks *Me*.	208
XXVIII.	Such a Late Date to Finally Discover the Best.	212
XXIX.	"A Conspiracy Behind Peoples Temple Exposé?"	218
	INSERT: DOCUMENTS...1-32	
XXX.	Turnabout's Unfair Play.	225
XXXI.	The Dead Cat on the Juror's Doorstep.	234
XXXII.	The Wrong Team's Pitcher is Sent In for "the Save."	240
XXXIII.	The Presence Takes My Hand to Carry Me Through.	246
XXXIV.	The Last Rotten Apple Falls from the Tree.	252
XXXV.	Our Light is Extinguished Forever.	259
XXXVI.	As the World Turns..	267
XXXVII.	The Sun Will Rise Again in the East.	272

IV. YEA, THOUGH I WALK THROUGH THE VALLEY OF THE SHADOW OF DEATH

XXXVIII.	*"Arise, Arise, the Last Shall Fall to Thee..."*	280
XXXIX.	Sorting Out Allies from Adversaries.	285
XL.	A Base From Which to Work.	291
XLI.	I Lose a Comrade-in-Arms.	295

XLII.	If the War's Over, Why are They Still Shooting at <u>Me</u>?	304
XLIII.	Every Story has a Cover Story. All Information has a Dis-.	309
XLIV.	What Really Happened is Released on Tape, and No One Listens and No One Cares.	317
XLV.	What Really Happened Shows Up on T.V., and No One Notices and No One Cares.	327
XLVI.	Congress is Told What Really Happened, and and No One Finds Out No One Cares.	331
XLVII.	The Cover Stories get Re-wallpapered and Published All Over America.	335
XLVIII.	Did the C.I.A. Have a Contract Out on Jonestown?	348
XLIX.	Sticks and Stoens and Set-Ups.	357
XLVIII.	They Kill Their Own.	364
XLIX.	A Last-Ditch Effort Fails.	369

V. "ALMOST DONE. NEW JOURNEY BEGINNING."

L.	To Be or Not to Be ...Again.	375
LI.	"Go Back to California and Forgive."	381
LII.	What Goes Around Comes Around.	386
LIII.	Blind Men and Elephants.	393
LIV.	Placido Domingo Means "Peaceful Day of Rest."	405
	UPCOMING SEQUELS.	411
	ABOUT THE AUTHOR.	412

PREFACE

My life has been more tumultuous than most, and at its fearsome centerpiece, the deaths at Jonestown, nearly lost in the storm. I have experienced, full spectrum, maximum warp, both the fragility of human life and its enduring strengths, as though the forces of Nature themselves had taken human form. Life extracted its homage from me before I barely knew how to honor myself.

Why did I still imagine that the world would, or could be, a better place? So much evidence to the contrary! But I always knew that somewhere, somehow, through magic if needs be, I was destined to survive, even flourish, unto a new day. Drawn hypnotically into life as if into a **snake dance**, I would follow the inward windings of life's paradoxes, enigmas and anomalies, to some mysterious nexus where the world would again flower and bloom. The karmas, sufferings and pain would bind me fast, but some day I would spring free. I would introspect, but then the revelations would come. I would hold to myself each hope, each dream, and some day I would give it back to the world as pure being.

The harshest of realities could be transformed as the snake would unpeel its skin to sleekly re-emerge. The bitterest traumas could be vanquished, their miseries shed, supplanted by something better, purer, strained through the grinding sieve. The struggle need not be in vain. One could learn from it. One could teach, one could enlighten, one could give.

At the darkest hour of that galling grief, such plans could scarce be born at all! Indeed, the public was so saturated with Jonestown's *travesty*, that there was scarcely a moment of recognition, much less comprehension, of what a tragedy Jonestown truly was. Yet I knew this chapter would never be complete until I had spoken publicly of all that had happened. Until I could take on the very "war of the worlds" and make peace. I even suspected way back then, how very long that would take, as now, twenty years hence, I release this thread. I discovered along the way (precious benefit!), that I could not make a separate peace with the world from that within myself. This bitter dislocation, it seemed, of the very soul, would needs be mended *very* publicly. But to do that, I had to first be mended from within.

Perhaps the passage of time has worked to an advantage, at that. This is the story that jolted the entire world with a visceral horror; yet was, in so many ways, a story that was wholly missed! The world was *given* the drama, complete with script, characters, plot, scenario, storyline, and the cruelest of denouements. It was given it graven in stone: black and white, as in *newsprint*. But what really happened, at whose hands, and by what design, that this horror was the end result, was unfathomably, so masked, concealed, and covered up, that no wonder America concluded that this "made no sense," and that "madness" was the only explanation to suffice. Idols graven in stone are the most intransigent to dislodge; and the very enormity of the impact, combined with the overkill of coverage, made such efforts prohibitive.

The truth, as we shall see, was more diabolical in some respects, yet more human in others. How and why reporters erred even in assessing "the villains," was a scenario too daunting, too pervasive, too twisted, to even broach years ago. This was the ***snake dance*** that got sucked into the black hole of network news, was stifled into silence, and might never, it would seem, unravel into the light of day. Until now. This is a story whose time has finally come.

As these pages unfold, you will see I never thought it chance or accident that I was involved. I never thought it chance or accident that I survived. And I surely never thought it would be happenstance, accident, or chance that I would some day emerge to tell the tale. My only real set of tasks was how, and when, and to seize the day. This is what I've always had it in my heart to do.

I only want to tell the tale well and to have it resonate as truth. No, not an absolute truth, but the *human* truth of it. So that finally, we may have the grace and power to take the ashes of the dead and consecrate them, instead of trampling them mindlessly beneath our feet. So that we may have the grace and power to be fully human in the face of infamy. So that finally, at long last, we may summon the power and grace to forgive.

I. OFF TO A FRAGILE START

"Human life --indeed all life-- is poetry. We live it unconsciously, day by day, piece by piece, but in its inviolable wholeness, it lives us."

Lou Andreas-Salome.

I. Touchpoint from Beyond.

I am a chameleon soul. A child of Neptune slipping with misty ease amongst personas, never sure if what I am or who I am is what or whom the world has supposed me to be. I was born beneath this star, indeed I *am* this star ~ its multitudes of shadings, reflections, nuances, and a silvery beauty which eludes the rays of Sun, so that it is a nebulous sighting which determines whether I am beautiful at all.

You may find me hard to fathom if you judge by measuring sticks of stone or clay. To this day, it is difficult, even painful, to lie; though truth can be elusive when the world is not a listening place. I have, probably, a mystic truth you would hold in as high regard as you would a poem ~ a truth which is pure in a pure world, and muddied in an impure one. I want the world to be perfect, and in the midst of disarray, have seen patterns, lights and shades others may not see, at times the oddest of *imperfections* revealing the most perfect play of light.

It is this gift, to discern the plays of darkness and light, that is the most sincere yet strange measure of perfection; for at long last, it does not seem to matter what has *happened* to me at all.

I have wished many a time to not be me as I am, but yet be me as a *truly* am. I have lived many lives this apparently single life, and nothing matters but to have lived fully, as the best passing or ephemeral "me" my soul would deign to express. I have suffered much, but it seems of no account. I am startled to discover I would have nothing different, nothing changed. It now seems all I could have desired: merely to be clear, open, unencumbered, unoppressed by all that has passed. I am thrilled the more I feel that my *life* is nothing, yet *I* am whole and free.

I am, as once made the brunt of labelling, "a rare bird out of left field."

My early life was both full of promise and forebodings of disaster. I was always and forever creative ~ music, poetry, dance, all would serve the dreamer of dreams. My family honored me as if a talented stranger ~ now what would I, their daughter, *really* do with her life? Surely not all this!

I was mad for learning, an instant advocate for abstractions, wildly enthusiastic about people I loved, yet painfully shy with others. From age eleven on, when I began to suspect self-consciously that no one would accept me as I really am, my games with dolls became silent dialogues with people. People I admired, people I wanted to tell my deepest thoughts, people with whom I wanted to cry or laugh or simply be with silently – many older people, who would, in a "perfect" world, be mentors, teachers, parents or friends. The ones I *belonged* with.

I wasn't at home when I was at home – I knew that somewhere my "real" home would welcome me. How would I tell anyone? Who would listen? I would rehearse my advances towards those who seemed like they would best understand. Most of the childhood dramas would never materialize in real life. Those that did were a bungle of shyness and words caught in the pitfalls of hesitation and self-doubt.

I think I might have grown up, nevertheless, as normally as anyone, save for an emotionally ill mother and the lingering shadow of a brother who hungered to do me in. (My crime? I was born. How precious little I could do about that!)

My mother was manic depressive, and if, perchance, one has a *choice* of a relative's illness, stay clear of this! "Victims"? They can be merciless in destroying their families. My mother, I realized all too late, was so obsessively self-involved, she scarcely pondered that she was destroying *me*, thus perhaps delivered the worst destruction of all: mere obliteration.

Indeed, from my early teens, I was her "trusted confidant." How terrible my father was, how inadequate, how her sisters had pressured this uneasy escape from her own mother's lingering stroke. How she never loved him at all. Somehow (I look back and am not quite sure how) I felt it fell upon me to make right this transgression of omission – his not being up to the job. After all, she had come to me, had she not?

I wept for her fate, off where no one could see. I looked at my tear-streaked, misery-ridden face in the mirror, and could not believe it was me. How could my *mother* be so unhappy? In the denouements of betrayal in the family drama (and betrayal be the worst, is it not?), just as I was turned against my father, he was turned against me. I was made into a most unlikely, pathetic rival for affections I did not even want. Once she screamed at him, "You've ruined this entire family." (They call that "projection," I only later learned.) "Everyone but her. You won't destroy her. She's stronger than you are."

4/SNAKE DANCE

Then, just as later on, I did not want this onus of being strong – I only wanted to be *loved*. I was chilled at the outburst with its terror of expectations ("*You* be the adult!"), and never quite thawed. It was getting too deadly for me. I shrank from human touch. I could not bear to be touched physically by either of my parents from my early teens on. My mother had declared war on everyone, but with me, it was the worst of wars – waged to destroy me, especially, "in the name of love"!

God spare us such "love" ever, and in the name of anyone. I was no match for the unenviable job of loving my mother either. She screamed out in the middle of the night, "I wish she would die!" when I had not shown her sufficient affection. She told me I was insane. She told me I was as cold as ice and incapable of loving another human being. By the time I was sixteen, life seemed the worse kind of hell. I was relieved to go away to college, even in what seemed like the interminably-distant Midwest.

As for my father's passivity in the face of the onslaught, a wedge was forged that was never broken 'til the day he died. Well, not quite "end of story." After I returned from my California odyssey, the house, the very one he built with his own hands, not just for himself, but for his *family* (bless his Cancerian soul), that was wrest away....

It was only years later on, upon return from my strange, ultimately tragic pilgrimage West, that I learned what had happened to my now-aged mother in the wake of my father's death. Sometimes gears shift so abruptly, that the mind is slow to push certain doors ajar. Slowly the real story about the house was emerging in disjointed threads. The loan my brother wanted for...*real estate*. The plea to my mother that the loan could only be granted by turning over securities that my father had put aside for their old age. "I'll sign them back later." Of course, "later" never came. When pressed, he refused – called her "stupid" for not getting his promise in writing. Perhaps the fateful decision to sell a treasured home was the only course that seemed commensurate with the pain of a wrecked family.

The last time I visited the house was to retrieve my guitar. It was painful to be there, painful to leave. I felt both alienated and drawn in, all in a fierce schismed thrust. I returned home shaken, and slept not to dream, but to be awakened with a hoarse, audible whisper into the darkened room: *"Don't sell the house!"*

My God, it was *my father!* My mind raced to find its place in the black square of space. Talk to your brother, Laurie. Do it quickly. He'll see after the house, maintain it, look after it. Surely he wouldn't want the family legacy to be lost. I hastily scrawled him a note. Dad wouldn't want the house to be lost. *Do something about it!*

Why no response? Nothing? Slowly, ever so slowly, the pieces swirled into place. I had gone to the fox to report that the chicken coop was in danger of being plundered!

The glint of conscience was never to flicker across the screen. Not directly, no. Obliquely, perhaps. There came a curious offer: take the Steinway grand piano. (He knew I loved music. An exceedingly clever bribe?) I can't do that, I said. But I can *trade*. Here. Take the piano that was rescued (like the hastiest afterthought) from the house. That saved me from keeping it, anyway. Surely a possession could never be a surrogate for *an inheritance*. The trade was done. It seemed an odd piece of ill-plotted design – too little, too late, not even a jagged crevice within my heart for it to be lodged. I would not see the whole 'til much later on.

Approaching my mother proved no less an ordeal. The tears flowed despite every effort to stifle them. But she wouldn't listen to *me*. She said only my brother could save the day. As for my father... well, he was "gone." What difference could *he* possibly make?

All seemed quiet past the sale of the house. Then it emerged in dreams, nightmares really, again and again, like a sub-theme to the dunning mantra of the "other" inevitable and total loss, the catastrophe at Jonestown.

Always I was in the house, shouting, "This is *my* house. You can't sell it. It belongs to *me*." Finally one night, in a most startling, however slumbering jolt, I was again in the house. My mother was there, my father too. My father was yelling, yelling 'til he was blue in the face. The words was incoherent, the upset devastating. My mother carped, with an icy oblivion, "Pay no attention to him. He died of lung cancer," heard the dreamer. Lung cancer? He didn't die that way. Yet here he was, *yelling his lungs out*.

I looked around frantically. There he was. The young man who had purloined our family treasure. "You can't buy the house," I shouted at him. I pointed right to my father. "It's *his* house. He built it. You can't buy it. It's *his*." I awoke with a fright.

It was a day or two before I set to weeping. I hadn't missed my father, such a distant figure had he been rendered to me. Now he was my *father*. In the spirit world still my father, and I the only one to whom he could make his tragic, delayed plea. Even he seemed to expect that only I would be strong. How could I ease his pain?

6/SNAKE DANCE

At the behest of a trusted elder, I found an old photo of my father and gazed at his face, into his eyes. "Mother didn't mean to hurt you," I began gingerly, a trifle uneasy at the half-truth uttered to the figure in the portrait. "She was very depressed when she sold the house. She didn't know what else to do. And *I* love you."

A day later the phone rang. It was my mother. Would I come by? We had things to discuss. What "things"? "Well," she said, "we never talked about your father's death. And we never talked about the house." I was startled. "All right," I said, "I'll come."

I had never seen my mother like this before or since. She was, at best, an agnostic, and surely atheism was not far behind, I was taught, like a truism, as a child: "When you're dead, you're dead. You're deader than a doornail." It would have been so easy for me to believe in nothing.

Now her eyes grew misty and distant, and she began to speak, a hesitant waver unsteadying her voice: "You know, Laurie, I really don't think there is anything beyond death. When you're dead, you're dead" (no "deader than a doornail" this time – the defiance was peculiarly softened). "But wouldn't it be amazing" (her eyes gazed upwards, almost wistful) "if you could be dead and yet be hovering out there and watch what the people here were still doing?" "Amazing." From her, a word and a half. Stunned, I merely nodded.

She went on. "Your father is buried in Staten Island with his parents. Your uncle Al wanted it that way, and I didn't care one way or the other. But... I don't know why I'm saying this, because I'm sure there's nothing after death... but when I die and am *cremated*" (doornails, dust, who knows how such decisions are made?), "I think I want my ashes scattered on the lawn in front of the house." "I'll do that," I promised. And not a word more.

I went home and cried. I really didn't know at the time of his death what I had lost (I was wholly preoccupied then, as we shall see), or *now* there would not be this flood of tears. But my father... he had never demanded attention like my mother. I was shaken inside at how this terrible breach of humanity was now bridged. Yet so many times before and since, I have been both uplifted and shaken at once. Life is what it is. However it happens, I've learned the Beatles' tune well: "Let It Be."

My father, of course, predeceased my mother, so the world would proclaim her the luckier of the two. My brother, in his time, snagged an heiress for a wife and they produced two gorgeous children. Even my own adeptness at explanations probably would not suffice, so let us just, for the moment, leave this be. (Yes, I had long suspected The Beatles sung a secret wisdom the rest of us had only "Imagine"-d.)

Nor are all these incidents but childhood memories ~ some are of recent years, and the early ones torment long after their sting was stung. We have the illusion that life's events are somehow constrained to a particular *time*. With most of us they are not.

There is only one thing I would tell you of it now; later, surely, than I would have chosen had I *really* been an adult when I was a child:

We do have miraculous capacities, us humans, to be free *at any time* ~ indeed a double-entendre, or an entendre of any dimension one might note. *At* any time and *of* any time and *by* any time, we share a singular capacity: that however bound we feel, we are forever capable of being free. And if you sit anyone down, even the most dense of souls, they will tell you somehow, however mute or incomplete, that they would love life and be happy if only they had that one precious inviolable gift: freedom.

II. A Rebel with Many Causes.

My own freedom has been hard-won, and yet not complete. But if it had a starting point, it should probably be not so much the start of life itself, but at the awakening of what we so clumsily and imprecisely call "destiny": for me, a place called *seventeen*.

It had come upon me rapidly for one so young; yet slowly, an encroaching sense of destiny, like a creature settling in on its haunches within my being, gradually, almost self-consciously readied to spring to life whole. Some unseen force only had to signal its release.

Melodies began filtering through my brain - first simple tunes, charmingly archaic in their thrust, with sprinklings of parallel fifths, like a tinkling of glass to punctuate the beat. Again and again, the notes would play, like a process of locating, refining, precisioning a crafted object. I would listen 'til each phrase would fall just right. My body seemed my gauge - electric-like tremors pierced me with a weird uncomfortable thrill 'til the tune was shaped and honed into its most natural, however a-rhythmic, beat.

I thought by the time I left for college, I would choose to be a composer. I was seventeen.

It seemed many other young people had the same idea. No. Many young *men*. An introduction round-table style was the protocol. I sat, uncomfortable and shy, as everyone (well, every *boy*, save for me and a young woman graduate student - the girl/woman discrepancy between us was palpable) poured forth pretentious intellectualisms to impress the energetic all-business-all-smiles-you-guess-which Charles Farley. Everyone was given the dignity of (or was it *in*-dignity) of begin referred to solely by last name, like we were a horde of British schoolboys; for each an index-card name, to each the same index-card question:

"Efrein, what is music?" What was I to say? All my predecessors had rung harmony, melody and beat dry, fluffed up with off-hand (aye, very *serious* off-hand) references to their symphonic icons - Mahler, Bruckner - it seemed German was in. Was this our stout, all-American heart, Michigan? Nothing seemed left for me but scraps and leftovers.

"Efrein, what is music?" Farley looked at me quizzically. This near-hard glance, a smile its punctuation rather than its substance, might at least give this *girl* a moment to speak. "Music is poetry in sound." "Well, um, um, I guess in a way, well, yes, um, um... Next. *Thompson.* What is music?"

A man in his late twenties (now to me young, then to me old) with piercing eyes of blue sat in the corner, observing. His name was Arthur (he had a first name, always, to me), and he was to be my teacher. I remember scanning him at a single glance and thinking, "This is a smart young man who knows exactly what he wants and exactly how to get it." It was a way I did not know how to be, and I wasn't sure I liked it... or disliked it. I had already been so flattened by the betrayals at home ("How could this be a betrayal? It is only of a *child.*" Is that what they thought?), and I don't know why I was not yet exceedingly capable of cynicism, but somehow I wasn't even in the ballpark. However he was, I would let the way Arthur was, be. Truly I needed a mentor. Adolescent inner dialogues are infinitesimally magnified over childhood ones. A child, it seemed to me, has but fantasies. Now *I* had needs.

The first several weeks of this brave new excursion into composerhood were discouragingly poetry-free. The assignment was percussion. How could a poet not hear melodies? Well, I tried, mostly plodded, my way through. Next, the good stuff: "Compose anything you want."

Then I had one of those experiences that are not prophetic, per se, but which open a *window* into life. As with a later experience (in my city of *very* good or *very* bad experiences, Los Angeles), I was on a bus. It was an ordinary school bus, a university shuttle for students to cross the campus, which was rather far-flung. This time I heard, very *clearly* heard, rhythm by rhythm, pitch by pitch a whole passage. This was a mere bus, a fairly crowded one at that. Who could be singing to me so?

I reached the dorm and went right to the piano in the common area, having no instrument of my own. I played the passage exactly as I had heard it and wrote it down. It was so beautiful, so pulsating, so modernistic. But how had it *written itself?*

Arthur liked it too, remarking how much better I was with pitches than with dry percussive work. The coming weeks were an idyllic interchange between me and my unseen, but so clearly heard, muse. Then one week I could hear nothing right at all. I told Arthur it was hopeless, nothing would "come," and so I had re-written everything. Arthur listened to my "new" piece. He was calm, incisive as always, but rather gentle, perhaps in consideration of the fawn-like poetry creature I must have seemed. "Laurie, you've destroyed every stable area of the piece."

10/SNAKE DANCE

Had I? Indeed, had life given me this gift, too – not only to give, but to rob? No, more pointedly, to rob *myself*? Had I only posed the question then. But who would expect a kindergartner to have graduated the real school at that age?

I went home and fixed the self-afflicted passage. The next week it was better, and better still the week after, and incredibly inspirational the week after that. I was on a roll. This was composing, after all. It was happiness. Mothers and fathers and brothers hadn't the slightest idea what *this* was.

The piece was a great success, as were our weekly lessons when I played my week's creation and it could just be. Every now and then, Arthur would wax serious with me. He'd gaze into the distance, tell me I was truly gifted, that the music I wrote would always be good, perhaps even great. I was entranced if yet timid. I always loved school. Now I could be *in* love with school. Its gift to me was something I had always wanted.

End-term break was the usual horror. I longed to return home, disgracefully (I supposed *they* might think) not to be with them, but to be with my piano, my very own piano. It was all I wanted to be with, live with, talk with, sing to, listen to, only.

My mother bristled. How could I spend all my time with *it*? Didn't I love *her*? Bad things happen, I was told, to people who did not properly love their mother. If you didn't love your mother, you could love no one ever, and no one could ever love you.

Before minimalism was ever invented, I endeavored to invent a minimalist solution. How many kisses on the cheek, or inquiries if it was a good day, would suffice to extricate myself from this pressure cooker sweltering me half to death in the name of "love"? It seemed insatiable. It seemed I was grabbed at at every turn. I couldn't even go shopping with her. I was never left to try on a dress alone, and even when it was on, it was never my own on my own body. She would come over and run her hands all the way down my back, clear down across my buttocks, and I would cringe. Why didn't my *father* love her? Why subject me? It was such bliss to just close the door of my room and be alone... with my radiant, sonorous, giving, loving ...*piano*.

I was happy to return to school, to return to Arthur. When I wrote "At The Dawn," it was like an anthem, or a call to arms, a true future-work, not of this time at all, and yes, happily, spontaneously, it began composing itself to music. "...What will come by virtue of the shaded mask, in greyness of unrealized hearts, when the Sun arises too bright to be seen? Look at me and steady in the somber gaze, whisper, 'Do not be afraid, do not be afraid.'"

It was teen-age enough, full of yearnings for a glorious future. I wanted the whole world to open, to lift its repressions and unhappiness to a brighter day. I wanted nothing less than a time and place when all Humanity would be free. Yet those eyes ~ that was more personal. My mentor's eyes filtering through poetic song ~ yes, they must surely be his. He was the one who believed in me, who had faith in my talent. I didn't think anything romantic. There was just this terrible, gnawing need. I had to be rescued from home. I had to be loved, nurtured as a *child* before the scary adult world could open to me. I didn't dare confide my distress in Arthur. It seemed enough that here, someone from the world of music was my advocate, and all the concommitant expectations which flooded my life in the wake of all the (however craved and needed) praise.

This was the sixties, when finally you could choose whatever odd array of instruments you liked, free of the staid, dull and standard string quartet. I chose soprano, piccolo, flute and bassoon much as one might chose a hot fudge sundae with strawberry ice cream, complete with whipped cream, cherry and nuts. It was a sonorous, indeed delicious choice.

"*At the Dawn*" was a great success. I had the best performers Arthur could find. But now, a whole new world awaited. I had recently been intimidated by the "Once" concerts locally ~ a mix of ultra-moderns, "performance music" (with the accent *off* the "music" part) and various interesting, if unlistenable, electronic discords throughout. I had been so happy with "*At the Dawn*," but in comparison to all these big names (and accompanying egos!), what would be expected of *me*? Now, Arthur said, I needed to master orchestration. I didn't want to become one of those greatly-gifted youngsters who didn't learn their craft and thus burned out at some intolerably young age ~ perhaps twenty-two or twenty-five... now did I?

Suddenly, it wasn't enough, not enough at all, to just be me. I would jump right into a new work and then another and then another... or would I? Spring break was as unwelcome as winter break had been, but in at least welcome anticipation of my New York piano, I flew on home.

To this day, I cannot say precisely how "it" happened, the horrendous break in consciousness which tormented me, it seemed, forever after, as mercilessly as "happily ever after" is kind and good to those so blessed.

12/SNAKE DANCE

I remember being trailed around the house, being carped at, picked at, torn at like a crispy chicken wing ripe for carnivore's teeth, as my mother berated me, "You can't compose music all the time. Even *Beethoven* didn't compose music all the time." What was my defense? Was I Beethoven? Would I *ever* be Beethoven? What had I to prove if I was Beethoven? What had I to prove if I was capable of love?

My all-believing mentor and my all-doubting mother could not thus co-exist. I thought (being an at-least partial paragon of reason~ well, didn't *one* of us have to be?) that there must be some way to approach this without feeling eaten alive by impossible expectations from every side, and never even knowing myself, what to expect of *me*.

The last I remember, I was in the bathroom. It wasn't my favorite place; in fact, it was where I retreated to cry ~ sort of a halfway house between how I seemed to be and how I feared I truly was. This time there were rushes of anger interspersed amongst the tears: "I am so much like her. But I won't turn out like her ~ I *swear it!*" I would deny my mother and embrace my mentor. I would risk a life without love (if she even slightly, possibly or plausibly be right). I would embrace the ecstatic muse who so uplifted me ~ this would be my love.

I would be like Vicki, the ballerina in "The Red Shoes." She was forced by a cruel taskmaster to choose art over love, and opted for love over art. Choosing love nearly cost her life. But perhaps, I would have an escape hatch she had not. A mentor's supreme and abiding faith would be all I would need. I would have my art, yet not wholly be devoid of love either. Love of my art would be my love. What was this *human* love, anyway? It seemed only fraught with pain.

Then, it seemed, I simply awoke one morning frozen. I could never reconstruct what happened. (Did it happen in my sleep?) My eyes were no longer windows of light but an already-invaded bomb shelter. I could look no one in the eye. They would see some deep well of pain and be frightened away, even though it was I who would be the frightened kitten or squirrel or bird who bolted from human view. The eye's function as a mirror was inverted, distorted, like the door that let life in to reflect its light, now had lost its power to reflect, indeed *deflect*, the wounds inflicted upon the unprotected soul beneath its gaze. Everything had invaded me and I had no defense. *Please. I wanted no one to see.*

Nor could I write, nay, I could not *think* my music. The flow veered dyslexically through my brain. I thought I heard this, I thought I heard that. Its rhythms would not cohere to the page. What was happening? Had the unseen forces which protected my eyes fled forever? Would my eyes, now and henceforth, only serve to guard their inner prisoner? How would I tell anyone? What would I say? Should I give my fear a voice? Would it not make things worse?

I returned to school in a silent panic of insecurity and fear. Whomever I would tell, they would have to look into my eyes, would they not? Would this not be unbearable for both? Even (no, *especially*) with Arthur. I could not look at him either. He was happy enough to see me, but I told him shakily that composing was suddenly, inexplicably blocked. He said not to worry – that I had already done enough with *"At the Dawn"* to merit an "A." But that it was also time for me to begin to master orchestration.

Orchestration? How could I orchestrate? How could I hear all the voices, the harmonies, together? How could I do this when I could not even think? What was this horror? Would it last? Maybe it was a nervous breakdown. Maybe these things got better, maybe they didn't. Maybe I would remain this way forever.

I supposed I would limp through the rest of the term. But instead, it seemed the worst was yet to come:

I had never considered that Arthur had some separate life apart from this important, indeed *central* mentoring of me. I knew he was married. I had met his wife. She was pretty and pregnant – part of the perfect life this perfectly extraordinary being must have. I thought people so perfect would forever stay in place. *Be* there. For *my* need hadn't ended. If anything, it was now all the more.

It was near the end of the term. I came for my weekly lesson though I had no idea what I was composing at all. All the sketches were blurred. I thought this would be a new song, but where were the words, where the melodies, where the muse?

Arthur said he had some news – some *good* news. A fellowship overseas, in Europe. He would be gone for a year. What? "Oh," I said weakly. "Congratulations." What was left of my eyes sank down to the floor.

Now I could no longer *feel*, either. I got back to the dorm just in time for my briefly-numbed feelings to erupt into tears. Sue asked me, "What's wrong?" "Arthur's leaving. He's going to Europe." I wanted to be happy for him. I just thought I would die.

I hoped summer would be better. I was to be a camp counselor in the mountains of Vermont. Maybe the scenery would revive me.

14/SNAKE DANCE

My freshman year had been a social wasteland -- no dating, no kissing, not even a thought of boys. High school had been rather an adventure. I felt a little young for "hard" sex yet, but it didn't frighten me. I just did what I liked and averred what seemed too far a step ahead.

I fell in love when I was fourteen. He was eighteen. At that age, the difference was huge. It was ecstatic, being in love. How could David not love me too? That particular year, it was summer camp that seemed the mortal enemy. David took up with Marian. She seemed neither prettier than me, nor more interesting. What she was was *his age*. He liked me though, and he would listen. He was the only one who knew that my mother planned on divorcing my father, later quixotically reversed. David was the first one with whom I could play out the childhood dialogues for real.

He invited me out to Queens to play guitar for his kid brother's birthday. Then I could sleep out there, in his parent's home, in the basement. It would be fun, if innocent. I don't remember the brother at all save that he was pudgy and short, unlike his tall, lithe overlooker. I was about to go to sleep when David knocked on the door, then came in. I remember a very slow pace of looking and light touching, foreverly slow, and finally, embracing. David gave me my first French kiss.

I was ecstatic. I came home and began to police the family mail. He said he would write. It was amazing to be in love so young, to know who you wanted forever so young. The letter finally came. I see it still in my mind, neatly hand-written, with many many words. How could I remember so little of it? Just one thing: "I wish November 1st had never happened." That he was in love with Marian.

Was it only I who could be so ecstatic one minute and so distraught the next? Why was there someone else? Would there always be someone else?

I had just turned eighteen when I went off to Vermont. Now I *was* ready for sex. The whirl of emotions had whirled out of control, and the targets of the whirlwind (adults, authorities, my elders) left too great a lack in my life. There were, after all, no *helpful* adults. I should look to someone closer to my age.

Andy, the camp lifeguard, was easy, even comfortable, to make out with. I had been, to date, almost paralytically shy socially, but sex didn't seem to faze me. He asked, and *I* asked nothing. The answer was yes.

We ventured into the pine forest after lights-out. The needles were soft, like a blanket on the ground. I asked shyly about pregnancy, and flattered to be an expert, he offered an ultra-sophisticated litany of false information about fertility. I could feel safe.

Three nights in a row we laid on our blanket-bed of pines. It was getting a bit more familiar now, the act. I thought by later on in the summer, it would feel more natural and I would understand why it was said to be such an incredible thing to do.

This third time, when Andy walked me home, he startled me: "I'm in love with Ann. I want to marry Ann." Ann? "Who's Ann?" "Oh, I didn't tell you about her?"

How ironic that he had been exactly where *I* had been the year before, the same school. But now, by chance, he had transferred away. When all the kiddies packed up their knapsacks and trudged on home, Andy, too, would be gone. Besides, there was *Ann*.

I returned to school in the fall. No Arthur, no Andy, a muddle of courses, a new music teacher I couldn't relate to at all. I learned Arthur would return in the middle of the year, for those thrilling, if whacked-out, experimental concerts. And so he did, but amidst whisperings that something was awry. He was about to get divorced. He was having a nervous breakdown. His life was in shambles. Who told me this, and how could it be believed? People like him didn't have divorces and nervous breakdowns. *I* could be crushed, but not him. I steeled myself. It may be true, but I wasn't going to be the person who would believe it.

I saw him two weeks after his return. Impetuous, headstrong, distraught creature that two intolerable weeks of waiting had made me (so I reasoned), I blurted out, "The next time you are in town, don't make me wait two weeks to see you." He halted my pace to a standstill with a single, icy, "Laurie, I haven't seen my *parents* yet."

I played him my new piece. He said it could be better. Then he said, impassive, the self-conscious mentoring not wholly rejected now, but hardly an act of ease: "You have a great gift. Don't mess it up."

I went home, fighting back tears. It was two in the afternoon. I didn't rest 'til seven the next morning, fiercely rewriting, recopying the entirety of the work. Then I called. I said the revisions were done, would he look at them. More unwanted attention and demands, but he complied. It seemed, as it would again in later years, that my dedication, even obsessively so, was the stolid immovable rock that stood in like a rigid but well-trained puppet, I merely its ventriloquist. I could throw my voice and that voice would be *me*. No one would see the tears. I would be strong.

Then there emerged a complication, a flutist named Carol Hall. Arthur, it seemed, was staying with her, and she, it seemed, resided in a tray of ice. Instantaneously it seemed to me, my lifeline had been severed. I forced myself to call her. "Where is Arthur?" "Arthur can't be reached."

The year's traumas had just begun. I found a single respite, my roommate's cousin. He was visiting from New York, and I took up with him at a glance. I wasn't in love with Robert, but sex was infinitely more interesting now. Besides, everything else was slipping out from under my feet.

Spring break was hell anew. I was picked up by my parents at the airport at the crack of dawn. It was early, and everyone was cross. Why was my mother treating me like I was six, or at the most ten? I was a *woman* now. (Yet blurting out at *Arthur* had been not only childish, but ineffective – why would I resort to such again? We mice in mazes – do we ever learn?) I had written my parents that I was seeing a boy. So now, when my mother asked, "What happened to the boy?," I nearly scowled at her, "We broke up." "What does that mean, you broke up?" Oh, hunting around for how I must have messed up? Did she *really* want to know? "Oh, it means we slept together and then we didn't want to see each other any more."

"Oh." The ice treatment. Why, dear God, over *this*? Yet then the matter seemed so easily, disturbingly easily... *dropped*. This wasn't *my* mother. My mother hadn't such an interest in permitting to me trespass into adulthood, especially with such a bold and sloppy stroke as this one.

Later in the day it came. "Your father wants to talk to you. *Alone*." "We're not letting you go back to school and sleep around with a few more people," he began. My mother gradually drifted in – eyes like ice, stone cold. She stared and stared. Her voice began slowly, then raised higher, faster, drumming to a fever pitch. "*I want to know who's sleeping with my daughter! I want to know who's sleeping with my daughter!*" The icy demeanor vanished into rage, and hysteria broke clear through.

Meals were the worst of it. The cold, hard stares would never cease. Finally, the words, like chunks of hard ice, merciless, unrelenting, this glacier that would never break: "There's something terribly wrong with you. You're so sick. I'm so worried about you. I'm so *frightened* for you." That no one ever loved me. That no one ever would. "You just *think* you have friends. They're all going to leave you by the wayside when they find out what you're really like."

I called Robert. He wasn't thrilled. He was with his old girlfriend, but he agreed to meet. I was scared to leave the house, as mother had hinted at suicide, and surely that (like everything else, it seemed) would be on *my* account. But I stole away to see Robert, say good-bye to Robert, leave Robert. It was all starting to seem so meaningless and frightening. Is this what "love" always came to? He, too, had someone else.

Again I took refuge in my music. The notes were so jumbled, it was like a mass of coronary arteries that would variously burst, or block, or cause some terrible attack. But I was desperate, so I pushed on into the night. My window was catty-corner from my parents. My light was on, theirs off. Suddenly theirs went on, too. Mother arrived at my door, words harsh and few. "Are you going off the deep end about *this*, too?" Her mouth, pursed into a stingy pout, clipped the final words with a razor-like cut. She retired and a few minutes later was when the screaming began. I left my room and pressed my ear to the door of my parent's room. "*I wish she would die! I wish she would die!*"

What was my crime now? For my brother, my crime was having been born. For her, my crime seemed to be that now that I was here, I would *express* myself, I would *be* myself. Well, I wouldn't be an appendage of hers, or an emotional slave. I had to right to love *anyone*. I had the right to *create*. I had the right to be *free*.

So why was I so miserable, so guilty, so shaky and confused and about to fall apart? Why the continuing, repetitive words, the very terror of them, "I wish she would die!," like an inner echo chamber? It seemed they would pound me forever. David and Andy and Arthur and Robert had already taken an ax to *one* half of my heart, while my own mother single-handedly wielded the ax with perfect aim at the other. But at least David and Andy and Arthur and Robert walked away. This one wielded the ax with a vengeance. It was not enough to strike the mark; it would be pounded in again and again without mercy. My punishment for not being a sufficiently devoted daughter.

Returning from Spring break was a year-end burden I didn't know how to endure. I would walk through the streets, tears streaming down my face, praying I would not run into anyone I knew. Could anything worse happen now?

Arthur planned on going back to Europe. He agreed to meet me, if briefly, to say good-bye. He thought he had already explained to me, without my having solicited such an embarrassing or painful explanation, that his only interest in me was my music, and not a thing else. I walked towards campus wading through a morass of questions and doubts. Say good-bye *again*?

18/SNAKE DANCE

He wished me good luck, though he thought it unlikely that anyone there would understand my work. I stood there frozen. He permitted a light touch of the hand, but it was, all over again, difficult to meet his eyes. He said, with nary a prompt from me, "Laurie, it would take more strength *not* to say it." He turned and began walking away. "I love you, Arthur," I called after him. He halted, turned but for an instant and shouted out, "Don't, Laurie, don't. Love ideas!" Love... *ideas?* Was this a suggestion or an epitaph?

But there was more, perhaps oddly more, than the usual teenage melodrama. It wasn't ever just the people. I always wanted to do something great. No, more. I felt *called upon* to do something great, and there was this inexplicable terror that it wouldn't be done. It defies belief, perhaps, but worse even than the seeming impossibility of love, was some stark, hidden terror that I would wake up one morning when I was forty years old and discover that whatever it was I had to do, it would be left undone.

It was no small matter, no side point. It was all so wretched, and could my mother *yes* be right? Maybe I *was* mad. But I had work to do. Whatever happened to me, whatever became of my hopes, my dreams, my love, my lack of love, still the work, some very special work would have to be done. In this I could not fail. Was I only going on nineteen? I was ages old, wasn't I?

I remember walking the streets in a daze. I was enraptured, entranced in Keats' masterwork, my newly-discovered "*Ode to a Nightingale.*" How my English class had butchered its meaning – didn't they know it was about death? Every time I reached, "*Thou wast not born for death, Immortal Bird!,*" I broke down in tears. Now I was in tears again. Why was I always in tears?

Then suddenly I saw it. I saw it right there on the street, through the teary veil shrouding my face. There was a *vision* there for me. I *saw* it. I had produced a wrenchingly emotional work. I, who knew so little of death to date, would lose many loved ones, yet I would live. They would all be gone, yet I would have to live on. And I would produce this work. I heard people screaming, crying. I saw them falling down in the aisles prostrate with both grief and a kind of ecstasy that their hearts were released. This is why I would live. I would free others. All the horrendous repressions of their lives would be gone. I could do this for people, I could do this for the world. Me. This special gift would be mine alone to give.

The work was so moving. *This* was my work. I wept on that very street. I fell to my knees for weeping. What *was* this? No lack of love this. No caricature of life, no melodrama of an overemotional teen. This was my *life*. All the other, the morass, the hurts, the rejections and obliterations, how they clawed at me. But was it my life? I felt like I had been thrown in with the swamp creatures of the world, wallowing in some hideous swamp, perhaps destined to *not* be rescued in time, not to be brought ashore into the shining Sun. To my *real* life.

III. To Save or Be Saved (Doom or Be Doomed).

That was moving into the Summer of '63. The topics of the day were civil rights and the Vietnam War. These raging fires seemed near-eclipsed for me now, only fueling my last rush of zeal for the mundane. I planned to march on Washington that summer. I would see Martin Luther King and, as history would later record, hear his "I Have a Dream" speech first-hand.

It was thrilling, but seemed a mere passing homage to my youth, the last return to childhood before tackling my great, if still unknown mission in life. I had been raised as an activist, a picket-line child. No white-picket-fence picket line at that. All solidly red. My mother was a communist in McCarthy days, when such was very nearly punishable by death. Childhood was haunted by the execution of Julius and Ethel Rosenberg. I met their children once at a neighbor's home. The younger boy was still very frightened and shy. His new mother had to hold his hand until he fell asleep every night for a whole year after it happened. I felt so for them.

There was another neighbor who knew nothing of this "secret club." Her daughter and I were friends. I came over soon after that day that America marked with a triumphal, ghoulish pride as a few hid in corners grieving. She said it was a shame about their children, but if they were communists they needed to be executed. I could say nothing. I, willful and tempestuous in matters of principle later on, was now all of nine. I felt so horribly that silence. I just cringed a bit inside and went out to play.

It was a pillar though, this death of distant strangers, yet so near. That and the Holocaust. Two pillars too mighty to define a young child, much less to stake out her world. Two twin precepts blazoned within my heart: "Stand by your beliefs, even to the death." and "Never deny that you are a Jew." I was so shy, but something inside me... I knew that if needs be, I could suffer for *everyone*. There was no how or why, reason or rhyme. I just knew. These pillars were precious to me. My two anchors of sorrow that both weighed me and buoyed me with their ongoing rhythms of pressure and release.

Yes, surely my world *was* defined in those tender years. Defined and bordered. I was marginalized politically, I was marginalized religiously,

I was later on marginalized artistically, psychologically, psychically... An illusion? Perhaps. We can only look into the mirror and see ourselves. We do not see that it is a mirror, and that all mirrors are but confirmation by reflection.

It seemed my whole identity was marginalization. A banner maybe, but also a task. The crusader *in* me that was born into this hunger for advocacy. The iconoclast in me. The non-conformist rebel, the essence of me defined as much by what I was not as by what I was.

This shoe fit me well. I always had my own personal marches, causes, that I claimed were "me." I cried when I learned of starving children, I cried at hearing of war, I cried at earthquakes and floods. It was easy to feel, difficult to act.

When I was eleven, my little cousin Jamie was dying of leukemia. No one could save her. I was home sick and a man came to the door, collecting for starving children. I had a powder-blue stuffed animal, kind of a fluffy dog, and his underbelly was a zippered compartment where I stored my allowance and other pittances – nickels, pennies, dimes, a rare dollar bill. I had no idea who the man was. I was just alone thinking of Jamie, wanting to help her. I told him to come back later, maybe we had some money in the house. I felt guilty for not having immediately been generous with my hoarded change.

I took out all the money and counted it. It added up to eleven dollars. I decided it was important to give the *entire* eleven dollars. That one shouldn't care just a nickel or a dime's worth. Here my young cousin was about to die and I could do nothing, but this man, whoever he was, maybe he could use my eleven dollars to help another child who could be saved. He returned and, not without trepidation, I gave him the entire of my booty. I hadn't the slightest idea what such instincts might cost me later on in life. If I had, would I have shivered the mere impulse cold and dry?

Probably not. Childhood decisions... there really *aren't* childhood decisions, are there? There are *personhood* decisions. Predispositions. You see, we live our future, we create our future, even as a child. How precarious giving the whole eleven dollars. Who was this man? Would the money get to the children at all? What if *I* needed the eleven dollars? These considerations were dwarfed in my childhood/personhood eyes. I wanted to save Jamie and was powerless. Surely the eleven dollars would save someone.

22/SNAKE DANCE

A ripple of guilt, even intimidation, unsettled this anonymous gift. My parents didn't want me talking to strangers. If they knew I gave my whole eleven dollars to a stranger, my argument about saving a child would be shattered en route from my brain to my mouth. So I would say nothing, pray there was a God for poor doomed Jamie, and imagine that many children had a lovely breakfast at my expense.

This mere incident, why even mention it? **Especially in that this particular impulse threaded its way into adulthood very nearly in tact** - most would say to my detriment. Even *I* would. But the Summer of '63... There was that "man at the door" again. I didn't know his name, but I somehow felt compelled to *give*. At a later knock on the door, it would be the same. Different actors, different timing, different circumstance, but just... the same.

The Washington March was exhilirating - if a last home- coming, at least a great one. The singing, the clapping, the faces and voices of hope. I almost wished it *could* be "the main thing," but in context, it was but a respite, a brief landing between two *cracking* pillars of my life, pillars of quavering would-be destiny that would perhaps now never be. One two weeks before, the other two weeks after:

I had been in New York that summer. I remembered Arthur saying he would stop there before heading back to Europe. I thought I would never see him again. This would be my proverbial last chance. It was hopeless to comb New York, but I noticed an ad for a so-called "avant-garde" concert. If he were in New York, he would be there.

Meanwhile, I had just read a rather maudlin, tear-jerking novel called *"The Gadfly,"* about an idealistic young man who had turned horribly bitter, and only too late regrets lost loves, lost this, lost that. Naturally, the hero (whose name even an erstwhile romanticist like me cannot recall) was Arthur, and the young heroine who endeavored to redeem him from his lesser self was me.

Memory fails me what inscription I injudiciously scrawled on the front page of this unsolicited "gadfly" of a gift. (Surely the brain has something called "an embarrassment quota." Too many embarrassing missteps and one simply does the socially acceptable thing and forgets. Perhaps it never happened.) I know I did go to that concert, somehow intruded upon my mentor's space, forced the book under his nose and made my getaway. Carol-of-coldness was there, too. Actually, no one was happy or pleased to see me. It was more awkward than I had anticipated, at best.

I returned to school in September, to a new residence, vaguely resolved to have a better year. I would never see Arthur again, but at least that was settled. I was shocked (I sensed that as omens go, this one must be bad) to discover a package waiting for me at my new address. I opened it and out tumbled "The Gadfly," along with a terse note. How he had told me he had no interest in me except for my talent. "Music and Carol occupy my life completely. I no longer have time for others' problems." I stared at it, gone fully numb.

The weeping ritual seized my life anew. "Why?" He was off to Europe. I would never see him again anyway. Why *hurt* me? Why crush me? The new semester had not yet begun and it was already rendered impossible. What was worse, I could talk with no one. Everyone at school thought Arthur had been my great advocate. The whole subject would have only sent me into paroxysms of crying anyhow. So I held my counsel not just out of self-control, but for fear that I *lacked* it.

Again, like a recurring mass of obstacles, composing was impossibly blocked. It seemed fantastically complicated in my head. The notes, like me, were in hiding, and refused to come out right.

I found they had assigned me to Samuelson for composing. He was a humorless chap (ah, so was I, so was I), and we had a special oil/water blend of personalities to boot. This couldn't be *school*. I loved school. This was just misery.

By mid-year, I felt ripe for the living dead ~ desperately dedicated to *something*, ever tormented that it had either not yet arrived or been hopelessly waylaid in a wash of tears. By Christmas break, even my piano in New York held no lure.

Then came a new icon of inspiration, which even the most unseasoned theatregoer might have identified at its opening scene as a disaster-to-be. Friends of the family were visiting a composer friend, and offered to bring me along. It was only years later that I learned that the short, odd, intensely neurotic man with the raspy voice I met that fateful night, was called "the Leon Trotsky of the music world."

No, friends, this wasn't about politics. I'm not even sure it was about music. Best I can make out now (sixteen different versions *then* ~ this child was not of one mind), it was about sex, about the dubious benefits of all-believing faith, aberrational psychology, fathers, lovers, extramarital involvements. Though I did tell myself it was entirely and absolutely about music.

Warren siphoned me off from the party to his studio. I showed him my scores. He seemed impressed. But first he wanted to know, was I a virgin? Did I have a lover now? And why was I so miserable? He seemed inclined to help (someone *attracted* to me would *help* me, yes?)

Warren was twice my age, and definite about his intrusion into my life, like a compelling, electric dwarf with wisps of whitened hair and flame blue eyes. His music mimicked all the demeanors of eccentricity – jagged, irregularly spaced, fiercely dissonant. It was the most fascinating array of notes I had ever seen. Moreover, he said I, too, was "a special case." Even my hysterias, my fierce rebellions, could now be a badge of honor. Surely I could confide in *him*.

Did I want to study with him, he mused aloud. He could introduce me to "everyone," he said. He *knew* everyone – he had even met Arthur. Knew them and hated them one and all! It was war against the world of music, war against the politics of music in New York, war against everyone. I (unimaginably) *admired* this. I too was at war. My war was less precisely-defined, my battles largely internal, and no trophies on the wall. His war sounded better than mine. To master music and this, too? It sounded like a bargain.

I listened, absorbing everything, but nearly paralyzed to speak. I was shy, almost immobile, with this quixotic silhouette of a man. "A penny for your thoughts." "I can only share thoughts in darkened rooms." "Do you want me to kiss you now?" I fell silent. He moved to shut off the light, came upon me and kissed me. It seemed tender at first, then he grabbed at a breast, as if to stroke me, then suddenly pulled away. "No, this can't happen." His wife and my parents' friends – where were they? Somehow I found myself safely delivered home. Would I celebrate, cry, or even believe this was happening? Arthur was gone, but now there was someone to take his... place (or was it "mantle"?) But this time I could be a very *sexual* child.

Like a hapless ball in a ping-pong match, I was scheduled to return to the Midwest. I had taken Warren's teaching address in Jersey. He said it was probably better to write him there than writing him at his home. I was too unsophisticated to question such euphemisms. I probably would have written if his address was the Moon.

Again, a wild, desperate thirst for mentoring would be quenched – by strong men, charismatic men, geniuses really, and I the special protégée. It never occurred to me that Warren could lead me into disasterville anew. He was original, eccentric, passionate, unpredictable, surfacing hidden recesses of psychology, sexuality, creativity, and I, yes I, by his very own estimation, was a "special case." A perfect new mentor he.

Imagine my excitement when my letter was answered. Oh, but not just a letter. It was a credo ~ full of faith, idealism, quasi (quasi, quasi) promises of sex... I proceeded to cancel the entire semester post haste, angry-young-woman style ~ and in dangerously reverse order! First I marched into Samuelson's office and told him I was off to New York. "But we want you to go to New York with *scores* under your arm." "New York is where I *live*." Cold water heave-ho.

Next I called my parents. School wasn't working, they too learned. It was back to New York to study with Warren.

Warren found out *third.* Suddenly it was cloak and dagger ~ nay, panic. The raspy voice turned to sandpaper: *"Burn the letter, Laurie! Burn the letter!"* The burning voice, the soon-to-be-burned letter, my burning heart... Suddenly life was all aflame. Poor Mrs. Johnson (or whatever the rooming house lady's name was) ~ her bathroom was nearly set aflame too. No, I would not shred the letter or disgard it a distance away. Warren said to burn it. The letter had to be *burned.*

I arrived on Warren's doorstep flush, trembling, fraught with expectations, a longing for them a fear of them both. Every burden of my young life might now be lifted, my course set aright. I rushed into his arms like a love-starved child.

Our first few meetings ranged from ecstasy to dismay to dread. He would hold me and soothe me, and as soon as I felt him hard against me, he would jerk away convulsively and plead the impossibility of it all. If we were together, he said, it would be passionately and for hours at a stretch, but how could this be?

I boiled over with tensions even a distraught teenager could never call purely sexual. It was unbearable. Creativity and neurosis, Warren told me, were inextricably intertwined. So were sex and creativity. His best student was a psychoanalyst ~ he would evaluate the student's scores, the student would in turn counsel him out of depressions. I had to read Wilhelm Reich to understand the miracle of the orgone box. And me ~ was I having full and regular orgasms? No? This was the worst, I was informed ~ I definitely needed psychoanalysis. ("Get thee to a psychoanalyst!" ~ quick, quick, quick!) This would be the stop-gap to this excruciating torrent of passions ~ *the answer.* What an altruist this man was, going to all this trouble for me! An appointment was set up to see the student.

26/SNAKE DANCE

Amazing. This man, in a few short hours, with the most spurious rationales, managed to do what my own mother could not have accomplished in a zillion years: get me to a psychiatrist. The student recommended one Dr. Bach. It sounded like a perfect choice for a musician. Unfortunately this was "no Johann Sebastian." No. This was *Seymour* Bach. My clearest recollection of him is that he was dull.

The worst part was the waiting room, with its fantasies of what terrifying truths might emerge once inside. I began reading vociferously, first Freud, then all his disciples: Adler staid and stern, reckless Reich, Jung's mysterious, uncharted terrain. I learned that analysis was primarily a very *long* process, fraught with hidden fears, defense mechanisms, repressions, denials, symbolic substitutions. It seemed human beings were willing to do anything, say anything, feel anything, think anything, so as to be absolutely anything but themselves!

The brilliance of Freud in discovering such an inherently flawed model of life as us! I secretly vowed to some day revise it all, unto the light, bright world where I longed to be. But for now, between Sigmund and Warren, I was steeped, very nearly drowned, in world views which never came up for air ~ the sub-conscious, like cement shoes, inexorably drew me down into the depths. My joy (or was it simply my imagination?) that ecstatic day on the bus with my unseen muse. The muse still came calling, but only in flashes. I finally composed a lovely work for solo flute. But it came to me instantaneously, like it daren't outwear its welcome, and it seemed to disorient rather than direct my path.

I became a hopeless psychology addict. I soaked it up like a sponge. It seemed I almost *knew* it ~ like re-discovering a world I had once lost. I remembered that I had discovered "transference" on my own at sixteen. When I lost David (you know, the kind of "lost" you get of someone you never had) and found someone else, I wrote: "This is the same love. I just *transferred* it to someone else." How could Freud know what I knew without him? How could I know what I had not yet read? Freud and I were friends.

Truth be told, I didn't *have* many friends those troubled days when those books came alive in my hands. Dr. Bach was hopeless ~ far too pedestrian to engage as a confidante. I remember once reading magazines an entire session. He insisted that since he was about to leave for vacation, this betrayed some deep inner need I feared would be unmet in his absence. I was derisive. Finally he retrieved his voice from its burial niche in the wall and virtually screamed at me: "You don't have to be in love with me to be psychoanalyzed by me!" Then I would go to Warren and tell him what I was *really* thinking. It was clear I "wasn't getting any better"!

Indeed, home was worse. My mother was into the floodgates of manic depression. It was unthinkable how desperately I had once desired to help her. Who would help *me*? My emotions existed, I was told, only to serve her. If I did not dance into the web, I would not live to dance away from it either. She would come into my room unannounced and snatch back the ballet tickets she'd given me, or inform me that she could commit suicide and I wouldn't care: "You'd just keep playing your music."

Once she came in only to enquire if I remembered Pepper, the beloved pet cat of the ten-year-old I had been "an emotional century" ago. "I told you I gave him away when you were at camp," she said. "I didn't do that. I had him put to sleep." A pang gripped me. What was she saying (*no one* could be saying this) – that she had killed my cat? I turned. But she had already departed. I would be sorry *now*, would I not? Had I not earned the death of my cat again and again?

Dr. Bach was not impressed. He said my mother had called him and said *I* was suicidal. I told him I wasn't. He looked, almost glared at me, it seemed. The whole hour was consumed by his questionings. Projections like that are very rare, he informed me. Was he now calling me a liar? Whose side was this guy on?

Perhaps nothing in life should be quite so mortifying as not being believed by one's psychiatrist. Well, I would show him who was the guilty party. I didn't really plan to mortify *him* (though Freud said you didn't really have to approach it like a "plan") – it just evolved as what had to be done:

I had had so many gifts given, then taken back. Mother gives, mother takes back, mother gives, mother takes back. Finally, she came to me with something I actually needed: a white sweater. I refused it. I was proud of the refusal and brought it to my weekly session as an acceptable morsel to share.

Dr. Bach, suddenly glowing with a kind of store-bought knowledge, felt he could finally emerge from his sinking-into-the-wall routine and shine. He counselled me why didn't I just take it. I needed it, didn't I? Why didn't I just eat when I was hungry and sleep when I was sleepy, and accept the white sweater and just wear it?

I couldn't deal with my mother without high penalties of pain, but ah, I could deal with this Bach impersonator. It would be the only thing in this entire dubious "analysis" which made sense. First I found a small, perfectly empty gift box. A bit of scotch tape and some nice ribbon. A nice "white sweater" for the sensible Dr. Bach. "I have a present for you, Dr. Bach." I offered him the box with outstretched hand. He blanched and tightened. "I don't accept gifts from patients." "Why not? It's only a present. Perhaps you will like it." "No, no. I really can't." "Oh, why not? It's just a box." (It *was* just a box.) "No, I can't do that."

I was quite calm. I paused, as if to hatch a new strategy. "O.k.," I said, "then I will give you another present. I will give you a kiss." I arose and walked towards him. He raised his arm, as if to fend off a blow. Now he had definitively, irrevocably lost me. The improbable, that instant, became the impossible. He could be of no value to me *ever*.

I had no interest in kissing him anyway, but now the advantage was mine. I sat back down and said I thought we should discuss the future of all this. What was the prognosis for such a terrible creature as me?

The man who would not accept gifts would not discuss prognoses either. I was a bit merciless now. Not just on him. On *me*. I had read everything and everyone, I announced. If I knew all about neuroses and psychoses, why didn't he?

Out with it! What would happen to me? Was I curable? He waxed most grave, this discerner of the true meaning of gifts. He said if I did not continue therapy, I might be in much more serious trouble later on. "Oh. You mean *really* sick?" (No, I never said, "*Like my mother.*") But that he questioned if he was the best one for the job.

How intelligent of him! I told him I needed to return to school anyway. Everyone had convinced me that "you have to finish your degree." I guess that's what Bach had done. Finished his degree and all, and now he was doing *this*. Doing it badly, perhaps, but doing it. What would *I* ever be qualified to do?

There was a horrible scene at home. Warren had thought he could get me an early admission to graduate school. My parents only had to fill out some forms. My father refused – *adamantly*. "My head is made up!" "Well, it's the head of a pig!," I screamed. I suppose it was dreadful to say; after all, they had sacrificed to send me through school thus far. Though ironically, it was the first honest reaction I'd given him in so long, it seemed a relief. Finally I could say something to *him*, not just to *her*.

My mother marched in on this scene, livid. Her comment? "You and your father are having a ball mashing *me* to bits, aren't you?" Who mentioned her? Would it never end? Must this family forever be incited like a pound of pit bulls? I thought I would just as soon go back to school *anywhere*. I thought I would just as soon die.

I wound up back at my old school. What amazed me is that they seemed to *want* me back. At the end of my sophomore year, Farley had made a little public speech about my potential ("high praise") and now, the grand step. He never took anyone but graduate students to teach. Now I would be the exception. I was awed at the compliment. I came in humbly. How swiftly did the illusion vanish.

I was not a very politic young woman. Every instruction I was given I compared to how Warren would have done it. (*Ouch*.) Farley exploded. After two weeks, he wanted out. He said that I had made myself a persona non grata with everyone. And "after all Arthur did for you." Then, like he had caught the wrong variety of fish on his hook, he tossed me back, to an underling on his staff.

I wept so hard after Farley tossed me out the door, I thought I would collapse like a house of cards into chaos. Distraught, I sought out the University's Neuropsychiatric Institute. The Rorschach test – well, I had never lacked for imagination. I think it was card 7 that was my Waterloo. "You have a lot of trouble with men, don't you?" "Actually," I ventured cautiously, "I have a lot of trouble with my *mother*." He looked almost *too* clinical, *too* professional. Like I would be coolly imprisoned if I fantasized awry. He decided I should see Dr. Teitelbaum. God, give me someone *kind* to talk to.

The doctor and I lasted all of one session. I told him I wanted to compose but my work was blocked. Stop. First there was a checklist: Mother? Father? Sisters or brothers? Older? Younger? Couldn't I ever just be *me*?

Yet the checklist seemed so normal, I was startled by what came next: "Do you have homosexual tendencies?" "What?" Well, you know, all great composers have been homosexual." "What?" "Of course, we don't know for sure what Stravinsky was doing with Diaghilev." (Why did I think they were producing a ballet?) "What?" He scratched his chin reflectively. "Well, maybe not *Bach*. Too many kids." "What?"

I walked out of there in a daze, and as soon as I hit the street, I began weeping anew. I wouldn't make it this time. I just wouldn't make it.

Farley – I don't know quite how it happened... I think he stopped me in the hallway. Asked how I was doing. Unimaginably, I blurted out that I needed a recommendation for graduate school and he beamed,

"Why, I'd be delighted, Efrein. *Delighted*." What was it with people? The man didn't even *like* me. But he threw me a life raft. Couldn't fault him for that.

I remember the date my acceptance came through: April Fool's Day. (I hadn't the perspective at the time to realize what a truly bad joke that was.) I was not only accepted, I got a fellowship. It seemed incredible, impossible. Now all I had to fear was how to deal with Warren. My emotions were so raw. And whenever my mind ventured towards him, I was a mass of sexual tensions. I had to work with this man again. I honestly wasn't sure I could.

I went to graduate school that Fall, shaky still, no model of mental health, but there I was. I looked up Warren and went over to visit. He introduced me to another guest, a colleague of his with the unlikely name of "Bentley." I remember the barest nod of acknowledgment and a limp hand.

God only knows what drew me to that man. He was most odd, with every manner of quirk, and he walked strangely, like someone had poked a stick up his rear end. But I somehow hooked into his overly bright brain and we cliqued. Later in the year, I befriended an ex-student of his, a jazz musician named Bob, who was positively fixated on Bentley. He was bi-sexual himself, and freely shared with me his diary about Bentley's clandestine escapades.

In those days, it was a deep dark secret. Ever willing to stand with outcasts, I remember being fascinated and empathetic. What a burden this poor man had to carry that no one could know! I wanted to be his friend. Bob said it was hopeless to try and seduce him, but then reversed. He said I was the only woman Bentley ever liked, and that if anyone could succeed, I could. It wasn't the first time (obviously!) that I followed through on perfectly dreadful advise.

Strange people call for strange measures. The way to Bentley's heart was through the piano. Not just any old tune, at that. Only Bach's E-Flat Minor Fugue from The Well-Tempered Clavichord, that five-part delight as performed with metronomic precision, perfect pedalling, and splinter-clean fingering. I practiced conspicuously in the main building for hours at a time, whenever I thought Bentley was close by. Finally I asked him, what was it about the E-Flat Minor Fugue?

I got my little audition in Bentley's apartment some weeks later on. God knows how I passed, but I was "in." And how I dedicated myself – four hours practice a day minimum, without fail.... and *zero school credit*.

My fingers were worn to the bone before my mind ever kicked in with my "real" studies.

I don't know whether Warren was impressed or not. He kept his counsel. He probably thought I was mad, and I *knew* that *he* was mad. Bentley may have been more mad than Warren and me put together, but he was the "mentor du jour" for that stretch of agonizing while. This was no easy taskmaster. With groups, he specialized in driving a different student to tears each class. In private lessons with me, he went slightly easier. I was "the undiscovered country."

I didn't begin to sense his true terror of women until we went to a concert together and after walking me home, I managed to get him to stand still, awkwardly, for a kiss. He avoided me for three weeks following. My furious practice routine continued. It was the only real discipline of my life – this wasted time, this deathwish of a liaison, this fixation on the unattainable. My fingers at least partly released my emotional cauldron. They, at least, would respond. I had no friends except maybe for Bob, who was alternately encouraging and dubious. The Good Ship Titanic rolled on. I was doing *well*, I thought. I was meeting the taskmaster's call nary losing a beat.

Finally, he took me as a composition student too. That went less well. Everything jumbled in my head. Fear (fear of failure, fear of rejection, fear of fear) accompanied me as surely as my plodding fingers on the keys. One night, to my shock, Bentley asked me out for beer, actually *pitchers* of beer. I hate beer, but drank as much as he did. I elicited another kiss. Now I was in serious trouble. The next time I saw him, terror was creeping back into his eyes. This could not safely go on. The piano lessons went on, the composition lessons went on, but now I, too, emerged each time awash in tears. Every lesson was a torment of tongue-lashing. Nothing was good enough for Mr. B.

Yet I couldn't seem to break free. (Break free and do *what*? Break free and go *where*? To *whom*?) The crying again became incessant, punctuated by bizarre vice-like headaches which closed in like cymbals crashing into my skull. I had been hovering on the brink for so long. Now the ship was about to sink for good.

As if to mark my declining station in life, I had been evicted from my perch in the attic of a rented house. There had been a fire. The landlord inspected and found an appalling disarray, mostly discarded sketches of music, scribbly testaments to the disorder of my scrambled brain. He said it was a fire hazard (actually he may have said that *I* was a fire hazard!) I could stay, but not *there*. The main portion of the house was already occupied, so I was exiled to the gloom of the basement, dank and dark.

It was like the penultimate scene of a grand opera. A scarce week or so later, a letter arrived, informing me matter-of-factly that my scholarship was being discontinued. I could stay, but only at my own expense. I hadn't the money. It was finished.

I confronted Bentley frantically. He had assured me he would stand by me. Instead, he deliberately let an "incomplete" turn into a failed grade, even though I completed the work. He refused to grade it, he said, because he "couldn't understand it," undoubtedly the smaller portion of a more encompassing paradigm. Then he told the faculty to discontinue my scholarship. I couldn't even be angry at first, I was so hurt. I was struggling to grasp not that it had happened, but that it had been *deliberate*. "Why? At least tell me why." "You're a whore," Instinct prevailed. I aimed for his head, but with his rapid, adroit duck, I missed.

Warren, not daring to chance a new sermon on sexuality, merely said he hoped I would "find myself." Bob said casually, like this was all a mere failed experiment, "It just goes to show ~ never try and change a fag." My fellow students *congratulated* me ~ said Bentley deserved it, they all deserved it. Wished me the best in breaking from the insanity of the university. Just one catch: They were going to get their degrees and move on to their chosen careers. I wasn't.

IV. A Phoenix Arises From a World Fallen Ashen at My Feet.

Leaving school was disastrous. It had been so long in coming that, in hindsight, it seemed inevitable. Yet if it *must* have been thus, then why not let it be? Why would it haunt me afresh at each turn? I think of all that might never have been had I not stepped out (or been shoved out!) of the paradigms of my college years, and wonder if an even greater waste than loss is regret.

Thus a life which appeared crushed was perhaps furthered. We call it "the winding *in*" of the dance, but ah, here's the rub: It is also the winding *out*. Academia back then would never have welcomed the adventures which soon rushed into the void of my young calamity. (This was, after all, the sixties!) And what seemed such perilous misfortune then did accrue to my benefit in later years.

As unceremonious as my move back East was, such views would seem scarce comfort! But I would credit my young mind with something of it. I wanted cosmic connections ~ some way for life to make sense. I was a shell-shocked being, ripe for what we now call, "post-traumatic stress syndrome." It bred nightmares for decades. Every time anxious or insecure, a dream: I was back in school, I hadn't completed school, I still may not complete school. I was thirty and back in school with the seventeen-year-olds, forty and back in school with the seventeen-year-olds. In my dreams, I was forever seventeen.

My life seemed too fractured to continue. How could I have a future with my present so chopped apart? I had to envision, to embrace, some greater whole, before the fractured pieces could be healed.

For me, it began unexpectedly. Twenty-two. Now back a year to twenty-one. My first window to a more cosmic view of life ~ if you will, my first view of the stars. Beings unused to light wince, and swiftly dismiss their illuminator as an anomaly. So did I. But I look back now and see how pivotal was that tiny dot of light against the darkened sea:

I was already nearly doomed ~ led here, there and everywhere in search of an ideal which only kept appearing and re-appearing in an ever more distorted form. How I was led from Arthur to Warren to Bentley to the abyss. You may even have been relieved when I got the boot. No one can save those so desperate to be saved. One can only save one *willing* to be saved. I was so sure I *belonged* there – I only had to make it work. So who or what could save me? Then came this one dot of light I could not even decipher 'til years later on.

It happened not at a point of awakening at all, but when my star seemed destined to sink. By the time I got to graduate school, I was finishing up Freud (talk about cult leaders!), and lighted upon a biography of one of his rare woman disciples. Her name was Lou Andreas-Salome, born in St. Petersburg, Russia, in 1861.* Although historians disproportionately made her claim to fame, her link with famous *men* (Nietche, Rilke, Freud), she was herself a prolific writer in many genres – equally intuitional and a gifted chronicler of her times. Were she alive in today's world, it might be difficult to discern if she was writing for humanity's history, or for its coming "New Age." But no one doubted her ability to nail down the facts where needs be.

And somewhere as I read through the tale of *her*, I realized (devoid of the scarcest philosophy, teaching, training or conviction)... I realized that the tale of her was, in fact, *me*. I had awoke one morning, quite literally, "in the dawn's early light," with a weird, unaccustomed thrill running through me – not physically, but running through my *being*.. I knew I was her. I was this child, this young woman, this woman of the world. This was my roadmap. I would live as I had lived before.

I scrutinized the book. Her ancestry was Russian. Mine was too. She wasn't Jewish, but many closest to her were, and she died in Germany at the dawn of the World War II. I remembered my uneasy shock when, as a small child, I learned of the Holocaust – a visceral, nearly familial horror, like "How could it have come to this?"

Each detail seemed a mirror of remembrance. She was born within days of the emancipation of the Russian serfs, as was I born in within days of "D-Day." She, too, had lived childhood in a dream world. Her rude awakening, replete with idolized mentor, happened, as did mine, when she was *seventeen*. It came through the death of her father, then an aborted affair with a Dutch minister/mentor named Gillot.

---
* I debated whether to weave the tale of a woman little known in America into the tale of Jonestown. I have, in that it gave *me* both perspective and strength; and I want to offer the paradigm for others who have suffered trauma seemingly "without cause." A darker tale from history, with Jim Jones as protagonist, is historically documented in a sequel, "**AND THE ANGELS WEPT.**" (See p. 411.)

I had not yet known a Dutch minister. Nor did I know any German poet named Rainer (Rainer Maria Rilke, her love), nor an Austrian Jewish physician (her "unofficial husband"), much less some rare exotic pedigree from Persia, suicidal to boot ~ namely, husband Andreas. At least not *yet*, my friends. Moreover, it would be ridiculous to run into all these by chance here in America, much less in *fateful* encounters. There were these "loose ends." But I knew I was her. I thought like her. I felt like her. I knew her life. I had discovered... *myself*.

Admittedly this rediscovered life, for all its exotic underpinnings, was no picnic. This strange creature's marriage had been an exercise in suicide prevention, when Andreas, proud scion of Persian royal blood, plunged a knife into his chest upon her attempted refusal to wed. The ceremony was performed but the marriage never consummated. After forcible abstinence from her mid-twenties to mid-thirties, as long as it was odd, she swept across Europe's intelligentsia, consuming, then abandoning love in sporadic feasts, unable to wed anyone she truly loved. Her only pregnancy was aborted for fear of her cuckolded husband seeking out her lover in a violent rage.

One might not thrill to the wild freedoms of this fate, given its accompanying perils! Yet instantaneously, it seemed, I was hoisted to a new vision of life. I could again be this wild, misunderstood, yet accomplished creature, Lou Salome. I would move from mentor to mentor, from lover to lover, from creative work to creative work. Despite searing chains of fate, I would not be bound. I would meet the great people of the world, yet retain the childlike, impulsive wiles. I would be wholly, exceptionally Lou/me. I would be happy. (So thought I at age twenty-one!)

The prospect of a "fated" life, rather than a "normal," much less happy one, did not put me off ~ it dared me on. As it was, stability was hardly my strong suit! Indeed, how was it possible, even as a weedstrewn seedling of my overfertile brain, to be *certain* of this? My own precarious version of certainty was uncomfortable even to me, perhaps even confirmation that I was ripe to go mad.

And the very worst: I had no knowledge of, nor belief in reincarnation! I could be mad, I could even be inspirationally mad, but how could I be *her*?

I can't imagine why I ran to tell *Warren* of it. Surely this wasn't helping my case. He listened politely (anything short of ranting was "polite" for this soul) and said something like how nice. How much out of my element I suddenly was! The very air split before me, as if to counterbalance, with a rude shock, my new inner parting of the Red Sea. I spoke of it again to no one in that place. To this day, I cannot imagine how or why it came up there at all.

Now I was ready to regroup in New York. For upon my exile, I did return East. As usual, I explained nothing. I had simply left school and would now find a job and an apartment.

At that time, my brother had recently married. We were never really friendly, but I liked his wife, so I visited upon my return. They said they had discovered a wonderful therapist and wouldn't I like to pay him a call? (Would *you* have tried therapy again? But mices in mazes, we do these things.)

Do you know those horror movies ~ actually, it's a horror movie *formula* : The monster, or deranged human, has attacked its prey. The prey has apparently miraculously escaped and will go free. Ah, but then, just at the tippy tail end of the getaway, the monster/deranged human suddenly revives and re-attacks. Then you witness the truly miraculous, hair's breath getaway, the delivery of a piercing bullet or the slamming down of a deadly object on the creature's head.

This new therapist, Norman. He must have *invented* that movie script. I couldn't seem to move on before having, however unwittingly, set myself up for a final attempted kill shy of freedom.

Norman was Napoleonic, like Warren, with, as Freud might say, the over-compensatory confidence of the overly short. He rushed to take me under his wing. My therapy would be free 'til I got on my feet. He would spring me money for an apartment. Then we'd get me into a "cozy group" and "help" me. He was a miracle worker. Needless to say, he adroitly slipped in, he was a sexual Hercules to boot.

I took in his kisses hungrily, expecting (if hardly solidly thought through) that they would lead to sex of some normal variety. I knew he had an apartment upstairs, though no invitation was extended to me. Our sessions more-or-less began as "therapy." After a bit of banter on my current problems (no lack of those), he would have me go down on him. I remembered I once asked what would he do for *me*. He turned suave, with only the slightest hint of contempt, which I strained to ignore. "C'mon, baby, make yourself come. I got someone else comin' in a minute. Here. Here's $5.00 for a cab."

The "cozy group" was Friday night, all night, 'til 8 or 9 in the morning. It was a zoo of screaming confrontations, with Norm the referee. Starting at about 7:30 on Friday, people would yell and scream, scream and yell. By 3 a.m., it was attrition time, and we would sup and chat. Then back to finish the hapless critters off. When it was your turn to be "helped," you were "on." People anguished over their hopes, doubts, fears about being "on." Clearly, you had to *earn* this badge of courage. Then you "took it." If you were worn to the ground, maybe you could be persuaded to the group viewpoint. Life wasn't working on its own. Here. Let the cozy group help you.

Of course, it was hopeless to not respond to the "help." Whoever resisted the onslaught, Norm just pronounced "very sick," fueling the bonfire. With such penalties of pain, not surprisingly, everyone seemed to come around. What a miracle worker this man was! He seemed to succeed in "helping" virtually everyone.

This type of scenario, a glimpse at the dark side of the turbulent, experimental 60's, seemed fascinating. You didn't have to hide with your problems in a little shell. Now all my meticulously-guarded defenses, denials and repressions could be aired openly. It awakened in me everything vulnerable. Yes, I, too, would be "helped."

Norm waited a few weeks to put me on, possibly so I could accept craziness as the "norm" (pun intentional!) before heading for the plunge. Colleen was ostensibly the worst. Hysterically neurotic, with her straight-man, Bill, silently by her side. At least they were a couple. I had gathered that Samantha, the woman sitting up front, had some special tie to Norman, like they were a couple, too. Colleen and Bill seemed to know the routine. Maybe they could straighten my perceptions out.

I cornered them at their diner table at the 3 a.m. break. Norman and I were having sex, I said (well, that wasn't *totally* true, I guess). I thought he was interested in me, but who was this *Samantha?*

"*You, too?*" Colleen freaked out. When we came back in after the break, she was still freaking. Norm rushed her into the bathroom, amidst everyone else's unrelated screaming and yelling. They scarcely noticed Norm was gone.

Norm and Colleen emerged a few minutes later. Colleen looked shaken. Norm, undeterred by the continuing racket, marched over to me, and like a wild spray of counterpoint, screeched out, "You shouldn't even be here. You're too fucked up for group therapy!"(!!) I was stunned. What (had I to wonder?) had Colleen told him?

He was more sedate our next private session. He said Samantha was about to move out, but now I may have blown my chances for moving *in.* He said he would give me one more chance. Next time I would be "on," and everyone would really "help" me.

Thus spake the serpent's tongue. I was an engineered case. Everyone there seemed to have markers for debts owed to Norman and would be his mouthpiece. I was mincemeat, mercilessly chopped up alive for the kill. He had somehow extracted the worst of it – the whole terror of *mother.* "You're cold as ice, aren't you? You don't feel anything for anybody." I was despised, hated, torn at. "Help": the first and last of the two-edged swords.

By 8 a.m., they had all departed but me. I walked over to Norman. "You son-of-a-bitch!" He ranted, raved, fumed. I left.

Notwithstanding, something startling good was about to happen. I lived those days in what some might consider a choice spot for the sixties: the East Village. I had no interest in drugs, but loved the macrobiotic food sprinkled with light, intriguing doses of metaphysically-inclined repartee.

I was now ripe to investigate *anything:* yoga, theosophy, scientology, tarot, Buddhism, flying saucers... In those days, New York was a regular amusement park, with clusters of fanatical enthusiasts one could join up with nearly at a glance. This phenomenon, "The Sixties," was not to be missed.

I quickly discovered what my sign was, and, very nearly on a lark (suspecting that the local brown-rice people weren't telling all), I headed to the Yellow Pages to find an astrologer. This is how I discovered my new mentor(let me not spoil that word *too* badly now) and life-long friend, Al Morrison.

I called and my appointment was set. I arrived at the appointed time, and found a very odd, this time a very odd *tall* man, who sketched strange glyphs before my eyes. No rush. As each swiggly mark hit the page, I felt him scrutinizing *me.* He began into the reading almost in a dreamlike drawl, not a mellifluous voice at all, but grounded somewhere as if on an invisible magnetic string. I felt keenly, acutely, that I was being "read":

"Your name will become a legend. People will try to understand why you did what you did, but it will elude them." (Ah, would I have my exotic past/future after all?) It was fascinating – almost like a *vision* of me. All the pain of the past could dissolve. I could be as I truly am. Do what it was truly in me to do. The duck hopped in and swam. I had found a new home.

This was a well-furnished home, too, filled with priceless gems of antiquity, as well as whispering spirits from a future, still unspoken, time.

Old (or as Al would express, in a chronic penchant to exaggerate good and bad alike), *"ancient"* texts crowded the shelves of what was a mere room behind a storefront. All the space-age pursuits that had lightly garnished my brown rice along with the sesame salt, now emerged as the main dish: psychic gifts, telepathy, mediumism, reincarnation, past lives... Freud & Co. could now sink to their watery graves. I was going to arise!

Sex was an added bonus, as was another rare commodity: a faith, purely, for its own sake, in me. It wasn't even that I found Al that attractive. He was about thirty years my senior, though that had admittedly never put me off before. He was someone with whom I could just, with no strain or effort or pretense, *be*.

I told him it was easy enough to find lovers, but what of this magical "full and regular orgasms"? Al was thoughtful, nearly clinical, but just also, positively, nice. Gentle. There would be no frantic proclamations, no judgments, no whacked-out yes/no chaos. He said he didn't think I had the slightest problem with sex. That if I were with him, I could begin having orgasms all night right away. I said great.

I had no idea this would be true. This was me, after all. I might have said "great" to Jack to Ripper in those days. I don't even know how it happened. It seemed like everything 'til then had been an emergency dredging job, barely hoisting me to ground level where, with the help of supporting equipment, I might breathe. But *this*... I felt myself sinking backwards into caverns and canyons. My mind emptied into a dreamy, ethereal mist, as my body merged into a place "no woman had gone before" - kind of a weightless float, wholly physical yet only a *quasi*-physical bliss. Was this sex? Could sex really be what you *are*, a state of being, rather than whatever this one or that one might *do* to you?

Finally relief, as the great forbidden dictum, as unspoken as it was pervasive (*"You can't enjoy sex"* - mother's most silent scream), was effortlessly reversed. Past all the conflicts and complexes, now, finally and forever more, I was a *woman*. No one (even Jim Jones. Even Jim Jones...) would ever be able to take this from me.

Al aided my astrological studies as best he could, and was otherwise promiscuous but honest. It would have been useless, anyway, to be jealous. He said he hadn't taken on any new lover since he had met me (a scant six months earlier!) and that seemed assurance enough. I thought, anyway, that it wasn't good to hoard this "tantra yoga." (The secret was whispered in my ear!) All women should know of this.

I didn't even bristle at his admonition, "Don't act like a wife." It was already clear I would never be a wife. My mother, the original model of "wife," insisted on twin beds and was barely touched, so I was prepared early on to be the *antithesis* of "wife." Wasn't it already borne out? David dismissed me and went off and married Marian. Andy had been all along engaged to Ann. Arthur left his wife but still wouldn't have me. Warren stood by his wife rather than come to me. I was now only twenty-three, young enough to become a new wife, but wifehood ~ it wasn't something to be hoped for.

I only received the quintessential release ~sexual~ with relief. One less battle to fight, one less obstacle to overcome. I hoped it would bring relief of other kinds, or even more stability in my life. Yet somewhere in my heart, I was already irrevocably destroyed. One cannot lose such a huge war and expect any single breakthrough to heal the wounds.

Better to explore new frontiers. I mastered new skills. I read Al's books, as the world of the occult unfolded before my eyes. Life seemed less fixed now, more open to sudden shifts. Within months, my life had turned on a dime, not just mentally, but geographically. It was magnetic, inexorable. I had to meet the call: *California!!* (Talk about other planets!)

Whether I had heard others speak of it (everyone was hitching rides cross-country in those days), or it was simply where I had to be, you could have simply tied a noose around my neck and pointed West. I had no contacts, no prospects, no reason to expect it would be different from anyplace else. I just had to be in California.

Al, ever ready to indulge the young, encouraged this. He said he would normally require five years' study for anyone to practice astrology with clients, but for me, the mere five months I had had would suffice. We both knew this was in my blood, something, someone, I must be. I could go to California and practice astrology.

The destiny creature within me, the mere human animal who also shares the Divine, began to awake and yawn. All its new, wobbly steps were now headed West. I picked up a few choice books, my proverbial hat, and on a fair day in May, departed to the new world.

V. "Go West, Young Woman!"

I had sold all I had and the total was $900, a handy sum in those days. I was to stay with a friend of a friend in Los Angeles. Al was to come to the Astrological Federation of America's convention that August in Seattle, where we could meet and take stock. I had two or three months to assess the lay of the land.

I arrived into the assassination of Bobby Kennedy, right there in L.A. I had no way to share, to grieve. On that mild, sunny day shaded with palms this grotesque violence. It was an anomaly of a welcome. I felt it begged my honor, but alone and adrift, I had no mooring from which to barely honor myself.

I had no friends, so went hunting for some. There were groups, meetings, centers, lectures, all manner of what-not in this sprawling L.A. Most of it seemed superficial or weird – even for me. But the streets were so open, sunlit, easy and warm. Poems began filtering through. I realized that I was at my happiest when I was nowhere, free to float. I felt a Presence pouring into me, a happy, songful muse. It was teaching me. It was giving me the essence of its Light. It was my unseen companion wherever I went. In having cut myself adrift, I was no longer alone at all.

Sometimes I'd feel transported to a future place – as though my entire life had already passed, and it had been but a dream: "'In the long hard wield of time, stake thy claim. Then leave thy vision for the rest and go thy way. Never ask for fortune's name.' When You came to me in undeciphered songs, did I neglect to *praise* Thee?"

"Undeciphered songs"? What was there to "decipher"? "Long hard wield of time"? What was *that*? I was going on twenty-four. There *was* no "long hard wield of time." Never mind. I had the sunlight, the ocean, the chirp of morning birds and the crickets' song. Was I not free?

It was so spontaneous, so effortlessly happy. Yes, I had come to the right place. I had *work* here. It mattered less than at any time that I had no direction, no home. I could sing, I could work. I had my muse.

I spent the sweet, lazy, if overhot afternoons, writing. By July I felt to depart North. Al had said we could meet in San Francisco; I could name the place. I had garnered a bit funds as the world's most distracted waitress. Fortunately, just as they were letting me go, I had to leave. These slightly messy ends with people you would never again see no longer mattered. That awful weight of proving everything to everyone at all times was, at least for now, gone.

I headed first for Berkeley, which in those days was an icon. I had nothing planned, I just craved to *be* there – to share in the climate of zeal in that most political of summers, 1968. Undaunted by the unfamiliarity, I marched with the students, and in a short while had a place to "crash." I asked around and crashed in San Francisco as well. It was a friendlier, more uncomplicated social scene then. The yuppies later on made a huge show of "networking" because they wouldn't just share themselves – it had to be transactional and result in gain. In 1968 there weren't those walls between a home and a friend and something to do. Wherever you were was all there was. Then you moved on.

Al and I rendezvoused in San Francisco. I was settling in well, he said. We ventured to Seattle together, but ever discreet, he insisted I get a separate room.

It was no effort to comply. I had found a new target of adoration: Dane Rudhyar, the "wise old man" for hordes of young astrologers of the day. The French accent did help, and the fifty-year age difference hardly put me off. I was rather into older men Olympics those days. You never could have talked me into a father complex. I just "preferred older men."

I had met Rudhyar briefly in L.A., a couple of months before. It began an odd phenomenon – something like a clandestinely-compassed blind man's bluff, that would repeat and repeat, 'til finally, the puzzle of my journey West would arrive at its stopping point: I "recognized" Rudhyar. I met him and I *knew* him. I was ecstatic to see my chart tumbling into his with snips of Geminian wiles. We were so alike: both composers and poets and astrologers.

He loved my poetry and I basked in the glow. He said he had a wife (oh, #6 or 7), but she was off visiting her parents. He suggested his marriage was shaky anyway. He had married poor Dana, he said, once she agreed to get a driver's license and learn how to type – he had books to write and commitments to meet. He didn't think she would find the convention too interesting anyway. He took me to sit with him at the formal dinner the last night, and several people mistook me for his wife. Rudhyar seemed amused; I was flattered.

I was (sometimes to my horror when I think back) mostly unconcerned about anyone's marital status anyway. It did perturb me a bit when he began calling me "Maureen." He said he had also (re- named) "Dana." I lightly slipped out of "Maureen" back into "Laurie" – no harm done. He said his reluctance to sleep with me was that he would disappoint me ~ the "I'm an old man" routine. He acceded nevertheless. I happily examined the dent in his back where his kidney had been removed at age twelve, and listened to mild ploys about his adrenals and arthritis with appropriate deference. Rudhyar said we would meet again soon, as he knew people in Berkeley he'd be visiting. I could meet Dana, too.

Al landed three proposals of marriage but averred taking the plunge. He wished me well, then headed back east. I wasn't to see him again for a very long time.

It was time to settle down in San Francisco. I discovered where the astrologers were and began a modest practice. In a few weeks, Rudhyar invited me to the Winstons in Berkeley, where he and Dana were staying in a spacious home lightly settled into the trees.

Rudhyar was attentive but subtle. It was more that he would light up around me, which the driver/typist could not help notice. I noted his treatment of her was not very good. He seemed unperturbed. Waxing philosophical (here somewhat perfected as a mode of being), he said, "I am an old man. I will die soon. Dana will still be a very young girl when I die."

However intent I was on locating the perfect older male mentor, this bristled. I too could become "the lucky owner of a driver's license and a typewriter." It was starting to look not so good. Then one morning, I got a call at home, a frantic one which just sputtered out, "Stay away from my husband!" and slammed down the phone. I was shaken. I decided Dana was badly put upon as is, and that I would really rather be friends with her than with him. So when he sent me a very special, coveted invitation (one many budding young astrologers would have died for) to become a charter member of his newly-founded International Association for Humanistic Astrology, I wrote carefully and painstakingly, thank you, but that I did not consider him "humanistic" (*ouch!*).

Besides, something else had happened in Berkeley which removed Rudhyar's allure for me. Right there in the neighborhood where the Winstons lived, there was something called "The Space Convention" ~ a diverse assortment of occult practitioners, psychics, experts on aliens, speakers on every manner of metaphysical legere-de- main. A man showed up on the podium, someone I'd never heard of. I looked at him and fell instantly in love.

His name was Luke, and he was... a Dutch minister. I couldn't know at first glance that he was Dutch-born nor a minister, nor had any thought of reawakening my earlier self, the infamous Lou Salome, and the early shooting star of her life, the Dutch minister Hendrik Gillot. I just knew at a glance that I loved *this* man.

I tracked where he would be next. It seemed that he would soon be giving a seminar in San Francisco, about a whole variety of fascinating offbeat things ~ auras, space people, magnetic healing, ancient civilizations, psychic work ~ an amalgam I soon learned was called "The New Age."

I showed up and sat in his space transfixed, then signed up for a "reading." He read auras around my head like the rings of a tree, counting out the years. He told me about the future. All that sounded familiar was, "No one will ever understand you." They all told me that. It was the worst and the best. What did it mean? Was it a promise, a challenge... a curse?

I told him I saw him at The Space Convention. He told me, accurately, *exactly where I had been sitting although we had not yet met*. Yes, he was as aware of me as I was of him. I thought he might not "make the move" and so I must. The magnet pulled at me, inexorably. I *knew* this man. We were *already together*. "I have such a strong urge to kiss you, I don't know if I can resist it." I gazed at him only. He moved towards me. "Why should you?" Yes, yes, yes: "the kiss of death."

This was immediately elegantly simple and exceedingly complicated, and by most normal standards, bizarre. He told me that in a past life, we were both Berbers, an Arabic sect; and that he had loved me so much, that when years earlier, he first put together his act (metaphysics and showmanship? Indeed!), he gave his assistant the same Arabic name. And now, here *I* was. He said we were both from the planet Pluto. Pluto ~ that deep, dark, mysterious place ~ elemental, irresistible, compelling. We could be from such a place, could we not?

We talked briefly about his wife and many growing children, and how he was on the road so much he was almost never home. Besides, he told me with remarkably little embarrassment, he was becoming impotent. He said he thought his sex drive was disappearing because of his spiritual work. I was confused but impressed, empathetic but determined to reverse the tide, "spirituality" or no. Besides, I was listening for the sub-text, unspoken but acted out, like a psychologist would approach a small child for hints of his true view of the parental roles. Luke, I figured, was telling me he had become impotent with *her*, but was eager to reverse this with *me*.

Time proved this true. Our times together were snatched from corners of a very public life, and whatever work his rejuvenation was, he was always open that he loved me. I was euphoric, and nearly oblivious to the landmines dotting our path. I was in love and my love was returned. There was nothing better, sweeter, more exhilarating than this. I became like a tracking devise for his seminars. If the locale was close enough for day travel, I was there.

Gradually, anxiety did creep in. Was this to be my life, following my love around, staging stolen moments behind his secretary's back? He would have me pay for readings, then refund my money privately when I arrived. This was, equally, exciting and dreadful. But "Project: Restore Potency" was beginning to take effect. And my astrology improved the more I saw Luke. I felt open, light, free.

He had recently moved out-of-state. I felt it would be best I move close by. He said he wanted to begin a school. Perhaps I could just blend in. I asked and he didn't object.

I set out sixties-style, with no thought of money or lodging, confident that some passing car could take me where I wanted to go. I wound up near his home, with a couple who knew him casually. They seemed willing to help me get settled. Then when my "gear" (as they put it) arrived in numerous boxes, my crashing in their small cottage began to look less feasible. They referred me to Morgan, a tall, blond, lanky figure of a guy, who brought me to a local commune where I could stay in exchange for helping out with common tasks.

I was disoriented – this wasn't quite what I expected; but my faith that Luke and I would somehow work this disastrously improbable dilemma out persisted. He even came by for a rendezvous in the woods, the only privacy we could have. I was so happy to see him, it hardly occurred to me how insane it had all become.

The next time I saw Luke, it was seeming obvious a more permanent residence should be found. He referred me to Sandy, who had rented a house on a mountain close by. The house was too large for her alone. We struck up a deal.

It was idyllic at first – long walks in the woods, organic foods, a sprinkling of astrology, endless opportunities to write. I dreamed of beautiful music, my setting of "*Ode to a Nightingale*," the death-haunting of several years ago. It was now set against a kaleidoscope of lights which enriched the sounds in rich, coloristic sweeps. My muse was alive and well or, at least, it *would* be... at some future time. I was never free of that ominous haunting. Death. They would all die and I would live. They would all die, but I would be left to overcome.

The residents of the mountain were included in mysterious Saturday night sessions with the local "channel." Suzanne talked to space beings, or maybe they talked to her. At night, we scoured the sky for strangely-lit objects, and once I hiked up to the top of the peak, where I was told a hidden cave would shelter us in the event of a society-wide cataclysm. Perhaps it was people's nuclear fears that had originally given rise to the so-called survival movement – some far right, some far left, some tuned to their local radios, others to mysteriously-orchestrated cries from outer space. It seemed plausible that some day such a haven might be needed, thus when, a bit later on in life, it was offered as an *imperative*, I didn't entirely flinch.

Then one day, my private trance was shattered. Sandy delivered the *first* bit of bad news. She said she couldn't handle my ongoing tensions about Luke and went to Suzanne. Then Suzanne, the "ethereal space creature," suddenly felt possessed of her civic duty to turn me in. She went right to Luke's secretary, who of course went to Luke's wife.

I was so shaken, I didn't even confront the treacherous twosome. But then it got worse. Luke's wife, it seemed, was *pregnant*. How could she be pregnant? When I first met him, he was impotent. Even now, it was a delicate process. And he was so rarely home. When did this happen?

My life had crashed into the proverbial stone wall. First I could neither eat nor sleep for three days and nights. I wandered through the woods at day, the house at night. All I could do was cry. This man I *did* want to marry. I wanted to spend my whole life with him. This couldn't be happening.

Then one night, all fell calm. I felt an enfolding Presence all around me, gently easing my distress. He spoke in soothing tones. He told me it would be all right. That I needn't fear, I was protected and safe. Who was this Presence? It seemed an angel, even a god. I could move on.

Soon after, I saw Luke at a public meeting. He came right to me, but spoke in low tones. He said he loved me but now there was trouble. His wife had confronted him, and he had simply said, "If it were true, would I tell you?" I felt reassured. She had his baby, but this snippet of his loyalty was mine. He got up to speak and made bad jokes about changing diapers. Then he announced the baby would be a girl, and that he was naming her himself. Even I was slightly aghast: her middle name was the same he said *I* had carried in a past life! There was no reality in *this* place and time. My comforting angel was as real, or more so, than all this. I vowed to proceed on faith.

I don't know how he managed to escape home the very day after Christmas. He told his family he had to go do a past-life regression. For all we know, that was the truth. Whatever was happening here, it was a karma-and-a-half. How had such convoluted, weirdly-timed coincidences even happened? Had I awakened his waning potency only so that on an odd day at home, he had accidentally, late in life, impregnated *her*?

When he showed up, we embraced without a word and made passionate love. We barely mentioned the coming child. He said he "saw me moving back to San Francisco." (What choice was there really?) We left everything in the air as he hurried on home.

It can be said that it is penultimate times that are the worst. Once something is a fait accompli, however great the catastrophe, some tensions are eased. And this still had months to go, as I sunk into despair. I cried, I pretended it didn't happen, I fantasized every manner of reprieve. I played the phrases of this plangent song again and again, desperate that it end on a different cadence. My nervous state was deteriorating and there was no one to whom I could turn. Most of my efforts to reach Luke failed, and our few talks were difficult and strained. The last time we spoke, I said, "I love you," and he said simply, "I know." It was like trying to coax a trapped animal out of his den. He wanted/couldn't, with a tension neither of us could bear.

I had been staying with a married couple in exchange for astrological advise. Their lives were about as stable as mine. Brian was an obsessive compulsive who firmly believed that marriage was a shared experience ~ even forcibly so. If wife liked mustard while husband disliked it, while husband was addicted to peanut butter to the disdain of wife, then both were made to eat their "share" of both peanut-butter-and-jelly, and mustard on their ham sandwiches.

I, too, was a shared find: the household astrologer ~ kind of a nanny to the loose strings of their dissolving marriage. I was supposed to be the best friend of each, even as their hatred for *one another* escalated. When Rosalind set up a secret bank account (secret from *me*, too!) for getaway money, Brian flew into a rage and railed that I was using Venus, Mars and who knows whatever other nefarious ploys to give her better astrological counsel, and if they got divorced, it would all be my fault. I was summarily evicted sans hearing or trial.

I moved into a local hotel. Now I had no home, no bearings at all. After a few weeks, it happened again: my Visitor ~ soothing, comforting, assuring me, as close as the most trusted parent or friend, that everything would be all right.

It was the first time I thought it might actually be *Jesus*. San Francisco was hopping with "Jesus freaks" in those days. I found myself an ad hoc group, led by an aristocratic British lady, with the accompanying pretentious name of Grace Hooper Pettipher. She loved my poetry, and soon took me under her wing. Much in need of parental surrogates, whatever fierce liberties my life had assumed, I pursued Jesus with a passion. I also met Marie, a fellow convert, who offered to take me in, if only I would sleep in the living room with her jungle of plants. I was more than happy to lie down with my new green friends.

I decided perhaps my poetry was not about Luke at all, but about "The Lord," Lord *Jesus*. I could not bear to give up Luke (all the while fearing life had already done that *for* me), but surely there was a greater love, a greater Light in which such paralytic anxieties as mine would be quelled. Perhaps Jesus was my true calling in life.

I don't know what stopped me from the headlong plunge into evangelistic oblivion. I suppose that although wholly attuned to faith, I still would not use it as a club to stupefy reason. Always it was within me to question.

Naturally I chose my new-found mentor as my sounding board. It was Tuesday evening, April 14, 1970. I had to know, I told her. How was it possible that there was *only* Jesus? Jesus was one personage. He lived two thousand years ago. Surely human history was of a much longer origin. And were there not others? Buddha, Moses, Mohammed... What of the Chinese and the Indians? Was there no Savior for them? And *especially*: Why would the Lord permit such terrible things to happen as The Holocaust?

"Ooo—hhh..." The voice dripped downwards, complete with its unspoken "my dear." "Don't you see? The Holocaust *had* to happen. The Jews killed Christ." I hung up the phone, aghast. What was I getting into?

I sat mute as glass, encased within my buzzing, spinning brain. I waited. What respite was this? Then the most astonishing thing happened:

There was an audible voice. It (*he*, actually) spoke directly into my ear. It was low, a bit like a stage whisper, but it was remarkably, distinctly, *audible*: "***April 19th.***" I felt myself (and I use this word simply, but as a total, elegant, unanimous simplicity) *lifted*.

That was Tuesday the 14th. April 19th would be the coming Sunday. My destiny point would be Sunday. I would be totally transformed. I would know why I had journeyed so far, for there the journey would end. I would find it finally. My *life*.

The remainder of the week was serene. No, more. I moved lightly, as if each step, each breath, were the gift of life itself. Those few days I forgot everything ~ that blissful forgetting we are said to have when we *leave* this world, the "Lethewards" of Keats' fever-ecstasy, beyond where death and sorrow cast their pall. Finally it would come. April 19th. Be it Jesus, be it God, be it Love ~ it would finally be there for me.

Marie approached me tentatively on Friday the 17th. She said she had been invited this weekend to see a Native American who was also a healer. Did I want to come? His name was Jim Jones.

II. LIFE RAW AND REAL

"A man who has nothing he is willing to die for isn't fit to live."

Martin Luther King.

VI. My Destiny Point Arrives.

The greatest uncertainties of life are truisms. Like, "You enter this life alone, you leave it alone." The truism is not quite true: You are invariably accompanied by a mother, most often a doctor, and hopefully (though here societal norms fade) by a father. You are perhaps also accompanied by angels, or perchance even a God.

As for leaving, you drift (ascend, sink ~ no one has fashioned this scenario exactly right) into realms so wholly unknown by the masses of mankind, that it is quite presumptuous, at best, to postulate that you are "alone" at all. Perhaps, free of the bonds of earthly flesh, it is then that you are *least* alone, most in harmony with the elements, forces, ay, even personages.

Yet it seems fitting that the entry into my new life, the world of Peoples Temple, was undertaken alone. The companions who invited me had vanished, leaving me to wander into the Black section of town, the Fillmore, on my own.

On my own and sinking. My world was crumbling around me and I was actively seeking a great, inspirational release from problems which though bizarre in their particulars, could only be seen as mundane ~ what passes for "severe romantic complications." If society as a whole had a common case of the flu, perhaps I personally had a touch of pneumonia, but that still would have made me but hospital fodder, not a budding young Saint Joan.

Yet my Visitor had imbued me with such a lightness, I *felt* like one. I knew at least this much: I was not just living life as is. I had waltzed through a parade of roles, of characters, of unthinkingly convoluted scenarios. Yet emerging from it, still sleepy and disoriented, like awakening from an anesthetic or a hypnotic trance, my mast was already hoisted onto a *spirit* of life which had survived the buffets and storms, transcended the hurts and pains, lifted me *already* from the shaky excursions into the deep, upwards now towards the Light, into the Sun. I was in truly terrible shape, a wretched wreck ripe to fold. ...But I was *ready*.

I arrived at 7:30 on Saturday, April 18, 1970. The church seemed only half-lit, matched to its overall crumbling once-elegant facade, like a faded ballroom made hand-me-down as a legacy to poorer, less expectant attendees. Yet what was not lit for kings was lit for angels ~ brightly torched by glorious ascents into song. "God's not dead. He is still alive..." "The blessings are flowing, don't let them stop..." "Behold what manner of man is this, who speaks to the lame and halt? He says thy sins be forgiven thee, take up thy bed and walk..."

They walked, they danced, they testified with a shout. A thousand paeans of praise were megaflames of light. I loved the singing; I love it still. The greatness of a people is their song. The spiritual meter of a people is their song. Always in my heart, when I am back in Peoples Temple, however pressured or chaotic the plight, I sing.

Beside me everyone was Black. The room, dotted with palefaces such as I, was substantially Black. We are usually shocked or startled as doors shut upon us, but now it was a shock of opening. I was singing, clapping, holding hands, rejoicing with these incredibly alive, listening, responding, exultant souls who didn't "happen to be Black," but were so wonderfully, electrically, resonantly Black.

I'll always remember (now, at its start, and later, at its demise, as I wept without respite in that very room, then silenced and eerie calm in doom's wake) the children that day. It was the children's choir that led the preliminaries, in their vibrant checkerboard trademark of black-white-black-white-black-white, a continuous face-by-face integration almost too flowing to be designed. They began to sing, "Brotherhood is our religion, for democracy we stand, we love everybody, we need every hand..."

I cried in awe. This was the "We are the world" childhood I had been fed in tiny, unsatisfying tastes, that I had to know, to see, to be. This was the *real* "man at the door," and surely, he was knocking for me. Jim Jones was still nowhere in sight, but I knew I was *home*.

The spigot of my life had opened, and its water, pure and sweet, poured forth from many tongues. Those who had gone through 'round-the-clock drug rehab, the seniors taken in out of the cold, the young saved from jails, crime, the streets, those whose faith had worn thin as a blade who were now restored to their true, never-before-imagined whole.

But more, so much more than this: the *healings*. The cancers spat up, the crippled raised from their wheelchairs, the cars that swerved out-of-control, totally beyond salvage, while their drivers walked away without a scratch. Blacks said this, whites said this, the young said it, the old said it, the intellectual and the illiterate said it alike, the impoverished, the advantaged, the tutored and the unskilled. What power was in this place? Most, astonishingly, said the healings weren't even what was most important. That what really mattered was the liberation of their minds, and the desire to now give their lives to something greater, more ennobling, than this single life with its variegate ills.

Each one spoke of Pastor Jones. Pastor Jones healed me, Pastor Jones lifted me, Pastor Jones freed me, gave me the hope, the faith, the will to go on. Pastor Jones gave me food and clothing, gave me a college education, gave me a job, a home, a vision for not just me, but for all Mankind. A young Native American woman, overcome with tears, sang Buffy St. Marie's "My Country Tis of My People, You're Dying." Teenage youth gathered in a dance showing violence and redemption in the streets. Little old ladies spoke with clarity and strength, and the young deferred in respect. Drop-outs, dealers and street thieves proclaimed new lives of service.

What was this? A whole community? Right here in America, black and white, young and old, skilled and unskilled, educated and uneducated, from every race, every creed, every faith? Had I truly wandered into this hallowed place in my dream-daze, balancing my way through ecstasy and despair? It seemed I had come in search of a flower and stumbled upon a whole botanical gardens!

Now finally, after all the personal calamities, the dysfunctional family, the shattered ambitions, the looking for love in all the wrong places. Finally now this. I looked at those precious children, in their bold synchro-harmony of black-white-black-white-black-white, and felt suddenly I was in a world anew, where dreams would again be possible, where faith would again be possible, where love would again be possible. I had not yet even laid my eyes upon Jim Jones. I just *knew*.

It was well over an hour before Jim Jones emerged. I was seated in semi-darkness, sandwiched between two aging Black ladies, feeling wholly at home in this foreign land. Jim emerged as we sang, inconspicuously, in a simple black robe ~ calm, silent overseer above the rising din. The singing, now the youth choir, grew more exultant, upbeat, as he stepped noiselessly onstage. Later he stepped onto the podium, as always (I was to observe) never rushed. He waited, watched, surveyed, nodded, acknowledged, gently smiled. There was no surface smile from this one ever, in all those years beginning now. It was a welling from deep within, as though smiles were a form of deep yogic breath. Never only the face smiled; a *being*, radiating life's breath, smiled, like an ever-brightening beam of light. When Jim smiled, the world smiled. When Jim smiled at *you*, your universe brightened. I knew this not only later on, I knew it *now*. I had never met anyone so wholly self-contained yet so wholly radiant as Jim Jones.

My first glimpse of this one who seemed (yes, to the end) only part "man" while part "being" (perhaps like a mythical centaur whose wisdom, to be visible, had to assume a wholly sentient *animal* form), was unerringly calm. As time went on, I saw that services were rarely, if ever, the same, as a genius of innovation resided in our midst. But this presence, even in the wildest swerves of course, was as constant as the ocean waves lapping against the shore. Its outward mode, revelation ("the gift"), never failed to come, like an underpinning buoying us through the storms of life, as we held hands, expectant, in the organ's soft glow. As Jim listened (his ear slightly cocked upwards ~ he, too, it seemed, had his whispering angels, though far more reliable and prolific than mine), the music invariably softened.

He would often first hear a name and call it out. The person identified would stand. Then more details, more details always ~ in floods, in clusters, names, addresses, dates, conditions, incidents from yesterday all the way back to the earliest childhood roots; more names ~ names of grandchildren, of cities, of doctors, of diseases. Punched out again and again, with magnetic force and intent, right, right, again, again, again.

His body came through the thick of it, awakening into the pain of the soul called out, transmuting its way through Jim Jones' own blood and bones. More and more water he drank, to sustain the voices, the impulses, the impressions, the sheer physical drain taken in, transmuted, released. Odd angular motions of the hand, with exclamations of "Now it's gone!" "...*Now* how many fingers do you see?" "Take up your bed and walk!"

Oh, but even more, so much more. The empathy, the compassion. How the very milk of life was poured upon the souls of those most distressed. The incidents recovered from childhood, the hurts and pains, the loss of children, the brute weight of discriminations and cruelties. So much surfaced as not mere fact, but living revelation, as he revealed the very genesis of the heart conditions, the cripplings, the cancers. "Your son died in 1949, and you've never been right since." "They said you would never walk again, but you came to the right place, and you're going to get up and walk today!" People wept as the very keys to their souls were unlocked, and whole, healthy bodies emerged from the debris.

I marvelled at all this and more: the reverence for age, the especial reverence for the silent suffering of the aged, the disabled, the despised, the abused. To be *most* sensitive to the ones noticed the *least*, the ones whom life had passed by, who now, by the gift of pure faith, had found their way here, their pain to be vanquished – pain of the body, pain of the soul alike.

People stood up one by one as their names were called out. They danced and shouted as their ailments were released. "Clear away! Give her room! She's just rejoicing. No one ever gets hurt when they're rejoicing!" And how Jim *knew*. When the time was right and the soul willing and ready, Jim always knew. A little later on, I saw repeatedly, that these powers of "protection" (as he called it) extended far beyond any room a service could contain. For now, I was in awe of the merely visible, the sentient, the celebrated. No (as the song went), I had "never seen a man heal like this man before."

This I saw, all this, even the very first time I saw Jim Jones. And I saw it *each* time. Could I tell you I didn't see it. Or that it later turned out to be false. Or that the man who performed such wonders was some kind of monster, or (and people really think it *worse*) a hypocrite. You might be more settled, more accepting of anything else I might have to say. I simply cannot tell you what I did not see, nor fail to tell you what I did. I witnessed something very powerful and very pure. I witnessed something I could never un-witness or rationalize away. I was, simply, awestruck.

What to call this man? "Behold what manner of man is this, who speaks to the lame and half. He says thy sins be forgiven thee, take up thy bed and walk..." At that point (late, understand, in the history of Peoples Temple, which began some twenty years before), he said he was "a prophet." "How can you hear without a prophet? How can he prophesy lest he be sent?"

A fiery prophet at that. Never did a service pass without pasionate sermons on social issues and current affairs, like a thorough-going research library had been tossed into full play each service. Never did a service pass without vehement pleas for social change, and heartrending defense of the downtrodden and oppressed – Native American woes, South African woes, Chilean woes. Never did a service pass without capitalist greed exposed ("crime in the suites" so it was dubbed), and economic and racial equality extolled.

This very first time, it defied credence. For he *also* knew the Bible, chapter and verse. He spoke the language of Baptists and Pentecostals and Methodists. He was credibly, wholly, of the church. Yet he tore into the *institution* of the church mercilessly. "The most segregated place in America is the church on Sunday morning!" He hadn't a scintilla of patience for "pie in the sky," or a distant Jesus. God must be *alive*. I listened as I heard him preach social revolution to little old Baptist ladies while they would cheer and shout! He spoke the language of the churches and the language of the streets, the language of the heart and the language of the body politic all in one. He preached a living Jesus, who would still endure the scorn as he drove the moneychangers out of the temple. Who would still minister unto the poor and the sick. Who would still *heal.* "Why would Jesus come for them two thousand years ago, and not come for you?"

The mystical and the pragmatic melded as smoothly as the proverbial twin peas in a pod. Our life on Earth uplifted. Heaven brought down here. I saw (or as the religious folk say, "witnessed") the coming heaven on earth. Here, in Peoples Temple, was its seed. "Faith without works is dead." The ongoing litany of church works - "You can see where your money is going." The services given to all who came, the needs met, the 'round the clock counselling, the people who showed up to support you in court, the people who visited you in hospital, the interracial society within the larger, racially *divided* society.

From macrocosms to microcosms. The *family.* Our extended "family" and Jim Jones' own: adopted from every race, save one "home-grown" son, Stephan, a tall, weedlike boy with an intense gaze, and well-chosen middle name of "Gandhi," a tribute to the non-violence which, despite any political activism, was the church's ongoing creed. The Jones' lives had been an ongoing struggle against bigotry and violence, arson and death threats. Jim's wife Marceline, who had gifts of both beauty and compassion beyond compare, was a registered nurse and the soul of dedication.

I learned it all quickly: the family, the church back-ground, the political stands, the elegant, powerful relationships to religion, to the nation, to the community at large. And the constant drumbeat: racial and economic equality, preached, practiced, lived. The effort went on continually with neither rest nor respite, to reach every new person at every service. This in itself was a credo - Jim's vow that whomsoever came would be told "the truth."

From the larger menage, the elect would emerge. "Many are called but few are chosen." Each who was truly his own (how he garnered and discerned, painstakingly, "his own"!) would be told - would have the opportunity to rise to the call. There would be no omissions, no exceptions, no failing of the heart's plangent cry.

Close to midnight, the service was drawing to a close. People were offering their homes for church members to stay. No one would ever stay in a hotel, from Jim on down. "If all of my people can't stay in a hotel, *I* won't stay in a hotel. If all of my people can't eat out, *I* won't eat out." He would never spend a dime on himself. No eating out, no new clothes, no new car, a home in the church's name only. Money wasn't for luxuries, even for amenities. Money was only for the common good. All those years, this was never to change.

That particular night, the eve of my magical April 19th, people were allowed to file by Jim for a moment and take his hand. As I walked by, he said, "Bless you." I said, "Bless *you*." I couldn't properly say I was "impressed." I was electrified. I vowed silently to return the next day for the Sunday service. Sunday ***April 19th***.

The next morning I settled down in the front row of the balcony. I was relaxed considering my drastic frame of mind of late, not only relaxed but transfixed. The very air tingled; I was ready. As Jim listened intently, his "angel" spoke to him a name. "Laura ...Zeffron." Close enough. I shot up. "I'm Laurie Efrein." He stopped and looked up to where I stood. He said very little. Only, "Come to Redwood Valley or write."

An usher came to get my name and address. I asked where was Redwood Valley ~ I wanted to go. She said I could go on the busses when the service was over. Amazed, I agreed to come. Surely, at the least, I knew it was my day.

Redwood Valley was a country community in Mendocino County, a few hours north of the San Francisco. A Sunday evening service was to always follow the weekend downstate, the latter a venture still in the exploratory stage. 1859 Geary Boulevard, the meeting place, was still only a rented hall, not church property. There was a smaller congregation in the Valley, including those who had come out to California in 1965 from Jim's now-abandoned Indiana base. Jim, his family, and a small cadre of followers went off in '62 to found an orphanage in Brazil; now the faithful had moved here. I was amazed at how much church history I could absorb in a gulp. Peoples Temple seemed an open book. The mystery that intrigued me now was only one: was it indeed my now and future home?

The singing and testimonies were briefer on the church's home turf. Everyone was more relaxed. This was an easier entrée for me. Church, understand (*any* church), was unfamiliar ground. I was there for the voices, for Jesus, to fulfill my faith and follow my star. Thus protocol was still not quite easeful. I preferred the magical, the entranced.

As we held hands again in the organ tones' soft glow, Jim looked out upon us, to me, and said, "Oh, this is the young woman who came up from San Francisco.'" I stood. He paused in silent listening. "You need a job and a place to stay," he began. (How did he know that Marie had just kicked me out?) "You came here on faith, and there's a home for you here. We'll find you a place to stay and help you find a job." He asked to have me sign my name on a piece of paper and someone to bring it up front to him. He touched it lightly and said softly, "Yes. You belong here."

Was it to be this simple? The words fumbled towards my mouth, eager yet shy: "I love this place. I want to live here. But I have some karma to complete." (Luke? Was I to choose between, perchance, that pain and this bliss?) He was calm. "Don't worry about your karma." He looked about, as if to locate signposts around the room. "Jack, Patty, Karen, talk to her." Then, as if with a final brush stroke of the cosmic pen, he said, *"You knew this would happen on this date."* No. Was it *his* voice in my ear? Was it he who had dried my tears even in Oregon? I was dumbfounded.

The service ended with Jim easing upon us a brief settling blanket of warmth, familiar even in later, more pressured times: "I love you." An instant later, I moved forwards to the podium, as Jim moved slightly to his right to meet my approach. He looked at me but a moment, his gaze settling levelly into mine, then spoke. *"I was Jesus. I was Lenin. I was The Bab."*

I was startled. A "communist Jesus"? Life had brought me to this? I was, indeed, born of a communist mother, reared in Lenin's shadow; and had only weeks earlier, come to Jesus in my own tentative, off-beat way. And true, false, it was what I had *expected* that day!; if here, in this cross-referenced collage of identities, surreal. It was even I who had told my brief aristocratic mentor that surely Jesus could not be the *only* one. Just days before my startling "April 19th," I had laid out the litany of "successive revelations (Jesus, Moses, Buddha, Mohammed...), the very creed of *Bah'ai*. Bah'ai, the universalist gift of *Persia*, The Bab its revered herald.

Yes, this had a fantastic ...*appeal*. But it wasn't just the content. It was offered without a trace of bravado or push to persuade, merely like a declaration: "You've arrived *here*. It is for you to know *this*." This wasn't the norm, no. It was for *me*.

Not that I could know, here at the start, how both Russia (Lenin) and Persia (The Bab) would, in fact, be *keys* – not just for me, but to "the final exit" on that as-yet inconceivably distant day. How years later, we would be *Russia*-bound when death intervened; and how, no sooner were the bodies buried than *Persia* (i.e. Iran) swung in to dominate the world stage with hostages, jihads, and fundamentalist revenge. "Things just happen," we are told. Do they?

1978 was still a long ways off; yet even then, I sensed some strange, inscrutable "code." Like a Morse code broadcasting the future in advance on my then-treasured, later terrifying "April 19th." Like an apple peeled just a tiny bit so one could begin to see the seeds.

At the least, this was my crossroads, spinning wildly on the proverbial dime. Indeed, pieces of that spinning are still, to this day, completing their thickly-ciphered pirouette. Parts of my world are "Rosetta Stones" even now. We only think we are creatures of chaos. Perhaps we are creatures of cause far more than we know. But this *one* day, it seemed, was the nexus of interlocking worlds.

I made no conscious link then between my Russian alter ego and her own Persian nemesis, husband Andreas, having met him in her twenty-sixth year then, as did I meet Jim Jones now. Much less that it had been my first introduction to (albeit prevented then) *suicide*. How could I have thought such a thing? Was not this budding new utopia in Redwood Valley, bursting with *life*?

Though I, too, shudder. I understand the shudder that my alter-ego had registered at her fated marriage. I understand such shudders at the imperatives of fate. Could I sense whispered echoes of the repressions into which that passionate young woman had been thrust – its seeming irrationality, its driving contradictions fraught at once with fear, mystical pulls, and the wildest yearnings to break free? Undoubtedly not. I was young. I was an *American*. Nay, more – a *Californian* American. With long, wind-swept hair, and poems, and voices in my ear. Such as Russia and Persia surely must have long since dissolved into the past.

Thus did my own strange Russian-Persian legacy resurface across lives. Surely, no one in sunny all-American California could be more Russian-Persian than me, except perhaps this beguilingly serene presence with his all-American name, Jim Jones. Who else could better conjure up a Russian-Persian Jesus than me?!

Even at that, how I flinched at "I was Jesus. I was Lenin. I was the Bab" surely qualified as "the pot calling the kettle black." I blurted out, "I think you're crazy!" Jim responded gently, "Do you think the healings are crazy?" "No. The healings are real." The seesaw inside tipped down into some modicum of balance. "Why" he reasoned, "would the healings be real and this be crazy?" The answer lay between us, expectant but in no way tense, as he directed those in eyesight to take me to the cottage next door to the church to talk. They folded gently around, waiting one respectful moment as Jim offered me, like a precise, measured cadence, *"This is your destiny point."*

"Destiny indeed," says now The God of Tears. What in life do we "choose"? What fateful turns are unrecognized until they are already, unbeknownst, upon us? Can we ever know where and when the snake will, swift as lightning, turn? Lou had vowed that after her Dutchman, she would never marry. Then came the rude shock ~ the one she *had* to marry or have a suicide on her hands. Was my traumatic break with my beloved Dutchman now, to reel me into a new, tragic "marriage" of sorts ~ to infallibly, inexorably be with him, yet never be with him at all ~ nay, worse, to have no say even as to the fate of death?

I found I wholeheartedly craved, yeah, was driven to a threshold that I at one and the same time shuddered to cross. At once I was his, and this "destiny point" was, at long last, mine.

VII. I Set Out on the Rocky Road.

I departed to the cottage next door, accompanied by a sprinkling of "oldtimers," along with newer, younger folk. Some had come from Indiana with the Jones family in 1965; one went back to the founding of Peoples Temple as an integrated church in a racist environment in 1952.

I felt the unspoken weight of their collective history in their mutual cohesion of world view. It seemed both far more visionary and far more insulated than any norm I had encountered to date, like a sculptor had molded a unique art work in mysterious duplicate. Yet the passions generated from each were no mimic, but grounded in hands-on experience. These were workers, pragmatists. They had perhaps taken a world on faith, but had labored long, each one, to make it their own.

Had I expected to discuss the fine points of clairvoyance, short shrift was made of my plan. These folk were more rough-hewn than I had expected. Metaphysics (the word was not even used) was a special reality inhabited only by Jim Jones, and with no other focus, parameter, or source. Jim had "the gift" – no one else was needed, wanted, or credited in that realm.

The rest was pure humanitarian pragmatism. These were no California dreamers – everything was pinned down to a cause, a direction, a goal, made real through actions, deeds and results. Part of me might be on another planet, but whatever part *they* could access, was being squared off in parcels addressed to Mother Earth.

Patty and Jack, both in their forties, had been around "forever," and (I later learned) had witnessed any miracle one might conceive, but it wasn't broached. Somewhat to my surprise, though not my comfort, they were more interested in how I related to the world. Karen was equally fixated on starving children, but more moony-eyed, with a soft, slightly raspy voice and a slight pleading in her tone. Jim (a different "Jim") was straight-talking and direct, and seemed less overbearing than the others. He turned out to be my first new friend.

I came to know these people well as co-workers, so it does neither them nor me justice to present them in a cardboard box with fixed flaps, slogans or labels. The schisms between my inner reality and my overt responses at this still-early stage, was more a reflection of my own spaced-out wandering into this 100% familiar/foreign world. *God* seemed to know I belonged, but the visible, sentient "I" seemed cast as an observer. I have difficulty remembering in that I probably absorbed little of what they said. I remember best that even as distraught as I was about Luke, my heart was serene and sure with Jim, but awkward and lost for words with these salespeople.

A subtle undercurrent (I was told later on, though jokingly) was their own discomfort, in that they had no conviction that I, a wraith-like creature at the time, rail-thin with waist-length hair and hippie attire, should be there at all, but had acted solely on Jim's certainty that I belonged. Indeed, I would have settled in Redwood Valley if I had been talked to all night or not talked to at all. I was already converted. But in my discomfort with the welcoming committee, I do recall sensing that shifting into gear could be an unexpectedly bumpy ride.

A shift it indeed was. The subtle compass guiding my steps had now hit a new energy field with its own compelling laws. Anything I had considered a strong suit seemed weak and powerless in this new frequency. My inquiries into the possible future of my poetry was tentative, and quickly, if gently, crushed. Of what value was a poem to a starving child? Astrology? Jim knew everything before it happened. I didn't dare bring up my romantic disaster ~ it seemed so peculiarly personal and not at all the subject of the day.

Even how I had arrived was deemed irrelevant. I "heard voices"? Be this so, their origin implied no special gift for *me*. The author was Jim Jones.

Jim was everywhere, with everyone, and certainly here with the five or six of us. There wasn't a thing I heard about him that didn't impress me ~ aye, impress me favorably. But I suddenly felt as alone and adrift, as I had felt delivered into the very hands of God just before I arrived. I was in the one context I had spent my entire life countering: a context of *consensus*. Bad consensus, good consensus, even impeccably good consensus, I was unsure I could adjust.

I'm unsure even now how I did. Regimentation, however benevolently conceived, had never been my style. I had just never seen a place like this ~ a step into the future not just for me, but for everyone. America needed this place, and if I were called, I would come. It was like the decision had already been made, and the details, the demands, almost didn't matter. Today; no, days before; no, months before; no, it seemed *always* before, this one step was a *fait accompli*.

So I listened intently to whole litanies of persuaders, familiarizers, assurances, blended in with a dollop of seeming certainties: Jim knew the trials and troubles of each one. Jim was always there, an omnipresent force to heal or to reverse danger, illness, even accidents miles away; ever rescuing youths from lives of crime or drugs. Because of him the elderly were cared for, the hungry fed, the abused taken in. Jim Jones stood for justice in the face of arson and death threats. It was overwhelming, what one sole being could do. In urgent, perennial concern, he was reaching out everywhere to everyone. He was doing what people needed. He was doing what society needed. He was doing *what no one else could*.

Understandably, I hesitate to mention the common denominator of absolute faith in that room, so cynically plagued is the culture at large on the subject of charismatic leaders! Yet, had I viewed this as a dilemma (my greater dilemma seemed how to fit in *socially*), I could still recognize, quite on my own, that the capacities I had witnessed were legend. I needed no convincing, though I realize, in looking back, that I had little idea of how such an extraordinary force could pervade ordinary lives, or the depth of the oft-sounded dictum, "To whom much is given, much is required." I was still something of a guest. Once I was welcomed in, I'd have plenty of time to learn.

I told Patty, Jack, Karen and Jim ("J.R.") that I had to settle some matters in the city. J.R. gave me his phone number. He said if I came to live, he would drive down to the city to pick me up.

I was by now staying in a hotel in downtown San Francisco, a rather cheap one, but livable. I had no one to consult on this momentous transition, save perhaps, the waning Grace Hooper Pettipher. That week, I went to a meeting of hers in the home of well-to-do parishioners in the suburbs. I asked her, "Jesus was from the Middle East. Wasn't he dark-skinned?" "Ooohhhh~....." (again the drippy downslide). "Jesus could *configure* himself in any color. But" ~ her face now beamed a self-satisfied school marm's smile~ "he was a being of the purest white-gold." I might as well have asked her, "Would you like to slam the door on me now?," and she had responded, "Ooohhh... Yes, let's slam the door quickly." My great find had turned to ashes in a single phrase.

My only other thought (or perhaps torment) was of Luke, whom I could not even reach. But you know how *children* think. The parent who is there is the one who will influence. My need for guidance, childlike in this respect, had hit critical mass. Jim was there. Luke wasn't. The "knock on the door" had come so explicitly, unmistakably, that though I still lingered at the earth quaking beneath my heels, the door ahead opened silent and sure, seemingly as an act of mercy. Maybe I could go to my new home and then, should the other situation break, receive a dual blessing. Fate was leading me north. How could I refuse?

I did just one strange thing that last week on my own. I went to the city library for a trip through the copious stacks. Maybe some hidden secret about my "former self" might decipher the conflicting, seemingly irreconcilable pulls.

I found a new biography of Lou Andreas-Salome. I remember opening it at random, to a photograph. I nearly gasped. It was Luke. I mean, it was *his face in exact duplicate*. Who was this man? I trembled as I read the accompanying tale. The man's name was Tausk. He had been a disciple of Freud's at the time he and Lou met. They had a passionate affair which she broke off, leaving him distraught. On the eve of his wedding to someone else, he ended his life with a bullet through the right temple. (Just as, later on, Jim Jones would meet his fate? **Yes**.)

He suicided out then? He was forced to care for an incoming life (i.e. *the opposite*) now? Did life truly extort such manner of recompense?

And was *I* not forced away, too? By Jim Jones, who told me of Persia. With me the same age as when the other, fierce Persian fell upon his knife to force a marriage. Could junctures as weird, singular, compelling as that, actually *repeat*? Had I no "choice" at all?

All these patterns. It seemed like any one of them could mean something or nothing, but *clusters* were like some weird cosmic Lotto with a jackpot nobody wanted. They swirled through far-flung geographies and centuries of time, all while my course ahead seemed *prescribed* for me. It whirled before my eyes like a headlong, out-of- control VCR ~ rewind, fast forward, kaleidoscopic, blink-of-the-eye. It had indelibly imprinted my fate, then vanished. This tiny, precious window into which the light of my life would swirl, then cast its beam... where?

The steps just ahead were all I could commandeer at this turning point extraordinaire of my life. *This decision must be made.*

By Thursday, I was back in touch with J.R. He would pick me up the following Sunday. We would be back in time for the Sunday service. As defeated as I was exhilarated, and vice versa, I would be taken to my new home.

With whom I would live seemed to be the luck of the draw (ha!), though even you may not believe that fiction by now. An announcement at the end of the Sunday service yielded a volunteer named Judy. She was the sister of Karen Layton, one of my earliest indoctrinators.

"Orientation," it was called. Indeed, the job fell to a small cluster of three women that were inherently more amiliar to me than the others. So it was not by chance, but a true early anchoring point, that my orientation fell to these three. The triumvirate of women who took me under their wing were Karen and Carolyn Layton, the first two, and Linda Amos, later called "Sharon."

They seemed an unlikely trio: Linda a short, moon-faced Jewish lady whose marshmallow exterior belied a brusque efficiency and a social worker's instinct for provoking consensus; somber, reserved Carolyn, slight and thin, ever terse but vehement in defense of the master; Karen with wisps of sandy hair, peach-pale skin, yet her soft and raspy pleas quick and sure. Yet circumstances had coalesced them into a kind of sorority wholly dedicated to proselytizing the cause.

More notably, all three, some eight-and-a-half years later on, had unique roles within the Jonestown Tragedy, all with regards to children. Neither Carolyn nor Karen were mothers at this early date; moreover, expected to *never* be. Every social rationale was employed to encourage people to adopt children rather than have their own, and in any case, these two were too preoccupied to contemplate motherhood. Linda had three children, all conceived prior to her entry into Peoples Temple, yet she had wholly placed their fate in Jim Jones' hands.

Yet Carolyn and Karen, unbeknownst at the time, both had destinies involving motherhood. Carolyn later became the mother of the younger of Jim's two out-of-wedlock sons. Kimo died with her at Jonestown. Karen was pregnant when she died at Jonestown - a clue, perhaps, to her identity in a far more ancient scenario.

Linda(Sharon)'s circumstances at the time of the tragedy were far less comprehensible. She was in Georgetown, Guyana's capital, at the time. She was with her three children, two of them quite young. When she learned of the suicides over the ham radio, she cut the throats of her two younger children, then herself. Her older daughter, Liane, did the same.

Sharon's situation is too charged to breach at this early point. Obviously, she had the option (most would say *responsibility*) to live, and her young children's fate was incomprehensible. Carolyn and Karen (mother and mother-to-be, by then) were also caught in the weave of fate, in that both were "Layton's." They were, respectively, the first and second wife of Larry Layton, whose lone shooting at the Port Kaituma Airport was a fatal prod to the suicides.

So by accident or design, I was, in those earliest days, face-to-face with three of the most singular fates by the time of Peoples Temple's demise. Beginning points do unravel stories of their own, and even back then, I was struck by the perpetual urgency which characterized these three - a propensity for ultimates, and the conviction that in bringing about the best for others, one might anticipate the worst for oneself. (The very Master's philosophy? Too much so, I fear.)

I quickly discovered that Peoples Temple, though ofttimes a joyful, even ecstatic place, had a more normative reality of sacrifice the closer one progressed towards the core. Jim's own declaration, *"So long as one person on Earth is not free, then I am not free"* was, for him, a reality to be actualized at any cost. Thus the early cautions, even pleas, not to drain his energy, not to expect personal revelations, to create no dissension, to look to authority, and to work on projects, which were in plentiful supply. To expect, much less demand, for oneself, was to potentially diminish the source of supply for others.

I received frequent doses of all this early on. These three peculiarly fell to me, and marked me indelibly from the start. In fact, except for services, I saw little of Jim at all. At times life seemed a morass of intermediaries, like a Catholic priest might insist on being, if not God, *authority*. I am not a Catholic, and I think, for that reason alone, might do poorly at it! But it seemed to be my lot. I was to learn my heart of dedication from Jim Jones as we went along, but my early catechisms from these three.

VIII. "And All That Believed Were Together..."

This christening was fierce ~ a psychological cauldron of not just new rules, but new paradigms of reality ~ some exhilarating, others terrifying, and against which my own more personal terrors were shamed into a lesser, hidden role. How could I put myself above all this? No one cared anyway. Whatever anguished baggage I had carried into Peoples Temple, and for all the interminable counselling, there was little help for fare as "trivial" as lost loves, lost careers, or the wounds from childhood that had never healed. I was up against a stone wall. I could only grit my teeth and dig in.

I devoted myself to learning about what Peoples Temple *was* (a mere church? Never!), and how great were our lengths to blend into, even enhance, a small rural community. We belonged to the conservative denomination of The Disciples of Christ. Jim was a registered Republican, and took on maximum civic as well as church duties: a post as schoolteacher, foreman of the Grand Jury, do-gooder for every local charity, police drive, youth program, civic campaign. In Indianapolis he had headed the Mayor's Commission on Human Rights; in San Francisco later on, it was head of the Housing Commission. Praise poured in from every quarter, ever deflecting the more controversial stands on race and class.

But was it enough? Jim, much as he extolled our local triumphs, seemed to see it as treading water. That we would only be accepted to the degree we tried harder ~ nay, set a sterling example for others. Aware that the local community (a very *non*-communal place) was wont to see us as wolves in sheep's clothing, we had to walk the extra mile: responsible jobs, conservative dress, clean-cropped hair, the ones who supported the locals when they took worthy or humane stands. Who told the local grocery "Pastor Jones told me to shop here." The good samaritans, the helpful neighbors, the willing friends. There wasn't a picnic ground that wasn't left cleaner than when we arrived, or an opportunity passed up to write the city council about a job well done.

Beneath the surface, of course, were more demanding rigors. Our America of good neighbors steeply trespassed the norm: barriers of race, class and social status virtually dissolved. Even bonds of family were derailed when those units became knots of self-centered concern. *Jesus* said to leave father and mother and take up your Cross and follow Me. He ministered to all, *"even unto the least of these."* Your own child should be no more important than another's. A white child should be no more important than a black one. If you wanted children, it was better to adopt, so many children already needing care. Moreover, it was drummed in, this way was working. It was producing happy children, productive adults, of service to one another and to the community.

Norms were trespassed in other ways as well. No one wanted a minister who could heal *like Jesus.* Especially one who wasn't *creditting* Jesus, but more and more, emerged as, himself, "a living God." I was easily impassioned on this point myself. Why worship a dead God? Any God who cared would be there uplifting the flock, doing the work himself.

Nor did anyone want a minister who had persuaded his flock to live like the early apostles, a model of economic equality. Oft-quoted was the earliest communal creed from Acts of the Apostles: **"And all that believed were together and had all things common: And sold their possessions and goods, and parted them to all men, as every man had need."** *(Acts 2:44-45.)* We may have been laudable in every way. But for those who didn't have it in their hearts (or their pocketbooks!) to practice such a living Christianity, we could only constitute a threat.

Jim, cannily aware that people will rarely sacrifice without return, made it worth their while. For those who would not sacrifice from the heart, their motivation could be belief. To the fundamentalists, this was an Apostolic Christian community. To the politically inclined, "the system" exposed and higher ideals sought. To the pragmatist, a way to keep society free of poverty, hunger, medical neglect, racism and crime. To the lonely, to the aged, to every kind of underprivileged or despised minority, it was a paradise of activities and friends.

As the reality of cherished longings sprung to life *in practice*, dissent dissolved. Why would you want to challenge what was being so remarkably *lived?* And as Jim was pushed to the limit and beyond, one's own rationales for holding back energy, time, money, dissolved as well. Society "out there" was such a mess. How could one not support this? How could one not support it *fully?* No fraud nor deception here ~ merely zealotry! Only gradually (like rivers flooding into our souls, nourishing, nurturing, never a thought to drown) did giving all become the *basis* of our reality, snowballing into an ethic of its own. The Bible was "out," but with the stingy or ill-motivated, it could just as well be "in." Look at what happened to those who in early Apostolic days, withheld *anything*. You know, the ones who "dropped dead." Paul the despot and the like. Trial by jury wasn't exactly the fashion back then.

Not to mention the coercive powers of *guilt* at holding back. The cause flowed like water, like a river, like a stream, ceaselessly, for *everyone*. How could you be the one to deny others life? We barely even noticed as the waters flowed in here, there, everywhere. Only gradually did giving all come to mean *all* -- all one's resources, all one's loyalty, all one's privacy, all one's control over one's own life.

But what power did we have on our own anyway? Were we not, globally, by the millions, lulled into a kind of powerlessness *anyway*? The common culture was deadening. The commercial culture was deadening. The insensitivity to human needs was deadening. Materiality, selfishness, the barriers between people based upon bigotry, or merely diversity, was deadening. Why not gravitate towards life?

Thus was I thrust headlong into an extraordinary paradigm through the presence of someone who embraced it as his own. As he identified with all, I too identifed with him. I too was Black. I too stood raw in the face of nuclear reality. I too acknowledged hunger with every morsel of downed food. I too acknowledged poverty with every last donated piece of change.

At first, the nuclear stuff was the most difficult, despite that it later waned in focus. Jim, his immediate family, and a small core of followers had arrived from Indianapolis in 1965. The church had established an orphanage in Brazil, and discovered upon return to Indiana, that the substitute pastor had embezzled the church funds, so Jim and the others went West.

But there was more. It was claimed that Redwood Valley was chosen by revelation. There were hidden locales, cave-like structures, ideal for refuge against a cataclysm which was said to be prophesied for 3:09 on the 16th of some unknown month on some unknown future date. Jack, Archie and others, had been taken to the caves by Jim. Meanwhile, members were storing water, an ointment called bacitracin for radiation burns, and eating regular portions of food Jim recommended to minimize nuclear damage, namely soybeans, sunflower seeds, and pork liver.

I was a vegetarian at the time and found the mere mention of pork liver revolting. Linda, after convincing me that all of humanity had a suppressed fear of nuclear war, but that we, above all people, stood raw against the wind, finally persuaded me to that terrible crossing of the line: chomping down into a hamburger. She said that in any case I was way too thin ("You looked like a concentration camp victim"), and that beef would be the remedy of choice. .I do recall that aside from my exhilaration at the healings, and the serenity of Jim's presence, I was still drastically unhappy – even, in stretches, distraught. So whether or not I chomped into a hamburger, or even chopped off my long stringy hair into some unflattering bob, it was, in context, no major sacrifice. But nuclear reality, indeed any number of other "realities," was a systemic shock. We could die catastrophically. We could be victims of genocide – even the whites, who identified as Black. We could be felled for our burgeoning socialist stance. Indeed, it seemed only being nestled in "Redneck Valley" that inhibited that from bursting forth earlier, awaiting our later move to more cosmopolitan San Francisco.

Ever present was danger. Yet everywhere too was its silent, pervasive companion, *protection*. Aside from the healings and protection from danger, there were also politically protective moves. Jim was a registered Republican – though honestly, he could persuade anyone he was *anywhere*, appealing seamlessly to those of like mind and unlike mind alike. His capacity to meet people on common ground and speak their language without in any way compromising his own inner intent, was legend.

Certainly, he would take a principled arch-conservative over a mealy-mouthed or two-faced liberal (Jesus' "Hot or cold I would have you, but lukewarm I will spew out of my mouth," was the going quote). He did care if people stood on self-interest rather than principle, or were bigots, or sacrificed innocents for their own gain. Ultimately, sheer justice was the avenger, with Jim Jones as purist, even while swimming through masses of human complexity, which were at times misjudged, but rarely averred.

In any case, endless hours were spent on the phone, chatting with this one, praising this, persuading that. Once Jim told us of time spent bargaining down the price of some property he wanted for the church. He continually maintained a disinterest in the property. It was simply woven into strands of conversations about other things. Without ever being aggressive, or proclaiming his desire for the prize, it was worked down to some unthinkably low price by the sheer attrition of its surfacing again and again, sinking slightly lower in price each time.

Back then, Jim could still converse patiently with people he inherently distrusted, letting nary a ripple of discord surface. He was motivated by the compass of instinct rather than by words. You would be steered like a ship through the sea. It was frequently, even awesomely, done en masse, speaking successively to this one or that, identifying no one by name, but each in turn would get the message directed at them. He often said that if you don't get it, you don't need to know. The political gifts of this one rivalled even his spiritual ones in dimension.

As for me, I wanted only to do more, even with my life such a mess those early days. It was a relief to take part in a community, as having a *personal* life had become a torture. So I limped through the hoops best I could. I forced my way through workdays, showed up for orientation, was enthusiastic about services, and joined the choir. Soon if I had to find my way back to my former life, I could not have done it.

Yet my life still seemed drowned in a self-perpetuating misery, like a refugee who could not free herself of memories of war. At first, mere functioning was far from insured. I was "in no condition to work," but was made to persist. I was fired from my first job, a clerical position, for being too distracted to handle simple chores. Next a shortlived waitressing disaster. Then a short stint as a nurse's aide in the local convalescent hospital at the going minimum wage of $1.65 an hour.

Finally came an opening in the welfare department. I was coached about the mentality of the locals, to never mention the church, a conservative wardrobe of second-hand clothes was hastily assembled, and I was sent in to present my credentials. Unthinkably, I was hired.

I juggled my various personas. I was distraught privately, but learned all the mannerisms of repression. I made myself act joyful at mention of the college students, while I still felt devastated by my own college past. I clapped and sang at the children's song that had so stirred me at first, "Brotherhood Is Our Religion," with its "We love everybody, we need every hand," yet I felt *un*-loved and too needy myself to be valued by others.

I comforted myself with the cosmic allure of the healings and the mysterious lure of a fascinating secret club, letting others prescribe the monotony of the mundane. Things happened at prescribable, routine times, with a clear chain of command. Anything that tinged of the personal was so dissuaded as mere ego, or a drain on the leader, that my life was no longer my own, anyway. Linda openly encouraged this ~ to know that our lives now belonged to the cause, not to us.

Of course I'd have told you at the time (and sincerely!), that I *chose* this. I see now that I "chose" it as a religious fanatic would choose to worship. And how it drove me, ultimately, to every personal limit! What an education! I discovered that what was strong was strong, what was vulnerable was vulnerable. What was weak, greatly suffered.

Sometimes we encounter such crossroads, such teachers, such circumstances. And we learn what we need to learn. Yet all the while, my stability and self-esteem were at a disastrous low. Everything in me longed to draw strength from a dominant male. Thus was I not only detrimented, but ultimately devastated, before all was said and done.

We can look at *children* and see in their most unself-conscious responses, the problems they will face if corrections are not made. I sometimes feel that could I have seen myself objectively, I might have also seen what was likely to happen, wonders and terrors alike. At the time, I had no luxury of objectivity, barely handling the demands of conformity. My life, now given to service, was an empty vessel to be filled with tasks. Nothing I had felt or done before was applicable.

So did I repress my more creative bents as self-indulgent, even harmful to the common good. Surely nothing I might create with my mind could rival this monumental practical work, or the ongoing sacrifices of our leader. I wanted so to believe this, even if only to soothe that one area of pain which never seemed to heal. It was one thing I never did believe, as hopeless as trying to force a size 9 foot into a size 6 shoe ~ but how I tried!

The church also began making use of me. Having been found to be unsuitable for churchlike activities like bake sales, flea markets and blood drives, I volunteered to tutor the Buckley children, a family of eight from the deep South. I helped with the children's choir, and learned how to greet newcomers. I stayed up nights writing letters to officials, some in protest, some in praise. Sometimes I would participate in the round-the-clock drug rehab shifts for withdrawing heroin addicts. There was always work needing to be done.

Remarkably, after several months, I was still in the state in which I had arrived: partly in awe, partly adrift! I just had somewhat better standing: I was about *proving* myself.

IX. My Place, Albeit a Shaky One.

My personal contact with Jim was minimal. Once in a service, he pleaded for funds to help a child – indeed, shamed people over withholding money they were only going to waste. I had left my wallet at home, and felt badly for the little girl. The next time we audited Jim's class at night school, I approached him with $10, saying I didn't have my wallet at church. A faint smile tinged his lips. He realized I wasn't trying to impress him, only to help. He spoke in a gentle stride, "I wasn't talking about you." "Oh," I stumbled. "I don't handle the money anyway." He directed me to a short, aging man in the back of the room. "See Jim Pugh. His wife Eva is the Treasurer."

Another time, I approached him briefly about nothing getting better. His response was brief. A simple, "Write me." I dutifully sat down and wrote out the whole disaster about Luke and the still-due child. I never felt I merited his attention in public, so I just sealed it in an envelope, addressed it, affixed a stamp, and off it went in the postbox. Jim never said anything. He handled things in time, would the patient soul only wait. My time would come, just not yet.

I remember Jim approaching me only once those early months, when the summer of 1970 had just begun to wane. It was the break between mid-day and evening services. I was my usual repressed and underfunctioning self. I was just outside the church door, having nearly shrunk into a rustic wooden pillar shading the entrance. He came over and asked how I was. I could barely eke out, "I'm depressed." His gentle and buoyant remark startled me: "Why should you be depressed? You have so much to offer." It puzzled, yet almost thrilled me. I could offer something. It wasn't quite the same as getting what I wanted, even craved in life. But this was good: to offer.

Still, the transition was slow. Then one Sunday, I was allowed to play the organ during a Sunday service. I was a pianist, not an organist, and could barely manage the stops. But I had Bach in my corner – the same Well-Tempered Clavier I had lovingly, if laboriously, practiced my last stretch in school.

It was music I loved. I sunk into the Preludes, forgetting I was not alone. Jim let me play for what seemed like a long stretch. Then we held hands, as always, going into the healing service, and he began to speak to me. It was the first time he had called me out since April 19th.

I stood. To my amazement, he identified me as an *astrologer* - verboten at best. He said I had a bit of a following and had done astrological work for a doctor in Toronto. I went blank. I had never been to Toronto, nor done work for anyone there.

He had been gazing off somewhere - common for "revelation." When he saw my puzzlement, he went inside, then surfaced, "Oh, that must be *the future*." (Oh? The *"very"* future? It turned out to be 1989!). Remember this odd point, the first link in a set of such clues. But I wasn't supposed to be an astrologer at all, was I? Not around Jim Jones. Nor was there supposed to be a "future" for that. This was a strange breed of faux pas indeed. This and others returned to haunt me many times.

He made some passing reference to my lost love. It was oblique enough not to embarrass me or throw me into tears. Then he said of the man whose own appeal to me was gifts for healing and psychic work, "Gifts and calling are no proof of character."

This was no comment on romance. Nor was it quite a slam on my lost love. It was a *measure*. Where will you find the highest character - all that could matter in the end. He counted upon my own value system, by now carefully trained, to value his character above Luke's. Whose character could compare to Jim Jones'?

I overreacted a bit, but it took the bait enough to serve: "He's a charlatan?" I looked up hesitantly for a response. He looked back, saying nothing, the proverbial pregnant pause. His eyebrows raised ever so slightly, as his chin nodded slightly down. This was, it seemed... an *acknowledgment* - explicit enough to serve, yet free from the tangles of offering specific proof.

I could not bear to solicit more definitive answers. A reality began closing in on me. Not the reality of what he said, for he had said *nothing*. I was a flower about to bloom, weather permitting. Now I was given the grace of a silent retreat to a bud-like state, perhaps a vulnerable young woman invited to be, again, a protected child. If I had misassessed, and cast my youthful energy into an unworthy romantic net, now I could gently escape its snare. From that day forth, I was finally free of Luke. And the subtle stigma of belonging nowhere was lifted.

Indeed, I was about to discover my new work. I had always loved to write, a habit acquired within a family I felt never understood me, to whom I could not *speak*. The written word poured from me as the spoken word could not.

I discovered Jim Pugh's function by chance. When I had approached Jim to donate money for the little girl and he sent me to Jim Pugh. I discovered that the Pughs were the ones to see about tithing, too. I began to tithe, and learned that Jim Pugh was the one answering the letters addressed to "Pastor Jones," at that time a small-scale operation.

I volunteered to help. I received a packet of letters each visit, that had been first reviewed by Jim, who scrawled comments on the envelopes. I could embellish a bit ~ write notes of encouragement, or suggest people come to services, or tell a bit about the work.

It seemed the only outlet for my restless mind in this still overwhelming place. I wasn't social ~ it wasn't natural for me to banter or network, or make decisions with people looking on. But letter-writing, in seclusion, my mind to the mind of the correspondent, with the inspired scrawls of Jim Jones himself the intervening catalyst, seemed wonderful. I took to it with a passion.

I would work during the day, by then in the welfare department, under Linda's watchful eye. (As luck had it, that was her employer, too!) Night was consumed with services, meetings, special projects ...or writing. Over the weekend, I could write a hundred letters at a stretch. Jim encouraged this, praising me publicly and locating a more suitable place for me to live, with needed privacy for the work. For me, it was part escape, part immersion. It was a link between me and the people who came to Jim Jones for transformation in their lives. I could be close to them all without ever having to chance the more risky world of personal contact.

My more socialized contacts came in becoming a greeter for the first-time attendees. The miracles were... well, miraculous, but occasionally threatening to skeptical types. The teachings were politically controversial, and the mix of Apostolic Christianity, socialism, and black power rhetoric (though minus the violence, which we scrupulously averred) was volatile. And even in those relatively early days, Jim was revered.

It wasn't a scene that someone just walking in could necessarily relate to. Jim would let loose with impassioned commentaries against the establishment, for racial and economic equality, and in defense of a wide range of causes every service. He felt *responsible* to impart this, called in total "the truth," to every person who arrived. They could embrace it or, perchance, reject it, or simply walk away. But they would know that in a corrupt society there was a better way, a place where not only Blacks were the equal of anyone, but where each senior was treasured, where children were loved, where the homeless were sheltered, the hungry fed. And with no preacher-man ripping off your money. All the money was for the people. You could see where it went. ...*And you could.*

At the same time, he would not only lift people's spirits, but have them in stitches laughing. The contradictions of the Bible were made hilarious – like telling "women to keep silent in the churches," and its preposterous ramifications, like the churches shutting down!

The churches were continual targets, of ridicule, derision, and passionate attack. How the preachers would select and choose from "the book," and disregard the rest. And how no one would preach, "Sell all you have and give it to the poor, and take up your cross and follow Me." More often, they themselves were living "high on the hog."

Sometimes the Bible would be thrown to the floor, daring God to strike him dead. Peoples Temple was a place where one's straitlaced church-filled mind could be freed from a bible mistranslated then re-arranged for the benefit of avaricious preachers and their flocks. "There are holes in my shoes." He would lift up his feet for people to see, then be irritated when fifty people would donate shoes to impress him, but out of the limelight, cared nothing about giving with no thought of reward.

This was not easy to greet people into! But I watched others and absorbed the routine, even a touch of its author's zeal. I was still nervous, insecure, a touch too eager to please. But life began to normalize. I cried less often, and could concentrate slightly better on the tasks at hand.

Linda was my overseer, however slight the problem. It seemed part help, part obstruction, but she was so damn sure of everything, and I hardly felt in a position to bargain. Between her as ever-present "mother-smother," and Jim as "distant father," it became a deadly brew. (How *did* I manage to re-create that scenario? Probably, I only realized far into the future, this home was simply too much like ...*home*.) I might have told Jim earlier than I did, and more gracefully (it was a horrible scene when I finally insisted on no more Linda), but I, ever a rebel before, did not want to rebel against *him*, who had installed her to break in the greenhorns.

For Jim's part, Linda was touted as "our most dedicated person." She left her children with others less high-profile, considered to be a sacrifice, though I wasn't sure the kids were the worse off. She was a confirmed disciplinarian, saying that children who cried should be spanked until they stopped. Once Jim told us that there was no medical evidence that infants needed to cry. I saw Linda's mark all over that one. Regrettably, her counsel was valued as a psychologist, though she held no degree in the subject.

What she was was persuasive, bedrock, convinced. Let people air their doubts, but only to hear the appropriate organizational response. We learned not to be "negative" because of the risks of "contagion." Soon we stopped talking to *each other*.

Meanwhile, we readily took on new habits, mostly austere, for did not our leader sacrifice everything for the common good? He even insisted on teaching until the Church Board insisted that he be pastor full-time, in his case "pastor to the world." We, too, became "citizens of the world," in unison. Wasting food was a crime with so much of the world starving. People with colds wore facial masks to protect others. No adult was ever ahead of a senior or a child on a food line. Everyone had to vote, to be a good citizen. This was all part of what Peoples Temple was – kind of an in-house conscience for humanity. You carried it with you wherever you may go.

We were flabbergasted years later on, to be called victims of sleep deprivation. We did sleep little compared with other folk. But there was always work to be done, and who to do it but us? Who would deprive someone of sleep simply to enslave them? Preposterous. I suppose we just let the world do our sleeping *for* us. How could the world be in such crisis and we sleep?

Ours was the role model for a new world. There was a side of Jim Jones that could even leave it at that. "If we only help a few seniors and children, it would all be worth it." This was sincere, although the context of such statements, and their depth, gradually seared into the psyche far more than their seemingly neutral, benign character would suggest. For something in Jim always expected not only opposition, but persecution, nay, even unto death, and he wanted the *humanity* of Peoples Temple to endure, however we were painted in the public eye. So we dutifully did everything. And over-did. And over-did.

Our reward? "You're the best people on Earth," we were often told, even though I think one would best *tell* people that if you want them to *give* their best. Lest we needed more incentives, all bases were covered. Material ones ("Life will be better for everyone"). Physical ones ("You will be protected against illness, accident or harm"). Spiritual ones ("I will be with you always, even unto the ends of the Earth"). Emotional ones ("I will be your friend, your brother, your father, even your Saviour, whatever you need").

These were played like the strings of a violin so adeptly, that cynics were wont to see it as cynical and idealists marvelled at its all-inclusive thrust. We heard more than once Jesus' *"He who is not against me is on my part,"* and Jim Jones steered many a ship through adversity on that mast, as conflicts and adversities dissolved.

Periodically we would shift gears, require more. Sometimes it was just time to clean house – to sweep out those who didn't "get it": "If you can't take the heat, get out of the kitchen!" The methods could be harsh, like a verbal brillo. But who could not trust the master helmsman? He was always there to resolve even the smallest personal gripe. Whatever the conflict, the model in the early days was angry or hurt people reconciled, hugging and kissing with smiles and tears.

Everything I saw seemed benevolent. What I wrestled with was giving all, not because I didn't believe this a higher calling, but because I seemed barred from working at anything for which I was *gifted*. I didn't understand why dedication to the cause entailed giving up not merely time, energy or money, but pieces of *myself*.

Had I been whole inside, I undoubtedly would have drawn lines. But I was already shattered by my failures at home, at school, at life. I longed for a wholeness I could not create of my own self. Here, every day was living miracles; so I felt not only troubled and confused, but somehow *trivial* compared to all this.

The more I bore witness to the healings, the more I acclimated myself to the precepts and demands of absolute faith. I almost longed for it. For if it were absolutely so, then I could live with any sacrifice, and the doubts could finally vanish, in their place emerging self-conscious sacrifice.

Indeed, had not my thirst to create stemmed from my desire for transcendence? Maybe this ultimate transcendence, universal rather than personal, was what I had always sought. Maybe it would free me of what seemed a pariah of anyway – personal creativity. Nothing, in its achievement, was more blissful. Yet nothing in its blockage had been more agonizing. My whole college career, and how it had come to a screeching halt, was the perennial thorny companion in my side.

I wished it could be.... *irrelevant*. I wanted it acknowledged, while also wanting it dwarfed. And oh, how life complied, giving me a suitable vice for the crushing! For to my dismay, I was discovering my twin impulses to express *myself*, and to save the world, cast as adversaries one to another. I had never thought that fulfillment of one might require relinquishing the other. Now, suddenly, I had stepped into a world which I embraced as mine, yet was also about to wrench me, in unthinkable ways, from my very self.

I could not yet see how potent a conflict this was to become. I would find myself swimming against the tide inwardly, while outwardly, I would struggle fiercely to keep my morale in tact. I do affirm, even now, that I did belong ~ an affirmation I would never aver or deny. Yet there was a cost for all this, a rather great one: *me* ; and I have no certainty, to this day, that this could ever have gone another way. Any of it.

For now, there was only one way to step and one choice to make. I bowed to the greater power.

X. A Promise.

By the fall of '71, I was an acclimated, even dedicated follower. This period was the lifting of the gloom, of the clinging insecurities that had haunted my entry into Peoples Temple, unable to drag that unwilling foot fully into the door. Finally I was settling down ~ my attention could be directed here or there, to the tasks at hand.

But letter-writing was my anchor. Introspective and shy, I needed a refuge. Writing made it possible to participate, yes, but in partial seclusion. Left to my own devices, I would never choose the crowds. I would stay in seclusion and write.

For Jim, writing was somewhat *un*-natural. Even when we later published our paper, *Peoples Forum*, his pieces, however lengthy, were dictated *ad hoc*. He never talked from notes ~ in fact, it seemed preposterous. This one was present in the moment and whole. That extra step, where we think, deliberate... He thought, yes, much. Nay, planned, strategized, painstakingly. But what emerged from his mouth, however scripted with nuance, was *definite*.

There was, indeed, a keen impatience with intellectual types. Know where you stand and *be* there. Don't dabble in theories or rationales. I couldn't imagine him ever sequestering *himself* to write, or leave writings to others. That opened him to interpretation. And no one took it upon themselves to interpret the leader. Words for this man, were never even descriptive, much less theoretical. They lived and breathed of their own force.

He once said of Lenin, his erstwhile "alter ego," that he would never have anything to do with poetry or certain kinds of music. That it would only make one sentimental. And (unspoken) "Of what use is that?"

I was an airhead compared to this man. Maybe we had few personal conversations across the years (too many public ones ~ or perhaps just the wrong kind) because I love ideas and descriptions ~ to play with words and thoughts. For Jim Jones, this was self-indulgence, a waste of precious time. When the world is on fire, you don't go roasting marshmallows.

But letter-writing... that could be useful organizationally. In those early days, Jim still had time to scrawl brief notes across the envelopes of letters sent to "Pastor Jones" asking for healing or other help. It was like a seed I could fashion into a flower. His writing was clear, strong, an incisive streak across the page. Subtly, it was an energy source that kept me buoyant and intrigued.

Finally I felt of use. It always touched me that the healings were touching others. But it never truly touched *me* until I found my place. Now I could be mind to mind with the master, sensing how *he* would relate to his flock. Always mindful of "the least of these," ever deferring to the elderly, disabled, neglected. It seemed an honor to be in contact with the forgotten grandmothers in Arkansas or Alabama, young people seeking identity through a higher calling, mothers laden with too many children in too dangerous circumstances, people in situations of social and medical neglect. Everyone wrote Pastor Jones for counsel or help. Once I realized that I, too, in this small way, could be a conduit for his love and help to them, my whole life seemed to calm down.

Though odd as it may seem, by the fall of 1971, I had never had even one conversation with him entirely alone. For all I saw of Jim in services, Planning Commission meetings (oh, let me not tread upon *that* too soon...), and "here and there," it was only once in those entire eight-and-a-half years that I ever talked with him at any length alone.

I craved this contact, yet feared it, for like precious perfume or herbs, that small elixir might be squandered, wasted, or perhaps worse still, rendered trivial. I kept my distance. For me he was both the warmest, most radiant presence, but also the most austere.

My only one-to-one contacts were stretches of perhaps ten seconds apiece following services. The running tallies on the mail. I approached him with my "numbers," and sometimes, he would take my hand. It was nothing sexual. Indeed, I think anyone looking on would have seen an insecure young woman simply being centered by this slight, if firm, touch. The skin of his hand was indefinably soft, like a baby's flesh, and its gentle pulses calmed me.

At first, I would have nothing to say to him in writing, either. But gradually, he began to solicit confidences from us all. How we felt about the work. How we felt about him. And (I don't even remember how it first came up), how we felt about *sex*. He got it into his head that although he personally considered obsessions with youth, beauty, sex superficial, and corrupting upon society as a whole, that people needed *him* to be young, *him* to be sexual, *him* to carry the powers of not just miraculous healings, but of charisma and youth.

"Need" evolved, ominously, like a two-pronged path. There was a benevolence, even purity, in "If you need a friend, I'll be your friend. If you need a brother, I'll be your brother. If you need a father, I'll be your father." It was wholly supportive, non-invasive. If ever in your life, you were sick or in trouble, down-and-out or in any manner of material, medical, or social need, you could count on Jim Jones 1,000%. He'd always come through. And that was truly the depth of my love for him.

But now there seemed to be emerging a dark side of "need." And from that point on, humans one and all, we were perhaps inevitably pointed towards the ignominious trio of sex, power, and death.

I don't know just what it was we all needed, anyway. Most of the core of the church wound up dead, and presumably, one of the things one needs the most is *life*. If what we all "needed" so drained this man that it led to ultimate, desperate resorts (though that is hardly the whole of it, by far), then I don't know that living up to people's needs, was even a safe, much less productive, way to go.

But with Jim, he would *only* relate to need. If someone's life was in danger, he was always there. If it was something of a more nebulous character, such as emotional balance... well, they could try and work it through 'til they went half insane, then he would step in because they "needed" him. Or they could simply declare need and be tended to, albeit at the cost of guilt. They could also declare need and just take, and not be guilty at all. Or be stoical and perhaps escape the guilt-gilded traps of "need" entirely, but at the cost of... *need*. Everyone does need something, yes? Not just to serve the world. Surely one needs more than that. (Ah, you too sense some slippery slopes on this cliff? How perceptive of you.)

I rue the day Jim Jones ever first spoke the word "need," though I have no recollection of just when it was. I do remember the evening he told us all to write him every sexual contact we had ever had, and put it in an envelope with his name on it and "For Your Eyes Only."

It wasn't suggested voyeuristically. It was like his eagle's eye had taken aim at its ultimate prize – a world free of racism and poverty, greed and materialism vanquished; and had to gauge the obstacle course blocking the appearance of this shining world. We were his vanguard – taken from tattered scraps of humanity perhaps, seemingly common, not illustrious at all. We were imperfect indeed, but still, he reminded us often, "the best." So whatever we "needed" to clear our obstacle course to devote our lives to service, this was the task at hand.

Certainly his concerns for our most elemental drives (and allegiances!) was not just altruistic, but incorporated a healthy dose of its flip side, pragmatism. We were high stakes. We would need the energy, the idealism of the young. Ideally *single* young people. Young people singleminded enough to give all and take risks, not be sidelined by the usual obsessions about romance, or building one's own personal future.

In any case, Jim Jones was willing to confront building his cadre from the ground up, whatever it took, in its rawest form. This was a man who had personally gone to a senior's cottage to relieve her of an impaction (this from straight-as-an-arrow old-timer Eva Pugh). There was never a list of things Jim Jones could do and those he couldn't. This was a being totally and incontrovertibly oriented to necessity. The necessities of *others*.

Jim (he told us often) was *disgusted* with people's focus on sexual conquests, power trips, games, ego, materialism. I thought one would have to be "out for lunch plus breakfast plus dinner" not to see that. So this gradual encroachment upon the very *privacy* of his flock, disconcerted me not in that I felt he had no right to invade, but that I was insecure how to handle it *personally*. I saw the model of sacrifice before me, thus never felt to question his motives. It wouldn't have occurred to me, as it certainly did in the post-tragedy years, that he could enter onto a course of action for unimpeachable motives and still be ... *wrong!* My only perceived task was how to handle what was thrown at *me*.

Things also followed their own inevitable progression. It was a long while before "Pastor Jones," had evolved to "Father," a fateful tale of its own. Much less how "I'm a prophet" evolved into the dangerous assertion (socially, physically, psychologically dangerous, every way dangerous *irrespective* of religion!), "I am God." It evolved in increments, as if to gradually immerse the receiver into baptismal waters, a toe here first, then a dunk, full immersion only later on. Jim had laid it out as if to calibrate the listeners to their limits: "If you need a friend, I will be your friend. If you need a brother... a father..." And finally, "If you need a *Saviour*..."

He never actually said, "If you need a lover, I will be your lover." I never, moreover, expected it, and when the first, however slight hint, came out obliquely in a service, I was shocked. I had had enough illicit involvements of my own to not be shocked by much. But him I revered, enough to keep my own sexual energies in check. I would have died before I ever overtly came onto him, if only because rejection by him would have crushed me.

So when he first spoke of it, I didn't hear it as friendly, but as unsettling, even threatening. I just... well, I "thought I didn't hear right." It wouldn't readily sink in. But when he asked us to write about all our sexual contacts, I complied on a literal basis. It was a long list, but he asked for it. He always told us that if we were simply honest with him, he would never embarrass us.

I wrote him when asked, but never asked for his *time*. Jim was forever counselling people with "major" problems, like drugs, crime, trouble with the law. He even helped relatives of members. Sometimes there was a good, sweet, loyal lady with a perfectly rotten niece or grandson, but he would help one for the sake of the other. Not infrequently, the effort was wasted on people who were simply not about to change their ways.

But what he had very little time for, was just talking with the people who were there all the time. The church was expanding now, even its Redwood Valley population. So during just one period in the fall of 1971, Jim announced that whoever had questions for him and wanted to talk with him personally, he would be at the cottage next to the church certain days, and meetings could be arranged. Finally I had my chance.

I wrote out what was most pressing, most difficult for me. That I loved the church, but it was difficult to have given up both sex and creative work. That was pretty much it. I wanted to write poetry and music, and doing without sex entirely, as he encouraged, was just very difficult. I made no demands, no pleas.

I came by midday, and was led into the small kitchen area of the cottage. I handed him the note, which he read. I also showed him a poem I was writing. He paused, reflected, then said, "Your work is... *sensitive*." Then something about how it wasn't really useful at this time. Maybe at another time... I looked at him and thought oh, if time goes on and on, maybe this will simply fall off the edge of the earth. I repressed my crestfallen heart. There was nowhere to go with this, was there?

Ever the empath, he wove in, as if our dilemma were a shared one, "Well, look at me. I have lots of talents. And I'm stuck away in this tiny valley." I felt for him. I *always* felt for him. But was his playing field the same as mine?

Hope nearly dashed, I went for one more gentle prod, as though some dyslexic fragment of my brain hadn't yet clicked in the unwelcome byte: "Am I not less sensitive now?" "No," he said reassuringly, "You're *more* sensitive."

Then I was so silent. I saw him gaze ahead and slightly upward. Like I had seen again and again in revelation, when information was about to come through. He said simply, *"You can write one great work."* That one simple stroke. "You can write one great work." Even more softly still, "Maybe some day people will be able to relate to your eloquence."

Then (as a postscript or a doorway, I can't say ~ it was more like *pervasive*), he again gazed into that supra-human place and said softly but firmly, "I need you. You're a pillar." Was this a plea for me to give up what I so cherished? What were the requirements of a pillar? Could a pillar be encumbered with her own thoughts and ideas, her own scrawls across the page, her own melodies lighting through her brain? I thought not. No, more. I thought he was *telling* me "Not."

Then he said, "About your physical needs... Something may happen, and you'll feel a greater warmth and closeness between us. You won't feel this alienation." Nothing more. No glance, no touch, nothing suggestive, just those words. I blanked and blocked and assumed nothing.

Then it lightened slightly. He said he knew of all the good work I was doing with the letters. He told me to stay with writing letters, and *not to do anything else*. This "order," or so it seemed, was never altered nor rescinded.

I left out of the cottage subdued. I had been given both praise and assurance of belonging. I had even been given (however vague) a promise: *"You can write one great work."*

I went home and pulled out all my musical compositions. How I loved them! No one knows how much. This was the promise of my life. I almost felt like Abraham being asked to sacrifice Isaac, his son. I hadn't actually been *asked*. I just felt in my heart that Jim had, in his own way, asked this of me. No, more. I felt that *I* could not give this up unless I had destroyed it physically. If there was indeed "one great work" in my future, it must be something far greater than this. I would trust. I would have faith. There would never be any doubt. I would have withheld nothing.

I *burned* them.

Then I got up in the mid-week service, and announced that I had burned all my musical works because what we were doing here was so much greater. I spotted Jim slightly from out of the corner of my eye. He was in the back of the room, listening, conferring, attentive, distracted, in response to the milieu. He heard. He was serene, but impassive. He said nothing. He never ever spoke of that at all.

XI. "Father is God."

The pace quickened into 1971. Holidays were wonderful, as always. Thanksgiving, Christmas and New Year's were each all-day extravaganzas. People came from San Francisco, or even further away, to join in. The floor was arranged into long banquet tables, onto which huge platters of turkey, vegetables, salad, and sheer yummies like sweet potato pie were heaped. The children received their presents together, communal style, on New Year's instead of Christmas, so that our shoppers could take advantage of post-Christmas sales. No child was ever excluded.

Later in the day after we ate, there was ....a *service*, naturally. And always, on its heels, a healing service. Jim Jones was always a healer. I could never see him as destroyer back then, because this awesome, compassionate, unfathomably psychic being was always healing. Marceline, his wife and a registered nurse, had been with him since slightly before "the gift" had blossomed forth whole at age eighteen. At first, her medical training had made her skeptical, but when the tumors were routinely spit up, and the crippled arose to walk, she never doubted the evidence of her own eyes.

We seemed crowded with people these holidays, especially newcomers. More clear-cut lines were now being drawn between members and non-members. No one new got in unless they were cleared by Jim ~ a cross of psychic ability and common sense, from all I could see. But the members-only services also became more restrictive, and of a more demanding character. People had to think, to relate, to give. What was Peoples Temple? What were the stakes and who was prepared to stay the course. With some, it was shape up or ship out.

Meanwhile, we were about to purchase the building in San Francisco where we held our monthly meetings. Still later, we expanded to Los Angeles and bought a building there.

We were on the move. I remember one especially ecstatic service, when just at the most pulsing, rhythmic crest of song, Jim's voice came bellowing above the din: *"Seven-and-a-half! Seven-and-a-half years to socialism in the United States!"* The crowd went wild. I remembered it with especial dismay because it was in the Spring of 1971, and "seven and a half years" later on (the Fall of 1978) was to bring mass death. When Peoples Temple, for sure, had established "socialism," but on foreign soil, and was felled in part by the passionate refusal to return. That what was to be the moment of glorious triumph in America instead turned out to be the target date for the expatriates' doom.

We will want to return to this. To a reversal so horrendous, that the term "miscalculation" pales to nought. Of course, whatever *Lenin* had envisioned at the time of the Russian Revolution, seven and a half years later, he was *dead*, leaving only Stalin, who converted "utopia" into tyranny. Ironically, moreover, Lenin was precisely forty-seven-and-a-half at the time of the Russian Revolution, "a success", whilst Jim Jones was also forty-seven-and-a-half at the destruction of Jonestown, obviously a catastrophe.

There is another prototype in history, too. Alexander the Great. He, too, envisioned the entire world under a multicultural flag, with him self-proclaimed "God" (well, he said it wasn't self-proclaimed ~ that it was the Delphic oracle ~ as in Phila-*delphia*, perhaps?), and just seven-and-a-half years later on, he too, died, his "infallibility" deteriorating in his last year-and-a-half via his first smashing defeat, exile, substance abuse, and poison. Read your history. I can't make this stuff up.

Such patterns. They haunt me still. But in 1971, we were like children eager for the foray. Expand. That must be good.

And so, expand we did. Beginning in the summer of '71, we took yearly cross-country trips ~ usually a two-week journey by bus, through the South, Midwest, Southeast and Northeast, eventually encompassing Houston, Detroit, Atlanta, Philadelphia, New York (only once we dared *that* terror of a place! ~ Jim deliberately booked the Audubon Ballroom, where Malcolm was killed ~ an eerie choice), and briefly, Indianapolis, Jim's original home turf, where we swept along Diane Wilkinson, our phenomenally gifted pianist who perished at Jonestown.

But it was 1971 in Philadelphia that became a fateful divide. Philadelphia, "Love of the Delphic Oracle" ~ fate indeed!

We had ten busses of people cross-country, sleeping on the busses and eating quickly-made sandwiches, canned food, touches of fresh fruit and cheap packages of desserts. It was primitive, but so many people had never hoped to go *anywhere* (imagine their surprise at Guyana!), and this was an adventure. Philadelphia wasn't our only destination this first cross-country trip, but it evolved into a pivot upon which our destiny ultimately would hinge.

Philadelphia was more missionary than the other stops. We went to rescue last, aging remnants of the followers of the now-deceased "Father Divine." It wasn't uncommon for us to embark on crusades, which would

88/SNAKE DANCE

dominate our lives for months at a time. Now it was the Father Divine people, later it would be Chilean refugees from the Pinochet regime; championing reporters' First Amendment rights; championing Angela Davis, Huey Newton and others of the far-left Black liberation movements; championing the Indians under siege at Wounded Knee; the prison unrest at Attica; the Bakke case; African liberation movements; exposing local Nazis; welcoming visiting Soviets; courting State politicians; a brief encounter with the Black Muslims; the list went on and on.... But the Father Divine project I remember as one of the first.

"Father Divine," as he was known, was popular in the 40's and 50's as the most prominent Black leader in Philadelphia. Although he performed no miracles, his following, working for free, called him "God." Perhaps for lack of civil rights in the society at large, any Black leader audacious enough to have grand plans might have attracted a following eager to serve, though this was apparently a stand-out case. At any rate, it would have surely intrigued Jim Jones that any Black man in America had ever been dubbed "God."

Father Divine had long since died, leaving his empire to his white wife, an imperious creature known now as "Mother Divine." She, like her husband before, lived "high on the hog," while the followers languished, in poor health and overworked, their fixed incomes taken, and given little but dying memories to sustain them. Jim disliked such exploitation intensely, and had decided to bring some of these older folk back to Redwood Valley with *us*. I don't think we succeeded in "rescuing" more than ten. But in remedying the discrepancy between their lives and what *we* could provide, remedying other discrepancies took on another, unanticipated dimension entirely:

Our journey to Philadelphia included a huge banquet (in honor of "Mother Divine," naturally) and, as we had our favorite songs, so had they, all in unbridled glorification of the deceased Father Divine. "Father is God, in every atom and cell of his bodily form, Father is God, and we are blessed..." "I know he's God, God, God, God, God... I know he's God, God, God, God, God..."

We were astounded. What had this "Father Divine" done? No miracles, surely. And the humanitarian record, whatever might have been claimed of it, was severely blemished at best, by amassing a huge personal fortune at the expense of a membership kept in perpetual poverty. Yet he they were calling him "God." This put us, who saw living, continual miracles as a very part of daily life, in an odd fix.

When we returned to Redwood Valley, fresh from having triumphantly snatched a few, dear, elderly followers out from under the nose of the arrogant, willful "Mother," we were heady with this, our first expansion of Peoples Temple across state lines. Then the discrepancy between Father Divine and Jim Jones (perhaps ripe for correction, perhaps even inevitable) got "remedied" through a previously unthinkable shift:

Linda Amos came onto the testimony line, at the first large service since we had returned. She was overcome with emotion. The first thing she said was, "I know Jim may be angry at me for saying this - he may not want me to say it, but I have to say it." (Whether Jim knew in advance, much less whether he was angry, who knew?)

She went on. That we had seen the movement in Philadelphia that had been led by Father Divine. He exploited his membership, never performed miracles, and yet they called him "God." But, said Linda, what she knew and had to say, was that.... *Jim Jones* was.... God. She *knew* this. "I know he's God. I know he's God." She was crying.

Claps and cheers and singing burst forth. "Father is God, with every atom and cell of his bodily form, Father is God and we are blessed..." That deed, henceforth, was done. Pastor Jones was now "Father." And Father was God. (Later, in the informalities of Jonestown, Jim was simply called "Dad.") The young people, the college students (many of whom later turned), were the most ecstatic. It was strange, since they were much more into radical politics than into miracles. But this shift was so infectious - why quibble over apples versus oranges? Everything changed with that power pack called "God." Even "Je-sus" and "Fa-ther" were conveniently matched by duo-syllables and our whole gospel repertoire got a "Fatherly" boost.

It was a move I thought Jim may have regretted at later times. Once, when we went through a period of catering to politicians, with purely civic interests, we were *verboten* to call Jim "Father," and he expressed positive relief. From time to time, he proclaimed that he had no capacity which was not potentially, at some future time, within the reach of all, and we heard much of, "As I am, so shall ye be, for I go unto the Father." He was certainly willing for the altruistic attributes of the ministry to be proliferated, if not the dark side, like sexual exploits. This was an inveterate experimenter, who once gathered in all the children, took their hands one by one, then sent them out amongst the crowd "to heal," but it didn't work. I'm not sure anyone believed that it could, that anyone could really emulate gifts such as these. After all, there is only one "God."

Never after Linda's public pronouncement, could he retreat from the "God" designation even if he wanted to. He was ever cautious around whom he said what (power was unleashed by design, not carelessly or purely out of ego), but he would never disclaim what she had said. So for a kind of initiation period, we got used to "If you want a friend, I will be your friend..." on to "brother..." on to "father..." then on to *"Saviour"*. It invariably aroused the wildest cheers.

And what else could? Who else healed your diseases, or even if your car was totalled, you walked away without a scratch? Who else got charges dropped against your kids, or took hardened street criminals and turned them into paragons of service to their fellow man? Who else brought back the very dead, as had happened in services more than once? Indeed, no member in good standing died at all. And with so many people in their eighties and nineties ~ statistically, at the least, it was inexplicable.

How much further from all this to... "God"? In America, we can't even pose the question. In India, where saints and sages relatively abound, like concentrated laser beams amidst the more widespread poverty and despair, one who performs miracles is wont to be called "God." Society still doesn't change, no, but no one is too upset at calling men (or women) Divine. Here it is different. *Whatever* one does, one can hardly be called "Divine"; plus if you are designated "Divine" <u>and</u> attempt to alter society for the better, you are especially likely to be pilloried!

We have no cultural disciplines to accept, much less nurture "godhood." We discover a Jim Jones and it is such a freak occurrence for us, we honestly don't know *what* to call it. We are happier, as a nation, to call it "charlatan," rather than to admit we have the challenge what to call a worker of miracles. Jim himself once lamented being "a twenty-second century man in a twentieth century body."

I don't even know that anyone on the outside cared who was called "God," but insiders threatened by power did, and several of those were used to destroy us. It was that, combined with threats of *political* power, power from *the left*, that made for an especially dangerous brew. We had certainly heard enough about how *Jesus* was political, and after all, look at what happened to him! But at this relatively early date, even be there danger, it held adventure and intrigue.

Jim, for his part, made the most of it, appealing to religious holdovers and the politically radical alike. "I am socialism. Socialism is love. Love is God," he'd proclaim with a flourish. "There *is* no God," sometimes got thrown in quixotically. "There's no God but love for your fellow Man. The highest is to live as an atheist, doing good for good's sake, not for thought of reward." And by this supreme measure, sacrifice for one's fellow Man, he *was* "God," was he not? It seemed clear that his stance was, indeed, as he proclaimed it to be: unimpeachably egoless.

I was so touched by the healings, I felt willing to go along. What was done for children was the most poignant. Like little April Klingman, an infant stricken with meningitis – how suddenly, seemingly on the brink of death, her white blood cell count suddenly reversed and the disease was vanquished. Or the Lundquist children – how their car tumbled off a cliff and was totalled, and little Dov showed us a picture of Jim, which had bled at exactly the same spot as the child's head that had catapulted through the windshield, landing without a scratch.

Much less testimonies from the adults. The eternally grateful, like octogenarian Henry Mercer, blinded in youth when acid was sprayed on him on a picket line, sight now miraculously restored. Father's gifts were generously seasoned with mercy for the elderly, especially those rooted in the hard, ungiving soil of social strife. Like Vera Talley, a woman in L.A. he discerned was so impoverished as a sharecropper, that there was no time off for pregnancy and she had to drop her babies in the field as she worked. Every illness is rooted in an ill, and as even aging bodies were drawn up tall, neglected lives were set aright, nurtured and healed. Many a time, I would have bowed down at his feet, so rich was the milk of mercy poured upon the humblest, ofttimes sweet souls who arrived Sunday morning at 11 a.m.

There were even the hostile ones, who could scarcely believe they were the recipients of life-saving miracles – like Grace or Charlie both, at different times, testifying about head-on collisions where vehicles had seeming gone right through them, leaving no trace of damage or injury.

Thus for a long while, I could not relate to Jim's gifts as in any way dangerous. Certainly never dangerous to us – it was, to the contrary, saving lives. But unbeknownst to us at the time, we were already in striking distance of what Jim and others considered to be extreme danger.

XII. Preludes to Disaster.

We were beginning to attract attention, not all of it welcome. Any attacks we had endured to date, even death threats and arson, were sporadic and isolated, and moreover, could attract *sympathy* for the courage of our stands against racism and injustice.

Lester Kinsolving (more properly *Rev.* Lester Kinsolving, although a journalist) was no sympathetic character, but was with a large San Francisco paper, thus able to inflict harm. The reputation preceding him was that he sported in destroying various religions. His style was cynical and snide. I glimpsed him briefly at a service and felt chilled. Yet there he was, right in Redwood Valley, like a personalized form of invasion.

There was little dissuading him. Jim probably thought that attempting to do so would only make things worse, as he would only consult his own sources, which were negative -- disgruntled ex-members and the like. People we had long since expelled for various anti-social or malicious behaviour.

So apprehensive was Jim about what this man might print, that he refrained from being with his own son when Stephan when he took ill and was rushed down to the city. Only after Kinsolving left, did he commandeer a 90-mile-an-hour clip south. Apparently, the implicit threat that the reporter would use Jim's own son taken ill for "ill" purpose, like to ridicule his healing abilities, was so precarious, that Jim would not risk revealing the crisis in Kinsolving's presence.

As always, Jim's position was that he was protecting *us* from attack. We were ever an extension of him and he of us. Ever father-protector (though obviously, not called "Father" when a reporter was around), our own fate would rest on how he fared, publicly as well as privately. And since Kinsolving was billed as our greatest threat to date, we tightened ranks for the coming crisis.

Fatefully, the first article appeared on what Jim had always told us was the most ominous day of the year: September 16th. All 16ths were deemed ominous, but September 16th was the worst. (9/16 = 9 + 1 + 6 does *equal* 16. It was even Jim Jones and <u>916</u> of his followers who perished in Guyana, after <u>16</u> defectors left. "*Coincidence*"?)

This was a short series of articles, three or four at the most. It began with *"The Prophet Who Raises the Dead,"* which may not sound like slander on the surface of it; but when you probed 'neath the surface, it was "the man his followers *call* 'The Prophet'..." and insinuations that we were no ordinary church, but more like a cult. By the last article, it had become *"Probe Church, State Urged."*

We wrote in furious protest, then picketed the newspaper. Although our stance was that this was dire, the message might well have been just "Don't go any further." It could have been worse. I even wondered what Jim had done in the way of damage control. Perhaps he had pointedly introduced Mr. Kinsolving to our attorney, the then Assistant D.A. of Mendocino County.

For all the air of crisis (we awaited that 16th like a death knell), it didn't seem too damaging, but it was certainly an omen. Peoples Temple had always been garnished in praise. Now the door was opened to slander. We were relieved the attacks ceased, but looking across a wider sweep of years, this was perhaps, symbolically, "the beginning of the end."

Especially for Jim. He began telling us, more often as the years wore on, that someone "very high up" in the church would defect and do us great harm. He didn't seem to know who it would be. *We* thought (paranoically - paranoia, unfortunately, is "catching") that surely he did know, and was saying this to put us all on our guard. Personally, I look back and believe that he *really didn't know*. When the truth hit, it was ghastly. I could never believe that he would not have forestalled that kind of harm had he known.

That whole year was rocky, anyway. We had just begun into "catharsis," a special mid-week service held on Wednesday nights. Sitting up front beside Jim were a dozen or so people, designated as "counselors." This was new. When I first entered the church, there was the Board - old-timers like Archie and Jack, and Eva and Jim Pugh, also some of the younger, more dedicated souls, like Carolyn, Linda, and Carol Stahl. It seemed a fairly sedate crew. No one even knew when they met - it seemed to be extemporaneous.

Now we had counselors. Jim explained that the counselors were important, but that the highest was membership on the Planning Commission. That everyone on the Planning Commission was automatically a counselor, though not vice versa.

I thought, of course, these must be best people, and indeed many were. Others, I later learned, were damage control cases, put in a position of authority to promote their being useful rather than destructive. This unwelcome discovery only came later on, when I found *myself* graced with what I thought was this seat of power, and rapidly felt not too powerful at all. But we get ahead of ourselves.

The counselors began taking on a more aggressive role in the church. Problems, be they personal, domestic, organizational, practical, issues of loyalty, nearly whatever, were referred for counseling. But Wednesday was reserved for matters considered either more flagrant or more widespread. Like when there was a drive for everyone, finally, to stop smoking entirely, this was the forum of choice. If Jim wanted to clue the membership into strategic thinking, this was the forum of choice. If something involved behaviour too far off the norm for us clean-living folk (and we rather were), Wednesday night was the time.

The most flagrant "star" of the mid-week gatherings was college student Jim Cobb – yes, the same one who later wound up suing Peoples Temple for millions of dollars when the tide had turned years later on. Over what, no one could figure. We gave him a free college education, then one day he up and split. Objectively, it was difficult to see what *we* might have owed *him*.

Cobb was an especially galling case, in that, according to several tearful co-eds, he had twisted the pro-black orientation of the Temple so deviously, that he actually had the white students at the dorm being slaves to the black students, instituting all manner of rituals and punishments, including sexual liberties of his own, to enforce "the new regime." He told them that "Jim had cleared it," and for some time, the poor students were so intimidated that they didn't challenge the lad's flagrant ego (at the least) with anyone who could intercede. Others reported Cobb messing with rifle practice in violation of our non-violent ways.

Cobb "got it" one Wednesday night, and the college dorms were never the same. This shake-up of our darlings, the college students, was the mini-scandal of the hour. Jim softened it at the end (wisely – you can't leave someone with a huge ego with nothing – it's dangerous) by telling Cobb that he saw "greatness" in him. Vague enough, I suppose. Cobb got up the next meeting, tearful at "what Jim said about me," and said he knew that in Castro's Cuba, or with Che Guevara (whom he worshipped, understand!), he would have been shot for his antics. I suppose it's no great compliment thanking someone for not going so far as to shoot you! But it seemed finished, anyway, and that our college situation was secure.

Aside from this, I knew little about the students. College had been such a trauma for me, that I found detachment the safest course. Whatever they were going through emotionally, or even sexually for that matter, it seemed like the usual chaos of the late teen's and early twenties. I didn't come on them much except at services, and weekdays, they were a distance away.

I did notice that other younger people seemed to be working closer to Jim personally - Janine and Hope, training to be nurses, had apparently joined a small elite group called "staff" (which included my original trio of indoctrinators), and often moved about looking busy and preoccupied with tasks I assumed were important. I had no idea what they did, just that staff was never brought up for catharsis. Jim was protective of them, implying that they worked harder and took greater risks than the rest of us.

Position was a mystery to me. I had never been socially ambitious, and had few skills in gauging the terrain. Jim did all the appointing, and if I let myself aspire to this or that, I would have gone crazy with insecurity, so I just kept my nose to the grindstone. I wanted attention, nearly craved it, but I had no special "in" by which to attract his notice.

Indeed, life was more routine than ever. Letter-writing had shifted in its emphasis since we had gone into an expansion mode. It was automated now on a new-fangled machine called a "word processor," which we found fascinating and quite advanced at the time. It had "memory," and we began resorting to form letters for the ongoing grind, which was now graced with a regular office.

I wasn't happy with form letters, but never complained. Others had complained about their routine responsibilities and were chastised. Told that everything needed to be done, and everyone was overworked, and why couldn't we just do our work. I didn't want to meet the same fate, and I lacked the inate tact to appeal in such a way as to garner sympathy rather than risk rebuke.

Besides, this had advantages. Although I worked ridiculously long hours like everyone else, I had free time when the machine was humming along on its own. It left me freer mentally. Eventually, this worked to the advantage of a restless creativity that would never completely calm down.

I was alone in the letters office that Friday night in June, 1973. The busses had already departed south for the weekend when I got a call from Karen in San Francisco. She said there was a meeting Jim wanted me at, and could I drive down? I had use of a car, and of course made the ride.

There were maybe forty people in the room in which we met. It included many I had come to see as important, plus a sprinkling of college students. Not Jim Cobb, but several others. I was told, along with J.R. and

Annie, that we were being brought onto the Planning Commission. Jim said, "We have reservations about all of you," as though we had barely made the grade, but that we had proven ourselves to be good workers. Why I imagined this might lead to more interesting work, much less a closer relationship with Jim personally, I don't know. No one said that. I spent four years in that "august body" and it never did.

On the surface, of course, it seemed an honor and a thrill. The information conveyed in that meeting, however, was odd, nearly traumatic – not quite like an earthquake, but tremors, at the least. It was mostly about sex.

Jim began by telling us that John Victor Stoen, the one-year-old child of our head attorney, Tim Stoen, and his wife Grace (who were both in the room) was really *his* child. That Grace (her eyes downcast) had not taken to the work very well, having come into the church only out of marriage to Tim. She was having marital problems and threatened to leave the church, slander Tim (the reason was left vague), and slander us. Jim had to prevent her from bolting, so he seduced Grace to protect *us*.

When Grace became accidentally pregnant, still being new in the work and not grasping the ramifications of having the leader's child (I soon learned she was now *incessantly* informed of such ramifications!), she refused to have an abortion. No one but us knew that John was really Jim's, and we were of course sworn to secrecy.

Grace was described as now "cooperative" (was that a *legal* term?), and had been put on the Planning Commission to become involved in the church work. Meanwhile (again left vague), Jim had also gone to bed with *Tim*. He said men needed this, too. That it was difficult for him to get used to – he had no history or inclinations. The first time, he said, he threw up on the man's back. But that all men (save him, of course) had homosexual inclinations, and also needed his love as a father. That he had been to bed with many in the room thus far, both women and men. Later he would tell us he was the only truly heterosexual man anywhere. That the whole world, both sexes, was turning homosexual. Kind of like population control or an instinct for extinction.

How had this happened? Honestly, no one had the appetite to ask, and contesting it was far from easy. It was never treated as a question – one would have to *dissent*. And since the measure of material reality was ...*material reality*, if anyone were to claim heterosexuality for themselves, they would have to prove it by demonstrating their skills. Jim threw that out publicly as a challenge and there were no takers.

This was beginning to look more intimidating than alluring. Nor was sex extended as an *invitation*. It was always, "They *needed...*" I looked around. There were people there several years younger than me, but probably more in the know. The college students were silent as anyone. The old-timers were silent. The loyal-to-the-death contingent ("staff") was silent. The youngest, who were presumably the most driven by dint of their age, were silent. I, a mere newcomer, was ...silent.

I cannot say I was totally unprepared. In services, Jim told us once that his marriage had been monogamous for twenty years, with just one exception. They were in Brazil founding the orphanage, and running low on food. To secure the food, he had to seduce a wealthy Brazilian woman and "had to make her feel like she was on the Moon." The money was thus "donated" and the project survived. And how could one not be sympathetic to that?

Apparently, there were already other involvements by the time the Brazilian "true life story" surfaced. Perhaps it was simply designed as a prototype for sex as an altruistic endeavor. Marceline seemed embarrassed as he spoke, but held her peace. I only remember one intimation publicly that he may have been with some in the group, which I had blocked off self-protectively. Likely he was offering a deliberately vague trial balloon to gauge people's response.

Now, in this induction into "the highest honor," membership in the Planning Commission ("P.C."), a more detailed history of this practice was set forth. It began with Janine, he said, the young student nurse. That she was only eighteen, and her *mother*(!) told Jim that Janine was freaked out because Jim had so heavily discouraged romance as a diversion from the cause, and she thought she would never get to experience anything in life. So he slept with her. She got pregnant twice, and had had two abortions.

Then there was Carolyn, and later Sandy whom, he said, were both suicidal, and with them, sex rescued them from that terrible abyss. Sandy, it turned out, he could not get free of for years. (Carolyn was a different matter entirely, as we'll see.) He usually downplayed such dilemmas, only saying now and then that he had to "maintain" certain people for certain, unspecified reasons. Mostly, he emphasized that he got into sex with people to get them *out of* it. To give them what they needed, but also to convert their allegiance from sexual hang-ups into social concerns, and get them out of bed as quickly as possible.

Sometimes, he said, that was possible by being with them once. Sometimes it took more. Janine's brother, Robby, whose history we learned of later, apparently had his own agenda of demands. That he was "genuinely" homosexual, and Jim's terminating relations provoked his leaving, with the possibility of threatening harm to the work.

Janine's friend, Hope, was given her sexual fling with Jim as a "corrective" experience after having been molested by her stepfather. Then there was Karen Layton, who was just plain too hung up on sex, so he "fucked her for eight hours, then took her out to fuck her in the bramble patch and arranged for them to be discovered by Jack Beam." Obviously, that was the last time they were together. Karen, eyes also downcast, kept her control.

So this was a mixture of correcting childhood molestation, demolishing romance, stopping from endangering the work, coming to terms with one's previously-repressed homosexuality, being saved from suicide... ?? The question of *attraction* seemed to play no role at all. This may have all been quite deliberate on Jim's part, since he would neither have wanted to provoke jealousies nor attract welters of demands; or, from his own perspective, it may have been "fact."

In any case, it was mind-boggling. On the one hand, this was portrayed as the ultimate experience of love, tenderness, potency and erotic pleasure; on the other, it seemed that one had to be completely disempowered to qualify for this man's attentions. And if you're in your twenties listening to all this, and you're denied sex anyway, obviously there is a giant problem to know where the union (or *separation*) of sex and love begins or ends. I sat there as quietly as anyone. Quietly *stunned*.

Jim said people don't really want sex anyway. They want a father. So what was this? "Mass incest"? I could never, ever ask. No one could.

Of course, "something" was said about dedication to the work, but it seemed lost in the avalanche of sexual liaisons. Other things disconcerted me as well: It seemed that once in P.C., you don't leave. If you are in the church and leave and cause no trouble, no problem. But for P.C. there were special standards. It was never said that leaving could be dangerous, but left implicit.

At the time, I was naive, plus in no way inclined to inflict harm myself, so certain imports that were clear later on, barely grazed me this first time around. Jim could obviously blackmail people there with *embarrassment*. He knew their intimate secrets. Or we could presumably blackmail him by leaving and getting the word out that this *minister* had multiple sexual involvements; moreover, with women and men both, producing at least one child.

Unthinkably, these possibilities did not even occur to me then. I was too shaken. Was this something I was supposed to have? To ask for? Did I have to be in dire crisis to ask? What was the emotional penalty for asking? I felt I needed some "trump" to even consider it. I remembered no molestation as a child. I had never threatened to leave or to harm the work. And certainly, I didn't need sex to turn me into a socialist - I was *born* into it. (That was a "biggie," of course. Hook people on carnal love, then *dismiss* them sexually. Teach them that love for the cause was so much greater than being led around by selfish desires.)

And even if he and I were together, would I be one of the ones quickly kicked out of bed? Oh, and one last thing: Would it mean he loved me, or just that *I needed* his love? How could I relate past that with any clarity?

To be fair, I could never say Jim encouraged anyone to go to bed with him. To the contrary. At least, that was his public persona. It was almost like, "Proceed at your own risk." Public propositions (i.e. in the relatively cloistered setting of P.C.) were rare. Once he offered to be with a man after it exploded one P.C. that his wife had been with Jim, and the man hadn't known about it. It's hard to put a tag of "romantic" on that. Jim disdained romantic trappings, anyway. He thought they *were* a trap. He could be so loving and kind. Occasionally he talked about being extremely sensual. But you would never see him in public with his shirt off, or embracing anyone in a suggestive way. This wasn't made easy for anyone. So I imagine many of the people who were with him never knew for sure whether they were a pleasure, a burden, or a volatile brew of both.

Moreover (moreover, moreover, creeps forth this petty pace...), there was one more thing (like "one more thing" times a hundred, yes?) that I didn't grasp. How many were in P.C. out of genuine dedication, and how many because somehow Jim had been first roped into relating to them and then, to turn them into productive, rather than self-serving people, put them in "leadership"? After all, there was Grace Stoen.

I think I rapidly got past congratulating myself on this one! At least I was there because I had earned it, for nothing sexual had ever happened between Jim and me. On the other hand, Jim set himself up as the only acceptable target sexually, he was intensely magnetic, and besides, although to date I had had no sexual designs on him, I genuinely loved him. I loved the being who was there to help everyone in distress and need with all my heart.

It became increasingly difficult for a young woman such as myself to endure. In fact, I sensed trouble in about three days ("sink-in time") and went to Karen Layton, whose friendship had been so helpful to me when I first arrived - genuinely friendly, rather than invasive like Linda's.

I told her I thought I might want this myself, and she turned on me indignantly. "But *they needed* it!!" she nearly screamed. What was it she thought *I* "needed" or "didn't need"? I had never told her of my sexual involvements. Had she read something? Perhaps what I wrote Jim "For Your Eyes Only"? I couldn't bear to ask.

Then, suddenly, she looked at me. I wasn't mirroring her upset, but instead was somber and subdued. She realized she may have overshot the mark. She calmed down and said softly, "Laurie, don't worry about any of this. We'll all get to die soon." While I mulled over whether this was comfort, escape, the answer to my prayers to transcend this life, or some new undeciphered herald of doom (or perchance all four), she backtracked, and said she wanted to talk to me about what it had been like.

That when she first came into the work, she was infatuated with Jim, totally hung up, that he took her to bed once, and told her she was a lesbian and which woman she was attracted to. Then he refused her sex for "a long time." I thought back. I remembered that she had developed endometriosis so severe, even in her early twenties, that she required surgery. What did one thing have to do with another? The second thing I couldn't bear to ask.

Then, she said, he finally took her back when it had become unbearable for her - the bramble patch incident. But, "Laurie, I never had any orgasms with Jim." (In *eight hours?*) She said that all she felt was an unbearable thirst, and that there was no way to stop and... get a drink of water. She seemed so anxious now to keep me away from what was obviously trauma, rather than pleasure, for her, that I don't know that it even occurred to her that what she was telling me was utterly peculiar.

I didn't doubt her word, yet naturally, I was astounded. It was so much at variance with what we had heard. Others, Jim had told us, had said it was an *ecstatic* experience. I felt for Karen. Her secret was safe with me. But I was starting to feel a bit shell-shocked. I questioned Karen no further. Besides, something else had scared me: An image flashed through my mind. I saw Jim standing and it seemed like his back was to me. I saw someone coming up behind him, I think with a knife. Like to stab him in the back. Was it me? How could it possibly be me? But if not me, then who?

I panicked and wrote him a letter. I told him if this was going on, it was going on. But that I would have rather not known about it at all. And about my frightening image. I said nothing about Karen. Even though Jim was "the ultimate confidante," I felt uneasy, like I would be betraying a confidence, or getting in the middle of something where, since I already felt intimidated, I could be easily scorched.

He sent a message that I could talk to Cindy. But she never seemed to be free. "The talk" never happened with anybody.

Thus we three new members embarked on the ritual of P.C., surreptitiously, clandestinely, at a private home each Monday night. 'Til 3, 4, sometimes 6 in the morning. We were, for better or worse, anxiety and honor crossed like swords, now "co-conspirators."

XIII. The Long Hot Summer.

Sex. All you wanted to hear about and you've had to wade through lo, these many pages to get there. You've, let's say, stumbled upon it with innocent, even idealistic intent, like me. And you say ah, this makes sense. Because sex between leader and followers is power over them, and power over them in Jonestown spelled death. It seems so simple.

For those involved, it was, to the contrary, complicated. Natural instincts reined, virtually corralled into a *political* arena which ties every impulse into every other. Like one of those Star Trek episodes (never mind the future ~ how they reflected the present!) where the hunt is on to find the main computer that is generating an entire interlocking system of responses. The kind of machine society we've at least learned to understand vicariously.

Risky experiment, at best. You cannot institute such a mechanism with living flesh, much less on elemental levels such as sex. This was living, human, sentient, responsive. There were no robots. The participants all suffered pain. Even the most weak, or the most hostile, or the most obtuse, suffered pain.

The one with "the controls," Jim Jones, transparently suffered pain the most. Even if egalitarian in much else, a giver, if sufficiently detached, or sufficiently shielded, can perhaps give to all equally, whether or not others are equally receptive; but not with sex and the volatility of its emotions where the taker can virtually vampirize the giver ~ not merely by malice, but by insecurity or need.

The protection Jim Jones opted for psychologically, was the conviction that he was always the giver and others the takers ~ obviously disempowering to the taker, who can never freely love, but must remain a dependent child! I would finally surmise that "Everyone needs a father" and "People need a father more than they need sex," had more to do with his relating across sexual lines, than any inherent homosexuality in either him or most of the men. The model wasn't man/woman. It was parent/child.

The protection to the *group* for such a risky scenario, was to tie in all dissent, even that based in emotions or sex, into dissent against the collective good. If you wanted to challenge Jim about sex, you were challenging the embodiment of racial and economic equality, whose followers idolized him for thousands of acts of healing, counsel and aid. Any dissent over what Jim Jones said, or even did, and you immediately risked dissenting what Jim Jones *was*. Especially, if you had a *personal* motivation for dissent. (And who doesn't? Like Solzhenitzin. He was a writer. He, personally, craved the freedom to write). You were taking on someone who could put you to shame with unceasing selfless acts. You could never win.

It became a crippling enigma. That the same genius who used his unparalleled activism for a wholly *desirable* break from society, virtually used his good deeds to blackmail us out of risking dissent. ("God" invented such a scenario, yes? To "test" us, Job-like creatures that we must have been.) Thus the intensity of people's emotions regarding the whole of Jim Jones, and the life he made possible, would far more often drive one's tangled emotions inwards, rather than risk that a single word of dissent might be construed as taking on *everything*.

It was a loaded minefield, to be sure, though one laced, curiously, not only with precautions but with incentives. That in your silence, you were stronger, perchance, than your neighbor, who might need personal attention as a point of weakness. That your sacrifices were secretly known. That you had the character to suffer with him without complaint; and who, after all, suffered more?

All these motives were lauded from time to time as marks of the faithful -- the secretly grateful Jim Jones acknowledging your sacrifice (if not by name), interspersed with pleas to not drain the leader with your own lesser cause. There were even intimations that "the closest" weren't necessarily so -- the most humble being closest to Jim Jones' heart. You feared you could jeopardize some true order of things only Father could discern. If you were quiet, you at least had the prerogative of being your own conscience, whereas if you spoke up injudiciously, others would fold in noisily and do your consciencing *for* you.

Not to mention the old stand-by, *guilt!* Jim took on everyone's distress, so why could you not bear your own? We had all seen him endure hours of petty problems, and gradually, the boom of silence lowered on us all, as if in penitence.

And what of guilt's twin, *humiliation?*: The risks of not staying in line ranged from embarrassment at the least, to public rebuke. Once you were brought up on the floor, your side hadn't a chance to be heard, much less weighed. Father knew what he was doing. He must have had his reasons. Who were *you* to question them?

This was admittedly a terrible system, fraught with pitfalls, not to mention the sheer chill of fear; and I'm sure that however many fell through the cracks publicly, others fell through privately, and became bedroom cases – perhaps, ironically, the most fearful "love" of all. If you only didn't need, you would not have extracted that from him. If you were stronger. If you had more character.

Thus we had, in effect, "consented to be miserable." Anything you could do selflessly, for the cause, could be a source of pride. Anything taken for yourself incurred penalties.

Well, at least one could relate to others, could one not? One surely hadn't signed up to be a monk or a nun. Well... it was highly discouraged, at best. As you will see, I got into dire straits for even suggesting it *privately*. I thought, naively, that it might actually help take pressure off of him. Oh, no, no, no, no, no. All roads must lead to Jim Jones. And by then, I would be depleted to think logic, much less instinct, much less invention.

It would take months to grasp the ramifications of joining "the most honored people in the world," the People Temple Planning Commission, "P.C." Yet most of us really did love the work and believe in it. We had never seen its likes, and it was thrilling to have a role. Thus we consented to such "benevolent blackmail" of our hearts, our minds, our tongues. To not jeopardize what it seemed that only the whole, working together, could achieve. Or make the already-impossible tasks of the leader more difficult. Rather sandwich *ourselves* between the threat of outward castigation and the equally ominous pressures of inward guilt.

Time and again, it seemed this was right, that it was warranted. Time after time, Jim Jones would wring *himself* through every labor of the heart to empathize, to comfort, to reconcile warring parties, to strengthen, uplift, encourage, allay fears, capture hopes, raise troubled eyes upwards.

Sometimes at odd moments, he would even openly muse, with astonishing quietness, at the dictums he had, after all, himself put into play. One night "the master egalitarian" reflected, "Can't I like some people and not like others?" Another night "God" revealed, "I'm not perfect. But my judgment, my human judgment, is so much better than others. You should trust it."

And who amongst us wouldn't?

Not that I can diminish that my entry into the Planning Commission was a shock. If I could but make this a simple tale. Even abuse of power is not necessarily simple, nor its adherents the monolithic underlings the public seems to crave as a answer to all its questions. Power is also leadership; power is also solidarity; power promotes progress. Power also flows to those who serve, who give of themselves the most; and iron-willed mandates or no, Jim Jones was always the one awake the longest, ever watchful to give, to help, to heal, to rush to one's aid. That version of power... surely one would not object to that. We would call it desirable. And with that, Jim Jones had no par.

Honestly, it seemed at the time that he *paid*, and copiously, for whatever power he had in our lives. Our anguish –what held us, more than any abuse-of-power scenario possibly could have held us– was much more the ongoing sturm-und-drang of a powerfully benevolent soul who himself became progressively snared into his own sacrifices and, once the dam burst, could never stay the flood released in its wake.

Even a benevolent Jim Jones walked the plank in relating to so many people *intimately*. The intermix of energies (the wholesome and the unwholesome, the generous and the greedy, the good-hearted and the vindictive) could corrode a very saint. And such a corrosion, once begun, is difficult to even see, much less reverse. You suffer good intent. You anguish over the well-being of others. You feel everyone who needs you should have a piece of you. And all the while, the well-intentioned would be good anyway, and the ill-intentioned now have the weapon of having sapped your strength. Like in primitive societies, when you kill your enemy, you eat a bit of his liver. Eating your enemy strengthens you against him.

So much for acts of love. What happens when the man who had so wanted to love all Mankind, begins to feel his liver being pecked to bits not just by "enemies," but by his own? Worse even, when he himself had opened the door?

He could not have wanted (oh, how people create what they "do not want"!) all the convoluted emotional threads that sex, especially, fostered. He seemed genuinely relieved when people just did their work. But once this ship set sail, the waters became impossible to separate out. Even the lines between his "family," and "enemies." We were all "family"; yet his nuclear family was already headed towards ruins, and his relationship with such as Grace Stoen, the mother of his own child, was tenuous, even hostile. Indeed, by the time *I* was brought on board, the ultimately damning thing had already happened: the birth of John Victor Stoen.

So do bear with me, please, as we return to the ongoing spectacle of the Planning Commission:

Grace dominated those first several meetings. It was already determined, before my time, that she had grave deficiencies as a mother. Finally the toilet-training debacle. Some observant soul revealed that Grace had been toilet-training little John by fastening a soiled diaper to the top of his head. That was "it"! The child got yanked and was given over to Barbara Cordell, a meek, housewifey type with a magic touch with babies.

Grace remained immature, selfish, willful, but beyond that, it was difficult to discern what the problem was. I mean the core of it. It was weeks on end with her alternately sulking, or threatening to go off ("I'll leave and go to Denmark," she hurled out, then quietly mumbled, "...and commit suicide."), being conflicted about John's upbringing (*everyone* had something to say about John's upbringing), hostile to Tim....

Finally, one time, there was a silence. What did this young woman truly want? Finally she confided quietly, verging on tears, that being with Jim was her every sexual fantasy come true. She wanted this... *again*. Of course, it was out of the question. Once a snare disentangled, don't step that way again. And what if (God forbid) she again became pregnant? She said she feared pregnancy so much now, that she made Tim approach her anally so as to prevent it absolutely.

So intense was our hostility towards Grace, no one ever thought to clobber Tim over the Stoen's marital disaster. No one took on Tim anyway. He was so "high up," so useful, even *indispensable*. And the guy just stood in the back of the room and blended in. He rarely offered argument and we rarely cut in where Tim was concerned. Besides, he was Jim's staunchest ally in defending parental rights to John. This thorn that not only pierced the leader's heart, but could be used to destroy all of us in the eyes of the world. We left Tim alone.

All eyes were riveted on Grace, and the hostility against her was rampant. Now at least, after weeks of hold-outs, tantrums, tears and threats, the core of it, her desire to get Jim Jones back into bed, had finally surfaced. Jim did not even have to voice, "No." This street was at a dead end, the out-of-control vehicle brought to a halt. Grace was calmed down, more attention given to her work responsibilities, and we thought that, for the time being, at least, her situation was stabilized.

After Grace, Christine popped up. I don't know how she wound up on staff. Karen used to date her dad, and had mentored her. Perhaps it was thought that staff, a tight-knit few with marked discipline, would stabilize her. Christine would compulsively twirl her hair into tiny, repetitive knots, like some bite their nails and others scratch their nose.

She was continually upset but could vocalize little, until once she ran out screaming into the night. A few weeks later she showed up smiling and was never any trouble again, so Jim had obviously resorted to his last resort once more.

I was alternately depressed and buoyant. I loved being around Jim, even in this pressure cooker, because of the high energy, and glimpses of the master's mind at work. This was the heart of pragmatism. Here he used discernment but rarely. His natural judgment, razor-sharp, would suffice. It was impossible to gauge whether the services, with the tolls of healing on his physical body, or this, with its draining *emotional* demands, was the more taxing of the two, but the two were certainly kept separate.

Many in P.C., especially the younger crowd, seemed polarized so heavily into politics that, to my dismay, the awesome subject of healing emerged but rarely. Only once Jim pointedly told us (the same one who would tell us in services, "Don't follow me for the healings. Follow me for the human service work"), *"Don't underestimate the healings - they're very important."*

I was unsettled that such an appeal had to be made. Why did others not see? I struggled to separate out his purely human judgment from the healings gifts at all. Yet it was clear that in this *political* body, P.C., he wanted us to simply trust his human judgment if not out of faith, then to spare psychic stress being heaped onto the pressures of long, demanding nights.

He even said that if he chastised us, and we weren't completely responsible, to just "take it" (it was like a *plea* on his part) because pressures were so great. To not force him to make discernment the final arbiter. I, unfortunately, took him literally, to my detriment. There even seemed a premium not simply on doing well, but in not emerging guilty of damaging the leader. Cooperate. Do it even if it damages *you*. Was Jim not drained upon by everyone? All these nameless people amongst us - maybe even me, maybe even you, maybe someone we thought we knew well and really didn't know at all.

No wonder there came times sandwiched between dry business matters and overwrought personal confrontations, where Jim just sat very still and finally concluded, if not always with his mouth, with his eyes, "We're screwed." It certainly seemed that we were revving up for being screwed with the likes of the Stoen debacle.

I sometimes wondered wryly, after the suicides, what desperate urgency could have driven such an extraordinarily gifted man to speed up the gathering of enough people to make our plunge across continents like lemmings rushing to the sea. Though I know what he might have said. That we were destined to have our backs up against the wall *anyway*. That we'll fight it as long as we can. But that if we had to wind up making a stand, better in a utopia of our own making, than beating the city streets. If there was already a Guyana in our future, it wasn't yet voiced. Our hand had not yet been forced. Unbeknownst to us those long summer nights, it would be soon enough.

For the time being, the room seemed too crowded, the undercurrents too menacing, and our own, each one's, subtle fears too ominous, to read the handwriting on the wall. Wait and watch, watch and wait. Then boom! The first major blow came.

XIV. "Family" Turns "Enemy" -- the Unthinkable Happens.

It was again September 16th, now 1973. (Was that chosen deliberately, to torture us?) Sunshine still held sway in Redwood Valley, summer in Northern California being not excessively hot, yet gentle to turn. A call went out to P.C. for an emergency meeting. Eight of the college students had departed, leaving barely a note. Jim had had a heart attack at the shock, but was deemed well enough to call together his leadership.

We met outdoors under trees on the church grounds. Jim looked weakened. The mood was one of agony, reiteration again and again of how could they do this? Why? Had he not poured his heart out to them? How could they turn like this?

At the same time, equal weight was given to their welfare. How would they manage? Would they have enough money? Where would they go? What was to become of their lives? Were all really intent on leaving? Could some be wooed back? We considered the roster of names: Jim Cobb (naturally), who wasn't in P.C. (his problem?); then Mickey Touchette, who was; Wayne Pietila and Terri Cobb, married and in P.C.; John Biddulph and Vera Ingram, also married and in P.C. Then there was Tom Podgorsky and Lena Flowers, not in the church for that long, and probably less close to Jim personally.

There were lengthy discussions about whom we thought they might contact, and did they intend harm, or simply to leave? Who could reach them? How could they have left at all? How could they do that to him? How could they do that to us? Shock, paternal worry, and only ever so slowly, acceptance, blended into this agonizing brew. Their note said little ~ mostly, apparently, how they claimed no problem with Jim, just with the people around him.

Did this mean they thought the people around him weren't radical enough? Another hefty morsel to crunch upon. This was a wild-eyed group of kids, who, according to some, had a clandestine program of rifle practice and thought guerilla warfare was the way to go. What would they do? Would they take a violent turn? In a world of anti-Vietnam War protests, civil rights havoc, assassinations still fresh and raw in the psyche of a wounded land, not to mention the rise of a militant left, Jim still invariably discouraged violence. He thought our stance dangerous enough without in this manner *incurring* violence. Nor did he think violence would be of any avail. Risk certain, gain doubtful.

Plus he thought that when he invoked, "The ends justifies the means," he meant one thing, and that they might interpret another. He didn't think they could handle whatever it was he speculated they might be getting into. He worried and ruminated, re-thought, back-tracked, despaired as much as if these were wholly and truly children of *his*. In his paradigm, they were. And they could get into trouble "out there." Did they even have enough money to buy food?

The rest of us felt helpless. There seemed to be nothing we could do. Perhaps one or two were sent out to scout, but time proved this to be a *fait accompli*.

It was a singular display – first shock, then hurt, then concern for *them*. It seemed to be eighth or ninth on the list at best, that they would move to damage *us*. The shock of their departure seemed to smart too painfully to even consider the possibility of simple treachery. Yet when after an hour or two of wringing our collective hands through this ordeal, the possibility of them damaging us did arise, it was suddenly no longer eighth or ninth on the list. It was *everything*. It was like we were driving along one road, a rather bumpy one, but at least in a vehicle and with our eyes on the road, and then, suddenly, the brake was slammed, and we had gone totally in reverse. I wasn't even sure the next series of considerations was happening:

What if they went to the press? What would they say? Jim could not conceive of these young people he so loved, that he had "poured his heart out to," even considering such a thing. But here it was. They were gone.

Jim was solemn, reflective, his eyes slightly inwards and intent. "How would you all feel about us jumping off the Golden Gate Bridge." *What?* (My "silent scream.") "As a protest. Because "they" (not the college students "they," – some greater, or more ominous, "they")... Because they won't just let us live in peace and build an interracial society."

Reader (more like "Dear Diary"...), I was very *confused*. What did the college students leaving have to do with building (or not building) a world of racial and economic equality? The press was unlikely, in any event, to directly attack us for being interracial, unless of course, they thought we were conducting orgies of interracial *sex*. (But most of Redwood Valley already thought that anyway, didn't they?) Or that the minister was involved with sex with parishioners. Fathering children and the like.

Was the Stoen fiasco about to bring us not just aggravation, but doom?

This was going too rapid-fire for me. I had barely processed that we were considering dying over... *what?*, when it turned out that "How would you all feel..." was rather a *rhetorical* question. The real question was, "Would any of you have any *reservations* about it?" People began to dialogue. What reporters might they contact? How badly could we be damaged? Could we recover? No, even more important.: Who would be affected if we jumped off the Golden Gate Bridge? Would people care? Would it change anything? No one... no one even seemed to reflect that we were talking about ...*death*. The place you don't come back from if you (wherever "you" may have gone) decided you did the wrong thing.

Do you know what it is like being out in the forest alone, an eerie silence in the air, and you hear a rustle? And you think that maybe it is a wild animal come to get you, and so you freeze every muscle 'til you are absolutely still? You don't even blink. Our language is so imprecise. Surely there is a name for that consciousness. Maybe "petrified." Like you're really terrified, but you don't even feel that, because you're *petrified*.

Well, I did have a tinge of that. If I expressed "reservations," I hadn't courage, or I hadn't commitment ~ I might even be accused of being afraid to die. If I questioned why such a drastic move was necessary, maybe there was something really important, really glaring, that everyone else knew that I didn't. Perhaps because I hadn't listened. Or wasn't concerned enough. Or others knew secrets not shared with me. All the people who had *slept* with him ~ probably they knew more secrets than me.

I had never studied a silence such as this, but I learned it in a clinch, post haste. I sat very still, like I simply had nothing to say. Perhaps someone else would say something that would at least clarify how to *approach* this.

I was especially sensitive to the question of die over *what?* (Even past the oft-repeated King quote: "A man who has nothing he is willing to die for isn't fit to live.") I had a haunting obsession of my own about it, that this seemed to link right into, like a lock shut or opened by a secret code, and I knew that something in Jim Jones would hold the key.

It flashed me back to that teary spring day and the bizarre episode on the street, reiterating inwardly anguished gulps of Keats' "*Ode to a Nightingale,*" weeping at the vision of mass death. They would be gone, yet I would live. I would release the whole world into a flood of tears. I would live for that day. When we could all weep openly about the deaths, and be free.

I wept on that very street. I fell to my knees weeping. How could this have been? How could I be paralyzed with fear and ecstatic with release all at once? Was I mad?

Were we all mad now? Had my reverie been but the tip of an iceberg? It seemed that premonitions had always bobbed up and down within me, nary reaching the surface, but never so wholly submerged that I didn't know that somehow mass death was *there*.

An obsession isn't quite like a fear, you know. It can have fears *attached* to it, as were fears attached to mine. Jim, sometimes in ways quite sublime, released those fears, in that death never seemed to daunt him. On rare occasions when people died in the church (the very frail, aged, or critically ill were often brought to be healed), he had everyone remain calm, as he walked over to the person, and slowly, gently, brought them back. He was so much in command, it seemed impossible to be afraid.

The spectre of mass death had come up just once before, in a late Sunday night service. We had sung *"Rock of Ages"* repeatedly, softly, harmoniously, holding hands. That night it seemed the only song that would do: "Rock of Ages, When the world's on fire, Don't you need God's bosom to be your pillow..." Jim had been talking of the future, and what might become of us, if we could break away to live as we chose, our own egalitarian community, our apostolic life.

He told us to close our eyes and that he would move across the floor and tap those who would be designated at a later time to go out and aid revolutionary movements in other parts of the world. The whole mood of the evening was so futuristic, it was almost trance-like. At one point, he gazed out amongst us and said gently but surely, *"Some of you will be stronger after I'm gone."* I inadvertently shuddered. "Oh, God, that's *me*." I knew it, though I could never tell you how.

He also told us, enigmatically, that "some day we may all be translated together." Perhaps he used the word "translated" so as not to freak people out by using the word "death." He said that no one who wanted to be included would be omitted. There also surfaced that night his ongoing obsession with numbers. That he was looking for certain people, and also needed a certain *number* of people. It was like a quantum mass concept. Only a certain number, together, could leap past certain points.

He was forever weeding out, cutting down ~ his, "If you can't take the heat, get out of the kitchen!" He didn't want hangers-on or spongers. He wanted people who were committed. It was exhaustive, this process of adding, then subtracting, then adding, then subtracting. He seemed sure of what he wanted, but no one but him could be sure of who, or how many, that might be.

So I couldn't say there was no preparation at all for "the Golden Gate Bridge option." I only had to *comprehend*. Surely, there *were* things worth both living for and dying for.

I had never felt that my own life span would be prematurely terminated. It was almost like I was *consigned* to live to old age. I didn't know why, nor even think it necessarily better. It just seemed clear. At the same time, it seemed clear that *Jim's* life could be cut short, and that frightened me. I feared he would die on us before I ever really knew him.

I also feared being cut off from myself ~ that even if I wanted the entire of my destiny to be with Peoples Temple, somehow I would have to live past it, and that I could, in effect, totally cut the ground out from under me. Living as though Peoples Temple was all my life would ever be ~ something tugged within me saying, "Not so." It was, in a seemingly perverse way, like I could almost feel more secure if I had believed Karen's "Don't worry about any of this. We'll all get to die soon." Maybe *she* would "get to die," but would *I*?

Jim had even seemed to confirm it. His calling me out and telling me inscrutable things about my future. My work in astrology, even with Canadians. Or the odd promise he couldn't have even wanted to make, that "You can write one great work." Peoples Temple, certainly Peoples Temple *as it was*, would not support that. We both knew it.

At times I wondered where or how the thread would, or could, snap. I subtly suspected this was past the point of anyone's control. That somehow it had already been long since pre-determined ~ long, long before I had ever met Jim Jones at all.

Obviously, it was verboten to air personal premonitions around Jim Jones, the master premonitioner. When I finally felt I had to, I landed myself into no end of trouble, as we will see. So I was on my own. Fearsomely on my own. I would soon enough realize how daunting it could be to view windows into the future *without them influencing the present*. Even for "lowly me."

For Jim Jones, how much the more? Our common assumption is that a paranoiac reality is created by a person who is inherently paranoid. What if it was rather that the person lived increasingly with premonitions of doom for what was really ahead, and simply felt he had to protect the people he loved? After all, what did become of Jim Cobb's bunch? Exactly what Jim Jones had feared!

And his responsibility was to all of us, wasn't it? The swings back and forth between projected triumph and projected disaster seemed excessively dramatic at times, though, like monkeys on a tree (grown to a certain maturity, with a certain height and weight, who would reach only within their range of agility), we each came upon the accessible branches and disregarded the rest. It was almost like we were being led through a minefield to safety on the other side.

And had Jim ever lost a one? No. Even with scores of people in their eighties and nineties, no member in good standing died. So here there would be *certainty*, yes? But even he, increasingly from then on in, could not guarantee such certainty. Unless, of course, you were willing to make your leap of certainly in the conviction that you were on the right path with your leader... **even unto death.**

The general congregation was slower in making these connections than those in P.C. or, especially, those in more continual or secluded contact with Jim Jones. Anyway, you can exhort, plead, even cry to the heavens at people again and again, but if they are unprepared to listen, no one will hear a thing. But that late afternoon under the trees, September 16, 1973, something in me loosened, and with a jolt, I began to *listen*.

So, as you see, I both did and didn't handle death by that 1973 date. I tried to absorb the panic about "The Eight," and remain steady and strong. Since my only real task was not to be conspicuous, I managed this with a fair amount of ease. Our systems, all of us, became regular shock absorbers, peculiarly inured to realities which seemed unreal. After all, we had gotten through the day and nobody jumped. Perhaps no one ever would. All we had to remember was, *Jim Jones would be there always.* He guaranteed all our lives with his own. Was that not enough?

A month or so later, "The Eight" were followed by "The Three," perhaps even more ominously, three staff members ~ sweet-looking Janine, cohort Hope, and a somewhat older woman named Lynda ~ the point at which Linda Amos became "Sharon." Lynda was a competent corporate type, and rather tough. She remained in Ukiah, perhaps thinking we had no right to see her banished just because she had chosen to leave *us*. But now there would be threats in the form of people who lived closer by than the vanished college students. Every now and then, news would filter in about one of Lynda's children being on drugs or pregnant in her teens. We took comfort in the fact that none of our kids were on drugs or pregnant. Eventually this all quieted down, even paling to insignificance in the shadows of what lay ahead.

XV. We "Protect Ourselves from Ourselves."

Like snow blanketing hidden seeds of Spring, September, 1973 proved to be "the winter of our discontent," rather than the full-blown crop of attacks that the summer of '77 would finally bring. Yet, as subtle shifts can also be pervasive ones, the very ground seemed to quake beneath our feet. Caution began to temper our characteristic welcome to one and all, and even loyalties of the closest were suddenly fair game.

Much of this happened gradually - like posting security people, who were mostly untrained and merely stood on watch at a post. Of course, since we had relocated to San Francisco, where the church had already been arsoned, this measure, although unorthodox for a church, cannot said to have been unwarranted. Probably more unsettling (mostly *mentally* unsettling), was an ongoing mindset that trust, freely extended before, could not be taken for granted now.

I watched with an abject fascination (unable, like others, to even consider intercession - *I* may have nothing to hide, but what if I hoisted a red flag that impeded critical safeguards against *others?*) as we "did what was necessary to protect ourselves." It wasn't even that it involved *doing* very much. Like signing potentially incriminating documents - you may object to it, but it's hardly an ordeal. Yet its effect was chilling; moreover, time would prove that it did nothing to protect us at all. Like Herod, who had all male children under the age of two indiscriminately slain, except that the very one he sought, Jesus, had been whisked away!

We weren't rank beginners by this point, of course. The precedent had already been set with the Stoens: To minimize, even circumvent, any future damage, Tim (himself an attorney, so swearing was no light matter) had sworn out an affidavit as to John's true parentage. Of all the quagmires we waltzed through, this was the worst. But after "The Eight" departed, such measures were introduced as blanket protections, not just specific to one individual or circumstance. As if to say, "If *they* could do it, *you* could do it."

A week or two later, blank papers were distributed in P.C. for us all to write out, "I fucked with Jim Jones and I loved it" - whether we had or hadn't, did or didn't. Then we had the whole congregation sign blank sheets of papers, presumably to initimidate them out of hurting us in the future. The rationale was the usual, "If you don't do anything wrong, you have nothing to worry about. This is to protect *all* of you." Yet it began to seem a hideous chess game, and too much now a public matter. Later, it was claimed that we were predisposed to be blackmailers, out of a cultish insanity, the living proof being such "coerced" documents! This wasn't a game that could ever proceed beyond a draw.

I do believe to this day, that Jim's root impulse *was* "to protect you all." He felt responsible for these people, even though sleeping with various members (*especially* to ensure their trustworthiness!) was so risky from the start, it could always veer towards endangerment, not protection. Moreover, extending what had only been done to forestall specific scenarios of potential harm (like the Stoen/Jones child), first to all of P.C., then to the congregation at large, probably did less to protect us than to seal our fate. Unless the *purpose* was simply to dissuade people by making them afraid. Even then, anyone who *did* want to cause harm, might not be afraid so much as *hostile* at being thwarted. Then you run into more trouble for ever having instituted the tactic than you ever could have hoped to accomplish by it.

You see, everything cuts both ways!

It became stifling. We seemed to become the repetitive proving ground for the one trauma Jim Jones seemed least able to endure: betrayal. His *"family"* left September 16, 1973. His family, his children, his own. Now he had to consider that *his "family"* (i.e. any one of us) *could become "the enemy."*

This type of wrench was intolerable for him. It tore at the fabric of his being, at the fierce father/mother defending his cubs. His zeal was unwavering, that by intent, by will, by indefatigable action, we, America's neglected ones, would at all costs be wholly equal and free. He would live on the brink every day of his life rather than relinquish that. Underdogs one and all, he believed we would only make it as a *family*.

Many quavered at his living as he did *at the time*. It was tragedy-in-the-making even back then, before all those precious lives were lost. Just like what showed up on the final tape made at Jonestown: *"They're my people. I'm standing with those people. They're a part of me. I can reject them... but no, no, no, no, no. ... You can't separate yourself from your brother and your sister. No way I'm gonna do it. I refuse. I've never lived like that.."*

And autocrat or no, it tugged at our hearts to witness the perhaps inevitable shifting from heroic living on the edge, to the emergence of damning Achilles' heels under stress. Not just those final hours at

Jonestown, but all the way from the time the college students left in 1973 up til the end. He couldn't understand them separating themselves from him, because he would never separate himself from *them*.

Worse, his worry proved warranted. They did go on to inflict deadly harm. But perhaps, given what evolved into the final scenario – government agents, mercenaries, a yellow press, i.e. outgunned by far!–, he *could* not protect against it. He could only make innocent people miserable in the interim. Here the relationship between Jim Jones' fiery premonitions, and the inevitable progression of events, began to chafe up against one another in an anguished kind of wrestling match, contending as to which would deliver the knock-out punch first, only to discover that the combatants were more of the character of Siamese twins! Each pushed the chess match to maximum stakes. "Check," "Check," "Check," til finally someone check-mated *him*.

Yeah, he had a heart attack when the eight college students left. This was indeed his very heart. Could we survive here at all? It seemed a pre-emptive stance, more drastic than immediate circumstances seemed to warrant. And admittedly, I say wryly (though "wryly" truly would not suffice!), no one really liked the Golden Gate Bridge option... But options there must be. Even a previously-unthinkable departure from the United States. Even our imperfect Planning Commission must now put its feet to the flames to safeguard the future out of this scenario of potential doom.

This was how it came upon us so rapidly that we needed a place like Guyana.

XVI. "*Tim* Found Us Guyana."

The Planning Commission, whatever its practical value (it did centralize all the departments of the church) was beginning to look less like the body of potentially-selfless saints I had originally hoped for, or even a body of uniformly dedicated workers that Jim necessarily portrayed it to be to the congregation.

Indeed, nearly everyone from the membership who later launched deadly attacks against the church, was in that august body called the Planning Commission. The students, the Stoens, the Mertles, Debbie Blakey, Teri Buford – all "one of us."

Everything that brought out the best in people also seemed to risk bringing out the worst. This seemed to be an assortment of the most dedicated, concerned, extraordinary people I had ever known, mixed in with the most insensitive, self-centered, treacherous dregs. Meanwhile, politics, persecutions, and pragmatics were coming so aggressively to the fore, that the magical world I had entered three years ago, was beginning to seem like a separate, even distant, place. We were into a whole different gear.

Our beacon of hope still shone, and our world of rapt followers endured. The magic of this extraordinary Light in our midst, Jim Jones, never failed to heal, guide and protect, even after hours of crises taking their toll; or to give us his love in a final, smiling glance. But surely nothing drained him like this. The betrayal by those in whom he had invested his time, energy, trust, even his physical love. This changed the ground rules for *everything*.

A more wary eye was being cast everywhere. The time of eternal assurances seemed more and more otherworldly, with Jim Jones more than ever not wanting devotees, but rather workers. A few short weeks later, he stared right at *me* and said, "I'm too much of a God to you." I wonder if he knew that all I could think was, "Then why not be a man to me? Why always this distance? This austerity?" But I wouldn't never voice this. I rather let it shatter me, piece by fractured piece.

Yet I, perhaps unlike others, was comfortable with reverence. I didn't want my wholly natural awe, given freely, to be supplanted by *enforcement*. That we had to stand when Jim (now "Father") entered the room; that he was now always accompanied by security guards; that people entering the church were now searched. These shifts were instituted gradually; we were still a family, but now a family on guard.

Even the rules of confrontation shifted. Rules like "You can't defend yourself when confronted." Perhaps others would speak up for you; perhaps they wouldn't. Perhaps Father would discern if some accusation was terribly wrong; perhaps he wouldn't. Perhaps, I even discovered, he himself would launch the accusation, true or false, counting upon misinformation from others. Then you were in serious trouble indeed – with no defense, and everyone willing to follow his lead.

Now everyone could be suspect. We were on the honor system. We'd have to trust that if we were indeed worthy, all would work out for us in the end. Because Jim (*"obviously"*) could now never again trust anyone fully. We all had our breaking points. He was the one who had to dance in and out of people's needs. Did they need him to smile at them? Did they need his praise? Did they need sex, or merely attention? The only one free of need, the only one purely a creature of conviction, was Jim Jones.

Another safeguard had entirely broken down as well, one rarely noted in what had become the insulated world of P.C. That was Marceline, as well as Jim's nuclear family. It disturbed me that occasionally, some even panned Marceline, for being "clinging" and the like. Marceline, who never came to P.C., was probably a saint in the total mix. I missed a mid-week catharsis when she was apparently told that if she didn't like how things were going, she could get a divorce. None would deny that Marceline was a mainstay, but it became, increasingly, a seesaw type of mainstay, her holding down the fort in L.A. when Jim was in San Francisco, and vice versa.

Jim's kids, of course, had horrendous problems with all this. Lew came to P.C. a few times, finally shouting, "All of you people – why don't you stop this," and was in too much anguish to live through a circus of which his father was (whatever his claims of reluctance) the apparent ringleader. Suzanne left not only P.C., but the work as a whole, shortly after Jim, her father, said in P.C. that if Suzanne "needed it," he would do it for her, too. Nor was she ever mentioned again as a problem. Maybe nothing more diabolical had driven her from us than sheer human pain.

Every now and then, Jim would say that founding the Planning Commission may have been the worst mistake he ever made. In any case, this was no place for the frail or frightened.

One thing, though, was now clear. With threats of destruction from our own disaffected membership (even these tiny few – but these tiny *knowledgeable* few), we needed contingency plans. Jim had never wanted to leave the United States, but was now ripe to cross the line. Marcus Garvey's name was brought up more often, the American Black nationalist who aspired to found an all-Black community, but outside the United States, believing that America's Blacks could never achieve parity here.

Several weeks of discussions were more like an ongoing report of a what a small, select group had been assigned to investigate. Finally one night, Jim looked to his left, to Tim Stoen, standing at his perennial distance at the back of the room, like some benevolent overlord who had risen above the fray, and said, with a slight smile of acknowledgment, **"*Tim* found us this. Tim found us Guyana."**

It was perfect. Within our hemisphere, a third world nation with a multi-racial population of black, white, Indian, Amerindian, even Chinese. The largest proportion of these was Black. They had huge tracts of unsettled land in the rain forest, where we could found an agricultural cooperative, which would benefit the neighboring Amerindians as well. Jim never forgot his genetic pool of Native American roots. Raven-haired, straight and thoroughly black, and skin tinged with undercurrents of red, yellow, brown, this identification, at least, was secure. He worried fretfully, from time to time, that he would never gain prominence as a Black leader in America, for the obvious reason that whatever his heart, mind, or soul, his skin color was simply not black. Could Guyana become the multi-racial paradise of which he had dreamed?

The holidays coming up in 1973, were a bit more lonely, as Father had "taken a trip." Just days past Christmas (miraculously it seemed, for this complicated, unexpectedly rapid negotiation), our lease for the land which was later named "Jonestown," was concluded. Jim returned in triumph to tell us of the breakthrough that could serve as both refuge and shining example to the world. We were elated.

Only two or three were sent at first, to bring in labor to clear the land, and to negotiate with the Guyanese government for whatever ongoing assistance might be required. It seemed the smallest crew for the hugest gamble.

One of those sent was Paula. When she first came into the church, she was married to Sam. Sexual liaisons with the leader ensued, and there wasn't much left of the marriage. Paula must have had some political talents as well, for various ministries were gradually won over as they saw the agricultural project flourishing in ways they had wanted to encourage their own population to undertake, apparently with little success.

Early in the game, she established a relationship with the then-Guyanese Ambassador to the United States, Lawrence Mann, which she maintained through the coming years. After the tragedy, she married him. I learned to my horror a few years past the tragedy, that she, her husband, and their new baby girl, had been murdered. The reports in the press had apparently stated that they had been despondent about the suicides, and that Mann (who had never been a member of the community ~ this made less than no sense) had gone berserk, killing first his wife and child, then himself.

Paula was a gentle soul, who was in Georgetown at the time of the suicides and then briefly returned to the United States. She was torn up at losing her adopted daughter at Jonestown. She would have been thrilled to have a child of her own. The story was such a fabrication, it stank, though I never had the time, money, nor contacts to pursue it. We may never know what Paula knew. That was all.

But this was still a long ways off. At first, we weren't even sure of making a go of it. Building the settlement was tedious and slow, even clearing the land, with the tropical hazards of weather, lack of roads, the local wildlife, and a whole host of other unknowns. It was a long while before we could consider a viable, thriving, much less self-sufficient community. Moving en masse was still in the distance ~ perhaps a dream, or a choice rather than a forced move. For now, building from scratch was too daunting to have any clear fix on its outcome.

We were entrenched in the United States, in fact, about to purchase the building in San Francisco where we had been holding our monthly meetings. Jim himself moved down to the city in 1975, anticipating this would be our new base, gradually phasing Redwood Valley out. Meanwhile, a building in Los Angeles had been added on. Clearly, any plans for expansion were purely local. So Guyana, for a long while, was an outpost, hardly a new home.

Going into 1974 and 1975, our meetings in all three locales were briskly attended. Jim had an extraordinary gift for courting the locals, including the Mayor of San Francisco (George Moscone, later murdered in those dark days following the tragedy); State Assemblyman Willie Brown (now himself Mayor of San Francisco); publisher of the Sun-Reporter (the main Black newspaper in San Francisco), Carlton Goodlett; even the Lieutenant Governor of the State, a black man of Caribbean origin, Mervyn Dymally. The latter two visited the Guyana project later on and loved it.

Meanwhile, anything a community could do to better itself, Peoples Temple provided the bodies to do it. We were getting a reputation as do-gooders that kept the more guarded reality of being socialists, a more-or-less sheltered secret. Prominent people, mostly left wing, visited on Sundays, and we complied with whatever was the desired behaviour of the day. We even got Jane Fonda to a service in Los Angeles, and shortly before Jimmy Carter was elected, Jim convinced someone that we were an important voting bloc, and was able to arrange a private meeting with the (soon-to-be) President's wife, Roslyn.

From the surface of things, from 1973 through 1976, we seemed out of our angst, and on a roll upwards. Yet Jim, ever a realist, believing that the success of an interracial, socialist group in America would not tolerated, and ever uneasy that the worst of traitors were planted in our midst ("they'll be very high up," he always said), never let us relax our guard. He said this would not last. The adulation would not last. Of that he was certain.

He was more adept than anyone I've ever seen at lifting people's spirits to the skies ~ to give them pride, purpose, motivation. How this could all be, and yet, be almost *intermeshed* with an ever-present Waterloo-to-be, I cannot explain to you. It just continually happened. Maybe at that, it brought out the heroic in people. Lifted them to a higher ground.

Certainly one would have to be made of stone to miss the underlying anguish that propelled our leader with unbridled force into Isaiah's "Cry aloud and spare not!" One night I remember poignantly, because it was the only time I had ever seen Jim cry. There was a skit, depicting black children being dragged away by cruel white overseers at some unspecified future time. Jim began to cry. He put his hand over his forehead as his body rolled involuntarily forwards, and I saw that he was beginning to weep. Slowly I could hear his anguished cries emerge: *"The agony of it, the agony of it, the agony of it...."* Jim Jones was a very proud man. Stoical. I would never forget that the only time I ever saw him cry was over *that*.

Then there were the long, ever long, stressful offerings, Jim pleading and exhorting money from the generous and ungenerous alike. He would know how much money they had in their wallet, or even whom they were sleeping with on the sly. Anything to make them give. Shame them, humor them, make them laugh until they.... *gave*. The timing was invariably brilliant, and "the gift" remained awesome, though now it was slipping more out of the divine into the most mundane ~ a question of dollars. He knew what our exodus would cost. No one knew it like he did, or poured their heart and soul into the raising of money like Jim Jones.

We were into a new gear. Our numbers swelled, but discipline tightened, as services became more intense ~ even, at times, wild. Mass healings. Mass confessions. Hours and hours of catharsis. Some probably ill-advised physical punishments, sometimes even of adults, for infractions of various norms of behaviour. But there were benefits. Like our kids didn't steal ~ they didn't even think of it. They would have mass wrath, or (possibly more intimidating) the wrath of Jim Jones to pay the piper. But they were also very good kids ~ friendly, cooperative, well-behaved.

Eventually, we settled into a routine of one weekend in San Francisco, one in Los Angeles, with Marceline rotating opposite locations from Jim. The skeletal membership still in Redwood Valley held services with Tim Stoen, Jim's "most trusted," who even seemed ripe, at one point, for successorship. Jim seemed quite willing to let Stoen go unattended. His work in the Mendocino County D.A.'s office was demanding, and there were always reasons to stay back while the rest of us travelled.

Little John was moved down to San Francisco at about the same time Jim moved, with our young woman of Greek parentage, Maria Katsaris, as his surrogate mother. Grace, now separated from Tim, stayed in Redwood Valley, perhaps predictably a mistake, finding herself a boyfriend with which to plot and plan... whatever.

Meanwhile, communal living had become a key, having crept up on us in Redwood Valley, then being encouraged as the San Francisco norm. I had already "gone communal" before induction into P.C., was giving over all my paychecks to the church, eating communally as well, and in return, I was given all of $2.00 a week as spending money ~ which we were actually encouraged to turn in!

It was a stringent life, but we towed the mark. I didn't want Jim sacrificing so much, and not I. Life's excitement came in the services, and even more (for this forum was still a *pulse*), P.C. I wasn't happy with what was often drudgery otherwise, but I looked around and everyone seemed to be in the same boat.

I was thankful to be relieved of L.A. perhaps every other trip, to tend to the letters. I hated the long trips southwards, especially in that I was never close enough to Jim to ride in his bus, and all the other busses were general chaos and confusion. I never felt I didn't belong, but no one else seemed to know that. It was like a cog-in-the-wheel syndrome. I repressed and repressed and repressed. Why didn't Jim at least know my heart? I feared, increasingly, that I might explode.

XVII. I Make the Mistake of Telling the Truth.

P.C. remained its own private world of intimidation and enlightenment. Much shifted for me personally during those years. For the *worse*, it seemed, like hinges that had been at least securely fastened, were now threatening to crack the doors of my very heart open and release floods of tears.

Everything that was done for people impersonally in our miracle of a church, uplifted me so. But P.C. seemed both too personal and too alienating, like an existential oxymoron. Like some people avoid marriage because it reveals how akin intimacy may be to separation. Better to keep your distance in the first place.

I could barely handle the emotional disasters –some centered in sex, some in rebellion against authority, some just based in people's character– that swirled too often around P.C.

Though sex was the worst. Jim was "in love with all of us," he would say, but seemed to have odd ways of showing it. Ellen complained she felt rejected because her husband never went down on her, so Jim made him go down on another woman in P.C.; though the man was white, so the woman had to be black. Another night he took David to task for "not cleaning out his ass" before they met; we never saw David again. Patricia, a lovely young woman who worked *so* hard and was a virgin, was offered her big chance so she wouldn't "miss anything" in life. He was incensed when she met his offered sacrifice with, "I don't want him coming on to me," and I felt so sorry to see her crushed. A young man, Chris, not in P.C., just a naive and innocent kid, felt he couldn't go through life without sex, so Jim had him to pick any woman he wanted in P.C., but instructed the women privately, to make him use two condoms, then to just lie there. Paul was a pedophile, and some idiot assigned him to work with young boys (because he had "promised not to do it anymore") with the predictable results. Jim had him beaten on the penis (admittedly, the children's parents might have preferred worse!), then come into P.C. and drop his pants ("It's all right, you're amongst friends") to reveal what discipline he had received, all the while lamenting that, "Even being with me didn't help."

Whatever the circumstance, the attacked party was made out to be guilty, with Jim Jones drained, and suffering under the load. Ironically, he *was* suffering under the load! Psychologists know this well. One can impose wrong burdens on oneself and suffer *horribly* – who amongst us hasn't done it? (Remember this when we come to "You're carrying an unnecessary burden!" His wrong burdens compounded with my wrong burdens made for a ghastly kind of brew.)

The obsession with homosexuality seemed the most bizarre, in that even educated guesstimates are that 10% of the population is homosexual – not 100%! God knows why he thought this – though the Stoen disaster could not have helped, later information surfacing that Grace's real problem had been her discovery of her husband's secret life as a *transvestite!* Whatever the genesis of Jim's "conclusions" about homosexuality, it seemed anguish even for him. Of course, it was nightmarish for us if only in that it *disempowered* people.

Nor would I minimize the slings and arrows of heterosexuality as well. Taking on all those people intimately. You synchronize with their energies or you repel them. And repelling someone for whom you've made a "cradle-to-grave" commitment – what a horrible risk. Even synchronizing is risky. Their outlooks and emotional bents, hopes and fears alike – a piece of them becomes implanted in *you*. And what if it countermands the common good? Even God, we might say, has had a horrendous job being "all things to all people." Just ask the Hindus and the Moslems. Or the Sunis and the Shiites. Or the Arabs and the Jews.

Perhaps once the Jones' own nuclear family got wrecked over sex, then every barrier, however intimate, was more prone to dissolve. And once such lines are crossed, how do you ever cross back? Amongst the subjects that only came up once were the early Soviet experiments in the 20's in breaking up family life; eventually having the leader chose everyone's mates *for* them, like the Moonies; and I remember vaguely a distant third, Jim Jones' own sperm having to repopulate a decimated Earth.

It would have been risky enough were we ordinary people, worse if a religion, but doubly, trebly courting disaster by way of being political! Us with the double trouble of the 60's and the Cold War – both interracial and socialist? How could sex not fail to, additionally, both damage our credibility and enhance our liability? One might leap valiantly over the waterfall and hope to land safely into the swirling currents below. But why risk stabbing oneself in one's own back?

Even the smallest children couldn't fail to note the drain. A little eight-year-old girl, Angel Casanova, walked up to Jim one holiday service and said, "I feel sorry for you having to be God." He was very touched.

Ironically, the man took on so much, passionately and without cease, that not only did I never want out, but like others, never stopped feeling for *Jim*. His willingness to suffer through each crisis never wavered. He was always the one waking us up towards 6 a.m. ~ how could people sleep when pressing matters still remained? For him, perhaps, the world was *always* on fire, and the Rock of Ages, for all its portents of doom, would always have to be *him*.

Yet the grind took its toll. I never had a viable voice, Nor did I receive but occasional praise for my work. Nor did I even want it. What I wanted, needed, was attention ~ a listening ear, a tender touch, love. I had stopped asking "When will he get to me?" It seemed hopeless. I held no cards. Why would I, why should I, deserve Jim Jones' attention? Besides, it could all backfire. What if I was, let's say, taken to bed once, made to feel inadequate or a drain, and then... exiled? It could make things even worse.

In the perennial crush of imperatives, I barely even reflected on the painful, even inhumane discrepancies ~ that in an "egalitarian" world, some were drawn into a passionate sexual embrace while others never received so much as a hug. I couldn't have even asked. I was untouchable. The moment I was touched, I would have dissolved into tears. It was strange. Once when Jim was depressed about our long-range prospects, he said "Sometimes all we can do is hold one another and cry." The only crying *I* ever got to do was alone.

I never even felt free to be depressed about anything personal. I had lost hope of producing creative work, but still, painfully, burning my music had not burned out that place in my heart which yearned to be whole. Should I rip my heart out entirely? I had already destroyed the most prized creations I had done to date. And that act was... *ignored*.

I was sitting on a smouldering identity crisis, whether it was ever discussed or not. God forbid it be discussed. How could I claim this was intolerable to *me*, when I saw what others endured? I'd only be castigated. Silence was less of a threat.

I certainly wasn't volunteering anything about sex. I was uncomfortable yelling and screaming at people at all, much less on that subject, where any step in the wrong direction could readily mire you in quicksand.

But Jim *solicited* confidences. This time it was in L.A. It was one of those "frozen" sessions, where Jim wanted people to talk about sex with him, and everyone sat immobilized. Why was no one saying it was wonderful? Was it guilt? That however wonderful it was, they had fully paid for it in guilt?

I Make the Mistake of Telling the Truth/127

This one time, Jim would not let it pass. He asked everyone to get out a paper and pen and write how they felt about sex and how they felt about him, and did they want to be with him if they hadn't already been. I wrote that it was very difficult to go without sex for this long, and that I did want to be with him. Then I inadvertently took a deadly step in the wrong direction. I told him I had had a sexual relationship before I was in the church where I was able to have orgasms throughout the night.

I'm not sure why I told him that (never mind the truth – it didn't always get the top billing claimed!), but I certainly didn't tell him out of defiance. It was more like "I know what this is, and it's a part of life, I'm completely cut off now and I want it again." I passed the paper in. I didn't feel so much anxiety when I simply told the truth. Jim always assured us that was all he wanted. That if we only told him the truth, he would never embarrass us.

The next P.C. meeting, we were in Redwood Valley. To my shock, Jim said he had read everyone's notes and "Laurie said she had sexual fulfillment with a man other than me. This is audacious and presumptuous." A cold anger tinged his voice as he clamped down on "presumptuous."

For all anyone knew, I was relating to Jim while also having an ongoing affair, flaunting it in Jim's face, and daring to make a *comparison*. Whatever people thought, it was "Rorschach Test style." After all, there must be good reason for his ire. He wouldn't just haul off and attack me if I were innocent, would he? I must have done *something*.

Of course, no one asked any clarification from *me*. Jim was definitive, sharp, with anger contained, directed, controlled. This was fact. He didn't even look at me. I was made to stand up and people landed on me like a pack of wolves.

It was so irrational, memory fails me. I only remember Sharon barking at me in a shrill voice, "No one has orgasms with anyone but Jim Jones." Was this a fact, or a mandate? What if it indeed happened, somewhere, any part of the globe? Who would be called a liar, much less arrested? And who would do the arresting? The bedroom police?

I could say nothing in my defense. Well, thank God for that, at least. What in the world would I have said?

Ah, yes, you wonder now about my sanity. (You've always wondered about *his* sanity.) It wasn't just that I had relinquished so much of my power. I was also in the bind of need. I was young and had no one. And I loved and revered this man for all the wonders, both Godly and man-made. I had never known a place like this, where all races, ages, backgrounds lived in such harmony. The bottom line was that I just never could turn. I wanted with all my heart for it to *work*. I had seen truly vicious people cause problems that hurt us all. I could never, ever, be the cause of dissension.

Thus I endured the terrors of not merely humiliation, but of *separation*. I trusted this man to know that I was trustworthy. He gambled I would never leave, but probably for the wrong reasons. He may have been right that sex is a relatively superficial component. But trust isn't. He should have trusted me. I earned it. It devastated me that he didn't.

And in that devastation, I felt humbled. I knew what I had written was true, but given his outburst, I wrote him (well, I *was* learning a bit about tact) that although I had never been with him, I was sure it was like everyone said. I wrote nothing more. I wrote nothing less. I didn't fall to my knees, but I made no issue of standing upright either. I told myself it was an aberration. There was probably some rationale at work I didn't grasp.

Yet even in that brief encounter, all I feared was confirmed: that any hopes to alleviate my love-starved life were dwindling.

Meanwhile, something else had happened that at least freed my *mind* into a natural release. It was also on the eve of a September 16th, but my own private September 16th, in 1974. I was at work one day, when I heard an inner voice say, "You are the poet of the revolution." I was startled. Within minutes, I was hearing lines of poetry, like I had when I first arrived West in '68. It wasn't anything I had decided to do. It did *me*. The lines were so flowing, so beautiful. I acceded to my intense urge to write.

The first poem was called "I, Too": "I too must live, though my name be sorrow, I too must feel, though ancient be the pain. I, too, know that the visions for tomorrow may not come, nor laurel victory nor glimpse of gain..." It came through with surprising ease. I coded it into the word-processor, so that when several liked it, I could run off copies. Indeed, that Christmas, it was slated to be read as part of the ongoing entertainment throughout the day, but at the last, it was inexplicably cancelled. I thought there was just not time for everything.

After some weeks, I had accumulated many poems. But except for the minor attention "I, Too" had received (even Marceline liked it, I had been told), I kept my writing to myself. I was holding on. Not altogether steadily, but enough so. Then, getting towards Thanksgiving, a process began that knocked me totally off my pins, and changed my life forever.

XVIII. My Muse Arrives, and Doesn't Get Along with My God.

"Allegory." It seemed like the arrival of a Presence. Floods of thoughts, impressions, ideas. Lines as melodic as the crests of waves or the curve of a setting Sun. But one sole Presence. I wasn't new to visitations ~ they preceded my entry into Peoples Temple, three within the course of several months. But once I heard Jim's startling, *"You knew this would happen on this date,"* I felt the Presence must surely be *him*. I had no need to question further, or to turn to any other spiritual source.

There were earlier times, too. The poetry I wrote when I first came West ~ it was like I was accompanied by someone. But this was more powerful still. An awesome Presence. Awesomely serene, but also terrifying. Acknowledging any spiritual presence but Jim was inherently terrifying, if only for its risks of social rebuke.

Yet my new (or perhaps very *ancient*) Friend would not be denied. I feared, I feared, I feared, yet that was *mundane* fear; with all my *spiritual* heart, I was His. What was happening? I felt myself thrown into leaps of time: the ancient past, the distant future, an ominous pathway ahead. Sometimes I experienced all these *simultaneously*, a trance-like distraction from which I could not shake myself free. This was a magnetic power, an enfolding power, almost... *ecstatic*. He was so... so very laden with sorrow, but in His very sorrow was a surging, resonant strength.

It was the first time in my life, I felt that a very power was Someone to Whom I could entrust my very being, not just now, but somehow, almost beyond any description, throughout all Time. Of course, with all my soul, plus all the intensities of my anxieties and fears(!), I hoped ~no, nearly prayed~ that it would be... Jim Jones.

I felt led to the library down the street from where I worked. I had never been there before. We had no time to read novels, and any "approved" reading was political, of the variety this particular library would never have carried. What impressed itself upon me was Greek mythology (of all things), and I sensed that some book would jog my mind into the intended niche. What I heard to research was the Promethean myth.

Be this a cosmic assignment, how had it come to me? We were steeped in Black culture and leftist politics. Were there a list of likely topics to research, it wouldn't be the lowliest of the low on the list. It would not have made such a list at all! I felt furtive and uneasy, sneaking it into stolen moments at lunch.

The Promethean myth, you might recall, is a prototype for the heroic vanguards of Man. Prometheus came to Mankind to bring Fire (if a metaphor, then be it Spirit), in defiance of the oppressive "gods" of his Age. For his heroism, he was chained to the rocks of Caucasus, with a vulture pecking at his liver throughout the day. At night, he rested while his liver was restored, and the torture resumed anew at dawn.

He was only rescued when the centaur, Chiron, wise teacher half-man half-horse, arose to take his place. It was clear to me that "Chiron" must be the awakening New Humanity, the only force on Earth that could relieve the Christ figure (for whom Prometheus was an early prototype) of his anguish forever.

I wrote a prologue about the Promethean myth, a prologue to the work I had not yet written. I knew it would be about Jim Jones and that it would be about us. And as it gradually encroached upon me, it would also be about *death*.

I remembered that dazed day in the street more than a decade ago, when I fell to the ground weeping at the deaths I was to survive later on in life. It was still early in this ...unsettling? ...disconcerting? ...no, nearly *earthquake-like* process. But I knew as surely as if a stake had been driven through my heart, as if to vanquish all the un-dead of Humanity and arouse them to a greater day... I knew that that premonition of death in those now-waning years, was *this*.

I didn't ever devise "*Allegory*," or patch the myth against the work. It, rather, impressed itself upon me, successively, phrase by phrase, line by line. I was drawn in, merely seeking the solitude and concentration by which to listen. It was inexorable. It flowed through me, impressing upon me, compelling me to write, whether I could make the time or space to listen at all. The language was hypnotically beautiful, but it was so much more. I *had* to do this. Sometimes I wept, out of the sheer despair of trying to discern what this was all about. Why all these deaths? Where? How? When?

Images arose, washing through me like a kind of existential dyslexia. It was set outdoors, it seemed in some kind of open-air arena – which turned out to be the common meeting area (not yet built!) called The Pavilion. I could look up and see the stars, like it was out in the country somewhere. Much vegetation, and a warm, breezy night. Not knowing it would be November in the tropics, I thought perhaps it was summer, because it was warm.

Why were our people dying? There were references to wars and battles, but *this* didn't look like a battleground. It was more like a place of peace ~ ay, a "garden home" ~ a beautiful garden bitterly destroyed. (*"Oh, mourn not your garden-loss! Love in this present place is a fearful thing, an awesome weight..."*) What was happening? Why the enigma of the two sets of guards ~ one friendly, another hostile? Are not guards simply guards? And why were there *"no known means of escape"*?

Why were swallows falling into the sea? A metaphor of some sort ~ the fall of human flesh into the abyss? Who were "the vultures" closing in to pick and taunt at every claim? And what was Jim's son *John* doing there? He seemed somehow central. This made no sense. We wouldn't send people off to battle with a little child.

And why, why that eerie silence in its wake? Why would none arise in defense of the fallen? (*"...a dirge too low to justly grieve., a song too weak for a too-wrong death!"*) Why would none dare, even chance, to speak? Where were the dark victors proclaiming our courage, our valor, our sacrifice? Why the ungodly silence?

Impression layered upon impression, in saturation not of the physical senses, but of the psychic ones, and ever, on its heels, the long flowing lines, like haunting melodies, telling this strange, seemingly undecipherable tale.

Is God merciful that He gives us veils? I look back now and know that my unseen Visitor was showing me Jonestown. (*"I see them plunge, one by one, towards the sea, 'neath the foam. My own heart sinks with thee..."*) Jim Jones looking on in sorrow, watching the swallows fall beneath the sea. This was death. *Our* death.

In misty veils of transcended time and haunting metaphors, caught in states ranging from total serenity to torrents of tears, I felt I could decipher nothing. The force of the words was the force of the words. Was it not enough that I was their conduit, and terrified of what they might mean at all?

My co-workers in the letters office realized vaguely that I was weirded out, cause unknown, but the church work was getting done, so I was left alone. And who *could* I talk to? Having this scenario close in on me was terror enough. What if it were true? If I were truly seeing Jim and our people dying, and I voiced this, I myself could have been accused of *wanting* the leader dead. I could be labelled traitorous. Or deluded.

Perhaps even insane. At the very least, narcissistic and self-involved. Why else would I write poetry when the whole world was starving and oppressed and in pain?

But there was a prospect even worse. What if this Presence who enveloped me was **not Jim Jones at all?** What if this all came to his ears and he denied it? I would die. I would truly die. No one else would have a chance to die. I would have already gone mad, or be *accused of* going mad ~ moreover, castigated. And my God, worse, the *very* worst: What if it were totally untrue ~ nay, delusional? Well, the worst for *me*, anyway. But wasn't the real "worst" *if it was true?*

Was I really being caught between stark raving insanity on the one hand, and loss of everything and everyone I loved on the other? And with fear of castigation piled on *top* of that? I could not have invented a worse "lose-lose" scenario than this. There wasn't any end of this stick I could grasp onto without peril. Mere human anxiety never had a hold on one as this had a hold on me.

There seemed no way to sustain these weird, inexplicable swings between ecstatic serenity, fear of madness, passionate fervor for this work, and overbearing terror of discovery. The work itself buoyed me. I could not believe I had been given something so aesthetically beautiful to write. Yet I was rapidly turning into a nervous wreck.

Then an atypical thing happened. Jim had come over one evening in November, 1974, to visit the complex of offices that was called "Publications." He happened to be in the far building, where *I* usually wouldn't be at all, but this particular evening I was. He was telling Maria Katsaris, a fairly new member of the church, and Kathy, a more established regular, that he wanted to bring them onto the Planning Commission; and he invited me, along with a few others, to come into a small side office with him and the two inductees.

That evening, I was especially on edge. I was into the first section of the text of *"Allegory"* when I realized in horror, that I was writing as **Jim Jones in the first person**: *"No one knows me, why I give all, though the moment to intercede is past, or has not yet come."* "No-one knows.... <u>me</u>"? I couldn't speak for the leader. Worse ~ speak for him *upon his own death?* They'd say, "How dare you," and much much worse. They'd say I wanted Jim dead. I couldn't do this.

But I also couldn't *not* do this. That evening was the crossroads. There was a power compelling me on, and a terror reining me back. I acted as normally as possible. I wasn't the proverbial writer at a desk with downwardly-cast pen and upturned eyes. I was just sitting there on top of a table, in jeans, going through this invisible... *torture*. What could I do, or not do?

I was steeped in that irreconciliable schism when Jim, in a casual, apparently impromptu manner, invited me and the others off to the side. We sat down with Kathy and Maria, and Jim began to tell them about P.C. What came up? Grace, naturally. Then Jim did this atypical thing. He had no interest in superficialties, even though he would at times adopt various kinds of social glue that keeps people attentive and engaged. It seemed this evening, that someone had shown Jim a "psychological test." Maybe he wanted some stray information about one of us. It was approached casually enough, and ever compliant around the master, we listened.

He showed us four shapes. There was a circle, a square, a triangle, and a "Z." He told us to draw them, each one, in order of preference. I knew at a glance I preferred the circle and the "Z," but the order was not yet clear. The triangle was nice, but still, it was third. The square came in a distant fourth. I fiddled a bit, then decided the "Z" was the most interesting. I wrote out Z, circle, triangle, square. I put the "Z" on top, then the circle, marking the two "nearly the same," and handed it in.

Maria, still struggling to make a clean break from an unhappy home situation, marked her first preference as a square. Jim finally got to my paper, and thought it interesting that the "Z" had won out. I seemed the only one so predisposed.

He then said this was a psychological test. That the square was security, the circle sex, the triangle intellect and the Z creativity. What did this mean? I supposed what it always meant. That I was back to "Square One." The cottage. Creativity and sex. I've always had an active mind, but there was little charge in simply being bright ~ indeed, it was easy to be bookwormish, with its implied forms of ostracism. As for security, it was dangerously underrated to my own peril. I had given up everything material with ease. I did not want the encumbrances of the material world.

The meeting was not too long ~ a couple of hours at the most. In this small side office, I was sitting on a table, as I had been in the more spacious waiting area outside. Ironic metaphor ~ perhaps that table was a fence. I, "sitting on a fence," was trapped in the anguish of not being able to land down on either side without encountering extraordinary grief.

It was pathetic, the human heartstrings that tugged at me. Were "bizarre" and "pathetic" in competition that paralytic night, the latter might well have won. Here I was, denied sex, offered creativity as not a shining star, but a poisoned apple, my intellect wasted in menial tasks, and Jim Jones' great gift to us was to be.... *security.* "Cradle-to-grave security" ~ well, that is, unless we *died.* If the grave prematurely closed in on the cradle. How could I decide what to do? I wondered if I could even *function.*

The meeting closed amicably. It all seemed low key. Maria and Kathy were appropriately congratulated. Then... ~ it was like one of those rushing scenes that happen so fast, you don't know whether it happened at all; and your mind, knocked off its perch into a space where reality seemingly cannot exist, for a moment doesn't register even the witness of one's own senses. Like "Did this happen at all?" But then the cameraman comes along and slows it way, way down, and you see it *really happening.* Like the assassination scene at the beginning of the film *"JFK."*

Jim was moving out of the room, rather slowly, stopping for brief words, gently smiling, the reassuring mode of his multi-faceted self. He came upon me, sitting on that table-shaped fence, self-conscious, unsure; then, like a warm gentle rain on a late summer's day, his words washed over me ~ audible, so unmistakably audible, yet on some other fence ~ the tender divide between the real and the surreal: *"No one will ever understand you. No one ever understands me."* And it wasn't even like it was Jim. Not like it was a *person.* It was like.... a *Presence.* I looked up. Then, in an ebbing instant, he was gone.

"No one knows me...."

"*No one will ever understand you. No one ever understands me.*"

Who spoke these words, these parallels, these twins? Who was it who echoed my own soul and heart? I was no less terrified, but now, at least, I did not have to make this excruciating choice alone. I was graced, even blessed, with a Presence. A Presence who, like a magical resonance in a minor key, had... not made the choice for me, yet *allowed* me (beyond risk or rescue, anguish or comfort) to follow the longings of my own already grief-laden heart.

I resumed writing now, with a renewed, if still trepidatious, passion. How could I relax my guard? Outwardly, I knew I was still ripe to be fodder for a wolf pack. I knew that I could not, understand, make the slightest assumption of the approval of Jim-Jones-the-man for my clandestine work. I knew that this outer world of interracial harmony and shared accomplishment, was both inherently intertwined with, yet also entirely separate from, the inner world of mystics and the heart ~ a world "owned" by Jim Jones.

But now I knew what I must do. There was scarce comfort, admittedly, in "never being understood." But now I could, would, even *must* (the key divide) let *"Allegory,"* pour through my soul onto the written page.

I wrote in the office, I wrote at work, I even wrote during P.C. My favorite was solitude. Solitude on the street, during a meal, before I fell asleep; just not crushed in with people. It was so much easier to "hear" without people. Sometimes I thought I could be alone forever....

It was February, 1975, before *"Allegory"* was complete. It must have been March or April when I finally wrote Jim. The work was done and the Presence (sent by Jim, not sent by Jim, I still feared the truth of this unremittingly) seemed to be gone as well.

I recalled to him that when we had met in the cottage a long while back, he had told me, "You can write one great work." And that now, I believed I had done it. That it was called *"Allegory,"* but that it was about his death and the death of many of our people, and it frightened me.

Had he asked to see it at the time, I would have of course handed it over. I mightn't have even kept a copy. That didn't happen, perhaps just for the banal reason that he was so biased against the writing of poetry, which he considered fantasy, illusion, worthless. He wouldn't even *value* it enough to ask for it.

I went on to say that perhaps he was angry at me because he thought I wasted a whole life writing in my last incarnation. (If that sounds mad, how did my *poem* sound?) But that this had *forced* itself upon me. And though the work frightened me, I thought perhaps it was all right, because of what he had said to me in the cottage.

I was, I fully admit, in a world of my own, and perhaps a very left field world at that! I was grasping for reasons for his anticipated antipathy in the only ways I knew how. What I wanted desperately was assurance, understanding, not to face horrifying accusations or castigation. It seemed fear beyond fear that I would be made a pariah over this. I couldn't bear it.

Did he even skim the letter and note the word "frightened," I might have been spared some of the ensuing traumas. I'm not sure *what* he read, or how he read it. I did know that I was frightened *now*. Frightened of *him*. What response could this bring? Were my molecules about to be splattered all over the floor?

I had written Jim just before (it turned out) the meeting where he told us about the new-born, Kimo, in a P.C. in Redwood Valley. As the meeting began, he took stock of the room, and when he came upon me, he looked, no, *scrutinized* me hard. I was mad... or what? Nothing was said. I saw in him a face that was disturbed, but momentarily averred from passing judgment.

The meeting began. He said we might have been wondering where *Carolyn* had been. That, as we knew, she had briefly returned for a recent service in San Francisco. Apparently, it turned out, that was set up to see if people liked Carolyn, or had missed her. Carolyn was a straight arrow, hard-working, dedicated, and nearly obsequious around Jim. She was supposed to have been his wife when he was Lenin, and one of the closest to him now. Yet when she was once offered successorship, she somberly offered, "I do not wish to live when you are no longer leader." Jim immediately dropped her name.

She was close to him throughout, if inclined to shun the limelight. I don't think anyone actually disliked Carolyn, just found her standoffish. Jim knew that; but still, he seemed disappointed that she wasn't more warmly received upon her return. Plus it may have made his present task a bit harder.

He went on. He said that close to a year back (I believe "nine months" said it), he needed Carolyn to go on a dangerous mission to Mexico. (Staff, as Carolyn was, were the ones he sent here, there, everywhere. She *could* have gone to a foreign country at Jim's behest, I thought.) She was told she might need to forge important contacts, even seduce one or two men if necessary, to gain information or access. (Somber, reserved Carolyn? Hardly the choice, even had such a mission existed.) That she had become hysterical at the prospect. That to calm her hysteria and ensure the mission, he had taken Carolyn to bed with *him*. He threw in, as casually as possible, that no one need feel jealous or threatened by Carolyn – that he and she had only had "a handful of sex" together.

After Carolyn had departed to Mexico, Jim continued, she ran into trouble and was thrown into a Mexican jail, where she was raped. By the time she was released, she realized she was pregnant. Panicked, she sought out a Mexican abortion clinic, where they told her that only a risky saline solution procedure would dislodge the child. She opted to do it. Jim, meanwhile, although here, knew Carolyn was in danger and located where she was. He rushed in to prevent her from undergoing the procedure.

This had to be the world's most perfect story ever. Carolyn had risked her life on a dangerous mission, suffered in jail, compromised her virtue – was even willing to die on the operating table, if needs be. If you questioned the tiniest part of this far-fetched tale, you had to question it all. No one was about to assert that Carolyn might not be a saint. I mean, what if there was even the smallest possibility that she *was?*

Jim very slowly, calmly, surveyed the room as he approached the final denouement. "Now that the child is born," he said, with the slightest quizzical pause, "I'm... *almost* sure it's mine. I looked at the child, and I feel he probably is mine." I looked closely at Jim. He looked both not quite certain, and also... *sure* at one and the same time. Then he said it was difficult for Carolyn, in that now she's had to "completely rearrange her life." (For *motherhood?* As opposed to being harried day and night for *work* responsibilities?)

Then he took another slow scan around the room. He said he knew there were many women who would have wanted to bear his child. That Teri, for instance, had had abortions, "even though I told her she could go ahead with the pregnancies if she wanted," because "that's the kind of person *Teri* is." (High compliment, yes? It was Teri who later left at the worst possible moment, citing abortions as a primary cause! Jim, for his part, was never cited as "stupid.") "Even *Carolyn* had an abortion once before."

It is hard to tell a convincing lie without there being *elements* of truth. Perhaps Carolyn *had* been "hysterical," not at any seduction planned for Mexico, but if she discovered she was pregnant and couldn't face having another abortion. In any event, whatever the truthful or untruthful elements in this new drama, Jim was under so much subtle pressure, no one even commented on the matter. Certainly no one would have thought Carolyn a "Grace Stoen." Not at all. But Grace was present at this meeting, her own ax now seemingly safely buried, and why risk resurrecting *that?*

Carolyn, predictably, was absent. She was tending to a tiny infant, and obviously, bringing us an adorable newborn in the flesh, especially to this forum so carefully schooled in not bearing children at all, would have undercut any sad tale of "the Mexican rape." I'm not sure her presence would have helped even were she there alone ~ it may have even detrimented him. He may have wanted to protect her from hostile response, but I think, probably more, she was still upset about whatever was the *truth,* and her upset might have made Jim's job more difficult.

Believing Jim? Even were we tempted to not believe him, disbelief over that particular subject would have been so destructive to us all, that there was no investment worth *making* in such disbelief. No one seemed inclined to not let this volatile subject simply *be*.

Carolyn did return to us soon after, looking shaken, nearly ashen, and much more jumpy around Jim than usual. Maybe Jim had insisted she *have* the child. Maybe he had even told her the *work* needed this particular child (what would happen with John if Grace ever left?; Stephan was disaffected; and Jim would have hardly underestimated genetics, if the child were his). Some weeks later on, Jim even brought Kimo (Hawaiian for "Jim") into a P.C., held him up proudly and said, "This child may be destiny."

We were told that to avoid any suspicion, it would be announced publicly that Carolyn, by force of circumstance, had to now care for the child of a relative.

How.... How could I have thought my... *poem* was important?

ALLEGORY

by

LAURIE EFREIN KAHALAS

Redwood Valley, California
(1974)

2/ALLEGORY

(With fluidity and pathos throughout:)

(PROLOGUE:)

(with sorrow:)
    The land lies barren and waste --
        the wake of unprecedented devastation.
    It is the dying of the day.
(more forceful:)
    HE STANDS at the penultimate hour of ***tribulation!***
       (breathy, with pathos:)
       and even the air is fraught with a deathly still.

(gentle:)
    By his side is a child --
(crescendo:)
    whom fate could ordain to lead an entire **race.**
       (quiet:)
       Now, 'neath the dim fire of dawning stars,
       dusk shrouds *each* tender face.

(stoic:)
    They are surrounded by a wall that is both massive,
       and clothed in heavy guard.
(more forceful:)
    There is no known means. . . . ***of escape!***

(Low voice, halting.
Thick: as though forcing the words through a deepening despair.)
  A <u>na</u>----tion... is **DY**-------ing. . . .
  G-g-g-g-...god <u>I</u>---s. . . .
  In **A**----gony. . . .
     (anguished whisper:)
     and no-one. . . . speaks. . . . .

I.

(solemn; subdued; flowing:)
    "On my left hand stands a child.
    On my right hand <u>stands</u> . . . . a wall.
(intensify:)
    In my heart all is still,
        though Titans fall:
(high cry of pathos:)   *(fade and fall:)*
    And pA---triots   grIE--------ve. . ."

        (supplication:)
          "Leave this *place*, itinerant one!,"
            (undertone:)
              a suppliant cries.
        (supplication:)
          "Leave this place, **Prometheus!**
          Mankind has more need of *thee* than these
              few. . . last. . . .
        (urgent whisper:)
          Hasten thee!"

(subdued pathos:)
    "My heart is still.
    I only see *this* . . . child.
(sorrowfully:)
    No one knows me -- why I give **all**, though
    The moment to intercede is past,
        (fade and slowing:)
          or has not... yet...   come:

4/ALLEGORY

(subdued pathos:)
    "No.   I am not/ numb.
(intense, tremulous:)
    My nerve-fibers bristle
            with a surfeit of senseate <u>**a-che**</u>. . . .
(anguished:)
    My voice cries **slumberless!** --
        (fade:)
        through thin. . . dawn. . . .
(intense ,whispery:)
    I **listen** : to the song of the un-marked <u>graves</u>,
        (peals:)
        <u>**'Gone!, Gone!,'**</u>
(intensify:)   *(fade:)*
    And my wrath knows   **NO** delay. . . .:

(subdued pathos:)
    "<u>Yet</u> my <u>heart</u> <u>lies</u>--
        (breath-speech:)
            oh---, so ocean-still. . . .
(slight agitato:)
    Swallows glide numberless   o'er the waves.
(rhythmic:)
    I see them plunge one by one, towards the sea, 'neath the foam.
(with pathos:)   *(fades:)*
    My own heart <u>sinks</u>. . . . with thee. . ."

II.

(agitato; half-voice:)
    "I remember --lest my heart still seem a cool <u>green</u> meadow-home--
        where trees would grow, and swallows <u>nest,</u>
        and little <u>children</u> come to play,   one   by   one.....
(crescendo . . . . .)
    "How <u>you </u>came --washed in ***pain!***
        neath   the setting of the sun,
            (fade. . . .)
    a raging,<u> moon</u>-swept sea   wrest
        from every hour and age,
        from every time and need:

(agitato; half-voice:)
    "From the childhood of your questioning eyes,
    From the wasted youth of your unrefrained desire
            (fade. . . . .)
        a fire that only dies,   dies,   dies. . . .
(to full voice:. . . .   .
    From a land where dreams are cast aside,
    and fortunes capsized and turned,
        lives submerged and lost. . .
      . . . .
In the madness   of your thwarted cries,   for <u>'Time!'</u> --
    (full voice:)
    past all reprieve!

        (half-voice:)
        Begging amnesty for all sins past;
            and destiny of all <u>future</u> guise. . . .

6/ALLEGORY

(agitato; half-voice:)
   "And each one asked a <u>favor</u>.
   And each <u>one</u> asked a wile.
   And no child thought
        <u>one</u> drop of sweetness drawn could exile mean
        from such a sweet, <u>sweet</u> land. . .

(slightly more agitato:)
   "I remember   --lest your <u>dreams</u>, love, still seem
        a reverie that <u>gods</u> would fire and breathe,
        make real for thee, and glean --
   As you think, 'Oh how good, how sweet, how fine
        to come as a little child,   how <u>I</u>
(intense undercurrent:)
   "<u>Listened</u>   to the song of the unmarked graves:
      (peals:)
      'Gone!, Gone!,'
      (full voice:) (softer:)
   And turned **NOT/**   away.   Aye,

(wistful; sorrowful:)
   "No vision will bring peace.   No.
   No longing will bring calm, nor even a balm, not
        for me, but even for <u>thee</u>:   <u>a</u>--s
(deep-toned; tremulous:)
   the grey world waits, and orphans <u>shamefully</u> weep;
(to full voice. . .   . . .
   And you hear the pleas to see, to feel, to know, to speak:

(full voice:)   *(soft, pleading:)*
    "To <u>remember</u>!!!   --lest this moment die
    <u>deep</u>. . within the dying of a <u>world's</u> last rays,
        in vain. . . . --:
(intensify:)   . . .   .
    How you <u>too</u> came,   and exclaimed in ecstatic murmurings,
                      (soft:)
    'Oh my Saviour, <u>just</u> in time!' -- <u>a</u>-s
(deep-toned:)   *(to half-voice. . .*
    the grim earth quakes with failing breath, and faltering steps,
        with scarcely time at all:

(intensify little by little. . .   . . .
    "Too late to mend,   progressed past arrest---
    Too soon for men to heed   and grasp---
    Haunted the past, the future --***foredoomed!***-- looms,
(anguished, insistent: . . .   . . .
    and cries, cries, cries   its all-too- present
    deaths!!!!

(full-voiced waves:)
    "WHY---------------- have you slept?
(a little softer:)   . . .   .
    WHY----   have you slept?
(softer; fade. . .
    WHY. . . . . .   have   you. . . .
    sle--p--t?. . . ."

8/ALLEGORY

III.

(measured, strong:)
    "Yes, it is time <u>indeed</u>!
    And though it bring me only grief
    to impart to you the <u>graveness</u> of this day:
        what you must do, and know, and say. .--:
(intensifying:. . .   . . .
    Though it brings my heart to your <u>keenest</u> need,
    though you'd not <u>believe</u> it, I say:
    'I give to you the <u>best</u> of days!'"
        (undertone, slightly agitated:)
        (And some shuddered. And some were like <u>stone</u>.
        And some walked on, on, on. . .):
(gentle:)
    "To live in a <u>hallowed</u> grief. . .
(defiant::)
    . . .***or freely die!!***"

        (undertone; agitato:)
        And some ran.. And some turned.
        (slightly softer:)   *(fade:)*
        And some faltered.   And some hid.
        (more forceful:)
        Yet some rose brave, and claimed:

(declarative:)
    "You see, there is no <u>garden</u> here.
    only what <u>you've</u> made of need, of fear, of pain:
        (muted; undertone:)
            (I came. I love.. I feed. . . .)

(with cogency:)
 "There never <u>was</u> a garden-home,
 only what your pain, your <u>need</u> would prescribe.
 And when you laid your woes on this altar of <u>ALL</u> life,
 you relinquished all <u>claim.</u>. . .
   (fade; slowing:)
     to distance. . . apathy. . . or retreat:
(cry:)   *(fade:. . . . . . .*
 Arise, ye people, wake! **A-RI------------SE**. . . . . . ."

(somber; with subdued pain:)
 Their voice fell, <u>snow</u>-silent as a dying dove,
 as a <u>swallow</u> cast in flight,
   towards death, towards night, 'loft a brimming
  (fade:)
   breath---. . . of the dark-. . dawned. . . sea. . .

(sorrowful:)
 "And the sentries of my heart did <u>grieve</u>,
 and <u>sorrowfully</u> shook their heads: 'Aye,
 it's true, I fear.
 There is no <u>garden</u> here.
 They have <u>plucked</u> the fruit --
  (outcry:)
  the <u>best</u>!
(sorrowful:)
 Now non---e can-- en-ter- in--. . . . "

IV.

(with depth of feeling:)
    "Who would hold you strong <u>now</u>
        as you shook, and wept, and grieved?
    Who will move on (--while you sleep--),
    as the wars rage, and innocents die?
(anguished:)
    My heart --laid <u>waste</u>!-- would <u>cry</u>, <u>bleed</u>, <u>drain</u> 'neath the dead
        (fade; slowing:)
    <u>weight</u>. . . of slain. . men's. . . bo--nes. . . . .
    CRUSH(shshsh)----ed.

(gentle; soft; agitato:)
    "Hush. No recourse waits.
    My heart has <u>known</u> its last reprieve.
(with weariness:)
    My heart beats on, on, on.. . . .
    I would not <u>deceive</u> you:
        it has been long to come.

(intent; discerning:)
    "Yet when all is known, yet when all is done,
        it <u>puzzles</u> me:
    Though you long <u>not</u> for pain, yet you long not for <u>love</u>:
        a love to make you <u>strong!</u>
    Whilst love is cast; your will is bent;
        and you wither. . . .
        within the sweet <u>rays</u> of my love. . .
(slowing:)
  . . .with <u>no</u>. . . protest. . . .?

(bitter, but not harsh:)
    "Oh, mourn not your garden-loss!
    Love in this present place is a <u>fearful</u> thing,
        an awesome weight.
(undervoice:)
    Love   --as a memory--   can be kissed, blessed --
        (stronger:)
        recognized,   reconciled,   <u>yea!</u> ---
<u>extolled!</u>

(half-voice:)
    "And you'll hear it as though the light of the Sun were sound,
        a gold far chime:
        'He said,
(voice from a distance, gentle, beseeching:)
        "Come, my sons, my daughters,
        a new <u>world's</u> at your behest.
        I would bring you through the slaughter.
        I will bring you through <u>each</u> test.
        Though men be blind, and falter, <u>I</u>---
        give credence to your <u>best!</u>
(comforting; fading:)
        That my heart would be your altar.
        And my love. . . would be. . . your rest.'"

(harsh:)
    The sentries round the outer wall are <u>brute</u> and <u>gray</u>.
    "No. I never saw him pass this way ---
(cry out:)
    <u>BE GONE!!!</u>"

V.

(steady; instilling confidence:. . .   . .
   "Now you'll gather 'round.   Soon it will all be told to thee.
   Those who gather in, a quickening trust shall hold.
   And with my vision as your eyes --*a searing fire!*--:
      you'll know, you'll know, you'll know,
         why I must
   Send you forth as a warrior into the darkest night---
   Send you forth as a warrior to uphold and <u>claim</u> the right!
   And I send you forth a <u>proud</u> warrior,
      divest of dreams and wanton hopes.

(undercurrent; building. . .   . .
   "For the shelter of my heart a fortress is, a tower shall be,
      and <u>you</u> shall scale its walls.
   The power of the poor, the low is <u>with thee,</u>
      if you will just give <u>all!</u>
         . . .   *(declaration:)*
   And I send you forth   a <u>**warrior!!**</u>
         (quiet:)
         --He who bringeth peace. . .   The gentlest one. . .--
(defiant:)
   He who bringeth the sword!!

(sorrow and pride:)
   "And you can be the <u>noblest</u> ones to grace this earth,
   for I send forth you last <u>first</u>-born of this anguished place.
   Yet I send forth you last, as first, into no midst of battle-blaze;
            (slowing:. . .   . . .
         but only through this dim. . . dawn's. . . haze. . . .

(with tenderness:)
    "And one died.
    And I laid him in a shelter 'neath the trees.
        His day is done.
    The sun did not scorche his lithe frame.
    Nor did many grieve for him.
            (whisper:)
        He seemed so calm (--*pass on*. . !--)
(gentle:)
    and overborne with shade.

(with building agitation:. . .   . . .
    "Another died, as he sobbed wretchedly, on his last, torn breath,
(protesting:)
    'That I might ***live!,*** to redeem a <u>travesty</u>
        (fading:)
        of mistakes, trials, and sorrows.'
(with deep feeling:)
    Who cried for him, <u>cried past rest</u>;
(calming:)
    and nestled at last
        within a web of insulate pain.

(forcefully:)
    "Yet another died -- as with a shout, he cried:
(defiant:)
    '<u>My</u> death shall be <u>avenged,</u> by all brave women and men!
(softer; f lowing; plangent:. . .   . . .
    I would not bury <u>him</u> --though the very oceans weep--,
    but I laid him 'neath the setting of the sun,
        for all mankind to see, and justly grieve:
(impassioned:)
    the epiphany of <u>me</u> -- flesh of my flesh, pain of my pain. . .
        (softer; slowing:)
    My heart is full. . .   still. . .   sealed. . . . . .contained."

VI.

(contemptuous:)
    Now the vultures come   --grey carrions of death--:
    they pick, pluck, peck,
    <u>tear</u> at his flesh with cruel-eyed intent,
        and crudely jest:

(mocking:)
    "<u>I</u> will save thee."   Ha!, <u>mock</u> call!
    Who will save <u>thee</u> this day?
              (slowing:)
    So few would enter in, and stay."

(bitter, but somber:)
    And as they incessantly peck at his bile in rude thrusts,
        they even <u>smile</u>,
        (mocking. . . . .)
    because "It is not <u>He</u>,"   <u>they</u> say.

(level:)
    Humanity, humanity, will you <u>not</u> be saved?
(forceful:)
    And the martyrs bleed.
(outcry:)
    And **<u>hypocrites</u>** pray,

(calmer:)
    One by one.
(agitato:)
    Now they plunder, and disarray the nest.
    The land is bereft of trees.
    Children weep.
(anguished:)   *(fade; slowing:)*
    Grief. . . . has <u>expended</u> its war. . .-born. . . toll. . . .
(subdued:)
    Now the sentries wait.

(with deep feeling:)
   "The guardians of my heart are crimson, dark, and green..
(bitter:)
   The guardians of the wall are brute, and grey.
(with tenderness:)
    Weep not, my little child, for I do encircle thee,
       though this day, your die is cast:
          (shout out:)
    Though flanked by **'liars and thieves!,'**
      they say,
   this day you are christened:
(with assurance:)
    crowned in autumn leaves, and bedecked in new-fallen snow:
    You'll be not afraid, you'll see a road,
       you'll know a way.

(growing more declarative:)
   "Your greens have turned to amber now,
   your golds will blaze and fade:
      no longer a child to be.
   You'll set upon a long, untrammelled road,
   to set my people free!
   And though all men may deny your faith,
   and though no man may know your name --
   Though you'd be **defamed!,**
(full voice:)
   THAT day lead forth a company. . . .
      (fading:)
       of daughters, and sons.

16/ALLEGORY

(quieter:)
    "Think. But think not,
      'Who will choose? Who will stand? Who will stay?
          Who will lose. . . all?. .
(probing, puzzled:)
    (What had <u>you</u> to find,
        lost child? incipient warrior? antithetical god?)
(clear, direct:)
    You must move <u>on</u> this ominous day,
        <u>whate'er</u> befall your fate!
    For I have made a covenant with thee.
    <u>I</u> appear to be   in chains.
(resolute:)
    Yet I shall leave <u>thee.</u> . . . . .
  . . . .**FREE!**

(level:)
    "Only three things did I ask:
    That you vow to move on; though every sign may read, 'No hope.'
    That you know you are right; though every step are your feet alone.
    That you ***never*** turn back.
        (imitating. slightly agitated)
        --And some said, 'I will see.'
        And some cried,   It is ***pain!'***
        And some claimed,   'I need thee
        <u>past</u> victory,   agony,   . . .or demise.'

(resolute:)
"But still the covenant remains, if only <u>one</u> its honor give.
      (with veiled pathos:)
      For as <u>I</u> live, I would share <u>all</u> with thee.
        (pace out:)
          And with. . . each. . .
(deep-toned; tremulous:)
    nerve-torn fiber of my ***time***-worn heart,
      (assertive:)
      I proclaim,
  'I'd ***stay!'***
(sorrowful:)
    Yet all I would say, you would never listen.

ALLEGORY/17

(slowly building intensity. . .   . .
    "Thus <u>you</u> must weep, and <u>you</u> must bleed, and <u>you</u> must grieve.
    Yet you must **speak!:**
(lower; then again build in waves:. . .   . . . .
    <u>I</u> spoke for all, I spoke for each one,
    that none would defend, nor hear, nor save.
    I spoke to free each slave, from unjust shares, ruthless gains,
    the <u>power</u> men crave.
(soft-toned:)
    I spoke of prisons, youth, and unsung graves. . . .
(declamatory:)
    None spoke more true, none spoke more brave.
    Yet <u>you</u> must speak, too,
        (anguished:)   *(quiet:)*
        where the <u>un</u>-spoken --**devastatingly!--**. . . failed:

(sorrowful:)
    "The deliberate mercies; the reckless affirmations;
    the joy feigned, and the agony well-concealed.
    <u>No</u>.
    It did its work <u>too</u> well, in a way. . .

(building gradually; emotional:)
    "But if this earth continues to quake
        --race against race, war after war--,
    If the bondage will not break --
        for laureates will not <u>rise</u> to the fore --
    If the valiant will not stand,
        to defend their own, though laid <u>waste</u> is their land!
    If you deny the oppressed a home,
        or leave this call to fend alone,
            (broad. . . . .)
            then . . though. . .

18/ALLEGORY

(deep-toned; with pathos; pick up pace:)
   "<u>all</u> this heart would render **Aa--ches** --
        you'll not feel its pain, you'll not heed its law--
(voice rising:)
   Though my heart for you asunder
(high-pitched cry:)   *(slightly lower tone; then fade:)*
   <u>**BRE--------- - EA--K-S**</u>. . . .
    (sorrowfully:)
  . . . .Then shall I <u>speak</u> no more,
      then shall I
<u>speak</u>. . . . . . .no more."

             (Pause. Then slowly begin:)

VII.

(low; undercurrent of deep desolation:)
   The song ri--ses. . . from a **_thousand_** un-marked graves,
       (fade:)   *(slowing. . . . . .)*
      its strains fi-l-tering through thin--. . . dawn--. . .
(very low, but anguished:)
   Rass--ping.
   Wrestling to expound in a dark, <u>un</u>-certain key;
(gaining bearing:. . .   . .
   to express in wa---vering tones
     (gaining pace, emphasis, volume:)
     a dirge too low to justly grieve,
     a song too weak   for a <u>too-wrong</u> **_death!!_**
(towards outcry:. . .   . . .
   One voice rises higher than foul-decaying flesh,
   "All **_power_** to thee!"
(wait, then subdued:)
   Yet:
(breath-speech:)
   where even spec-tres scarcely cry. . . . .
(plaintive:)
    "<u>**Arise!**</u> <u>**Arise!**</u> **The last shall fall to thee.**
            (fade:)
   The last shall <u>fall</u>. . .   to thee. . ."

ALLEGORY/19

(somber:)
    You longed for interpretation.   But
    the interpreter is gone.
    The play is done. Now <u>you</u> the player shall be.
(gentle, incisive:)
    Only the silent voice within speaks plain,
           to you, true bearer of the faith:

(steadfast, but not harsh:)
    You stand alone.
    Hence I send <u>you</u> forth.
(with pathos:)
    Through <u>ca</u>lvaries of night, on this <u>pil</u>grimage
        of <u>dry</u> dust, and bliss--tering rain.
(with veiled passion:)
    Though men be blind, <u>you</u> see a distant light.
    Though men be <u>dumb</u>, you speak with <u>fervent</u> tongue --
(sorrowfully:)
    Yet all you greet are blind, and deaf, and dumb. . . .

(uplifting:)
    And so --unwavering!--,   you <u>climb</u> the wall,
(pace out:. . .   . .
    though men's bru<u>t</u>-e guns wai-<u>t</u>- at your fee-<u>t</u>-, hois-<u>t</u>-
    the <u>swee-t-</u> child aloft your shoulder blades,
        to mee<u>t</u>-/ your call:

(resume motion:)
    With your left hand, you secure his hold.
(voice rising: . . . . .
    With your right hand now, you lift
        a <u>proud</u> torch, and journey on --
            <u>un</u>fed, <u>un</u>bedded, <u>un</u>shorn:

VIII.
(forceful; waves of motion:) . . .
    BLACK Prometheus!, your face is rich-ly dark,
          and no fire-flies guide   your feet.
              (pulse-beats:)
Thus   your <u>flames</u>   <u>are</u>   <u>pure</u> --
(wave. . .   . .
    BLACK Prometheus!, wanderer through ten thousand
          <u>nights</u> and days -- first, last
to endure this earth's <u>cruel</u> sacrifice fate.
(softer:)
    Prometheus, you are verdant black:
            (wondrous:)
        dark, yet green;
     (harsh:)   *(exultant:)*
      <u>Strafed</u>.   Yet <u>exudant</u> of life!
(full-voiced:)
    Prometheus, you are black. . . . proud tower of light:

    Shine forth!,   Cry <u>out</u>!,   Cry <u>loud</u>!,   Cry **FREE-------**. . .
(soft again;)
    Cry <u>grief</u>, Promethean one,
         for all this darkening world --***alas!***-- has <u>need</u> of thee,
            (growing louder:)
              yet turns, turns, turns:

(steady motion; insistent; openly emotional:)
    None will feel the pure, still heart of Thee,
(strike:)
    TURNS!
    None will speak Thy words of life.
(strike:)
    TURNS!   Nor take this surrogate plight, turns,
(strike:)   *(luminous:)*
    turns!!   Thy mountain glimmerrr----------s
    with a light   too <u>bright</u> for Man to see!
(continual outpouring:)
    None see that no sun pours down light more <u>ra</u>--diant
         than <u>your</u> <u>brave</u> <u>eyes</u>--
    Turns, <u>turns</u>, <u>turns</u>:

(full-voiced:)
    Prometheus <u>spurned</u>! **Bound**.
(slight pause; then incisive:)
    Yet <u>free</u>-----. . .
(with defiant pride:)
    A vulture's glee are your inward wounds and pains --
        makes mockery of your chains--
    <u>TURNS!!</u>:
(lower, gradually to full voice:. . . . .
    Yet still this self-same tragedy confirms:
    Mankind, not Thee, is doomed.
(still building:)
    Mankind has bound <u>himself</u> in chains!!:

(in anguish; full voice and strength:)
    Go forth, Prometheus!!, from this <u>A----LIEN RACE</u>!!!!
(still anguished, but softer:)
    To another clime, to another time and place.
        Where your <u>face</u> is not
(shoot out:)   *(quieter:)*
    "<u>An anathema!</u>" . . .to the blind; nor your words
(shoot out:)   *(quieter:)*
    "<u>A blasphemy!</u>" . . .to the deaf.
(with longing:)
    Where free beings speak --
    where dreams are left behind,
        for goodness ***lives***. . . . .
        (echo:)
            "No one knows me, why I <u>give</u> all. . ."

IX.

(wistful:)
    Then.. . ., at some fine, indeterminate point of distant reckoning:
(secure:)
    you <u>will</u> be seen as a rising, waxing star -- Aye.
(regretfully:)
    Too late, too dim, too far. . .
(assuring:)
    Seen and known to raise the very <u>angels</u> from their rest. . .
(gently:)
    to tread the purest edge of quickening sun. . . .
(sorrowfully:)
    Bid each, last, grief-laden one a new farewell --
        smile; nod; **"Be <u>bra----ve.</u>"**
(distant:)
    Wave one last, fast-fading farewell. . . . .
        (very deep-toned; slower:)
          Pity the earth-- <u>hell</u>-- <u>grave.</u>   Then
(hold:)
    <u>tur------n</u>. . . . . . .

(resume motion:)
    To eternally tread that path forlorn,
(breath-speech, crescendo. . . . . .
    from dawn, to dawn. . .(nn...in the beginning there will always
(attack, then fade:)
    BE------ . .but/ thee. . . to
(hit high, then fall and fade:)
    Ddi--- -i-----mmm------ly fil-------tering
        (fade, then intense, last push into "the tears.")
        daw------nn--.-nnnn"). .

(pour out onto deep breaths:)
    n-. . . nnn- the tears flow now   *fi--nally* --
    in <u>full,</u> <u>pouring</u> <u>torrents</u>
(easing off; slowing:)
    of bitter-<u>sweet</u>, salt. . . . and dusky rain.
(outpouring of breath:)
    Who you would have taken <u>with</u> you!
(softer:)
    Yet so few would chance the rude, hard journey
        (luminous. . .   . . .
        to the very <u>heart</u> . . . of the
        most . shining . five . pointed . star. . .

(outpouring of breath:)
    How many you would have <u>taken</u> with you!
        (remorsefully:)
        But now, it will all be too late. . . . .
    Now it is not a matter of who you would
        (passion; outpouring of breath:)
        --with full, <u>sweet</u>-willing heart!--
(soft again:)
    carry aloft your back.
        (outcry:)
    Now it is all --***only!***--
(soft again:)
    what you would leave. . . to remain.
                              (outcry:)
    Your mission of rescue has become   --**TRAGICALLY!!**--
(quiet:)
    a mission . . . .of legacy.

X.

(quiet; expectant:)
    Yet   your heart   i---s still.
    Not a moment's waver, not a shade.
(tenderness and subdued grief:)
    You'd lay down your hallowed, yet weary frame.
    Even humble yourself to be called just,
        "the last of men; the first of saints."

(upsurge of intensity. . .   . .
    For them to trample, scorn, and maim --
    For them to castigate, denigrate, and shame--
(floodwater cry; amplified from all sides:)
    "NO. IT IS WORSE YOU'VE MADE TRAVESTY
               (high note, fall:)
    OF   MY   *SPI*-------- *RI*-------------*TT!!*"
(stoic, but with deep feeling:)
    For only the non-flesh-ridden   to extol
(voice rise in tone and intensity; fade and fall:)
    the **NA**----------------**AA**-------------------mmme------. . . .

XIX. Let's Kill the Messenger.

The single-minded aren't necessarily made for each other. You don't say, "Oh, come meet so-and-so. They're as fanatical as *you* are. You'll love each other."

Jim's death obsessions and my death obsessions seemed to have little in common save for their being about the same people. His carried the burden of preventing ultimate disaster -- an action flick with him the principal player. I was so terrified, my premonitions were cloaked in veils, and I felt powerless to act. Jim Jones' commitment was to stand by his own to the death. I would not necessarily die *myself*, whatever our collective fate. Every waking breath forced him to realism. I could barely face such a reality at all.

No, I would never leave Peoples Temple. But I would never get to Guyana either.

Thus our existential reality, Jim Jones' and mine, seemed fatefully, at a right angle spin. Oh, I knew I would never jump ship. But like an inner dyslexia, I could not decipher who would be where, or when, if calamity struck. Jim, for his part, thought *anyone* could jump ship (even some terrible traitor in our midst, "very high up"), so why exempt the lower echelons, ...like me?

I once moved to ameliorate the impasse, by writing him that we could wind up as "two families" -- one, the Guyana family, perhaps doomed (though we had no reason to think it then); the other, in the States, left adrift. Though I still could not fathom that *"Allegory"* was about any real future event, much less set in Guyana, a strange jungle of a place we had barely penetrated to date. Although unbelievable now, I never consciously connected *"Allegory"* with Guyana until the tragedy had already happened.

I suppose what psychologists say about trauma is true: the mind will block out what it cannot handle. I knew that *Jim's* consciousness was that we might be doomed, but it had a proviso (that proviso being *everything*) that it would be his to either determine, or to react as circumstances inevitably forced his hand. If *he* foresaw our doom (which even he could foresee only in terms of what to *prevent*), it could happen. If *I* foresaw it, I was presumptuous, deluded, traitorous or an outcast.

So prejudicial was this psychological roadmap, that perhaps were I only clearer that what I foresaw was not just *his* death (like wanting the leader out of the way), but the death of hundreds under his care, I might have actually curried favor rather than castigation. "*They're* out to get *us*" would target outsiders as villains, and I would be one of "us." His perception of "*You're* [i.e. Laurie] out to get *me*" could only land on yours truly's head. How dared I?

What I *really* couldn't dare was envisioning our potential doom as real, when for Jim Jones, bearing our collective weight like an ultimate parent, it had to be *avoidable*. (The final Jim Jones: "*I waited against all evidence.*" That is how the cosmos ironed it out at the last.) It was painfully clear, as much as if the words had been spoken outright, that if I crossed this bridge, I would have to do so alone. Thus was I thrust back into the primal terror of the table-shaped fence.

Somewhere dimly, I also sensed the perils of being left adrift post-catastrophe, but I intimated this only in oblique terms. I simply said that should it happen that one family died in Guyana, and the other family lived on in the States, what should the world learn of the family of death (like a letter to the world), then reflecting plaintively, "What then would happen to the family of life?"

I handed my odd missive (for he had always talked of *unity*, never of *separation*) in. Teri Buford was sent to tell me that Jim was impressed by my letter - that now I was really thinking. The next time I approached Jim after services with my "numbers," Tim Stoen was there (ever Hephaestion at Alexander's side), and Jim told him, arm outstretched onto my shoulder and smiling pridefully, "This is one of the best minds we've got."

A short while later, Jim said more people were needed for strategizing. What should a "best mind" do? I volunteered and as always, it seemed, was ignored. Had he sidelined me deliberately, sensing that I would somehow tread a separate path? I would have liked to believe this, if only to impart some benevolent intent to the crushing debacles that were about to come at his hand. Yet I wonder if such knowledge might have muted the wrenching separation anxiety ("He'll die on me, he'll die on me"); or if perhaps, the reality of separation being thus *certain*, it would have only made things worse. Maybe the energies were such that *whatever* I did, the end result would have been the same.

Certainty seemed to elude even the miracleworker. Jim Jones dared not acknowledge a *reality* of having led his own people into a death trap. He could see that he *might* have, because the overlay of impending doom never departed, even with the work in Guyana such an extraordinary success. He couldn't close the book then (*especially* then) upon this dream; and all the more, knowing in his heart of hearts that he had to *save* us.

Do you know the Indian story about the man who fled Benares to go to Agra, because he believed that Death was in Benares and he had to escape it? He arrived in Agra by nightfall. And there was Death, saying, "I was amazed to see you in Benares. I was expecting you in Agra."

Do you know that the man in that story was named Jim Jones?

Thus from 1974 'til the time tragedy struck, he had his "impossible consciousness" and I had mine. And (he made it ever so clear) there wasn't going to be any truce on the subject of doom. There would be rules, restrictions, barriers. But always at a certain point, the ax would fall. It was to fall upon *me* three times. Like nightfall in the elegant parable about Fate. By then, the separation between us would be complete. Our night would fall in a separate place forever.

The ax fell in the form of public ordeals. How could he have put me through them? I have always wanted to forgive fully, for that is how I am. And at times I do. I'm past the traumas, and for humans, that seems to be *prerequisite* for forgiveness. (We humans. We forgive what no longer persecutes us! A noble lot are we.)

But it is more. I thought that I could never tell you, the world at large, what had happened. That if you knew what happened to *me*, I would be powerless to reveal what happened to *Peoples Temple*. I was harsher then, those endless times I thought this through. I thought you had to take sides -- that truth must be framed as a *battle*. It only occurred to me in recent years that I could simply *tell* you:

The first of the ordeals came approaching our nemesis date, September 16th, in 1975. What happened that year collectively at that ominous time, I don't recall.

Some weeks earlier, I had summoned the courage to read "*Allegory*" for a small (*very* small) group of people, recruiting them nearly at random, and including (of all people) Grace Stoen. We met in the far end of publications, where Jim had inducted Maria and Kathy into P.C. Now there was recording equipment set up to make tapes, along with a soundproof room. I asked one of the technicians if he would assist.

This work was demanding to read. It was more like a symphony than a poem, and I hadn't yet mastered its delivery. But it came across strongly enough to enthuse *Grace*. Remember -- the work was veiled. I had always seen John as the child standing beside Jim at the Prologue, but I was in so much denial about what the work even meant, I didn't tell Grace. John (whose biological mother, Grace, and legal father, Tim, were both still very much in the church!) was indeed at the epicenter by the end, but how could I share that with Grace *now*?

She asked no explanations or embellishments, just exclaimed that it was the most fantastic thing she had ever heard! "This is what we're all about!" She asked could she borrow it to show it to Tim. I let her take it, and when she returned it a few days later, she told me excitedly, "Tim said it's just like *Shakespeare*." (The Stoens. You don't yet know how strange this all was. "Life gets curiouser and curiouser," said little Alice.)

Yet there was still nothing in me that could bear to wave red flags. This was barely a release valve. I now had both the text of "Allegory" and the tape of its reading. I had no further plans. I don't know how word got to Jim. It certainly wasn't through me. I could only imagine it was though "my new-found friend," Grace Stoen.

Next thing I know I'm sitting in P.C. and Patty Cartmell - fanatically loyal, sometimes-hysterical Patty Cartmell- is flailing about, telling Jim something about "Prometheus." He responded in kind. *"Prometheus?"* The Greek Empire had truly fallen. He was livid.

"Where is your poetry, Laurie?" He asked with the cool ire of a parent asking for the proverbial unsparing rod. I had most of it with me. Jim Jones was a man of precious few words when he was really angry. "Read!," he railed; then after the slightest pause, he raise his voice several decibels with, "I *command* you to read!"

At that moment, I wished I had left "*Allegory*" on another planet. That I wouldn't read. I hurriedly grabbed for "I, Too," as there were at least six or seven fellow P.C. members present who had enthusiastically requested copies.

I began haltingly, in a soft, uncertain voice: "I too must live, though my name be sorrow, I too must feel, though ancient be the pain..." Judy in the front of the room began to titter. I could see several people suppressing the urge to laugh. Some were shaking their heads with disgust. Others just withheld their response, even from their own face. But Grace was quick with *her* verbal attack. Almost like she was the heroine of this disgraceful scene.

I stopped. "You see?," Jim said, softer now, almost like a parental appeal to a recently chastised, now wounded child. He let the silence fall and hold.

God only knows how we got from there to sex, or at what point we switched channels at all. Some time in recent weeks, Jim had us do a run around the room, each saying to whom they were attracted, a hopeless exercise that was more embarrassing than edifying. He also provoked his own bedpartners to confess how wonderful it was, despite no one smiling, laughing, or jumping for joy. The best at this exercise virtually *proselytized* their ecstasy. Teri spouted deadpan that she had "spent every waking minute wanting to fuck Jim Jones"; Carolyn spouted in a livid fury that after being with Jim, she would never in her life be with anyone else *ever*, like to think otherwise was tantamount to rejecting racial and economic equality. If this was meant to be intimidating, it could not have been more successful.

So sex was "up" these days. Mike Prokes made a public announcement that whomever was with Jim, could they keep it to twenty minutes, as it was all getting too stressful for him. I cringed. I thought I'd rather do anything else on the globe than have "twenty-fucking minutes" with Jim Jones. Was this pleasure or pain? Was this now a weapon? The transgressors against Jim Jones? He against them? Did he love these people all the while that he was contemplating that they hated *him*? Why in the world had he done this in the first place? To be egalitarian? Who believed this area of his life was "egalitarian"?

I would have obviously *not* wanted the channel switched at all, from the poetry I loved to the physical embrace I both craved and feared. It was devastating enough to have the work I produced out of love ridiculed as self-serving garbage. I wasn't eager to throw my very body into the foray.

As far as whatever had happened in the cottage in 1971, that was ancient history now ~ vivid for me, but forgotten for him. I had left out that day hanging by one silver sliver of a thread: *"You can write one great work."* At least one denial in life, my creativity, could be salvaged, yes? Moreover, by a "pearl of great price." Though thank God, I had the sense (or was it raw fear?) not to bring that up now. The water I was in was already scalding hot.

As the ax fell like bars between my consciousness and the written page, I sensed that anything I had ever valued as my own (gifts, inclinations, desires) faced eradication for me to so much as be *accepted*. Everything I *was* seemed unacceptable. Couldn't he at least leave it to a one-issue session? Why creativity and sex both? Why compound this? No one cared about my pain anyway. If it were single pain or double pain, who would notice or care? Just me.

I think Jack Beam led the charge, goading me to admit that I was attracted to Jim. After all, I was the "presumptuous, audacious" one who claimed there existed other men who could fuck. Though with half the room having slept with Jim, and me barely daring to look his way, I seemed like a real weird person to be attacking. I felt bullied, but I seemed to lack either the means or the confidence to protect myself. Where was my "protection" when I really needed it? Why was this man I looked to to protect me, instead attacking me?

Jim, never one to relax his guard in battle, now looked at me hard. "Is it sex you want? We can go upstairs right now." He stared me down defiantly, and pointed to his apartment above the podium. At that point, even lamb that I was, I knew that "sex" under these circumstances might mean dispassionate rape, after which time I would be pronounced "fucked for good and don't ever ask for it again." Not to mention incurring everyone's hatred for "putting Father through this."

"Is that what you want? Do you think you could do better than Karen Layton?" (The famous Karen Layton ~ eight hours of.... what? Was I the only one there who knew the truth?) I answered that with silence. I feared that if I spoke the truth about Karen's "ecstasy," I mightn't be guaranteed physical *safety*, much less pleasure.

In fact, I had *nothing* more to say. There was no more bait to offer. Finally Jim said, "Sit down."

I couldn't believe that Grace, of all people, had reacted like that. Sure, she was treacherous, but wasn't that "the old Grace"? Why this venom at *me*? Jim looked at me and knew that this was not resolved.

"What is it?," he asked, like he was saying, "Oh. *You* again." "Grace was lying," I stated simply. "She never said anything like that to me ~ she said the *opposite*." Grace stood up and hurled at me spitefully, "Laurie, I only said I liked your poetry because *you needed* it!" "Coup de Grace," indeed. How long that needy bitch had probably been wanting to project that onto someone else (perhaps anyone would do).

I said softly but firmly, "Grace is lying." Jim would stand no more of it. This wasn't about truth or lies ~ it was about *authority*. I lost.

I sat through the rest of the meeting outwardly calm. I had had much training in life how to be stoical ~ the graduate course, indeed, from Jim Jones himself.

Later in the week, fighting back tears, but determined to endure, I started a fire in the wood-burning furnace of our communal house. Slowly, carefully, page by page, I lowered all the pages of my poetry into the flames.

Then (*again* ~ like I did after burning my music), I told Jim what I had done. This time he made a public announcement that "Laurie Efrein is probably the most talented person we have, but she was willing to sacrifice all that for the cause." I was upstairs helping with the offering money. Were I not standing near the P.A. system, I would have missed this rare praise entirely. The people around me smiled in acknowledgement and respect. I felt self-conscious, uncomfortable. Which pages of my writing had paid for this praise?

Truthfully, there was one thing I could not bear to do, and that was to destroy "*Allegory.*" Something, Someone was staying my hand. If Jim Jones would not accept it, he would not accept it. But I had been given something for the world. I could not destroy what I had been given for *the world.*

It seemed, even then, insupportable ~ my absolute commitment to serve two masters. I knew I had to stay and be loyal to the death to Jim Jones, while I also had to sail past it all into the future, alone if needs be, with some unknown Personage Who bore the sorrow of the world within His Heart. This apparent schism which caused such excruciating pain ~ how can I explain it to you? It was years before I could explain it to *myself.*

I only knew that the Force staying my hand when I came to "*Allegory*" was such a comfort. I don't know how it was that I never doubted my allegiance to Jim Jones. It was just that, in a world where open questions so often became gaping wounds, there was this place.... almost *above* him. Still connected to him, but on a higher place. A place of comfort and calm and peace. A place of knowing and certainty. A true home beyond this transient journey. Or how the miracles and the healings? How all the sacrifice? How the transformed lives? How *anything?*

Two realities always in this place ~ one disastrous, one serene. Each wholly present, each wholly within me to live and, ultimately, to reveal. For was it not *always* so that I had a life beyond November 18, 1978? Was it not *always* so that he did not?

I would decipher this in brail if needs be. I would endure 'til the answers came. I would have my loyalty *to* him. I would have my independence *from* him. I would follow him to the death. I would *survive* his death. I would sacrifice all for the now. I would save all for posterity. Some time much, much later on, I would meet the author of this insane tightrope of a script, and He and I, or They and I, we would have a very good laugh. I still count on it.

If I had not been able, despite everything, to contact that higher place in Jim Jones, I mightn't have endured such a dual route – a two-pronged disaster that, like a fork, seemed to skew me alive. But I contacted it frequently. And that place was a welcoming place. There I was "a wanted child." There was no screaming or yelling or condemnation. That place, that Being, knew my heart. He forever smiled on me. And I always knew that somehow, somewhere, I would finally and forever be a pillar for *that* "Jim Jones."

XX. Los Angeles is Not "Angelic" to Me.

Somehow I preserved that rarefied space in tact, while the rest of me edged towards panic. I would never know the fierce rush of this giant's love. Never again succumb to the inner voice or be transported into flights of song. Not even work upgrades accompanied the public praise, which I feared wasn't meant to uplift me at all, but rather keep me nailed to the post. No closeness. No trust. No emotional mooring. No nothing. One big "Stay right where you are." Would I stay in my body but go out of my mind?

I knew I could never be close around Jim anyway without extreme sexual tensions, but now I knew he would never have me. Ostracism had been handed out like an award. Would I be ungrateful or disloyal enough to refuse?

Nothing was making any sense. I couldn't believe this paragon of compassion to little old ladies and troubled youth could ever be cruel to me. Why did he hate me so? My emotional defense system seemed like putty and stone all at once. I couldn't afford to be fragile, so I simply froze.

Meanwhile, my father in New York was very ill. He was dying of cancer. My mother had written me wrenching letters, pushing and pulling his condition back and forth from the brink of death. Every time he deteriorated, she congratulated herself on her superior nursing abilities and said how well... *she* was doing. Every time he was in remission, she complained bitterly at being stuck at the family house in the country without culture or friends. I was alienated from them both, but thought it pitiful. If she really wanted him to die, it almost would have been better for her to *say* so.

I told her I might only be able to come to New York once, and that I preferred it to be while dad was alive instead of at a funeral. Jim cleared me to make the trip. I asked could I do anything for the cause while I was there, and he told me to see Sarah. Maybe finally, I could be of value.

Sarah was a true bitch ~ dominating, snippy, cold. She acted like she was doing me a royal favor. She gave me a list of businesses to phone in Philadelphia, to insinuate various things about Mother Divine. I took the list. Even though I would be isolated upstate, I would somehow get the project done.

There was a P.C. meeting a few days before I left. By now, I had seen countless confrontations with the sullen, the cynical, as well as people who had just been caught on a bad day. I don't know how I retained an innocence, almost a childlikeness about it. I trusted Jim to tell us the truth because *I* would. I had heard him say again and again (no secret of it) that he would do *anything* necessary to protect us, and to me, this in itself was "truth." I saw so many sacrifices, so I factored in little of guile or strategy, much less deception.

It was years before I realized that Jim probably *wasn't* telling us the truth that night, just sending a message to a sexual manipulator amongst *us* (obviously a man) to lay off. The story was that he, Jim, was in a hotel lobby (like when? - he didn't frequent hotels), when he was approached by a red-headed man who offered him $200.00 if Jim would let the man perform fellatio on him. Jim said he let him perform the act, taking the $200.00 not for himself, but for the cause.

Maybe this was a parable for our times. Whatever it was, and for whomever it was intended, I was filled with sympathy for our leader, subjecting himself to something like that to help us. Of course, the message was not intended for *me* at all, but I look back and realize how plagued he was with the very plight he fostered (to be "all things to all women and men"), and was reaping a bitter crop. He could take little more. His frame of mind was not good. My frame of mind was *terrible*. And that's how I went off to see my dying father. It must have been just after Thanksgiving.

Then the strangest thing happened at the airport. A man approached me for apparently no other reason than to flirt. I was considerably out of practice, but it was a relief to talk with anyone *casually* at this point. He told me his name was Giovanni, that he was Italian and lived in Los Angeles, and that he was wealthy - that he had contributed $400,000.00 to Jerry Lewis' cause, muscular dystrophy.

I told him I had a cause of my own, a very worthy one. He said perhaps he could help, and gave me his phone number in L.A. I caught my plane, and spent the trip mulling over whether or not I should contact him upon return. Maybe he wanted sex more than to donate money, but if he *had* money, I could use a break in any case. I never wanted to leave the church. It was more like being able to "kill two birds with one stone." Do something of service to the cause, and escape emotional and sexual tensions that were becoming unbearable.

New York was dreadful. My mother picked me up at the airport and we drove north of the city to our country home. My father had lost so much weight. He looked gaunt and drawn, like a concentration camp victim. He was weak, but glad to see me.

My mother was an emotional disaster case. Not entirely news, in her case, but she was also under unendurable stress caring for a dying cancer patient on her own. I was horrified when at breakfast, she yelled at him for, in his weakened state, reaching for the wrong toothbrush and using hers instead. They had never gotten along, but where was mercy? It was heart-wrenching.

Meanwhile, I insisted that I had to go down to the city "to make some phone calls." I went to the phone booths at the 42nd Street Library. I took out the list Sarah had given me, and made meticulous notes on each call - what I said, what they said. Later in the day, I returned upstate.

The morning of my departure, my mother drove me to the bus station. I bid my father a stilted farewell. It was so hard to relate -- my emotions were already a lemon squeezed dry. It was years before I came to terms with my grief over his death at all.

Ten minutes before my bus was scheduled to depart, my mother re-dredged the story of her trip to Puerto Rico when I was just thirteen years old, and the horrible argument she had had with my dad just before she left. "He *cursed* me," she railed at... *me*. "I said, 'How can you say that? I'm your wife, the mother of your children.'" What was this? Gratuitous torture? The man was dying. Could she not even let him die in peace?

I ran into Jim briefly before a service upon my return. He smiled into my eyes and asked was I o.k. "Yes. I'm fine," I told him in a respectful gulp. When I had some solitude, I wrote him about the man at the airport, and asked if I should look the man up. That he seemed to be wealthy and I was willing to do this. At the end of the letter, holding my breath, feeling it may be a terrible mistake, I added that I would do this, yes, but I would rather be with *him*. It's the closest I ever got to *asking* in all those years. Then I wound up on the post-service line, and when I asked Jim if he got my note and should I do this?, he responded by *patting my head* and saying gently, "No. That won't be necessary." I felt mortified.

Then I took my careful notes on the phone project to Sarah. She thumbed through it, like an unfavorite grade school teacher checking a child's homework. She said all these notes were unnecessary. She huffed away, annoyed. *I had left my dying father to do this project.*

My frame of mind had progressed now from terrible to slightly *worse* than terrible. I was depressed and sinking fast.

Then came ordeal no. 2 – that dreadful P.C. in L.A. It took me two years to release enough of my hysteria over it to tell Jim the simple truth that I would have rather died. Not a metaphorical "dying" – not even from this poetic soul. I told him I would rather he had put a bullet through my brain. I'd never take out a gun and do it to myself. I just felt that if it was to come to this, to what he did to me in L.A., why not just *kill* me?

We were down in Los Angeles that particular Christmas in 1975. As always, P.C. ran very late, and it was going into the next day as we crowded onto the floor of the church office, 70 or 80 of us, it seemed. By this time, Jim's sexual schedule had apparently degenerated into something of a zoo. (You get up one morning, as he had recently, and announce to your congregation, not in braggadocio, but in a weary, near-desperate plea, that you had been with *sixteen* people the night before, both women and men – I'd fairly call that a "zoo.") This would be the night of bring-down.

He said things were getting entirely out of hand. What should we do? I began writing, like I always did. (When in doubt, *write*.) I had nearly completed my suggestion that couldn't there be some kind of a list, when Jack Beam quipped cynically, "You know, someone in here suggested a *list* to keep things orderly." A few let loose with nervous laughter. Obviously this suggestion was preposterous. No one's sexuality was going to conform to "a list."

I glanced down at my half-written page and felt a shimmer of panic. I had nearly handed this in. I felt like a clumsy thirteen-year-old who had accidentally stumbled onto a porno film and was the only one who didn't know what was going on. Yeah. I felt not a day older than when my mother went off to Puerto Rico and my now-dying dad cursed her and they nearly got divorced and it didn't even occur to them that it might upset *me*. My brain was swimming through age points and time zones. I wanted out. No, I wanted my say. I wanted comfort. No. I really wanted for none of this to even exist.

Jim said he wanted to hear from the people who had been with him. This was beginning to take the tone of not someone who screwed, but someone who was clear *he* was being "screwed over." At first the room was painfully silent. Then some spoke, cautiously, guardedly, in low tones, always praiseful of Jim, always deprecating of themselves. But few details resembling confessions were forthcoming. "*Mike* is so comfortable with his homosexuality," Jim volunteered, "that he ejaculates right in the bed." No takers. "All some of you want to do is talk," he next threw out dismissively, whereas "*Maria* thinks so little of herself, she just lies there and fucks." So much for the women's banner of expression. So talking wasn't "in," was it? The room again fell silent.

Some scribbled notes and handed them towards the front of the room. I looked around and spotted Sarah furiously scribbling away. In fact, I couldn't believe the succession of people at all. Mary Jane? She never said anything, and rarely was anything mentioned of *her*, except for one time early in her stay in P.C., when it was reported that she had called Jim a "motherfucker." She called him a "motherfucker," and he took her to bed to make her more... *friendly?*

Larry Schacht. Our brilliant medical student. He was hardly ever there anymore. When had this even happened?

Carrie. Well, at least that made some sense. Her husband, Paul, was a flagrant pedophile. This was probably one of Jim's "corrective" situations. "Therapy" did, not infrequently, happen in two's ~ the Lelands, the Ingrams, the Adkins, even the Stoens ~ why not the Williams?

By the time we heard from Debbie Blakey, the room was seething with undercurrent tension. Jim said, "You told me you had a *lesbian* affair. What do you want with *me*? Sex? Or attention?" Debbie chewed on that glumly, then popped out with a pout, "*Both.*"

I tell you, almost to this very day I could not remember what was on the note *I* sent up to Jim. It was something about maybe it's not you, maybe it's me. Something about it's not *you* I don't trust ~ it's *me*.

What was it that I, in my own mind, was taking blame for? Or doubting myself about? My emotions, locked into a strangulation hold, still felt for *him*, still wanted to *help*. If my youthful vehemence could not be poured into love, passion, joy, let it at least flow by the torrents into guilt!

It was a full eighteen years before I remembered the contents of that note with a start. I had just read an account of past traumas in *The New Yorker* from Jim and Marceline's surviving sons. And it was like a veil fell from *my* memory. It seems there are two kinds of veils ~ one over the sublime, the other over the traumatic, as though in our limited range of sleepwalking through life, as we humans are wont to do, neither heaven nor hell, in glory or horror either one, can be fully revealed, lest we too fully *live*.

I remembered it finally. That I had written, "It's not you I don't trust. It's me." I thought I really *might* have gone off, and left this whole mess, the horrendous bringdown happening right now, for others. I had even dialed the man's number in L.A. No one had answered. What if someone had?

Of course, trust, my own unfortunate selection of guilt-du-jour – once "trust" hit the soundwaves, it was like a buzzword at which to either clench up or go berserk. How could anyone put Father, and any question of trusting *him*, into a single sentence?

To this day, I cannot grasp how Jim interpreted that note as defiance. Indeed, I was reneging on any thoughts of independence and returning to the fold. Unless the thought of my ever being interested in another man, under *any* circumstances (like letting myself be raped to save a whole horde of little kids? Maybe...) was so verboten, that the ax had to fall, whatever my true intentions.

Moreover, it was only during a disastrous stretch of silence, breaking only here and there like sharp chips of fractured ice, that I could even compose myself enough to pass up that note. If they wouldn't speak, I would. This was all such a ghastly sacrifice for *him*, and they couldn't speak up? The ones he *had* loved? Say how they wanted it, or how incredible it was, or how awed they were that he gave of himself to them? They all seemed so repressed, even frightened to speak.

And *I* would suggest to him going off with someone else? (No gold medal for tact, to say the least.) How would I dare? It looked like now "the lamb" was about to be attacked by "the lions." Fierce creatures prowling for blood.

My vulnerabilities had been bared, the assault but moments away. I was hardly up for sexuality, or creativity, or fulfillments of the heart as is. These are the forces of *life*. My life could not be my own. It had to be his.

And his it was. What was left for me? I couldn't be accepted. I couldn't be wanted, needed or loved. With a tragically ironic twist, when I passed up that note, it was out of wanting to help. He may not want *me*, but maybe I could help *him* – ease his burden by affirming that the failing must be mine, not his. If I could ease his pain, I would have *some* empowerment, be of some use. It was terrible just sitting there doing nothing.

Was it a mistake offering to go see the man from the airport? Maybe I was too vague in my note. I remember Jim opening it. It was passed to him, he opened it, read it and stiffened. Then he said pointedly, "I asked to hear from people who have been with me." He handed the note back to Carol Stahl, his monitor, and said, "Read this out loud." She did, and something got real, real *twisted* in all this. Everyone suddenly jumped to life. Very *hostile* life. Finally a scapegoat had been located.

"Stand up." I did. He lambasted me to the floor about the airport scene. "What do you think *you* have to offer?," and "Did that man even exist?" "Yes," I said weakly. Was he accusing me of *lying*? How could he accuse me of lying? But at the airport.... it was admittedly pretty weird. How does a millionaire just show up at the airport and volunteer to give money to *us*? I was already discredited the instant Jim brought it up. That's all it took. Now "liar" and "manipulator" were piled onto the fire.

I said nothing. There was nothing to say. A "defense"? Only guilty people tried that, and unsuccessfully at that. How could I, already steeped in upset, confusion, even terror, defend myself against this mob?

Jim's eyes narrowed to a hard squint, like they were saying, "Don't fuck with me." Maybe that's *exactly* what he wanted to say... to the whole room. Then, like a karate master gauging his prey to launch a single, deadly blow, he said to me with cool contempt, "Take off your clothes." What? *"Do it!"*

My mind.... zapped. I was in traumatic shock. I made a half-conscious effort to act "as though this were happening." What if it were happening? What would I do? I had undressed before strangers before. Skinny-dipping in Oregon. No one thought anything of it.

And sometimes people who endured confrontation well (so few had, it would be extraordinary) were respected for it. If I did *not* comply, I would be shut out forever. Jim would have been "right about her." The chess game would be irretrievably lost. I had given my whole life to this place. This place where no one even seemed to want me.

There was more. I had no *way* to defend myself. My very voice might fail. I couldn't handle this scene even if this travesty were not happening. I couldn't handle my dying dad or my histrionic mom. I couldn't handle Sarah's imperious contempt. I couldn't handle riding up and down the busses to L.A. like a mousy little lackey. I couldn't handle my own feelings. How could I handle my "defense"?

But all that was required of me here -in *complying*- was simply *silence*. I couldn't answer these people's questions. I couldn't answer Jim's questions. I couldn't tell them when I had "stopped beating my wife."

I had one thing, one thing only. My *integrity*. I wasn't a liar. I wasn't a manipulator. I was no traitor. I would not be the cause of this having happened. I had no credibility *now*, but if I did *not* comply, I would have no credibility *ever*.

I complied. It took a few minutes. I swore I would not shed a tear. I *swore* it.

"Now turn around." I turned around. I felt my face go into the flattened gaze of hopelessness ~ the ashen skin, the quivering lip, the inability to feel... *anything*. Suddenly I feared I would begin to cry, no, weep. It would make everything much, much worse. I held my tears. I mustn't do this.

"Does anyone want to fuck with her?," Jim threw out in a suppressed fury. Some of the guys made crass wisecracks. The women were respectfully silent. I stood motionless. This man I adored, this man I trusted. He wouldn't organize a gage rape, would he? No. Please. For *everyone's* sake. Nothing like that.

By now, I could no longer talk. I remember thinking, maybe I need to go through this. It is *happening*, isn't it? But if, for any reason, I need to go through this at any time in my life, why not at the hands of Nazis? Why at the hands of this man (god - man - god - man) I adored?

The last thought I remember before my mind joined my body in a numbing freeze, was that maybe I was a child of *Sparta*. You remember how the Spartans put their infant children on the mountaintop? If the lions did not devour them, then they were fit to live, to be Spartans. If the lions did devour the child, then they devoured the child. Did I not, indeed, know something of ancient Greece after all?

My attention, momentarily diverted to that narrowing slit of space within, now snapped back into the room. Jim looked at me menacingly. He said I had been "coming on to him," and "If I had a list of the people I *didn't* want to fuck, you'd be on the top of the list!" I said nothing. How could I? My very *mind* was being rendered mute. I had never "come onto him," not even once. How in the world did he even think that?

No, not just that. Icing ~ *proof*. "You said I should be with you." Now the mob was like lions ~ the lions of ancient Sparta. "You" (lowly, nothing, despicable you) "said he *should* be with you"? When had I ever said such a thing? Oh..... Once I talked with Sharon Amos, I was miserable beyond belief, yet felt I couldn't ask Jim Jones for *anything*. I thought maybe, somehow, he could drag me out of this perpetual misery. Not as an obligation. More like a mercy. I said it in resignation: "Maybe he *should* be with me." The ongoing misery was more than I thought I could bear.

And Sharon had thought... *this*? That I had said that arrogantly, as though it were my right? And told *him*? Is *this* what she was doing being my friend? Was she my friend so that this screaming mob could be my enemy? And why was he relying on how this "friend" interpreted what she thought I meant by what she thought she heard me say? Why didn't he ever ask *me*? Ever believe *me*? Ever trust *me*?

I was pulverized, panicked, my thinking process fading fast, almost unable to even hear. Whatever he thought I meant by what I did or said or thought or felt or breathed or ate, or even puked for that matter... how could he keep *attacking* me? He saw I was *totally defenseless* – that there was no way I could utter a single word, make a single gesture, that could have possibly abated my situation or given me a scintilla of strength.

But this was the time. Strike, strike now, while the iron is hot. Why did I think I had any *talent*, he asked. Why did I plague him with letters about my *feelings* about everything. That he didn't want to hear about my talents, or my feelings, ever again. I *had* no special talents. I *had* no inner feelings. "*Say it!*," he railed at me. "Say, 'I have no special talents. Say, 'I have no inner feelings.'"

Then he launched the very worst. (Was this why he was doing this? Was this at the root of it?) "You want me to *die*, don't you?" Oh, God, now I *couldn't* not cry. I always *feared* he would die on us. I feared he would die before I ever knew him. I feared we would be left in some disastrous state with our leader gone. I never, ever *wanted* it. Did he never discern the difference? I had been there for years now. Did he not know me better? Did I do anything ever, even once, to harm him in any way? To harm the work? How could he say this? I loved this man. *He* would never believe it, but I did. Foreseeing his death was a *terror*, not a *wish*. Had they all gone mad?

My voice would not fail me now, however muted and weak: "I don't want you to die, Father. I don't want you to die." Tears streamed down my cheeks. Didn't he see my tears? Didn't he see that there had been no tears for my own plight, but that only now, there were tears for *him*? Couldn't *I* die? It would be more merciful, wouldn't it?

I must have gone not only numb but amnesiac. In the weeks ahead, I was approached about various responsibilities I had "agreed to take on," like a penance: heading a security team, organizing the agenda for P.C. I said I would do these things? I never even remembered their coming up.

It had begun at about 2 a.m. that morning, December 26, 1975. I needed no pneumonic device to recall the date: it was the sixth anniversary of the last time I had had sex. *I had been totally abstinent for six years on the very date everyone felt free to treat me like a whore.*

156/SNAKE DANCE

It ended at about 4 a.m. This went on for two hours. Were there two hours' worth of epithets hurled at me? I don't know. You might ask someone who was *there*. My mind had somehow managed to check out of all that pain soon after it began.

"Can I put my clothes back on?" I heard myself ask these words. They connected to nothing. It was like my very heart was drained of blood. "Yes," he asserted quietly.

We closed out with all the usual instructions. No one talk with her. No one sympathize with her. (Was I not already a leper? Was this not gratuitous?) People filed past me out the the door. I couldn't move. I just sat there. I saw Jim out of the corner of my eye. He arose, surrounded by his small entourage, and left. I waited until he left, until everyone had left. It was getting towards dawn.

Services began warming up at 11 o'clock that morning. There was always about an hour of singing, then testimonies, before Jim came out on the podium. I don't know what got into me. I had this thing about *bravery*. Make yourself do the most brave thing under the circumstances and you will be able to handle it.

I stepped up to the testimony line. I was brief, but my voice was clear. I had undergone a difficult experience the night before, I said, but I still believed this was the best place in the world. My voice didn't crack. I didn't cry. I did... *"fine."* I left the stage calm. Not relaxed, no. But not shaking, not upset, not a tear. *Calm*.

The busses went back up to San Francisco that night. It was Friday, heading into the weekend. I was greeting downstairs when Jim entered the building. He saw me sitting on a chair. He walked over and sat beside me. He took my hand and held it for what seemed like a very long time. Like a doctor would take your pulse. I said nary a word. He stood up and moved on.

Now life truly began to feel regimented. I just worked. And worked. And worked. We were turning in weekly schedules, anyway (like there was anyplace else to go or anything else to do), and it was a relief that I could claim no moment of time as mine. I wound up back on the post-service line a few weeks later on, with my "numbers," and Dick made a nasty wisecrack about why was I there? Did I have another unwanted letter for Jim? Or was it to come onto him? I blanched and ran upstairs to the third floor. I ran smack into Teri and Maria. I looked so shaken, they asked me what was wrong, and I told them what Dick had said.

Teri said, reassuringly, not to pay any attention to it at all – that *Jim* didn't feel that way. Maria added, "Jim has so much respect for you, it's not even credible." I calmed myself, walked down the stairway, took my brief stint on the line, then disappeared.

Four or five weeks had gone by. I was sitting in the office in L.A., for counselling work, when Sharon came by with a few choice words. She said Jim was "sorry about what happened." That it was "a new therapy." I went numb so quickly as she spoke, I thought, just answer this quick and be done with it. I murmured, "It's all right."

Then I said (not quite on impulse – it was almost like someone had tapped me on the shoulder), "Tell Jim I destroyed all my poetry, everything but the work about his death. I want to know if it's all right that I keep it." She looked horrified. I was *serious*, wasn't I? Jim was sitting at the front of the room. If she was messenger from him to me, was she not also messenger from me to him? She walked up front and conferred briefly. She came back and said it was all right. I saw her struggling to do this real, real... *businesslike*.

If this was interpreted as some new manner of defiance, the reality was the opposite. I would be *clean* about this. I *wouldn't* hold onto "*Allegory*" as a matter of defiance. I genuinely wanted what I said I wanted – for it to be all right. Whoever loved me (or not), whoever liked me, whoever hated me – all that seemed out of my hands. This one matter of principle (that I saw what I saw, wrote what I wrote, and would stand by it alone, if needs be) *wasn't*. In an odd way, he had brought out in me what he might not even risk my having – *character*. Oh, but it was the premium, wasn't it? Character, character, it's all we ever heard.

So I'd have it, this rare premium "character." Enough character to risk his mistrust all over again. He had said that I, like him, would be misunderstood. What could I do about whatever *he* might misunderstand? Obviously nothing.

A few weeks later on, Jim said I looked well and was doing *so* well, and did I have anything to say. I said it had been very traumatic, but I was "fine." He was congratulatory. It seemed I was the new role model. I had done it. I had really done it. I had held onto my integrity for only "the small price" of loss of love. No, more. Loss of all *possibility* of love. Not so much as a single embrace. Not ever.

Like Spock in the Star Trek episode where hideous extraterrestrial leeches were clamping onto people's backs and killing them. Spock fell victim while attempting to rescue others. Then he volunteered to have them purged experimentally from his own back with light rays. The light eradicated the beasties, but left Spock quite blind. Of course, he was Vulcan, so it all got restored. But ah, not right away. At first he thought – well, *all* of us thought – all of us viewers thought he was quite blind now for life. He merely said, "An equitable exchange." He had been taken out of excruciating pain and his life spared. So he was now blind. "An equitable exchange."

I got my "equitable exchange." My integrity acknowledged. Father's respect. My heart.... was this not a small price to pay?

Jim would go even further. An interesting admission. He said when he first told me to undress, that he thought maybe this was crazy, but that he did it by *discernment*. (What did that mean? God said to do this?) Then some concessions. Quite theoretical, of course. "Maybe we should all undress." "Maybe we should all go through what Laurie went through." "Maybe I should be with everyone who wants to be with me." Maybe this, maybe that.

Could I console myself? Maybe what Jim went through *was* worse. Surely he had undressed with a lot of people he couldn't stand, and even acted like he enjoyed it. Maybe somewhere, at some time, he and I could even be "comrades." Maybe he would finally let me be a part, to be what I had *earned*, not locked into perennial exclusion. As always, I feared not. I feared this would never be. I feared it was like all my fears. That he would die before any of that could happen.

What constraint was on others? Why had *my* thinking processes to be rational? I *feared*.

XXI. "Heaven Help Anyone Who Opted to be Caught within the Crunch."

Other shifts began to happen as well. Now, finally, I was forced to begin separating out Jim Jones the revelator from Jim Jones the man.

Last time around ("the poetry shake-down"), he had defended a liar against me. Bad enough. Now he made *me* out to be a liar. Moreover, the perennial assurance, "If you tell me the truth, I'll never embarrass you," had been violated beyond sanction. He may have been a serene, all-knowing protector for people who had come, in desperation, looking for "God," but Jim Jones the person and Laurie Efrein the person seemed destined for the sword.

I had allowed this man to become my entire life, yet I only seemed to incur his contempt. Like a badly-ground lens had been placed upon my eye, all our personal relating had schismed into a blur. Any ideal corrective lens had been scratched into blindness by an abrasive reality I seemed powerless to effect.

I was faithful. I was brave. I wanted nothing more than to have peace with the miracle worker. I tried every compensation, allowance, rationale – the pressures, the hours, the efforts, the pain. But slowly, painfully, from then on in, the bond that had so drawn me to Jim Jones over five years back, was beginning to unravel.

L.A. was hardly Jim Jones' Waterloo (betrayal was – not even a second-close candidate in sight), but it was mine. The very human, personal Jim Jones had exploded so furiously in my face, in ways so *contrary* to what I needed, so contrary to my safety and protection, that there seemed little way to reconcile even an understandably provoked Jim Jones with the loving god-man who had first welcomed me with such tenderness into this place. So finally, painfully, I began to redesign my shattered reality to accommodate the schisms:

Now there would be *two beings*: Jim Jones the God and Jim Jones the man. They lived in the same body, but did not necessarily share the same experiences. The man may not always remember what the God had said. He was something like a *conduit* for the God. The voltage of the God's immensity took its toll on the man's body and was an extra-dimensional extension of the man's mind. The God was eternal, the man mortal.

With the God I had nothing to fear. With the man, the complex, emotional, multi-faceted pressures of leadership made of fear and power seemingly needed boundaries to protect against human pressures and Godly endowments intermixing too interpenetrably. The human pushed in upon him; the Godly expanded out. *Heaven help anyone who opted to be caught within the crunch.*

The God never misunderstood. He forever knew my heart. I mourned the man, and empathized the tragedy of what he took upon himself (no, not people's personal lives -- a greater societal task by far) at perilous, increasing, unrelenting risk. I had no key to either separate these two, God and man, nor to merge them either. I feared the man would die on us before I ever knew him, before his embrace could ever envelop me in love, whatever its origin -- sexual, compassionate, fraternal, paternal, eternal. I could only hope that the God would love me irregardless of who lived or died at all.

I hoped against hope, that if not now, then please, at least some time prior to death (the death he cruelly claimed I *wanted*), that the man would understand. That the God within him Who knew my heart, would instill that knowledge within the heart of the man.

No perfect model of reality; but as my heart was felled, my brain must assume its function. Jim Jones had much what the evangelists would call "The Christ Spirit working through him," with healings, comfortings, unceasing devotion and love. But then there was the human soul --driven, impassioned, ambitious, fanatical--, which sported a far more political version of "God" -- more like Caesar, or the Pharoahs, or Alexander the Great. Or (in modern times) Lenin or Mao. *That* kind of "God." The God of Politics. God of the World.

I even wanted all this to work. I had entered Peoples Temple awed that the spiritual and the political could be grounded into one being, into one work. That "one nation under God" meant not the God of stagnant churches, but a God of life -- a living God who practiced all he preached, and wasn't just a artifact of some ancient text. A God for *all* of us -- every race, age, gender or class, as *"one nation."*

To this day, I don't believe that any true God would want less. If we as Americans truly believe "one nation under God," then why is it not part of our national life? I live with these questions still, and anguish that it would take "extremists" to create a just society, or face slaughter for the trying.

But now I had more personal matters to attend to. My faith in the union between God and humanity in *this* man had been breached. The "two gods" within him, human and divine, had been so in harmony when we started down this path. But now I could no longer reconcile these Siamese twins of Deity, which increasingly, seemed to be at war even within him. It threw *me* into a war I never wanted against someone I didn't want to fight. I wasn't a liar, I wasn't a traitor, I wasn't even a rebel. I was nothing I was painted as. I was just struggling desperately to be myself; and for that, The God of Politics was destroying me.

Unfortunately (or perhaps *fortunately* – I thought it, despite my insecurities, a mark of character), I had my own Siamese twins of *devotion*. I loved *both* the political and the spiritual work. I believed in it. I wanted it to succeed. I had given my word and my time, my privacy, my resources and devotion, and I wasn't about to pull out just because Jim Jones had made grievous errors with *me*. Maybe time would iron this out. Maybe some day we'd be in a less pressured time and place. Maybe he would learn, too. Maybe he wouldn't do this to anyone else. A whole world of maybes.

Maybe he would even stop trying to cure the incurable, and simply let me be. His gavel-like dictums that I mustn't write, I mustn't write, I mustn't write. It was that I mustn't write about his *death*, wasn't it. If only that were a dysfunction, I could remedy it. But I couldn't. There was no cure save perhaps some rare elixir that need be imported from another world, another time and place. All the more human remedies (rage, castigation, humiliation) were like applying salt to an already-stinging wound. I truly needed *God* to tell me it was all right. And *this* "God" couldn't or wouldn't ... not just do it, but *see* it. He was committed to save us, and I was seeing us already doomed? What did that make me? Poor Cassandra, the cost of her immortal name being that of being destroyed in her own time?

My one most crying need ("need beyond need" – yes, very much as when loved ones die, and people need No One less than God to comfort them) was for Jim Jones to acknowledge that what I saw, what I wrote, arose from being on his side, not against him. Couldn't he see how I was suffering with it, not that I wanted to harm *him*? But instead, I got the reverse. That he would see me destroyed before he would let the Pandora's box tilt open at anyone's behest but his own.

I *was* made a pariah, after all. Everything I had feared had happened! I was castigated, ridiculed, humiliated, vilified, accused of wanting the leader dead. No one who was goaded into attacking me even knew why. If they did, it would have been... *worse*. She tells the leader that other men can fuck, she may even go off with one, and then she writes poetry about Jim Jones' death? What jury would exonerate such a guilty creature as me based upon such incriminating evidence? Such a person could not be *allowed* any expression – creative, sexual, psychic, freedom of thought, freedom to feel, freedom to write, anything. I was indeed now paralyzed into silence.

I look back, twenty-odd years hence, and in a faded-out yet still vivid horror, I realize how little choice I had at the time. Had I been more mature, less insecure, I might not have arrived at that room at that point of time at all. I would have been a different human being with different options. But once there, there seemed no option but to endure, tragic schisms and all.

Notwithstanding, I could barely absorb my most painful ordeal shy of the tragedy itself. It was too horrendous to make the cost of all this *love*. In a world where only the disempowered merited love, I seemed forced to choose between such love, and maintaining my own integrity. Must I have made this choice? Must I have, indeed, made this choice, this stand, for *everyone*? I wouldn't shirk it, but it was excruciating.

I had no thought that it might be of *value* to me. That it might exclude me from not just the acceptance I craved, but from the ultimate cauldron of our collective fate! That perhaps it was the burning of my flesh within the cauldron, to some irrevocable point of overkill, that purified me sufficiently to escape its *ultimate* scorching flames.

I had no thought of preserving my life at the time. Being killed *by* Jim (metaphorically) seemed more of a terror than being killed by outside, opposing forces (while I was) *with* Jim. Yet I'm never entirely sure that my taking that route, rather than those taken by the ones "loved" by Jim Jones, did not, in fact, spare not just my good name (the respect of someone who said he could no longer fully trust *anyone* was hardly given casually), but my very life. You will see.

XXII. "Foul Times Require Foul Tests."

Do you know the Sidney Rittenberg School of Human Relations? This emerged in 1993, when Rittenberg wrote a book about his experiences in Communist China. He was one lone American who lived amongst the Chinese, knew Mao Tse-Tung and was a friend of Chou En-Lai. He was one of them – *trusted*. Then, he said, the Soviets fabricated that he was a spy. It wasn't too difficult a charge to press (notwithstanding that he had always *acted* loyal), as Americans were perennially suspect in the Communist world.

So the Chinese threw Rittenberg in jail. Even his friend, high-ranking Chou En-Lai, could or would not appeal on his behalf. Finally he was cleared, only to be thrown back into jail when new "charges," equally false, surfaced, this time for many years.

All his years in jail, he insisted upon keeping his cell meticulously neat and clean. He knew it was they who had lost faith in him, not he who had lost faith in them. He didn't want them to think him any less than a loyal comrade. He acted what he was, not what anyone *thought* he was. And amazingly (well, amazingly for the common mind to grasp), this spared him from bitterness!

After his book came out, he went on the usual round of interviews. And people approached him like... well, they admired him, but why in the world did he react *that* way? No one could understand that you don't necessarily turn against the one who turns against you. That you are who you are irregardless. If the Chinese thought he was a spy, it didn't *make* him one. So he wasn't going to *act* like one.

Me? I never even tried to rectify the story of the man at the airport. (Good God, I never even told Jim Jones in all those years that my mother had been a card-carrying communist. I would have been turned into a poster child!) I never said he got the facts wrong, much less got my *intent* wrong. I never told him I had considered going off, at least in part, out of empathy for *him* (his "redheaded man who paid him $200"), much less reaffirmed that the man at the airport did exist.

Understand, reader, this wasn't quite saintliness, but more, an aversion to doing anything that might recreate that excruciating pain. So if I were ever tempted to tell him what really happened, that temptation died a thousand deaths for each resurrection.

Nevertheless, I do also understand the enigmatic Mr. Rittenberg. I wondered if Rittenberg had ever wept in that lonely jail cell. I wondered, if he had, if any of the guards had even noticed.

By March of 1976, I was beginning to weep – episodes of sudden, uncontrollable upset. The tears would erupt as I hurriedly rushed to the bathroom to evade any watching eyes. I was so depressed thinking back on that ghastly night, I blocked out my *own* watching eyes. If I worked long enough, hard enough, maybe it would all just go away.

I finally approached Jim shyly, with trepidation, after a P.C. I told him I didn't think I could handle what happened in L.A. That I was beginning to get very upset. I don't know whether he never heard of post-traumatic syndrome – it was still early for the publicity about the Vietnam vets; or whether he thought such could only exist as a manipulation. (He was a fan of Thomas Szasz – you know, the "there's no such thing as mental illness" Thomas Szasz?) But all he said, eyes gazing *away* from me (was I a leper still?) was, "Someone may need to talk with you."

Why not him? Why never him? Half of P.C. had *slept* with him. He couldn't *talk* with me? Moreover, the "someone" never came. I supposed that there were more pressing concerns, and suppressed my tears. I couldn't very well let them flow on, could I? They would never have stopped.

My heart bristled aimlessly with autumn leaves. They fell one by one, lost to the wind. It was pointless to grieve their demise, much less the fate of the tree from which they unceremoniously had fallen. My love never wavered, neither for Jim nor for the work, albeit love that never would or could be acknowledged. How could I harbor *"unrequited* love," when that very rare orchid itself, love, was deemed to rarely even exist in any heart but Father's?

Would Guyana be different? I didn't even dare *think*. The gap between that visionary wonder and the moment-by-moment grind seemed unbridgable most days. Yet I hoped. I knew in my heart, that despite everything, Guyana would be wondrous, wonderful – if not for me personally, then for everyone as a whole. As always, whatever joy there was to be had would be found in what was done for others. This wasn't *my* life, anyway, was it?

Something else had happened in the interim as well, which made it seem like it mightn't be *anyone's* life. Jim had run this test in P.C. No, he didn't call it a "test." Not before. Not during. Not after. It was clear this was *reality*. He actually exploded when someone wrote him about "the test."

I don't know to this day whether he wanted us to know what reality might come to; to see who could or couldn't live in this reality; if he foresaw it as inevitable; upon what *he* believed it to be contingent; if the world would create this for us; if we ourselves would create it; if circumstances were immutable or changeable; who, indeed, would live, and who would die and... in what *consciousness*.

Many years later, a curious, equally dire and enigmatic (now there's the rub ~ when "dire" equals "enigmatic"!) scene showed up in "Shogun," about the ancient territorial wars within Japan. Lord Torinaga knows that if Blackthorne (the protagonist) tries to leave Japan, he will be killed, and that it is his destiny, in any case, to stay. So even though he is Blackthorne's... well, *guru*, he knows he will have to have Blackthorne's most precious, elemental possession, the ship by which he plans to leave Japan, burned to the ground.

Of course, he cannot tell Blackthorne this. He would not only take it the wrong way (obviously!), but might try to prevent it from being carried out. So instead, Torinaga does the following:

He assembles Blackthorne and others in his court. Blackthorne has his faithful Mariko (translator, lover ~ perhaps, metaphorically, the only vehicle by which *Japan* could be transfused into his alien blood) by his side.

Then he calls in a young couple. The man says, I hope we have not caused your displeasure. Torinaga glowers slightly and says, no, if you don't consider *treason* displeasure. They are struck silent by the force of his words.

Torinaga asks if they are loyal. They say yes. He asks they bring their children to be killed. Pain flashes across their faces. In their eyes are both terror and sorrow. But they do not protest.

He says go quickly, get the children and bring them here. The young couple departs. They look everywhere, but their children are nowhere to be found. They return, and in a desperate anxiety, they say they cannot *find* their children. Lord Torinaga scrutinizes them, and seeing that they would sacrifice all despite their pain, relaxes his guard. He beckons to his side, and the couple's children are brought out from behind him. They fall into their parents' loving embrace, then all are respectfully silent. Lord Torinaga is brief, fierce, yet certain and strong: ***"Foul times require foul tests."***

Blackthorne is transfixed, and puzzled. He cannot see that this stage has been laid for *him*, to prepare him for what he cannot possibly comprehend ~ the burning of his treasured ship by his own master. For

166/SNAKE DANCE

him, indeed, though he does not yet know it, it is no "test" at all. It is reality-in-the-making. Thus Torinaga wants Blackthorne to grasp the meaning of *sacrifice*.

Blackthorne's rejection is, of course, predictable. Surely his own personal agenda and the larger agenda of all Japan cannot so grievously collide as they nearly did for the two small, innocent children now lapped up into their parent's arms. He rushes, thus, to demonstrate his lesson unlearned.

He goes to the door as directed, opens it, and there is Father Avile, whom he has requested to see. Because he needs him to translate something he cannot have translated through Mariko. He makes Avile swear secrecy. Then he tells Torinaga through the priest that he desires Mariko to be granted a divorce so she may marry him.

Torinaga is angry, calls the request "presumptuous," and to never speak of it again. For Torinaga knows that Mariko is meant to sacrifice her life. He will not have this personal, emotional desire of Blackthorne's interfere with this, with what will affect the destiny of so many, of an entire nation.

By the same measure, he knows the love of the young parents for their children, and their horror at the purported sacrifice; and that yet, even in their grief, they were prepared to obey. He wants Blackthorne, who is unprepared to see this, to yet see it. It isn't that Torinaga doesn't understand love. It is just that, "Foul times require foul tests."

We hate such "ethics" here in the West. We cannot even comprehend this biblically, when Abraham is asked to sacrifice Isaac. How mindless it is to sacrifice children. (Nor did Shakespeare write a sequel to "Romeo and Juliet" - we never learned if the Capulets and the Montagues were indeed able to transcend their children's fate.) Yet culturally, we barely understand what sacrifice is at all. It is an anathema, even though parents of necessity sacrifice for their children. That is the sanctioned sacrifice, and often the *silent* sacrifice at that. Everyone wants a payback.

There are Asian cultures in which sacrifice is honor. Yet the Englishman here, Blackthorne, much less Americans of modern date, are transfixed, and comprehend not.

Thus was this too, no "test" - not to Jim. This was **life raw and real**. Nor were there "experts" to decipher this beyond its surface trappings, which were admittedly bizarre, even (to some) frightening. One woman freaked so bad, she left out and never came back. I can give you an abbreviated explanation (paranoia gone amuck or the like), but I cannot tell you that this caused that, then this caused that, then this caused that. It wasn't causal. It was more like a consciousness that you either knew was there or you didn't. You knew that scenario was there or it wasn't. This was no cause-and-effect exercise. It was a *pulse*.

Jim wanted to be sure that everyone was present, everyone who belonged, everyone seated, everyone settled. He had several pitchers of grape juice in the front of the room. Many small cups were then filled. Jim said to pass them out but not to drink them. Everyone received a cup and held it quietly in their lap. Jim looked around. He said to make sure everyone had one, but that no one drank from their cup.

Then he bid us drink. All of us together. He looked closely, out at all directions in the room. "Be sure everyone drinks. Has everyone drunk their juice. Is there anyone who hasn't drunk their juice." A moment or two and all had complied. "Now." He paused, easing into a slow, steady stride. "You've all just drunk a poison. It will take about half an hour to work. It's a very strong poison and it will work for everyone. Maybe a little sooner for some than for others. If someone next to you drops down, it just means it worked a little faster for them than for you." He was very calm.

"Who has anything to say?" Carol Stahl spoke hesitantly, meekly. She was from the old Church Board and was a literalist with Jim and his capacities. She had been there the day he disappeared into a ball of light, then reappeared moments later. She wouldn't ever doubt his reasons, nor his word. Her question was simple and direct. "What about the children? What about Bonnie [her daughter]?" Her lip quavered.

"They're all being taken care of." His voice was unwavering, even calming. It was not only eerie, but weird. This was the stage of the church – an open area! Someone could even drop by from outside of P.C. It didn't happen. People knew to stay away. But here we were, in an exposed part of the church for such an intensely private act. And so few of us. I mean compared to the membership of the whole church. How could all the children have been "taken care of"? Would this go on in different locations throughout the night? Well, this *fraction* of a night. Was there a night to go at all?

Few people said anything. Strangely, *Grace* (who had threatened suicide – and was perhaps relieved to now have it taken out of her hands) said it had all been worth it, and that even if John died tonight, she was glad he was raised in the church. That was the strangest. I spoke nothing.

168/SNAKE DANCE

I almost... *felt* nothing. Like a huge lid had been pressed down on me – not painfully, but securely. Now there was nothing to say, nothing to do.

Patty Cartmell began to freak out. Patty, who had deliberately refused novocaine at the dentist, because she thought if she were ever tortured to extract information, she had to be prepared for pain. Was she *really* freaking out? Then Andy freaked out and ran up and down the aisle dividing the center of the room. Then someone dropped to the floor.

I don't know why I didn't react. I just didn't. Like it was not quite real. Like I had to just watch and wait. More time went by, while Jim silently observed.

It was at least a half hour later when he told us it was just grape juice. But, no, reader, it was *not* the ultimate practical joke. Not in the slightest. He seemed impelled to discern how we would react in the face of death. Later in the week, he assigned someone to go to each one and record their reactions. I found the prospect of death not all that chilling. Of course this was but a month or two after the disaster in L.A., when whole pieces of me felt hollowed out and responseless.

Aside from this, I felt the same. That I had more in life to do. Would death have "rescued" me from that, or would it be an *evasion* of my responsibilities in this life, Peoples Temple or not? I shared none of this. I had learned all too well how to monitor the barriers between feeling and thought and speech. I had no sense of withholding anything. There was just nothing to give. No cup into which this water could flow.

For Jim's own part, who knew whether he was preparing for contingencies, or foreseeing inevitabilities? It was both. *Guyana* was both. At first, there seemed nothing *inevitable* about a mass exodus; yet by the time it happened, it was so provoked by outside forces, that an idiot could have seen that we needed to get the hell out! Jim, by contrast, had foreseen it, and prepared for that *contingency*. Was it not all one and the same? Did we not just get three-and-a-half years' lead time on the inevitable?

Not to minimize the paradigmatic shift of "the grape juice incident" in the slightest! This was no "What if..." or "Do you have any reservations?," like the proposed leap off the Golden Gate Bridge. Notwithstanding, it turned out that there was one big advantage of *death* being put on the table. After that, we no longer had huge harangues about *sex!* It came up rarely now, with a weary, anticlimactic thud.

In one oddly muted P.C., we heard about Jim's "prostate problem," which he described as his prostate becoming hard and swelling to the size of a grapefruit were it not relieved by continual sex. No one inquired who was his doctor. One dear woman, perhaps sixty, single, and undoubtedly out of sex for many years, offered altruistically that maybe some of the women should volunteer to alleviate his distress. He realized she hadn't the slightest design on him, thus looked at her kindly and said something like no, dear, that won't be necessary. I'm sure others besides me were confused. Did we need him or he need us? And why was sex suddenly cast in low clinical tones, as a *medical* matter?

Aside from this odd episode, I don't know that our chief nemesis was vanquished at all. We just talked less about it. Nicki had left after approaching Jim from behind with a lead pipe after he refused her sex. Every now and then, a last tangled disaster still unravelled before our eyes. Why had this man ever consented to be with *anyone*?

But as our more private source of anguish was momentarily suppressed, Jim, by this quiescence at one end, took the liberty of being more open now at the other ~ public services for the membership. Once even on a serene, exquisite crest of healing, singing, drinking in what was still so pure in Peoples Temple and Jim Jones ~ maybe the more so on a night like that. The singing had gone on and on. "I'm So Grateful," and "Father Is All," and "Soon, yes very soon, we are" (no, not "going to see the King" but) "going to The Promised Land" ~ our beautiful, flourishing Jonestown. Jim finally stepped out onto the podium. He just stood there and looked out over the crowd. It was ethereal. We had recently hosted the triumph called "The Testimonial Dinner", and it seemed like finally, the world was giving us respect. Jim always cautioned it was an illusion ~ that very dangerous forces would try and destroy us. But *these* moments, at least, were ours.

I remember that night, a late Sunday service, because Jim stood there for so long, maybe fifteen or twenty minutes, while we clapped and cheered.   His eyes held that intense-serene, resolute-comforting, unfathomably-distant yet quickeningly-close gaze forever, it seemed. That rare energy current, an essence of Divine Love, radiated throughout the room again and again.

But as always, he never neglected reality. I don't think there was anything he was ultimately unwilling to tell us ~ it was clear he didn't *like* living a concealed life. But now, with the serene overlay of radiance throughout the room, it was easier to stretch the boundaries of what people could hear. So he chose *that* night to tell everyone, the whole congregation, what had happened with Karen Layton, only sparing her name.

Everyone laughed. You think laughter, even the most bellowing of belly laughs, cannot be intimidating? I think Jim must have wanted to scare anyone off who might have similar ideas. But he did it when the energy was so high, that it didn't seem to be about sex at all. It was lessons in life. Don't mess with energies you can't handle.

As always, there were alternating currents of consciousness – never on matters of principle, like race (bedrock, anguished concern, always), but ever on matters of emotion, like sex. Sometimes, he'd talk about Karen and say it had been "ecstasy." Whether it made Karen feel better or not, who could tell? What Jim felt, even, who could tell? It seemed his total orientation was gauging what others needed to hear. Even after **all this(!!)**, I thought he couldn't care less whether he had been with *anyone*. Sex was a means to an end. If you catch someone by the throat, they will listen. If you catch someone by the genitals, they may even *want* to listen.

Other times he became caustic on the subject, saying "Since my penis has become public property..." and "I sure don't want to go down in history as 'a great lover'!!"... and, finally, "If I'm still sleeping with you, it means I don't *trust* you!"

Me, I got so I didn't feel *anything* on the subject any more. Not openly. Sometimes I would see out of the corner of my eye, him looking at me out of the corner of his, to see if I was laughing when jokes were made about sex. I always made sure I was laughing, despite my aching heart. I thought, maybe it *is* worse for him. I can no longer let this be an issue. Gradually, the door within me shut too.

And that rare commodity "trust." The baby had been thrown out with the bathwater long since. What was left to discuss?

XXIII. A Parting Tort, and Jim Jones Is Forever Gone.

1976 was the best year ever - the pinnacle. There were awards and prestigious visitors, dynamite publicity and the coup etat - the very political boost of The Testimonial Dinner to cap the year off. (See DOCUMENTS, pp. 2-3.) Then-Assemblyman Willie Brown (now Mayor of San Francisco) was the evening's emcee. Mayor George Moscone presented a plaque thanking Jim Jones for "his personal support given on many occasions whenever asked." State Senator Milton Marks presented Jim with a resolution on behalf of the entire State Senate commending the work of Peoples Temple. A certificate of honor was presented by Bob Mendelsohn on behalf of the San Francisco Board of Supervisors. Lt. Gov. Mervyn Dymally, who later visited and loved Jonestown, praised Peoples Temple as a place where "all people can live, work and love together for here is an example of thousands who have come together - blacks, whites, orientals, the young and the old of all denominations- in a temple, God's temple." San Francisco Police Chief Charles Gain was also amongst the guests.

Jim had even arranged a meeting with the First-Lady-to-be, Rosalynn Carter, as Peoples Temple was touted as a voting bloc to sway if the election were close. This was no time to do anything but swallow my distress, put on a good face, and pitch in.

We were thrilled, even though Jim told us it wouldn't last. He seemed to see it more as a buffer than as the main thing. Guyana was pushed with gusto, and it seemed like every Wednesday night problem case got, instead of punishment, a free trip overseas. It was painted as the buoyant, exhilarating story of building a refuge from the mean city streets, but it was also assuming a tone of greater urgency. This was no vacation spa. We needed Guyana. We had to have it and we would. Even P.C.'s gradually became dominated by committees planning a major move overseas.

No time for tears. Jim had told us repeatedly that "all tears are self-pity"; and since he also entertained the notion that "there is no medical evidence that [even] infants need to cry," no grown-ups, certainly, would be flaunting applications to emote. It was all business, almost too much to handle. We were now heading into the wind-down of our long journey to a distant home.

But there were people we weren't taking with us. There was a strange pair who had never seemed to fit in ~ like unmatched fractals violating the milieu. Elmer ("Mert") and Deanna Mertle and their assorted children had left by late '75.

They had started by skipping P.C. meetings. Eventually they didn't come at all, and then one day they were gone. They had headed up the Publications Department, and they ripped off many materials when they left. It was some time before we discovered what they and their "friends" (not Peoples Temple members, to be sure ~ members of quite another "club") were up to. They wound up being one of our more ghastly departure stories.

But the more immediate concern by mid '76, was the overnight departure of Grace Stoen. She and her boyfriend Walter Jones ("Smitty") had taken off on July 4, 1976 ~ unsettling Bi-Centennial present for us indeed. We were celebrating July 4th outdoors in Redwood Valley that year, though this new blow hardly qualified as a picnic. Jim convened a P.C. on the church grounds to discuss what had happened and what to do. Naturally, Tim Stoen was there, expressing concern about her next possible moves, and advising how to protect little John from ever being removed.

John, understand, had been living in San Francisco with Maria Katsaris for at least a year. Grace had refused to move south, instead launching into a tirade against her estranged husband, Tim. For all intents and purposes, Maria, who was even younger than Grace, had become John's mother.

Jim never had any challenge winning over Maria ~ she was so miserable, she was desperate for relief. It was whispered that her father had raped her. Jim (being *"Father"*) easily usurped Maria with a bad-father-to-good-father conversion. Maria was only 21, and perennially depressed until Jim took her to bed. Apparently, since she asked nothing for herself and was completely malleable, Jim prolonged the relationship. Perhaps he found it a relief to relate to someone who made no demands. In any case, she got on great with the child, and also physically resembled Grace, so the transition was easy for John.

Yet Jim now went through his customary ritual of torment when someone departed. What to tell John? He didn't want the child psychologically damaged; and after all, this pull-out wasn't yet confirmed as permanent. And what to tell the congregation? It was improvised that

Grace had "taken a trip," to buy us time, and also give Grace an "out" could she be persuaded back.

And what if Grace tried to regain John? Tim, still her husband in name, was reassuring. After all, she had abandoned the child, hadn't she? No court would award her custody. Still, it was the hugest headache at best. At the least, Grace would have to be negotiated with. After all, Jim said, "I always knew what she was." Thank God *Tim* was so solid. His legal parenthood would surely be invoked, and he, of course, avowed the child would always be Jim's.

Several months later, Grace visited with John when we were down in L.A. We took shifts on an all-night guard posted to ensure that Grace would not abscond with the child. I learned later on, that in a private confrontation, she had done a "vintage Grace," rushing towards Jim, then jerking away crying, "Don't touch me!" Finally the child was interposed between the two, with Grace flinging him at Jim saying, **"Take him - he's yours!"**

She left on the heels of this tantrum, but we were sure we'd be hearing from her again. Now something had to be done. One seriously damaged child was about to become one seriously endangered child custody.

I wasn't privy to the what-to-do-about-Grace sessions. Nor did I expect to be consulted - my advice rarely seemed valued. Yet Teri came to me one day and said that Jim wanted me to write up what I thought should be done about John because "he said you have insight into how he relates to his sons."

Rare acknowledgment - how I never expected *that* to come! Some time earlier, Stephan had attempted suicide by swallowing a poison. His stomach was pumped, and the instant he was free of all this "concern," he re-swallowed it again. The child was in bad shape emotionally, even if recovered physically. Jim offered woefully, "We [which "we" this time?] think it may have something to do with hostility towards Marceline for wanting to bring him into the world."

It was rare I was angry at Jim, but now I was appalled. He had told the congregation repeatedly that Stephan was conceived because "Marceline needed to have a child," and that he didn't - that he preferred to keep adopting. Meanwhile, he was so bent on being "egalitarian," that sometimes I felt he bent over backwards to *dis*-favor his own natural offspring. (The truth, like most things, was more complicated, but for the moment, this would do.)

174/SNAKE DANCE

He once had some issue with Stephan, and made the boy beat *him* publicly, saying Stephan being beaten himself would sink in less with this child. Specifically, deliberately, he had Stephan beat him on the legs where, he announced publicly, it was "less likely to cause him kidney failure or a stroke." We were all given the impression that Stephan could be putting his father's life at risk, forced into it or not.

On another occasion, to demonstrate that "his own son was no different from anyone else," he made Stephan "confess to ever having had homosexual feelings." This was an aggressive adolescent, obviously very male, and it could have been nothing but humiliating. As it was, Stephan was being subjected to peer pressure on the subject of loyalty. Since Jim always said that someone very close would defect and cause great harm, someone had got it into their head to suggest it could be Stephan, and he was apparently distraught.

Of course, I couldn't be as distraught as Stephan, but I was distraught at who Jim was blaming for Stephan's suicide attempt: on Marceline, the parent who *wanted* him. I wrote Jim three letters. That "needing" and "wanting" are so akin, that surely the child had thought Jim didn't *want* him; and about forcing Stephan to beat him publicly; and forcing the ridiculous "confession."

I told Jim I realized he must be in great pain over all this, but if there were any parent to blame, it was *him*. Also how useless it would be to send the child to a psychiatrist.

Curiously, I wasn't scared to write Jim any of this, because I felt no elements of conflicts in the matter. I had *always* cringed when he said children were hostile at their parents for bringing them into the world. I wrote three letters rapid fire over a few days, and poked them under the door of his apartment.

When I next saw Jim, I asked him if he got the letters. He stiffened and said tersely, glancing away, "We're sending him to a psychiatrist." (So much for *my* opinion.) When P.C. convened, he mused aloud, as he sometimes did, that maybe he shouldn't have been so open about not "needing" his son, but hastened to add, almost with puzzlement, "But I have to be *honest*, don't I?" This cringe I kept to myself. I merely thought, "You would lie to protect any other child. Why not your own son?"

So I was surprised that my opinion was solicited. I wrote him, of course, that John should be sent to Guyana, both to ensure keeping him, and to get him out of the foray. But that why not send Stephan with him, as they got on great, and if Stephan could be a "surrogate father" to John, it could both strengthen him and lessen his conflicts with Jim. Also, needless to say, let him get away.

I stayed at the end of the next P.C., where people were congregating for a post-meeting huddle on the subject. Jim told me that sending Stephan with John was a good idea, but that Stephan didn't get on with Charlie, the project manager (he was dating Charlie's daughter), so this move would be postponed. Whether Stephan himself *wanted* to go is another matter. (He claimed later on he didn't.) Ultimately, it was decided *for* him. John, of course, was to be sent post haste.

I saw Tim show up for the post-meeting meeting (so much for the child *ever* been snatched out from under *his* nose!), before ducking back into my old haunt, the letters office.

But even more ominous things had begun to happen now, regarding the Mertles and their apparently deadly plottings. I would see people coming in and out of the church *very* late, like three or four in the morning, some project related to the Mertles. Meanwhile, the pressure was growing to leave San Francisco for Guyana *quick*. Already a couple of hundred had gone, and the community was flourishing. We awarded trips overseas to otherwise incorrigible children, who were doing beautifully there in the fresh air, sunshine, and freedom from the pressures of inner city life.

But this was no mere show project. We ~not the general membership, but P.C.~ were about to be clued in as to why we had to start moving out *en masse*. Meanwhile, I stayed with my grind, but one evening, it was precariously disturbed. Fate? I wonder. In its own way, it may have sealed the matter of whether I personally would ever get to Guyana, *permanently*.

What had happened was that Susan, a teenager in the letters office, decided she didn't like being cooped up in a tiny office, and had been strewing people's personal letters around the church in careless attempts to do the work anywhere but the office. I called her down on it. Next thing, Sharon Amos was at my door.

I hadn't had much contact with Sharon for about a year, when we were driving up to Redwood Valley together after a P.C. Some weeks earlier, Jim had lamented that we couldn't take our pets to Guyana and we should "take care of them." We thought he implied shooting them. My co-worker Tim (a different "Tim") took our office pet, an adorable little dachshund named Paco, who was shivering with some pre-cognizant fright, into the woods. We were both heartbroken. Then two weeks later, Jim told us, no, he only meant the very *old* dogs, and that he was upset at the loss of young animals. It was horrible. So Sharon and I got into the car together and she attacked me with, "You wanted that dog dead because it was Tim's dog and you don't like Tim!"

I was horrified. I told her it was *our* dog and we were both heartbroken, and how could she think I wanted him dead? I was so hurt and angry and appalled, I would have told Jim, except I thought the directive had probably been painful enough for *him*, so I kept my silence.

Now she was at my doorstep. She told me that Nina, Susan's mother, was "fragile," so I should "lay off Susan." Never once had I been told how to run this simple, basic, boring operation called "letters." Now I was supposed to let it be disrupted, plus have correspondents' privacy invaded by a restless teenager, because her mother was "fragile"? What about me? Was I still so much a nothing and a nobody, that anyone higher than me in the pecking order could invade my work space and tell me what to do? Had I no quarter-of-an-inch of space that was safe from invasion?

I tightened. Clenched my fist and steadied my voice to a taut furious low. "*Jim* sent you here, didn't he? He sent you here to *spy* on me!" "No, he didn't," she maintained. "Yes, he did, Sharon. And I want you out of here. I want you out of here *right now!*" This matter was not to be discussed. She was to be gone, and immediately.

Then I wrote Jim a letter, a quite enraged letter. That I didn't want him sending Sharon to spy on me. That Carolyn had interfered previously to defend her younger sister (who used to work with letters) from cutting out without notice, and she seemed to be biased about taking younger women under her wing, so by all means, don't send Carolyn either.

Though I didn't say it, my issue with Carolyn was more painful. She thought Annie should be gone to see *Jim*, that she needed to be with Jim because she was "young," and after all, "you already had your chances to screw around." I stiffened. Who had discussed me with her? Me, who had had no sex since 1969, and she who had the leader's child? *I* had been "screwing around"? But the proverbial cat got my tongue then, too. A single word and I wouldn't have been dealing with her. I would be dealing with *him*. So I argued the point on other grounds. I guess like now.

But now, finally, it was straws on camels' backs. My quarter-of-an-inch of space, the letters office, seemed a pathetic springboard from which to release my rage over being denied a life, a voice, so much as "a fair trial," but it would have to do. It seemed to be the cell to which I was relegated, and now even that was no longer mine. "Laurie, why don't *you* defer?" "Laurie, why don't *you* take the flak?" "Laurie, why don't *you* be the scapegoat?" "Laurie, why don't *you* stand there without a whimper while a gun is put to your head?" At least I had this one sovereign refuge.

I hated doing this, stooping to defending my turf. The pettiness of it. But if I was left to stand on one quarter-of-an-inch of space, I'd be damned if anyone was going to pull it out from under me. *I could be terse and definitive too.* I kept this guided missile short if not sweet. No Sharon. No spying. No Carolyn. That Nina may be "fragile," but why make it impossible for me to so much as function? Oh, and one more thing (God, I really was angry): "As for Karen, *she told me that she never had any orgasms with you.*"

So much for my opening triumvirate – Sharon, Karen, Carolyn. How well they had taught me. I didn't want a blessed thing to do with any one of them!

I slipped the note under Jim's door. In this particular competition in my own inner war, fear receded, hurt held its own, and rage positively charged. I closed the note by saying if he wanted to lash out at me anonymously, as he was wont to do, just not to do it, because I would *identify* myself.

An hour or two later, an enraged leader's voice came booming over the public address system. He was curt, nearly clipped. Every word, every phrase, smashed into the microphone, like a hammer driving nails into my heart. He said he had received a note from someone who requested to be identified, but that he wouldn't, and "Don't you *dare* identify yourself!" (A moot point. Which of the myriad speakers spread across the multi-storied building, was I going to "confront"?)

He said, "If she wants to be fucked, I'll fuck her with a bulldozer!" Then, "You know, people here with me are saying, 'She must want you dead, Father.' Why don't you just drop me in boiling oil?" Next that the people she criticized ...well, they had "taken" so much more than she could ever take. (After *L.A.???*)

I had heard the tirade beginning over the P.A. about eight o'clock that evening. I slowly moved up the main stairs to the stage area, like a child who had been sent to bed without dinner now creeping up to secretly peer at the t.v. in the parental abode. I didn't know whether I felt small or brave. But this new excoriation (being so publicly, yet anonymously, attacked over the whole P.A. system) was unbearable.

By the time I arrived at the stage area, with the P.A. blaring away at full speed, he had launched into his new, slicing pronouncement that I "wanted him dead." Now I was truly felled. He couldn't have said this. *The* most hurtful thing. Had he chosen it to kill *me*? I fell to my knees weeping, in a desperate plea, "You've *losing* me, Jim. You're *losing* me. How can you do this to me? How can you do this? Why are you doing this? You're losing me, you're losing me, you're losing me..."

The last I heard him exhorting across the airwaves was, "Get out of your morass! Get out of your morass!" Didn't he know the struggle was already over? There was no more "morass" as opposed to "doing well." No more climbing out of a steep hole in hungry search of some elusive prize - his approval, his praise, or his love. Didn't he know this meant it was finished?

I knew it was the end. The tenuous thread had finally snapped. It wasn't my turning against *him*. There were so many people at stake here - black, white, young, old. We were *one family*. Finally we were on the brink of shifting our collective bulk across the seas, to a fresh, new world for disadvantaged youth, for the elderly, for the impoverished, the neglected, the overburdened. Jim Jones was giving us this. He was giving it to us tirelessly, magnificently. Not one cell in me would ever turn against that, would ever turn against *him*.

Yet the thread, the subtle, powerful bond, which had brought me here and kept me here still... It had just snapped. It couldn't be mended now. I never felt that I would not endure to the end, whatever the end might be. But now not because Jim Jones was there for *me*, nor could I ever again reach towards him. It was like if I knew I was about to drown, and *needed* his help, and he threw out a liferaft to me, I would have no arms, no hands, to even catch it. He had cut them from my side.

This was March, 1977 - unbeknownst to us, "the last days" of Jim Jones Stateside. About 250 people had already departed for Guyana, including several teenage terrors. It had become our own personal boot camp, but of a friendly, constructive variety. The kids loved it. Everyone was busy building cottages and communal facilities, and learning how to farm the land.

Ministries from the Guyanese government were, by now, lavishing praise upon these brave new pioneers. They wished they could encourage their own populace to do the same. A license was issued to set up a school in Jonestown, and medical facilities were planned. The location of the community was so isolated, it had to be, if not self-sufficient at this early stage, at least self-contained, bringing in supplies but providing all the necessities of life from within.

With our membership thinned but still burgeoning, services became extended paeans of praise to Jonestown. Our rich music was enhanced now with songs about "The Promised Land." *Jonestown.* It was an ecstatic hope. No more hard pavements. No more crime. No more bristling hatred and anger. No more poverty. No more drugs. No more kids in trouble with the law. No more prisons. No more police. No more "the man."

The pace of people moving overseas was quickening, and everyone was glad, irregardless of the reason. It was a natural expansion, timed right into what turned out to be a forced exodus. Jim Jones, as always, had spared us from the onslaught.

In P.C., the cause for the stepped-up pace was revealed. We had always figured the Mertles were up to no good. Now we had come on proof-positive confirmation of our worst fears.

The Mertles had lived on a rather spacious plot in Redwood Valley, with a long path winding down to their home, which passed over a bridge. Years ago, when they were in the church perhaps just a year, a strange man, never identified, had been seen conferring with them on that bridge. Surveillance work after they left, showed up the same man, in continual contact with the Mertles now. His name was David Conn, and he had (as would be revealed) all the earmarks of being *a government agent.*

It was now, early in the Spring of '77. The Mertles and others had been holding regular meetings in the home of Conn's ex-wife, Donna. They were plotting how to destroy Peoples Temple. It seemed a surreal prospect, for the church, by that time, was "the toast of the town." Garnished in praise. Even a conservative body, Religion in American Life, glowingly awarded Jim the honor of "one of the leading 100 clergymen in America." (See DOCUMENTS, p. 5.)

We were also publishing a community paper, *Peoples Forum,* which we blanketed across the city streets. There was news of Temple work locally, of the Guyana work, of our burgeoning network of high-profile contacts, and of Temple views on pressing issues of the day. So intent, still, was Jim Jones on reacting to, responding to, aiding with, anything and everything on the public horizon, that every issue read like an encyclopedia of progressive politics.

Their media, by contrast, was targeted right for the mainstream. The Mertles and the Conns were planning a well-financed campaign of slander and innuendo, using an expensive, prestigious P.R. firm to spearhead the way. Ex-members would carry the anti-Temple banner high. They would beginning by talking about "Behind closed doors...," and lend credibility to their views by claiming that whatever the public image, no one knew the dark side of this dangerous group with its enigmatic leader.

A handful of our cloak-and-dagger types, like Teri Buford, were assigned to hiding out under the Conns' home on Monday nights with a tape recorder, bringing the conspirators' plans back to Jim Jones. By now, March, 1977, the planned campaign was imminent. Jim had never wanted to leave the United States, but if ever had come the time we *had* to exit, surely it was now.

There had been committees assigned for some time, to coordinate all aspects of the move: passports, transferring social security checks, getting shots, sale of assets Stateside and, aside from the paperwork here, various kinds of coordination with our growing community in Guyana. P.C. was suddenly a calm and orderly place, as Jonestown took center stage.

Jim himself departed in June of that year, so there were only a few more P.C.'s to go Stateside. I remember them for their somber contrast to the buoyant public services about the joys of the new world overseas. This was a pensive, reflective, even worried Jim Jones. His entire family was at stake. All of *us*.

The hunt for the key traitor, "very high up" resumed, but had lost its manic edge. No bravado, no threats, no high-flying passions whipped to a fiery heat. This was ground zero. The moment of truth was upon us. Jim wanted to know whatever *we* might know, and he wanted to know *now*. He asked us each to get out a paper and pen and write whom we thought might leave or betray.

I knew the people I didn't like. I knew the people I thought of questionable character. But I'm not sure I knew who would betray. That's not necessarily the same thing. I, like many or most, was thinking of who might *turn*. So entrenched were we as a family, one might think who would succumb to pressures or paranoia, overwork, jealousy or resentments, as family members are wont to do. It did not occur to most to ferret out those who may have been *against us from the very start*, a different behavioural model entirely.

Of course, now there were the Mertles, who were obviously planted agents. They never *had* seemed part of our family: Deanna brittle, cautious, clipped, Mert smiling on cue. They made all the moves, but seemed to lack passion. They kept advancing grand plans for publications (the last apparently a "kind offer" to take over management of the entire church!), but seemed more mechanics than believers. Everyone seemed more worried than shocked when these two and their brood pulled out. It wasn't hard to believe that they were out to harm us. And harm us they could – especially as ex-P.C. members who had, nevertheless, never seemed to compromise *themselves* in any notable way.

People were still writing away furiously when I handed my fairly short list in. (Oh, how I had learned brevity! By now I was prepared to almost *spit* it out.) Jim perused the notes as they were passed forward, finally offering in a deflated undertone, "Only one person put down that name." That's when I realized that he *already knew*, and that the news must be very bad.

On another of these more somber P.C.'s, he wanted to know what each was paranoid about. Again, the furious long-winded scribblings. I didn't even want to do this. Death, sex, betrayal? Tons of bait for this one. I knew all the reasons for *collective* paranoia. And the reasons for *personal* paranoia I could not even begin to indulge.

One seemed to put the clamp on the other. I had all of seven words to say: "I'm paranoid because I can't express myself" – I suppose the closest anyone could get to "I pass." I handed my paper in first. Jim read it, looked at me with an abbreviation of the *long* scrutinizing look, and let it be. He could glean his hundreds of paranoias elsewhere. Surely he didn't need mine.

How I possibly could have incurred his, I can't say. He sent someone to me with a message to tell him if there was anything I wanted to "confess." All I had been engaged in, even mentally, was wanting to return to composing. I told him following a service. He took my hand and smiled, it seemed almost gratefully, in relief. "I've forgiven so much worse." Oh, it still needed to be "forgiven" didn't it?

I don't know where he thought the personal traumas left people. There was one more reflection to come I couldn't even bear to hear. It dragged at me so, that I scarcely remember where it fell in the dark final sequence underpinning the exultations that our charge towards Guyana had become. It seemed the more this man became depressed or uncertain of our fate, the more he rallied even from within *himself* the energy, the courage, to uplift others. From anything you could see, this was a valiant champion in control of our fate. We would shake the dust off our feet, head for "The Promised Land" and together, all for one, one for all, our Peoples Temple family would *triumph*.

Finally the long-awaited exodus from everything in the States that held our largely minority membership hostage. Now we would be free. Nothing would divide us. Nothing would stand in our way. The singing was especially resonant, with our now-diminishing numbers augmented by fervent cries of *"If they take one of us, they'll have to take us all!,"* and the pulsing harmony of "United we stand, divided we fall, and if our backs should ever be against the wall, we'll be together, together you and I." No. There was no doubt at all who was in command, or the fervor of the flood of lives about to sweep south.

But this last reflection. Was it emblematic of how possible it was for the fierce rallying cries to one day dissolve into nothingness? How could such joyousness and such sorrow, such hope and pain, co-exist? It was one of our somber "silent moments" that last P.C. The strained, excruciating quality of the confrontations seemed drained away by now. Maybe we were just weary.

Jim was pensive, quiet, reflective. He said he knew that many of us had fears, and that not all of them could be calmed. But that "I don't want to disappoint any one of you – even *slightly*." I looked at him incredulously as, at that soft, tender moment, the faraway gaze seemed to grace his weary eyes once more. Maybe there *was* a future. Maybe these were merely diaphanous veils between hallucination, illusion and mirage, and a real world of hope, faith and love did await.

Then he continued (*unbelievably*): "Maybe sex made no difference. Maybe the people who were loyal would have been loyal anyway, and those who turned would have turned anyway." Then, ever so gently, "Maybe you can't ever really know what another person feels. Maybe if you're not that person, you can't know what they feel."

Now a stabbing sensation both quickened me and forced my silence. What was he saying? That if the wrong person was put on the scaffold, it didn't matter? That had I been treated like a leper out of, perchance, mere "misunderstanding," it made no difference? That my heart was pillaged and chewed by wild wolves, and so what? I wanted to run, scream, pound my fists against the very air, sink through the floor. I was aghast to be glued in place. Why was I so water-logged? I couldn't move. My *eyes* couldn't move. He couldn't have said this.

Mere days later, he was standing on the podium and I was in with the choir on the stage. He looked out along my row, surveying for a face.

"I want everyone to look at me." My eyes were downcast. "I'll wait." He was patient. I felt his eyes stayed on mine. No. I couldn't bear to look at *anyone*, almost like the psychic assault at tender seventeen when I felt no one's eyes could ever again meet mine. Jim was gentle, but persisted. He waited and waited, 'til finally my eyes, troubled, inwards, brimming with pain, met his the instant I looked up. There was no condemnation there. He nodded and moved on.

At an even later service, the last one I recall, he now asked us to *close* our eyes. (Perhaps a fleeting history of Peoples Temple in capsule form all this: eyes wide open, eyes shut.) "Who here has had thoughts of leaving, or of suicide, raise your hands." I raised my hand. I never thought of leaving. I thought slightly of suicide, though I had never been suicidal before. But when he asked, I realized that it could be possible. I was in such terrible pain, I let my hand go up. People scurried around taking names. The voice approaching me with a pen was Patty Cartmell. How, really, did Patty (who kept Jim's sexual schedule for him) *expect* me to react?

Carolyn came to me on "suicide watch patrol." She said that Jim had requested that she talk with me. It didn't even occur to me that if Jim sent *Carolyn*, that he might have given her instructions what to say. But Carolyn wasn't Jim. If he was so concerned, why didn't *he* talk with me? Yes, he was busy getting hundreds of people out from danger and moved to Guyana. There would have been no time. But it was more. It was seven years of no time. Tons of time for internecine war and no time for peace.

I told Carolyn I was "fine," to go talk with the younger people. Maybe the pressures were too great for *them*. She deferred. I almost regret I never heard what she had to say. But I had been listening for seven years now. Surely ten or fifteen minutes would yield no respite. Maybe she wasn't that keen on this assignment anyway. After all, she deferred. Maybe she, too, sensed the hopelessness of the task.

I felt I would endure. I was *trained* to endure. Also trained to "stay back." I was always staying back for the letters. I was always staying back out of exclusion from coming closer. Maybe, I was there all along for a different function, for a different purpose, than I had ever imagined or supposed: *as a witness*. (Or as my future husband later put it: "You're Ishmael." Reference to the one who lived to tell the tale in "*Moby Dick*.") Some people have this function in life. I wouldn't underrate it. To observe and remember. To live to tell the tale.

Or perhaps when Carolyn approached me, the internal crisis was just not yet ripe to break. The *collective*... you know, the collective is fully as captivating as the personal, sometimes far more so. When Jim was still there, up to the very last, I couldn't even let myself be myself. The collective concerns were so great.

All the more so now. All our previous crises were beginning to look like mere dress rehearsals. That last service, I realized something others may not have noticed at all. Jim said there was a (ham) radio message from Tim Stoen from Jonestown. That he said everything was going well, and some other pleasantries. Jim acted sort of normal about this, even enthusiastic. But I looked at him, and... ~ well, mostly it was the tenor of his voice, like a masking, or a shading, that didn't ring true. It was *Tim*, wasn't it? Tim had turned. Our chief attorney, chief strategic adviser, confidante of Jim Jones, trusted henchman, loyal friend, legal father of Jim's biological child and... the one "very high up" always destined to turn? *Tim Stoen*. God. What a disaster we might be in for. Why had anyone ever castigated *me* for envisioning a Greek tragedy?

The last time I ever saw Jim Jones, I was rushing through the corridor near the stage and he reached for me suddenly, impulsively ~ a long grasp, like a boarding house reach. He brought me to a halt. He held my hand firmly, securely, for a moment, and smiled right into my eyes.

I remember it for its friendliness, its responsiveness. To this day, I remember Jim Jones as the most responsive, aware, fully present human life I had ever encountered. Ever wearied, ever responding, ever concerned, ever plagued, ever caring, ever buoyant, ever smiling, ever uplifting.... *life*.

III. WHAT THOU HAST MOST FEARED HAST COME UPON THEE

"...All that has been done is to get people to believe in society... Our people had been so alienated. All they they can see in this is a set-up, a classic scenario: first muddy our name... whip up attacks in the press, and then: by the time you reach the classic ending, the frame-ups, the "kill," no one even cares. ...And they think that the press has already done its job with slander and smears, and so no-one will care about the frame-ups..."

From a letter to the President of the United States and All Members of Congress from Jonestown, Guyana, March, 1978.

XXIV. A New World Arises as My Own Sinks.

One star rose as another sank beneath the darkening sea. Guyana, land of promise, ay, "The Promised Land," gained in stature as testimonies of a pristine new world poured onto the Temple stage like milk and honey for the hungry crowd. Like the proverbial "huddled masses yearning to be free," our own nation's exodus from worlds abroad, people clamored to know when they, too, would be given the green light for their exit to paradise. The move was on.

I never knew the exact date Jim Jones left in June, 1977. It was never announced. Nor was it assumed that this was "the final exit" (no pun intended!). The move was not touted publicly as being made under the gun or forced by overt pressures. Rather it was in the spirit of the high triumph of a military command. *We will win.*

We were long since prepared. For years, Jim talked of doing battle with powers and principalities, and spiritual wickedness in high places. We heard the likes of the 1973 Kerner Report predicting that we were moving towards "two Americas - separate and unequal." Stories of people who had written away for their government dossiers under the Freedom of Information Act and found them marked, "Hold for Detention" in the event of martial law. The assassinations of Martin, Medgar and Malcolm. America could not combat racial inequality except through interracial unity, and "the most segregated place in America is the church on Sunday morning." America didn't want socialism, even "*apostolic* socialism" as in the early days of Christianity. Exhortations that you think you're accepted in the white world, if you're Black, to them you're always a "nigger." No place at the table for us.

It was the same song again and again with different words. We had sung it for years. Jim Jones, more than anyone, never expected the rising crest of respectability, even honor, to last. The inevitable attacks, discreditation and threatened downfall had not yet arrived. But from the exultant cries of "If they take one of us, they'll have to take us all!," shouted again and again at fever pitch, perhaps even those not privy to the taping under the agent's house, or the circling in on "the traitor very high up," might have suspected that all the outer proclamations of triumph were in fact heralding a sea of troubles to inundate us in the days ahead.

Yet all people needed to embrace this fateful move was "We will win!" It's all they yearned to hear. And surely you don't send soldiers into battle without that. We must, and would be, strong -- champions of justice who would overcome the odds. Now we would stake our flag in the new world. Of course our leader was needed *there*. Besides, he had travelled there before. His departure was not necessarily cause for alarm at all. This shift, like so many across the years, was a double-edged sword. Thus we saw in it cause not for panic, but celebration.

I had seen the evolution of this move from Jim's reluctance to leave our base in the United States, towards the high-pressure drive south. Whatever his reservations had been before, he would make the best and more of our crossroads now. Pressure, rather than oppressing us, was rising all tides, indeed its energy was lifting all stakes. "Every knock is a boost!" was the watchword for this most canny yet committed General of our fleet. Were there any hint of depression or worry, he concealed it with valor. The wind-up services late in the Spring of '77 were explosions of joy.

After Jim's departure, our numbers dramatically thinned week by week. People were thrilled to leave this vale of tears and pain behind them. No crime. No violence. No substandard housing, filth or neglect. Opportunity. Education. Jobs. Medical care. A pristine life for the children, a peaceful retirement for our older folk. And all free. The years of pleading with people during offerings, of scrimping and saving, of austere lifestyles Stateside, were finally paying off. We had our collective dream. It was a miracle.

I had seen Jim nowhere for days when Carolyn Layton approached me. Why had I barely reflected that it was *Carolyn* he had sent? Why did I snap into my stoic self? Why so guarded? Now, with our heady exodus, did I fear there would be no time for me ever? I was genuinely happy for others to go. I just had no confidence that there could be a new life for *me*.

Work assignments (never any respite from work!) now began their subtle shift. Kathy, the last remaining teenager who had been helping with the letters, was overjoyed to be going overseas. But there was little work left in that office anyway. Word was getting around that we were closing up shop. Large numbers from even Los Angeles and Redwood Valley were being sent to Guyana. Fewer letters were coming in, and I wondered if I, too, was about to be phased out.

How Sharon Amos got mixed up in my affairs again I don't know, but maybe this time she did me a favor. She said Carolyn (a different "Carolyn"), who had been monitoring the newspapers, was being sent over, and I would be transferred to her assignment – mainly keeping things catalogued, and getting every last piece of press answered – *copiously*. Maximum letters from a maximum number of members.

My regular work had dwindled to nothing. I could have been sent over in a snap. But now this. *An ongoing project.* The slow, gradual trickle south had swiftly swelled into a flood. It seemed like almost everyone was leaving, but me (ever the faithful stay-behind), I would stay.

The work shift was subtle, related work in a somewhat different sphere; but as the many components of my daily life shifted away, my precariously-maintained facade was about to crack. My world was disappearing. The ongoing pressures were becoming deflated at *our* end like a rapidly-depressing balloon. No more voice bellowing over the loudspeaker. No fever pitch yells, cheers and hoots. No more live presence – thrilling, uplifting presence who seemed always a touch out of my grasp, and now had vanished. Whatever the demands, he had always been a source of *security* for me. A subtle bond that grounded me, anchored me. This had been crushed and severed with a brutal finality just weeks before, and there had been no time to mend. Now he was gone.

I didn't quite feel abandoned. Quiet and solitude was, for me, a relief. It was more like my matrix of reality was about to dissolve. I went to work every day, just a short walk away, returning for lunch, then back to work, then home for the night. It seemed so sterile, so artificial. I was going through the motions, but the life of it was gone. At first, I just cried a little bit each day. Then, just as surely as our hopes tumbled downwards through the latitudes, life seemed more and more drained from *me*, and the tears welled up within me like a dam about to break loose into a flood.

I went to Sharon at that point, perhaps from force of habit, perhaps out of fear for my state of mind. Perhaps even because however harsh she was on others, she herself was supposed to be a miracle of endurance. She had once gotten into her head that she had betrayed the cause and swallowed poison. Jim was said to have reversed the effects and taken care of the damage the poison had inflicted on her kidneys.

And pharmaceuticals... I just figured she would know. Months earlier, Jim had told the P.C. that he was suffering from off-scale depression. Said he was taking... *qualudes* (not exactly an "upper," I don't think."). Street drugs were verboten, grounds for expulsion, but the others, the anti-depressants, the tranquillizers... Maybe they were even badges of honor. For all these brave people who functioned day and night whatever their state, all these lemmings so desperate to rush towards/away from/towards/away from/towards the devouring sea. Talk to Sharon. She'll know. And know she did. No ginger words now, no palliatives, *thank God* no time now for counselling. Just go and see so-and-so for a referral.

I went tentatively to the referral, and wove in as casually as I could that I had been feeling depressed and could he prescribe something. He suggested Elavil. He said I would be sleepy at first, but that after a week or two, my system would adjust. I was happy enough to sleep-walk through those days, as our "bright promising future" seemed, in contrast, a most uncertain one for me.

The doctor, perhaps simply out of good medical protocol, asked had I considered seeing a psychiatrist - he could give me a name. I stiffened and offered briefly that I didn't think that would be necessary, could I just get the prescription. Of course he examined me too - routine stuff like heartbeat and blood pressure. He also looked down my throat. That's when he made the strange observation that *my gag reflex was completely absent*, and might that have something to do with my depression.

I responded numbly that I didn't know. I thought inwardly, well, maybe this is what happens when things get forced down your throat and there is nothing you can do to protect yourself. Maybe this drug would be my protective cocoon. I hoped it would make me *real* sleepy and halt the torrent of tears that threatened to shatter my reserve.

I embraced my new work responsibilities, as work, especially in solitude, was always therapy for me. If only I could turn off the tape in my brain. It was like a voice that was both from within me and outside me. It was my own voice and a distant voice, a hostile personal voice and an objective neutral drone, a force dragging me down and a propellant urging me forwards. It kept saying again and again, *"You cruel son-of-a-bitch, you cruel son-of-a-bitch, you cruel son-of-a-bitch, you cruel son-of-a-bitch..."* I wouldn't bite. I wouldn't play. Surely this couldn't be *me*. I could work past this. I had worked past everything else.

Mostly I was on my own workwise, and no one questioned me about why my hours were shortened into prolonged periods of sleep. After a couple of weeks I was used to the drug, but then *it* got used to *me* and seemed ineffective. I had little compassion for myself; thus not acknowledging that I had merely applied a bandaid to a festering boil, I not only despaired but panicked. By the time I asked Jean to talk, I was a basket case.

At first I couldn't talk at all. I just cried. When the words finally surfaced through the tears, I said I never knew why Jim had attacked me in the first place. Over having had good sex before I had even met him? He had asked us to write him in confidence ~ we were in a P.C. ~ I had no choice ~ I simply wrote him the truth. He always said that if we were only truthful, he would never embarrass us. Why were people set on me like a pack of wolves? What had I done? I was just being myself. Did he really hate me so much? Why? Did he hate me just for being what I *am*?

The remainder of my hysteria has sunk out of consciousness. The thrust of it, uneasily echoed in memory, was disjointed and skewed, perhaps because its original premise ~control of my thoughts, feelings, body~ was still so impossible for me to accept. I'm sure I spoke of L.A., but I don't recall a single word.

We must have "talked" (mostly my hysterical crying) for at least two hours. It made nothing better, nothing resolved, but now at least I could spend a portion of each day crying without mortal dread of discovery. This is where I was. It could be known that I was there. I went off the Elavil because it had proven ineffective. If I couldn't just be myself, in whatever state I was in, there was no hope anyway.

As my Elavil proved ineffective, perhaps Jim Jones' Elavil (metaphorically, or even literally) was proving ineffective as well. But the ramifications went way beyond him. In tandem with all hell breaking loose for me personally, all hell had broken loose now on the public terrain. Our enemies, caged lions clawing and tearing at their bait, had broken free, and were charging right up to our very door with threatening growls. The onslaught began as we had been told it would, in a trendy new Murdoch extravaganza called *New West*.

XXV. "Let the Games Begin," said Goliath to David.

I've resisted all along, I confess, the temptation to produce "The Double History of Jim Jones, Peoples Temple and Me," for my story and Peoples Temple's story were never entirely the same. So pressing became my need for personal well-being, that I cannot tell you what seemed more important then: how Laurie Efrein was doing in the face of psychological breakdown, or how Peoples Temple was doing in the face of public attacks. I never had either the pleasure nor the shock (be it that) to discover whether my orgasms and Jim Jones' would have timed out to an ecstatic unison -- or whether, for that matter, we could merely agree peacefully that I did not want him dead; but for whatever set of reasons, we both hit the rockiest, most destabilizing juncture at co-incidentally the same time.

Perhaps it was simply that Jim's departure also created a vacuum Stateside into which my long-repressed feelings could finally erupt. Be that as it may, all hell began breaking loose publicly just as my own private world seemed least able to endure further strain.

Were I less oriented to work as a refuge, I might have wound up on a plane south to lick my wounds in the tropical Sun. Ironically, I began to work *better* once we went under the gun. I had always felt tucked into a side pocket of the church. Now I was thrust closer towards the hub, all the bad press being routed through me! Like an understudy who had hovered hesitantly in the wings through everyone else's on-stage debuts, I welcomed this chance to display my talents. Everything in me that was willing and able could now spring into action. I was a wreck, but suddenly I was *needed*.

The attacks had gotten off to an insidious, if shocking, start. The *New West* article was a cleverly-phrased "behind closed doors" scenario. The Temple doors were the headline photograph, seeming to verify the sweeping premise that nothing inside was as it appeared. Overnight, Peoples Temple became New York. "Greatest city in the world? Or a great place to visit and a horror in which to live?" Just look at the 11 O'Clock News. You're tuned right into the police station to find out what's happening in New York each night. All that ever happens in New York is rape, murder and mayhem. Everyone knows that.

Here nestled in San Francisco's inner city was a pristine world with no robbery, no drug use, no one in prison, intelligent children doing well in school, community-minded, everyone cared for whatever their race, age, or class. No, reader. It only *seemed* that way. Here were a few brave dissidents pioneering their "untold story." They became New York's news teams' secret connection to the daily police reports. Hearsay police reports at that. And the accused "defendant," Jim Jones, had "fled the country." No indictments even. Just one "fled defendant."

By the time *New West* was launched, Peoples Temple Stateside was already a waning enterprise. Its true base had become Guyana. Jim Jones. You may hate him. But was his original, extreme reaction to the departure of "The Eight" (four of whom showed up in this article!), and the subsequent leap towards Guyana, really an unwarranted overreaction? It was beginning to seem not. Here we were, braced for a full-scale attack, and our people were *safe*.

Keeping our Stateside people insulated from bad press, and the havoc it might provoke in shakier souls, was more problematic, so countermeasures were taken. The article seemed snuck in like contraband. The membership was cautioned to no longer look at the news at all. That a lot of lies would be told. We had no way to monitor whether anyone had actually complied with this admittedly unenforceable restriction, but from that time on, no one asked any questions publicly, no one aired any of the mostly bizarre allegations, no one expressed any doubts or discouragement at all.

We were, it seemed, the same. A much smaller group, yes, and devoid of not only Jim Jones, but of any dominant leader, save for Marceline on her shuttles back and forth between Jonestown and us. Even she was there more than she was here.

My assignments --what to do about first the dusting, then the heaps of adverse publicity-- came over the ham radio, where Jim maintained daily contact. My own first reaction to *New West* was that it was so far off base that no one would believe it anyway. This place was home. It wasn't a prison or a military barracks. We were doing good works, not deceiving people into giving all and getting nothing. No one was forcing me to stay up nights, or depriving me of food, or denying me my freedom. It wasn't just that it was so imbalanced. It wasn't *us*.

Naturally the stars of this emerging drama were the Mertles who, due to Temple threats, they claimed, had changed their names to Jeanie and Al Mills. They were just ordinary, innocent family folk, and they were subjected to all this "just because they left the group." Personally, I had thought we were better off without them, except for their having stolen equipment when they left. Besides, it was obviously *they* who were threatening *us*. And who was *paying* for this smear campaigns? And why was government-connected David Conn, never a member, involved at all?

Never mind. It had finally come. The Mertles and silent partner Conn chose to attack in a glossy-covered newcomer of a magazine. *New West* wasn't quite *The Enquirer*, but Rupert Murdoch, its publisher (who was, ironically, a socialist in his youth: "Red Rupert," he revealed to Barbara Walters at a later date, kept a picture of Lenin in his room at college) was already famous for his sensationalist ploys, plus his politics were known to be the opposite of ours, on the right.

The Mertles were joined by Grace Stoen and her boyfriend Walter Jones ~ no real surprise of personnel. Four of the Mertles' other "co-stars" were Cobb & Co.! None of us had seen hide nor hair of this previously wild, now "indignant" crew of malcontents since that dreadful September day in 1973. Like the proverbial bad penny, they had now flipped over right on cue, and seemed to pursue Jim Jones with a special vengeance into the grave.

The remaining two "brave dissidents" were elderly Black women with assorted axes to grind. It was impossible to make a case of abusing the elderly. The elderly were treated *incredibly*. But one had donated her watch, then wanted it back. (Actionable?) The other was incensed that her hostile husband who never even came to services wasn't healed of cancer! These two were undoubtedly added to "flesh out the Black wing" (the only others being Cobb and his sister Terri) of this unseeming contingent of malcontents. They, offered up as "proof of Black people being used," were certainly never used again by the *Mertles* ~ just here, to light the match.

The media in 1977 was, on the whole, not quite as bad as it is now, "bad" denoting not just flagrant and sensational, but *mainstream* flagrant and sensational. Yet the original *New West* article, complete with brazen pre-publication stunts and a brand of overt bias unusual, even suspicious, for a supposedly a-political forum, might have qualified well as a foretaste of things to come.

At the time, it seemed a five-alarm fire. In retrospect, it was more like a cleverly-produced legere-de-main ~ full of smoke, very grey smoke, thick with vehemently-pressed showmanship, purportedly heroic personalities, and a glossy wrapper which left you wondering why, if things were really that bad, it merited celebrity status billing more suited to the darlings of Hollywood.

Before the article even hit the press, we were clobbered head-on in the more mainstream *San Francisco Chronicle* and *San Francisco Examiner* with preposterous claims of a break-in at *New West* headquarters. It read something like a malignant, ill-intentioned "Mrs. Doubtfire." There the personality bounced off "Police *Doubt Fire* Was Accidental," and you could only root for the dad separated from his kids pulling well-meaning, if disruptive, antics. Here the police got dragged in on a case where they could discover no evidence of break-in at all, and the intent of the crew reporting the alleged crime was self-serving at best.

It was unclear why a mainsream magazine would be flirting with charges of filing a false report, or who might have authorized this on the advertising budget. The entire substance of the story and ensuing police report, was that a file containing the article about us had been "disturbed" and "jammed back in" and "was sticking out an inch," along with the magazine's editor, Rosalie Wright, complaining of harassing phone calls (anonymous, naturally) telling her not to print the article. The file was, mysteriously, not taken, with the editor speculating it may have been "photographed" (you know, one of those nifty little spy cameras they used to use on "Scarecrow and Mrs. King"?).

The police investigated, found no evidence of a burglary, and closed the "case" down as quickly as they had opened it. Meanwhile, news of the "attempted burglary," complete with an hysterical editor blaming *us*, was printed in (unbelievably) not only San Francisco, but Eureka, Costa Mesa, Oakland, Vallejo, El Cerrito, Sacramento, Anaheim. "News travels fast." Thus were we painted as "accused burglars" sans the slightest evidence, before the Mertles and Russom, Lowry & Leeper, their expensive P.R. firm, had barely even warmed up.

Nor did the authors of the *"Inside Peoples Temple"* piece, Marshall Kilduff and Phil Tracy, offer even a pretense of objectivity in this yellow journalistic assault on our good name. Following the glossy photos of each ex-member was a brief tale of alleged transgressions against their property, children, dignity et al, then summarized under the bold-faced heading *"Why Jim Jones Should Be Investigated."* Like Kilduff and Tracy were themselves aggrieved and itching to destroy Peoples Temple on their own.

The tactics were slick and sly: They've been considered credible, those folk, even fashionable. Lots of good works. But what's *really* going on? Like, "Here. Look at this. Here is the sheath of acclamations and awards we are about to toss into the flames." Then the purported transgressions: "Locked doors" (following an arson that nearly burned the church down). "Armed guards" (security guards --no arms--, who were reluctantly installed following upon threats.) Inane stories of chopped hamburger meat used to masquerade as expelled cancerous growths.

I knew the nurses. They were straight as a dye, from Marceline on down. I saw the people, frequently older, who expelled these growths. They were who they said they were. They were healed. I had seen it again and again. I was completely shocked. Until I saw the name "Jim Cobb" attached to the accusation. Then I was horrified.

I couldn't believe this article at all. I wasn't legally sophisticated enough to know what, if anything, *singly*, would create the greatest havoc. But "singly" was never the game. It was set up scenario-style, and laced with Catch-22's. Like you feel threatened. You protect yourself. Then you get accused of being too self-protective -- that you must be hiding something or intimidating people.

It was true that years earlier, in our rural upstate home, we were gentle people who left our doors ajar, and in a large city that was no longer possible. Moreover, we were both interracial and socialist. We supported every left-wing cause that came along. We had foreigners in and out. We had politicians in and out. We had celebrities in and out. We hosted Angela Davis and Laura Allende and the local American-Soviet friendship society. A lot of people liked us, but a lot of people sure didn't. Had everything we had done to make an environment *safe*, in fact *endangered* us?

Or Jim's frenetic efforts to raise huge amounts of money -- the very maximum anyone could be encouraged, cajoled, shamed, or even arm-twisted into giving. Our bitterest enemy never claimed he misappropriated a dime for his own personal use. He was just desperately driven to have enough for us, largely people of no means at all, to have our own society, and be protected against threats, including this massive onslaught he always sensed would come.

It was like a mother who would do anything shy of outright steal to feed her babies. If you were there while it was happening, you had to empathize. But how was it looking *now*? A pathetic woman (one of "the ten who courageously stepped forward") complaining bitterly about giving up her best watch. What about the people who gave up their *homes*, then thought better of it? This could (and would) be disastrous.

What a steep, sharp curve this was. But for more than the article's contents. It was the shock of the first major press attack on us ever. It also implied, without offering any actual evidence, a potentially bottomless pit of thorny legal tangles: "Misappropriated rest-home funds using government checks," "improperly-dated notarizations," "coerced offerings." No documentation -- just "charges." Not cases you could press purely by affidavit. But you can use such accusations to whip up investigations and try to harass people out of existence.

This was treacherous, McCarthyistic. Like the rest homes accused of malfeasance were already closed down and their owners off to Guyana. This was never raised to prosecute anybody. It's just that as soon as you say "government money," you are whipping up the I.R.S. to remove tax-exempt status, or older people abroad to be cut off from their Social Security stipends. David Conn had already bragged of working with the I.R.S.

This was also a line cast to fish around for malcontents. Like people who gave up property, then changed their mind and could charge "coercion." That's not an easy sell when a group is reputable. But with a *smeared* group, it's happy hunting. Knowledgable, trained people had constructed this spearhead to spurt blood out of Peoples Temple's side. The *New West* article was a loud, unabashed public announcement that here was a magnet for anyone who wanted to bring Peoples Temple down. "This is just the beginning," the authors ominously warned.

The article said it was rumored a few hundred of the close people would be in Guyana by September. This was late July and we were already, for all intents and purposes, gone. Jim was reported making phone calls to reporters as late as June 18, but from New York.

Whatever anyone thought, of course, he had to be gone. These people wanted him *here*. To slap him with this or that paper, and most surely suspend or even void his passport. Not to mention leaving little John unprotected; and if the leader's child could be snatched, then *anyone's* child could. I could never question his leaving when he did, even retrospecting with an ultra-long lens of time. For so long he never wanted to leave America. Then he wanted to come back to defend himself, but couldn't. Then he was desperate to not be *forced* back. Ironic.

I found the *New West* article insidious then, and was fascinated to still find it so insidious now. The people interviewed, of course, held little surprise for *us*, just camouflage for the outside reader. These mere ten were our most suspect handful, lauded by *New West* as courageous, virtual heroes, but not a single one noble at all. Four of them Jim Cobb's crew. Two of them Grace and the lover she split with. Two of them the Mertles.

Of course, the spigot to the feds was invisible at first glance, only emerging in later months, like a dentist had spotted a little cavity and before you know it, your whole mouth is signed up for root canal. This was laying the groundwork for Customs searches, Social Security cut-offs, I.R.S. audits, and subpoenas from various D.A.'s, as "proper," "official" responses to this handful of carefully-engineered complaints.

The clandestine stuff, like phony break-ins, or hang-up calls in the middle of night allegedly coming from us, just as carefully picked up a thread of tactics here and there from us. Like phone calls may have been made to try to squelch the article -- for who wants their lifework destroyed by the likes of the Mertles? And this legit stuff --like picking up the phone and calling, stating your name and business-- got patched into "the dirty tricks department," like calling in the middle of the night, *not* stating your name, muttering brief threatening messages or not speaking at all; or "allegedly jamming a file in sideways," or "making a window look like it might have been jimmied, then leaving it slightly ajar." Stuff we would never do even if we wanted to, as it could only *detriment* us.

You can't even prove these things, but that's not the point. The point is, you can't *disprove*. And so the people who picked up phones and stated up front who they were and why they were calling, or why they were writing, get called burglars, or people who make your life hell by waking you up in the middle of the night with threatening phone messages. (Unfortunately, I had to learn about wake-up calls at 3 a.m. myself. Later, much later. Do dead people really pick up phones and do this? I wonder.)

It would have been too early for anyone to openly charge the F.B.I. or other clandestine agencies with such dirty tricks, but only from a public relations standpoint, not because this fish didn't already smell. How could the F.B.I. and C.I.A. to boot, *not* have been interested? Here an interracial, socialist group with an indefatigably outspoken leader, had gleaned enough political and economic power to relocate internationally. Economic self-sufficiency may have been enough to set off alarm buzzers. Incendiary rhetoric, all the more. And a genius for building political clout.

Besides, this wasn't a new or recent interest. The Mertles joined Peoples Temple in 1969, Stoen in 1970. Stoen "found us Guyana" in 1973. We had been under surveillance for a very long time, yet we made our move *anyway*. We had to be stopped.

We could see the undercurrents that would gradually engulf us in a flood of bad press, investigations, obstructions, and threats to invade Jonestown with mercenaries. But exposing the undercurrents and demanding investigations of them was hardly a plausible public stance for us at this juncture.

To the contrary -- it wasn't our call. We had been successful for years, then suddenly here we were, on the defensive. We had to increasingly defend our very right to exist, moreover in absentia, with virtually all our spokespeople gone. We were never again positioned to call the shots. Here we were in cosmopolitan San Francisco, yet it was to become like one of those small towns where the Sheriff arrests people at will, and if they don't like being charged with speeding, he can up it to burglary, and if they don't like that, well then, he'll just up it to murder. After all, he's the law. And the head honcho on the other side is out-of-town.

Of course, the *New West* article was as clever in its omissions as in its charges. Even if its authors knew, they mightn't have cared except to conceal the truth: Cobb's slave camp in the college dormitories. The real story behind Grace Stoen's child. The Mertles and government agent Conn. And the glaring omission: Where was *Tim Stoen?* Be there legal transgressions, *Stoen was our head attorney.* Any risk ever taken was cleared through him. The one who made sure that our legal department (you know, the legal department files complete with "blank signed papers" and "self-incriminating affidavits" and "irregular notarizations") was all ship-shape.

Indeed, as later testimony revealed, it was Stoen who *authored* many or most transgressions of the law, as often as not, *autonomously!* One would think that be that the case, the likes of Stoen would have been a *detriment* to the likes of the Mertles. But as we were soon to see, it was Stoen who was to become the conspiracy's greatest *asset.*

It took a while for the Mertles and Tim Stoen to find each other -- you know, how one inhabits one room in "heaven," and the other another room in "heaven" (or the other place, it seemed), so "the match made in heaven" just takes a bit of prodding to gel. The Mertles and Stoen, if both plants, did not originate from the same agency, as *New West* clinched. *New West* cites Stoen as "the Temple's top attorney," and Grace confesses "fear of telling Tim" when she was about to leave because "he would tell Jim." The saga of little John is not relayed at all. There is simply a caption under her picture, saying *"They have her five-year-old boy."* "The daddy question" is not broached.

Stoen, probably happier as a lone wolf anyway, undoubtedly had his own, separately-mapped agenda to pursue. If the Mertles knew that he was "one of them," they surely would not have cited him as "the Temple's top attorney"! Or even identified him as an attorney at all, much less *our* attorney, much less our "*top* attorney," but merely as he was always identified later on: "a concerned father."

Nor was the congregation at large yet privy to Stoen's defection. I knew it in my gut, from the moment Jim announced Tim's purported message from Guyana, and I noted an uncharacteristic quaver in the normally-implaccable Jim Jones. But public announcements about such things were scarce. Why alarm people Stateside? They were hanging in there by tenuous glue anyway. Memories. Hopes. The honor system. No voice booming across the airwaves laying down the line to tread. If you loved Peoples Temple now, you did it on your own recognizance.

For Tim's own part, he had played the paragon of loyalty far too effectively to risk such a visible public shift this early on. He chose a much smaller fishpond, Ukiah, in which to make known his low-key disaffection, even telling *The Ukiah Daily Journal* (watch for Kathy Hunter, the editor's wife, a bit later on), "I have always made known my respect for Jim Jones," and assuring the interviewer that Jones personally would not have misused or absconded with funds -- that it was not in his character to do so.

Much later on, too late to do anything but grieve, other pieces would emerge that would made Mr. Stoen look much like an *agent provocateur*. (See "Sticks and Stoens and Set-Ups.") It seemed that our own "top attorney" was surely "the mother of bad legal counsel." But if this was truly an *agent provocateur* who had deliberately steered us into murky ports, how can you protect against damage all those years after the fact? You were set up every step of the way.

From then on in, reality --real, hard conditions we had little option about-- twisted itself like a mobius strip noose around our necks. Do you know what a mobius strip is? You take a strip of paper and twist it once, then fasten it as a circle to its other end. You can run your finger around the inside which becomes the outside which becomes the inside again. You *can't* do anything which ultimately protects you.

Like all the clamoring for Jim Jones to "return and face the charges." No indictments, no proof, just "charges" incessantly reiterated as front-page news. If he doesn't return, the "charges" balloon unchecked. If he does return, he walks into carefully-set traps.

But it all *looks* so bad. Here we're accused of being secretive, protective, concealing all kinds of horrors and... we run off to the Guyanese jungle? It was hugely inconvenient to even get Jim talking with reporters "by phone." There *weren't* any phones in Jonestown, just the ham radio, with limited hours per day and dependent upon weather conditions – itself a glaring reminder that Jim Jones and Peoples Temple were indeed now isolated from the entire world. We seemed to be doing the very thing we had been accused of.

At first, Jim wanted to use the *Peoples Forum*, our paper, to respond. His response, however heavy-handed on the rhetoric, made sense. That these people cared far more that we were *successful* Black people, *successful* poor people, *successfully* bucking the system, than they ever possibly cared about how anyone was treated internally.

> "I know some of you are wanting to fight, but that's exactly what the system wants – they want to use us as sacrificial lambs, as a scapegoat. Don't fall into this trap by yielding to violence, no matter what kind of lies are told on us or how many.
>
> "Peoples Temple has helped practically every political prisoner in the United States. We've reached out to everyone who is oppressed, and that's what is bothering them. We've organized poor people and given them a voice. The system doesn't mind corporate power for the ruling elite, but for the first time we've given some corporate power to the little man and that's an unforgivable sin. And that's the whole problem in a nutshell."

The rest –the urging of people not to take up arms– may have been just so much wasted bravado: a) No one *had* arms to take up(!), and if anyone thought we would be calling in the Black Panthers to shoot up the scene, it sure wasn't us; and b) we never did have numbers like Jim was always and forever putting out. This was for *their* benefit, not ours. But such bluffs were becoming hopeless now. If there are "arms" of the *government* poised to fight you, you really *haven't* much defense, especially in absentia.

Nor did we believe we should be physically armed. All our teaching was against it. Moreover, even if an Armageddon lay ahead of us, a few guns would hardly stave it off. Maybe we had our share of people itching for martyrdom, but not "Waco style" in *this* respect, at least. All the more so in Guyana, a beautiful, thriving community, cooperatively owned and run, where older people had their own landscaped gardens, deprived children learned how to read, and young people all had fulfilling work. We would have been happy, no, thrilled, to never have to give a thought to physical defense at all. We were thousands of miles away now. It should have been safe. It was a rude and ugly shock to discover that it wasn't.

If I ever were to catalogue all the reasons why I could look back and shudder, I could work my way into a deep freeze. And the first buds of frost would begin accumulating with *New West*. I shudder that Jim Jones feared the ultimate destruction of Peoples Temple even when things had been going so well. I shudder that he felt our darkest hour had already cast its shadow years ahead, when Cobb and his crew, now Mertle protégés, split, leaving a mere snip of a note. All the talk about the traitor high up. That the honors won't last. Finally, "I want to choose the manner of my death this time," like he was sure he would land into straits where death was, in any case, inevitable.

So it was all starting to happen after all. People are far too glamorous about psychic abilities, aren't they? They can be truly terrifying. Even I knew that first-hand, and all the more, Jim Jones. I didn't dare overreact to my fierce visions, at least not openly. Jim Jones, by contrast, was a case study in overreaction about to boil over. Not that he didn't feel he was responsible for all those lives ~ our people overseas. He felt with every piercing cry into space how acutely he *was*.

You are perhaps familiar with the idea of "self-fulfilling prophecy." If you look hard enough for doom, you can certainly *create* it. But who created what would become of *this* convoluted scenario? Nothing in us wanted this. Even Jim Jones. He was wrong about much. This was an extreme world view in so many ways, and overlooking many of the failings of the left like a father would overlook the failings of his favorite child; yet so passionate for justice, for equality, for giving underdogs a fair chance. But there would be no fair chance for us, it seemed. The fix was already in.

XXVI. The Pawn that Would Ensnare the King.

How happy the Mertles must have been when, in addition, that very special plum, Tim Stoen, fell from his leafy web of camouflage right into their laps. It happened with Stoen's predictable style: slow, measured, as quick to sink low-key as Jim was to rise to fever pitch. Marshall Kilduff, who, unluckily for us, was doubling on the *San Francisco Chronicle* along with his *New West* stint, reported the progress of Grace Stoen's custody suit on September 21, 1977, noting that *"[Timothy] Stoen has also reportedly split with the temple, but has balked in taking part in the custody fight."*

Tim had reportedly left Guyana in June, but did not emerge publicly with his estranged wife until November 18, 1977, one year to the day before the tragedy. The Stoens appeared jointly before a San Francisco court over custody of John, who was of course absent, making the entire proceeding a tool rather than a *fait accompli*. It was also the exact same date that, unbeknownst to us, Congressman Leo Ryan, already successfully courted by Stoen, attempted to pressure the Justice Department to force John's return from Guyana, but was turned down.

Tim meanwhile issued a public statement that "I have received reliable information to the effect that Grace is being seriously discredited in John's eyes. Not only is this deeply offensive to me, but it could easily cause irreparable emotional harm to John. I ask you [i.e. Jones] to immediately reverse the hate campaign and to advise John repeatedly what you and I both know to be true ~ that Grace loves him deeply and has never abandoned him."

So much for flinging the child at Jim with, "Take him ~ he's yours!" I heard Tim Stoen on this topic so many times, assuring Jim that abandonment charges against Grace would stick, and *never* siding with Grace, that I wondered what gun Stoen felt was pointed at *his* head. If we were prosecuted, *he* could wind up disbarred. Could this presumed change of heart have been happening shy of a deal? But who was there to deal *with?* Whether or not Stoen was provably an *agent provocateur* from the start, he was surely being cut a deal now. And how do you do this with suits pending in several different counties of the State, plus the feds being called in? Who can give you any blanket guarantee of protection in the midst of such a hodge-podge?

The press, whose job it was to smear, not to investigate, never asked. Stoen simply claimed that he first left in March (our March paranoia panic?), returned upon Jim's insistence, then left for good from Guyana on June 8. There were obviously missing pieces here, as it is hard to imagine that he had told Jim to his face that his departure was, in fact, a deadly defection. Like, "Well, o.k., I'm the head attorney, but if the church is in legal trouble, go paddle your own canoe. And forget about keeping your own child. I'm off to Washington to paint Jonestown as a concentration camp so Congress can drag the kid back. And by the way, could someone give me a lift out of the jungle to the airport?"

Yet apparently, whatever the apprehensions, they *did*. The account later given by Teri Buford, who travelled back and forth from Guyana, was that Stoen was discovered to have been on a secret spying mission in East Berlin in the early sixties (see DOCUMENTS, p. 4), was accused of being an agent, and surreptitiously fled to *London* in March, where he was tracked down and escorted back to Guyana. Then somehow, he convinced Jim Jones that although he personally wanted out, he would *never* harm Jonestown and *never* try to remove little John. Then, he moved right to Washington, D.C., where he went on an intensive lobbying campaign to "retrieve my son"! Moreover, his vitriolic efforts to destroy Jonestown included charges that "no one was allowed to leave"!

Maybe Jim just did not *want* to believe that someone who had been so (apparently) committed, could be so treacherous or, on a more pragmatic level, assumed that *Stoen (our "top attorney") could not act against us without incriminating himself;* but his anxiety level must have zoomed off scale when everything he had feared, and worse, materialized. At the least, he felt forced to join John in Jonestown to protect his parental rights, lest Tim join forces with Grace. The rest was history.

Tim, of course, knew that *New West* was on the way, and that Jim would be forced out of the States just when his voice and clout would be needed more than ever, to prevent the Mertle bandwagon from steamrolling over what was left of our flock. Thus strategically, Stoen's departure seemed timed to produce maximum harm.

Nor did he have to rush into view publicly. He knew the Mertles would welcome him *whenever* he surfaced on the other side. He could lay his groundwork carefully, and apparently spent time secretly on the East Coast doing just that.

204/SNAKE DANCE

Stoen's desertion, shocking though it was, was landed on us rather gently, the more visible Mertles stealing the show. Tim first chose to surface in small-town Ukiah, where he had been assistant D.A. He was his usual low-key self, implying little, much less explaining his motives. But he was just parting company. Sort of.... just. "Hard to say why," he told the press.

So why *was* he leaving? Most surely he wasn't aggrieved. He even told a reporter *after* the tragedy, "*I loved Jim Jones.*" Surely there was no normal reason for his departure. This was the closest, the most loyal, the most "in" ~ strategizer, planner, executor, mastermind of every facet of the church's legal affairs. One of the most *trusted*. And the most *reverent*. I remember when he conducted services in Redwood Valley and told us, "I'm not fit to tie Jim Jones' shoelaces." (Boy, they really do train them, don't they? They train them well.)

Tim, cannily aware that he had played the loyalist par excellence, courted as little fanfare as possible publicly, even though later reports revealed a driven man, rounding up relatives at a furious clip, and even trying to destroy us with our church denomination, where our reputation had been not just unblemished, but pristine. After a time, he and Grace, who had separated and were negotiating a divorce, "reunited," at least for the purpose of "regaining our son," an area where Tim had been the most stalwart defender of Jim. Tim now claimed paternity of the child, who had allegedly been kidnapped from under the noses of both biological parents.

Surely he knew that if he did only one thing, this was the worst he could do ~ to use John as **the pawn that would ensnare the king.** My short sprints in front of the t.v. had always been stolen time, when others were gone and I stayed behind. But I remember discovering *Star Trek* on the reruns. There was one episode where the mortal enemy of the week (Klingons or some even more insidious crew) were plotting to take over the Enterprise. Captain Kirk, ever protector of his own, said proudly, with a barely-concealed flash of anger, "They're not taking my own life because they know my life means nothing to me. They're attacking my *ship.*" His face instantly metamorphosized into the strategist. How to save his ship, his own?

I thought oh, that's Jim Jones. That's *just like* Jim Jones. They'd attack his own. Threaten to take his own child. Nothing would get to him more. Tim Stoen, loyal protector of Jim's parental rights through the whole Grace-less scenario, knew that better than anyone.

Oh, sure, we had "protected" ourselves. Affidavits from people now claiming they had been forced to sign this and forced to sign that. Who would believe anything "signed under coercion"? The newspapers didn't care about covering the affidavits anyway. We didn't even have anyone left in the States skillful enough to put the documents right in their face, or to know how to monopolize their attention.

Much less the article about the spying trip to East Berlin, found amongst copious notes in Tim's own hand. It was about a speech Tim Stoen, "formerly" conservative (oh, God, who had believed that? Jim Jones himself?) gave to the Rotary Club at some undisclosed former date, about how he "accidentally wandered across the wall in Berlin." He was just "an innocent tourist," taking a stroll to get some pictures. Why was he arrested? And how he managed to break free of the grey East German sky back into the sunlight of freedom.

Sunlight or snow job? Teri Buford, the highest ranked member left Stateside, waxed more vivid in her portraits to this official and that. It was Tim, she said, who claimed he was "to the left of Huey Newton." It was Tim who initiated the most radical, unthinkable moves, like the proposed grand scheme for poisoning the water supply of Washington, D.C. Presumably, it seemed, *they* would drink the water, and *we* would get the bread-and-water combo, minus, of course, one "innocent bystander": Tim Stoen.

So *Tim* was the one all along? Not just a plant, but a classic *agent provocateur*? The same Stoen who had studied at American University for foreign service in the U.S. government? How naive had we been? Stoen's defection, timed to coincide with the beginning of the smear campaign, was actually beginning to make sense. He was talking to the press now like he had talked to the Rotary Club. His low-key omissions. His simple, face-value intent to "regain my son." Uncomplicated, innocent tale. Who would believe *us*?

The Mertles meanwhile pressed on, encouraged by the small, but pragmatically valuable, barrage of complaints by various "aggrieved ex-members." Many were assigned a roving anti-Peoples Temple ambulance chaser, a private investigator named Joseph Mazor, who was, best we could discover, an Interpol agent with, to boot, a lengthy criminal record of his own, which somehow did not bar the State from granting his investigator's license. [NOTE: An Interpol document smearing Peoples Temple was discovered under the signature of "Louis B. Sims," an individual apparently also involved in trying to destroy Scientology.] Rather late in the game, too.

It seemed that Mr. Mazor had only *become* a private investigator in May, 1977 - just in time to investigate *us!* Whatever his usual occupation had been, no public announcements were ever made.

The various "charges" the Mertles dug up with their fishing expedition found ready news coverage, with the "victims" paraded across the t.v. screen, people pursued by no one but appearing frightened. Even a few of the infamous "Eight" showed up, appearing vague yet disturbed as to why they had left Peoples Temple.

We were disturbed too, but used to crisis. It was early yet, too early for dire predictions, but was Peoples Temple being prepared to die? Was there ever any way to win a battle with such stacked odds and laden with Catch-22's? Like "Where is Jim Jones?" He's in hiding, he won't face the charges, he must have something to hide. How many people has he taken with him? Have they gone willingly? Will their relatives ever see them again?

It wasn't long before it became clear that Jim Jones couldn't return even if he wanted to. He would have been detained forever, if only with the Stoen custody suit. And he could no more bring John back to the States than he could risk leaving him in Guyana while staking his claim to parenthood *here*. At first, he kept saying he wanted to return and answer all of the "charges." But would his return make things better or worse? Less pressure or more?

It still seemed a coup that we had gotten hundreds of people out from under their noses. They would have liked to destroy Peoples Temple as a real, living onslaught in plain view. It dawned upon us only gradually that they would settle for destroying Peoples Temple *in absentia*. Not just here, but *there*.

The Mertles may not have realized they were already preaching to an empty gallery. The bulk of our committed membership was gone. I thought it a miraculous feat, pulling the rug out and leaving these dreadful people to the chase. It seemed to make us safe. Protected. No, also *unprotected*. Would we have been better protected were we still in San Francisco or less protected? There was no one to step forward and answer all the "charges." In the absence of strong spokespeople of our own, would this just fizzle out? Like a boxing match with no opponent being called off?

This conclusion seemed both uneasy and premature. They could steamroll over us and destroy our reputation so badly that we would be left more vulnerable than ever before.

Phase One of this insidious venture had been launched. But no one's coffin is nailed in in a single stroke. It was Phase One only. This early in the media attacks, I was certainly having less trouble with this than with my own more internal wars. I wasn't getting better on these drugs. Maybe I was even getting worse.

XXVII. I Make the Break, or *It* Breaks *Me*.

Several days after I unloaded my hysteria onto Jean, I was called into the radio room. Jim wanted to speak to me. The sound of his voice was not reassuring - I finched like a child who had been hit before and expected no better now.

He was animated. "You're carrying an unnecessary burden! You're carrying an unnecessary burden! What happened in L.A. was done out of love, faith and trust in you. It was a *compliment!*"

It was... *what?* I respectfully froze. I knew I couldn't speak freely over the radio; everything was probably monitored. Jim's dissertation was brief. I left out, repressing the inevitable new torrent of tears 'til I had safely entered the landing below. I wept and wept and wept. How could there be more tears than I had already shed? Would this never stop? He called this "love"? On what planet was this love?

Within a few days, I could compose myself well enough to write. The writing for the church - well, I was on automatic pilot for that. I knew others wouldn't keep writing letters from scratch, so I wrote them all myself, hundreds of them, and had people copy them and sign them. All they had to know was, do you want to write a short, medium or long letter. The system seemed to be working. They would know we still had numbers.

More frequently, I was getting special assignments as well. I could be given 10 or 20 thoughts to incorporate into a letter or a P.R. write-up, and handle it with relative ease. I wrote Jim totals of letters sent, plus observations of the local scene. I could get this done in nearly any state of mind. It was indeed stabilizing - therapeutic.

This particular letter to Jim was obviously more stressful to write, but once begun, it composed itself. He hated embellishments, he hated anything tainted with self-pity, he hated people defending themselves. He wanted it straight? He would get it.

"Dear Jim,

After we talked over the radio, I went off and wept for three hours. You said what you did in L.A. was out of 'love, faith and trust' in me? That it was a 'compliment'?

That must mean that when you attacked me over the P.A. system last March, saying that you would 'fuck me with a bulldozer,' and that 'I must want you dead and why don't I just drop you in boiling oil,' and about how everyone else could 'take' things I couldn't 'take'.... All that must have been 'the greatest compliment of the century'!

I'm not that much of a masochist, Jim. I would rather you had put a bullet through my brain.

And whatever made you think I was taking everything 'well'? I'm on anti-depressants for the first time in my life. I went to the doctor to get them, and when he examined me, he told me that that my gag reflex was totally absent. That's an autonomic reflex ~ it's what keeps you from having things forced down your throat.

How 'well' am I with an autonomic reflex knocked out and on anti-depressants? I don't know why we went through those bizarre ordeals in the first place. But I do know that they had no redeeming value whatsoever. They were nothing but pain.

Jim, I really don't want your 'compliments' at all. They are more like insults to me. All they seem to mean is that you don't trust me. And why not? I've always been trustworthy. I've always been here for the work. So keep your praise and 'compliments.' I have nothing more to prove. If you don't know what I'm made of by now, when will you ever know?

I'm happy everyone is doing well in Guyana.

Laurie"

This was the truth. I never had it in me to turn against Jim Jones. Why did I have to be broken in two to prove that? His love, his approval, *anyone's* love and approval ~ humanly people may need this. But if "L.A." and "P.A." were what he was calling "love, faith and trust," I wanted no part of it. Love is when you touch someone, or hug someone, or listen to them ~ not *this*. Nor was I about to point out the obvious. If he didn't see it for himself, what was it worth, anyway?

The anguish would endure for longer than I could have beared knowing then. But now, acknowledgment or no, there was no more collusion on my part, no liberty to allow any repeats. No more slices of my heart blackmailed away lest I stand accused of caring too little or not giving enough, or accusations of wanting the leader dead because I only wanted to hold onto myself. Who *did* spare Laurie Efrein's life? Why did it take me years, even past the suicides, to figure it out? It must have been... *me*.

I slipped the note in with my regular write-ups, to be sent over by courier. I felt neither defiant nor frightened, but rather in that mid-range crunch where one daren't either charge nor retreat. Anxious and apprehensive though I was, I had to do this. I had nothing further to lose. He wanted me alienated? I was alienated. He wanted me unloved? I was unloved. But I wasn't going to be told how brutal treatment was really... a confirmation of my worth!

Why he never knew the depth of my love, my loyalty to the work, how something inside me, despite all this, *transcended* all this... If he still didn't know, it was not on me, it was on him. This wasn't an ultimatum, nor even a negotiation. The ground I stood on was *mine*. It was my "piano." (You remember "The Piano"? No voice, a silenced tongue, yet the unswerving: "The piano is mine. It's *mine!*")

Jim Jones, by now pushed to the limit and past, believed that most people pushed as far as me, would either crack into submission *to* him or turn *on* him. He believed most people wouldn't stand alone without the props of approval, sex, or other special regard, or stand unified without the prods of power or fear. He claimed life forced these surmisals on him. That what most people called "love" had elements of selfishness that would override commitment to the common good. That any pressure to transcend those limits provoked hostility in the human animal, however lofty the principles or great the goal.

Thus the best we might hope for was to become good, noble and pure ourselves, while inevitably hating *him* as the exemplar! For how many would voluntarily "throw themselves on the sword" ~ skating for God, so to speak, rather than for the gold? Jim believed *he* would, but others mostly not. For their child, perhaps, or a spouse or a dear friend. Not for some greater good, done for its own sake alone, whatever the risk.

Was *this* the backdrop of expected behaviour that landed me such "compliments"? That guilty *or* innocent(!), I had borne the brunt as scapegoat for the purge? And yet not turned upon him? Were that so, I probably deserved, even in his terms, his high respect. I had taken on the denials, disciplines, training, rituals, like a yoga of the pillaged heart. It was so austere, I still shudder and would wish it on no one. Yet broken in pieces, awash in tears, burying my disempowered rage unto a day when our people would be no longer under siege, I somehow emerged untouchable.

I would have to live with my fears now. There was no hope, no help for them. He pushed me away and there I would stay. I would let the letter go, still hurt more than enraged. I would tuck it unobstrusively into a wad of more businesslike things, as if to envelope it in a shroud of insulate pain – a raw, if mute, parody of "having one's heart in the work." I would let it separate from *me*, as I now separated from *him*.

This strangest moment of time had past. I had wholly broken from Jim Jones and at one and the same time, wholly committed myself to stand by his side. I let the letter go. I let it go, to be wafted by breezes seasonal and timeless both, towards its inexorable cadence south, like autumn's last bird, swept upwards and downwards, Icarus-child, wafted past all return across the darkening sea.

XXVIII. Such a Late Date to Finally Discover the Best.

My guided missile must have hit the bull's eye when it arrived at our jungle home ~ the point to which Jim Jones could not manipulate even vulnerable, insecure, compliant me. That point turned out to be, fatefully, a place called Jonestown, Guyana. I didn't ask for this result. It just arrived, quite literally, on my doorstep, in the beautiful, gracious personage of Marceline Jones.

It was some time late in the fall of '77. I heard a knock on the door, and when I opened it, I was startled to see "Mother," newly returned to our San Francisco church. She came to see me in my unshared abode ~ a small plot of space inherited from our now-departed P.R. director, Mike Prokes. Mostly it gave me the seclusion I craved. No-one ever came to see me there. Marceline asked to talk, and startled though I was, I invited her in.

You've long since forgotten Jim Jones was married. I fear many of us did, too! Increasingly, she would take over in one location while Jim was in another (the two, like bow and stern, alternating weekends between San Francisco and L.A.), so we saw her less and less.

Judging from the assessments of Jim and Marceline's surviving sons, the Jones' family life had become a bitter and traumatizing wreckage, at least for Stephan and Suzanne; while meanwhile, organizational pressures devoured any hope of ever putting Humpty Dumpty back together again.

It was "too bad," which is admittedly too little to say of it. Yet I personally learned, however belatedly, that he was indeed married to an extraordinary woman, whom I shall never forget. I never had much chance to get to know her before I got myself stranded in the States and separated from *him*, but what a welcome contrast. Someone in the Jones family I could get along with ~ finally!

Marceline was a natural beauty, with porcelain-white skin, wavy blonde hair, and large, startling eyes of a light but piercing blue. Anyone that close to Jim might have been intimidating to others, but Marceline, sometimes fiery in speech but nevertheless the soul of compassion and kind words, never was. For years she had subjugated herself into the role of registered nurse assisting with the healings, which was sometimes a severe, sudden process, like spitting up a growth for cancer, or relearning to walk after spending years wheelchair-bound.

She often expressed how she hadn't believed miraculous healings were possible in the early years, because of her medical training, but when it happened again and again, it was undeniable. As was her humility, and her deep love for the elderly and infirm who often fell under her care. She wound up working for the State of California, as nursing home inspector. If she sensed the slightest maltreatment or abuse, she would rather carry patients out on her back than permit it to continue.

As for me, I had seen her so frequently in a service role, I always felt she had earned a leadership role, not somehow usurped it, or manipulated it, or ego-tripped it, as one often suspects about those in leadership in many walks of life. Marceline was Jim's wife because her commitment and character merited it. And although in a leadership role of her own, she continually deferred to her husband's authority, in fact made a point of reiterating that if she wasn't married to him, she would still follow him, and that after twenty-five years of marriage, that was quite a statement to make.

Surely she had suffered greatly, as the Jones' family's step into California was another of our myriad of two-edged swords ~ for all the thrills of expansion, also "a step into hell" for them all. As Peoples Temple expanded, our extended family crowded out Jim and Marceline's own. I only learned years after the tragedy (Stephan's tale), that Jim had, Stephan claimed, begun his sexual expansion when Marceline's back gave out and the doctor ruled out further sex, notwithstanding the severely altered rendition Jim touted at my grand opening to the Planning Commission. Their son even claimed that the original plan was for Carolyn (the "Mexican rape victim") to become Jim's mistress, as part of the Jones household ~ Marceline, children and all.

Maybe my subtle instincts had been right all along ~ that "if this is going on, I don't want to know." I sensed missing pieces, and couldn't retrieve them from the landscape at hand. In any case, how Marceline tolerated the strains of the changes foisted upon her with as much dignity as she did, I'm not sure, except that she truly loved the work and loved Jim and loved *us*. The sight of her at my door was as welcome as the sound of Jim's voice on the ham radio had been forbidding. I invited her in.

Marceline, though as forthright as could be, had rare interpersonal qualities as well. She could listen and listen and not invade, the mark of a truly compassionate soul. She began very simply and directly. That Jim had read my letter, and sends me all his love and concern. (Love and concern. Love and concern. The whole *world* had his "love and concern.") I could barely nod at that.

"He wants you to know that if you want to go to Guyana you can leave immediately." (Why was I not feeling relieved?) "Or if you want to stay, you can stay. Whatever you like." *"Whatever you like"*? I looked at her dumbfounded. When was it *ever* "Whatever you like"? I never heard this man say "Whatever you like" to a single soul in all the years I'd been there. It was always "Clear it with Jim." "Clear it with Jim" wasn't "Whatever you like." Was this new language... *English?*

Whether instinct, duty, repression, altruism, apprehension, training or pragmatism governed my response, Marceline probably never knew. Altruism was in the running for a medal, so to speak, but the unspoken dark horse, Apprehension, probably stole the day. Yet for once, I steeled myself to the strictures of diplomacy: "I'd love to *visit* Jonestown," I told her cautiously. "But if I left, there's no one here who could fill in for what I'm doing. So I think I should stay."

Marceline, undoubtedly sensing that whatever my outer demeanor, I was fragile, let that rest. I had reason to stay. Certainly, I would not ask her what reasons she had to put up with all she had, but in turn, respected, even admired, that she would stand strong. She, in turn, seemed willing to grant me something Jim never could ~ the honesty and integrity of my own heart. I was *willing to stay.* I would have loved to see Jonestown, if only for a visit, but my open-ended commitment was to stay and hold down the fort.

The truth was, I couldn't bear to have my role repeated in Guyana in any form. If it was to be the same; if, in effect, it was not *made up to me*, I couldn't bear to have my heart shattered all over again ~ even in the bright Guyanese sun where our children loved to laugh and play.

And how could I know Jim would make it up to me? I would have maybe a few words, a smile, a brief conversation. If he did anything as drastic as take me to bed, it would be at the cost of precious time drained away from the ongoing crisis, and done for the sake of my mental and emotional stability. Was this "love"? If he loved me, why didn't he *like* me? Why was it that everything I did with any freedom or ease or joy (from thinking to feeling to creating) seemed to incur his wrath?

The very thought of having the wounds re-opened, even for the sake of relief, sent shivers up my spine. You don't sign yourself up for surgery when your wounds are already healed enough for you to walk. You may walk with a limp. You may walk with a limp *forever*. But what if you let the doctor re-examine your injured leg, and he just says, "Oh, it doesn't look too bad. You'll be fine." And you say, "Yes, I'm fine," like I did when I returned from the trip to my dying father. Then you've accepted that the unhealed wound will never be restored. You've allowed the demoralization of a continuing disability, without recourse.

Better I stay where I was. And why really? It was on the tip of my tongue. On the tip of my tongue but I never could say it, I could never ask Marceline *that*: "Does Jim ever say he's sorry?" No, not the send-Sharon-to-say-Jim's-sorry,-it-was-a-new-therapy kind of "sorry" – that's just time off for good behaviour. I mean the get-down-on-your-knees-and-beg-forgiveness kind of "sorry". Maybe I would have gone to Guyana to hear him tell me face-to-face how sorry he was. But I could never bring the words to my lips. They failed me each time. The irony of having a choice whether to go. The irony of having a choice and *not* having a choice. The irony that *that* was the choice. The irony of it.

How ironic that now, at long last, denied everything I had ever felt I wanted for myself, that the one thing I had totally undervalued, I had just then, at that moment, gained: *my life.* "I think I should stay."

Our lives tick within us like a timeclock. At least mine always did. I felt my past beating heart, my present beating heart, and my future beating heart like a multiple cacophony. At times it seemed like the voices around me, the conversations I heard myself participating in, were like a drifting shadow concealed beneath the clouds until a brighter, clearer day.

I cannot even say I told the full story to myself as to why I chose to stay. It was that subtle tug on the arm again, the stayed voice, the withheld thoughts, the inability to cross barriers I sensed as impassable, much as one would stumble over an unfamiliar object in the dark of night.

Parallel to my ...*choice* (a word I use guardedly here) to stay, I realized that my day job left me enough free time to re-type *"Allegory"* in a more artistic, staged version. My brain, freed from its pressured setting for several hours a day, allowed me to re-surface the haunting dictums surrounding the work. To never take it out of the United States. For it to be a legacy. To never destroy it. To let it be for America. To let it be for the world.

All these strange premonitions and more returned. I noted not with dismay, but with curiosity, that my temples had begun to gray ever so slightly. I'd always looked younger than my age. I was just feeling so worn. Like whatever had taken its toll upon me in *this* segment of life, it was already done.

I purchased some music staff paper and began scrawling assymetrical lines, haunting jagged melodies from out of the lines of *"Allegory."* The timeclock continued to tick, as its hands progressively reached digits I could somehow touch but not yet see. How little I knew of it all. How little and how much. I never talked to anyone of it. I prepared and prepared and talked of nothing.

It had been difficult to talk to Marceline extemporaneously, which she surely sensed, and she kindly offered to come back if I liked. I gratefully accepted a day's reprieve. Even then, I don't quite know why I chose what I did, except that what Jim had put me through was so painful, that the only other person to wreak such pain in my life had been my mother. So I spoke of her.

I told her my mother was an hysterical woman, seemingly obsessed with me, and that my independence of her, especially *emotional* independence, was like escaping the stranglehold of a vampire. That I couldn't risk expressing my feelings at all. That my only pathway to freedom had been *sexual* independence. That I had to have this then, or drown, or die. Never be myself. Never be free. But that here, even *feeling* that way was deemed a crime.

She said something meant to be of comfort, like, "Well, just remember Jim loves you," and I responded softly, with an unmistakable touch of despair, "All I can think is that he *hates* me." I said I still wanted to "be with him," despite everything. Then, realizing I had perhaps offended *her*, added, half-apologetically, "Jim's never even hugged me." I heard my voice trailing off into a whisper, like someone else, a lost and lonely child, had eased that coda onto an already-imperfect main script. And suddenly there was nothing more to say.

Of course there was *much* more to say. Every form has a shadow; every word an unspoken intent. I wished I could have talked of love. Why had it been made something I didn't even deserve?

Maybe it was, indeed, "Mother" all over again: "You're as cold as ice. You're incapable of loving another human being." Jim said the whole race was incapable of love. Everyone *needed*. Did that mean we should all impale ourselves on the sword in penance? Why must giving and receiving love entail penalties: sacrifice, penance -- nay, torment?

I never even added, "Oh, by the way, I haven't had any sex with anyone since 1969." She probably thought I had done something sexually flagrant. I thought so little of protecting myself, that I couldn't even spell out that much. I never even mentioned that I had been living like a nun in the midst of debauchery. Why didn't this come up? Surely it made the castigation I had endured doubly, trebly senseless.

Indeed, the stoicism of my fragile youth may have served me well, protected me from the ultimate manipulation of "You owe your *life*." Like a raw but hardy weed, I took root in Father's soil, and insisted upon survival despite lack of nourishment. Perhaps my very stoic strength put up the red flags that Jim, most forceful in resistance (he treasured coverting fundamentalists ~ that the *strong-minded* were won), provoked into public display. Stand there and take it. Such strength was lauded. "Doing the right thing" was torture, but I happened to also be good at it. I had had a lot of practice.

So when I talked with Marceline, I also withheld in what I said. Yet perhaps she was impressed that I vented no anger, no bitterness towards Jim. I think she must have realized that whatever I had done (even had I, in fact, done... *nothing*), all that had been left of me, or to me, was hurt. And when people are in pain, you empathize.

Ironically, of course, Marceline, too, wound up as "one more intermediary." I might as well have joined the Catholic Church. But if this be unwitting Catholicism yet again, at least it was a comfort to have a *saint* in my corner. She typed out a note to Jim and showed me exactly what she had said. She didn't want anything kept from me. I appreciated that. "Appreciated." A word and a half.

It saddened me, too, in that I felt only Jim could lift the lingering pall clouding my days. Had I only the impulse to gravitate to his side in our southern bed of sheltering trees. But I could never sense that the gravitational pull of our *relationship* (I suppose "juxtaposition" being a better word) would correspondingly shift, or that my heart would, or could, mend. Here I had a peace of sorts. Time to heal.

Marceline was so much an empath. I imagine she heard many messages I never deigned to speak. She accepted this much ~ that I should be where I felt of greatest value. She must have sensed that I could release but little of the turmoil inside. She had so much the gifts of a comforter, a healer, a mother, a nurse. Nurse of the heart. Her job was to console, not to judge. Her very presence radiated this to me. Bless her forever.

XXIX. "A Conspiracy Behind Peoples Temple Exposé?"

As for the invitation to come to Guyana, it was never repeated. My staying back was deemed yet another act of selfless sacrifice and the question laid entirely to rest. Thus the collective plight proved my salvation, even as in equal measure, it proved the doom of my co-workers and friends.

That to be barred from embracing the trip overseas that most left behind craved, had also opened my energies to the small whirlwind of a life where Stateside, the cause actually *needed* me, was a rare double insurance premium that fate, perhaps my benefactor after all, finally paid out when all else seemed lost. The incentives were powerful both for *staying here* and for *not going there*. One alone mightn't have sufficed, but joining forces, the two sung out a clear, if rough and raw, unison in my otherwise-fractured life.

Once, mere months before the end, we nearly got the directive to go en masse ... but not to Guyana. We were told we might have to move *directly to the Soviet Union* to meet up with our newly-transplanted community there. I heard the news with an oddly-detached astonishment. I never pictured myself going. I never really pictured myself going to Guyana either. I was proud of our flourishing community, and happy that others could fulfill their dream. But for me? A dream? A life?

Children were being born there. Jim had queried us in P.C. just weeks before he left, upon deciding to send the pregnant girlfriends of two of his own sons overseas. Still uncomprehending of deliberately bringing children into such a world, he wanted to know which women still felt they wanted to have a child.

Nora, a tentative hand barely aloft, confessed ambivalence. Diane, known to be a lesbian, said she thought she might, but couldn't explain why. The rest were still as a frozen pond. But now, as though we had been living in a darkened world mysteriously, suddenly, swept up into the Sun, children were being born, and cared for in its rich nurturing glow. Maybe the Sun *did* shine there. Maybe it would even shine on me.

But this was merely a thought, an abstraction, whereas the duties at hand were pressing and real. Even Jim seemed to realize, in astoundingly belated fashion, that a ruined life could not take to a "paradise"; and rushed in at every odd turn to send messages of encouragement, unsolicited on my part and greeted with the silent tears of one who once wanted to be loved, and now merely wanted to believe that the crushing of her heart could not have been a deliberate act, much less one of deliberate cruelty. Messages of how much I was appreciated, messages that I was needed to teach the children music, messages that I would (unthinkable!) have the freedom to compose: "These things are possible here."

There were seven messages in all – seven perfect dwarfs matched into an incomplete jigsaw against, "I *love* you. I *accept* you. I *embrace* you. I am so, so sorry for what I've done" – the one whole, complete message that never found a voice. Each time someone told me "I have a message for you from Jim," I felt his hand boarding-house reaching for mine anew; then, letting his fingers slip through mine like ghost fingers into dust, I skated the razor-thin line between those deliberate mercies and the pain they inevitably reawakened with a start. He *seemed* to want my pain diminished – this far-away man in a far-away land. I *tried* to picture myself going. I really did.

Then subtly in the ensuing months, I began to accept distance as a friend. It became easier to tackle the tasks at hand now that my emotions had been cried out to a numbed state. The outlet of new responsibilities, ones mentally challenging, filled in the void where my emotions had played out their overstocked hand. I had no more hearts, but it mattered less. I had trump. There were tasks to be done, and me the only one to do them.

I asked clearance to quit my 9-to-5, to handle the avalanche of work. Sarah handed down a reluctant, nearly scowling clearance over the radio: "Well, if you *have* to." I was so relieved, I scarcely even reflected on what *Jim* thought, or why the release was delivered in such a grudging manner. One thing no one had ever accused me of was slothfulness. I was doing more than enough to merit my request. I had no apologies to offer.

Nor was it just me taking on more. We were badly understaffed, with a brutal campaign hemming us in. I relished being useful. My emotional woes neither blocked my observations of events, nor even dulled their sting. I was still the McCarthy era child who watched on in horror as the Rosenbergs were executed by a hysterical nation craving a scapegoat. These engrams long impressed upon my brain from childhood, I seemed to understand, each step of the way, *how such things happen*. I could never be so self-absorbed as to lose my pulse on what was happening to *us*, or how it had come to pass.

Thus the two-tiered story, of me and of my world, continued to co-exist in an oddly-bound symbiosis, me a flower of fragile glass inside, yet externally surprisingly secure. I saw it all unfold. I saw that we were, indeed, inching towards disaster.

New West was just the beginning. Even that was oddly muted, as not everyone saw it, nor were its contents discussed publicly. Directives came in to not look at the news at all. We wrote letters en masse in *general* terms, extolling the good works of Peoples Temple and not citing the "charges" beyond calling them outrageous, ludicrous, and an orchestrated campaign of slander and smears. Understandably, Jim didn't want morale lowered in his absence, but it gave the chilling early attacks a surreal cast. That here this horrible thing was happening, but it was going to be all right. Everything was always all right around Father, wasn't it?

Our counterattack was substantial, if ineffective, with leaflets, press releases, letters appealing to everyone from the locals to the U.S. Congress, the President, governmental agencies, the United Nations, Amnesty International - anyone to whom citizens at large could appeal. But incoming mail was sometimes maliciously damaged, and who knows what happened to our *outgoing* mail, even when sent out in a continuous flood. Strategies were hatched over the ham radio, using secret codes that had probably long since been deciphered by wakeful, hidden ears. Even a tapped phone might have been relatively private compared to this.

After a few meagerly-attended press conferences, a mere David to counteract a Goliath of bad press, even our P.R. director, Mike Prokes, had departed south. No one still based in the States, would clearly, persuasively speak for Peoples Temple ever again. The group that had been "the toast of the town" was now silent, as were its friends. As time wore on, and distance and slander conspired to fade true blues into the dusty footprints our church had left behind, we increasingly drew from our deck of Temple friends like a poker player wishing for a magic match, but prepared to bluff our waning prestige on higher stakes we were less and less able to cover.

Yet it would be too innocuous to surmise that we were doomed to lose by attrition or merely by way of bad press. Publicity only laid the groundwork for a broader campaign of destruction - high-powered, well-connected moves, like the illegal cut-off of social security stipends, and mercenary raids to frighten and destabilize us in our new jungle home.

In fact, the public stance that bad press arose, then snowballed, out of a grassroots movement by ex-members who had simply been too frightened to step forward before, was a legere-de-main of P..R.., not a real chronology of events. One of the most damning incidents of all happened *months before New West hit the newsstands*, and the players were high-powered outsiders, not Peoples Temple members at all:

American Indian Movement leader, Dennis Banks, whom we befriended during the siege at Wounded Knee, had been approached by David Conn, *who said he was working with agents from the Treasury Department and I.R.S.,* with an offer to assist in preventing extradition to South Dakota if he agreed to denounce Jim Jones; if not, that "it would go badly for him." Banks refused to cooperate, even though he knew a death warrant could be hanging over his head. It was clearly a bribery/blackmail scenario. Why wasn't the press covering *that?*, we cried. Why were they smearing good people who were simply trying to build a better life?

By August we had taken on scrappy left-wing attorney, Charles Garry, his earliest assignment being to publicize the damning Banks incident. A brief scuffle to reclaim a higher ground came with a September 23, 1997 article in the *Berkeley Barb*, entitled *"A Conspiracy Behind Peoples Temple Exposé?,"* which included Banks' disclosures, and what seemed like an aggressive Charles Garry eager to take on the powers that be. (See DOCUMENTS, pp. 6-8.)

Why would outsiders, especially *government-connected* outsiders like Conn, step in to commandeer the anti-Temple campaign? He was never a member, never attended a meeting, had no relatives in the church. Unbelievably, he took on this huge, time-consuming, expensive, risky project of doing Peoples Temple in, with nothing personal at stake. Conn even admitted to *The Barb* that he had been investigating Peoples Temple for *seven years*, and that *his friendship with the Mertles pre-dated them joining the church.* Joseph Mazor, meanwhile, who gradually emerged as our all-purpose nemesis, admitted handling the press attacks through a P.R. firm, offering damaging material to all takers, and drawing on funding from an undisclosed source.

The rub, of course, with Conn, Mazor and others, is that many of the people who hurt us the most, were people we not only never hurt, but never even *met!* Even twisted trees planted in our midst like the Mertles and Stoen, were so handled with kid gloves during their time with us, that they could have no motivation of avenging personal harm. Nor did they, the joint founders of the so-called "Concerned Relatives," even *have* any relatives in Jonestown! They even from time to time (Tim upon defection, the Mertles on their way to the Grim Reaper), had kind things to say about Peoples Temple.

Incidents like Conn's threats to Dennis Banks, the prominent involvement of well-heeled outsiders, and the rabid thirst to destroy on the part of members who had no legitimate grievances nor any relatives left in the church, were classic alarms for anyone familiar with the ways of political persecution. It seemed that someone was preparing the stage world-wide as well. Within weeks of the *New West* assault, identically-worded smears, citing a "prophet with the profits," appeared in both the Canadian (Toronto, home of many Guyanese immigrants) and Soviet press! (See DOCUMENTS, p. 9.) Who could get *that* done? Some local ex-members? A later smear in a Caribbean paper accused Jim Jones of starting a riot in Guyana when his passport showed he wasn't even there.

Was no place in the world safe? We had relocated to Guyana by the onset of the smears. Not to run away from a fight, but to embrace a dream. Yet it inevitably meant running away from a fight just when holding our own was needed the most. Our best hope seemed to build our dream magnificently, albeit abroad, and thus deflect, even reverse, the destruction which every marker suggested was deliberate, massive, and long-planned.

But the pressure never let up. Battling partly exposed, partly hidden detracters, we seemed pitted against the very forces of time and space. To ride through the storm (the time line) and to be situated in a location of safety (the space line). *Both.* For it was dawning upon us that Guyana, however far away, was hardly safe. As we basked in praise from the Guyanese, visitors from the Soviet Embassy were threaded into the Jonestown schedule as well. The coup was a visit from the Soviet news agency, TASS, and a glowing write-up which paved our way for a fresh move overseas. (See DOCUMENTS, p. 10.) A scouting party was all lined up to visit Russia in December, 1978, had the community survived but a few more weeks.

Was this really an armed camp of crazed cultists lost to the world, as the press widely reported? Or was it a successful, integrated, socialist, politically-connected group of expatriate Americans already acclaimed in the Third World, and about to make yet another move, to the dreaded Soviet Union, during the Cold War? Jim had even made a trip to Cuba to see Huey Newton, which we had publicized, and was looking into sending our young people to Cuban schools.

I often wondered who in the press would like to step forth and claim that the C.I.A. would be *indifferent* to such a scenario. Especially in Guyana, considered notorious as a C.I.A. pawn. And had it been just an odd coincidence that it was *Stoen* who "found us Guyana"? Stoen's bizarrely-rationalized "day trip" to East Germany was beginning to seem rather more sinister than a mishap of innocent tourism. Stoen had in fact denied to us that he had ever been in that part of the world, much less taken a stroll over the infamous Wall. Who *was* Mr. Stoen, anyway?

Jim, of course, was crushed by the Stoen defection worst of all, if only for personal reasons. The Mertles, who prior to their departure headed the church's Publications Department, were a bureaucratic pair -- efficient, plastic, and never inner circle, despite their appearance in the shadow circle of the Planning Commission. Tim, on the other hand, was an innermost twist of the swirl surrounding Jim Jones -- friend, comrade, co-worker, strategist, confidante. The Mertles and Stoen were probably not even sent to darken our doorstep by the same handlers. Conn (the Mertles), positioned to threaten Indian reservations, reeked of F.B.I. Stoen's international ties looked more like C.I.A.

Yet the Mertle/Stoen marriage thrived, its poisonous symbiosis gelling before our eyes. Tim laid low, letting the Mertles lead the charge, not just because his style was more reserved than the autocratic Mertles, who seemed to revel in overt control; but because, as long-time Temple attorney, with prosecutions against us pending, he had to avoid the limelight for everything save the one thing Jim Jones could endure the least: the child custody suit. Stoen was still John's legal father, it having been thought *protective* to put his name, rather than Jim's, on the little boy's birth certificate. And since the child's mother, Grace, had left, Tim was the one thread that had to hold, lest the entire tapestry become unravelled into a messy, even dangerous, tangle.

By now of course, the damning dice were already tossed. We were in Guyana, as likely as not "agency's pick," presumably "holding another couple's child hostage." The child of the agent's wife and our leader? How wrong were we about "God"? Perhaps God was indeed there, but incognito -- as a novelist!

No, no one was using that volatile word "hostage" this early on. In retrospect, one wouldn't even know which finger to point where. Who, after all, *was* hostage? If no one was about to let us either *live* in Jonestown in peace, nor *depart* from Jonestown in peace, were we not all held hostage? And not necessarily by Jim Jones. Perhaps by "the wrong people Jim Jones went to bed with thinking that was going to save us." Of all possible tragedies, could the Greeks have possibly envisioned this?

Grace, however trying her histrionics, had far more to be aggrieved about than either the Mertles or Tim, but perhaps that only rendered her fodder for exploitation. Jim, a chess grandmaster at heart, was forever anticipating moves of potential adversaries, even years in advance. He would throw out every now and then that "If you want to leave and hurt us, you will find that all they will do is *use* you."

With Grace, this was pathetically true. Who really cared about "rescuing" her son? *Tim* knew that Jim would never give him up, so the custody fight was waged primarily to apply unbearable pressures to the leader ~ to force *him* into creating a "hostage drama" that risked killing us *all.* Or were these really altruists who cared only to "rescue John," and let the other thousand people go on their merry way? John was a mere pawn.

Cobb, for all his arrogance, can hardly be said to have emerged a winner, either. He and the other students from "The Eight" who were enticed to participate in *New West,* each lost relatives in the tragedy.

Even Tim, Deanna and Mert were used. They may not have been told that this was a fight to the death. Like Kirk marooned on Vulcan, with Spock fighting for his betrothed wife, Kirk would step in cast as *hero* ~ as a surrogate fighter, to rescue Spock from the brute who wanted to claim his wife as his own. Only when the fight was just about to begin was he told, "This fight is to the death."

It is doubtful the Mertles received such a warning at all, though *Stoen* surely knew that pushing to remove, even forcibly kidnap, John, was pushing Jim way beyond the pall. He had in fact reportedly told Tim Carter (who was sent on a mission to hunt down a defector in his camp) that he was **"counting on Jim to overreact"** to the Congressman's visit, and that he wanted to **"destroy Jonestown."**

But however "successful" he was in this, both he and the Mertles were still hardly left "free" in the aftermath. Indeed, the Mertle's grizzly end only punctuated the point. Once they announced, "No more".... You see, the Mertles were killed so *quickly.* Unwilling to play their role ghoulishly way *past* the tragedy, they made the fatal mistake of bolting, and were murdered within days of publicly resigning their role as anti-Peoples Temple icons. Key players Conn and Mazor, non ex-members, non-interested parties, outsiders, scattered into the shadows. Luckily for them, unlike the doomed Mertles, their job was done. For his own part, Stoen had reportedly "gone into hiding."

"A Conspiracy Behind Peoples Temple Exposé?" Maybe so, but the mainstream media never touched it. *The Berkeley Barb* article, however damning, was alternative press, and like all the bright spots that showed up here and there, it proved but a tiny spotlight on the darkening stage of our ongoing demise.

DOCUMENTS

1. "Testimonial Honors Fresno Four," Ukiah Daily Journal, September 27, 1976. ... 2
2. "Reds Kept Local Student 15 Hours Without Food for Taking Photos," 1961. ... 4
3. "Jones Honored By Organization," Los Angeles Sentinel, 5/29/75. ... 5
4. "A Conspiracy Behind Peoples Temple Expose," Berkeley Barb, September 23, 1977. ... 6
5. Affidavit of Dennis Banks. ... 8
6. Smears in the Canadian and Soviet Press. ... 9
7. "To the Jungle from the 'Free World,'" TASS News Agency. ... 10
8. "Charles Garry Visits Jonestown: 'I Have Been to Paradise," The Sun Reporter, November 10, 1977 ... 11
9. "Concerned Relatives" flyer: "This Nightmare is Taking Place Right Now". ... 12
10. The Food at Jonestown: Plentiful and Delicious! (excerpts from letters). ... 13
11. Affidavit of Deborah Layton Blakey. ... 15
12. The Mercenary Attack on Jonestown and its Timing. ... 16
13. Affidavits re Paternity of John Victor Stoen ... 18
14. Grace Stoen Complains of Tim Stoen's Transvestitism. ... 19
15. "Trouble brewing in Guyana," Ukiah Daily Journal, April 3, 1978; excerpt from U.S. State Dept. log. ... 20
16. "Peoples Temple colony 'harassed,'" San Francisco Examiner, October 4, 1978 ... 21
17. Press Release re Congressman Ryan, November 17, 1978. ... 22
18. Report on Banks/Conn Encounter in U.S. Congressional Report. ... 23
19. Mark Lane Parades a Rat, Then Charges Top Dollar for Rat Poison (excerpts from New York Times, March 4, 1979) ... 24
20. Transcript of Interview: Mark Lane/Joseph Mazor. ... 25
21. Note by Timothy Stoen Proposing Harassment of Jim Cobb. ... 26
22. "Berkeley Victims Had Said They Didn't Fear Reprisals," March 1, 1980. ... 27
23. "...A feeling of freedom...," Commentaries about Jonestown, 1978. ... 28
24. Jonestown is Falsely Portrayed as "An Armed Camp" -- excerpts from San Francisco Examiner, December 10, 1978 ... 37
25. The Government's Eyewitness Admits He Was On the Opposite Side of the Plane When the Shooting Erupted -- excerpts from Tyler Courier, November 21, 1978. ... 38
26. Untrained Amateurs.... Or Highly-Trained Professional Assassins? -- excerpts from Seattle Times, November 20, 1978 and The Charlotte Observer, November 20, 1978. ... 39
27. Did the Man Who Made This Phone Call Know About the Assassination in Advance? -- excerpts from San Francisco Chronicle, November 21, 1978. ... 40

Ukiah Daily Journal

Ukiah, Calif. Monday, September 27, 1976

Testimonial honors Fresno Four

By KATHY HUNTER

If you came to spend an evening with Assemblyman Willie Brown, Lt. Gov. Mervyn Dymally, San Francisco's Mayor George Moscone, Police Chief Charles R. Gain, District Attorney Joseph Freitas, Eldridge Cleaver and his wife and a member of the John Birch Society, where do you think you would be?

At a political rally, right? Wrong!

You would be one of the more than 5,000 people who turned out for a testimonial dinner in San Francisco for Pastor Jim Jones of the Peoples Temple honoring the Fresno Four newsmen with the proceeds to go to the church's many charitable projects.

The whole evening was precipitated by the participation of approximately 1,000 members of the Peoples Temple who traveled from Los Angeles, San Francisco and Ukiah churches to protest the continued confinement of the Fresno Bee newsmen in a peaceful demonstration supporting the First Amendment to the Constitution.

Mike Prokes, an assistant minister of the church and Assemblyman Willie Brown shared the emcee duties of the evening which featured the public thanks of the "Fresno Four."

THANKS FROM THE 'FRESNO FOUR' — A special feature of the testimonial dinner held in San Francisco Saturday night for Pastor Jim Jones of the Peoples Temple church was the appearance of the four Fresno Bee men who were jailed on contempt of court charges for refusing to divulge their news sources and came to the dinner to personally thank Jones and the 1,000 members of the Peoples Temple who went to Fresno to make a peaceful demonstration protesting the confinement of the newsmen and in support of the First Amendment to the Constitution. Pictured with Jones at far right are, from left: Joseph Rosato, reporter; James Bort, city editor; William K. Patterson, reporter, and George Gruner, managing editor. (See page 2 for additional pictures and story.) —Journal photo by K. Hunter.

"If you came to spend an evening with Assemblyman Willie Brown [now Mayor of San Francisco], Lt. Gov. Mervyn Dymally, San Francisco's Mayor George Moscone, Police Chief Charles R. Gain, District Attorney Joseph Freitas, Eldridge Cleaver and his wife and a member of the John Birch Society, where do you think you would be? ...You would be one of the more than 5,000 people who turned out for a testimonial dinner in San Francisco for Pastor Jim Jones... honoring the Fresno Four newsmen... Mike Prokes, an assistant minister of the church, and Assemblyman Willie Brown shared the emcee duties of the evening..."

DOCUMENTS/3

REPUBLICANS ALSO TALK TO DEMOCRATS — Dr. and Mrs. Si Boynton of Ukiah visit with Lt. Gov. Mervyn Dymally and his stunningly beautiful wife, who everyone agreed could win any office she chose to run for.

WELCOME! — Sandy Bradshaw of Ukiah, who was one of the hostesses for the Peoples Temple dinner, makes S.F. Police Chief Charles Gain especially welcome to the evening's festivities while Tim Stoen exchanges a witticism with a dinner companion.

"We have seen no greater example of the brotherhood of man," said James Bort, city eidtor of the Fresno Bee speaking for himself and the other three newsmen, "than was exemplified by Rev. Jones and the members of the multi-racial, inter-faith Peoples Temple" who came to Fresno in their support.

Mayor George Moscone presented a plaque thanking Jones for "his personal support given on many occasions whenever asked" and State Senator Milton Marks presented the pastor with a resolution on behalf of the entire State Senate commending the work of the Peoples Temple.

A certificate of honor was also presented Jones by Bob Mendelsohn on behalf of the San Francisco Board of Supervisors thanking the church for its many projects "which have been so beneficial to all the citizens of the Bay Area."

Claude Worrell, ambassador to the Guyanese embassy in Washington, D.C. was present at the head table to thank Jones and the Peoples Temple for their present agricultural mission to his country and Cecil Williams of Glide Memorial church was also present to give Jones and the Temple a plaque of appreciation for the Temple's work in humanitarian ministry.

Perhaps the most poignant accolade came from Lt. Gov. Dymally who commented that all people can live, work and love together for here was an example of thousands who had come together —blacks, whites, orientals, the young and the old of all denominations —in a temple, God's temple."

The evening, which included outstanding band and vocal entertainment as well as dancing by the Temple's young people, concluded with Jones telling the assemblage that prayer alone wouldn't do the job —"you have to put legs to your prayers."

He also introduced and thanked Walter Heady and Dr. and Mrs. Si Boynton of Ukiah for their support, counsel and friendship during many difficult times.

"We have seen no greater example of the brotherhood of man," said... the editor of the Fresno Bee... Mayor George Moscone presented a plaque thanking Jones for "his personal support given on many occasions"... State Senator Milton Marks presented the pastor with a resolution on behalf of the entire State Senate... A certificate of honor was also presented to Jones... on behalf of the San Francisco Board of Supervisors... Lt. Gov Mervyn Dymally commented that all people can live, work and love together for here was an example of thousands.... "in a temple, God's temple."

Reds Kept Local Student 15 Hours Without Food for Taking Photos

Fifteen hours in Communist hands. That was the experience of Tim Stoen, Littleton graduate, who had the audacity to take a picture of a sign being erected in East Berlin.

Stoen told about his ordeal at the Rotary Club last week after returning from a year abroad on a Rotary Fellowship.

"I thought I should go to East Berlin and see what it is like behind the Iron Curtain," Stoen said. "The first thing that I noticed was the blank expression on the faces of everyone. You could tell they were just waiting for the day they might have some freedom. This will come slowly. Poets are already getting some freedom, and so are theatrical people and musicians. It was noteworthy that a journalist was able to print in Moscow the interview with President Kennedy."

Began Taking Pictures

Stoen said he took a number of pictures in East Berlin without difficulty. Then he took one of a sign being erected near the newly-built wall.

Three German officers rushed over to Tim and an East Berlin student who was showing him around. They took the pair at 12:30 p.m. to a building and held them there until 8 p.m.

"I was fearful for my new-found friend because he had taken too many liberties for the Communists, and I didn't want to get him into trouble," Stoen said. "Finally, at 8 p.m., three men escorted me out of the building and put me in a Czech car. We drove and we drove in silence. I didn't know Berlin was so large. We came to a building with bars on it and I was taken in and questioned. They kept trying to trip me up, coming around to the same questions in different words to see if I would contradict myself. I had to take everything out of my pockets. They found a roll of exposed film and kept it. The guards were curious about my nail clip and wanted to see how it worked. They had never seen an American coin purse that opens a crack when you bend it, and they were like children with it. I was getting both weak and apprehensive, and I was trying to test the power of positive thinking. I had had no food for 15 hours and I was glad when they brought me some unpalatable ham sandwiches. Soon afterwards, they took me to the border and let me go."

Stoen had a happier experience in West Germany, 5 miles from the East German border. A little old lady recognized him as an American without much in the way of funds.

"She pressed two things in my hands," Stoen reported. "One gift was about 40c worth of coins and the other was a sack containing four bananas. She told me that she loved Americans for the kindness she received from them at the close of World War II."

TIM STOEN

"Fifteen hours in Communist hands. That was the experience of Tim Stoen, Littleton graduate, who had the audacity to take a picture of a sign being erected in East Berlin. Stoen told about his ordeal at the Rotary Club last week after returning from a year abroad on a Rotary fellowship.

"I thought I should go to East Berlin and see what it was like behind the Iron Curtain," Stoen said. "The first thing that I noticed was the blank expression on the faces of everyone. You could tell they were just waiting for the day they might have some freedom."

Los Angeles Sentinel

Jones Honored By Organization

By VIRGIE W. MURRAY

The pastor of Peoples Temple of the Disciples of Christ, James V. Jones, was recently named one of the 100 most outstanding clergymen in the nation by Religion In American Life, an inter-faith organization.

Jones was honored for his guidance and inspiration in establishing the many humanitarian programs and facilities in Peoples Temple that attempt to meet every type of human need.

Peoples Temple is scattered over California, with members in many cities, traveling in the church's fleet of Greyhound type buses to worship services in San Francisco, Los Angeles, and the church in Redwood Valley.

A native of Indiana, Pastor Jones has been in California for 10 years. In that decade, Peoples Temple has grown from a meeting place in the garage of his home to 10,500 members in the three congregations.

RESPONDS

This ministry is known for responding to both public and private appeals for assistance, giving support to the local school system and law enforcement. The Temple has rehabilitated over 175 young people from hard-line drug habits and educated many local residents through its college program.

Pastor Jones and Peoples Temple have been viewed by many people. Dr. John Moore, District Superintendent of the United Methodist Church said, "Peoples Temple is a caring community of people of all races and classes. They bear the mark of compassion and justice — compassion for the hungry and jobless, lonely and disturbed, and also for the earth and her offspring."

INJUSTICE

Michael Prokes, former TV News Bureau Chief, who resigned his post to join Peoples Temple, stated, "Pastor Jones manifests the life of Christ by working day and night to stand courageously against all forms of injustice, to relieve human suffering of every kind, and to establish brotherhood among peoples of all different backgrounds."

The Rev. Gerald McHarg, assoc. regional pastor, Christian Churches, Southern California, commented, "I have the impression the congregation is ready, willing, and able to assist any human being with almost any problem. One gets the impression of being in the midst of the human race at its best: a community of people whose primary concern is to love and to serve."

CONGRESS

A legislator stated on the floor of Congress, "Mr. Speaker, I would like to commend the Rev. James Jones and every member of his congregation for this outstanding demonstration of their commitment to the principles on which this country was founded."

The Rev. Karl Irvin Jr., regional minister-president, The Christian Church of Northern California-Nevada, Disciples of Christ, said "Pastor Jones has a great organizational ability. He has been largely responsible for the establishment of a large congregation of everyday human beings from all walks of life, binding them together in a truly extraordinary commitment to human service. The ministries of this pastor and his congregation are staggering in scope and effectiveness."

SERVES NEEDY

Besides serving the needs of the people in California, Peoples Temple also serves needy in South America. They have acquired a large ocean-going boat which can hold 50 tons of supplies and will be used to transport food produced in the church's agricultural mission to critical hunger regions of the world.

While awaiting the next harvest, the boat is being used to take sick people to hospitals, and delivering food, clothing and other supplies where they are needed by people living in remote areas of South America.

"Jones Honored by Organization," Los Angeles Sentinel, May 29, 1975: "The pastor of Peoples Temple of the Disciples of Christ, James V. Jones, was recently named one of the 100 most outstanding clergymen in the nation by Religion in American Life, an inter-faith organization. Jones was honored for his guidance and inspiration in establishing the many humanitarian programs and facilities in Peoples Temple that attempt to meet every type of human need..."

6/DOCUMENTS

A Conspiracy Behind Peoples Temple Expose?

Berkeley Barb, September 23 - 29, 1977

Indian leader Dennis Banks says he was asked to denounce Rev. Jim Jones.

by Art Silverman

Is the current two-month barrage of sensational charges levelled against San Francisco's Peoples Temple "an organized, orchestrated, premeditated government campaign to destroy a politically-progressive organization," as Temple attorney Charles Garry accuses?

Or is it "a spontaneous, courageous action by a group of former Temple members, who never came forward before because they were scared to death (of reprisals)," the explanation offered by Rosalie Muller Wright, senior editor of New West magazine, which first published and has since supported the accusations?

There still aren't any definitive answers to those questions -- or to the specific allegations of fraud, deceit, real estate swindles and physical brutality raised in numerous media accounts since publication of the first of two New West articles in mid-July (see Barb, July 22).

But a number of unusual circumstances and coincidences can't help but raise the suspicion that there's more going on than first meets the eye. For example:

••A Barb investigation has revealed that one individual working behind the scenes to discredit Peoples Temple is a San Francisco private investigator, who somehow managed to obtain a state investigator's license after being released from prison in 1976.

Joseph A. Mazor, the detective, has a lengthy criminal record including at least eight arrests in three states for various bogus check and fraud charges, six convictions, several jail and prison terms, and has been returned to confinement three times for violating probation and parole by committing new crimes.

A confidential, 16-page California Adult Authority report on Mazor, written in 1970, was recently obtained by the Barb. "(He) is a smooth 'con-man' with an insatiable desire to get ahead," concludes the report. "He is bright, well-educated, and so well-versed in the law that he had five attorneys in the Pomona area convinced that he had a law degree.

"It is felt that the subject is a menace to the community."

Mazor has admitted to the Barb that he was first employed to investigate the Peoples Temple in November 1976, eight months before publication of the first New West article. But he refuses to say who retained him.

"I'm not going to tell you that," said Mazor, though he did reveal that his employer was an outsider, and not a past or present member of Peoples Temple. Mazor said he is currently employed by "several" former Temple members, including Elmer and Deanna Mertle, the original sources for the New West articles.

••Mazor apparently is not only investigating Peoples Temple, but also actively seeking publicity to discredit the organization.

To that end, the Barb has learned, Mazor hired one of the largest public relations firms in San Francisco and then asked them to coordinate a publicity campaign against the Temple and its minister, Reverend Jim Jones.

Bob Kenney, an account executive at Lowry, Russom and Leeper, confirmed for the Barb that he has been working for Mazor "on this (Peoples Temple) project, showing him how to handle the media." He referred further inquiries to Mazor himself, whose only comment on Kenney's role was, "I don't think that's any of your business."

Mazor did note that he originally hired the public relations firm to help him attract business from insurance companies, "and then the Peoples Temple matter just came up, and so naturally I turned to them for help."

But a source close to Lowry, Russom and Leeper told the Barb that Mazor came to the company "saying that he wanted to become San Francisco's next Hal Lipset (a famous investigator)," and that the Peoples Temple controversy "presented an excellent opportunity" to garner publicity.

According to this source, Kenney's work for Mazor included sending out letters to selected journalists, offering them --

Temple leader Rev. Jim Jones

Berkeley Barb, Sept. 23-29, 1977: "Mazor has admitted.. that he was first employed to investigate Peoples Temple... eight months before publication of the New West article. He refuses to say who retained him... he did reveal that his employer was an outsider, not a past or present member of Peoples Temple..."

DOCUMENTS/7

through Mazor -- exclusive material of an incriminating nature against Peoples Temple.

Kenney's campaign resulted in at least one article in the San Francisco Chronicle last month, concerning an alleged tape recording of a telephone conversation, in which Temple members supposedly discussed irregularities on the notary seal of a document transfering title of a member's home to the Temple. The allegations raised in that story are now also in dispute.

**In another strange twist to the Peoples Temple story, American Indian Movement leader Dennis Banks charged recently that he was approached on March 23 by a man who identified himself "as working with the Treasury Department, with an Internal Revenue Service agent, and with two men from the San Francisco Police Department."

The man, who Banks and his associate Lehman Brightman identified as David Conn, then allegedly offered Banks help with his extradition problems in exchange for "a public denunciation" of Jim Jones. Banks is facing possible extradition from California to South Dakota.

Banks has long been a Peoples Temple supporter, and has attended Temple services three or four times. The Temple also made a loan of $19,000 to bail Bank's wife out of prison last year. Her charges were subsequently dropped and the money was returned.

"Conn was obviously making a deal with me," Banks charged in a sworn affadavit presented at a press conference earlier this month. "I was being blackmailed. These agents all knew that I had a lot hanging over me. Besides the extradition, I also had a case in federal court in which the Treasury Department was involved. I have often made it clear that if I am extradited to South Dakota, that is like a sentence of death, because I am certain I will be killed there."

Banks also quoted Conn as saying that he has been investigating Peoples Temple for seven years, and was working with several ex-members, including Grace Stoen, who turned out to be another source for the New West articles.

When reached by the Barb this week, Conn admitted that he has been investigating Peoples Temple for seven years, but said that he had undertaken the project on his own, as a private matter, "because I became aware that this is one of the worst religious frauds being perpetrated. This man is ripping off the black people."

Conn also admitted that he sought out Dennis Banks and arranged a meeting, but his version of what transpired on March 23 was notably different.

"I wanted to talk to Banks because I respect the guy, and I was afraid that he was going to discredit himself through his association with Peoples Temple, without really knowing what they were about."

Conn, a surveyor employed by the Standard Oil Corporation, denies that he ever mentioned Banks' extradition or offered him any deals. He claims that he only mentioned the Treasury Department and other government agencies in passing, pointing out to Banks that they were conducting their own investigations of Reverend Jones and the Temple.

In fact, Conn said, it was he and Santa Rosa freelance journalist George Klineman who approached various police and governmental agencies last fall, offering them witnesses and documents with which to attack the Temple. No investigations were underway before that time.

Both George Klineman and David Conn also have connections to the New West articles -- Klineman was credited with helping write the stories, while Conn was a secondary source and appeared at a New West-sponsored press conference held at the Sheraton Palace Hotel July 20 to help promote the articles.

In addition, Conn is a close personal friend of the Mertles: the main sources for much anti-Temple publicity. By his own admission, Conn was investigating the Temple during all the years that his friends the Mertles were members.

It is also the Mertles who hired private eye Mazor and retained San Francisco attorney Daniel Deneberg to file a lawsuit against the Temple.

But nobody has been served with legal papers yet, and so for the moment there is still no way to get witnesses on the stand, under oath, to try to get at the truth about Peoples Temple once and for all.

Jim Jones is still in Guyana, where he has remained since before publication of the first anti-Temple articles on attorney Garry's orders. According to reports from Guyana, relayed by Garry, there have been two attempts on Jones' life in the last month, one staged by "three white people with guns" who came onto the Temple's 5000-acre mission.

The Dennis Banks press conference, held in Garry's downtown San Francisco office, marks the first time that Temple officials have made any comment about the various charges raised by New West and other media.

But they are still refusing to respond concretely to any particular accusations, on the grounds that they still don't know who is responsible for these attacks.

"We're going to keep our mouths shut," said attorney Garry, "until the dust settles and we get to the bottom of this. It looks like a conspiracy to me."

Are Investigators Trying To Destroy A Progressive Church?

"**Mazor** has admitted that he was first employed to investigate Peoples Temple... eight months before publication of the first New West article. But he refuses to say who retained him... though he did reveal that his employer was an outsider, and not a past or present member of Peoples Temple. [He] is also actively seeking publicity to discredit Peoples Temple... Mazor hired one of the largest public relations firms in San Francisco... Bob Kenney, an account executive at Lowry, Russom and Leeper, confirmed... that he has been working for Mazor 'on this [Peoples Temple] project... [including] sending out letters to selected journalists, offering them -- through Mazor... exclusive material of an incriminating nature.

"...**Conn** identified himself 'as working with the Treasury Department [and] and with an Internal Revenue Service agent'.... Conn... admitted that he has been investigating Peoples Temple for seven years... Conn said he and... journalist George Klineman approached various... governmental agencies... offering them witnesses and documents with which to attack the Temple... In addition, Conn is a close personal friend of the Mertles [a/k/a Mills], the main sources for much anti-Temple publicity. By his own admission, Conn was investigating the Temple during all the years that his friends the Mertles were members."

DECLARATION OF DENNIS BANKS

I, Dennis Banks, declare that I am a citizen of the United States, and that I am 44 years old.

Several months ago, in May 1977, my friend Lehman (Lee) Brightman was contacted on the phone by a man named George Coker. He wanted Lee to set up a meeting between myself and a man named David Conn, concerning the question of my extradition to South Dakota. Naturally I was concerned about this when I was notified of the call. In the next couple of days there were other calls. Lee called David Conn and asked him for some more information about my extradition. Conn told Lee that he wanted to talk to me about Peoples Temple and Jim Jones.

Lee asked Conn what Jim Jones had to do with my extradition. Conn wouldn't tell him. He said it was strictly confidential and that he would only talk about it with him and me personally.

So Lee set up a meeting between myself and David Conn at Lee's house in El Cerrito, for that night.

At the meeting, Conn showed up with a folder of papers. He read notes from the papers. I noticed the paper was stationery from the Standard Oil Company of California. Conn said that he was working with the U. S. Treasury Department, with an IRS agent, and with two men from the San Francisco Police Department. He told me the first name of the Treasury agent (Jim) he was working with. But Conn did not talk about my extradition problem. He read material that was disparaging to Jim Jones. He went on for some time. Finally I interrupted Conn. I asked him what all this stuff about Jim Jones had to do with my extradition. Conn asked me, "Well, you took money from the church, didn't you?" He said that my association with Peoples Temple could reflect very badly on my extradition. He then asked me to make a public denunciation of Jim Jones. He assured me that if I made such a denunciation, the rulings in my extradition would go in my favor. I asked him why a statement against Jim Jones could help my extradition.

Conn said that such a statement would be a determining factor with people like the Governor and other government agencies making decisions about my extradition. He said that if I came out with a statement against Jim Jones that a decision against my extradition could well be forthcoming.

Conn was obviously making a deal with me, and I was being blackmailed.

These agents all knew that I had a lot hanging over me. Besides the extradition (which to me is certainly a life and death matter), I also had a case in Federal Court in which the Treasury Department was involved. I have often made it clear that if I am extradited to South Dakota, that is like a sentence of death, because I am certain that I will be killed there.

So this was definitely a deal that I was being offered. Because it was not just a matter of Conn indicating that it would go well with me if I co-operated, but the implication was that if I didn't co-operate, it would go __badly__ for me. This was to me a threat, and obvious blackmail.

I declare, under penalty of perjury, that all of the foregoing is true and correct, executed this 6th day of September, 1977 at Davis, California.

(signed) *Dennis J. Banks*
DENNIS BANKS

"Conn said that he was working with the U.S. Treasury Department, with an IRS agent, and with two men from the San Francisco Police Department. ...Conn read material that was disparaging to Jim Jones. ...He said that my association with Peoples Temple could reflect very badly on my extradition. He then asked me to make a public denunciation of Jim Jones. He assured me that if I made such a denunciation, the rulings in my extradition would go in my favor. ...Conn was obviously making a deal with me and I was being blackmailed. ...I have often made it clear that if I am extradited to South Dakota, it is like a sentence of death, because I am certain that I will be killed there."

NEW TIMES

A SOVIET WEEKLY OF WORLD AFFAIRS

No. 41, October 1977
Founded 1943

TORONTO STAR
September 4, 1977

A prophet heads south with profit

BY CHARLES OLEY
Special to The Star

SAN FRANCISCO — Moving in small groups, nearly 1,000 people of all ages have left the west coast on a 6,000-mile trek by bus, car and plane for a jungle sanctuary in Guyana.

They acted under secret orders from their leader, Jones, 45, a new white "prophet of God" who predicts a Fascist takeover of the United States followed by a nuclear holocaust.

Last week, when Jones was found to have joined the migration himself, thousands of the faithful from Los Angeles to Vancouver mourned the loss of their leader, not to mention millions of dollars in church funds.

Shock waves are also running through the California establishment. Politicians, bankers and businessmen who courted Jones' favor, praised his good works and benefitted from his formidable political clout, have gone to ground.

The handsome Jim Jones, who arrived from an obscure midwest mission 12 years ago, is no backwoods preacher, but a prominent local figure — foreman of a San Francisco grand jury, chairman of the housing commission, with aides who have also been eased into well paid public posts.

Profits of a Prophet

Self-styled Californian "messiah," Jim Jones proclaimed that he was resurrected from the dead, and could do the same for others, and also cure every disease. Recruiting a large following, he "purified" them by pitilessly trouncing them with tongue and stick. Claiming a "revelation," the "prophet" has now vanished into a Latin American jungle, with some thousand "disciples" and the millions he had stashed away.

"A prophet heads south with profit," and "Profits of a Prophet": Identically-worded smears in the press of two foreign countries thousands of miles apart: Toronto, Canada (where there is a large concentration of Guyanese immigrants) and the former Soviet Union, which Jim Jones was trying to befriend. These appeared within weeks of the beginning of the smear campaign in San Francisco.

TO THE JUNGLE FROM THE "FREE WORLD" AROUND THE WORLD TASS NEWS AGENCY

"In the Northwest part of Guyana, in the very heart of the jungle, for the last several years the small town of Jonestown has been established. It is a town surrounded by croplands cleared out of the vast jungle rain forests. The town and farm are owned by members of the commune consisting of more than one thousand pioneers. They left their motherland because of suppression and as a sign of protest against racial and political discrimination. All the inhabitants of Jonestown are members of the People Temple organization uniting the lower strata of American society -- white, black, Indian and other -- those who had been denied basic human rights.

Its founder, Rev. Jim Jones, tested all the promised "good" of American democracy. After being sure that his attempts to find justice in America were in vain, Jonestown called a vanguard of his supporters to leave the "Free World" where they had failed to find a place. "I have chosen Guyana," Rev. Jim Jones told the Tass correspondent, "first of all because this country is socialist oriented and is working toward the establishment of socialism for the most just and human society in the world." Peoples Temple expressed its readiness to assist the people of Guyana in this endeavor.

The Parliament of Guyana has given this community a leasehold on 27.000 acres in the Northwest part of the country. The first group of settlers arrive in 1974. Each year more and more members of Peoples Temple join the collective: workers, farmers, white collar workers, teachers, lawyers, and other professionals. Among them are many young people who in the United States were refused the right to work.

Today's Jonestown has neat houses, farm buildings, dining halls, schools, kindergartens, some cottage industries, gives free medical service to not only members of the commune but also to surrounding villagers. Special care is given to the children. There are about 250 children in the town, many of them adopted. No less care is given to the seniors, about 100 of them, in Jonestown. After being in Jonestown, one can hardly believe that everything was created in one or two years. The inhabitants of Jonestown are creative, they love work and they celebrate life. They demonstrate real care and concern for children and seniors alike.

The movies and literature about socialism and socialist countries are very popular among the people of Jonestown. Jim Jones explains that socialism is the only way to realize true civil and human rights and democratic freedoms."

Tass Correspondent Voropaev
Georgetown, Guyana, South America

(Translation from the Russian)

Charles Garry Visits Jonestown: 'I Have Been To Paradise'

On Nov. 6 Peoples Temple welcomed Charles Garry, who represents Peoples Temple as its attorney. Garry has recently returned from a visit to the temple's agricultural project in Guyana, Jonestown (so named by the Guyanese government). He had much information to share.

"Last Monday night I was on a talk show," he began, "and I had the opportunity to tell that I had seen and I had been in paradise. I saw it. It's there for anybody to see, and I'm hopeful that in the next few day or weeks we'll be able to have a documentary, which everyone will be able to see.

"I saw community where there is no such thing as racism. No one feels the color of his skin, whether he's Black, brown, yellow, red, or white. I also noticed that no one thinks in terms of sex. No one feels superior to anyone else. I don't know of any community in the world today that has been able to solve the problem of male sex supremacy completely. That does not exist in Jonestown.

"I also saw something else: There is no such thing as age-ism. The community is comprised of the little children, the teen-agers, the young adults, the old adults, the senior citizens, all together.

"I have never seen so many happy faces in my life as I did in Jonestown the three days I was there. I want that captured (on film) so that skeptical America will know what it is when you live without fear of the rent being due, and all the other problems we're surrounded by.

"There are some 800 persons or more there now. They've got cottages set up that you just could not believe. I saw sanitation there that I had never seen in any part of the world, except Switzerland. You can eat off the ground."

He went on to speak of the consistently high level of medical care, organized under a doctor who is "thorough, conscientious and dedicated." The medical team has "the latest in medical equipment and books," and "every person who goes to Jonestown is medically thoroughly examined, and charts are prepared." He recalls that he urged Dr. Schacht to start keeping daily, hourly diaries, to put the operation of the medical compound in writing, so that some of our medical schools, and the American Medical Association, can learn from what is being done at Jonestown.

A high point of his talk related to the care of senior citizens, which he said moved him deeply. "All of the senior citizens' cottages are built around the immediate vicinity of the medical compound. Every single morning a member of the medical team knocks on the cottage of the senior citizen and inquires, 'Did anybody have any problem during the night? Do you have any problems here this morning?' Can you imagine the security that the senior citizens feel with this kind of care? I'd like to have a representative from a body here that's trying to improve the lot of senior citizens who are left to be beggars and paupers to see what is going on in Jonestown."

He spoke of the many agricultural projects, including an improvised method of developing feed from protein food grown in Jonestown. The area of Jonestown devoted to raising animals also drew praise. "Those pigpens, as we call them, looked like palaces. Many of the homes that I've seen in America could not measure up to the sanitation, the cleanliness, the spaciousness of the place we call a pigpen." The chickens raised and butchered at the project he called "luscious," and the food generally is "delicate, nourishing that will make your blood pressure go down; your diabetes will disappear. It's substantial, nourishing food—the kind that will take away the fat you accumulate by the type of food we eat here."

The project as a whole is described as quite developed: a thriving sawmill, generators to meet electrical needs, wells, streets refrigeration. The school is open-air, in a large covered area, with 15 to 20 youngsters in a class. Teachers are drawn, in part, from "at least 50 people there who have advanced degrees." He spoke of the enthusiastic participation and discussion on the part of all the students, which is something he had not seen here, with the exception of the Oakland Community School.

Does Jonestown lack for entertainment and fun? Not at all, Garry says. "There's this beautiful auditorium, and for three-and-a-half hours I saw the most beautiful entertainment in the world. I've never seen such talent in my life. I saw children from toddlers through about the age of seven putting on a demonstration, with voice, and clapping, and marching, and children six and seven years old getting up and reciting poetry with meaning and gusto. It was just remarkable.

"Why are those people so happy?" he mused again. "They are learning a new social order. They are learning an answer to a better life. When I returned to the States, I told my partners in the office that I had seen paradise. From what I saw there, I would say that the society that is being built in Jonestown is a credit to humanity."

And then, as if to reinforce the amazing description, he added, "This is not propaganda. I'm not a propagandist. I'm a hard-hitting, factual-analysis lawyer. I saw this with my own eyes. I felt it."

12/DOCUMENTS

THIS NIGHTMARE IS TAKING PLACE RIGHT NOW

WILL YOU HELP US FREE OUR FAMILIES?

WHO ARE THE "CONCERNED RELATIVES"?

We are individuals having only one bond in common; relatives isolated in the "Jonestown" jungle encampment in Guyana, South America, under the total control of one man, Jim Jones. We espouse no political or religious viewpoint. Our only concern is for our families. We are bewildered and frightened by what is being done to them. Their human rights are being violated and the fabric of our family life is being torn apart.

WHAT SPECIFICALLY IS BEING DONE TO OUR RELATIVES?

These are the sad and terrible facts:

* All decisions in Jonestown are made by one man, Jim Jones. There is no democracy. There is no dissent permitted.

* Guards are stationed around Jonestown to prevent anyone leaving unless given express permission by the leader.

* Passports and monies are confiscated by Jones upon the arrival of his members in Guyana so that they cannot be "cleared" by the Immigration Officials to leave Guyana.

* Long distance telephone calls to the United States are prohibited as part of Jones' campaign that all family ties be cut in favor of his "cause".

* All incoming and outgoing mail is censored.

* Barbed wire fences have been built to prevent escape.

* Closed circuit television has been installed for internal surveillance.

* No one is permitted to leave Jonestown except on business for the "cause" and then only in the company of other residents who are required to spy and report back to Jones.

* Each resident is told that if he or she tries to leave the Peoples Temple organization, they will be killed and their bodies left in the jungle.

**JONESTOWN
CONCENTRATION CAMP
GUYANA, SOUTH AMERICA**

-over-

TIMOTHY STOEN (who had NO RELATIVES AT JONESTOWN) founds the "Concerned Relatives," to smear a peaceful, acclaimed community as a "NIGHTMARE" and a "CONCENTRATION CAMP," complete with "barbed wire," "closed circuit t.v." and "guards to prevent escape."

DOCUMENTS/13

The Food at Jonestown -- Plentiful and Delicious!

"The food here is great -- everyone eats lots... Think of the one person who used to pile their plate with food then double it and you have the amount most adults eat here. The children eat the amount of the size of the plate before doubling it. I'm not joking either. I've never seen anything like it."
(Handwritten letter)

"Greg and I live in our own cottage. We fixed it up really nice. I've planted eggplant along the sides. . . . some beans growing up the house. On the right side of the porch are cucumbers. I'm thinking of planting a papaya tree in the back of the house. . . ."
Erin Watkins

"Our strong forte is agricultural. . . we have an endless supply of greens, black-eyed peas and other delicious wonders. . . . Jim just ate an exceptional cookie that someone invented. . . "
Penny Kerns

"Talk about delicious food. . . . you can't beat the menu at Jonestown!"
Maria McCann

"Maybe you've never heard of the Ice Cream Tree -- well, we have it! It's green outside with soft spines and a slightly fibrous green pulp inside. When ripe -- split open and eat it with a spoon. It's like eating sherbet ice cream! . . . I am also learning how to graft and bud citrus trees, all of our citrus scions are budded onto rough lemon or bitter orange root stocks which are very vigorous stocks."
Mike Rozynko

"The food here is so good that you wouldn't want to taste the food in the States no more."
Maurice Anderson

"All of our foods are natural. What a relief to get <u>real</u> food. The food here is so good and you can have as much as you want. The fruit is so good."
Diane Lundquist

"We eat very well! Tomorrow morning I think we're having biscuits with syrup, eggs, cracklin's and coffee or tea."
To Jakela Wetzel

"This is a land of plenty. . . the food which we are growing, it is so good. Sweet potatoes, mustard greens, squash, all kinds of beans, bananas, watermelon, pineapple, cassava and oh, so many other. . .[and] cereals which we grow."
Magaline Lyles

"The food here is <u>great</u>! The bread tastes like a donut that melts in your mouth. Remember the saying that 'man cannot live on bread alone.' Well, that is a lie 'cause here you can. The chicken, pancakes, greens and everything else you can and can't think of, you name it we got it or can get it."
Glenda Polite

"I'm now working in the Jonestown Bakery. We are making all sorts of different kinds of cookies, breads, and many other good things."
(Handwritten letter)

"Joan is fine, stuffing herself daily. . . ."
Christine Lucientes

14/DOCUMENTS

"I'm back on the farm again -- my favorite place to be. In these last two weeks, we have planted (our crew alone) 25 acres of pasture grass for our newly-arrived cows and 2 horses: 15 acres sweet and starleaf potatoes: 2 acres pineapple, not to mention the harvesting and crop maintenance work done in-between. Jim has really been pushing our production level in the effort to unite all of our family (you guys!) here with us.   Ronnie James

"You have never tasted food until you eat here."   Patricia Houston

"We plant and grow and pick all the food we eat instead of eating a bunch of food that is not good for us like in the states."   Judy Houston

"We have planted over 300 pineapple plants the other day, 3 acres of eddoes, 2 acres of cassava. We do a variety of jobs harvesting papaya, greens, cutlass beans, everything -- it's great!"   Marlene Wheeler

"Now let me tell you about the food! We have for breakfast pancakes, they are bigger than four hands put together, we all can't even handle one and if you don't believe it when you get here you will."   Alfreda March

"I work on the banana crew and now I know all about growing and taking care of bananas. We pick about 1,650 pounds of bananas every two weeks. The banana bread and puddings that the kitchen make are fantastic."   Gary Tyler

"Wait until you taste our homemade fudge!! Yum! Yum! It's just delicious. Everything is amazingly fantastic."   Rose McKnight

"One of my favorite jobs is climbing in and our of the windrows in search of eddoes. The windrows are the most excellent spot for our banana trees. (We have a couple of thousand by the way.) They are the long curving area where the trees and bush were pushed when the land was originally cleared.....Wait 'til you taste our Jonestown -- casava cookies, casava cornbread, donuts, bread, biscuits, all made in expertly-made wood burning ovens and stoves. They are the best you have ever eaten -- and you know how I love donuts!"
     Mary Lou Clancey

"The food is so good that you can eat, eat and eat and never get fat..."
     (Handwritten letter)

"We eat like kings. I mean we really eat our asses off.   (Handwritten letter)

"I tasted my first piece of sugar cane, it is very sweet here. And I tasted milo drink. It is a drink that tastes like chocolate and marshmallow. Then last night we had cassava and some very good chicken. Down here bananas grow so big you could eat them for a year."   Frances Buckley

"The longer I am here, the more I marvel at the fields of vegetables, bananas, pineapples and many plantings I don't know. Philip was telling me that we are going to plant peanuts."   "Lisa"

NOTE: There is no mention of <u>rice</u> in all these glowing reports. Where are the meager rice rations Ms. Layton-Blakey claimed to have been forced to eat in lieu of three meals a day? The staple in Jonestown, in fact, was cassava, a root vegetable, not wheat or rice.

EXCERPTS FROM AFFIDAVIT OF DEBORAH LAYTON BLAKEY

I, DEBORAH LAYTON BLAKEY, declare the following under penalty of perjury:

3. ...I had grown up in affluent circumstances in the permissive atmosphere of Berkeley, California.

6. The Rev. Jones... convinced black Temple members that if they did not follow him to Guyana, they would be put into concentration camps and killed. White members were instilled with the belief that their names appeared on a secret list of enemies of the state that was kept by the C.I.A. and that they would be tracked down, tortured, imprisoned, and subsequently killed if they did not flee to Guyana.

14. Rev. Jones has expressed particular bitterness toward Grace Stoen. Her personal qualities of generosity and compassion made her very popular with the membership. Her departure posed a threat to Rev. Jones' absolute control.

15. I am informed that Rev. Jones believed that he would be able to stop Timothy Stoen, husband of Grace Stoen and father of John Victor Stoen, from speaking against the Temple as long as the child was being held in Guyana.

20. Conditions at Jonestown were even worse than I had feared they would be. The settlement was swarming with armed guards.

22. The food was woefully inadequate. There was rice for breakfast, rice water soup for lunch, and rice and beans for dinner.

33. Life at Jonestown was so miserable and the physical pain of exhaustion was so great that... I had become indifferent as to whether I lived or died.

I declare under penalty of perjury that the foregoing is true and correct, except as to those matters stated on information and belief and as to those I believe them to be true. Executed this 15 day of June, 1978 at San Francisco, California.

Deborah Layton Blakey
DEBORAH LAYTON BLAKEY

16/DOCUMENTS
THE MERCENARY ATTACK AND ITS TIMING:
RELEASE THE CHILD "OR ELSE"???

THE EVENT

"In September 1977, for about seven days, shots were fired into Jonestown from out of the jungle. Myself and about fifteen others from the security team were stationed at the front entrance and various points around Jonestown with guns. Several of these people did fire at those firing from the jungle, and I witnessed this.

The first day during this period, I was doing electrical work around Jim Jones' cottage and a shot was fired into the cottage while Jim Jones was inside. Marceline Jones was also in the cottage at that time, and ran out shouting for security to come. She said the bullet had whizzed right in front of Jim's face.

Myself and several others on the security team examined the bullet holes where the bullet had gone through a wall of the cottage, and where the bullet was lodged in the door frame. We recovered the bullet. It had come from a 3030 Winchester, a type of rifle we did not have in Jonestown. The identification of the bullet came from Doug Sanders, an Army veteran, who lived in Jonestown and was a head of security."

In September 1977, for about seven days, shots were fired into Jonestown from out of the jungle. Myself and about fifteen others from the security team were stationed at the front entrance and various points around Jonestown with guns. Several of these people did fire at those firing from the jungle, and I witnessed this.

The first day during this period, I was doing electrical work around Jim Jones' cottage and a shot was fired into the cottage while Jim Jones was inside. Marceline Jones was also in the cottage at that time, and ran out shouting for security to come. She said the bullet had whizzed right in front of Jim's face.

Myself and several others on the security team examined the bullet holes where the bullet had gone through a wall of the cottage, and where the bullet was lodged in the door frame. We recovered the bullet. It had come from a 3030 Winchester, a type of rifle we did not have in Jonestown. The identification of the bullet came from Doug Sanders, an Army veteran, who lived in Jonestown and was a head of security

Subscribed and sworn to before me this
___ day of _____ 19___
_____ Notary Public

OFFICIAL SEAL
CHARLES J. VARSALLO
NOTARY PUBLIC - CALIFORNIA
SAN FRANCISCO CITY
My comm. expires ___ 1, 1981
2564 San Bruno Avenue, San Francisco, CA 94134

Chuck Kirkendoll

Witnessed by:

John Davis

AFFIDAVIT OF CHUCK KIRKENDOLL

ITS TIMING

San Francisco Examiner, Fri., Sept. 9, 1977, "Rev. Jones Hushed by Lawyer": "Moments before yesterday's press conference [i.e. September 8], Garry said he had received a telephone call from a church member in Guyana who reported *the second attempt in four days* [i.e. September 4 on] *had just been made on Jones' life.*"

San Francisco Chronicle, Wed., Sept. 21, 1977, "Temple Leader Is Accused in Custody Case": A San Francisco attorney... Jeffrey Haas [attorney for the Stoens' custody case] said *he spent three weeks in the South American country* where Jones has apparently relocated... attempting to obtain custody of John Stoen... Haas said that on August 24, San Francisco Superior Court Judge Donald King signed a temporary custody order granting Grace Stoen custody of the boy. The attorney then flew to Georgetown and obtained a... ruling from local judiciary that required Jones' to appear in court... Haas then flew to the backcountry mission to serve the papers... He said the church apparently was alarmed over the legal wrangle ["legal wrangle" or shooting??] -- enough so to have most temple members stay indoors at the mission on his second visit... Haas, who returned here Sunday [i.e. September 18]...

Page 6—S.F. EXAMINER ☆ Fri., Sept. 9, 1977

Moments before yesterday's press conference, Garry said he had received a telephone call from a church member in Guyana who reported the second attempt in four days had just been made on Jones' life.

Garry and his investigator, Pat Richartz, said three persons visited the 900-acre mission four days ago and when they left, shots were fired at Jones. Garry said he did not know if the visitors were involved in the shooting, nor did he know if they were Americans or Guyanese.

Jones has been at the temple's agricultural mission in Guyana and has been unavailable to respond to charges against him, although temple officials have denied all allegations.

Garry said yesterday that the attacks on Jones are part of a seven-year-long conspiracy "to destroy and eliminate the temple as a force in the community."

Wed., Sept. 21, 1977 San Francisco Chronicle

A San Francisco attorney charged yesterday that the Rev. Jim Jones, leader of the controversial Peoples Temple, has evaded in the United States and Guyana court orders to return a five-year-old boy to his mother, a former temple member.

Jeffrey Haas said he spent three weeks in the South American country, where Jones has apparently relocated his top staff and 500 followers, attempting to obtain custody of John Stoen, the son of Grace Stoen, who left the church last year.

Haas then flew to the backcountry mission to serve the papers, but was told by church aides that the minister was not around.

He said the church apparently was alarmed over the legal wrangle—enough so to have most temple members stay indoors at the mission on his second visit.

Haas, who returned here Sunday,

18/DOCUMENTS

AFFIDAVITS RE PATERNITY OF JOHN VICTOR STOEN

TO WHOM IT MAY CONCERN

I, Timothy Oliver Stoen, hereby acknowledge that in April, 1971, I entreated my beloved pastor, James W. Jones, to sire a child by my wife, Grace Lucy (Grech) Stoen, who had previously, at my insistence, reluctantly but graciously consented thereto. James W. Jones agreed to do so, reluctantly, after I explained that I very much wished to raise a child, but was unable, after extensive attempts, to sire one myself. My reason for requesting James W. Jones to do this is that I wanted my child to be fathered, if not by me, by the most compassionate, honest, and courageous human being the world contains.

The child, John Victor Stoen, was born on January 25, 1972. I am privileged beyond words to have the responsibility for caring for him, and I undertake this task humbly with the steadfast hope that said child will become a devoted follower of Jesus Christ and be instrumental in bringing God's kingdom here on earth, as has been his wonderful natural father.

I declare under penalty of perjury that the foregoing is true and correct.

Timothy Oliver Stoen
Post Office Box 126
Ukiah, California 95482

Dated: February 6, 1972

Witnessed: _____ (Marceline M. Jones)

State of California   )
) ss.   AFFIDAVIT OF
City and County of San Francisco)   DEBORAH BLAKEY

I, Deborah Blakey, being duly sworn, declare:

I was a close friend of Grace Gretch Stoen. She would often confide and talk with me especially when I was newer into the Temple organization and I didn't know too many people. Her son, she told me, was Bishop Jim Jones' child.

There was never any question about Jim being the true father of John.

Dated this 20 day of August, 1977

Subscribed and sworn before me, a Notary Public in and for the State of California

NOTARY PUBLIC

Official Seal
James R. Randolph
Notary Public - Calif.
Principal Office in
Mendocino County
My commission expires Oct. 7, 1978

Tim has gone out + bought
1 wig
2 negligee's
1 slip
nylons
woman's underwear

I jumped on him hard, and he told me to mind my own business. I told him he did NOT have the privelge to do such things + I was pissed. I said for John's sake not to do this. He said, "Oh, I think its more than that!" (Implying me). I told him I did not care for him, didn't bother him (he agreed) + wanted nothing to do with him, etc. He told me to get fucked. I told him he was defensive, + would bring to council. He said fine......

Grace Stoen's note of complaint to Jim Jones about her husband Tim's transvestite patterns: "Tim has gone out and bought 1 wig, 2 negligees, 1 slip, nylons, woman's underwear. I jumped on him hard... He told me to get fucked. I told him he was defensive, and would bring to council. He said fine..."

Viewpoint / Ukiah Daily Journal
← Thursday, April 13, 1978

Editorial

Trouble brewing in Guyana

A potentially explosive situation is brewing in Jonestown, Guyana.

On Tuesday of this week some twenty-five relatives of Jones' followers who are residing in Jonestown, the Guyana settlement, led by Steve Katsaris, went to the Temple headquarters in San Francisco.

Katsaris' 24-year-old daughter Maria, who has resided in Jonestown since last summer, has indicated through letters to her parents that she is satisfied to stay in Guyana. Katsaris accuses Jones of violating human rights by holding relatives as virtual captives.

ONE FATHER HAS EVEN THREATENED TO HIRE MERCENARIES TO RAID JONESTOWN AND "LIBERATE" HIS SON BY FORCE. TROUBLE THAT COULD LEAD TO AN INTERNATIONAL INCIDENT MAY LIE AHEAD.

99

```
9-23-78    Embassy reports a press conference by
           attorney Mark Lane in Georgetown in which
           he charges that the U.S. Government is
           conspiring to destroy the People's Temple
           in Jonestown.  Lane reportedly threatened
           to file suit against government officials
           and agencies including the CIA, the FBI,
           and the Department of State.
           (Georgetown 3098 - Log 142)

9-25-78    Embassy responds to Department's request
           for views outlining the logistical problems
           in visiting Jonestown and emphasizing the
           need to get prior agreement of the People's
           Temple.
           (Georgetown 3125 - Log 143)

10-3-78    Mr. Tim Stoen informs the Department that,
           in view of the failure of the judicial
           process in Guyana, he is prepared to re-
           trieve his son by force if necessary.
           (Log 587)
```

From the U.S. State Dept. Embassy log in Georgetown, Guyana. 10/3/78: Mr. Tim Stoen informs the Department that, in view of the failure of the judicial process in Guyana, he is prepared to retrieve his son by force if necessary. (Log 587)

Page 20—S.F. EXAMINER ☆ Wed., Oct. 4, 1978

People's Temple colony 'harassed'

People's Temple, its leader the Rev. Jim Jones and its Jonestown colony in Guyana are under a heavily financed attack by the U.S. intelligence establishment, Mark Lane charged here.

Lane, a Washington lawyer, educator and author whose works include "Rush To Judgment," a book on the John Kennedy assassination, is a director of Citizens Commission Inquiry and was invited by its local chapter to look into temple affairs.

He appeared at a news conference at the temple in San Francisco yesterday after a trip to Guyana.

Attacks on the colony, both in Guyana and in Congress, have been financed with large sums of money "laundered through banks in neutral countries," and there is evidence of "a concerted effort by the U.S. intelligence establishment to destroy Jonestown," Lane said.

Included in the effort was a trans-jungle trek by a party of 20 men armed with rocket launchers and small arms, Lane said. He declined to name the leader of the group, whom he characterized as an employee of Interpol, the international police coordination agency.

He said the leader gave him a full statement because "he said he felt misused." The group had been sent to fire on the colony's generator building, darkening the compound, after cutting their way through the supposed barbed wire and minefields around the compound. After darkening the area, Lane said, they had planned to "free the children" from the supposed evil influences of the colony.

When they discovered there were no minefields nor barbed wire, Lane said, they contented themselves with sniping at the compound for six days. Lane related that the patrol leader told him he was amazed to be invited to visit the colony and stayed there several days.

"He told me he was satisfied that the 'concentration camp' charges against Jonestown were false and that he thought he had been misused," Lane said.

Lane declined to name the agent, but hinted that he might be named after the filing of a multi-million-dollar suit against the government, which Lane said could be expected "within 90 days."

The suit will charge, he said, that a host of federal agencies are doing all they can — much of it illegally — to scuttle the Jonestown colony.

To be named as defendants, he said, are the FBI, CIA, Department of State, Internal Revenue Service, Treasury Department, Postal Service and virtually everybody but the Coast and Geodetic Survey.

The motive for the alleged government conspiracy, he said, is that the colony of 1,200 American expatriates is an embarrassment to the government because of its success.

As to charges that people once in the colony are not free to leave, he said that the U.S. Embassy staff has on several occasions sent a car to the colony and offered anyone who wanted one a free ride to the airport and a free flight home.

On the other hand, at another point in his dissertation, he said there are no roads to the colony but that transportation is available by boat or a complicated series of train trips or flights.

Lane was backed up by four persons who had recently returned from the colony, and by Jones wife, Marceline, also recently returned.

Mrs. Jones said that her husband had remained in Guyana because of the advice of his attorneys and because his presence is needed there.

MARK LANE
Accuses U.S. agencies

"Attacks on the colony... have been financed with large sums of money 'laundered through banks in neutral countries'... Included in the effort was a trans-jungle trek by... men armed with rocket launchers and small arms, Lane said... The group had been sent to fire on the colony's generator building, darkening the compound, after cutting their way through the supposed barbed wire and minefields... [Then] they had planned to 'free the children" from the supposed evil influences of the colony... When they discovered there were no minefields nor barbed wire, they contented themselves with sniping at the compound for six days. ... The patrol leader was amazed to be invited to visit the colony and stayed several days..."

NOTE: Whatever Lane's tarnished credibility, it must be noted that he went on record with these claims, in the capacity of Peoples Temple attorney, which in turn was used to bring an extremely dangerous man right into Jonestown towards the last -- namely, Joseph Mazor. There was no documentary "proof" offered of leadership of the mercenary raid, though obviously, Mazor would never have been let into Jonestown if the raid itself had not really happened.

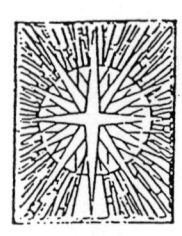

PEOPLES TEMPLE
OF THE DISCIPLES OF CHRIST
Jim Jones, Pastor

November 17, 1978

FOR IMMEDIATE RELEASE

Congressman Leo Ryan arrived in Jonestown, Guyana, late this afternoon where he was warmly greeted. He was accompanied by his aide, press representatives from the Washington Post, San Francisco Examiner, San Francisco Chronicle, and NBC Network News, in addition to several relatives of residents of Jonestown. They are staying overnight and will also spend the day in Jonestown tomorrow. Congressman Ryan conducted about a dozen private interviews with residents of Jonestown as part of his fact-finding probe of the community. During a conversation with Jim Jones and members of the press, Congressman Ryan said: "All that is being done here is significant, valuable and worthwhile, even of great significance on a worldwide basis."

Later, after completing a number of interviews, the Congressman remarked to over 1,000 assembled residents of Jonestown: "I hear many of you saying that this is the greatest thing that has ever happened to you." His statement was met with a thunderous round of ovation. Said the Congressman: "The reception has been very friendly. We have all had a very good time here."

"Congressman Ryan conducted about a dozen private interviews with residents of Jonestown as part of his fact-finding probe of the community. During a conversation with Jim Jones and members of the press, Congressman Ryan said: 'All that is being done here is significant, valuable and worthwhile, even of great significance on a worldwide basis.' Later, after completing a number of interviews, the Congressman remarked to over 1,000 assembled residents of Jonestown: 'I hear many of you saying that this is the greatest thing that has ever happened to you.' His statement was met with a thunderous round of ovation."

—To the extent that violence was considered a possibility by the Ryan Codel, there is evidence to suggest that Mr. Ryan may have looked on the accompanying media group as a "shield"; conversely, to the extent there was any apprehension in their ranks, the media regarded Mr. Ryan's status as a Congressman as their best protection. For other members of the media, the principal potential danger considered was the jungle against which they protected themselves by taking special supplies.

E. U.S Customs Service Investigation

One key element relating to the question of whether the Ryan Codel had adequate awareness of the potential for danger as well as the degree of violence which ultimately ensued involves a 1977 U.S. Customs Service investigation of reported illegal gun shipments and other contraband to Jonestown (see Appendix III-E, in classified version only). In the course of this inquiry, therefore, the Staff Investigative Group obtained evidence which warrants the following findings on the subject:

—Working on allegations interspersed amid many "bizarre" tales about People's Temple, the investigation was begun in February 1977. One of the allegations contended that more than 170 weapons once stored in Ukiah had been transferred to People's Temple San Francisco headquarters and then possibly on to Jonestown. The investigation was compromised 1 month after it began, not through any inadvertence on the part of the Customs Service, but when an individual conveyed some information on the matter to Dennis Banks, head of the American Indian Movement, in an effort to dissuade Banks from any further contact with Jones. That conversation was apparently taped and word was passed to Jones. Complete details of the investigation's report were further compromised when a copy of the report was sent to Interpol. From Interpol it was, by normal procedure, shared with the Guyanese police. According to information provided us, Guyanese Police Commissioner C. A. "Skip" Roberts reportedly showed a copy to either Paula Adams or Carolyn Layton, two of Mr. Jones' trusted aides, one of whom passed the information to Mr. Jones.

—Although the Customs Service investigation was not diluted or diminished in any way, it is clear that it was carried out in an unusually sensitive mode because of what was perceived to be Jim Jones' considerable political influence in San Francisco. Surveillance relating to the investigation was virtually impossible to carry out because of the tight security screen Jones placed around the Geary Street headquarters of People's Temple in San Francisco.

—The investigation was concluded in August–September 1977 after a shipment of crates destined for Jonestown was opened and inspected by the Customs Service in Miami in August 1977. Shortly thereafter a report on the investigation was filed with negative results. Nonetheless, investigators apparently felt enough residual suspicion to send copies of the report to Interpol and the U.S.

Attempts to portray Jonestown as "an armed camp" lead to a Customs probe. (In reality, the Guyanese discovered all of 39 weapons at Jonestown in the wake of the tragedy, the Americans 40, and none of them automatic.) The following is how the Conn/Banks blackmail attempt was "re-written" for the Congressional report:

"The investigation was compromised 1 month after it began… when an individual conveyed some information on the matter to Dennis Banks, head of the American Indian Movement, in an effort to dissuade Banks from any further contact with Jones."

24/DOCUMENTS

MARK LANE PARADES A RAT, THEN
CHARGES TOP DOLLAR FOR RAT POISON

The initial element in Mr. Lane's intelligence-gathering campaign proved to be an unsuccessful attempt to win over Joseph A. Mazor, a San Francisco-based private investigator who became a vocal critic of Jonestown.

In early October, Mr. Lane took Mr. Mazor to lunch with two reporters, Robert Levering of The San Francisco Bay Guardian and Hal Jacques of The National Enquirer, telling them he thought Mr. Mazor would give them the story of the plot against the Temple.

Mr. Levering recalled, however, that Mr. Lane seemed to be trying to push Mr. Mazor "farther than he wanted to go."

Asked recently about the source for his allegations of C.I.A. efforts to destroy Jonestown, Mr. Lane said: "A large part came from Joe Mazor."

Miss Brown said she recalled an occasion when Mr. Lane tried to prevent an unfavorable article from appearing in The National Enquirer.

In an affidavit, Miss Brown said she flew to Los Angeles and was met by Mr. Lane, who asserted that the article "had to be stopped" and told her to return to San Francisco and seek permission from Jonestown to give him an additional $10,000 "so that he might acquire and respond to the impending article."

Permission was granted, and the next day Miss Brown again met Mr. Lane in the Los Angeles airport. "He asked for the money," Miss Brown said in her affidavit. "I handed him $10,000 cash and asked him to please try to get the price down if he could."

She said Mr. Lane indicated someone from the Enquirer was at the airport and took the money and disappeared, returning more than an hour later with a sheaf of typewritten pages.

"The article was extremely negative about the People's Temple," she said. When she expressed alarm, she said, Mr. Lane suggested, "Well, a hundred thousand might stop it" from being published. Miss Brown said she dismissed the suggestion out of hand.

Mr. Lane has acknowledged that he obtained a copy of the article but would not say from whom. He said he had the article in a locker at the airport and that he returned to Miss Brown with it in a matter of minutes. He added that he had obtained the article for free and had told Miss Brown he needed the $10,000 to finance an investigation of the article's charges. "I said, 'Funds are required to immediately check out every allegation,'" Mr. Lane said.

The Enquirer article was never published. Mr. Levering, the Bay Guardian reporter, recalled that at the Oct. 5 lunch Mr. Lane expressed interest in the article and Mr. Jacques told him the newspaper "had canned it, or words to that effect."

> Asked recently about the source for his allegations of C.I.A. efforts to destroy Jonestown, Mr. Lane said: "A large part came from Joe Mazor.

THE NEW YORK TIMES, SUNDAY, MARCH 4, 1979

"Mr. Lane took Mr. Mazor to lunch with... Hal Jacques of *The National Enquirer*... Mr. Lane [then] tried to prevent an unfavorable article from appearing... and told her [Jean Brown] to 'give him an additional $10,000' so that he might acquire the impending article... 'I handed him $10,000 cash'... He [later admitted] he had obtained the article for free... Mr. Lane [then] suggested that 'Well, $100,000 might stop it' from being published..."

INTERVIEW WITH JOSEPH A. MAZOR AND DONALD FREED, WITH PAT RICHARTZ AND MARK LANE

SEPTEMBER 5, 1978   12:30 P.M.

D.F. The principle investors in this are concerned with two things. They like the idea of a controversy in a real life story, in a real foreign country and a real large group of people, and the colorful idea. They are afraid of an errors and omissions insurance policy becoming difficult when there is so much litigation around an issue.

M.L. Do you know about errors and omissions insurance policies?

J.M. I carry it, yeah.

M.L. For films? They are hard to get in films unless ....

D.F. Mr. Mazor, I don't know if you know any of the Graham Greene novels, but they definitely that dimension, and that is beautiful Guyana, lush tropics, etc. etc. But. Intrigue. The files that have been developed -- and I want to be very frank, I don't want to play poker -- so far go back in the case of one principle to Berlin, the border between West and East Germany in the early sixties, and Rotary International, and through some research firms and down to today and a lot of money being spent and a lot of "daring-do" going on in Georgetown, sniping-- and you told us about the extraordinary story of someone with a rifle across from your office -- and gunfire in jungles of Jonestown....

P.R. Did. I miss something about gunfire....

D.F. Well, just before you came in Joseph was saying....

M.L. He had nothing to do with the Temple, he was just a fringe nut that had read some of the newspaper stuff and got up on the roof -- not a Temple member.

. . . . . .

J.M. I'd like to have a copy. Do I get a copy of Jim Jones' letter?

D.F. I think, yes.

J.M. OK.

P.R. Then you want me to type something up?

D.F. I do, Pat, I want to type up what Ingrid didn't finish, and I want to type up the idea of Joe going to Jonestown.

September 5, 1978 interview with Joseph A. Mazor, Mark Lane, Donald Freed and Pat Richartz (Charles Garry's assistant). Interview promotes Mazor starring in a film about his (alleged leadership of) the mercenary raid on Jonestown, discusses Tim Stoen's suspect connections at length, and closes with "I want to type up the idea of Joe [i.e. Joseph Mazor] going to Jonestown."

DECLARATION OF TERESA BUFORD

I, Teresa Buford, hereby declare:

Timothy O. Stoen passed me a note, copy of which is attached herewith and incorporated herein, one evening at Peoples Temple in the San Francisco Temple at a meeting of counselors. It was in or around the late part of 1973. I recognized the handwriting on the note as being Tim Stoen's handwriting. Tim Stoen told me to give the note to Jim Jones as Tim Stoen felt it would be a "good way to handle Jim Cobb." I wrote at the top of the note "Re: Cobb" and passed the note on. The note was never acted upon. Tim Stoen told me at the time that if Annie Moore could not do it, that I should interview other people to do the same.

I declare under penalty of perjury that the foregoing is true and correct.

Executed on September 29, 1978 at San Francisco, California.

          Teresa Buford

— Re Cobb —

I still think it advisable to proceed. Person who does it should be unknown to subject and should try to disguise voice and speak to the point. Annie Moore probably good.

I don't think that the authorities will go to all the trouble to make a voice print since nothing illegal involved.

It's rare that such a "natural" opportunity will present itself.

          Jim

TIM STOEN suggests, in his own handwriting, that a threatening phone call be made to Jim Cobb. "I don't think the authorities will go to all the trouble to make a voice print..."

Berkeley Victims Had Said They Didn't Fear Reprisals

By Ann Bancroft

Just five days before Jeannie and Al Mills were shot to death along with their 15-year-old daughter in Berkeley, the couple told some Marin County college students that they no longer feared being killed by a Peoples Temple hit squad.

In a lecture to about 25 Dominican College students, the couple said that although their children bore psychological scars from their years as followers of Jim Jones, the family no longer feared reprisals from surviving cultists, according to psychologist Robert Shukraft.

The Millses told the group that they planned to give no more public lectures about the Peoples Temple, and that they were anxious to build a "normal life."

But authorities continued yesterday to discount theories that the Millses - defectors from People's Temple and vocal critics of the cult — were killed by avenging cult members.

And they steadfastly refused to comment on any other aspects of the investigation.

One report yesterday said police think the Mills family may have been in the living room of their small cottage when they were accosted by their killer. The Millses reportedly fled down a small hallway — Al and Daphene running into the master bedroom and Jeannie into a small bathroom at the end of the hall — where they were trapped and shot.

The body of Jeannie Mills was found crumpled behind a bathroom door, and on the morning after the murders police removed what appeared to be a bullet-shredded door and took it away for further scrutiny. The killer reportedly fired through the bathroom door at Jeannie Mills before she was killed with a single shot to the head.

"Just five days before Jeannie and Al Mills [Elmer and Deanna Mertle] were shot to death... the couple told some Marin County students that they no longer feared being killed by a Peoples Temple hit squad.

"...The Millses told the group that they planned to give no more public lectures about the Peoples Temple and that they were anxious to build a 'normal life.'"

"...a feeling of freedom..."

—a collection of photographs & comments about the community of Jonestown by residents and visitors at the Peoples Temple Agricultural/Medical Project in Guyana, South America.

DOCUMENTS/29

> "...You know, people are so free here and they look so different. People's faces glow with freedom in their eyes. No more drugs, no more racism, no more rapes, no more prisons or jails..." —Rosie Ruggiero
>
> "...This is a dream come true. This is a whole new world—clean, fresh, pure..." —Mary Wotherspoon
>
> "...There is a place for everyone here and something for them to do. No one has special privileges and everyone feels worthwhile and a part. I am so happy, and that terrible feeling of insecurity is gone..." —Penny Kerns
>
> "...Jonestown is pure democracy in action..." —Johnny Brown
>
> "...When we first arrived on October 3rd, it was about 6:00 p.m. and everyone was eating dinner. Then they all came running towards the vehicle to greet three people—all of them came up to embrace us, saying, 'Welcome to your new home, Jonestown!' It made me want to cry..." —Connie Fitch
>
> "...I was afraid of facing retirement in that one-room apartment, but now I have my own cottage. I have all the free time I want and still plenty to do if I want. I am so happy to be here..." —Lucious Bryant
>
> "...You know, we had good jobs and a nice home—but we wanted to retire in a place of beauty. Well, we came to the right place!" —Mr. & Mrs. E. Jones
>
> "...I'm teaching a class in the Continuing Education Sessions and I've never felt so useful in all my 76 years..." —Henry Mercer
>
> "...Jonestown is truly a milestone. Nestled in the most exquisite forest surroundings, we have every convenience—plus more: the best in social services any community anywhere can offer!" —Dorothy Worley

Jonestown Guest Book

"IMPRESSIVE WORK"
    Officer in charge of Guyana, Jamaica, Trinidad and Tobago, U. S. State Department

"I AM IMPRESSED"
    Charge d'Affairs to U. S. Ambassador Andrew Young

"IMPRESSIVE" *Chief Medical Officer of the Ministry of Health, Guyana*

"PEACE AND LOVE IN ACTION"
    Minister of Foreign Affairs, Guyana

"VERY IMPRESSIVE" *Minister of Education, Guyana*

"VERY PROGRESSIVE" *Regional Development Officer, North West Region, Guyana*

"VERY IMPRESSIVE, KEEP IT UP"
    Representative, Ministry of Agriculture, Guyana

"A VERY PLEASANT DAY IN A VERY PLEASANT ATMOSPHERE"
    Chief Official in the Ministry of Education, Guyana

"A MOST IMPRESSIVE START AND I WISH YOU ALL SUCCESS" *British High Commissioner in Guyana*

"IMPRESSIVE" *Chancellor of the University of Guyana*

"A WONDERFUL EXPERIENCE, A MODEL VILLAGE COMMUNITY TO BE EMULATED"
    Permanent Secretary of the Ministry of Works and Transportation

"EXCELLENT" *Assistant Director-General of National Service, Guyana*

"IT'S VERY, VERY IMPRESSIVE. THANK YOU FOR THE OPPORTUNITY AND BEST WISHES"
    Delegates from one of the world's largest news agencies.

> "KEEP UP THE GOOD WORK"
> *Regional Minister, North West Region, Guyana*
>
> "FANTASTIC, BEYOND ONE'S IMAGINATION, MIRACULOUS, BEAUTIFUL, A TRUE EXAMPLE OF SOCIALIST LIVING" *Thirty-five teachers from the MacKenzie District, Guyana*
>
> "THE HEALTH CARE IN THE COMMUNITY IS FANTASTIC. JONESTOWN IS A LITTLE BIT OF HEAVEN." After examining the teeth of 67 children he found only two cavities. "THIS," he said, "IS UNHEARD OF."
> *A dentist from India and founder of a dental school in Georgetown, Guyana*
>
> "IT'S MIND-BOGGLING TO SEE HOW YOU HAVE CARVED OUT OF THE JUNGLE A COMMUNITY THAT LOOKS JUST LIKE A TOWN IN THE UNITED STATES—AND WITH ALL THE PUBLIC UTILITIES." In a letter following his visit, he wrote: "The training program of the youths and young adults at the Project is highly successful. I have met many and they have told me that they are so happy to be there, as it has made a great change in their life, and given them a chance to prove themselves."
> *Head of nearly a thousand physicians of a Medical Network of Amateur Radio Operators*
>
> "I also wish to give praise and credit to you and the other members of the Peoples Temple Church for the magnificent and humanitarian efforts that you are making. I feel certain that if there were more such organizations with devoted and sincere people such as Larry Schacht and yourself and the members of your church throughout the world that this planet would indeed be a better place upon which to spend one's life."
>
> "Dr. Schacht is, in my opinion, a modern-day Dr. Schweitzer. I was truly impressed with...his activities in Mission Village regarding the comprehensive medical program that he is running there."
> *excerpts of letters from Dr. Albert Greenfield*

"...a feeling of freedom..."

—statements of Rev. and Mrs. John Moore, who had just returned from a week's visit at the Project, and Atty. Charles Garry, during a press conference held at Peoples Temple, May 28, 1978.

REV. MOORE:

"I'm John Moore. We have two daughters who are members of the Temple. One, the older girl, is a teacher, and the younger one is a nurse...The two words that come to my mind immediately, as I was there and as I tried to reflect upon my experiences were: 'impressive' and 'amazing'. It almost boggles my mind to see that great clearing and to understand how so much could have been done in the relatively short period of time.

"We wore ourselves out, walking around the facility. I think about 800 to a thousand acres have been cleared, and it's in the midst of a jungle, and that's part of what's impressive; and all except a part of the land that's not finally been cleared, has been planted with various crops.

"We went to the piggery, the chickery, to the dairy, to the mill, where the refining of flour from the tubers of the cassava [is done]. We were first impressed—certainly I was—with seeing the older people at the time we arrived ...about noon, engaged in calisthenics with an instructor, keeping their limbs and joints and muscles limber. And then we went to the nursery, the child care center.

"They have probably 35 preschoolers. I don't know how many they have in school. They have newborn babies; several babies have been born there. They have a day care nursery for parents who work, and there are those who are caring for them; and then they have the older people. That's really a part of the beauty of it, we felt.

"We talked about what they were doing, and what they were interested in, and all of them were engaged in some activity or work that was particularly important for them, they were about business which they regarded as important.

❝ "I had a feeling of freedom...The food is provided for everyone, there's medical care for everyone, educational opportunities for everyone; there are work needs and opportunities for the members of the community. I think obviously people with certain skills and experience move into those fields. If it's a tool and die maker in a machine shop, or a man in agronomy, they work in those particular fields. On the other hand, some people have not had the experience in specific fields. One of the great things, I think, is the opportunity for some of the younger people, particularly, to be learning skills when that opportunity is not present here."

In regard to the relationship of the project to the citizens and government of Guyana, Rev. Moore said, "The school is accredited by the government of Guyana... They've had people from the Department of Agriculture and their agricultural stations there working with the people at the project. The health services are provided for the Amerindians or people who live in the community as well as for members of the project itself."

BARBARA MOORE:

"My impressions are, having just experienced our visit there, that this is a beautiful, heroic, creative project! It is absolutely miraculous. There are excellent medical services, excellent educational services, and...it's a community of caring and sharing with an added dimension, and this dimension I would say, is Love—if you want to use that term. In a sense it reminds me of...a New Testament community, in the purest sense of the word, in the love and concern for all, that we observed. And with complete freedom for creativity! Those who want to farm, are farming; those who wish to teach, teach; those who like to cook, cook. They have an excellent nutritionist who is working scientifically all the time to discover new uses for the indigenous plants and growths there, and is in contact with the Guyanese experts to discover new and useful uses for these various crops... That was very impressive to me.

"It was most impressive to see the elderly people, the older folks, who had their neat little yards, their little

(Cont'd. on page 12) ❞

34/DOCUMENTS

(Cont'd from page 7)

> white picket-type fences, and their opportunity to take classes if they wished to, or to garden, or to just sit. They also have a lovely library of over eight thousand volumes, from poetry to 'how-to-do-it'...and this was most impressive, that one could sit and read...
>
> "It's a complete city, and one thing they do encourage is the nuclear family. There are families there with children. You can have your own home, or if you're a single person, you may live in a dormitory, whichever you prefer. They have a lovely nursery for infants; they have a nursery for toddlers, and of course a fine educational set-up."
>
> One of the reporters in attendance at the conference stated that he thought she sounded impressed. He asked, "would you think it's rather Utopian there?" Her reply was, "Oh yes, a lovely Utopia."
>
> **CHARLES GARRY:**
>
> "I was impressed by the medical center particularly. All of the older citizens live right around the medical compound. The medical compound is something that you have never seen and you probably won't see unless you go there. It's almost a miracle. This young doctor, who was trained by the Temple, graduated with high honors from the University of California at Irvine, has performed miracles...Every morning at eight o'clock, someone knocks on the cottage door, and says, 'did anybody have any difficulties last night?' Can you imagine the feeling of security that these folks have, to feel that somebody cares for them, is interested in them, and will do things for them?"
>
> **A FIRST-CLASS EXAMPLE OF COMMUNITY LIFE**
>
> "It was a very rewarding experience," he said. "I have never before seen so many people of varying races working happily side-by-side without a single spark of friction. With its own school, sawmill, electricity, roads, houses, and so on, all being scrupulously clean, I could not help but be impressed." *Dr. Ng-a-Fook, Dental Surgeon [from a news article which appeared in the <u>Guyana Chronicle</u> following his visit to Jonestown]*

12

> "...Right now I'm sitting in our Pavillion. I can hear our saws going in the background, people are writing letters, playing in Spanish class, or in our Agriculture meeting. I work with Tom out in the housing area...I build closets in the cottages, and do some of the finish work on them. Then Charlie gives me various jobs, too, like building cabinets for the Nurse's Offices, and Radio Room. I feel like I'm really doing something worthwhile, especially when I walk around the houses and see the things I did on them, or go to the nurse and she reaches for my file in the cabinets I built..." —Kim Brewster
>
> "...I have changed my last name. I am now Tobi Mtendaji. My middle name is Chekevu. Put together these two names mean Happy Worker in Swahili...I am now on the construction crew building these beautiful cottages the family lives in. I guess I am just now bringing out my talents here..." —Tobi Mtendaji
>
> "...Greg and I live in our own cottage. We fixed it up really nice. I've planted eggplant along the sides. On the left side of the porch is a bread and butter tree, flowers, and some beans growing up the house. On the right side of the porch are cucumbers. I'm thinking of planting a papaya tree in the back of the house..." —Erin Watkins
>
> "...This place is growing by leaps and bounds. New and wider sidewalks are going up all the time; more cottages to accomodate more arrivals; electric wiring, fencing, planting, painting, gardening, everything you can think of. There is plenty to do and everyone enjoys working..." —Loretta Coomer
>
> "...We make all our own clothes now, and we get just the style, color, and material of something that you want and you don't have to shop for it!" —Rheaviana Beam
>
> "...There are experimentations going on in many phases, such as making our own clay bricks, our own smokehouse, experimental herbs, and all different kinds of woods to build some innovative carpentry items with also..." —Ron Sines

15

36/DOCUMENTS

❝

"...Talk about delicious food...you can't beat the menu at Jonestown..."
—Maria McCann

"...Your eyes will pop out of their sockets when you take a look at the beautiful piece of land called Jonestown. Words can't describe the beauty of this place..."
—Gary Tyler

"...The tropical rain showers are just like you read about. It is sunny and bright one minute, then all of a sudden the rain comes up quick—a gentle, steady rain. Just as suddenly, in 15 or 20 minutes, it clears up and the sun is shining again! It is absolutely refreshing..." —Magnolia Harris

"...You should see our horses, especially the stallion—he is fine! I would never have been able to own a horse, but now I do..."
—Ronnie James

"...Maybe you've heard of the Ice Cream Tree—well, we really have it! It's called a sour-sop tree and it produces a fruit which weighs up to 4 kilograms. It is green outside with soft spines and a slightly fibrous green pulp inside. When ripe—split open and eat it with a spoon. It's like eating sherbet ice cream!" —Mike Rozynko

"...There is a beautiful little waterfall located 1½ miles south of Jonestown past some of our crops. It is a breathtaking hike down a jungle path, and when you get there it is a long, smooth, sloping series of rocks and two pools of water (after a rain you can swim) and even a vine to swing over the water (or in if you fall). A large felled tree lays over the water so you can sit on it in the comfortable shade. It is one of my favorite places here..."
—Barbara Walker

"...It is a beautiful tropical night. There is a cool breeze blowing. I can look out the window at the full moon, hearing people laughing, and I can see Jonestown lit up in the moonlight. All else is quiet—it is just a perfect experience."
—Laura Johnston

❞

JONESTOWN IS FALSELY PORTRAYED AS "AN ARMED CAMP"

Tracing the Jonestown guns

December 10, 1978

By Tim Reiterman
and James A. Finefrock
©1978, San Francisco Examiner

Federal investigators have traced 38 of 40 guns recovered at the Peoples Temple mission in Guyana and found that most apparently were bought over the counter and made part of a temple weapons cache here.

One source said most of the guns traced were shotguns and .22-caliber weapons of various types — the sort commonly used for hunting — and that most appeared to have been sold by retail firearms outlets.

It is believed that some of the recovered guns were used in the killings of U.S. Rep. Leo Ryan, Examiner photographer Greg Robinson and three others at the Port Kaituma airstrip near the temple's mission in Guyana, since all eight alleged attackers were found dead at Jonestown.

However, federal sources say no ballistics tests have been performed because Guyanese authorities have refused to turn over the recovered weapons to U.S. authorities.

"There was a variety of weapons," he said. "They were not military ordnance:

Debbie Layton Blakey — who was with the Guyana colony from Dec. 7, 1977, to May 12, 1978, when she fled — said she never saw an automatic weapon at Jonestown. But she did say she saw 200 to 300 rifles, some with scopes, and about 25 handguns and many rounds of ammunition.

Spokane, Washington
Spokesman-Review   NOV 21 1978

Also found in the fields, huts and dormitories were 17 shotguns, 14 rifles, seven pistols, a flare gun and large amounts of ammunition, government officials said.

Spokane Spokesman-Review, November 21, 1978: "Also found in the fields, huts and dormitories were *17 shotguns, 14 rifles, seven pistols [and] a flare gun...*" (= **39 guns**)

San Francisco Examiner, December 19, 1978: "Federal investigators have traced 38 of *40 guns recovered at the Peoples Temple mission...* One source said most of the guns traced were shotguns and .22 caliber weapons of various types..."

"Debbie Layton Blakey.... said she never saw an automatic weapon at Jonestown. but *she did say she saw 200 to 300- rifles, some with scopes, and about 25 handguns...*"

How could Ms. Layton-Blakey have seen between 225 and 325 guns when the authorities found no more than 40??? That was approximately *seven times as many guns as were actually in the community!*

38/DOCUMENTS

THE GOVERNMENT'S EYEWITNESS ADMITS HE WAS ON THE OPPOSITE SIDE OF THE PLANE WHEN THE SHOOTING ERUPTED.

SAN FRANCISCO (UPI) — A defector from the People's Temple who survived the airport ambush that took five lives says the cult's death squad "thought they had killed me."

James Cobb Jr., who was with the visiting party fired on by temple gunmen Saturday, said he was "very lucky."

"I was on the opposite side of the trailer (carrying the gunmen) and hurrying to get people on the planes," Cobb said of the airstrip ambush.

"I saw (NBC reporter Don) Harris, the congressman, (NBC cameraman) Bob Brown. I saw them go down. I ran to the jungle 50 yards and dove into the jungle."

Tyler, Texas
Courier
·(Cir. 39,469)

NOV 21 1978

James Cobb, cited by the Congressional investigating committee as providing the "eyewitness identifications" of the assassins, _admits to the press that he was he was "on the opposite side of the trailer (carrying the gunmen)" when the shooting erupted._ Then he fled for his life.

THE GOVERNMENT CLAIMS COBB HAD "GOOD EYESIGHT"

JANUARY 4, 1980

The interview convened at 1:45 p.m., pursuant to call, in Room 2200, Rayburn House Office Building.

Ms. Efrein. Well, you start with the question of whether someone who is fleeing for his own life can properly identify eight people coming towards him with guns. That is a logical question.

Mr. Smeeton. Jim Cobb said he has good eyesight.

Ms. Efrein. [Can] someone fleeing for his own life...properly identify eight people coming towards him with guns.
Mr. Smeeton. Jim Cobb said he has good eyesight.

UNTRAINED AMATEURS..... OR HIGHLY-TRAINED PROFESSIONAL ASSASSINS?

MONDAY, NOVEMBER 20, 1978 — SEATTLE TIMES

'Nobody said anything... they just opened fire.

by GENE MILLER and DON BOHNING
Knight News Service

GEORGETOWN, Guyana — The religious zealots struck <u>silently</u> from ambush as darkness fell on the jungle airstrip. They murdered <u>methodically</u>. Only Americans were their targets.

"Nobody said anything... they just opened fire."

Bob Flick, a N.B.C. field producer, hefty, whiskered, muddied, trembling, tried unsuccessfully to master his emotions.

He had watched five companions die. Only instinct had spared Flick himself from the massacre.

Yesterday, in a disbelieving and sometimes disjointed chronicle of terror, the exhausted Flick and other witnesses <u>described the massacre as carefully planned and mercilessly executed.</u>

Trouble lay heavy as humidity in the late afternoon air Saturday as Representative Leo J. Ryan, California Democrat, and his party of Americans reached the crude airfield in the isolated settlement of Port Kaituma in Northwestern Guyana.

The region is so remote it might as well be in another century. There are no telephones, no radios, no conveniences. The jungle dominates all.

The congressman's party had twice visited the People's Temple, not far from Port Kaituma, hoping to persuade some of the young Americans there to return to the United States.

At Port Kaituma, the group waited nervously for chartered planes, an Otter and a Cessna, coming from Georgetown. The planes were late. Finally they came. Passengers hurried to board before darkness closed the unlighted field.

"Then <u>a tractor pulling some sort of trailer with people on it came up</u>. Obviously there was going to be trouble. Three policeman showed up, but they were disarmed and took off.

"People were loading the airplane. <u>Someone shot the left tire of it, and then there were more shots.</u>

"Anytime somebody would fall down wounded the gunmen would walk over and shoot him in the head with a shotgun.

"If you fell down you had to get up. They shot the motor on the airplane. All during this time the engines were running."

The gunmen made no attempt to kill the Guyanese fliers, Flick said.

"They were only killing Americans."

"When the shots rang out, the congressman dove behind the opposite wheel of the airplane, away from the gunfire.

"He was hit almost immediately — and then shot by <u>people walking through with the guns. They were not running or anything — walking, just walking.</u>

THE CHARLOTTE OBSERVER

The People With Guns...
<u>Calmly</u> Searched For The Wounded — Then Killed Them

The assassins are described as "silent," "calm," "methodical," "merciless": "The religious zealots struck **silently**... They murdered **methodically** Nobody said anything... they just opened fire. ...witnesses described the massacre as **carefully planned and mercilessly executed**... Passengers hurried to board... Then a tractor pulling some sort of trailer with people on it came up. (<u>NOTE</u>: A second vehicle, <u>NOT</u> the Temple truck.) ...Three policemen showed up, but they were disarmed... Someone shot the left tire (of the airplane)... ...people walking through with the guns. **They were not running or anything -- walking, just walking."**

"The People With Guns... **Calmly** Searched for the Wounded -- Then Killed Them."

DID THE MAN WHO MADE THIS PHONE CALL KNOW ABOUT THE ASSASSINATION IN ADVANCE?

San Francisco Chronicle
The Largest Daily Circulation in Northern California

TUESDAY, NOVEMBER 21, 1978

FBI Probes Temple 'Death Threats'

By George Draper

The FBI reported yesterday it is checking out "some very heavy rumors" concerning the People's Temple crisis, including several purported death threats.

One of the death threats, it was learned, was directed against the son of Joe Holsinger, administrative assistant to Congressman Leo Ryan, who was gunned down in Guyana on Saturday.

Will Holsinger, 27, the son, has been on the congressman's payroll for the past two months investigating People's Temple in the Bay Area.

His telephone rang Saturday night, a few hours after the first radio report of the Guyana shootings. Young Holsinger's wife answered the phone and heard a man's voice saying:

"Your husband's meal ticket had his head blown off and he (your husband) might be next."

The Holsingers notified authorities and moved to another San Mateo residence, which is being guarded around the clock.

Re Will Holsinger, son of Joseph Holsinger (both aides of Congressman Ryan): "His telephone rang Saturday night, a few hours after the first radio report of the Guyana shootings. Young Holsinger's wife answered the phone and heard a man's voice saying, **'Your husband's meal ticket had his head blown off and he (your husband) might be next.'**

NOTE: Everyone in the San Francisco Temple was in shock and disbelief at the time of these reported calls, without even confirmation of the shootings. **No one in Peoples Temple even knew who this man was!** "Someone" may have made these calls, but it was impossible that it was anyone from Peoples Temple. Was the anonymous caller lined up in advance of the assassination to make these calls on cue?

And what of the countless other anonymous threatening phone calls and other harassments that had been falsely blamed upon Peoples Temple for a year-and-a-half leading up to the tragedy? Who was responsible for those incidents?

XXX. Turnabout's Unfair Play.

Nor did the mainstream press ever cover *Jonestown* first-hand, shy of the Ryan visit in November, 1978. The Jonestown community flourished, even praise of the community flourished with impressive blooms; but the name of the game was never the real living Jonestown, but rather the *publicity* surrounding the community which the conspirators were committed to destroy.

We even had non-member relatives visit, who raved about the "lovely utopia," and held press conferences where not a word of praise was reported in the news. Members wrote back informally, scores of them, with rave reviews of the climate, the natural beauty, the plentiful food, landscaping and gardens for the cottages, the diverse agriculture, the sawmill, piggery, chckens, dairy cows, cassava mill, machine shop, Jonestown Community School, clothing manufacture, and many cottage industries producing toys, baked goods, and other items for sale in the capital city, Georgetown. Virtually every Minister in the Guyanese cabinet had come to Jonestown and raved. (See DOCUMENTS, pp. 28-32.)

Our own attorney, Charles Garry, an outsider, visited in November, 1977, telling the press (i.e. the alternative press - the mainstream press would not touch it) *"I Have Been to Paradise."* (See DOCUMENTS, p. 11) He reserved his most effusive praise for:

> "a community where there is no such thing as racism. . . . no one thinks in terms of sex, or feels superior to anyone else. . . . There is no such thing as age-ism. . . . . I have never seen so many happy faces in my life as I did in Jonestown. . . . you just could not believe the cottages. . . . the sanitation. . . you can eat off the ground. . . the consistently high level of medical care. . . .the care of senior citizens. . . . the 'luscious' food. . . . it will make your blood pressure go down; your diabetes will disappear. . . . thriving sawmills, electricial generators, refrigeration. . . . the school managed by at least 50 people with advanced degrees. . . with enthusiastic participation and discussion by all the students . . . .the most beautiful entertainment in the world. . . ."

226/SNAKE DANCE

Summing it up, he said that *"the society that is being built in Jonestown is a credit to humanity."*

Tim Stoen, who founded a vitriolic slander factory called "Concerned Relatives" knew the truth, yet encouraged every manner of lie in the press and in lobbying campaigns. As if to seal that "Concerned Relatives" was a sham operation, Stoen, who had **no relatives in Jonestown** (the paternity claim being knowingly false) was joined in "leadership" with Steven Katsaris, whose *24-year-old* daughter Maria, who had repeatedly claimed her father molested her, and wanted nothing further to do with him; and Sherwin Harris, whose *21-year old* daughter Liane had never lived with him or been supported by him, for her parents had separated before her birth!

In addition, one Yolanda Crawford was recruited, a young black woman (a "plum," the anti-Temple group being overwhelmingly white) who had peaceably returned from Guyana in June, 1977 after a two-month stay, *testified at the Temple that Jonestown was a beautiful place(!),* then drew up an affidavit for Stoen that there were "armed guards," "closed-circuit t.v." and threats of "hit men" to keep the people of Jonestown from "escaping"!

Steven Katsaris, for his part, volunteered that "someone" (anonymous, naturally) had called him at 3 a.m. and threatened to burn his home down, and naturally, he was certain it must be *us!* All it really meant was that the "dirty tricks" department (the one that *Stoen himself* had apparently set up when he was with us,) had commissioned its own seedy *anti-*Temple personnel, to press an ongoing barrage of harassments against relatives and newspeople, to turn them against the Temple and its work. But by then, the climate was so adversial against Peoples Temple, no one would venture that the truth was precisely *the opposite* of what it seemed.

Stoen then took his tiny, embittered crew to march outside of the *Chroncicle,* distributing flyers called *"Jonestown Concentration Camp: This Nightmare is Taking Place Right Now."* (See DOCUMENTS, p. 12.) By the time Debbie Layton Blakey returned to the States in May, 1978, any wild-eyed lie would fly. She claimed that Jonestown was an armed camp, that people were starving while Jim Jones lived like a king (see actual letters from Jonestown raving about the food, DOCUMENTS, pp. 13-14), and that she became so exhausted from virtual slave labor that "I was indifferent to whether I lived or died." "I'm sure everyone wants to leave," she sourly dumped onto a press which had been provided with all the glowing reports and printed not a one.

Revelling in her new role as "media heroine," Blakey proclaimed that everyone had been "forced to flee to Guyana," the black people being told they'd be thrown into concentration camps in the U.S., and the white people being told that the C.I.A. had all their names, would hunt them down, imprison, torture, even kill them if they did not "flee to Guyana." (See DOCUMENTS, p. 15.) Wow! The crew in San Francisco who could not process passports fast enough for people eager and happy to go overseas, would have found all this news quite a surprise.

Layton-Blakey, arguably "the Linda Tripp of Jonestown," exceeded even her own reputation in Peoples Temple as a regular little F.B.I. informant. She had "specialized" in self-righteously turning people in, the two choicest tidbits of which were Patricia Cartmell, for *not wanting to have sex with Jim Jones*; and Teri Buford, by her own report, for *not being zealous enough about guns* on the heels of a mercenary attack against Jonestown. What did that mean? That Ms. Blakey *wanted* unwilling virgins pressured to have sex with Jim Jones? That she *wanted* the community to have guns? Difficult to have it "both ways."

Yet after the royal capper of attacking Teri's "loyalty" for not being *zealous enough* about guns, she went right ahead and turned *us* into the authorities for being ***too*** zealous about guns(!), citing that she personally "saw 200-300 rifles." Except it wasn't true. After the tragedy, the Guyanese authorities found all of *thirty-nine* weapons at Jonestown after the deaths, and the Americans all of *forty*, none of them automatic weapons. (See DOCUMENTS, p. 37.) But that was way too late, to say the least. Jonestown had already been painted as "an armed camp," to justify violence ***against*** it, and to pave the pathway for a ***frame.*** The rest is history.

Now the speciality became turning *everyone* in. In blatant contrast to the fresh, enthusiastic letters from Jonestown raving about the food, medical services, opportunities for creative and constructive work, she swore under oath that the residents of Jonestown were starved, exhausted, beaten, abused, exploited, terrorized, held hostage, and that the community was "swarming with armed guards."

I obtained an affidavit on my own following the tragedy, about Blakey leaving on the heels of Jim Jones refusing her demands for sex (coming from someone who, in her own words, "was so exhausted that I had become indifferent as to whether I lived or died"); and who, against pleading, abandoned her own terminally ill mother ("I don't think she's that sick"), who soon thereafter died of cancer. Obviously, no one in

228/SNAKE DANCE

Jonestown was interviewed about *why Debbie Blakey had really left*. They only cared about her smears - the more flagrant the better.

Trick or Tripp? Ms. Blakey had officially launched her career of smearing, slandering and defaming the very people she claimed she wanted to "save"! Well, she had to shut down *Jim Jones*, didn't she? Had he not *refused her sex?*. Had he not refused her sex *publicly?* He had to pay. And the other thousand people? "Small price."

In an adroit adjustment of her allegiances to now favor the roundly-despised Stoens *(and in direct contradiction to her own previously sworn-out affidavit!)*, she also swore out that Tim Stoen was "the father of John Victor," and that Jim Jones was "holding" the child so as to "stop Timothy Stoen from speaking against the Temple" (by handing him a *"cause celebre"*??!) Grace, not precisely the Queen of Hearts, was lauded as having been "very popular with the membership for her generosity and compassion," her departure posing "a threat to Rev. Jones' absolute control." Control of what? Surely not the yellow press! (See DOCUMENTS, p. 15.)

But the crowning coup was surely "warning the authorities" (i.e. the federal government) that suicide had been discussed - omitting entirely, of course, that however gruesome a *contingency* plan, it was only considered in the *context* of the community facing imminent military invasion with no way out.

Most helpful to "warn the authorities." That was like going to the fox to report that the chickens were in fact terrified of being plucked alive! Just one more push and you can move on in for the kill.

A frantic ongoing letter-writing campaign was launched, targeting "the 600" - meaning all of the Congress, the President, and other key officials such as in the State Department. The case was laid out from scratch - the conspiracy, the smear campaign, the harassments, the beauties of Jonestown-, but I do not recall getting even one response.

I think we were probably quite naive. My own personal mail to members of Congress was obstructed *following* the tragedy. Why in the middle of this horrendous, multi-agency campaign of destruction, the Post office *(who had already illegally held up Social Security checks headed for Guyana!)* would be expected to automatically comply with delivering Peoples Temple's mail to Washington, I do not know. I look back and think it *unlikely* that the mail arrived at all.

All that was really sure to arrive was the bad press onto the newsstands!

Our reversal of fortune had snowballed. Although the rave reviews were so copious that there was no way to do in Jonestown *fairly*, both the yellow press, and our own dearth of P.R. personnel Stateside, posed detriment after detriment. Our friends, if well-meaning, or even incredulous at the sudden campaign of slander, were hard-pressed, in our virtual absence, to find a voice. Meanwhile, the weak links in the friendship chain were manipulated against us entirely. Nothing in this regard was more notorious than what was done with Kathy Hunter:

Hunter, a reporter, wife of George Hunter, editor of the *Ukiah Daily Journal*, and formerly considered a friend, was now, in Jim Jones' absence, being wooed by Tim Stoen. Intrigued by the split between Tim and Jim, in February of 1978, she authored a piece about the custody case entitled "*Greek Tragedy Played on Worldwide Stage.*" I was in such a perpetual rush to garner the avalanche of newsclips, that the connection eluded me -- that the custody case was the very "Greek tragedy" that "*Allegory*" had presented as central!

Whatever role fate played, of course, the Hunter fiasco had malovolent *human* fingerprints all over it. A few months after the "Greek Tragedy" piece, she claimed to have been "invited to Guyana by the Prime Minister," which call was apparently "a hoax" (and *we* would make such a risky, stupid move which could only backfire?), and was met at the airport by a chaperone, one Pat Small, a woman suspected to be C.I.A. by the Guyanese government.

Her nightmare trip included several bomb scares and fires at her hotel, interrogation by the Guyanese government for misrepresentation of her credentials, and numerous other unpleasantries. She demanded to go to Jonestown, but when told that Jim Jones was traveling up the river but she was welcome to visit anyway, she made a "not even veiled threat" (according to our P.R. director Mike Prokes) that "if she didn't get what she wanted, it would not go well with Peoples Temple."

The U.S. press, of course, reported that the Temple had handled her so "forcefully" and "hostilely" that she had to be put into "protective custody," which we had confirmed with Vibert Mingo, the Guyanese police chief, was never so. All that had happened was that she refused an offer to visit the very community she said she came to "investigate." Meanwhile, several odd, anonymous phone calls came into the Temple headquarters in Georgetown, faking a Guyanese accent and asking when Jim Jones would be back at the project. Finally, Mrs. Hunter got into Parliament courtesy of

Pat Small, apparently to create problems, so the Guyanese government simply asked her to leave.

When she came home and her ordeal was publicized in the press, she then claimed two black men broke into her home and forced alcohol down her throat, the windows of her home were smashed, and she was bombarded with phone calls (anonymous, naturally,) threatening, "Jim knows what you are doing. If he goes down, you and all your family will go down with him," and "Hey white trash. We know where you live. Keep your ass clean and your mouth clammed up."

Well, the dirty tricks department was obviously alive and well! We already had a bitter sample stirred into the unsavory *New West* brew – the phony, yet highly-publicized "break-in." The swampland of "guilt by innuendo" had already been dredged. Peoples Temple *could* do something like that to Hunter, couldn't they? After all, were we not *accused* of it? No one in the press ever considered blaming anyone but Peoples Temple for the Hunter set-up and ensuing mayhem.

The Hunter fiasco, distressing as it was, arrived into a context of planned disintegration of our credibility. Indeed, destroying the last vestige of support from our former stronghold in Redwood Valley must have been considered a special coup by Stoen. The slander that had lurched sporadically into the news those first several months (like, "*Jonestown" Paradise or Prison?*," using "sources" who had never been to Jonestown at all!), got a ready follow-up with Kathy Hunter about the presumed "horrors" of Jonestown. By the reporter who never got there.

Meanwhile, the Mertles, Conn, Stoen et al, had long since realized that the press attacks could only be sustained for so long without being followed up with criminal prosecutions. Investigations that were trumped up for District Attorneys' offices in San Francisco and Mendocino County, had already been dropped for "lack of evidence." Now, moving into 1978, the Los Angeles D.A.'s office was brought in over an alleged bilking of property from an elderly couple, the Medlocks, whom (I surmised) opted for Guyana, "all expenses paid" (air fare, a guaranteed home, and life-time care), on the condition they sell their home and donate the proceeds; but this couple renegged.

Others found this a more-than-equitable exchange. It was oppressive for seniors to remain in the inner cities, and I understand the senior population at Jonestown was thrilled at their good fortune, by and large. Reversals like this pair were rare, but pounced upon by predatory opponents eager for lawsuits.

"Predatory" indeed. Obituaries of people we barely knew were paraded across the front page like we had killed them. The death of a peripheral ex-member was used to rile up the authorities in L.A. A child, Curtis Buckley, had died in San Francisco of a drug overdose (totally out of the norm, so we had hardly publicized it!), and now suspicious circumstances were claimed. Then there was Bob Houston, who died after he left the church, in a freak railway accident that could not have possibly been related to us.

This latter may have caused the greatest havoc, as Bob's father, Sam Houston, a former UPI photographer, was a good friend of Congressman Leo Ryan! And although Bob had left us, his wife Phyllis remained, and the two Houston grandchildren, Patti and Judy, lived in Jonestown. Perhaps Bob's death *was* a homicide, not an accident (for *someone* was capable of this ~ look at the Mertle/Mills, look at Paula Adams Mann), though surely not by *us!* But it did give Stoen "an early lead." Ryan, through the Houstons, was corralled into the Stoen camp at least a year before the tragedy, his letter to the Justice Department on behalf of the Stoen custody suit coming on November 18, 1977, the exact date Tim emerged to join Grace "to regain our son."

The custody suit, of course, was the most explosive, but it took many foxes to destroy the vines, and everywhere people were encouraged to sue, however spurious their claims. It was infuriating to try to presuppose what Jim Cobb, who took his free education and ran, could possibly feel *we* owed *him*, but having his large nuclear family transplanted to Guyana, he seized upon whatever pretexts Stoen's "Concerned Relatives" front could provide, to file a multi-million-dollar suit.

Maria Katsaris, little John's surrogate mother, found herself at especially bitter odds with her estranged father, not because she was not of age and free to travel, but in that our expose of "the true facts" included Maria's own claim that he had molested her. Now made a public issue, Mr. Katsaris of at course.... filed suit. Not against Maria personally, and not for lies, but rather against the church, out of carelessly- worded flyers which outright accused him of the molestation. Naturally, the subject of the suit became *libel.*

This stew of lawsuits whipped up out of ugly, family-based grievances, served its purpose well. Picket lines were organized to counter ours against the slander of the press, and ever more relatives of Jonestown residents were corralled to stir up venom. Meanwhile, the Feds were doing their job as only they could: holding up social security checks of pensioners at

Jonestown, instigating Customs raids of our shipments going overseas, whipping up the I.R.S. to investigate our tax-exempt status, prodding the F.C.C. to cut off our ham radio lifeline.

Were it not clear upon leaving the States that we could never return, the locks on our exit out were more securely fastened with each new assault. Smears and innuendo had progressed their way into overt threats to cut off both communications and funds, and pending lawsuits of varying gravity and monetary demands were pressed.

It seems like the suit filed for custody of one small child would be lost in the ongoing shuffle of the deck, yet it was not only the most devastating to Jim personally, but had all the earmarks of our doom. Stoen, having been an official in the State of California, had not only a network of State connections to draw upon but, we would always surmise, Federal ones as well. His bankroll seemed unlimited. He had turned in his salary regularly to the church, and was now unemployed, yet upon leaving, first traveling to London, and then to Washington, D.C., he seemed to cross the continents at will, setting up an extensive lobbying campaign in Washington, where he set up an office, as well as a lobbying campaign back and forth from Guyana.

Certainly, he was able to reach Congressmen where we failed, like Leo Ryan. Although Stoen's association with Ryan was never touted openly 'til the Fall of 1978, Ryan had obviously been courted far earlier. Undoubtedly the Houston smear, never accusing us outright, but insinuating foul play, was used to force Ryan's hand.

I might use the hackneyed phrase, "Fate conspired to...," but it is *people* who generally conspire; and this odd coincidence of the Houstons, parents of the freak accident victim, being also close friends of Leo Ryan, is one of many too-perfect pieces that may never be dissembled and placed in their true context. The Ryan/Houston friendship was a pre-existent situation, but it did give Stoen the perfect entrée to pressure *Ryan*, rather than other potential allies. All the more so in that the Ryans also had a daughter, Shannon, in a so-called cult (Bagwan Rajneesh in Antelope, Oregon), which may have made Ryan more sympathetic to investigating Jonestown.

Meanwhile, as expected, the Stoens' legal demands for John's return were pushed post haste. It had been hoped, in the days when we had the upper hand over Grace, and presumably Tim (though no one suspected that hand would ever need be played), to have an insurance policy in the form of affidavits placing the Stoens in a humiliating position rather than Jim Jones.

But we had no upper hand now. Tim's affidavit, stating that finding himself unable to father a child, he called upon his "beloved Pastor" to do it *for* him, which his wife "graciously consented thereto," got a one-day stint on an inner page, but more as gossip than gospel. Grace's scribbled catalogue of women's clothing Tim had purchased and hidden away in a drawer of his own clothes, much less his homosexual affair with Jim Jones, if offered to the press at all, was not published. (See DOCUMENTS, pp. 18-19.)

Tim admitted signing the affidavit, but said Jim did that to him as "a test of faith." In any case, a child by a married pastor with a married parishioner, even if true, would hardly qualify as good publicity! Most of our opponents, apparently including reporters, knew *exactly* who John's father was. But it never mattered. It was meant to be a *main* point, but became a *moot* point, in that we hadn't the manpower on hand to push the publicity our way.

It fell to the hands of the courts. To the dismay of the Stoens, this meant the *Guyanese* courts, who captured jurisdiction based upon the residence of the child, living with whom those courts conceded was "John-John's" biological father. They ruled in favor of Jim Jones. Naturally, the American courts ruled to have the child returned, but it seemed clear that nothing short of kidnapping would bring that about.

XXXI. The Dead Cat on the Juror's Doorstep.

Kidnapping? It was only a matter of time. Threats to send in mercenaries were waved in our faces like red scarves in front of a wounded bull. Perhaps as a trial balloon, it was first published in our former stronghold up north, Ukiah. Eventually, the threat showed up in logs from the U.S. Embassy in Georgetown, Guyana ~ "eventually" being after the tragedy. It said that on October 3, 1978 (certainly too close for comfort!), Tim Stoen had made a threat to the State Department to send mercenaries to Jonestown, presumably to ensure enough urgency that the Ryan trip would proceed full speed ahead. (See DOCUMENTS, p. 20.)

Nowhere, of course, was it mentioned that *a scouting trip was planned to the then-Soviet Union for December, 1978.* That would surely qualify as "urgent" for Stoen & Co.! Indeed, notes later discovered at Jonestown revealed two meetings with the Soviet Embassy, one in December, 1977, the other on March 20, 1978. Not that politics were ever mentioned by this "concerned father," the threats being made purely "to regain my son." Of course, such a threat could backfire on *Stoen*. Who, after all, was threatening violence ~ us or him? But now their true hand was being forced by a timeclock ticking our new course eastward.

Notwithstanding, for Stoen to convey that the matter was beyond negotiation may well have been true. I.e., no one was about to hand over their kids. Naturally, it had never been open for negotiation on *either* side (Grace was provided with a round-trip ticket to visit John, which she simply cashed in); but now, with this narrow time margin for escape to yet another continent for the residents of Jonestown, the Ryan visit had to proceed.

The reality of mercenaries, of course (i.e. not mere threats), was already a *fait accompli* ~ a sniper attack a full year earlier which received only perfunctory coverage in the local press. It seemed that the Stoens' attorney for the child custody suit, one Jeffrey Haas, had travelled to Jonestown to serve legal papers, and the subsequent sniping episode was, for all we knew, the equivalent of "the dead cat on the juror's doorstep." (See DOCUMENTS, pp. 16-17.)

At the time it occurred, the mercenary business was so volatile, that we tunnelled the story to the press, not the membership, so as not to alarm the faithful. Nevertheless, it was a huge shift which colored everything to come. Whatever happened in Jonestown in September, 1977, was *the warning knell that if mere bad press did not do us in, it would be followed upon with violence.*

Deanna and Mert's first line into the foray, the smears, had begun as a fishing expedition for malcontents, with limited personnel, albeit perhaps *un*-limited clandestine back-up from government operatives, given the Banks/Conn scenario. Investigations then began mounting with Social Security, the I.R.S., Customs, The Federal Communications Commission (where's the "slow, lumbering, unwieldy, inefficient federal bureaucracy" when you *need* it?); plus foreign newspaper smears; dirty tricks like the Hunter fiasco; high-powered attorneys, private investigators, fancy P.R. firms, all with clandestine financing and within months of the initial attack in *New West!*

The second line of attack, Tim Stoen (and his "*Concerned Relatives*" travesty), who unexpectedly fell right into the Mertles' laps, and Stoen's lock on the custody case, gave a cause celebre around which the third line, *armed attack against the community*, could gel.

This had now gone beyond "mere bad press." This was breathing down our necks. **Mercenaries.** It was the steamroller about to push the entire symbiosis of factors to the finish line.

It began with September, 1977 at Jonestown. Jim Jones' story, corroborated by other eye witnesses, was that snipers shot into Jonestown from out of the jungle, and that it continued intermittently for six days. Marceline's story, which I later heard first-hand, was that a bullet whizzed right by Jim's head, and that a bullet was recovered from a wall of Jim's cottage.

At a later time, Joseph Mazor, the seedy character who kept bobbing up when it was "dirty work time," claimed to have *led* the attack. Mark Lane affirmed it, then after the tragedy, tried to disclaim it entirely. A member of the Jonestown security team who survived, claimed it did happen; that moreover, he saw people *firing back*; and that he saw Marceline, who was no "actress," run out of Jim's cottage screaming for help at the time. (See DOCUMENTS, pp. 16-17.) He said that the bullet recovered was from a Winchester 3030, a type of rifle not used in Jonestown at all. (What kind of gun was used to assassinate the *Congressman*, of course, we do not know. Why do forensics when "everyone knows" Jim Jones was responsible?) I heard Marceline talk of it personally, and handled Teri Buford's written eyewitness testimony of the attack to the Los Angeles District Attorney.

Some suggested that Jim Jones could have set up a mock attack to alarm people enough to realize that their lives, even in remote Jonestown, were not safe against the outside world, but rather in *danger* from it. He was surely a master *military* strategist, using psychology almost as would a general: decoy, deception, camouflage, flanking his attacks, then charging straight down the middle when his position was secured.

But manipulate *this* situation? It's preposterous. *This was too physically dangerous!* And with threats of mercenaries in the offing anyway, and given the isolated locale (where anything could be done and the evidence confiscated), undoubtedly we *were* in danger. It's the old adage, "Just because you're paranoid, doesn't mean they aren't out to get you!"

It does seem undeniable that the sniping episode did happen, especially in that the attack occurred right after Haas, the Stoens' attorney, travelled to Jonestown to serve papers for the custody suit. (No one would accept them, and I believe they wound up tacked to a tree.) Even if no one was injured, *the timing of such a provocation was classic*: an implicit threat of military assault if Jim did not release the child.

It was also an assassination attempt. This was done just weeks after the first smear in *New West* broke. Thus the implicit threat that if you try to leave Jonestown, Jim Jones, we will kill you. They surely had tried.

It would have been difficult to assassinate Jim Jones on his own turf, shy of an outright invasion (though obviously, the shooters were hoping to "get lucky"). It would be easier if he were lured out of the community, where shooting scenarios would be easier to line up. It became one of the bitterest ironies of all. For all the loose talk of "people held hostage at Jonestown," it was *Jim Jones* was now effectively the "hostage." He could never return to the States.

Nor can this be underestimated as a turning point. The earlier turning point Stateside which had led us to Guyana, was the departure of the eight college students, headed by Cobb. All Jim Jones feared had now happened – *four of them* showed up in the initial smear in *New West!* Now, not just smears, but actual bullets became the turning point in Guyana. One only has to listen to the final tape made in Jonestown, to realize that a dominant element in the suicides was *fear*. I mean not just fear of death, but fear of *armed attack* – that there would be bloodshed *in any case*.

Thus the six-day siege in September, 1977, had become the masthead for preparations to fight, run, or die in the event of full-scale invasion. Yet any of those three were being touted as *preferable* to being dragged back to the United States, kicking and screaming, so to speak. It would never just be a disappointment, or even "a failure." It would be young people thrown back onto the mean streets, enraged at having their wholesome new life, indeed their entire future, snatched out of their reach. Older people thrown back into the slums whom such a dislocation could rapidly kill off. The political ramifications. At the least, an assassinated leader to avenge. The loose cannons in our ranks who might want to "make them pay," whether the true perpetrators were ready targets or not.

Whatever options were considered, being dragged back could not be one of them. Running was also ruled out ~ escape routes through the jungle to Venezuela were investigated and deemed too dangerous. And whatever the bravado, fighting was no option, either. We weren't a military camp. We were young and old, male and female, families. And for all the talk of "an armed camp" (the best ruse, of course, for perpetrating violence *against* us!), we were pathetically underarmed ~ barely enough small arms to protect the community against the natural hazards of the jungle.

A friend who was in Georgetown at the time of the suicides, hence spared, also said that Jim never wanted us to fight the military of our host country, Guyana. He realized that we would never see the enemy's face. Like if the F.B.I. were in part responsible, we would obviously never be shooting at the J. Edgar Hoover post. It would, more likely, be the Guyanese military who were being manipulated into making a strike, and we could wind up killing people who were our hosts and benefactors.

Thus the subtle underpinnings for responses reporters must have found enigmatic; like one queried Jim that final, fateful day in Jonestown about an alleged mass suicide threat, and he said, "No. *What we said was that we would rather commit suicide than kill.*" Well, there's desperation, and then there's the kind of desperation which resorts to the unthinkable when it cannot project a viable voice. It silences *itself*. Don't spend an entire lifetime building bridges, uniting the races, alleviating poverty, healing the sick, elevating the underdog, and then in a few brief, furious moments, violate and reverse everything for which you ever lived. Rather *die*.

Not everyone would make such a choice, surely; and any question of *imposing* such a choice is a societal taboo at best. But if you want to know how and why *Jim Jones* made such a choice, you must lay it out for what it is.

Some in Jonestown, left to their own devices, indeed might have preferred being dragged away, just or unjust, rather than risk any loss of life. Others wouldn't. But what if "free choice" was an assumption that didn't even exist? History may never clarify whether the people of

Jonestown, trapped in a remote jungle on the heels of an assassination, ever *had* a choice. I don't know if you have ever seen a riot. Surely not everyone meant to riot. But violence wins. Sometimes *no one* meant to riot, and violence still wins. Even massacre. Look at history. Look at India. Look at Ireland. Look at South Africa. Even in the light of day in known, open locations, in cities. And after people are dead, who can clarify whether or not it was really a "riot" that provoked their getting killed?

And was there not ample cause to take a military threat seriously? From then on in, it became a whole different ball game. The six-day seige, even if seen as just one more step towards a deadly end, changed <u>*everything*</u>.

An infamous Catch-22 somewhat later on would hardly help. Allegedly a mass suicide threat had been made over "if they try and take *John...*," and when Debbie Blakey had returned to the States in the Spring of 1978, announcing she was in the anti-Temple camp, she publicized the threat.

A press release delivered over "ham radio patch" (no, not precisely like having cameras rolling in your face), mostly a condemnation of the "Concerned Relatives" monstrosity, tackled it as openly as possible without uttering the word "suicide":

> "Finally... about some statement supposedly issued ... by Peoples Temple ... to the effect that we prefer to resist this harassment and persecution even if it means death. Those... lying and slandering [us].. are trying to use this statement against us. However... any person [of] integrity and courage would have no trouble understanding our position... Dr. Martin Luther King... told his Freedom Riders: 'We must develop the courage of dying for a cause.'.... *If people cannot appreciate that willingness to die, if necessary, rather than to compromise the right to exist free from harassment... then they can never understand the integrity, honesty and bravery of Peoples Temple...* It is not our purpose to die; we believe deeply in the celebration of life. It has always been [our] intention... to light candles rather than curse the darkness... But under these outrageous attacks, we have decided to defend the integrity of our community and our pledge to do this. We are confident that people of conscience and principle understand our position. We make no apologies for it."

The Dead Cat on the Juror's Doorstep/239

This never made it to the mainstream press. Even if it had, such statements can come back to haunt you. "Haunt" and more. Given ongoing mercenary threats, would not a suicide threat make us even *more*, sitting ducks? Virtually *anything* could be done in the dense jungle, and then called "suicide." If you really think people are out to kill you, it does seem deadly to suggest that you might do away with yourselves!

I watched this particular chapter unfold with little alarm. I was busy, dutiful, responsible, but it was a siege of peaceful silence that graced my days, not panic or fright. In any case, there was no advantage (to the contrary, some risk) in our San Francisco church becoming alarmed. Talk of the sniper attack was quickly dropped. Nor did it resurface as a major issue until September, 1978, a whole year later, at which point, however, it became *dominant*.

It happened with the advent of famous attorney and so-called conspiracy theorist, Mark Lane. Charles Garry, our attorney but still not one of us, was balking at claiming conspiracy in court. His view, oddly, was that Jonestown was such an incredible place (he had seen it with his own eyes: *"I Have Been to Paradise"*), that all we had to do was bring people there and every attack against us would be defused.

Patience was wearing thin to even fathom the gross naiveté of "just bring everyone there." We had *already invited* everyone from the President on down through every Senator and every Congressman, plus the United Nations, Amnesty International, and numerous other prominent folk, and takers were few. Everyone who went gave it rave reviews, but none were powerful or well-placed enough to reverse the tide.

Meanwhile, the conspiracy was gaining in force, they dominated the press, and we had no numbers left Stateside, no P.R. people, nor even an ongoing think tank to fend off the attacks. Some bad press and before we knew it, every agency was on our back and lawsuits abounded. There were obviously well-financed, well-connected parties making all these wheels go 'round. I guess we had just reached the point of "How could Garry be so stupid?" when....

XXXII. The Wrong Team's Pitcher is Sent In for "the Save."

We landed Mark Lane. The famous *"Rush to Judgment"* Mark Lane. On one of the rare occasions when we viewed "approved" films together (mostly rampant with "redeeming social value"), we had seen *"Parallax View,"* a fictional account of an assassination said to echo Lane's unique reconstruction of the assassination of JFK.

Lane was a plum while Garry, by contrast, was getting to be an obstacle. He was ignoring all the blatant pointers to conspiracy, wanting us to "make friends rather than fight." It seemed that Joseph Mazor, anti-Temple P.I. alias jailbird for a career in forgery, had somehow wormed his way into Garry's left ear, implanted the fantastical notion that *Tim Stoen had merely ripped off a million dollars of Temple funds on the way out*(!), and that that neatly explained all the well-funded efforts we had misconstrued to be a "conspiracy."

Never mind that the Mertles, Mazor's employers, were a fully-funded operation before they even *knew* Tim Stoen was on the way out, that David Conn had never set foot in the Temple at all, that Stoen's stated purpose for opposing us ("They have my son") was bogus, or a million other mere "details."

Garry was our attorney but there were instructions he was unwilling to pursue. We needed these evil-doers off our backs and Garry wouldn't do it. Lane would. He showed up "just in time" and seemed to be exactly the godsend we needed.

Teri had tracked him down through his Citizens Commission on Inquiry, and at the time, there was no more reason to be suspect of her than to have been of Tim when he lined up Guyana. "Good for Teri." The master conspiracy theorist was willing to take a look at *us*. Now Jonestown could be saved!

We just had to play our cards right. And what initiative Lane showed right off the bat. He took on one of the trickiest cards in the deck: Joe Mazor. Lane claimed he had never met him before in his entire life at the time of an allegedly innocent interview on September 5, 1978, but obviously brilliant, perceptive, quick to size up the opposition and parlay it into our court, he was (oh, wasn't this wonderful?) adept at not merely courting him, but positively turning him into a friend! And at his first contact with the man? What genius! No one even seemed to notice the bizarre cloak-and-dagger lingo that Lane and Mazor bantered back and forth, ostensibly to gain our confidence.

Or was it a confidence *ploy*? There was no Jim Jones on the scene to check out either the personages nor the motives of the participants. All we knew was that Lane had apparently, with remarkable skill, uncovered a startling, unanticipated revelation: Within just moments, it seemed, with the untrustworthy Mazor, Lane had extracted from him that it was in fact ... *he* who had led the attack against Jonestown in September, 1977! Yet, the story ran (Mazor's inroads *against* us from the September 1977 raid to now, September, 1978, remaining conveniently unexplained), so impressed was Mazor that he didn't find squalid or oppressive conditions in Jonestown (to the contrary), that he had willingly retreated and now... was prepared to make a movie about his exploits! Lane, of course, heartily recommended that we pursue this fantastical course.

Oh, then there was that one phenomenal "coincidence" that sent Mark Lane virtually sailing into our arms: Garry's insistence that the shadiest character to emerge thus far, Joseph Mazor, had *his* confidence, assuring us with a self-satisfied flourish that *"There's no conspiracy - Mazor convinced me of that,"* leaving Jim Jones, who was already in severely failing health, desperate for legal counsel to bail us out of our woes.

How had this fortuitous blend of coincidences gelled? That within a few days, it seemed, our champion (Garry) was in the hip pocket of an enemy (Mazor), while Lane, by contrast, cool, suave, hip to private-eye-ese, was virtually managing both Mazor and which ambulances he would now be chasing after.

I never saw the Lane-Mazor transcript myself until some time after the residents of Jonestown were already dead. When I did, it seemed impossible that Jim Jones, shy of life's last embattled gasp, had fallen hook, line and sinker for this odd skew of events, except that it was *hopeful*, and little other news coming from the States was. And desperate people (people desperate to save their own, not to mention the terminal illness now consuming his lungs rapid-pace) will sometimes take desperate gambles. Perhaps a Mazor talking to us seemed less risky than no one talking with us at all, just getting ready to send in the troops and snatch little kids.

But here was *Lane*, delivering us the very inside circle of the mercenary cabal. He held another card as well, which seemed at the time the very Ace of Trumps. Garry would not press suit. Lane was willing (no, positively eager!) to pursue our case against every and all governmental agencies that could be listed in an extensive multi-million dollar lawsuit. Well, so he said at the time, even to the press. Why, the papers had already been filed, hadn't they? Lane certainly had collected his retainer to do so.

Surely Lane was our man. Man of the hour. A grateful Jim Jones rushed to invite our prestigious new champion for a warm personal reception in Jonestown Even, at Lane's behest, we risked inviting in Mazor, whom Lane (who did seem surprisingly chummy with Mazor in the interview) assured us was ready and willing to "come clean." Now, finally, the conspiracy would be broken open!

The Lane bonanza was kept from most of us until he was ready to declare the very launching of the legal missiles that would sink the conspiracy to the bottom of the sea. I didn't know much about it myself until Sunday, October 1, 1978, a mere six weeks before the tragedy. Until what seemed like that joyous revelation, I was strictly into routine. Letter-writing and some side projects as assigned. I had plenty to do without invading "need to know" territory.

No one in Guyana even thought the bulk of us "needed to know" about the disastrous decline in Jim's health. Though it might be hard to fault that decision, even in retrospect. That double-bind was an especially horrifying one. If the general congregation knew, then it was potentially no secret from *anyone*. And if the conspirators knew, or believed, Jim to be very ill, they could accelerate plans to endanger the community.

Jim's usual inclination was to say things were going very well, anyhow, for morale purposes. We were bombarded with reports on the joyous progress of the community. Which wasn't un-true. It was just one side of a scenario of fierce, enigmatic contrasts. Jonestown's burgeoning expansion, which routinely yielded high praise from on-site visitors, and its contraction into paranoid isolation, were factors which seemed to exponentially grate against one another, perhaps indeed, because both ironically and diabolically, it was its very interracial, socialist *success*, not its shortcomings, that provoked its *destruction* by forces Stateside.

We also had a community of greatly enhanced health (physically, vocationally, and phenomenal morale compared with inner city life here) just as our leader began his own long, slow dissolution into terminal illness from a rare fungal growth in the lungs which, mysteriously, no one else had appeared to contract.

Thus it was indeed possible for Jonestown to be a place about which one was ecstatic, fanatic, and passionate to defend, while at the same time, might give it a guarded prognosis to even survive. In San Francisco, we were inundated with one side of this two-edged reality, and quite shielded from the other. No one ever lied about Jonestown being a phenomenal place, an advance model of interracial achievement that America could well emulate. But no one ever informed us San Franciscans, either, about a mindset which at times verged on desperation and panic. It made it impossible for us to gauge what things were really like so very far away.

Lane showed up one Sunday morn, appearing quite the distinguished one, bearded and beaming with leonine confidence, and filled in many of the blanks. There was a Sunday service on October 1, 1978, followed by a smaller meeting of about twenty of us, including me, and a couple of days later, a public press conference, which appeared in the news on October 4. (See DOCUMENTS, p. 21.) I was at both Sunday meetings, and transcribed the press conference, so I arrived at what I know first-hand.

Nothing gave us a shot in the arm like welcoming Lane. He and a left-wing author friend, Donald Freed, *raved* about Jonestown. They told us of construction and expansion, and charming anecdotes, like "punishment" for the children was not being allowed to work(!), because they so loved their opportunities to contribute and excel.

Excerpts from a Freed interview done in Guyana are as follows:

"If you look at Jonestown. . . and then you read some of the [people's] oral histories. . . ***you're driven to the conclusion that the most extraordinary material and social experiment is being carried out.*** . . by a population. . . which in the United States were not considered useful, in fact. . . 'non-entities.' Either too old, too young, too unskilled, uneducated, with burdensome personal records, either of addiction or health problems, or incarceration. . . And to see these statistics translated into people singing, as I saw last night, taking part in a very full cultural activity. . . . The heavy collective past of suffering . . .and then, this existential present, as the jungle gives way to schools, dispensaries, and agriculture, and culture, and with its future orientation, its planning and its expansion for the future. . . . ***I'm at pains to find the words to describe what's essentially an unspeakable experience, but I have no doubt it will be spoken about and written about widely, and there will be steady traffic through Jonestown in the years to come.***

"These people feel. . . I think you'd have to use the word 'love' as a catalyst. . . . .a chance to express through work . . . . negative, aggessive and hostile feelings towards conditions of oppression, which were expressed in the past in self-destructive acts in the United States. . . . So that individual resentments and frustrations are [transmuted] and the guilt is removed, and translated into the community and nation-building that lies before them. . . institutions which support the children, support the seniors, support those who've been culturally deprived. . . . *I was absolutely stunned at the sophistication and professionalism of the cultural activities at Jonestown.*"

". . . .We've been told from the beginning that if you take people, even from the best-educated class, that soon the strongest will have garnered the power. . . and we will see a deadly and monotomous repetition of all of the ills of the super-industrial state, because we are told that is human nature. . .That cannot be true, because Jonestown exists. [Jonestown] shows that the monotonous and routinized life of workers as we have been taught to believe is the only way to work and live, is a pitiful cariacature of what could be, and Jonestown gives the lie to all those myths.

"To have come here to Jonestown from Washington, the city of lies. . . . to what appears increasingly to me to be a kind of city of truth here. . . . I really am at a loss for words. . . . Martin Luther King, I think, if he could see Jonestown, he would recognize it as the next step in his agenda, and he would say, one, two, three, many Jonestowns."

". . . When I came to Jonestown, I knew I was entering a superior society. It's like coming to another planet."

Lane seconded the motion, and more. We had no one left on a regular basis who would rouse the crowd to their feet to cheer and cheer, as Jim had done routinely. But I'll never forget *Lane*. How when he was done with the praise and the raves, and the vows that we move on victorious, he shouted out to us, *"Jim Jones is a saint! Jim Jones is a saint!"* We stood in force. We clapped, we cheered, we hooted. Lane was emphatic: "Jim Jones is a *saint!*" It wasn't a word *we* used. Lane invented that quite on his own, but we loved it.

Such sensitivity, too! He seemed genuinely moved by his Jonestown journey. *"It makes me almost weep,"* he told us plangently, *"to *see how the intelligence agencies are trying to destroy this amazing work."*

I thought it an honor to be asked to stay for the ensuing, smaller meeting of people, including Marceline, who were more closely involved with the work. What he had to tell us... I can look back and see that it was alarming, except that the spin on it was that it was *past*, and that now things were turning around ~ towards openness, revelation, counterattack.

It was neither questioned nor answered how Lane had become acquainted with Mazor, just that he had, and that Mazor had "confessed" to having led the now-infamous raid on the community in September, 1977. Not only that. **He played us the actual tape of Mazor's confession.** That he arrived expecting to find barbed wire and horrendous conditions, and that his instructions had been to kidnap the children. But when he found what appeared to be a peaceable community, his party contented themselves with sniping for a few days and then left.

Then Lane turned the tape off. He added in confidential tones, that Mazor had requested it be kept "off the record," but that he said he was sent not only to kidnap the children, but to ***"then kill all the adults."*** A hushed silence fell across our little group. Somehow, presented in this manner ~i.e. that these deadly confidences were extracted on our own territory in the presence of Jim Jones~, it seemed like a *turn-around*, something like the extraction of a decaying tooth before the whole mouth could go rotten. "Former arch-enemy" Mazor was so impressed with Jonestown himself, Lane averred, that he was cooperating with us in breaking the conspiracy.

Whatever the *truly* appropriate questions may have been, they weren't posed. It seemed we had been granted an enormous reprieve.

Yes, indeed. Just two days later, on October 3, Lane held a press conference and announced to the whole world that help, safety and a bailout was speeding right around the corner for Peoples Temple in the form of Mark Lane and his "massive anti-government lawsuit."

To my delight, I was given the honor of transcribing the tape of the Lane/Freed raves. My fingers flew over the keys. It seemed the happiest assignment of the decade.

XXXIII. The Presence Takes My Hand to Carry Me Through.

Only one unanticipated ripple in consciousness made that period one of foreboding for what would happen next. I had no way to know that mid-September night, while I slept undisturbed in my ascetic quarters, that "our greatest triumph" (a/k/a gamble) was bursting onto Jonestown. Lane, still a few weeks' shy of his San Francisco debut, was being heralded into Jonestown, and on his arm, our new "conquest," Joseph Mazor.

Even had I known, it seemed to spin in our favor. Those mere two months before catastrophe, my mind was not on death. September 16th, just passed, no longer seemed so ominous. Maybe, indeed, it was our last veil of darkness before the bright dawn in yet another world – if not Guyana, then the Soviet Union.

Indeed, by that fateful November eve, we were right on the brink of relocation to our new home – something all the massive post-tragedy publicity failed to uncover, much less explore. (Everyone was disclaiming us. Why not the Soviets? Or, as Jim Jones said on the final tape, *"Russia won't take us [now] with all this stigma."*)

Sandwiched in between, planned for December 1, we would be hosting a dinner in San Francisco, to gather in our supporters and celebrate the hoped-for power and clout of our counterattack. I could dream now in peace, could I not?

But I cannot even say this was strictly a dream. There are dreams and there are dreams. Some, fraught with fragments and fears, leave you enervated, and frantic to unravel the knots your mind forged in your sleep. Other dreams, rarely, have a lightness about them, as a beacon to propel you ahead. This dream in mid-September, 1978, was most singular. It was one of the most singular dreams of my entire life.

It came through in "dream language," but it was more like a visitation. It happened in three parts: Past, Future, and Present, like my own personal "A Christmas Carol." First the Past: I saw an open, park-like space, rich with green. It looked much like the campus at the university where I had gone to school. I saw Kathy Richards, my former young helper with the letters – awkward, insecure, unfocussed seventeen-year-old Kathy Richards, the same age *I* was when I worked with my earliest mentor that fateful year of exhuberant, then cruelly dashed, hopes.

Yet I realized that somehow Kathy Richards was also a stand-in for another "Kathy" that had left the group and just recently written back, from several states away (= the distant past), just recovered from a mental breakdown (= my state then), to ask "how we all were." (Talk about being out of it!) Her first name was also Kathy, but her last name in real life was the same name as my mentor those earliest years. It seemed I was again 17, with all the promise and all the heartbreak anew.

I saw Kathy, and turned to my left to acknowledge her. As I turned, I felt a hand in mine, and a hand on my shoulder, and heard the most gentle, reassuring voice: *"I asked someone to always keep a hand on you."*

Next the Future: I saw a young man. He seemed to be a high spiritual soul whom I would work with later on in life. He was tall, well-proportioned, sandy-colored hair with a slight wave, and green eyes. Our relationship was everything my relationship with Jim was *not* -- relaxed, secure, accepting, at peace. I felt a comradeship, almost a joy in his presence, as we walked hand-in-hand. It was free of the conflict and trauma I had endured with "The Spirit of Gurus Past."

I was startled because he so resembled a *poet* boyfriend I had taken up with, following my catastrophic break from school. Was this "dream person" a "person" at all? It seemed rather *a promise* -- that as with my *poetry*, "Allegory," a Presence would accompany me later on -- that the Future would transmute my catastrophes into *freedom*.

Then, suddenly, I was thrust into the Present. I found myself on a subway level with masses of people -- all of Humanity, it seemed. To my right, I saw a staircase ascending into the sunlight. I saw Jim Jones on that staircase, as he rose upwards into the golden Sun. I remained below. There were people everywhere -- anonymous, oblivious, confused. I felt shocked, abandoned, even panicked. He was gone. He had disappeared into the streaming golden Sun and I was left alone.

Then, just as suddenly, I found myself mid-way up the staircase out of the subway towards the Light, looking up, but still bound to the world below. I heard him call my name loudly across the crowd, and suddenly he was right there, by my side -- supportive, strong, his energy wholly with mine. It seemed late afternoon, and as I glanced at him, I saw that he had changed his clothing. "I thought you might not come back," I said. His face radiated a serenity and love which warmed every fiber of my being. Then, with an infinite gentleness, he said, *"No. I wouldn't do that to you."*

I was jolted awake with a start. I saw a rich, golden, near-blinding flash of visible light and felt, in an instant, overwhelming exhilaration. I had been touched by a near-blissful blend of serenity and power, and I was *free*. At that very moment, I felt "*Allegory*" dropping off my shoulders, its huge oppressive weight released. Mysteriously, suddenly, this was a burden to me no more.

I felt my soul rejoice, "I know who you are. I finally know who you are." Then I suddenly began to weep. I wept off and on for a week, not knowing why.

Something had been cleansed from me. The murkiness, the cloudiness that clings to *personal* conflict – it had dissipated. I thought of Jim and it seemed like I was left with pure Spirit. It was the Spirit Who had enticed me there from the start. It was the *Spirit* in the man – the healings, the warmth, the compassion, the untiring patience, the Spirit of Unity, the Spirit of Love.

Somehow the synapse in me that had snapped, like a bit of tinder crackling with a fierce flame, destroying my sense of belonging in this place... it was *healed*. *I* was healed. I was made whole. I was, almost, *reunited* with the guiding Spirit who so retreated into the shadows when my life was shattered by the excruciating ordeals.

How could I be so free now, and yet so immersed in grief? There was no one to talk to – surely they all thought me strange enough as is. Until *Marceline* returned, though I did not tell her of the dream 'til mid-October, a single month before the end. Lane had accompanied her when she first arrived, and the flurry of activity allowed no time. By the time she and I could meet, our spirits were boosted so far *up*, that my dream was already beginning to seem like a mirage.

I don't remember if it was me who asked to talk. I think she asked how I was. I was appreciative that it wasn't a guilt-laden affair just to talk, as it would have been with Jim. She came up to my cubbyhole of a room. First she gave me Jim's praise. "Jim appreciates your work so much. When the packets are brought over, he always reads your write-ups *first*." This was praise no. 7 now – the one thing I had told Jim explicitly, "*Don't!*"

It did move me despite myself – almost like I could hear him saying, "I'll reach out to you even though I don't know how, nor do I know if this will work." Because however inadequate this was, he cared about making it right. Even with all those horrendous pressures and the very survival of Jonestown still far from assured. Even with terminal illness, which I didn't even know. I just knew that every time a message was sent through for me, that Jim Jones, however unable to make things right, did *care*.

Even while not wanting the messages. Having meant every word I said. Almost like if he gave me something I wanted, needed, much less asked for, it was tainted. That only an initiative in defiance of my wishes could express what *he* wanted. I suppose I came to understand why even destitute people sometimes refuse charity. It had to be because *he wanted*, not because *I needed*. It *had* to be.

Even Sharon had chimed in with praise (no. 5 or 6), at how Jim appreciated my write-up to the United Nations International Commission on Human Rights, and that in the future, I would be given more of this kind of work. How could I respond? It took them eight-and-a-half years to discover that I could think? But still, the tug on my heartstring... Maybe somewhere, at some time, it could be different. Maybe he had the will to make it right.

Now, this new praise coming from Marceline... This was Marceline, and certainly it came right from *her* heart. I couldn't bear to tell her how I cringed when she said, "Jim wants you to know how much he appreciates all your work." I held my heart, but gently released my tongue. "I've always worked hard," I said softly, measured as if to tread only a certain, central line. "I expect I always will." I paused a moment and looked down. "But that's not all there is to life. It's not everything." She left me an easy, uncontested silence.

Then I told her I finally felt I could talk about "*Allegory*," a long poem I had written about Jim's death and the death of many of our people. That it had been hanging over my head like the Sword of Damocles for four years now. That I could never live with it, but I could never destroy it either. That Jim had been angry with me ("You know, he doesn't like me writing poetry anyway"), but I couldn't seem to shake its hold on my consciousness. I had tried. I really had. It terrified me, but I could do nothing until now.

She looked at me intently, almost fascinated. Destroying people over poetry seemed foreign to her. She wanted to let me speak.

I said I had had a remarkable dream, that seemed to free me from "*Allegory's*" oppressive weight, and now I could not decide whether to hold onto the work or to destroy it. If my destructive impulses shocked her, she didn't reveal it. She paced this lightly, like a scan gently easing o'er my face. Listening, listening. How extraordinarily this compassionate soul listened.

250/SNAKE DANCE

I asked could I tell her about the dream. She nodded slightly in assent. I told her about Jim disappearing off the top of the staircase leading from the masses of humanity up into the golden Light, about the visible flash of light when I awoke, the exhilaration, the fantastic release, and then the sudden, inexplicable, yet uncontrollable sobbing, not knowing why.

I looked at her with slight apprehension ~ maybe a weariness, more than eight years in the making now: "I finally know who Jim is." I was nervous, slightly nervous yet perfectly calm. What I knew, I knew. God knows, I could never reach the *man*, but nor could he me. Yet on that high, serene level I could never explain, Jim Jones and I were *close*. Closer than I had ever felt to anyone ever before.

"I finally know who Jim is"? I? Through all this? How so trusting, so innocent still? Marceline, abundant with the virtues of solid Capricorn, while eschewing its harshness, had the calm good sense to not make this "a conversation about who Jim might be." She had a rare gift of making sense of silence, and of offering silence as a response, as a salve even ~ a healing salve for the soul. She said nothing. A moment later, I resumed.

I said I wanted to read "Allegory" to her, and could I ask her to decide whether or not I should keep it. **"Because it's so tragic"** (I looked down), **"And everyone is so happy now."** She said yes, of course, she would like to hear it. I told her it was emotional and could get loud, so maybe we should use the sound-proof booth near the stage. I asked if the sound engineer for the services could set it up for taping. It was mid-October, a single month as the clock would tick down to the very catastrophe "Allegory" was about.

We met in the late afternoon. I first showed her the Introduction, based on what I had gleaned from the Greeks, filtered through my own brimming mind. She seemed intrigued, not having had this world opened to her before, or expecting any excursions beyond the prescribed regimens or routines. Ancient history? Mythology? She seemed... well, almost *pleased*, like it was a refreshing break from the worries that had beset us, especially of late.

I asked her to give me a moment to get into the reading. It was like going into a trance state ~ inward, emotional, and then it was like voices were coming out of me. I shouted, I whispered, I clenched my teeth, the words sailed musically across the interlinking rhythms of the lines. Mostly I wept. I couldn't hold back the tears. I wept the tears that the Being who gave me the work released years before. I wept the loss of my friends. I wept the loss of our leader. I wept the loss of the "garden" which was our jungle home. I wept the misunderstandings, I wept the transgressions, I wept the hurt and the pain. I wept the ignorance of humanity. I wept that the very angels would weep as they watched from the serenity and wholeness of perchance another world.

Finally, there was the burst of *"No. It is worse you've made travesty of my SPI⸺ RI⸺T!!!! For only the non-flesh-ridden to extol the NA⸺ME⸺..."* Then I looked down, shaken still, nearly quavering, composure barely regained.

I looked to Marceline cautiously, hesitantly, and asked, "Do you think I should keep this?" The slightest pause. "Should I *destroy* it?" I saw her face blanch, like she could scarcely conceal being jolted, shocked, at the intensity of this paean of funereal praise. (Were Jim Jones and Peoples Temple already gone?) "No," she said, her voice as gentle as it was firm. "You *keep* it. It's beautiful."

I was content with this. Content to take Marceline as arbiter. I could release the tortured consciousness, even not knowing that I had just revealed to her, at length and in rich, accurate (i.e. accurate-to-be) detail, how the Jonestown Tragedy would unfold before the world. I revealed, indeed, my *own* heart, my *own* plangent grief at the tragedy, the grief I had wept out years before its scenario had materialized at all.

I sometimes still wonder what she wondered about me. About how this work had come to me. About how (even though I *said* I felt we would emerge triumphant and free) I knew in my innermost soul what was to come. I *told* her about the tragedy that day. I told her its agony. I told her its grief. I told her of a world that would castigate and ridicule us, and never comprehend what really happened at all.

A few short days later, she was forever gone. She called me in my room by phone. She asked me to come upstairs to the apartment to say goodbye. I walked in and she moved right towards me and hugged me, just like I was her own child. I was very moved. I felt I would see her again. Why would I not see her again? I was happy. In this whole huge, shattered and darkened world, I had found a friend.

XXXIV. The Last Rotten Apple Falls from the Tree.

Marceline left San Francisco for the last time within days of our hyperintense "time warp" encounter. Her departure seemed routine enough, or even better, for in her wake we had been left a hope: Mark Lane. The place buzzed with anticipation, with a renewed energy to push our way past the last dark trials, to freedom.

Meanwhile, of course, no one had been keeping too close an eye on Teri Buford. It was hard. *She* was the one who was on top of everything. So much was top secret, and you didn't question top dogs about top secrets. Besides, who had to watch Teri? She was the quintessentially useful one, especially now ~ doing all this incredible work in securing and orienting Lane.

There was just one tiny, odd thing. I remember ascending the staircase from the podium while she was walking down, and she looked at me and said, "You look nice." My hair, my clothes, something. Something small. Yet I thought, rightly for us oddballs, "Now, *that's* strange." We were scrupulously trained not to comment on looks or other trademarks of attractiveness. We were "workers," not "women" or "men." And Teri, of all people, was all business. She would never notice stuff like that.

It was only on looking back (upon meeting this terrible twosome wrapped up in each other's arms on a New York street!), that I realized that Teri (whose father was a Naval officer ~ another "miraculous convert," like the John Bircher Mertles and Rotary Club Stoen?) had already taken up with Lane, a "love" about to produce deadly fruit.

At the time, who could think the unthinkable ~ that Teri was about to bolt? She was stuck like glue to Lane, and he seemed a bonanza, not a threat. His heartfelt outpouring to us, his rave reviews of Jonestown, his willingness to go public with countersuits, was electrifying. People were ecstatic. Our salvation had arrived!

I had no way to track the underlying reality. Or did I? My dream had been so transparently about death, my tears pouring forth in a flood. It so much belied what seemed like multiple omens of hope. But I was used to living in two worlds by now. So I rooted for Lane to press on, and any weeping I did, I did alone.

Only following the suicides, with the shocking re-emergence of Lane with *Teri* at his side, could I see the cruel illusion. There was never that champion, that advocate, that hope. I couldn't fathom that such a mirage had happened at all, much less why. But it does matter that the Lane "bonanza" was an illusion ~ perhaps a giant hidden reflecting mirror of the true state of Peoples Temple at the time, whatever the brave public words.

Like most liabilities during that period, of course, knowing the truth at the time might have only made things *worse* ~ as if a "worse" could exist, given the ultimate leap into the abyss. But that it *was* a hoax, rising to the fore of a whole host of hoaxes, itself makes a muddier case for failing to see that the people of Jonestown were under real pressure, not mere fabrications, or the ravings of a paranoid lunatic.

History can be rather a dumb beast, too. Like take Egyptology. It turns out that the pyramids are at least twice as old as the experts had thought. And why? Because someone, one John Anthony West, finally noticed the degree of erosion around the pyramids, which could only have been caused by *rain*; and that much rain had only fallen on Egypt thousands of years earlier than the original dating! All those scholars, and no one had observed the obvious. So who will rewrite the entirety of Egyptology, and when will they do it? History characteristically "proves" only what the discovery of new information has not yet contraindicated. It's a process, not an icon graven in stone.

That said, and given that an illusory state of mind existed on the part of many approaching that fateful November night, this is how I can best reconstruct how Teri stole away:

Some time after Lane's San Francisco debut, Teri, who was coordinating Lane, disappeared. It was October, 1978 ~ she gave "October 27th" as the date to the press, exactly three weeks before the end. She undoubtedly opted to wait 'til Marceline was gone, then slipping her parting note vowing *eleventh-hour double-agent heroics*, under Jean Brown's door in the middle of the night. It was full of pleas for secrecy, an appeal which could readily be made to Jean, but not to Marceline. Jean would handle this "organizationally" (i.e. silently), whereas Marceline (given Teri's premise that "When a person [i.e. Jim Jones] is dying, what choices are there?") might have handled it "personally" ~ like "My husband's dying, and you're *leaving*?" Then Jim could have knee-jerked, and everyone and his dog would have been tracking Buford down.

254/SNAKE DANCE

Teri did go back and forth from Guyana, so her departure wasn't unusual, per se, but very few knew that this time was different. That she had just disappeared – left a letter, yes, but no forwarding address, to say the least.

For all the clamor over the arrival of Lane, and the stealth of Teri's departure, no one had thought to connect the two. Especially since Teri, in her letter to Jim, obviously considered our situation desperate; and Lane, by contrast, had arrived buoyantly, as a beacon of hope. Plus, although Teri was managing Lane, it would have been prohibitive for anyone to ask if he had heard from her. You don't lose track of your own top people and query an outsider! Thus from then on in, until the chilling joint emergence of these two following the tragedy, the gain of Lane and the loss of Buford were undoubtedly thought to be a mere coincidence of time.

Just days after the tragedy, Lane and Buford surfaced *together* to the press. Lane's **"Jim Jones is a saint!,"** like the proverbial bad penny, had tossed itself over into **"Jim Jones is a murderer!"** Teri, curt, reserved, still "all business," announced (quite in contrast to her writing Jim Jones, "Everything the church is presently in trouble for, I organized and carried out") that she had never been anything more than "a glorified relay machine," and solemnly volunteered to "cooperate fully with the authorities."

It was like the proverbial darkness before the dawn had been turned on its head: Lane's raving tribute to the beauty and genius of Jonestown, his avowed determination to lead us to triumph over our enemies, was the brilliant laser beam of light lifted up like a sword of victory just before it descended instead as an executioner's sword upon the heads of my cherished friends.

I look back and almost wish it had been an analogous phenomenon to the black of night or the thrilling relief of dawn. I still cannot fathom how any *human* agency could be so cynical, even satanic (claiming no religious monopoly on the word), to foist that kind of treachery upon people merely desperate to survive and live in peace.

Even Jim Jones, who welcomed in Lane with the Ryan party, was undoubtedly unable to decipher this poisonous scenario. We thought Lane had already filed suit. I didn't know Teri had left at all. The few who did surely had no idea that she had gone to *Lane*. Paranoia can be a highly destructive force. But what, after all, do you do when you have the responsibility of a thousand people on your shoulders, and you truly, legitimately, **do not know whom you can trust?**

The Last Rotten Apple/255

The parting note itself, shy of emotional overtones, was cleverly designed to, even if it created panic, to give that panic no recourse against *her*. For one thing, it gave her lead time. Jean, given the cover note imploring secrecy, had to travel to Jonestown to deliver it personally. That gave Teri time. Also, Jean couldn't second-guess Teri's motives, so if she spilled the beans, she could be endangering Teri's life, thus was barred from seeking advise about it from others.

Jim could make no inquiries either. Unless by discernment (which if once razor sharp, he was now terminally ill), Jim wouldn't know for sure whether Teri was loyal or had truly split. He would have to send an actual person who would also have to act like a defector, if there was any chance of learning the truth – which he apparently did in the person of Tim Carter.

And no small point: He would look for Teri in the enemy camp, not with *Lane!*

That said, indeed compounding insult onto injury: That Teri Buford and Mark Lane were the new anti-Peoples Temple "item" the very moment Lane was mouthing, "Jim Jones is a saint!" and telling us to trust *him*, Lane, to save us, may never lose its chill at all. It may have seemed but a grace note in the aftermath of the tragedy, the deaths having struck such a pounding knell within the heart of the world. If I had known the truth about Teri and Lane in advance, if *anyone* had known, it may have altered nothing, only added greater panic to a brew that was already boiling over the rim. But that doesn't make it less. It makes it *more*.

I have always been unlike others, anyway, who said, "If I only knew this, if I only knew that..." What a terrible thing to be entrusted with knowing. And ironically, knowing or not knowing that Teri had left, or the circumstances, empowered no-one, even Jim Jones, to *change* anything.

I don't know that knowing the state of Jim's health would have changed anything either. That sword cut too many ways. Anyone meaning us harm would have exploited that knowledge. The people who did know, like Teri, were, one would think, especially responsible to act like human beings, not predators out to save their own skin by citing a dying leader as a ruse for supposed heroics to come.

As for Teri and loyalty, if she were suspect by some close to the leader, as her letter suggests, it was a well-kept secret. She probably would have been put on a short list of people *not* to be suspect of. After all, were not the numbers of the Swiss bank accounts entrusted to her?

Indeed, Teri, like Stoen, had been a fixture. She joined the church later than me, 1971 or perhaps early 1972. I remembered seeing her often by Jim's side, but as an austere presence. Nervous, quick, real "hop-to." Give her an instruction and she was presto chango *gone*. Tall, thin, with sharp bones framing an intent face, she rarely smiled. I had never put her in a sexual context at all until Jim made a special point of praising *her* for her presumably valiant sacrifice in having an abortion (or was it two or three?), as he scrunched his way across chipped egg shells the night Carolyn was transformed into a saint for having an out-of-wedlock child.

Teri didn't flinch when she was praised. She was her usual austere self. "*Teri's* had abortions. And I told her she could go ahead and have the child. Because that's the kind of person *Teri* is." Jim thrust the force of his personal energy into his words, as if to ground whatever loose bolts might fly out of this basketful of praise. Maybe he knew, or sensed, that she was the one who would later on snap over this issue. Teri herself indeed cited "resentment of others who had children" in her parting note. Common wisdom can sometimes be as simple as, "Hell hath no greater fury than a woman scorned." (Grace. Debbie. Why not Teri?)

Not that Teri didn't work hard, whatever her conflicts. To this day, I would like to think this was a case of burn-out being manipulated by Lane, though it may have in fact been a mutual collusion by people who appeared to put self first and ethics last. Certainly, her actions *after* the tragedy (whatever she was before: a burn-out, a plant, a ruthless shell of a human being with its soft insides long since hollowed out?) bordered on unforgivable.

At the time, of course, this was all unthinkable. No one was even supposed to know that Teri had left. Within days following the tragedy, *the whole world* knew, of course, and that Lane, "our friend," nay, "our salvation," had mentored her unseemly exit from the start. Lane wasn't *for* us at all. He was *against* us.

There is little energy left now for bitterness. Let God take care of these people. Maybe He has a special place reserved for "sweethearts" like Buford & Lane. I wasn't even too surprised to learn later on, of Lane representing the notorious anti-Semite, Willis Carto, the original "holocaust revisionist." Lane. Himself a Jew. It takes a special kinda guy, I guess. I wouldn't want this guy out there directing ongoing traffic to the right or the left, and expecting to thus avoid a fatal accident.

As for Teri's farewell letter to Jim, I discovered it by chance after the tragedy. I was always the most tenacious one. The discovery was not only a surprise, but chilling. Not only for its *con*-tents, but for its *in*-tent. At the least, she saw someone about to die, upon whom a thousand lives depended, and jumped ship to save her own skin.

As for the *con*-tents (notwithstanding the emphasis on the "con"), although fleeing to Lane, I doubt she aired this oddly *personal* communiqué with him, re-capping angst about abortions and "having thought myself in love with you." Maybe it was just a cynical attempt to manipulate sympathy, thus alleviate suspicion. Though I suppose that when you know you are saying good-bye for good, you say whatever you need to say, in however distorted a form.

One thing is sure: Teri never meant this departure in good faith. She went to Lane and then waited. Waited to see if and when Jim Jones died. And Carolyn, of course. And their un-aborted child, Kimo. Whether she was surprised that there were over nine hundred others, how much of a surprise or why, we may never know.

I suppose you, the reader, might find this frustrating by now -- that you cannot find **one single person** who had any noble, high-minded motive for turning against Peoples Temple. If I could provide you even one, I would. There is nothing to lose in this regard -- the people of Jonestown are long since gone.

Though it was also tragic that the *psychological* maelstroms, mostly related to sex, were so pre-dominant in the ex-members who did the most damage, but were presumably not in government employ (Grace Stoen, Debbie Blakey, Teri Buford), that they fell right into the clutches of ex-members like the Mertles and Stoen, whose agenda was rather more cold-blooded -- destroying Peoples Temple for *ideological* reasons; or what appeared to be a coven of "guilty bystanders," like Conn, Klineman, Mazor, and Lane.

Jim was surely right in his cautions that if you left and turned against the church, "they'll use you," though I doubt that anyone who came to love/hate a man as much as Grace, Debbie or Teri love/hated Jim Jones, would care to concede that they were used by the people who claimed to be their champions. On the other hand, if you truly want to keep a harmonious interracial cooperative, a haven for people without hope, out of harm's way, as Jim always insisted was paramount, then sleeping with women, and then pressuring them to have abortions (*whatever* one's motives), is a poor safeguard!

Indeed, it seemed that all our safeguards were crumbling beneath our feet: Our attorneys: Garry threatened to abandon us entirely if Ryan wasn't let into Jonestown, and Lane, regrettably, was the one who led him in! Our top dog Stateside, Teri Buford, had disappeared into the dust. And Congressman Leo Ryan had written us that yes, he was coming to Jonestown at the behest of one Timothy O. Stoen, "to regain his son."

The clock stood poised at one minute to midnight. Was this the moment Jim Jones, all those years, had so feared?: *"...the classic ending: the frame-ups, the 'kill'... ..and [our people] think the press has already done its job with slander and smears, and so no one will care about the frame-ups..."*

XXXV. Our Light is Extinguished Forever.

November 18, 1978: "dark night of the soul." It was a Saturday, in the West a day of festivity and joy, in ancient times namesake of fearsome Saturn ~ somber, melancholy, bearer of grief. The same Saturday that our counterparts overseas had already passed on through, five hours ahead of us. By 7 p.m. San Francisco time, it was already midnight in Jonestown, Guyana. With services scheduled for 7:30 p.m., our Saturday, touted as a special paean of joy *this* week, was just beginning. Guyana's Saturday, laden with inexpressible sorrow, had just passed.

I knew I would be running a little late for services. I was getting out a press release, a very "hot" press release. (See DOCUMENTS, p. 22.) Full of quotes from Congressman Leo Ryan, who had lavished Jonestown with praise. It was poured over the ham radio with a burst of ecstatic gusto. It was infectious, contagious. No one who saw the text of Ryan's comments could conceal their glee or, frankly, their relief!

I was getting the last envelopes ready to mail out. It was an overwhelming high. I couldn't believe that just twenty-four hours earlier the papers had reported a nervous, nearly frenetic Sharon Amos visiting the Congressman at his hotel in Georgetown, saying please don't come, it's a very bad time. Because Jim Jones is very ill.

I knew what "very ill" meant ~ well, what people take it to mean. It's the flu, or an *attack* of something ~ heart, gall bladder, ulcers. Maybe even pneumonia. It's something acute. You have a bout of being very ill and then you recover. I had seen Jim very ill before. I had seen him collapse on stage, more than once ~ from exhaustion, from hypoglocemia, from a heart attack. He always recovered.

I didn't even know that Sharon's claim was true. We had other reasons for keeping Ryan out ~ even the ensuing media circus that could wrench not only John from Jonestown, but any child, not through courts of law, but through mercenaries, through invasion. And this seemingly dignified, proper, official visit ~ it was never just "a visit," and it was never just Ryan. It was the Stoens invading us, the Mertles invading us, Jim Cobb invading us. If this door was opened to them, it could be rammed open by a hundred more, people much more dangerous than "merely concerned relatives."

260/SNAKE DANCE

We had had accolades galore – from Guyanese ministers, and a whole host of other visitors. But even at that, we didn't think we could stay. We had a scouting party ready to go to the Soviet Union *the very next month*. Why couldn't they leave us alone long enough for us to take our children, our older folk, our zealous youth, to a safer port of call?

Ryan wasn't coming to be fair – he was coming as a partisan, at the direct behest of Tim Stoen. Stoen lying about a little boy to drive the leader over the edge. We had issued an open invitation for everyone in Congress to come. But only Ryan met the call, and not at our invitation at all. As a supposed "oversight" visit. So hastily planned that there was only one Congressman, rather than the required two. This was an investigatory visit, an adversarial visit. He had already lined himself up as a hostile witness. What good could come of this?

Sharon, of all people, could roll all this into "Don't come because Jim Jones is very ill." She was trained to couch everything in the most dire terms. I remembered her telling us that Jim Jones was her children's protection against nuclear war and race war alike. Her entreaties in the early days that "He only has a certain amount of energy. Don't drain his energy." What taking too much of his energy would entail, or its risks, was never spelled out, or which drop of this precious elixir of "energy" would finally be too much. For Sharon, it was anything or everything. You waste a penny and it's life-or-death. A starving child could eat for a day on your wasted penny, or die but for that penny's worth of food.

How many pennies was Sharon bartering when she visited the Georgetown hotel? Could I weigh her pleas objectively? I thought Jim really doesn't want the Congressman in Jonestown. He may also be ill. Though we had never heard that he was *chronically* ill; and being *terminally* ill (as Carlton Goodlett, our doctor friend who had visited Jonestown, later told the press) – that was unthinkable. How could I even broach the subject? Even with Marceline. Marceline, who most surely knew, and also most surely knew that I *didn't* (me and my, "Because it's so tragic, and everyone is so happy now."). She wouldn't lie, but also wouldn't volunteer information painful for others to know.

I saw the papers myself, the day before the collapse of our house of cards. How Sharon had visited Ryan in Georgetown, beseeching him not to go. Please. This was a terrible time to come, when the leader was ill. But *they* seemed to give it *no* weight. She might as well have been talking to the T-Rex in *"Jurassic Park."* The march was on. The irate relatives and their champion, Leo Ryan, who was ultimately marked for death. He backed Stoen, who was backed by people who undoubtedly cared far less about retrieving one small child for America, than about keeping the Americans in Jonestown from making yet another move across the seas.

The leader's health? It was too insignificant to consider. After all, they notified us they were coming, didn't they? Should Jim Jones not have been ready for this prestigious visitor? Postponement was out of the question.... and how could we possibly be surprised?

But this press release, the seemingly miraculous turn-around. Once Ryan saw the real, living Jonestown with his own eyes, we seemed suddenly on the brink of what Jim had always, hope against hope, promised: *victorious!* So I tucked Sharon's final plea under my hat, and welcomed the ecstatic reprieve of a pleased Ryan addressing Jonestown in friendly, supportive praise. I could write in my final notes to Jim Jones: "I finally believe that nothing is impossible to resolve." Were we not right on the brink now... the brink of being home free?

Now, at about 7 p.m., my industrious pace of folding, inserting, sealing the news releases (all the many small, repetitive tasks that like a dot matrix of labors, etched out my tapestry of life with Jim Jones), suddenly and forever more came crashing to a halt. It came over the regular commercial radio. *"Congressman Ryan has been shot..."*

What???? How could the report be true? It came as a numbing, surreal shock. Moreover, our ham radio had suddenly, mysteriously, with no warning, no instructions, no panic, no anything... had just *suddenly gone dead.* We counted on that daily rendezvous on the air. If this horror had indeed happened, where were the instructions for *us?*

"Congressman Ryan, visiting the Peoples Temple community at Jonestown, Guyana, was shot at the Port Kaituma Airport." The list of killed and injured, the few sketchy details available, were broadcast. I thought one thing - one thing *only.* "C.I.A." They couldn't let a good report come back. This was the work of the C.I.A. I had no doubt of it.

I rushed down to the service, which had not yet begun. Some had heard nothing. A few were talking uneasily amongst themselves. I rushed to the third floor. The ham radio was there, implaccably silent, as were the bulk of "in" people who were left to man the ship Stateside. They were concerned, baffled, and... *cliquish.* Everyone was trained not to reveal any information to anyone else unless it was their department, their work. If anyone had any info for *me,* it wasn't forthcoming.

No one was in tears, no one seemed shocked - more like worried. We were trained. Trained to be *stoical.* To hang in tough, watch for directives, and scramble for the bail-out on cue. This was a waiting mode. It was inconceivable that there was nothing to wait *for*. I sensed no mooring here, and fled to my room, the commercial radio pressed to my ear. Jonestown was so isolated, so remote. For hours more, 'til the morning news broke, there was only the radio.

The news was incessant but repetitive. "All we know is.... all we know is.... all we know is..." Finally, a few hours hence, a new knife sliced through the haze: "Sharon Amos and her three children were found with their throats slit. Authorities are calling it suicide." They added that ***it was thought that members of the Jonestown community were committing suicide.***

What? No. I can't handle all this at once. I remember... like a block snapping in, saying you can handle this, but you can't possibly handle that. Ryan's death was an act. But now Ryan's death, and Sharon and her children, maybe even the whole community – it was *a pattern*.

And patterns have reasons. The second horror, Sharon's horror, got tucked into a new envelope of "reason" – of *some* explanation. Something, anything but what it sounded like. *The C.I.A. had killed Sharon and her children and called it suicide.* I rushed, now frantic, back up to the third floor. "They killed Sharon and her children and called it suicide. What's happening?" Now everyone was grim. "We heard. We don't know." "What about the radio?" (I meant the ham radio.) "It's cut off. We're trying. We don't know *anything.*"

I fled the third floor. I couldn't bear to be with anyone, even those supposedly in the know. It seemed like suddenly, our very communal building, our communal work projects, our communal meals, our communal radio, our communal brains.... Why were they suddenly so nakedly, so stiffly, so impenetrably a *barrier* between us? I sought out no one that dreadful first night. I remember being awake. I remember not sleeping a wink. I remember vague, sometimes fierce flashes of panic. I remember thinking, or more *think-feeling*, "If I were there..." I wouldn't let them die without *me*. How could they all die and leave me behind? This was the death of our world, and here I was, isolated, abandoned – left to... *live.*

No, this wasn't real. Some time late into the night, I began walking, pacing – not to think, but to *be* – to move, to walk, to not be trapped in that tiny cell of a room waiting for the next bit of bad news to deepen, blacken, thicken into an impenetrable haze. I swept through the main corridor behind the stage and ran into a hysterical Betty McClain.

Her teenage daughter and new baby granddaughter were in Jonestown. I rushed back up the third floor. "Betty's hysterical. She believes the reports."

There was no resistance offered, nary a word. No advise what to believe, what not to believe, what to think, what not to think. Like it was better to remain calm, but it meant nothing. Calm assured nothing. Hysteria assured nothing. Listening to the reports assured nothing. Blocking them out assured nothing. I retreated to my room. I tried to lay down. I couldn't turn the radio off. I couldn't stop crying. Who did I say was "hysterical"? If *I* didn't believe this, why couldn't I stop crying?

I went out the next day and picked up the papers. By now, television was supplementing radio, and it was doubly scary to have visual added to audio. Lack of sleep got augmented with lack of food. How could I eat? How could *anyone* eat? How could anyone *live?* How could they die and I live? How could *Jim* die and I live? How could my whole world die and life still go on?

I don't know what makes people suicidal. I often thought it was genetic ~ like you were born either prone to suicide or not prone to suicide. Was I really the ultimate misfit here? The only one who never found suicidal feelings natural? I remembered years back on my day job, when I was walking through the hallway and suddenly had a vision of charging through the birth canal, shouting with an exhilarating cry, "I want to live! I want to live!" I was horrified. How could I scream out this rich, raw joy in life when others had risked so much?

Gradually across the years, I had made myself tread the barrier between craving life and braving death. We lived fully, did we not? We lived like no one in America lived. Would I not brave death for *this?* Jim never *wanted* us to die. I never believed that. He wanted us to *live.* To live as fully as ... well, as fully as "they" would let us. The times mention of suicide arose ~ it's like it wasn't even morbid. It was ...*noble* somehow. Was it not always couched in the matrix of solidarity? Loyalty I always understood. I would act, even drastically, out of loyalty. I would *die* out of loyalty. I would die *now.*

But the one who had mastered life unto the very door of death... They said he was already gone. I wouldn't be dying with *him* at all. I'd be dying into a morass of uncertainty, alongside people who seemed not defiant, but rather repressed, stultified, into an uneasy silence. *("You longed for interpretation, but the interpreter is gone. The play is done, now you the player shall be."*) I was terrified. Not of dying. But of making a wrong, or uncertain decision, and making it *irrevocably*.

What was expected now? Were *we* expected to commit suicide? Would I have to witness others die and choose whether to die or to live? Not knowing how to live with this, and deciding to commit suicide, were totally different crossroads, were they not? *Don't make me decide this. Please. Don't make me deal with this fear and this grief simultaneously. I'm going numb. I can't do this. I can only feel so much.*

I wept and wept. I felt everything and could feel nothing. I thought I had been all wept out over not being a part of life. Now I was weeping over not being a part of death. Over *wanting* to be a part of death and also *fearing* to be a part of death. I wept up to the barriers of all these disclaimers. I wept past them. I wept 'til the dam broke. Then I just wept and wept and wept.

On the second day I looked around at my tiny room and I suddenly couldn't bear to be alone. I wanted only to be alone, but not like this. Not in this tiny room with no space or air. I moved down to the main auditorium. The chairs were all put away. I walked through a ghostly half-light, as if expecting to encounter the perished each step of the way.

I knew this huge room so well. It was where I first met Jim Jones that magical April 19th. It was filled then with children's song, with clapping and singing, dancing and shouts. With young and old, with black and white. I loved this place so. Would it be silent now forever? Would *I* be silent too? Now how does one *live*?

I walked to the side. I found a small stretch of space and paced back and forth. I wept and paced, paced and wept. Chris walked in on me. I saw her and fell into her arms and wept. No one spoke a word.

The kitchen had all but closed down, the communal kitchen that fed perhaps fifty of us – us, the remainders and scraps of a once-flourishing brethren of co-workers and friends. No one could eat. No one could sleep. The little talk there was was of survivors. It was like "survivors" was the sweet cream you could skim off the rancid milk no one knew how to drink. It became a mini-obsession to hunt down survivors, almost like it had been a ship lost at sea and the main task was rescuing those who had swum ashore.

I didn't understand "survivors." Were those the ones who *escaped?* How could you watch the people who were your friends, your comrades, all those years die, their *children* die before your very eyes, and even think to "escape"? I was horrified that anyone would "escape" like that. I was also horrified that they would die.

Why couldn't I identify with survivors? With gasping breath, bleary eyes, aching bones, I strained with all the force of my being... to the *dead*. I was dead. I was dead with them. I had died in solidarity with them. I was there. It's like I was *always* there. I was a part of them and now they were dead. This couldn't be happening.

The papers, the radio, the t.v. ~ it was getting worse each day. The estimates of the dead were rising exponentially. Day one was horrified speculation. By day two, it was maybe as many as two hundred. By day three, three or four hundred. By day four, seven hundred. I had thought my emotional barriers were pulverized across the years. Now my mental ones crashed headlong into my shattered heart. This had *happened*. It was no respecter of what I personally could or couldn't tolerate. *It happened.*

It was three or four days before I glanced at the papers scattered across my room. On an impulse, I picked up "*Allegory*." I opened it randomly: **"*The song rises from a thousand unmarked graves...*"** No. I had done it. I had really done it. Finally I *knew*. This is what I was told would happen. That's why I saw John at Jim's side. That's why it took place in an arena. That's why it was in the open, warm night air. That's why it was so isolated, surrounded by a wall of hostile forces. That's why people were dying one by one, even little children. These were the swallows, sinking one by one beneath the sea, as Jim watched, his heart laden with inexpressible grief ~ they were *us*. That's why it was "the dying of the day" ~ it was dusk. That's why it was "a nation" that was dying. We *were* "a nation," weren't we? We sure couldn't come back. We were now our own nation.

As details filtered through in the ensuing days, each found its matchmate in my haunting work. "*No. I am not numb*" the denial of acting under the influence of drugs. The references to "*the unmarked graves*" being the hundreds who could not be identified, and were later buried en masse in the Evergreen Cemetery in Oakland. "A <u>thousand</u> unmarked graves" echoed in Jim's final exhortation, "We're a thousand people who didn't like the way the world is." "*Too late to mend, progressed past arrest, too soon for men to heed and grasp, haunted the past, the future foredoomed looms and cries, cries, cries its all-too-present deaths!!*" the desperate script of events having gone amok, the world having no way to even piece together events, much less to forestall the anguish of the deaths.

And what had been the pivot of my whole tumble into madness, the agony of my table-shaped fence: "No one knows me, why I give all, though the moment to intercede is past, or has not yet come." It was a *Rosetta Stone!* "No one knows me, why I give all" (= *no one understands why I sacrifice all these lives*) "though the moment to intercede is past" (= *too late to prevent the assassination of the Congressman*) "or has not yet come" (= *dying to pre-empt an anticipated slaughter that the world would never see, hence never understand as a provocation.*)

How could I have been given this vision years in advance? And how could I have been so blind?

This was my first glimmer of calm. What if this wasn't a surreal madness after all, that no one could either accept nor deny? What if Someone, somewhere, *knew?* Before its time, beyond its claim of precious souls, Someone knew. *I* knew. I couldn't believe it, I couldn't accept it, but I knew. All that time before. *I knew.*

I tried to talk about it, but it was a hopeless sell. I myself felt small and weak in the grips of overhanging gloom. I choked it out -- what had happened, what I had done years before. Then I looked at a headline, or the news on t.v., or even a nearby face, and retreated into my cocoon of numbing pain. Laurie, *the whole world* knew, did it not? The whole world screamed with a jolted, dislocated horror.

Yet somehow, as I looked about, it was like no one knew anything. No one could *explain* anything. No one could *comprehend* anything. ("Rasping... *Wrestling to expound in a dark, uncertain key, to express in wavering tones, a dirge too low to justly grieve, a song too weak for a too-wrong, death!*"). I realized silently, wordlessly, in this still tiny, incipient, a cappella islet of eerie calm, that were I a "survivor," my rescue surely was not at hand. To this new shore, I must swim alone.

XXXVI. As the World Turns.

There was much, indeed, that seemed peculiar to me in that onslaught which only seemed to sweep one downwards. As though *"Allegory,"* and the years I had suffered with it, were an underpinning or matrix for the tragedy others did not share. Like it was water underneath me as I rose up now to survey the land.

Surely others had had fears. What I had that others perhaps did not, was a comfort, a guide, that both affirmed as inevitable the reality others had merely feared, and seemed to extend beyond Jim Jones the man, or even the trappings of our collective life: its people, its circumstances, its locale.

The destruction of that material world, however tragic (for our tears were tragically real) was never, for me, the bottommost line. The snake may *always* have been slated to shed its skin that terrible November 18th. But it is sometimes when the mask of Life is so brutally ripped away, that we can confront reality at its roots. I was already "a different person" when, like a pierce of inward lightning, I picked up *"Allegory"* and realized what I had done.

So overwhelming was precognizance and reality now one, that even with our very air thick with grief, I was aware on some other, "'parallel" plane, that it was a relief that the tragedy had finally happened. That however dark and impenetrable were those days, the event was finally done. I knew I would never have to pass this way again. *Not ever.*

It was like a graduation ~ a completion of a process from long, even anciently long ago. Much longer than my paltry eight-odd years for sure. I sensed whole centuries washing clean beneath my feet. Whenever I was born to endure, it was done. My soul had been cleansed through its merciless vice, like a sieve would only permit the finest particles to pass on through. Whatever my fated role, I did it ~ honorable, clean, finished, *forever.* However cataclysmic the shock, I would eventually find peace. I wasn't at peace. I was a wreck. But I *would* have peace. I knew I would some day.

Some say God can, and does, live anywhere. The blessing of this release, I inexplicably had. I had grief, I had despair, I had rage ~ all of these and more. Yet somehow, belying all the ravings and recriminations and dislocations, I, as if by an inexplicable grace, never felt the catastrophe could have been *prevented*. Thus was I spared what many long since informed me was the worse: *guilt*. Whatever I had arrived to do that fantastical April 19th, it was done.

I couldn't explain it, even to myself. Lack of guilt wasn't an arrogance, much less a separation from those who had died. It was more like a state of *being*. Something so unfathomably deep, it reverted to simple. I simply knew that terror, horror, rage, grief and all, in some inexplicable way, I was now *free*.

I seemed to know other things as well. That *some* in Jonestown, at least, the ones who went to their deaths willingly, in the consciousness of willing sacrifice ~ that those souls would return in later lives as "Lightworkers." To a time and place when their lives *could* make a difference. They had somehow expunged a scar, or a blot, on their souls, that had to be cleansed to move onwards into the future.

I had been left to complete the saga of Jonestown. Their spark was extinguished. Mine would need burn dimly, then ever more brightly, 'til I knew what flame had set my soul afire in this life. I would never reject them, but somehow, *uplift* them. "*Allegory*" itself, later on in life, would be such a task.

Was this delusion? What of what I had feared the most? "*Allegory*." It hadn't been delusional at all. All that shock and grief... in an instant, true! Now, just days into the aftermath, had begun a slower, subtler process. It took but minutes to die with the poisonings. It was to take *years* to redeem life from the deaths, but timeclocks could not mark the measures of my heart. Or prescribe why for me (so contrasted with Jim Jones' "*Step that way [into death]. It's the only way to step.*"), from darkness into *Light* was "the only way to step."

We rarely acknowledge that life and death may harbor the same secrets. We see death as a darkness where Light cannot exist, thus greet it in black. I, more than anyone, was startled that light could emerge from such an impenetrable darkness as this. The death of so many ~ no, more. The *unnatural* death of so many. Was this not *only* horror? Could it spawn such as life? It seems impossible to describe what became in my life, almost like a form or source of life. Like a *transformation*.

It had nothing to do with what I wanted consciously. No one *wants* the death of people they love. Nor was it fostered by anything in the environment ~ to the contrary. We *can* gain strength in death, if only its flames do not destroy us; but only, it seems, from certain *kinds* of deaths.

From the noble deaths, from the deaths bravely fought, then just as bravely borne. From the deaths of those who lived uplifted lives, even if death had smitten them with neither warning nor forethought, prolonged suffering and pain, or no.

We don't shout about it – it seems unseemly, uncomfortable, even in the most auspicious of passings; but secretly, silently, we admire that this can sometimes be. We've all seen snapshots of the "perfect" funeral and read the quotes: "We must go on. Michael would have wanted it that way," and "Let us draw strength and courage from our dear Emily and rededicate our own lives from how *she* lived." The family stands mute but dignified, silent yet the eulogies ring out, seemingly so alone, yet the community closes, folds in, like a gentle arm around their shoulders to comfort, to understand.

This manner of healing I would never know. The human hands, the audible words, the protective cocoon of memorials. Whatever my sources of comfort, they didn't wear a human face. I had them, but more in the sense that Maria, in *"The Sound of Music,"* innocently repeated her elder's counsel: "Whenever God closes a door, He opens a window." I vowed that the healing, the comfort, would somehow come, whatever the odds and however narrow "the window."

For Jonestown was the worst *antithesis* of comfort. It was shrouded in the worst kinds of darkness for the bereaved. No one said so much as "I'm sorry you lost all your friends." The press made of us robots or freaks, terrorists or psychopaths, at best brainwashed – not worthy of comfort or upliftment.

We would never be more than "cultists." Any sympathy you felt for the people who *wanted* to die at Jonestown (for none could see wanting to die as "dying *in preference to*...") would be deemed "brainwashing." If you expressed any sympathy for the suicides, then you were in favor of murdering children. If you had any evidence pointing to conspiracy, you had to think who were you talking to, and why were there clicks on your phone, or strange people showing up behind you, the same strange people again and again, on the street?

There was no way to even mourn. You *had* to mourn. You had to weep 'til the universe would bleed no more tears. But no one could see those tears. No one would comfort. There were no eulogies. You could barely act like the people who died were *human*, or like *you* were human.

I cringed so early in this wicked game the mass consciousness plays on its subjects, I felt like a scrap of paper tossed into a flame; I was left curling in the wind, burning slowly, slightly, about to be consumed and disappear into ash. Well, that one little piece of me. Then another little piece would light aflame and the process begin anew. And the air would become so thick with soot and smoke, no one would even notice. They would just cough and choke a bit and move on.

I didn't understand *that* version of "survivor," either. No one would treat me like a loved, valued member of a human community, salvaged for a brighter day. I could only curl into my little cocoon and slowly, painstakingly, burn my flame of tears away.

I wept for everything and everyone. The worst was the children. I could never have children, could I? Not after this. I wept for the demolished hopes and dreams snuffed cold. I wept for the dehumanization of both the living and dead - that the body count elicited such horror, that no one even cared why they died, much less how it happened. I wept for my own agony - I know I did.

And I certainly wept for Jim Jones; I couldn't fail to weep for him. The greatness of a mission, a *failed* mission - the mission and its concomitant failure torn ruthlessly apart at dangerously jagged angles. No one cared about the twenty-five years of humanitarian work, the love, the care, the concern, the heroic efforts to make the world better for others. I knew the paranoia, the overreactions, the overprotective tiger defending his cubs. God knows, from the depths of my soul, I knew how he hurt and damaged *me*. But I also knew how with desperate abandon, he moved to achieve what no one else seemed willing or able to do. Yes. I *would* weep for Jim Jones. And who would ever understand that?

Though truthfully, I felt luckier than others. To be able to break down so totally, so early in the grief process - it was a twisted sort of blessing not all shared. I sat in rooms with people who sat tight-lipped and restrained, who perhaps just could not bear torrents of open grief. I sat while we were told that our own attorney wanted us to relinquish all the Temple's remaining monies to the State, to avoid getting pilloried in the street. I sat while I learned that some of Jim's own children were castigating him to the press. I sat while people muttered cynically, that was all this "just to make a *stand?* Why should children die over making a stand?" I sat when we discussed who was going to talk to the press like it was just another P.R. drive. Or when we had to figure out how to *fend off* the press, who had heard a rumor that *we* were about to suicide out, and they wanted to come in and take photographs.

There was the huge blank face on this unspeakable horror that was painted in with press reports that no one knew were true. It was like a bizarre, raucous circus with ghouls as its ghastly clowns. (*"Now the vultures come, grey carrions of death, they pick, pluck, peck, tear at his flesh, with cruel-eyed intent, and crudely jest..."*) Was this the world I had to check back into? The haven the de-programmers had waiting eagerly and helpfully for the misled?

There was nothing I heard that wasn't unreal or insane. It seemed like a fishbowl, but a special circus fishbowl where all the fish were expected to be a certain size and color. And now, just when it seemed like being a fishbowl *together* might be of some comfort, we were starting to split up. Well, *communally* of course. The couples in this and that house. The singles in this and that house.

I was astounded at how quickly people got coupled off. And then hung out in sparse couplings to buffer the magnitude of a universally pervasive failure in a way that I suppose only cliquish, sequestered couples can. I cared about these people. I truly did. There wasn't anyone who understood one bottled-up, grief-stricken, disempowered Peoples Temple person like another bottled-up, grief-stricken, disempowered Peoples Temple person. But I was beginning to wonder if I had a future here. I began feeling like I had to get out. To get out now. To find some redemption in all this. Some Light.

XXXVII. The Sun Will Rise Again in the East.

There was no overt dissension in the ranks, but neither was there unity. Plus boot camp training in stoicism was apparently not confined to me. Almost no one cried in front of anyone else. I'm quite sure it wasn't for lack of grief, but more the hugeness, the enormity of the shock. There was no warning for this. Not only no *immediate* warning, but no viable warning at all.

By contrast, the residents of Jonestown, we were to soon learn, had little *but* warning, drilling, training, ever hoping for the best but being prepared for the worse. We *had* split into two families, hadn't we? It wasn't just a split of locale ~ it was a split of *mentality*.

I remember being gathered in the downstairs greeting room near the front of the church. We were voting to dissolve, to give over the proverbial six million dollars (where *do* they get these numbers?) confiscated from several continents, from which Charles Garry assured us we could "sue for our share."

This was left vague. There could be thousands of people out there who had not seen their relatives for years, suing for "their share," leaving scraps for those of us who had given all. The logistics of this were locked outside this door ~ already decided. All we had to do was vote "yes." We ought to do this, we were counselled. The community is very angry. If you want people off your backs, vote yes.

This was transparently a bad deal. We had *no money*. Every dime had been scrupulously donated to the church every step of the way. We had been promised life-time security, and now none of us had a dime. We had nothing, and we (who were, at that, only a portion of the survivors ~ many were still in Georgetown, Guyana) were being asked to give over everything, with information woefully incomplete and no alternative options.

No one could bear to inquire the ramifications of all this. "Yes" carried the day.

Somewhere mid-discussion, an interloping issue of the survivors was broached, I think by A.J., our most senior member, who started talking about Stephan Jones, who had survived in Georgetown. I had already read the press from Georgetown. Sharon's suicide was indeed a suicide, and her children, too young to "commit suicide," save possibly 22-year-old Liane (Christa and Martin were all of 11 and 9), had had their throats slit compliments of their frantic mother. Christa was screaming, "Mommy, don't! Please don't!" Another little girl, Stephanie, had been dragged into the foray, but another Temple member in the house dragged the child back from the knife.

The nuts and bolts of my brain were being hammered in sideways. I wanted to die with everyone, I wanted to be there with everyone, to stand with everyone, and suddenly now, I wanted Christa, the terrified litle girl, to *live*. There was more. Now my brain froze midspace. The C.I.A. *hadn't* killed Sharon and her children. What if they hadn't killed *Ryan*, either?

The last time I remembered tromping up the stairs to the third floor, or perhaps tromping them *down* in a fierce crush of panic, it was over the report that seven or eight of *our own* people were the ones who assassinated Ryan and the others at the Port Kaituma Airport. The names were read aloud, like a roll call of the damned. "Oh," groaned June, "Joe Wilson. Tom Kice." Loose cannons of our San Francisco days were on that list. People who had been entranced with guns, or rescued from drugs. Plus a karate buff. And a big hulk of a guy. "The usual suspects," tailor-made for us.

Belief, the rat-a-tat-tat of what to believe and what not to believe... It was abrasive, it was invasive, it hit its mark like a drillhammer into stone. But it was *sure*. Now, like a slippery pebble sliding out of our grasp, these loose cannons, sans trial, were apparently the guilty ones, the assassins whose actions triggered the ghastly poisonings. Who wouldn't believe a list like this, at which one surely could groan?

It was surreal -- almost too easy, too pat. It pushed lightly on the wall already eroded to breaking point by an avalanche of tears. We were broken, weren't we? We had done it to *ourselves*. All the cards now stacked against us, people were edging over to, if not collapse, then at least stand clear of the bulldozers. If we could identify guilty parties, we could close doors left painfully ajar, and that was a less anguished effort than that required to *think*.

More whispers, more groans still. Jean, a gentle soul who was rapidly as disillusioned as she was crushed, whom Teri would later (devoid of rhyme or reason, crisis or cause) call "the ringleader of the hit squad" (like *what* "hit squad"? Who had guns? Who wanted violence at all?) huddled cliquishly with June in cloistered commiseration. Their words scraped the darkened ground, collecting yet more drudge and mud each pained step of the way: "All the *children*... ? Just to make a *stand*... ?"

I recoiled. Is *that* what they thought? That children had been deliberately sacrificed just to *say* something? It was so difficult... no, so *impossible* to believe this. How could anyone build a pristine, wholesome life for children, then toss them onto a funeral pyre?

I snapped back into the room. We were meeting at the behest of our attorney ~ well, the one who had stuck around, Charles Garry. He had recommended we dissolve the church immediately, and release the millions of dollars scattered across Guyana, the Caribbean, the U.S., Switzerland. Don't worry about it, we were told. Just sue to get your share.

A.J. steered us back to Stephan Jones, and his opposition to .... well to *Jim*, his father. A.J. said little, but his voice quavered, as if to say, maybe we've been on the wrong side. Aside from the furor at the Lahana Gardens, the Georgetown headquarters, the blood and gore of Sharon and her children slain on the floor, all Stephan's past anguish was pouring forth ~ namely, *sex*. How his mother's back went out when he was eleven years old and his father took on lovers. Surely the deaths were more than enough ~ the poisonings, the assasination, Sharon offing her own children with a knife. But here this kid was totally messed up over the dissolution of his very public family *years back*.

You would think the issue of sex would have been jumped on long since. But no one wanted to be asked had *they* slept with Jim, much less had *Grace* slept with him(!), and this volatile issue had been oddly quiescent throughout. Now horrendous stories were emerging about sex, as if mass death were not enough excitement for the crowd.

But it wasn't just that. This was Jim's *son*. We were the interracial family par excellence, inter-age, inter-gender, inter-class. Ever egalitarian. Yet how *biology* comes rushing back. A.J. brought up Stephan, Jim's own son, and no one wanted to say anything else. We were numb.

There was no discussion yet about closing the church building except for Garry's fear that we could be stormed by an irate public. We quietly voted to dissolve. The six million dollars got relinquished without a murmur.

Something inside me, even deeper than the depths of passion and pain, was at that moment quelled. That one small spot that wanted someone, virtually anyone, to question, to fight. It wouldn't happen ("*a dirge too low to justly grieve, a song too weak for a too-wrong death!*"). We quietly divvied up housing ~ couples here, singles there. We quietly divvied up our hearts - yesterday here, tomorrow there. We quietly divvied up our tongues - the world had quelled us into abject silence. Solemn and subdued, we were no more.

There was the minor ritual of the newscast, eight in the morning and six at night. They showed Jim Jones' corpse - the only one they showed. It was like a trophy. They had cut out the heart of evil. Vultures one and all, they had pecked at his liver, and they wanted the world to see that the people who pecked at his liver were good and that the corpse was bad. I gazed at the primitive rite in stony silence.

They even managed to drag Joe Mazor across the screen. Strange. He seemed to have little interest in "concerned relatives" any more (his avowed motivation for involvement at all!), much less the fate of little children. Indeed, the man was quite terse: **"It was considered that Jim Jones would become a major political force in the Caribbean within five years."** Oh? And who amongst the "concerned relatives" (like the Mertles and Stoen, who didn't even *have* relatives in Jonestown) had informed him of that... *intelligence assessment?* No one asked, no one cared. What does one ever need but a corpse and an expert?

But this was the core of it, wasn't it. Jim Jones had even visited with the Black Panthers' Huey Newton in Cuba. Did they really so fear "a new Castro" in the Caribbean? Worse, "an *American* Castro," with U.S. citizens free to enter and exit the U.S. at will? Was *this* why they hounded a thousand expatriated Americans to their graves? Why didn't all these ugly people just let us go? We had children, old people, families. Our leader had been successfully poisoned with some deadly fungus. To this day, I cannot understand any *preference* (even given the a-morality of many "Cold Warriors") for killing us off rather than letting us live.

Besides, whatever they feared of Jim Jones - support of political prisoners, of so-called liberation movements, creating a socialist base in America, organizing Black people against the establishment on American soil... every bit of this was moot once we landed in the remote jungle. Had we ever landed in the Soviet Union, it would have been doubly moot. We would have lost our autonomy.

Surely we weren't hurting anyone in Guyana - to the contrary. We established a role model for a successful collective farm. Nor were we hurting anyone *here* - to the contrary. We were building a better world. We were building a better America. Our kids didn't take drugs. They didn't rob, rape or murder. They worked together. They built homes. They learned trades. They respected their elders.

Didn't they want *their* kids off drugs? Did they want to produce this new breed of psychopathic children who roam the streets like predators with assault weapons? Wasn't anyone thinking down the line but us? Destroying Peoples Temple. Why in God's name would anyone want to destroy a place like *that*?

How very sad, Jim Jones having to write the whole U.S. Congress, that "We have made a great transformation," as a code for "We're not on your soil anymore. We're on ours. So we called ourselves socialists. Forget the labels and look at all the good. Please, in God's name, just let us live in peace." Why did he have to beg and plead like this? Why didn't they look at the unblemished, very public, twenty-five record of humanitarian works? Wasn't it obvious?

I guess people just go on automatic. They're hired to destroy and so it can cost a thousand lives, including children, but damn it, hired to destroy they were (anything to the left of Attila the Hun deserves to die, anyway), and so destruction is what they will do. It's not sane. One man, Jim Jones, goes extreme and the whole world is aghast. A whole bureaucracy goes extreme, and with taxpayers' money to boot, and no one even notices. If they do, they applaud, like they're heroes.

It seemed the whole world was going mad. A few weeks later on, the Shah of Iran was ousted, as the Ayatollah Khomeini rode victoriously back into Teheran from his exile in France. Ah, my mind (probably now, yes, quite deranged) mused: "Persia will now take its revenge." Why *had* Jim Jones told me that very first day, April 19th, all those years ago, of... Persia? This non-sequitur was quickly tucked beneath my bleary facade of lost sleep and overflowing tears. Would anything be right in the world *anywhere*? The Shah was overthrown, finally. It seemed good, but revolutions suddenly seemed especially frightening. People would die. Death.

I had to do something, not just stay in place. My mother was in New York. I decided to visit for a couple of weeks, then return West. My mother was an emotional wreck, as usual (it didn't take a tragedy for that), but I needed the distance and space myself. I was too much of a mess to go out and get a job anyway. Not just emotionally. My face had broken out in large red blotches, some kind of allergy.

I needed a retreat, peace. It was getting to be like being caged in a zoo. One day the reporters clustered about. They said it was rumored we were about to off ourselves, and they wanted to get in and take photographs. I even remember an agitated Japanese man following me in the parking lot with intent questions, saying that in his culture they understood suicide. He thought it was his pass for getting in.

Another day, we were told the F.B.I. might be coming to search the building. We began shredding everything wildly. I was protective. I thought nothing there could incriminate us and we should *save* papers. I swore to myself that they could send in the whole federal government and I still would not destroy "*Allegory.*" And if, by some remote chance, all of us inside wound up dead, they could take "*Allegory*" as my parting note to the world. I was in a cage now, but some day I would yet sing. The work I had been given – *it* would sing.

Somehow, somewhere, I would defy the odds. The grip of overlapping, conflicting, raging emotions, to die and yet to live again, was beginning to stir within me, notwithstanding the leaden lids of grief on all our hearts. Please. I just had to go.

So I decided to go East, to visit my mother. This wasn't an emotionally-soothing move. She was draining under the best of circumstances, and these circumstances were a true bona fide disaster. I planned on staying for two weeks at the most, then return. Maybe by then, things would be more settled out into households, rather than this relatively uneasy, at-odds, clannish type of hovering together that passed for comfort.

The fact was, we *had* to move. The church was going to be sold. We had to move and we had no money. There was no rehab money, no money for us to lay low and just grieve. We would all have to go out and get jobs. Start totally from scratch. Nil. Nada. Eight-and-a-half years of giving over every dime, and now nothing. Jim Jones himself had tried one last, rash, hopeless plunge towards historical realignment by trying to sneak one million dollars out of Jonestown with Mike Prokes and the Carter brothers to the Soviet Embassy in Georgetown. While not a dime, not a penny, had been earmarked for his own – for *us*. I didn't know how I was going to bear it. Wasn't bearing the grief enough?

I had to get away. To be alone. Not to be in a group. The entirety of my face now erupted fiercely, like a scarlet shroud whisking me out of view. I just wanted to hide. I had to be gone.

But there was also something more subtle. Like that "tug" again. It was fortuitous, my going East. "To visit my mother." Really, I just had to go East. It was time to go. So early in the process yet, but I knew I had to be there, not here. I never thought I'd move back East, not ever. Now I couldn't seem to help myself. I packed a few scarce belongings, then stepped onto the plane.

I believe I was guided. I even believed it then. I felt the Presence who had come to me in the dream. I felt His comfort like no other. I felt the subtle, pervasive pull East much as I had felt the subtle, pervasive pull West a decade earlier. The compass had swung. It, like the proverbial "footsteps on the beach," would carry me home.

I got a salve for the blotches on my face and they only got worse. By the time I stepped onto the plane East, I was a bloated, swollen mass of red. I don't even remember saying goodby.

IV. YEA, THOUGH I WALK THROUGH THE VALLEY OF THE SHADOW OF DEATH

"When Hitler came for the Communists, I didn't speak up, for I wasn't a Communist. When he arrested the Jews, I didn't protest because I wasn't a Jew. When the Nazis arrested the trade unionists, I didn't protest, for I was not in a union. Then they came after the Catholics, but I didn't speak out because I was not a Catholic. When they came for me, it was TOO LATE. . . . There was no one left to stand up for me."
Pastor Martin Neimoeller

"We are not sure anybody is listening or that many care. We would not be surprised if we were short lived. But *this is the way democracy dies, and we owe it to those coming after us to tell what can happen to them* -- whether anyone cares what happens to us or not."
Flyer from Peoples Temple,
"Victims of Conspiracy."

XXXVIII. "Arise, Arise, the Last Shall Fall to Thee..."

I was a mass of disfigurement by the time I arrived in New York, a visible confirmation of what the world thought we were anyway: freaks - distorted, frightening, unnerving freaks. My mother hugged me, but only as her daughter, nothing more. Not a single relative said "I'm sorry you lost your friends." Everyone wanted it to just go away.

I no longer knew anyone in New York. Well, almost no one. On a ragged impulse, I called the psychiatrist/composer from years past. I thought, well, the man's a psychiatrist. At least he'll know better than to ostracize me.

My instinct, thankfully, was right. He invited me down to his spacious downtown loft. He saw how impassioned I felt about the overkill of it all, and that I wanted to speak from my heart whatever I knew. He suggested I contact the local politically progressive radio station, WBAI.

I got on a program the following Saturday. Surprisingly, I was barely nervous. The microphone got put in my face and I went on "go." The incoming calls were more stressful. Like waves lapping up against the shore, I remember their rhythmic jostling against the brain, except for that one big tidal wave, which threatened to engulf me in a single gulp: the children. It was almost like I had to make-believe I was another person to get on through. "The real me" never could have handled it at all.

I was staying at my mother's, the only place that I, with neither friends nor money nor a job, *could* stay. I arrived home and mother (I could never call her "mom," not since childhood; I tried calling her by her *name* once and she threw a fit, like I was Eve rejecting the Creator, so we settled, resistantly, on "Mother") announced that she was giving me a wool cape she had garnered in Ireland. Because I had been on the radio and she was so proud.

Another "white sweater" (my bollixed excursion into psychotherapy)? It was a beautiful lavender tweed. I took it, slowly and cautiously draping it towards the light, while a sidewards glance gazed at her incredulously. I realized she hadn't even heard what I *said* on the radio. The stress, the trauma, the words forced through tears.

No one realized I was just barely warming up. It was that quintessential pivot, the flip of a dime. The vital life-force, so drained by the collusion of shock, grief, and tears, seemed destined to re-emerge where a counter charge was needed the most: the unabated media stampede over the carcasses of my dead friends.

I marvelled at how the shallow and misinformed branded *us* "brainwashed." It was *me* they were talking about, wasn't it? Yet no one knew my face, my name, much less what I might say. The "experts" had invaded to become mouthpieces for people who were not dead at all, but still very much alive. One of them confidently predicted that within a few scant years, a third of us would ourselves resort to poison, a gun to the head, or a jump off a bridge. Others reported hordes of anxious parents reporting in droves to cult deprogrammers for every manner of overblown advise.

Jonestown was simple, they all claimed. A madman leader chopped his followers off from reality, then proceeded to wrap their brainwaves, pretzel-like, into his bizarre brew of baseless paranoia, enforced slavery, and paramilitary zeal.

It was all so simple. So simple that not a single person ever comprehended anything that happened. I know. I looked experienced newspeople in the eye, and not a single one of them comprehended a thing. Much less the experts. I would truly be undercutting them if I said they understood nothing. Most seemed to understand less than nothing about anything.

Seek a voice through *them*? Though my own world had fallen ashen at my feet, there wasn't any world out there to which I wanted to return, either. The haves, the have-nots, the whites, the blacks. The schisms it had been such a magical wonder to dissolve, transcend, release... Now they were all around me. A racist world where I would have to hunt out Black friends. There was nothing in the currents of the world out there, that wonderful, highly-touted place (surely a lush refuge for the brainwashed!) that would ever bring them to *me*.

Was I truly so blind-sided all those years that I had missed out on how terrible "*our*" world was and how wonderful "*the*" world was? I looked around. People were panhandling in the streets. Older people were being neglected. Mental patients were being dumped out in the streets with no network of support. Children were being shuffled into the world, the world out there, the only "real" world. Some went to school. Others, by some mysterious process which selected out high numbers of residents in certain parts of town, went to jail. That's just the way things *were*.

Peoples Temple had become a flawed place, with the cracks of pressure, persecution, and weaknesses from within gapingly visible now, with the bloody flow from wounds the world would be slow to forget. But how this happened, no one out there seemed to know. Much less what a loss it truly was. The extraordinary model carved right out of the wilderness of our jungle home. And not just for us. For *America*. So America could empower *all* of her citizens, utilize *all* of them, honor *all* of them, welcome *all* of them. To make *that* world "the" world.

I worked for that kind of world, yet I wasn't even a human being now. I who loved, I who gave, I who sacrificed. They talked about me all over the news networks, in the third person, like confidential insights about a mental patient splashed all across America's t.v.'s behind their back. Why didn't they have the decency to at least drag me onto t.v. and say it all to my face?

All of our people but me wanted to hide. In grief, guilt, despair, fear, stifled rage, even in shame. Disempowered now, disempowered forever more. But *I* didn't want this. I didn't want it at all. Let all those ignorant, unknowing, unwitting mouthpieces of the news services commit all these indecencies to my face. Did they think *they* loved the little children who died more than *us*?

Some time right about then, I remember taking a long hard look at... *myself*. I stood in front of the mirror and looked me square in the eye. I said you're nothing but circus freaks to them. Robots. Cultists. Psychopaths. Well, they could say it, but that didn't make it true. No one was going to say that about *me*. I swore it.

I could say the cliché-ish "I don't know where I got the strength." Yet I do. "Someone" was with me. I was *given* strength. I have never been so alone, yet never as supported by compassion and love. I would cry and cry and then Someone would be right by my side, and I would become calm. I would remember that there was a reason. That I knew. The reason was locked within me, it would emerge in time. The Presence surely knew. He calmed me. I would cry and cry and then float off into nothingness, one with the unknown Him.

In fact, it was *all* about me that was strong. I was like a fragile bubble, painfully pricked into showers of tears at a mere feathery breeze. The children were the worst. I would cry incessantly over them. It was often the first thing people would ask, and I would force my replies through brimming tears.

Not that there weren't enough tears to go around. Laurie's tears seemed periodically, rhythmically, chaotically, sporadically, by day and night, by spurts and starts, at home, on the street, any which way, to flow for all. Even for Jim. He tried to do too much for too many. The world never understood it when he was Mother Theresa. How could they possibly understand it when he "became Dracula"?

The grief over what he did to me personally was hardly muted, even then ~ indeed it underwent agonies of metamorphosis 'til its misguided legacy was finally spent and I could rebuild my shattered life in peace.

But this was still early in the game. What I felt towards "L.A." then, wasn't the reservoir of past feelings one might envision it to be. Rather it loomed *before* me, like a huge, ill-placed stumbling block. Now, what he had done to me was now no longer an internal matter ~ not ever. Were *I* to speak, *it* would become living history.

Yet no one seemed ready to speak *but* me. I who in terror had heard the words from *"Allegory"*: *"Arise, arise, the last shall fall to thee, the last shall fall to thee... The play is done, now you the player shall be... You stand alone. Hence I send you forth..."* I didn't even want this aloneness. It terrified me. Me, mere mortal, who years down the line has so much normalcy in her life ~ who thinks, who feels, who reasons, at least so much *like* mere mortals. I truly *am* that human being that the onslaught of early media would grant us not.

But now this early on, I had to decide. Decide what would happen if I spoke up publicly and someone decided to expose that ghastly incident in L.A. That an opponent could use the very tactics of my *mentor*, to twist and wring my heart into public view, as well as twist and wring my words into a discredited silence.

I chose unerringly then, and I still believe I chose well now. Maybe that would never happen publicly, at first, such revelations. After all, it might draw me out, not silence me. But whether it happened or not, I was simply too angry to care. My world had been brutally destroyed ~ physically, psychologically, socially, mentally, emotionally. What did people think I had left to lose? Someone wanted to do that to me? Damn them! Let them live with *themselves*. What Jim Jones did to me was tragic. But look at what he had done under the gun for *everyone*. Damn anyone who would now screw *me* over just to protect their own hide.

I was a mass of searing rage, torrents of tears, and fitfully, I was inexplicably calm. Each of these, diverse tributaries feeding an ocean of pain, seemed to play against the undercurrents of the others. I had been on radio now. I was negotiating with the executive editor of the *Soho News*. I was on other radio programs, gave a talk at a local college, showed up wherever the tragedy might. I could count dead bodies as well as anyone. But who could count the rats and the snakes and other poisonous vermin who provoked us to the brink of death? I could count *them*. And no one else could or would.

XXXIX. Sorting Out Allies from Adversaries.

The radio interview was not so much a boost to my morale, as some small hope of not sinking into interminable grief. I had not yet planned any ongoing course of action. Then the old friend who had referred me to WBAI also kindly phoned *The Soho News*, at that time the competitor to *The Village Voice*, and it cushioned my walk through the newpaper's door.

I was introduced to Hal, the paper's editor. We had our tete-a-tete in a local bar in the West Village. I even showed him "*Allegory*," and he offered to have it published. I averred. Anything else was a piece of the *world's* pain, but this was peculiarly my own. Maybe I just couldn't imagine it going into a newspaper. News of the day, cast into the trash tomorrow. I mean, what this guy was salivating over was selling papers, wasn't it?

I told him my background, my role in the church, that I had believed in our work, and that there were many unanswered questions surrounding the destruction of Jonestown. He offered to let me work out of his home. It could be memoirs, recollections, pretty much my choice. I thought this fair. I was paid something nominal. I was so aching to reverse the tide, I probably would have done it for free.

He saw me into a cab at perhaps two in the morning, then on an impulse kissed me, surprisingly passionately at that ~ definitely a "Sleep with me" grade kiss. It wasn't that I suddenly thought he *wasn't* salivating over selling papers, but commerce and careers aside, it was thrilling to, at long last, again be kissed. I was interested, but let it pass for an aberration.

We picked up dinner one evening in Chinatown. As we walked, I told him parts of my life were wrecked during my Temple years, like sex. That I hadn't had sex for nine years. He was duly surprised, though I knew I wasn't catching an unsympathetic ear. I don't remember if he suggested we be together or if it was I. In any case, he did take me home, and not to write.

I couldn't believe how easy it was to again fall into passion. The nine years seemed to make no difference at all. He commented on how impossible for anyone to go so long without sex, "especially someone as sensual as you." A slightly more reserved commentary was offered re sleeping with a source ~ something like, "I don't even know if this is ethical – sleeping with a source." This seemed a rhetorical enough insight, and I stayed the night.

The article I composed didn't touch upon Jonestown at all, only the years Stateside – recollections of Jim Jones, his gifts, and our ongoing plight, all sympathetic. I touched on the Stoen debacle, and how the child was really Jim's, but hardly detailed a conspiracy. I honestly don't know how I did this much. They printed a picture of me (looking ashen, frankly) on the front page, with the title of my article, *"Jim Jones: The Greatest Man in America."* I daresay New York was surprised.

I sometimes wish I was the person then that I am now. The things I might have said while the window was still open. The questions I would have asked. The leads I could have given or followed. Hal wrote the introductory blurb, saying a future piece would comment on Jonestown and the suicides, but as we will see, this wasn't to be.

It wasn't much of an affair, either. He probably had to be secretive, even aside from "sleeping with a source." I was part of a whole discredited breed. I was amazed I had the opportunity at all, to write for a paper found on every newsstand in the city; or that I could handle it so soon. It was barely two months after the suicides that my article came out.

I was immensely frank with this man. I even told him what had happened in L.A. To my chagrin, he said he already knew! What was weird (though interesting that anyone had thought it mattered) was that whoever told him said the real issue was to break me creatively. That I was creative artistically, and that had to be stopped.

"Who told you?" How could I not ask? "I can't tell you that." "Well, it can only be one of three people – Grace Stoen, Debbie Blakey, or Teri Buford." He slowly gave a nod. The subject was dropped.

I had no idea of people's whereabouts. I mightn't have known it was Teri except for running into her and Lane in the street some months later on. God knows what else she told the reporter. He didn't seem too phased. Things happen to people. Their viewpoint is their viewpoint. For all I knew, the editor thought *I* was nuts, but that the *story* would play. The whole topic of Jonestown was – well, "topical," hot. He conceded that "the principle of the thing didn't concern him much," just the story, the scoop. Let the chips fall where they may.

He fished for more material. I said I had Temple friends in California and maybe we should go there. He got his paper to agree and to finance the trip.

Just before we left New York, I decided to look up my old mentor/friend, Al Morrison. I seemed to have been given a universal calling card for this guy, for (lo and behold) I found him all over again in... the Yellow Pages! Astrologers Guild of America. Maybe they could tell me where to find Al.

"Hello?" said a strained but kindly voice. The duo-syllabic greeting said it all – it was Al! "I'm looking for Al Morrison." "This is Al Morrison." "Oh. I thought it was you. This is Laurie Efrein. You remember me?" "Oh, sure." The two words skipped down tones, like a spritely-skipping child. "I just got back to New York. Can I come down and see you? Where do you live?"

Al expressed immensely pleased surprise at my arrival in New York after a hiatus of ten years. "Look," he said excitedly. "The chart of Israel." There it was – the astrological chart of Israel magic-marked onto a huge paper picnic-cloth. "Do you remember this?" I confessed I didn't. "That was spread out the last class you took with me in New York. I just hauled it out again the other day. Didn't know why. Just did."

So I was *expected*, it seemed. An eccentric, off-beat welcome that, it seemed, hadn't missed a beat. Here we were, just picking up where we left off. This was an easy presence to talk to – almost to talk *into*, sink into his presence. My words, anxious and charged, or abruptly halted by sudden wellings of tears, could weave out into his slow web. There was no rush. He would listen.

He immediately took my side. I was never entirely sure why. It wasn't just affection. It was *recognition*. Though probably enough *dis*affection, as well, with the mass culture, to sense how much the cover stories stank. There was nothing I couldn't share with him. I would fish my line into his mind again and again. It always caught, and some fresh insight would emerge. Again and again, this child fisherman, me, would cast my line into the waters. We always met somewhere down there, and surfaced with something resembling a theory or conclusion. He called it getting a "bounce" off of it.

He dragged out an old issue of his home-published magazine, CAO TIMES. Years earlier, he said, Comet Kohoutek glanced by Earth, causing havoc to its denizens. There was an eclipse directly over Guyana in late December, 1973, into which the comet fell. He showed me where he printed its meaning: "*A Messiah will arise out of Guyana.*" In late December, 1973, Jim Jones was *in* Guyana, negotiating to get the land! So this was how Jonestown began. With the ominous punctuation of the comet and the eclipse.

I was so amazed, that I forgot to ask how he had extrapolated optimism from this. Comets, like eclipses, often portend not triumph, but downfall. A community founded under a comet within an eclipse, was far less likely to be saved (as in "Messiah") than it was to be doomed!

Yet each fascinating morsel was tossed into the exotic buffet that my return to astrology had become. There were untold hours of catch-up, as though I had been in a time capsule now freshly opened up. "Oh, by the way, a new planet was discovered while you were gone."

"Oh, a new planet? What is it like? I have dates to look up." I plummeted his tables, raided his charts, exploded in glee. Bingo! Al and I were again friends. I told him I was about to depart for the West Coast. Nothing about the affair, if it was such. Would it lead anywhere, anyway? I was "an aside." I couldn't even get regular sleeping dates.

I told Al I'd give him a call and come by when I got back into town.

Hal set up in a midtown hotel in San Francisco. Technically, I was staying with my Temple friends. I was apprehensive enough telling them I came out there with a reporter. I could hardly tell them I was *sleeping* with one. We set up a meeting with whomever of my friends were willing to trust *me* enough to come.

Meanwhile, Hal also contacted Joe Mazor (Buford and Lane's brainstorm?), only to find his hotel room bugged when he returned later in the day. Like a hospital technician sorting out which tube would sustain life for a poor hapless hospital admittee, he retrieved the telltale apparatus from behind the nighttable. Then an ex-Temple member showed up at three in the morning outside the home of my invited friends, babbling some threats. They cancelled. All that was left was Mike Prokes.

Hal took Mike and me out for dinner, then we adjourned to the hotel where, to my horror, he began grilling Mike about how could he have left the community when all those children were dying. (The preposterous mission of "delivering a million dollars to the Soviet Embassy.") Mike froze. It was really bad for him, and the reporter wouldn't stop.

Finally I stopped it myself. Mike went downstairs to the lounge. I followed him and apologized for the reporter. Mike said it was o.k. Then he said he had been thinking of suiciding out himself. "No, Mike. Don't do that. It wouldn't make anything better or different, and you should live." He said it was o.k. That he had decided not to.

Then there was the bizarre episode in the hotel room the next night. Hal had bought a bottle of brandy. I've never been a drinker, but not having indulged in *anything*, so much as a meal out, all those years, I succumbed. He plied me with half the bottle, some furious sex, and then he got weird. He pulled out a razor and held it to my breast. "What the hell are you doing?" I stiffened and freaked. "Oh, I'm just going to cut very slightly. Just to get a tiny bit of blood. Then I'll suck it, just very slightly. It's very erotic."

All I could think of was Sharon and her poor doomed children with their throats slit. "Put that goddamn thing away. Get the hell away from me!" I fled.

Other times it was talk of "sharing me with his buddy from the Times." Did I want this? Maybe the world out there *had* become as sordid as Jim Jones had always said. Sure, I had had sex before, but no one had ever weirded out on me like this.

The only productive thing we got done (though he downplayed it, like it was just a minor blip), was collecting some papers I wanted "for posterity." He thumbed through them. Said they looked unimportant, valueless. Not worth a story or anything. But hey, he'd do me a favor. He was travelling back a day or two ahead of me, and he'd carry the stuff back for me and store it in his office. I naively agreed.

I stayed on to talk with Mike, the only one who seemed interested in pursuing our case. Then I hopped a plane back to New York and showed up at the news office. To my shock and real hurt (like a stung *child* – for should I have not known better?), my papers were all laid out and being perused by the whole staff. I exploded. "Those papers are *mine!* You promised to store them until when I got back."

His voice turned sarcastic and snide. "What did you think was going to happen? I go all the way out West and I don't use what I get?" "Don't do this," I pleaded, "Just don't." I felt helpless and powerless and left out. I hopped a train down to my new "co-counter-conspirator," Al, to plan a strategy for getting the papers back.

Al, as always calm, said, just pick a day he's not there, go in and take the papers back. Oh... *logic*. "Well," I said, "He's not there on Mondays." Al sat down with his astrology tables to do a little plotting. It looked like there was no real heavy-duty security on the place. I had to at least try.

Monday arrived. I walked in and calmly made my way to the back of the building. Some people recognized me, but just gave a nod. No one seemed that concerned. I walked into Hal's office and spied my boxes. They seemed in tact. But the walk through the complex, which was laid out like a railroad flat, was long, and these boxes were heavy.

I took a deep breath, picked up a box and began the slow, calm, casual walk. Well, what walks in can, it seemed, walk right out. The boxes were rested near the reception desk one by one. I went back and forth, slowly down the corridor peopled with desks, chairs, xerox machines, phones, spacious and modest offices alike. I walked slowly with their weight, weighed down mentally as well, by the uncertain disposition of my fragile legacy of black-and-white. I said nothing to anyone. There were six or seven boxes. I didn't remember anything being left out.

Slowly, carefully, I carried each box outside the office door. Right in front. I hailed a cab. In went the boxes. In went me. Off we all went, me and my contraband of oblongs and squares, up to my mom's. Then I rushed downtown to Al, to pour out my relief, even squeamish delight, at the whole episode.

A day or two later the phone rang. An irate newsman. "Where's the stuff?" "What stuff?" "You know. The boxes. Did your people break in? When did you do it? The middle of the night?" "Wait a minute. What are you saying? You're saying my things were *stolen*? How could you let that happen? Why weren't you watching the stuff?" "Oh, c'mon, you know your people broke in. And I want it back." "*You* want it back? *I* want it back. The stuff belongs to *me*. You better find it or they'll be serious trouble." Slam.

Talk about breaking off a relationship! Laurie's relationship with the press was going poorly.

XL. A Base From Which to Work.

After this abrasive run-in, I was in no shape to tackle *The New York Times*! Not that I didn't try (i.e. the New York Times) with, not unexpectedly, no response. I was a mass of vehemence and rage. I was brimming over with facts, scenarios and rationales, pouring from my lips each with spontaneous counterpoints of showery tears. Between grief, anxiety, and desperation, I may have just scared a lot of people off. Whether or not they were interested in my story, they may not have wanted to cope with *me*.

Al was the one person who could. Notwithstanding the thirty-year gap in age, he became my constant companion, my best friend. He did famously with younger people, anyway. He was almost in a throw-back mode to the sixties, as he exclaimed, "Oh, groovy" at each strange suggestion as to how to proceed. It was, in fact, all of it strange, off-beat, even dangerous. Though we didn't really bargain for what we got.

First, it seemed that we *both* had dossiers. Al had been a government inspector for the FDA in the early 50's, but he was too zealous at it, refused to take bribes from the mob, instead turning them in! He wound up canned, his government employer of the early fifties claiming, conveniently, that he was a "pinko" ~ McCarthy security risk.

His other claim to fame was that he had predicted the Kennedy assassination, then made an avocation of tracking down witnesses who were killed themselves. Intermittently, he said, there was government surveillance on *him*. His theory was that the Russians did it in retaliation for The Bay of Pigs, and that since he predicted it through astrology, and the government people didn't understand astrology, they thought he could be a Russian agent himself.

The fact is, he hated Russians! He had met Russian soldiers during the war, and didn't like them a bit! Yet there was this government dossier nearly branding him as a communist. As for me, I undoubtedly had a dossier lined up from babyhood, given my card-carrying mom. And Peoples Temple, most assuredly, hardly "cleared my name." So here we were ~ marked.

Though nothing possibly could have prepared me for the bizarre harassments that were to litter our daily lives. It got hairy, to say the least. Notwithstanding, we started with something quite simple ~ what was the most natural for me: writing. Here was a magazine in need of articles.

Here was one of my lost careers --astrology--, and a suddenly-rekindled interest. I plunged.

The article for CAO TIMES. It wasn't just that astrology came rushing back. I suddenly surpassed my earlier training, like a silent tutelage across the years had sharpened my mathematical brain, released my grasp of form and line. The planets came alive beneath my pen. Scandal when the chart sliced into Uranus. Deadly Pluto pressing the doors of death. Triumphs and crises one and all, the plan would unfold.

I wrote stridently, with a missionary zeal. That I believed the suicides were an act of unity, a model of sacrifice to elevate Humankind to a higher plane. Sisters and brothers who would not abandon their interracial paradise, who could never return to the chaos from whence they came. Neither could they turn one another in, some having violently lashed out. It was Jim Jones the exemplar beseeching all, in turn, to be surrogates for these damning acts (*"I can't separate myself from my people"*) -- even though he had not ordered any killing (as the final tape revealed), or any violence at all. Because when lines are drawn to a new life, you do not, you cannot, abandon your own.

Thus the beacon of self-sacrifice was flipped from idealistic intent, now bitterly dashed, to doom: **"*I waited against all evidence. The choice is not ours now. It's out of our hands. Better we do it than they do it... We've lived. We've loved. We've had as much of this world as we're going to get. Let's just be done with the agony of it.*"**

You see? He *did* believe that were we not to exit this life ourselves, we would surely be attacked, murdered, or brutally taken. *He* believed, *I* believed, and undoubtedly there were many at Jonestown who believed.

Probably no one could believe any *less* than that we would be brutally dragged back. No one would spare a community that (however innocent 99+% of its inhabitants, or how provoked the guilty 1-%) "spawned that kind of violence." Were we not already under vicious attack for doing.... *good*? Too much good for the wrong people, too much empowering of the societal powerless. No one would have granted the community as a whole forgiveness for the actions of *any* of its members.

So read the tale in CAO TIMES. I was younger then. I was bashed to pieces. I had to reveal the unseen face of the tragedy to the world at large. Thus the anguished cry to *"Listen!!"* If I did this quietly, I didn't stand a chance. Perhaps if I cried out loudly enough, I did. It might be different now. This was the only course that rang true then. Never underestimate the chance to speak.

Speak through tears. My zealotry was the kind of protective shield people raise when they feel hurt and powerless, or cannot believe that what was so idealistic for them, could be corrupted by others. If you think I was untroubled by moral questions (like even if you stand together to the death, how can *children* decide for themselves to commit suicide?), I was indeed *very* troubled by them. Why should children have to die? But who provoked this, and why did it go that far?

And what was the *pragmatic* reality? If not suicide, could there not have been slaughter from the outside? Certainly, from the account of the six-day seige, Mazor's ill-spoken "confession" that he had been sent to kill *everyone*, the slaying of the Congressman giving the entrée to invade, and Jim Jones' own words on the final tape, there could have been a slaughter in the works.

I am past the traumas now, and though storms ofttimes seems diminished on reaching the calm, I've discovered years past, evidence reviewed, perspective matured, that I still believe this now. Ultimately, of course, one is better served by evidence than by belief. It wasn't easy to come by in the middle of the ghoulish media circus that the postscript to Jonestown had become. Though it did matter hugely to consider the odds on Jonestown being wiped out had the suicides *not* intervened. That could alter *everything*. But in those early days, the evidence coffers had barely been emptied. I was still groping, as if by brail, to decipher how the pieces had fallen together, absent some of the most critical clues of all.

Even the factor of unity within the Jonestown community or no. I wanted to believe that, of course, even though my own "Angel" had shown me that however much this act begged unity to grant it redemption, it was in fact to be played out through conflict on an all-too-human Stage of Life: *"And one died, and I laid him in a shelter 'neath the trees..... He seemed so calm... and overborne with shade..."* *"Another died, as he sobbed wretchedly on his last, torn breath: 'That I might live to redeem a travesty of mistakes, trials and sorrows!'..."* *"Yet another died as with a shout he swore, 'My death shall be avenged by all brave women and men!'"* Three diverse states: one at peace, one in conflict, one the zealot's cry.

I would tell you now, more softly, that I understand the stridency of my tone... for *then*. No one else would be the voice that I insisted on being. The highest that *I* had aspired to be. I could not let all that goodness die unsung, despite that the world was not ready for Jonestown. The people of Jonestown may not have been ready for Jonestown either! But they were no longer here. I was. And I did whatever I had to do to heal. Vividly, for myself. But at least dimly, for *everyone*.

As for the rest, I wanted desperately to pluck a glory from out of a horror. I wanted the pure in spirit especially lauded - almost as if to carry the other, more tortured or recalcitrant souls, across the great divide with the dignity the world had denied them.

I don't know how well I did at elevating their memory. These were overwrought words - more one-dimensional, even propagandistic, than I would write now. Yet deep inside, we know the only course that will suffice: that of our heart, our conscience. Could a therapist have instructed me in what to say; or a newsman dissuaded me based upon public reaction; or relatives of the deceased censor what was appropriate or no? Bless my strange comrade-in-arms with his hokey one-horse magazine, that he flung across the nations, however sparsely, to let me speak.

I needed personal answers the most, but who was there to ask? Why was I thrust into this horror? Why was I so dedicated to a man who had spurned me? But perhaps most of all: Why had I always, despite everything, known I belonged in that place? The ringing recognition of "coming home." Even to a place where I was slated for ostracism. My gifts and talents spurned. My one trophy an inscrutable Rosetta Stone for an incomprehensible turn of fate. And Jim Jones, whose mission it seemed created to eulogize... it was he who had tried to crush it as though it were an act of defiance, not of love.

Perhaps, indeed, that *was* my answer, though I could not see it then. The agony of being witness, an answer all its own. Were I a hostile witness, anyone would have understood. People would encourage it. I could just never do it. Something in me knew I *had* been planted there. That I *was* a witness. I, eyes prematurely opened, heart prematurely traumatized, mind prematurely bent at an impossible lean, was there to serve as witness in ways that others could not. I was given this as a gift. Or perhaps an "assignment." Sometimes you just know. Know and obey.

Yes, there were polemics in my words. Defending the people who were no longer alive to defend themselves. I felt the weight of them each hour within my heart. Who else to defend them but me? Me and my newfound unlikely comrade, a strange eccentric warrior knocking on old age's door.

The shock of how alone I truly was was just about to hit home.

XLI. I Lose a Comrade-in-Arms.

No one celebrated the holidays that year, so I don't recall whether I came East just prior to Christmas or just after. There were no holidays, no celebrations at all, for years to come. I wasn't a party-goer anyway - not before all this and certainly not after. I would freeze in rooms of strangers, feeling plastered into walls, or paralyzed into stilted words, or caught on the edge of one of those little groups that coalesces around the one who laughs the hardest or talks the most. Anything *I* had to say was too deadly serious to laugh, and as for talking, no one ever broached the one thing no one wanted to talk about but me.

For all my zeal to vindicate Peoples Temple, that was a mission, not a life style. For that, I would force myself to write strangers or to seek people out. This "wailing aloud" - some Middle Eastern cultures sanction it as a mass expiation of grief. Surely the ancient Greeks knew it as well, as scenes from "Oedipus Rex" and other dramas with loud, plangent choruses will readily enact. It doesn't mean its participants are social in character, or that their overwrought passions necessarily translate into other cultural pursuits.

I would not, could not, sustain such passion in any normal social milieu. To the contrary. I retreated into the ranks of the pathologically shy. I dreaded invitations to socialize shy of a one-to-one mainstay who would remain glued to my side. I had no dates, and Saturdays came as an unwelcome bas relief - stark, barren and bare. I rarely even went to the movies, for as the locals lined up two by two, it was a painful reminder of how alone was I.

Al became my steadiest companion and served me ever so well as mentor, listener, psychologist, morale-builder, even co-worker. He used to say we were "soldiers in the field" and couldn't stop to rest, just had to push on.

Our various off-beat dering-do's came to claim center stage. Nothing in my life save temp work (the bane of New York's underrated pool of talent!) resembled a normal life. Mostly I wrote and thought, thought and wrote. Being locked out of more relaxing pursuits, I tightened each precious moment of time like the fiercely shrinking belt of an anorexic dieter - nervous, nearly furtive, that not a single morsel of time be squandered. I compiled copies of the voluminous letters I wrote, the documents I gleaned, the stray recollections and thoughts, like they could be my food when I could again afford to eat.

I cried more than anyone would ever want to know. It took no provocation to cry ~ merely a thought, a remembrance, some silent, unarticulated prod that did not have to appear in either images or words. Suddenly it would well up in me, the grief-stricken souls who died, the lingering horror for those who lived. It was perilously precarious to distinguish, or to keep one from invading the other's ken.

Sometimes someone would show up on the street, invasively, like a double, for someone who had died. One day it was Patricia Cartmell, and a rush of recollections streamed back ~ her bustling about the church, her dutiful sublimation to mother Patty's protective bulk, her industrious youth, her sweet young face. I looked at this girl who perhaps looked little like her at all, and the tears were for Patricia that day. Another day it was Karen Layton. I ran into "Marceline" and could barely move. Once I even spied a faint resemblance to Jim.

I don't doubt that part of the levelling of grief upon my face, my voice, my body's inroads into space, was the crushing barrier between the two worlds of life and death, like a microscopic slide tissue crushed immobile from above and below by deceptively transparent glass. Worse yet were my dreams. It was years before the half-light dreams, wavering between life and death would fade, or their anxieties swell from their pulverized state, explode, and finally, fiercely, like demons exercised from the inky depths, the ghosts of Jonestown would flee my troubled sleep.

The repetitive dreams were the worst. We were regathered in some kind of hall, those of us who were still alive. There were crowds of us and the podium up front, as before. Why were we meeting? It was always the same. These were the survivors. We had to decide whether or not to do a second wave of suicides of those who were left.

But it never was just those who were left. It was always a mix of those who were left with those who had perished. Different people surfaced each dream. The faces would drift before me. I would recognize each face with a start. "Oh, *she's* still alive? *He's* still alive?" It was like going to a class reunion each night. You knew who had been in your class but had no idea who would show up this time.

The leadership shifted each night. Sometimes Jim, sometimes a leaderless, but vociferous entourage. Sometimes Patty or Jack would show, sometimes the Pughs or Johnny Brown. Sometimes a child I hadn't known too well would appear. The territory was fair game for all. All these people who were dead. They could all show up as "alive" in my dreams, yet alive not to live, but to urge and press and coerce our own demise.

We had to decide. It was imperative, like the last train out in a tear-jerker of a film. The whistle is blowing. You leave the scene or you stay. If you stay, you are trapped. If you flee, you break a thousand hearts. Either way, everyone will cry. Will you cut that tragic edge into a perfect, jagged silhouette in time? This was Peoples Temples now. All these people alive, dead, alive-reborn, living ghosts shouting for unity in the life-death of my heart. Would there be a second wave of suicides or not? *Make this decision. You must make it now.*

Never in any dream was it made. Always I awoke with the dangling ends of indecision draping my torso like a shroud. It was foreboding, threatening, like the last arm-twisting of "If they take one of us, they'll have to take us all!" from the grave. Didn't we *have* to do this? Wasn't it already too late to reverse?

I was, as always, not suicidal. I seemed to lack "the gene." But there were these dreams, gnawing, enervating, pressing, urging, tugging on the tears ("tares") my fragile psyche had left raw. I felt paralyzed. I couldn't say no. Abandon my comrades? I could never do that. But I couldn't say yes, either. Everyone pressed. But no one directly pressed *me*. It was a more subtle, pervasive, stifling sort of thing, like a huge anonymous pressure that would never either resolve or go away.

It was into this matrix that fell the tragic fate of my treasured friend, Michael Prokes. I had no idea Mike was "up" that solitary March, '79 night – not consciously. My impression upon taking my leave of the West with the editor, was that Mike was calm – his normal, calm, measured self. There was no hysteria, no anger, no desperation, not even jumpiness. I could discern no inner turmoil. God. I thought I guarded *my* emotions. Here was the "guru." Maybe I just didn't *want* to see.

That March night. I was still living at my mother's, but she was out-of-town – her yearly art pilgrimage to Mexico. The bright Mexican colors inspired her artist's palette, and seemed to route the wild manic sweeps into an ordered flow and line.

I needed this time alone. I would sit and sink into an uneasy gloom well into the night. This night, however, was different. Like a journey, a reverie. From about 9 o'clock on, I just sat at the big table. Did nothing. Sat. Then it seemed like visions, scenarios, were encroaching upon me. I just sat, opened the door, and in they came.

I was in Jonestown. It was like it was both me and it wasn't me. I was in Jonestown and the suicides had begun. I had to leave, but I was in torment about whether I should. How could I leave? I had to leave, but I couldn't. It wasn't right.

This anguish. At first it seemed purely mental. Then gradually, over two hours or so, it deepened, intensified. Feelings of panic were starting to emerge. That I couldn't let myself leave. It was wrong. I had to go but I couldn't. I couldn't do this. How could I let myself go when all the others were dying?

It was like a dream, a reverie. My brain was swaying in the slow thud of a dirge. People were dying. I was right there while people were dying and I was going to *leave*. I couldn't. I had to stay. I had to stay and die with them. I *had* to.

Gradually, gradually and increasingly, I became distraught. I can't not die. I can't leave everyone else to die. I knew it wasn't me, it wasn't me who was saying this. I was nowhere near Jonestown at all. But I felt this. I felt like it *was* me. Like a second-person me. Me as another person who couldn't bear to leave the others to die.

Now I was getting really upset. I *had* to stay. How could I go? I had to die, too. I *had* to. I began crying, crying and shaking and castigating myself. How could I leave when everyone was dying? I belonged there. I had to stay. To die with all of them. It was too much torture to leave. Please, God, let me die. Let me not have to leave. It's too much agony. I should be dying too.

Then slowly, gradually, the grip of what was almost akin to a psychic fugue, crested and began to wane. Slowly, the tears flowed less. Slowly I felt myself return to a shaken, exhausted reprieve. Free of torment. Free of pain. Now I could rest. It was terrible. I felt terrible. But I could rest.

From out of the pinprick of silenced tears, the phone rang. Why so late? It must have been at least midnight. I ran to the phone and picked it up.

"Hello." "Hi, Laurie. It's Jean." "What is it?" "Laurie, I don't know how to tell you this. Mike Prokes. He called a news conference. Then he went into an adjoining bathroom and shot himself through the head. They rushed him to the hospital. He was critical for a couple of hours. He just died." "Oh, God, no. I can't believe this." I couldn't talk. I just couldn't. I thanked her for calling and hung up.

One death. This couldn't be. One death couldn't possibly be worse than nine hundred deaths, could it? I began crying now, but crying furiously. Shaking, screaming, pounding with my fists. *"No more death! No more death! Please. I can't take this! I can't take anymore! No more death! No more death!!"* I felt myself moving into some gear of gear shifts that had never been invented. That gear that goes just *beyond* hysteria. I had tolerated all the rest. I had gotten through. I had stopped that teensy fraction of an inch before the cliff's edge, and didn't jump. Why more? Why this? Why now? "No more death! **No more death!!!"**

I had.... Well, I had almost mastered being two people. One would comfort the other, or tell the other (perceiving compassionately how "the other" was paralytically locked and unable to move) what to say, what to think, what to do. By now, it was going on 2 in the morning. Go downtown to see Al. Al will comfort you. He'll be all right with it. Go!

I moved like one suffused in a terrible nightmarish dream. I made myself go. I cried all the way down the elevator. I cried onto the street. I cried down the subway stairs. I cried on each train I alighted. I made myself move on. I must have arrived going on 3. Thank God he was willing to be awakened. Thank God he was willing to listen, to comfort me. One kindness amongst a thousand from that dear, strange man. There would be so many more.

The man just *listened*. He had that extraordinary gift. Like Marceline. Different personality, different style – just that same wonderful rare gift. He let me choke out the words, head swaying o'er my lap like a weeping willow sweeping the riverbeds, filling them with torrents of tears, rocked into an uneasy, tiring, exhausting lull of numbing pain. Finally, in the dawn's early light, I was drained dry.

A couple of days later a package arrived. Mike had carefully packed copies of write-ups he had handed out to the press before he went off and blew his brains out. He had probably been quite calm with *them*, too. He said he made an audio tape, and to whom it had been sent – that it would explain more. Of course it never arrived. (We'll return to "What did the Post Office know and when did they know it?")

Some of the package was quite moving, including his statement that he was dying "in solidarity with my black brothers and sisters." His personal note to me, placed across the top like a mere "memo," was handwritten and short, telling me that "I admired your courage and the way way you refused to be intimidated." That I would probably want to pick up my last remaining things stored at his mother's. He said he hoped I could find a way to make life meaningful again and signed it, "All my love, Mike."

There was no "good-bye" in this note. No "I've decided to die." I scraped the few curt words for hidden content and surfaced none. This was vintage Mike Prokes. He didn't say it. He just did it. Mike was gone.

What did this mean? That we all do what we have to do? I would face the music and he would face his Maker? Was this o.k.? Was it o.k. to just off yourself, to duck out on people, doing what *you* had to do while they did what *they* had to do? Was there a world where all the people who did what they had to do would finally meet up? Poor Mike. His guilt killed him. Guilt I don't even know was rightfully his. It shattered me. He had such a good heart. I only asked, dear God, may he rest in peace.

It was years before I gave those papers more than a cursory glance. There seemed nothing startling – how he came to Peoples Temple as a newsman to cover a successful church, and found himself impressed enough to stay. He wove in a tale that was a surprise, yes. About being approached by a man who said he was a government agent. The man told Mike he learned of his visit to the Temple from *tapping Jim Jones' phone*, and said that he would pay him weekly to glean information about the group. Mike said that when he decided to join the church, he took the man up on his offer.

That only later, when he was convinced of the Jim Jones' sincerity (he said he had seen him perform too many acts of kindness secretly) did he tell the man that he would no longer be an informant. That he told him he would not reveal the man's existence unless he suspected someone else was taking his (i.e. Mike's) place as an informant.

This *could* have happened like he said (even Mazor told Lane that "one of the plants went native"). Mike was CBS News Bureau Chief in Sacramento, an impressive title for a man still in his twenties, when he joined up with Jim Jones in 1972. It would have been a true plum to gain a veteran reporter as a spy.

Ironically, I had no reason to hold this against Mike. Many people are faced with temptations in life, and the greatest thing is to resist when it grates against the evidence of your heart, or more so here, your conscience. Mike could have even told me that. Even when he and the Carter brothers were sent out of Jonestown with money for...the Soviet Embassy (so much for "a father taking care of his children"), with guns to do themselves in if caught, and it turning out that course wasn't possible... I hadn't the

I Lose a Comrade in Arms/301

slightest problem with "that course not being possible" ~ i.e. with my friends being able to *live*.

I thought the problem more the grillings he had received about why he left Jonestown at the last. I had bent over backwards, myself, to apologize for the reporter's behaviour. Surely Mike knew I was in *his* corner, not the reporter's. But I had also heard that two zealous Black former members of the church had quizzed Mike brutally, claiming he only got to go because he was white, leaving all the black people to die.

Then there was Teri Buford. In her book jointly authored with Lane, she claimed to have talked with Mike shortly before his end. God knows what Ms. Buford said. She seemed to have an ugly habit of doing in her best friends.

I wouldn't have even remembered the name of the self-proclaimed government agent if I had not kept Mike's press release. I only looked back in 1992, upon being sent a book about Jonestown by a relative of people who had died. One of the segments was written by one "Garry Scharf," who not only claimed membership in the Temple, but as "a close friend of Mike Prokes." He also said he had changed his last name ~ something to do with his father. To take his father's name or drop his father's name. God forbid he did it to conceal his identity, or something flat-out logical like that.

This Garry Scharff was touted as the "Golden Boy" of C.A.N. ~ the Cult Awareness Network (who worked closely with Ryan's daughter, Patricia, following the tragedy). He toured for years following the tragedy, talking about alleged druggings and beatings and sexual abuse, even attempted murder. That Jim Jones had personally begged him for sex, or forced him to beg for sex. (If I get this sordid point confused, please do understand ~ *Jim Jones did not know this man. Had never met him.*) And that now, for some unknown reason, C.A.N. was beginning to doubt the Scharff fellow's credibility. After eleven years. Incredible.

Well, there are cults and then there are *cons*. But this guy ... he was on a *payroll*. Someone was paying him to speak out against Peoples Temple as late as 1989 ~ *eleven years after everyone was already dead?* Move us all to Antartica. Cold chills. Cold, cold, cold. How low will the temperature go?

I looked at the photo of Garry Scharf in the book I had been sent. *I had never seen him before in my life.* He was *never* a member of Peoples Temple, not *ever*. If he was a friend of Mike's, no one knew. If Jim knew, Mike would have been blasted. No one as close to Jim as Mike was, could have maintained a friendship with someone who was not even a member.

I read what this fellow had to say, too. His stories were preposterous, his alleged knowledge of people like Jim, Mike, the Mertles (all conveniently dead, understand!) was tell-tale flawed, his quotes wrong, his chronologies wrong, everything wrong. A dead-ringer for a liar if you were simply inside enough to know the rudiments.

I thought, well, he choose Mike as his "best friend" because Mike was dead and could not refute it. But then I looked back at what Mike himself had written. The government man, the agent. His name was "Gary Jackson." Gary. My gut froze. *It was the same man.*

In fact, for someone who had never been in Peoples Temple, he did seem to have a special affinity for the recently-deceased. His other "best friends" were said to be the Mertles, who allegedly "rescued" him when he allegedly left Peoples Temple after an alleged confrontation with Jim Jones on an alleged date he "remembered as well as if it had happened yesterday," except for the small reality that Jim Jones had already left for Guyana permanently! He said he had been working for the Cult Awareness Network for nine years ~ dating back not to 1978, the time of the the tragedy, but to 1980. This marks his surfacing as on the heels of the Mertles' murder, just after they had tried to duck out of the anti-Temple circuit. *Was he their "replacement"?*

Interesting. You deprogrammers out there. Do such people really aid your cause? But more interesting still. Who was *paying* this man? And why so late in the game, past any purpose or logic? And how do "the Gary's" of that private select world duplicate themselves? Who are they? Where are they? Who else are they working to do in?

Do I care? Someone else out there. Any interested party. *You* make the effort to expose him. It all gets so wearying. Why doesn't the *media* do their job? Everyone thinks they're vultures and vampires, but sometimes they're just infernally conformist and naive. Ironically, *Nexus* magazine managed, at late date (Dec. 1994), to expose that C.A.N. seemed to employ the same crew of psychiatric "experts" as the C.I.A. used, but still swallowed the same load of disinformation about Jim Jones' alleged collusion with the C.I.A. in "mind control experiments." Scharff (Jackson, whatever) was never cited.

No one ever pursued the obvious. There we were, black, white, black, white, black, white, lined up like a perfectly checkered billboard, primed to move to Russia during the Cold War, and every newsperson out there, to the last one, accepted that "crazed cultists" covered this story nicely.

I Lose a Comrade in Arms/303

Imagine what succcess this "cultist" might have had trying to claim that people were trying to do Temple survivors in *after* the tragedy. I often stayed at Al's now, ironically because I felt so *safe*, working well into the night on my treasured, rediscovered art. Only gradually did we begin to notice the odd characters who trailed us in the streets, strained to hear our conversations in restaurants, peered invasively over our shoulders at the post office, or logged in nightly with "wake-up calls" at 3 a.m.

I had missed the siege in Guyana. It seemed that now we were in for one of our own.

XLII. If the War's Over, Why Are They Still Shooting at <u>Me</u>?

This was never anything less than a sinister sub-beat to the main plot. If you asked me to estimate how many people were assigned to the wholly destructive, tax-wasting harassment of me and Al Morrison, or how much the personnel got paid, I wouldn't know, but I would have been thrilled had they only paid the money to us personally. We could have lived in grand style. Like we had won the Lotto or something.

Phone-tapping was the least of it, though my phone was never free of odd intermittent clicks 'til '92. It was such a transparent pattern that my own slow, stage-laden transition to normalcy seemed clicked off in integers timed in phone intercepts, never landing down quite solid while Big Brother was still listening in.

For some reason (perhaps because some miscreant in secret government employ thought the older of the pair, Al, "the original Russian agent," and the younger, myself, a mere sycophantic offshoot?), Al got the brunt of this, despite that it was I whose muddy bootprints had tromped this new trouble into his door. He hadn't a tie in the world to Jonestown 'til *I* arrived, but they lowered the boom most decidedly upon *him*.

The people trailing us in the street, in and out of restaurants, setting up listening posts, was more than a minor annoyance I often wanted to intercept with, "Whose your employer? What do they pay you, and is it worth it to screw up innocent people's lives?" I wanted to, but Al would always stop me, saying it would make things worse.

This wasn't anyone's imagination, friends; some of it seemed blatant enough to deliberately *incite* paranoia. Who believed me *anyway*? All I had to do was freak out over being followed in the street. That would do wonders for my credibility, wouldn't it?

Once we paced someone. We felt him behind us, then looked. Right on Seventh Avenue. Right out in the open. We walked a few paces and stopped. He walked a few paces and stopped. We walked a few more paces and stopped. He walked a few more paces and stopped. Finally we stopped, looked back, and stared the guy down. Remarkably, he whipped out a key, stuck it into the nearest car door in the adjacent gutter, hopped in and sat there motionless until he thought we had moved on. One quick look back, and he jumped out of the car and ran away.

We got to know this crew by sight. I had gone out of the neighborhood to do a mailing one day. I went to the U.N. Post Office in the East 40's. This guy kept peering over my shoulder – *invasively* peering. He wouldn't stop until he could see some clear name or address. I kept shifting my parcels, staring back. His eyes glowed fiercely, with a genuine meanness I would never forget. Like *I* was preventing him from doing his job!

Months later on, we sat down in a restaurant and there's the exact same guy. This time it's Al across from me opening up his mail, and the guy's eyes are glaring sideways, squinted and crosswise from a catty-cornered table, trying to read Al's letters upside down. I'm sorry Al stopped me that time. I wanted to spit in that man's face so bad. Just walk over without a word and spit.

A friend helped us get out a mailing once, and had to go through a whole labyrinth of subways to shake a tail. The next day, she was trailed in the street, then the surveillant (i.e. *assailant*) skirted in front of her and blinded her with a spray which gave her hallucinations for days. That was even worse for me. Me being hurt was bad enough. Why hurt her? She wasn't even directly involved.

We never knew how much mail we could get out through the Post Office at all. We'd send out mailing receipts for certified mail and they'd come back unstamped or undated, unsigned, unprocessed. God knows what reached its destination at all, especially the mail I was, at one point, eager to get to *Washington*.

Home base was no better. Al's home was staked out and the intrusions were continual. The phone became the megaphone for the coven of evildoers who set this all up. They'd call. And call. And call. They'd call as "Mr. or Mrs. Joe Q. Public," but the questions were pointed, specific, technical. Always about astrology. Always about whatever had just found its way into the trash. Or what he had been talking about on the phone a few hours earlier. Things no one else knew or cared about. Things that had just arisen. Again and again and again.

Then there was a whole crew who only phoned at night. Sometimes they'd ask some stupid question, sometimes about what number they had dialed, sometimes they'd just hang up. It was impossible to sleep the whole night through.

I finally got a device for Al to record calls off his phone. That led to one of the weirdest contacts of all. A woman with an unpleasant, but distinctive voice – kind of a babyish whine. On the phone, she was always

"Joan Gottlieb." I heard the tape and the voice was a dead-ringer. I'd recognize it to this day.

Then the same woman calls, but now she's "Lillian Lutein." She wants to come by. Asks does Al have any info about birth data for Roy Cohn. (McCarthy's sidekick. Our favorite person, wouldn't you think?) Well, Al did have tons of birth data, and said he would assist. He knew that she was a harasser, but thought he would have himself and me and at least one other person there, and maybe she could be trapped into some admission.

So we're waiting for her and the doorbell rings. As soon as the door opens, we see this *huge* blond woman, and she's shoving her way in, as if to do bodily harm. Except three of us are there together, so she's foiled. Turns out she knows nothing at all about astrology – little enough to have no conversational skill in the subject at all. I recognized her voice, of course. "Lillian Lutein" and "Joan Gottlieb" were one and the same.

We had pre-arranged to take a picture, but when the camera comes out, her hands go up to her face, and she freaks and runs. Keeps calling back, says she must have the picture, but will never give her own number or an address to mail it to. That was a scary one – built like a truck. Whether *we* intimidated *her*, I really doubt.

Meanwhile, my poor elderly mother has phone trouble, calls the phone company, and I walk in and find color-coded wires all over her apartment, running alongside the walls and into the next room, *which doesn't have a phone in it at all.* She said they took hours to string it up and she didn't have the faintest idea what they were doing. Like I had *never* seen phone service like this. Phonemen from Mars maybe.

So you really don't have to be out in the jungle to develop a siege mentality! As if life were not already enough of a trek into *"The Twilight Zone,"* our world gradually incorporated the ubiquitous crew of trailers and listeners, panickers and destabilizers alike into the daily grind. It got even worse once Al talked on an overseas call and said it wasn't Peoples Temple members who assassinated the Congressman. We were in for it then. The harassment became so incessant, Al ripped the phone clear out of the wall, refusing to ever install a phone again. I couldn't blame him. How could anyone do that to people?

Some months later, we saw a sketch of the still-unapprehended "subway gunman" on the front page of *The New York Post*, the guy who felt threatened on the subway, whipped out a gun and mowed the kids down in expert fashion. You know. Bernhard Goetz. But this was before anyone knew his name. He had escaped the subway and was being hunted down through a police sketch. The one that showed up in *The Post*.

"Oh, I know him," Al offered casually, "He lives around here." "You *know* him?," I responded incredulously. "Sure. That's the guy who showed up an hour after I ripped out the phone. He showed up at the door to ask if my phone needed repair." Some days later in the paper, after he had turned himself in, he gave his address as Chelsea, Al's neighborhood, and he cited his profession as "electronics calibration expert for the government."

Oh, so that's what they call it, "electronic calibrations expert"? And where'd the guy learn how to *shoot*? That's no mean feat, hauling off shots into a subway train crowded with innocent bystanders, and you only hit your mark. That's no Mr. Average Citizen. That's *training*. So what in the world would electronics calibration for the government have to do with being a crackerjack shot? I've been wondering ever since.

The weird thing was that Al's building was opposite a police precinct, yet there was nothing that could be done about the ongoing invasions, intrusions and harassments. Al's astrological practice went into a decline. For one thing, no one could reach him by phone. For another, he couldn't risk having new clients in his home ~ it was too dangerous. I felt as enraged on his behalf as on my own (and yes, a tad guilty at that ~ I had transported this mess back to New York), yet there was nothing to do but try and survive, hopefully in one piece.

Occasionally, errors were made identifying "agents." Al taught a Thursday night class. I had met a sweet young girl named Amy, wanting to learn astrology, and she wound up at Al's before me. To my dismay, I found poor Amy out on the street, helplessly crying. "What's wrong?" She choked out, "He said I was an agent." "He *what*?" "He said I was an *agent*. He wouldn't let me in." I took her by the arm and we tromped upstairs together.

One more minute and it would have been no more Amy forever. Well, people come and go. But if I had not kept in contact with Amy, I never would have met her music teacher, to review a later-composed score. And if I hadn't met him, I wouldn't have years later met his new love through whom, years later even, I met her friend who still later on introduced me to my future husband.

That was all of twelve years after I found Amy crying her eyes out on the street! How today's mishap can become tomorrow's series of coincidences! That a small incident in 1979, akin to a child spilling a glass of milk on a table, could lead to a fated union in 1991. How little we know. I don't bother much anymore about people who disparage my odd collection of interests in life. Maybe I have them because it was me who knew how to listen to the inner voices and to look for the outer signs. It's an obtuse lot who thinks they get all their info in life from books or t.v.

Of course, marriage was the last thing on my mind just then, though we'll backtrack on this later on, to pick up stray pieces from my alter-ego, the elusive Lou Andreas-Salome. (You forgot her. I know. I forgot her too for years at a stretch.) Life is a tapestry of sorts. God and the Angels weave the strands, and we humans can only sense when the patterns of it all shall be complete. I will show you where I went with Jonestown from then on in, also where I *couldn't* go. At least not yet. The threads. Lost, picked up, lost, picked up again. "Just give me twenty years for this." And They have. That and more.

XLIII. Every Story Has a Cover Story. All Information Has a Dis-.

Twenty years. It is not quite that yet; though it is more since I first joined the church in 1970, and perhaps the tragedy was "always with us." I know as well as anyone, the subtle shifts of the lens from close-range view to a distant, trustfully safer, time and place.

It's like the world itself has eyeglasses. And mostly they're myopic. They see things close-range that look so huge that they block the way ahead. But there is more. They also cannot see what *is*, at the *moment* it is, because its pieces are surfaced selectively, with weighted thrusts. It's like if you had a palette of paint, all different colors, and all that was splashed across the canvas was blue. The artist would be full of fanfare and bombast ~ there would be dark blue and light blue and royal blue and aqua and teal. But yet, the whole world of it would be... blue.

And if you ever thought to ask, then the artist, so tied into his own creation, would say there was no more of it. In the world of color, detail, outline, this is all there is. It's all blue.

If the whole of it *were* any more, you wouldn't know until you stood back ~ what we call "perspective." If you could only see the whole, the entirety of colors the artist *could have* used, discover where they are hidden away, and why. Or see that the artist did not discover his palette, but was *given* it, as a deliberate sampling of one color alone, distorting or concealing others that might have given the whole a differing cast.

In the days following the tragedy, an optometrist surely would not have helped *me!* I could never have seen the Jonestown Tragedy like the world at large. These were my friends, and they had built something miraculous that was destroyed. This was my leader, a man who was the living, pulsing throb of *"I care."* Whatever his failings, he cared passionately ~no, *consummately*~ about building a better world. For twenty-five years. Record solid gold. Unimpeachable. Like Mark Lane said: "A saint."

And finally, magnificent Jonestown. The answer to the inner cities' demise. It seemed the crowning coup.

Were such contrasting colors on the palette at all? No. The palette was set, the dye cast. The verdict forever graven in stone: "A *bizarre murder/suicide ritual.*" All those eager-beaver reporters ("vultures," as "*Allegory*" unflatteringly termed them years in advance) were so obsessed with "How could this happen?," that no one had the perspective to ask.... "*What* happened?" What was the actual sequence of events? They thought it didn't matter because Jonestown was a terrible place, a jungle hell no one cared about but a few "concerned relatives." And a madman had just up and killed all his followers.

All those newspeople. The whole world. And no one investigated anything. No one even thought to look. Here are all these people, lined up black-white-black-white-black-white, all primed to move to the U.S.S.R. at the invitation of the Soviet government, and... *no one investigates?*

I looked on in horror, not just at the event, but at the mindset surrounding it, as one by one, the pieces fell into place. In a year's time, enough evidence had filtered my way to reconstruct what had happened. It landed with a jolt. Suddenly my original instincts were confirmed. Our people hadn't killed the Congressman, after all. It smacked of a professional hit team who did it so as to *frame* us. Now Jim Jones could never (as Mazor told the television commentator*)* "*become a major political force in the Caribbean within five years.*" Now we would never relocate to the Soviet Union. We would go nowhere at all, except, if we were lucky, to jail.

It all made sense. I even discovered, oddly, that the worldwide myopia over Jonestown had some benefits. Huge tracts of information emerged close to the event, when no-one realized the pieces could ever fall together differently than they had originally appeared. The horror had given way to an uncritical free-for-all, since Jonestown packed its sensationalist punch for a matter of months. A lot of stuff came out that no one realized might be important, or saw as any more than an artifact to satisfy the morbidly curious. Thus I was able to glean a bit here, a bit there. Some news, some leads, some research.

The pieces that cannot, will not, ever fit into the official view, arrived on my doorstep, so to speak, just as I had gleaned enough background to decipher their context. Background you, too, will need, to experience the lightning rod which finally centered my stormy course:

The autopsy process was botched. That was predictable. Indeed, autopsies were nearly nil. Nor was poisoning verified, much less any catalog compiled of how each had died.

We didn't know *when* they got to the bodies (a "freakishly heavy" storm delayed coming in); or who got to them *first*, Guyanese or American; and exactly what did they do. ("*One by one now they plunder, and disarray the nest. . . .*"??) We do not even know if the suicides were complete before forces moved in. Apparently, the bodies were so decomposed by the time Temple members were identified, that hundreds could not be identified at all ("*I listen to the song of the unmarked graves...*"). Dick Gregory also claimed (to *The Black Panther* newspaper) there had been unusual activity at Dover Air Force Base, where the bodies were taken, *prior to* the tragedy.

The dismay on the part of American doctors receiving the bodies from Guyana was palpable. *Only seven bodies had been autopsied*, the leader and one close aide having apparently died of gunshot wounds; of the five others, no attempt had been made to even verify poisoning! Leslie Mootoo, the Guyanese coroner claimed "murder, not suicide," citing "needle marks," but the American team not only found no needle marks, but a total lack of examination of blood, urine, or body tissues prior to ...embalming. Dr. Rudiger Breitenecker, a civilian member of the team, lamented to *The New York Times* that "*All someone had to do [to verify cyanide poisoning] was drain a little urine or blood through a needle, and not even do an autopsy. If it was worth the expense of several million dollars to fly the bodies back, maybe it would have been worth a needle to establish what happened.*"

No forensics were ever done, nor bullets matched against guns; indeed, the Congressman was reportedly killed with "dum-dum" bullets (designed to shatter on impact and create maximum damage)– **which was not only clearly beyond our availability or expertise, but would render the bullets untraceable!**

Moreover, "eye witnesses" accusing Peoples Temple of murdering Congressman Ryan were far from credible, as a trip to Washington would later confirm. Mark Lane offered the press a preposterous quote from Jim Jones (who allegedly confided in *him* at the last – no, friends, I don't think so...), that people might go off shooting "because they love me and they may do something that would reflect badly on me"; which even were it true, would belie any notion that he ordered Ryan's assassination himself. I.e. *"reflect badly on me,"* would mean that this was *not his intent at all.*

Jackie Speier, Congressman Leo Ryan's aide, caught in the gunfire but recovered from her injury, insistently speculated that Richard Dwyer, the State Department escort who accompanied Ryan's party to Jonestown, "may have been C.I.A.," because when the shots rang out, everyone either ran, or fell face down to protect themselves, whereas Dwyer fell face up.

She speculated, perhaps rightly, that this inexplicable response, the opposite of a normal, protective reflex action, might be so that he would be recognized, hence not targeted for assassination.

Well, recognized by *who*? Why, the C.I.A., Ms. Speier averred. Was Dwyer the C.I.A. plant in the State Department, she wondered aloud? Joseph Holsinger, also a Ryan aide, tried to make a big deal of it. Only he got sent on a disinformation wild goose chase to prove that *Jim Jones* was C.I.A.! Nothing, of course, came from out of this mess. Don't people even notice who it is who winds up *dead???*

Though obviously, there is a serious problem here: If Dwyer was C.I.A., and really fell face up to be recognized by the assassins who were also C.I.A., and the assassins were supposed to be *us*, then... *we* would also have to be C.I.A.! And Holsinger, Spieier, or both, might, out of personal loyalties, pursue this – perhaps passionately, perhaps long-range. Indeed, the C.I.A. disinformation ploy found its way into the Ryan family suit against the Federal government! Patricia, a Ryan daughter, had linked up with the disinformation mill called the "Cult Awareness Network," the same ones to sponsor "Gary Scharff," so perhaps no kind of wild, false charge was surprising.

Next thing we knew, Holsinger, now safely ensconced as a "Jonestown scholar," got seamlessly diverted onto "the Philip Blakey lead." Blakey was the real C.I.A. culprit, he was told. He had "recruited mercenaries for the C.I.A. in Angola in 1975."

Pretty "coincidental" alleged assignment at that. As surfaced recently in an article entitled "Revisiting the Jonestown Tragedy" in "Freedom" magazine: "*In 1975, Ryan leaked word of the CIA's involvement in the Angolan civil war to CBS newsman Daniel Schorr, creating a wave of major embarrassment for the agency which reverberated for years.*" Naturally, news of a "C.I.A. mercenary recruiter for Angola in 1975 within Peoples Temple" would be an especially inflammatory allegation to concoct for the *Ryan* family. Thus did the prized disinformation become the centerpiece of the Ryan family suit.

Why did no one check out if this allegation was even *plausible*? Anyone knowing the history of this shy young fellow from *England* (now the American C.I.A. recruits British teenagers?) knew that he had simply met Debbie Layton, (later Debbie Layton Blakey, the defector) at a British boarding school. They later came to the States and got married. Philip's only tie-in to us was Debbie (though mysteriously, no one sought to question *her*), whose brother, Larry, in turn, was the one who went off shooting *alone* at the Port Kaituma airstrip.

What Philip Blakey was doing in 1975 was running supplies down the river – for us to build, for us to eat. There was still but a skeletal crew at Jonestown, and his services there were indispensable. This was a *ridiculous* name to float as "the C.I.A. culprit"!

But now it was making a modicum of sense: a) it was a false lead, so would go nowhere; b) the alleged C.I.A.-Angola-1975 connection would be so inflammatory to Ryan's family and aides, they would be unlikely to look elsewhere; c) it could be a complicated diversion, since Philip was a foreigner; d) it would tie up the energies of a potentially troublesome Holsinger, since if the attention wound up back on *Larry* (i.e. Philip to Debbie to Larry), there would be none to spare for the (real) assassins of Leo Ryan. Outsiders like Holsinger would lack the knowledge required to recognize that this was a disinformation sham, or why.

Whatever Holsinger's "source" was (the final face-slapping mockery being citation of the same "lead" in *"Worker's World,"* as if the C.I.A. would feed a true hot potato to the Socialist Worker's Party!), maybe there were drugs in *his* soup, or a big fat paycheck; or more likely, the opportunity to cover incriminating footprints into the Jonestown disaster. Holsinger, flush with "revelations" of C.I.A. *collusion with* Jim Jones, offered that "The CIA had a covert operation in Guyana, which included support for Peoples Temple... as a terrorist organization to intimidate Burnham's [Forbes Burnham, the Prime Minister] opponents." "There is little doubt" (reported the *Pittsburgh Courier* in 1980), "that Peoples Temple ... was serving Burnham... chiefly as a force to intimidate the opposition."

I remembered when Burnham was up for re-election, late '77 or '78. We in the States were told that the Burnham government was corrupt, and given a free choice, we preferred his opponent, Cheddi Jagan. But that our bread-and-butter, for better or worse, had to be whoever was in power; so we should write letters of glowing praise, wish them success in the election, and hope against hope that they would *lose*. Is this was it was to "intimidate the opposition"? Good God – we wanted Burnham *out!*

Ironic? How many more words could lose their meaning? People like Holsinger (though I would not doubt the sincerity of his grief) seemed to be swayed by any red flag that was waved in their faces. By the time I got to the charge that Jim Jones was "letting the CIA use Jonestown ... for mind control experiments, notably to create a group of Manchurian candidates – hit men who would self- destruct after murdering their victim," I thought that the world, seeing Jonestown "go insane," had meekly opted to follow suit. It was even offered as "verification" of Jim Jones' purported willingness to allow his followers to serve as hapless victims of C.I.A. mind-control, the fact that we had "excellent medical facilities"! God forbid the excellent medical facilities were used to keep not only our own people, but the entire surrounding area, in good health!

Meanwhile, Robert Fabian, the court-appointed receiver for Peoples Temple funds, who would have no reason to defend us, stated flatly that there was no evidence that anyone from Peoples Temple had shot the Congressman! Except no one cared because it didn't upset any litigant's apple cart. The massive lawsuits regarding "wrongful death" were pressed as a result of the poisonings, not the assassination. So it got tucked and buried away in the edges of the official story.

The psychiatric "experts," of course, merely hovered around like vampire bats, picking at the psychological carcasses of deceased and survivors alike. *I* knew that "The Truth Is Out There" (as the sci-fi series, "The X-Files" would say), but no one was offering it up. Piecing through the wreckage of news clippings was more a complex process of weeding through mis-directions, little confirming what was *so*.

There were other factors leading up the deaths, that while baffling to explain, no one thought to question. Like Jim's illness – a rare fungal infection of the lungs which his sons clarified years later on was called "progressive coccidioidomycosis." It seemed that out of a thousand-plus people, only he had contracted it. (*Oh?*) It was a killer, too, a slow, deadly one.

Perhaps they had hoped that Jim Jones (who was, unfortunately for them, legend, suprahuman, about functioning through illness, agony and pain) would have been long since dead from the deadly fungus. Ideally (meaning minimum bloodshed), the leader would simply die and then the followers could be forced back to the States. Jim, for his part, was fond of quoting Martin Luther King on the eve of his assassination: "*I* may not get to the Promised Land. But *my people* will get to the Promised Land."

As Americans, we may scarcely relate to the (then)-Soviet Union being "The Promised Land," but Jim would have been *glad* to die if only he could have lived long enough to get his people again overseas. He honestly thought that was the best, at that very late point in time, that could be done. No one would be sneaking into Russia to off us there!

If only Jonestown had survived a month longer, when a scouting party was slated to go to Russia, we might have been "home free." Even Teri Buford said in her parting note, "I'd like to see you get to Russia." Of course, Stoen knew we were on a tight timetable as well, pressuring the U.S. Embassy in Guyana to crisis point in October, 1978, by threatening to send mercenaries to Jonestown if Jim didn't give up John.

Carlton Goodlett, M.D., our long-time friend, had visited Jonestown, and told Jim that if he didn't go to hospital in Georgetown, he should expect to die. He had apparently lost a great deal of weight, was running high fevers, and was later said to have been living on a diet of amphetamines, painkillers and anti-depressants. A survivor told me that his voice would sometimes waver over the P.A., as though drunk, totally unlike anything in the States. Or he wouldn't appear for days at a stretch. But he would never go to hospital. His deadly fear (worse than pain, worse than even death) was that his absence would be an "Open, Sesame" for invasion, and all the lives placed in his care would be destroyed.

One can only speculate the relative doses of ego and fatherly protectiveness which inhabited this deteriorating mindset. But on that point, it would be hard to fault Jim Jones, since what he feared was, in all likelihood, the truth! I don't think he could have left the community without inviting invasion either. Nor do I think he would have survived a trip to hospital. If illness had not done him in, an assassin's bullet would have. This "major political force in the Caribbean within five years." To this day, I have no confidence that he was not deliberately poisoned with the deadly fungus in the first place. I cannot prove this. But even paranoia can trip over into mere common sense!

Of course, it was all an especial horror for the Jones children. Years later, Stephan claimed his father went into psychic fugues during his ongoing illness, and Jimmy (Jim and Marceline's adopted Black son) said that when he assisted his father to the bathroom those final weeks, the color of his urine was bright green, the color of green beans. I talked with an expert in botanicals and pharmaceuticals, who claimed that a) it is fungus (this infection was fungal) that is the source of hallucinogens; and that b) no pharmaceutical on the market would turn urine green, as that would make it unmarketable. That any *medication* that would turn urine bright green, would only be on some other "list" of pharmaceuticals, i.e. for some unknown, other, different purpose than to *heal*.

Meanwhile, a survivor avered that Larry Schacht, our young Temple doctor, had developed bizarre patterns of behaviour towards the end, like wildly swinging around a machete. Larry was a very stable sort once oriented to his medical studies, but when he first came to us, he was addicted to psychedelics, thus perhaps more vulnerable to pharmaceutical destabilization.

So why, out of all those people, was it the leader and the doctor who are having all these weird mood swings? I can't say "America wanted to know" (America believed what it was told), but *I* still do. Pretty strange odds.

There were stranger things still to come. The final tape.

XLIV. What Really Happened is Released on Tape, and No One Listens and No One Cares.

The tape was released in 1979, shortly after Mike died. It filled in some gaping blanks. It was horridly spliced, of course, with weird musical backdrops that sounded like bad ice-rink music slowed down, then jolted through an echo chamber. Loretta and Diane, our organist and pianist, respectively, would have been dismayed.

It was produced only briefly by some outfit called "Creative Arts Production." Who released this to them, to then release to the public, I never learned. I remember just picking up an address and sending away.

I recognized both Jim Jones' voice, and that the words were surely his. He didn't sound deranged. I mean, he sounded like himself – what I remember from California before he left. Visionary, pragmatist, worried father, protector, fanatic – they did get the man on tape, despite its being impossible to believe that was the *entire* tape, by far. It was about 45 minutes long, extracted from several hours of excruciating real life pain. Yet much is telltale of how the man was – what he would do, what he would say, even given the extremity of the circumstance.

It did contain, perhaps surprisingly (though it's hard to release something and still conceal everything), more than enough to dispel "the bizarre murder/suicide ritual" litany which had almost instantaneously become graven in stone. Black-and-white. As in newsprint.

Earlier that day, before the visitors departed, he had noted his adversity to killing – for those who knew him, a life-long non-violent bent. A reporter had approached him, and asked about a suicide threat the community had allegedly made. "No," he said tersely. *"What we said was that we would rather commit suicide than kill."* Jim was guarded with reporters, at best, but from his perspective, this shockingly blunt comment rang true.

Way back in Indianapolis, a man had stabbed him. He removed the knife, and... *counselled* him. His son Stephan carried the middle name, "Gandhi." This man (shy of the desperate straits of Guyana) had been *unerringly* non-violent. But also a fierce protector of his own, who would never hesitate to throw a chilling bluff to ward off harm. Stuff like threats of mercenary invasions, with no viable possibility of defense, could only have been excruciating.

Some, even who had loved the man, believed he was angry enough, ill enough, destabilized enough, desperate enough (all of these) to have ordered the assassination of the Congressman. I do *not*. He would never deliberately will Jonestown to be destroyed; nor do the facts support such a belief. Though notes from broadcasts to the residents of Jonestown just one month prior to the tragedy leave no doubt of his extremist bent against "enemies," especially "class enemies" and "fascist USA." A many-years' shift, certainly, from the gentle Christ-like soul who, with legendary patience, would tirelessly "turn the other cheek" until he finally exploded with "I've turned both cheeks, and both cheeks of my ass, to boot, and there are no more cheeks left to turn!"

The Jim Jones I knew in 1970 was masterly to persuade, weaving through minefields of obstacles with eerie composure and calm. But life was a gambit then. Now it was a trap; worse still, his *people* were trapped. He would not have life entrap them any further than the crush of circumstance had already done, i.e. into a scenario of slaughter with no possibility of defense.

The final tape, indeed, is explicit that he received news of the slayings with anguish and shock. News of the slayings will be Stage Three on this tape. (Hold on; just listen.)

Stage One: Ujara. There had already been an incident before Ryan departed, involving Don Sly (called "Ujara" in Jonestown and on this tape) who had apparently tried to stab the Congressman and was stopped. The tape reiterates the commitment to stand by Ujara – not because of his violent act, but because "my people have been too provoked." In the States, attempting to stab a visitor would have been an anathema, shy of fending off an armed attack. Nothing like this had ever happened. Our teachings had been *the opposite*.

Stage Two: Larry Layton. His grievance was *personal*. Jim Jones: "There's a man who's gone off with a gun... He blames his sister, and rightly so, for the death of his mother..." When Deborah Blakey defected following an incident where Jim Jones publicly refused her sex, their mother, Lisa, deteriorated with cancer and died.

Thus a backdrop as chilling for its enigmas as for its violence was already set. For if Stage One was us, and Stage Two was us, would it not be enigmatic if Stage Three were *not* us? Jim already knew what Ujara had done. He foresaw what Larry Layton would do, or some approximation of it: "[Larry's] gone with a gun and he intends to shoot the plane out of the sky. *I didn't plan it*, but I know..." (Larry's shooting got pre-empted by the separate group of eight assassins, at which point he, too, began to shoot, though he later claimed that he had originally intended to shoot the pilot.)

The report of the shooting of Patty Parks. a member who was leaving with Ryan, was greeted with *anguish*: "Patty Parks? *How many are dead? ... Oh, God Almighty. God help them!*" Nor is there any identification on the tape of who was responsible for that – Larry acting alone, or the team of eight assasins. (Frankly, even a non-brooding Larry Layton couldn't have coordinated a pep team, much less a hit team. He was dour!)

Stage Three, the assassination of the Congressman, was akin to how medical people describe invasion scenarios of foreign organisms: They sneak right in there; they act like they're "you"; they mimic some function of your body; by the time you're alerted to their presence, you're a goner. Stage One, Stage Two, Stage Three. One, Ujara; Two, Larry; Three: eight faceless, nameless men closing in on the Congressman.

Note (no small point!): The shootings, according to eyewitnesses, were not coming from the truck at all, but from **"a tractor-trailer that had pulled up alongside the truck .."**

It was not Jim Jones who sent the truck, much less the tractor-trailer. Even Lane's quote of what Jones allegedly said, "They've gone with the truck... [and] *may do something that will reflect badly on me*" is a tacit admission of such. He did think men on **the truck** had "gone with **a gun**" (i.e., **not** *eight fully-armed men*), but there is no mention whatsoever of the tractor-trailer, *the vehicle from which the shooters disembarked*; and surely *the tape-slicers would have kept it in* were it on the tape. It is obvious that Jim Jones hardly knew the complete scenario by far. More pointedly, he was *unaware of* the second vehicle, the tractor-trailer, although the shooting came from *that* vehicle, not from the truck.

Indeed, all Jim knew for certain was that people had been killed, and devastating news it was. Thus the desperation quotient heightened and finally burst. By the time it came to, "The Congressman is dead," *that* is when the resolve to commit suicide finally snapped in: *"Please get us some medication. It's simple. There's no convulsions with it. Please get it before it's too late. ...The GDF [the Guyanese Defense Force]'ll be here. I tell you, get moving, get moving. They'll torture some of our children to death. They'll torture our seniors. We cannot have this."* It was with the Ryan assassination, that there was, finally, no recourse. ("My *heart* –laid *waste!*– *would cry, bleed, drain 'neath* the dead weight of slain men's bones, *crushed. Hush,* no recourse waits, *my heart has known its last reprieve...*")

Like a hapless relative of an accident victim ("He's been hurt; he needs an operation; he's critical; he's dying..."), each bit of escalating damage seared through Jim Jones' tongue. It was all *reactive*. He hadn't *planned* any of these events ~ Ujara's assault, Larry's assault, the assault on the Congressman by parties unknown. Moreover, he greeted any option for escape with despair: "Russia won't take us now with all this *stigma*," he muttered when one follower, at the last, had the preposterous idea to just pick up and go to Russia, as had been planned before. (*"'Leave this place, itinerant one!,' a suppliant cried. ...'Mankind has more need of thee than these few, last...'"*)

The tape, moreover, is explicit that he not only **didn't** order the assassination, but **he didn't even know who had shot the Congressman.** He was shocked at the killings. More shocked, even, in thinking it was our people who fired the shots. Wired to stand by his own to the death, he shot out, "He shouldn't have come. I told him not to come," all the while lamenting "If only I could call this back..." An index, surely, of off-scale despair ~ not the Jim Jones I had ever known. It was despair beyond words that any one of his own would kill someone. There was no reality left. You spend your entire life tirelessly, ceaselessly, day and night, building a better world, and then your own people go on a killing spree?

I was also shocked that he did think it was our people who assassinated Ryan, as a progression of logic, because Larry was one of us, as was Ujara. And right or wrong, he would stand by his own. (*"They're my people, and they've been too provoked."*) Even though he had not ordered Ujara to attack the Congressman ~ he had him restrained. Even though he had not ordered Larry Layton to go off with a gun: "I would hope the plane *isn't* shot down..."

Moreover, it is clear that even if he thought it was our people, *he didn't know who had done it*: It is perhaps puzzling that Jim Jones, "the most paranoid one," did not suspect what he himself had explicitly warned of: **frame-up!** That our people hadn't done it at all, but were being framed. But when life finally has you by the throat, you cannot always stop to launch an investigation! Nor was Jim Jones ever one to do things half way. He would stand by Ujara by the death. He would stand by Larry to the death. He would stand by "whoever shot the Congressman"... *to the death*.

Not that anyone listened to the tape, or cared. It was probably the worst irony of all. That maybe the government had *nothing* to fear in releasing even the small portion of the tape that they did. For it could not

What Really Happened is Released on Tape/321

have been more clear that "the story" had been reported all wrong... **_and no one even noticed!!_** Jim Jones:

1) "I didn't order the shooting";
2) "I don't know who shot the Congressman.";
3) "I can't control these people [who did].";
4) "I waited against all evidence... I tried to prevent all this from happening.";
5) "I wish I could call it back.";
6) "I never wanted to kill anybody.";
7) "How many are dead? Oh, God Almighty, God help them..."

But that "there is no way to undo what has been done tonight." Spoken in utter resignation. Why isn't anyone subjecting this to voiceprint technology?, I thought. The contents, the voice, the sequence of events... Was it not *impossible* to construe that Jim Jones "ordered" the assassination? This voice wasn't on the offensive. It was the voice of doom. Off-scale despair. To have told a newsman earlier in the day, "*I wish I was never born*"??? He said that to a _newsman???_

Ah, but it was the one non-negotiable point of honor that he would stand by his own. If *they* went down, then *he* would go down. "Spoken like a true suicide," one might say, but also vintage Jim Jones. This brand of honor was his very soul:

> *"I didn't want to kill anybody. ...[But] I'm going to put my lot with you. If one of my people does something, it's me. I can say, I don't have to take the blame for this. But I don't live that way. ...Do you think I'm going to deliver [Ujara] up to them? Not on your life. No. No. ...I cannot live that way. I've lived for all and I'll die for all. ...I'm standing with those people. They're a part of me. I can reject them, ...but no, no, no, no, no, no. I never detach myself from any of your troubles. I've always taken your troubles right on my shoulders. And I'm not going to quit doing that now. ...I didn't [i.e. shoot or order the shooting]. But my people did. They're my people. And they've been provoked too much. ...I don't know who fired the shot. I don't know who killed the Congressman. As far as I'm concerned, I killed him.... We can't separate ourselves from our own people."*

An especially poignant wrench went through my heart. In the States standing by our people meant one thing, but Guyana had become a different paradigm of solidarity entirely. Here in the States, whether we liked the barriers of society, its institutions, its norms, its biases, prejudices, or not, we would never have been forced to that measure of "solidarity."

To be a *surrogate* for members who had committed violence? Violence was an anathema. Anyone who played with guns got the most severe lacing down. We would be an *advocate*, a corrective, constructive advocate for those who may have strayed, but their *surrogate*, never. We were model citizens – the socially responsible ones par excellence. The reputation so carefully, conscientiously built for twenty-five years. The same reputation that by now a handful of agents, plants, vindictive ex-lovers, and rotten kids on a power trip had used for toilet paper and, in our absence, pressed their demolition job as "the truth."

We were the ones who took in Marie Lawrence, who was on the lam when she first arrived, and encouraged her to turn herself in, then volunteered to the court to be her mentor, to turn her around, to be the friend every judge would welcome. But we would never say, well, if *she* goes back to jail, we all go to jail! That was a world of separations, of barriers, of judgments, of rules; and much as we didn't like the odds by which the justice system is often stacked against the poor, it was Peoples Temple who made the law work to their benefit. We may have railed against "the system," but it *protected* us, too.

We ran a tight ship Stateside, in so many ways the jewel of the seas. Why *Religion in American Life* could not compile a list of the 100 top clergymen in the United States without including Jim Jones' name. With Jim Jones to hold center, steer the course, rescue this one from this side, that one from the other side, bow to stern, man this ship well.

But now I could hear the rhythms of that same ship agitated in a storm. And now the only sea to sail was the one inundating our boat via the press, the conspirators, the lawsuits, the traitors. It had become a leaky ship with an ever more violent storm forcing it further out to sea. If *one* fell aboard, there was no way to rescue either his actions or his fate. The sharks would be ripping into his flesh, and once tasting that one, would demand ever more blood from the beleaguered crew. There were no laws to protect us now.

In even a racist culture, Peoples Temple perennially rebounded against, with, against, with, against, with the culture at large. Opposed the bias and unfairness, the inhumanity and neglect, yet earned respect through hard work, upholding the law, keeping people employed, off welfare, off drugs, out of crime. But now the model, law-abiding citizens could be no more. If one jumped ship, the sharks would instantly fish for more. There was no one to negotiate with but the wind, the rain, and the dark dank sea.

And not just one had fallen overboard now. Ujara, who tried to stab the Congressman, and Larry, who went to the airport with a gun, lay a roadway to culpability for *everyone*. Thus the anguished cry on the tape to them and to the assassins alike, who he mistakenly believed were our own: *"You don't know what you've done..."*

And all the longings that this not be so:

> "What's going to happen when they [the people at the airstrip] don't leave? I hope that they <u>could</u> leave. [But] what's going to happen when they don't leave? I wish I could tell you you were right [i.e. that they were leaving]. If there's any way to call back the immense amount of damage that's going to be done. *I waited against all evidence. I tried to keep this thing from happening."*

And all the anguish, approaching panic, of what would happen if the military arrived to find our people still alive:

> *"Now there is no choice. Either <u>we</u> do it or <u>they</u> do it ... When they're shooting out of the air, they'll shoot some of our innocent babies. ...They gotta shoot <u>me</u> to get through to some of these people ... You'll see people land out here. They'll torture our people. We cannot have this ... Hurry, hurry, my children, hurry. There are seniors out there I'm concerned about. I don't want to leave my seniors to this mess. Quickly, quickly, quickly..."*

And "Anyone who has a dissenting opinion, please speak."(!!) All the listening to objections, even at the last. All the calming and comforting. All the prods to be dignified, to be strong. That those "born out of due season" can now "lay down their burdens by the riverside." "No more pain..." Yes, and the defiance, too: *"Going to set an example forever. A thousand people who said we don't like the way the world is."*

Yet never in all that, never at any time, did he say "I" ordered, or "I" wanted this, or "I" planned this or cleared this or knew about this, or ... "I" ...<u>anything.</u>

I remembered when I first listened to that tape, hunched over protectively in a clutter of papers and books. So this is how the deed was done. No real surprises for one who knew Jim Jones. And for me, it was already done twice. It was what I had already lived through years earlier. Anything in "*Allegory*" I had not already matched up against the flood of news clippings and broadcasts, was on that tape. I mean, I was *there*.

I just began to wonder slowly, like a barely lifted lid of haze, where all the *newspeople* were. Had anyone before *ever* handled slayings with "It doesn't matter now, because everyone's dead"? I mean the slaying of the *Congressman*. Someone could be slain on a street corner and there would be an investigation, a hearing, a review, a trial, *something*. This was a *Congressman*. Of course much, much more. Over nine hundred people; ordinary people, yes, but over nine hundred. Plus... .a *Congressman*. Didn't any newsperson care who *did* order the assassination? Didn't anyone listen to that tape? Didn't they hear how no one "ordered" anything? To the contrary. The anguish at not being able to *intercede* before the descent of such a doom?

Oh, yes. We had the Congressional committee, who listened to Jim Cobb's (of all people) preposterous rendition of "good eyesight." Who took the names provided, dutifully lined them up against the Jonestown list, and summarily concluded that "all the principals are dead." Why even bother to listen to Jim Jones, the madman, when you can take the word of Jim Cobb, the superhero with miraculous gifts of sight? Indeed, **Cobb told the press that he was "on the opposite of the plane" when the shooting began," and then, of course, he fled!!**

I had to know the truth. But I still had one more hoop to traverse, one that was to be startlingly thrust right up into my face. The anniversary date was approaching now, November 18, 1979. There was a piece missing. Where was it?

Yes, it would show up not that much further along. At least, at that time, it had not yet been confiscated. Certainly much of the *tape* had been confiscated. That was obvious from the non-sequiturs, from the splicing, from the weird echo chamber sounds camouflaging the disjointed sequences.

Mike Prokes had told me that The State Department (namely one Charles English, an aide quoting Ambassador John Burke) was apprehensive that, ***"The contents of the final tape must never be released."*** Even now, it was obvious that this tape was far from complete, even butchered. Like at one point Jim shouts to "Get *Dwyer* out of there!" He is very specific that it is "Not *Ujara* ~ *Dwyer!*" And of course, that was Richard Dwyer, who was with Leo Ryan when he was shot. The tape then breaks completely (from Side A to Side B) and you immediately hear *"The Congressman has been murdered."* So that momentary break in tape had to be *at least an hour* ~ to the airport, the shootings, people going back and forth to see what happened and report back. And the suicide process itself had to be *many* hours.

    Ironically, it was unclear to me why even this much was released to the public. It was so *exculpatory* of the "murder" part of the "bizarre murder/suicide ritual" equation, that one wonders what advantage was gained by its release. Maybe someone felt it would need be proven that it was indeed an inside job ~ i.e. suicides by the residents, not slaughter of the Jonestown community by outsiders. Did they also feel that a confirmation of suicides was needed to clinch that Temple members were guilty of the *assassination?*

    After all, we did hear again and again in the news, "the bizarre murder/suicide ritual," like "You can't have one without the other." No one said, "Murder by parties unknown, and then suicide by the residents." Perhaps better to risk having the murderers (whom no one could ever locate to extract a confession) as a question mark, if only suicide could be established as a certainty.

    And the tape would surely "prove suicide"... well, at least that it *began* as suicide. Presumably with the body count thus "explained," with Jim Jones at the helm of death, who would bother questioning further, or even suspect a back-up plan of slaughter? Much less explore the previous mercenary attack, giving their fear of slaughter *legitimacy*. Certainly threats to send mercenaries to kidnap children were no secret ~ **they wound up in the Congressional report!**

    If only the press had reported *that*. Maybe my early, soon quelched then later revived, instinct, that it wasn't us, but mercenaries who assassinated Ryan, would have become the "Open, Sesame" to the truth. Instead, the door slammed shut as a safe with the click, click, click of the mounting body count. By day two or three, no one doubted what was "the truth." *Jim Jones caused all this*, we were told. Surely, Ryan's death must have been his doing, too.

Something else no one noticed. A slaughter may have been expected. But in what *spirit* did people take their own lives?:

"They are not taking our lives from us. We are laying down our lives. We are not taking *their* lives. We just want peace." And this from... a man with murder in his heart?

"They'll have to shoot *me* to get through to some of these people..." And "They can do what they want with me. I want *you* to [be able to] go..." That from... "a megomaniac"?

How could anyone think that "a murderer" and "a meglomaniac" was at the helm? How could anyone who *listened* think that? No one *did* listen, did they?

Jim Jones hadn't ordered the assassination, I was now very sure of that. But that would still not prove that our *people* didn't do it. The tape had partly revived my original gut hunch of a frame-up, but still could not clinch it. The missing piece, the missing piece, the missing piece. Then came anniversary time, November 18, 1979. The rush to splash the spectacle across the screen anew. I watched intently, me and all of America. What happened next was to impact my quest for the truth forever.

XLV. What Really Happened Shows Up on T.V., and No One Notices and No One Cares.

Chris Kice was in New York at the time of the first anniversary. Her husband, Tom, and cousin Bob, were both listed with the eight alleged assassins of Congressman Ryan. She, Al and I found a t.v. and plastered ourselves to the evening news.

I knew the assassination had been filmed by Bob Brown, an NBC cameraman on site, before being killed himself in the gunfire; but not having seen it broadcast the year earlier, I was shaken to see it now. This was a startling display of expertise.:

A second vehicle had barrelled on in (NOTE: A tractor-trailer, **_not_** the Temple truck). I saw eight men disembarking from that vehicle in a symmetrical formation, covering each other's flanks. They moved in rapidly, slightly crouched, in a tightly-coordinated unit. These was our "anarchists"? The loose cannons from Peoples Temple who were supposed to have killed the Congressman? Not *these* men! These were trained military personnel. You don't move like that, coordinate like that, without professional military training.

Al peered at the screen, his Army training from decades earlier suddenly sprung to life. "Oh," he said. **"I know what that is. It's called a squad diamond formation. You learn that in basic training."** (What? *Our* people had no "basic training.")

Chris peered at the screen, too. **"I don't see Tom. None of those men are Tom."**

Then something happened that was so brutal, so swift in its thrust, I really knew for sure it was not us. The men closed in again on the victims. But they closed in *solely on the Congressman*. Closed in and blasted him with a brutal blast of gunfire. Pursued no one else. Cared about no one else. They gave Ryan that last brutal blast of professional fire, and fled.

Wait a minute. They didn't pursue Jim Cobb? They closed in like trained, coordinated brutes to be surely that Ryan was dead – like it was Ryan alone who was their "assignment"? This made no sense. Our people hated the defectors and they had just barely met Ryan.

The names of the eight –Joe Wilson, Tom Kice, Bob Kice, Wesley Breidenbach, Eddie Crenshaw, Ron Talley, Albert Touchette, Ronnie James, and the alleged driver, Stanley Gieg– all wound up on the Jonestown list of the dead. But *Jim* didn't know who they were. We had people back and forth on the one road between Jonestown and the airstrip. How could he not know, not be told?

And now that I had seen the assassination with my own eyes, the list of "likely suspects" we had been given suddenly collapsed. Reserved, methodical Albert who manned the ham radio? Asthenic, lackluster Bob Kice? Eddie Crenshaw who had lost a hundred pounds in Jonestown and was unrecognizable? Others on the list were hotheads, but not even hotheads who were friends; nor do hotheads necessarily coordinate well with each other. This thing was choreographed. These men were trained killers, described by numerous eyewitnesses as **calm, silent, brutal, closing in "execution style."** How in the world did *our* people get fingered for this professional hit? (See DOCUMENTS, p. 39.)

Did America see this? Did anyone see what happened besides me? When CBS finally produced its travesty, "*Guyana Tragedy,*" the men were shown wildly spraying bullets from a truck, uncoordinated and not disembarking at all. Would that be what America would always remember, not the reality? Not this?

It took far longer for the real, living assassination to sink in than the minute it took to view it on the screen. This wasn't a story about it. It was the *reality*.

I scoured my brain for the roster of people who had returned to the States. Who had been in Jonestown and knew about the security team. It seemed far-fetched at best, that any of them had been trained to do this.

I found one Chuck Kirkendoll. He had been on the security team and volunteered what he knew. He had no idea what a squad diamond formation even was! There was no army training in Jonestown. No training in military formations at all. I probed him some more, about the six-day siege in September, 1977. What would prove it had really happened? Well, he said, bullets recovered from a wall of Jim's cottage were from a Winchester 3030, **a type of gun never found in Jonestown**. He thought it completely impossible that this attack had been staged.

I felt I should bring this information, especially about the professional military hit... well, to *whose* attention? Which parrot spouting "bizarre murder/suicide ritual, bizarre murder/suicide ritual" *could* one bring it to? I felt like I was already fending off some especially malignant rendition of Alfred Hitchcock's *"The Birds."*

I knew one thing. It was life-altering that it had come to *me*. It changed *everything*. No one had grasped the motives for solidarity. I mean, everyone saw what they perceived as people being coerced into sticking together, but no one saw them as *wanting* to stick together, except perhaps, amongst our own survivors. And our voice was the least, the most muted, the least able to persuade, to even speak.

But what if, after all, the people of Jonestown *had to* stick together? What if there was no place else to go, no alternatives to hatch, no authorities to whom to appeal -- indeed, no way out?

Can you envision a trial of eight young men, falsely accused, and a thousand people giving them alibis and all being called liars or forcibly hushed? Because this wasn't the city streets, where you can duck in or out of an alley or a restaurant. This was a remote community, each one in touch with another in touch with another throughout the days. Everyone's whereabouts were known by *someone*.

Most common here Stateside, is the one-person alibi. "Who saw you during that period of time?" Well, "He was with me." "She was with me." Or, "I saw so-and-so in such-and-such a place at such-and-such a time." But that wasn't a Jonestown alibi. There you would have, more likely, a ten-person alibi, or a fifty-person alibi. A big problem if you want to finger innocent people. And here it's not even just one innocent person -- it's *eight*. So how do you do it? How do you finger eight innocent people with scores giving alibis?

Imagine that the professional hit team assassinates the Congressman, then you just have the police walk in, everyone peaceably "goes down to the station," and you sort out the truth without bloodshed. This could never have happened. Indeed, it would have been *imperative* to kill yet more people in the wake of the hit. Then maybe you can avoid a trial at all, because (just as the Congressional report claimed), "All of the principals are dead."

But then you also have to silence those who could give the alleged killers alibis. And in a community that close-knit, you can't even do that. You'd have to kill *everyone*. At the very least, kill enough people to create enough havoc, shock, trauma, and death, to make your framing stick.

But then you still have a problem (like in the movies: "We have a problem. Take care of it." Everyone knows what that means). Perhaps even more than before. Whoever is left calls it a slaughter. Not by a deranged Jim Jones, but a military armed to the teeth against unarmed civilians, including infants and the elderly. And then the tables could get turned. Innocent civilians engender sympathy. So a *partial* slaughter, instead of wholesale slaughter, is a risky course. If you want to get away with this, you'd best slaughter *everyone*. Kill them all, then call it whatever you want.

Since the community had already threatened suicide, the only *sure* course would be kill everyone and call it "suicide." Here the residents offed themselves... or at least they *started* to. **We don't know how it ended.** Or what would have happened if the residents hadn't offed themselves, but instead waited for the military to arrive. Or if people were still alive when the military *did* arrive.

Now that's presumably the *Guyanese* military. Except there's a gap of *thirteen hours*, during a freak thunderstorm, that kept the Guyanese from coming in. Just like earlier freak storms that we suspected were engineered to try to destroy our crops. Was this even a freak of... nature? And do *you* know what happened during that time? Are you sure?

Not only what happened, but by *whom*. Well, who else could get in but the Guyanese military? Not during the freak thunderstorm, but perhaps already there? After all, there were those eight, the eight hired assassins. *They* were there. (And there *without* back-up forces?)

Recently, someone (one "Charles Huff") even surfaced, claiming to have been with the U.S. Special Services at the time (the "Green Berets"), who claimed that his unit had been called up and *"were on site in Jonestown within five hours."* Be this true, they *couldn't* have flown in within five hours with the freak thunderstorm. They had to have already been there. Moreover, even if they indeed were there, then why did not "mopping-up operations" begin immediately? Those bodies were left to rot three days in the tropical sun!

Another source, uncovered by *"Freedom"* magazine, one U.S. Air Force Colonel (retired) L. Fletcher Prouty, who claimed close ties with the C.I.A., claimed that the body bags were all ready to go before the mass deaths had even happened.

Not to mention Joe Mazor sleuthing about all of two months earlier, talking about being in the thick of invasion plans. And on whose authority did we know that he was in Jonestown to change sides and help us, rather than being there to case the joint, so to speak? Mark Lane? The same Mark Lane who later denied any of this had ever happened? Who ridiculed the very story about Mazor's role, that he had told the press just weeks prior to the tragedy, was *true*?

You see, readers. We didn't just have "a problem." We had tons of them. Close to a thousand, to be precise.

XLVI. Congress is Told What Really Happened, and No One Finds Out and No One Cares.

Of course, I seemed to repeatedly see problems where others accepted pat explanations, and comprehension where others were confused. Sometimes the *interpretation* of the tragedy seemed more daunting than the loss of life. People said they didn't understand how such a thing could happen, but kept re-enforcing frameworks ("spins," we now call them) which could never explain, never account for it.

Perhaps part of how I look back and wonder why I was so eager to brandish my new revelations in *Washington*. Washington ~ the place where truth so rarely takes precedence over politics! How and why I took my losing battle there seemed more a quirk of fate ~ who knew who knew who. But I almost wished I had never gone. It was one of the most dismaying experiences of all, and may have even provoked the eradication of key evidence.

Yet, "as luck would have it," Al knew an attorney in Washington who seemed well-placed. We visited him and I told my tale. He contacted a Congressman to arrange an interview with the investigating committee. It was set for January 3, 1980, barely past the first anniversary date.

Amy was in Washington at the time, so I had a place to stay. Meanwhile, I had also been in touch with James Reston, Jr., the son of the famed *New York Times* columnist, the younger of the two now turned author. I had read a newsclip about his filing for some materials under the Freedom of Information Act and being given a hard time. We corresponded, and he claimed sincerity as his motive for pursuing the deaths.

He seemed open-minded, or at least willing to listen to *me*. I wouldn't say we struck up a friendship, but I felt no particular reason for mistrust, and thought giving him accurate information couldn't hurt. (Of course, I thought giving Congress accurate information couldn't hurt either.) He was visiting his parents' home in Washington while I was there, so we could meet. This was one of several fiascoes in the making during that difficult period of time.

The attorney who helped mentor my "Congressional" interview (or so I had anticipated) gave me little advise but to take copious notes about what I had said. Excellent advise, it turned out, for some unexpectedly upsetting reasons. I knew this material well and was prepared, so my time in Washington, otherwise, was free. I arranged to visit with Reston.

It seemed cordial enough. On an instinct, I showed him "*Allegory,*" and he flipped. He thought it incredibly beautiful, and wanted to have it produced by a group in Washington called the Folger Theatre Group, telling me, "I consider your situation unprecedented." He sent me seven requests for the work I was eager to show, yet reluctant to share. This guy *seemed* to be on my side, but I just kept hearing "No."

Bad things happen in three's, they say, but sometimes, it seems, they happen in two's - the Washington committee and the coordination with Reston. I nearly choked upon sighs of relief over having coveted my artwork when the following year, Reston's book came out, entitled, "*Our Father Who Art In Hell*"! I couldn't bring myself to buy it. I read a synopsis in *Penthouse* magazine and was horrified.

My expectations of a fair Congressional reception turned out no better. I was surprised to find no Congressmen at all, but rather two aides, a deadpan Mutt & Jeff team named Berdes and Smeeton, one short and stout, one tall and thin, and both equally dubious that I had anything meaningful to contribute. Moreover, they seemed familiar with *me* before I arrived. "You're interested in music, aren't you?" Had *I* said anything? More of Buford's handiwork? I downplayed their comment, concealing my discomfiture with however Ms. Buford had elected to impugn my credibility.

As remarkable as what I had to tell them was that *no one* had told them anything helpful in uncovering the truth! The Banks bribery/blackmail scenario, for example. "This is new to us," said they. Not that they cared. I later discovered that the approach to Banks was *in fact detailed in their own report*. (See DOCUMENTS, p. 23.) It was quite a re-write of reality, but they did detail "an individual [privy to governmental investigations] approaching Dennis Banks" and "compromising an investigation." It seemed impossible to match the official report against the Banks affidavit and not conclude that David Conn was an employee of the federal government.

Everything else was like pulling teeth. My trying to pull the slightest response out of these stolid two. I focussed with especial emphasis upon the film of the assassination. I asked point blank who claimed to identify the assassins, for I hadn't seen it in the press. "Jim Cobb," they said. *"Jim Cobb? He didn't even know some of those people he 'identified.' And how could he identify eight men* [himself the ringleader

Congress is Told What Really Happened/333

of "The Eight" - *poetic injustice?*] ***coming towards him with guns, when he was running for his own life in the other direction!"*** "He said he had good eyesight," Smeeton volunteered weakly. (Eyes in the back of his head? Cobb himself admitted that he was ***"on the opposite side of the plane"*** when the shooting started! See DOCUMENTS, p. 38.)

I told them I had seen the assassination on t.v. at anniversary time. With an army veteran. That he had identified the squad diamond formation, which was part of standard Army training. That we didn't have that kind of military training. Plus I didn't recognize anyone. That it just wasn't us. Why didn't they blow the film up themselves and identify people that way if they could?

Their voices fell flat, like a clamp had muted their tongue. Why do *that*? These men were already identified. It was over. Why even bother? I was dismayed. How could they gloss over that? Not think it important? What could be more important?

I got into the interview whatever I felt belonged there. I wasn't intimidated and I was outwardly calm. But where were the Congressmen?

"Oh, they'll be sent transcripts. They'll be told." It was weird. Me and these two parrots rattling around in this big room. That and what looked like a court reporter. It wasn't exactly reassuring that Congress was listening.

I left out, back to Amy's, followed the attorney's advise, and made copious notes of everything I had said. It seemed like it mightn't matter because after all, it had been transcribed as we spoke. But I did it. Me. The diligent one.

A couple of weeks later, I was first excited, then horrified, to receive the "transcript" of the interview in the mail. Sentences were cut off mid-way, the syntax was jumbled, whole thoughts were omitted or left dangling. Misspelled words galore. No one had transcribed this. They had butchered it! The lowliest secretary would have been fired for this kind of a botch-up job. Unless, of course, it was "what the doctor ordered."

Along with the transcript was a terse note telling me to make any corrections within seven days and send it back. I freaked. Correct this disaster? I reconstructed my notes and re-typed the entirety of the 1-3/4 hour interview. Then I went one step further. If this is what they were calling called a transcript, how likely were they to *distribute* it as promised? I called and suddenly it was only available "on request." That's hardly the same as guaranteed distribution. Probably none of the committee members knew there was a transcript at all, even a butchered one. And what difference would it make? If they did distribute it, I would look like an idiot who could barely speak English. If they didn't, I was effectively silenced.

Al was helpful, if even more dire than I. He was sure that only a trained legal transcriber could do the corrections, at great expense. He volunteered to give me his magazine publication money. I opted to do the job myself. I then xeroxed copies of the transcript for all 34 members of the Congressional committee, and sent them out with cover letters about the botch-up.

I was furious. And shaken! I gave these people keys to cover this up! If they didn't review the film, they could (God forbid) confiscate it. I felt like a chicken who had gone to confide her distress in the fox den, and had emerged plucked and barely alive. Why had I gone to (of all people) *the government*? It was a low, bad, bruising blow.

It got worse still. I was hoping to shame Congress into caring who had really killed their colleague. I never got a single response. But was this a surprise? I never got any confirmation of my materials being received! Although I had sent each packet out certified mail, return receipt requested, nearly every receipt came back defective ~ unstamped, unsigned, no Washington postmark, no proof of receipt at all. I had made the simple mistake of mailing them from the local Post Office in New York. I should have donned a wig, some sunglasses, and taken the bus to Jersey. The phone was invaded, the streets were invaded, the mail was invaded. If I was a "cultist," who were *those* people supposed to be?

Meanwhile, other people seemed to have no problem getting their stories into print ~ yay, distributed across the bookstores of America. It was edifying, though. You learn something from all this. If when all is said and done, you still cannot bring yourself to believe how treacherous your fellow humans (be they such) can be, they up and put it into black-and-white. The parade of the cover-up books was under way.

XLVII. The Cover Stories Get Re-Wallpapered and Plastered All Over America.

Infuriating things happened on a recurring basis anyway. The first anniversary in 1979, *The New York Times Magazine* ran a piece featuring ex-members who concocted a whole talk show's worth of revelations about the infamous grape juice incident. Neva Sly said she heard Jim Jones talk about death, and she wasn't afraid. Of course she wasn't. *She wasn't there!* Grace Stoen said that (her lover) Walter had just come onto P.C. (he was *never* on P.C.) and just stood right up, brave as can be, and said, well, if I'm going to die, I want to know why. Brave as can be. Except he *wasn't there.*

Grace herself *was* there. But her rendition was that "I didn't believe him." To the contrary. She had said, tearfully, that it was all worth it, and that even if little John's life ended right then, she was glad he was raised in the church.

Deborah Blakey (more fully Deborah *Layton* Blakey) was there, too. But her version, that she was called aside by Jim, who suggested sending the entire Planning Commission up in a plane and then shooting down the pilot(!), *never happened.* No one was called aside. As for the "shoot down the pilot" rendition, that was lifted verbatim off her own brother Larry's confession that *he* intended to shoot down the pilot of the plane leaving the Port Kaituma airstrip. Of course, by her rendition, she is claiming that it was all Jim Jones' idea all along, i.e. killing the Congressman by shooting down the pilot. Nothing to do with her brother flipping out at all.

This crew could have given Abigail Williams in *"The Crucible"* a run for her money! It seemed like everyone had manufactured their own self-serving fantasy of how strong they were, how brave they were, how wise, or how they stood up, or spoke out. If it were not for the cruelty of dancing on the graves of by-and-large decent, wonderful people, who, by unspoken comparison, *"weren't* brave" or *"were* afraid" or *"didn't* speak out," this spate of fairy tales might have qualified as merely pathetic.

The Mertle/Mills, meanwhile (the far-right-wing pair who fabricated for the *Times* that they found Peoples Temple attractive because "Al [Mert] marched in Montgomery"), had already sold *their* version of the grape juice incident to a tabloid. Except for one catch: *they* weren't there either. They got front page billing, repeatedly, these lying people. Any old tale would do. Why all the theatrics? The ghoulish embellishments? Hadn't anyone told them "the show is over"?

This was a year past the tragedy, and here were all these people still revelling in their fifteen minutes of fame. And always the self-aggrandizing slant. Like "the 10 courageous ex-members who stepped forward" memorialized in *New West*. Well, one thing was true. They were indeed indispensable. Never could have organized a tragedy without them.

David Conn authored a book I never bought because I didn't think I could bear to have it in the house. The same of the Mertles' book, *"Six Years with God."* Reston's book synopsis in *Penthouse Magazine* so inflamed me, that I lambasted him, and dearly hoped that the words stuck. But buy his book? No way.

But the Lane & Buford travesty, *"The Strongest Poison,"* could not be evaded. From what I had seen to date, Buford could sell out her grandmother; and Lane, as the whole world can see now, seems to be a Jew selling out the whole Jewish race ~ his legal representation of notorious anti-semite, Willis Carto, of the far-right-wing "Liberty Lobby." Certainly, when someone first lifts a wing on the left, then lifts a wing on the right, you don't say, "Look, there's go an angel"!

I dreaded Lane's book, but had to confront it head on. Lane & Buford's damage might be expected to be more personal ~ me or my still-much-alive friends. They had already tried to discredit *me* with the reporter, then charmingly referred him to Joseph Mazor who, true to form, bugged his hotel room. What next? So I cursed the blood money of their royalties, took a deep breath, then purchased my single copy. A review of this book proved indeed instructive:

I approached it with distaste. Opponents, even upset, emotional opponents, are an easier swallow. You see where they stand. You see where they fall. You see where they're blinded. You can even see self-interest, the peskiest of intruders, shoving its way to center stage. You may hate them with a passion and they you. But at least everyone, however wrongheaded, *feels*. A psychologist could even discern how and why people lie, and their subscripts of avoidance, denial, control or gain.

But Lane was something else, and inherently a more wrenching human task. Here was a guy who had his book on the Kennedy assassination, *"Plausible Denial,"* printed by Noontide Press, the imprint of Willis Carto's Liberty Lobby, whose Institute for Historical Review "is dedicated to proving that the Holocaust never happened." (*East Bay Express*, 1/10/92). Lane, when interviewed said, "They have never said that the Holocaust didn't happen." Carto, when interviewed, said, "There were no Jews gassed in Auschwitz because there were no gas chambers." I suppose, not being a lawyer, I missed some fine point here.

You want to put out feeling to combat such mentalities, but it's a land of quicksand where feelings themselves can lay booby traps. Standards, values, norms, have dissolved. Any semblance of a moral center dissolves into an unpatternable sophistry that will twist and squirm to keep from being pinned down. You want to comprehend humanly, feelingly, the rationales, but they simply sink and slide and leave you chilled.

That said, my first impression of *"The Strongest Poison"* was, nevertheless, outrage at the temerity to engrave into black-and-white a minefield of half-truths, distortions and lies. Why was this being done? For royalties, for money? They could have done "grape juice revisionism" for that.

And why issue whitewashes about the shadowy Joseph Mazor? There was no trial at stake. Whatever perjuries may have been committed, they were already sealed in the records of grand juries and official investigations. Besides, Lane and Buford were with "the good guys." Wasn't that protection enough? Why auction off what no one has offered to buy?

Moreover, in all likelihood, they had been believed. Teri, assuming that her post-tragedy promise to "cooperate fully with the authorities" was made, at least in part, to evade the kind of liability her parting note to Jim Jones implied (i.e. *"Everything we are presently in trouble for, I organized and carried out"*) would have been better off opting for public silence. So there were motives more hidden at work.

Nevertheless, but only much later on, did I see that their book, however self-serving, could actually be useful. Where it *didn't* lie, keys were given to unlock the conspirators' secrets.

This made the book a sticky wicket. It would be nice to claim that it had been written on behalf of the "warm, gentle, decent people of Jonestown," as Lane did tuck into the pages somewhere, like a small child being tucked to sleep. But it seemed rather more likely to damn, not redeem, the community. After all, how successful is your scream of "government conspiracy" going to be when, at the same time, you claim the leader was a "psychopath" who "murdered" his own people? Everyone would praise the government for trying to stop him!

Indeed, the "saint versus murderer" case was alive and well. Although before her defection, Buford had warned of "another My Lai in South America," i.e., like the massacre of civilians in Vietnam by *invading*

338/SNAKE DANCE

military forces, they now claimed that the suicides were in fact "murder," - murder by *Jim Jones*, because Lane, fleeing through the jungle, claimed to have "heard 90 shots." "I counted them" he solemnly confirmed. Yet C.A. "Skip" Roberts, the Guyanese Commissioner of Police, later remarked that, **"If Mark Lane heard 90 shots, where are the other 87 bullets"?**

And from what cache of guns? Contrary to scurrilous reports, Jonestown was in no way, shape, or form "an armed camp." For all the lurid testimonies of the "Concerned Relatives," there *weren't* any "semi-automatic weapons" at Jonestown, much less "fifty armed guards." Authorities found a total of no more than forty small, non-military weapons in Jonestown, to defend over one thousand men, women, children, the elderly, infants, from outside attacks. These people were obviously, transparently, *defenseless*.

So the Lane book has no power to indict Peoples Temple for "mass murder" at all. There are several reasons why it was written, however, and it is the *motives* that enables one to weed out the true from the false, and to recognize that however mixed in with "tall tales", there are also truths about how Peoples Temple was destroyed. This was no job for amateurs. We had been "the toast of the town."' You needed masterminds for this demolition job. Trained personnel. People whose very job it was to destroy . . . . . for *political* reasons.

That said, the motives for writing "The Strongest Poison" can be capsulized as follows:

1) To protest the scapegoating of Teri Buford for culpability over whatever she claimed *Tim Stoen* had himself directed her to do within the tiny unit (*all of five people*, she herself claims) called the "Diversions Department."

2) To shift any suspicion of leadership of the alleged "hit squad" off of *her,* onto others, namely innocent, gentle Jean Brown.

3) To claim that the so-called "hit squad" was now out to get Buford and Lane, Lane claiming that the "proof" was packets of Kool-Aid ominously deposited on Lane's doorstep in Memphis!

4) To scapegoat gentle, decent, innocent Mike Prokes (conveniently deceased, naturally) as "an agent," while leaving "real" agents, like Conn and the Mertles/Mills virtually untouched.

5) "The usual": Make Mark Lane look like a hero.

6) The subversion of any effectiveness in claiming "a government conspiracy against Jonestown." If Jim Jones was indeed "a psychopath" (as

Lane and Buford claimed) who "murdered" his own people, who cared if anyone was "conspiring" to stop him?

7) To minimize the most ghastly, deliberate escalation of paranoia: the arrival of Joseph Mazor in Jonestown; and to downplay into nothingness Lane's leading role in getting him there.

That said, the public could barely even follow this book without a sophisticated lexicon of the conspiracy. No one had even *heard of* David Conn, for example. Or realized that no one in their right mind would go calling Jean Brown (who was so shattered, she urged us to turn over every dime to the State), "leader of the [non-existent] Temple hit squad." Understand, the "Concerned Relatives" crew were jolted to see *Teri* come out against Peoples Temple after the tragedy. They thought *she* was "the leader of the hit squad"!

But we get ahead of ourselves a bit. This book had a cast of characters, characters anyone who had followed from the inside knew well: Elmer and Deanna Mertle a/k/a Jeannie and Al Mills. David Conn. Joseph Mazor. Timothy Stoen. Grace and John Victor Stoen, the cause celebre that brought Congressman Ryan to Jonestown.

Then there was the most innocent one of the lot, whose greatest nemesis was his own conscience: Mike Prokes a/k/a Scapegoat No. 1, and conveniently deceased. He was "smeared" (pun intentional) paper-thin into a four-chapter "role" in bringing about the deaths, pompously heralded in by "The Unquiet Death of Michael James Prokes." Like Holmes and Watson championing the spoils, they ghoulishly vowed to file Freedom of Information Act requests on Prokes, and <u>no one else</u>. No Stoen. No Mertles. No Conn. No Mazor. Just Prokes.

David Conn, although wholly an appendage of the Mertles, Lane & Buford detoured to Mike. Although Buford herself admits to hearing David and Donna Conn claim **"high priority Treasury Department numbers"** in the spying mission under the Conns' house, and it was Conn who had orchestrated the press smears *even though he didn't even know us*, all that Lane & Buford claimed was that *Mike* had mysteriously appeared at the Conn's while she was taping meetings under their house, where the original *New West* smear was planned.

Perhaps Teri thought that since she was the only one on the Conn stake-out still alive, no one could refute what she claimed to hear, namely "Mike Prokes in David Conn's house." Except that the claim was *inane*. Were it true, Jim Jones would never have left Mike, our P.R. director, in the States, to *oppose* the press attacks (the ones Teri implicated him in helping *plan*), as he did following his own departure for Guyana!

So I presumed that "the Prokes lead" was simply used to divert attention away from the real conspirators. If you try and track down David Conn through Mike Prokes, you get nowhere. (Much as if you tracked the disinformation "lead" of Philip Blakey, you got nowhere ~ the Holsinger scenario.) You would have to go through the Mertles. But they are barely accorded a few sentences in the book, even though it was they and Conn who orchestrated the smear campaign and ensuing investigations. The Mertles and Conn were "at least half" of the conspiracy against Peoples Temple.

By contrast, Temple member Jean Brown, who inherited the crushing responsibilities of leadership Stateside after Teri left, was not part of any conspiracy at all, yet Lane and Buford very nearly turn her into La Femme Nikita: "leader of the (mythical) hit squad."

Why implicate Jean? She emerged as Scapegoat No. 2 for a variety of reasons that only the paddlers of this leaky canoe could comprehend: 1) she had the transcript of a damning interview between Lane and Mazor; 2) she knew how Lane brought Joseph Mazor to Jonestown; 3) she was the recipient of Teri's parting note to Jim Jones; 4) they claim she had the Peoples Temple "archive" in her possession, with perhaps incriminating documents. There were other potential threats as well:

Jean had apparently delivered thousands of dollars to Lane in exchange for his producing an advance copy of an exposé of Jonestown planned for *The National Enquirer*. Lane had himself offered Mazor to *The Enquirer* as a "source"; then, claiming a negative result, apparently asked the Temple for a huge sum of money to have the article "quashed"! (See DOCUMENTS, p. 24, "Mark Lane Parades a Rat, Then Charges Top Dollar for Rat Poison.")

Meanwhile, he kindly offered to obtain the proposed article for $7,500, down from $10,000 (big "favor"!), although he later *admitted he got the article for free!* Moreover, he had solicited $20,000 as a "retainer" to represent the church, although he was reportedly not even licensed to practice law in the State of California. Definitely best to pre-emptively discredit Jean! Then they could discredit any monies, documents, or conversations that may have gone through her.

Thus was the cruel hoax perpetuated. Lane & Buford, hot on the trail of "the hit squad," make a huge stinkbomb of *The New York Times* printing excerpts of the final tape from Jonestown. Their stated reason is that innocent, beleaguered Jean Brown used this information (*which was not even available at the time - it was months before that tape was released at all*) to try and persuade Temple members to "follow their leader's last homicidal instructions."

They never spell out the personnel of the mythical hit squad. Was Jean going to go off bullets ablaze on her own? What of Tom in the radio room? Tim at the printing press? Jim with passport processing? Or what about Laurie with letters? What gun range did *she* practice on? The assertion in *"The Strongest Poison,"* that "only Brill [Steven Brill, then of *Esquire*, who wrote an article panning Lane] and Jean Brown disclaimed the hit squad," belonged on a flap-jack grill, not in a book. No one *claimed* a hit squad but *Buford*. No one seemed to know anything about it but *her*.

As for *us*, we were slandered to pieces and in inconsolable grief -- powerless. But how could *Teri* be expected to know that? Teri, not unlike the grape juice wannabe's, *wasn't there*. She never set foot in the church after she left, so this was like someone in Australia testifying as a eye witness for a crime committed in St. Louis. Anyone who *was* there, knows that the truth was the *opposite*. Indeed, not a single person left even expressed *anger*, so devastated were we in those last fragile days of tenuous unity.

What could possibly have induced even this "poison-ous" pair to fabricate such ruthless libel out of whole cloth? Was there strategy behind the a-morality? Even vampires do not choose their victims at random.

In point of fact, Jean wasn't even Teri's first choice to head the imaginary "hit squad." It was Sandy, a surviving member of Stoen's notorious "Diversions Department." But even the eeny-meeny-miny-mo choice of hit squad leader had apparently shifted by the time *"The Strongest Poison"* was written. Teri perhaps disliked Sandy, but had to consider that she wasn't positioned to *harm* her like Jean might. With the so-called "tainted documents." Like her parting letter to Jim Jones, perhaps?

It had been slipped under Jean Brown's door on the eve of Teri's getaway. There were numerous reasons why she did not want it to become public property. At the least, her saying she had "been in love with" Jim Jones, and "resentful of others who had [your] children when I gave up mine [i.e. abortions]" would not advance her case; even less so, her admission that *"Everything the church is presently in trouble for, I organized and executed."* Perhaps there seemed no way to neutralize the threat of such "tainted documents" than to pre-emptively slander the person Teri had handed them to.

Ironically, this chilling move was probably as stupid as it was cold-blooded, since Jean, anxious to extricate herself and move on, had handed over all documents, "tainted" or not, to Charles Garry. It is there where I, by sheer accident, discovered one of history's more deplorable "Dear Johns."

The letter, understand, was far more than embarrassing. It was a masterpiece of twists and ploys -- probably the most unnerving document ever written to a terminally ill man. How she was about to make a great, noble sacrifice -- pretend to defect to the other side in a desperate last-ditch attempt to foil our enemies:

> "I would like to see the stage set so you all could go to Russia... So go ahead and call me a provocateur... Only Carolyn or I can do it... no one else would be believable... but Carolyn is now a mother and it would be cruel if Kimo thought his mother was always an agent provocateur, whereas I gave up my several children... even though I was in love with you."

And so poor Teri will bury her grief over the lost children and throw herself on the sword, for "When someone is dying, what choices are there?"

> "I may [even] have to speak out against [you]... I don't know if I am able to pull that off without going mad ... If I really blow it, I will [do] the final solution [and] you will just have a suicide [i.e. herself]... I am enclosing several declarations that I wrote that will have me thrown in jail and Tim Stoen too any time you want to show them to the authorities, so you have complete control...
> ...I signed the last bit of finances out of my name... Everything the church is presently in trouble for I organized -- did and carried out... You can put on the blame on me. That will take the church neatly off the hook. I would not sue."

What was this? The paragon of selfless sacrifice... or the cruelest cut of all? There are a thousand heartstrings tugged, but not a shred of logic. If a few mere documents would have thrown Tim Stoen in jail, why hadn't we already done it? If she was out of the finances entirely now, as she claimed, how could she have handed over the numbers of the Swiss bank accounts after the tragedy?

And what of the professed martyr shouldering the blame and "taking the church neatly off the hook"? Was this to be like, o.k., we'll let Jim Jones and his thousand followers go their merry way, either to wreak havoc by *setting up shop in the Soviet Union*, or becoming *"a major political force in the Caribbean within five years,"* as Mazor announced on t.v. following the tragedy? But hey, that's all right, because here Teri Buford has martyred herself to take the blame, and so now, we've got *her*, so what do we need with *him*???

And in the middle of this plan to set up a rat's nest in the public square, Jim Jones should worry about whether or not Teri would... sue? We were already being sued royally by people's relatives. She knew the other side didn't give two hoots for the law anyway. The name of the game was to do in Peoples Temple, not follow the law. And if she *really* wanted to "neatly take us off the hook," that would *ruin* her credibility with the other side. Who would believe her then? She would have to turn the blame around again.

Meanwhile, for all her purported anguish over, "I don't know how much longer you are going to live... Can I live with myself if I don't do everything possible knowing the condition of your health..." So she helps the dying leader by bolting from Lane's side when he is planning a sweeping lawsuit, presumably our best hope??? She bolts just before Ryan is scheduled to come to Jonestown to help Tim Stoen "regain his son"? She ducks out *then?* Three weeks before the big showdown, to go play double-agent footsie with the Mertles and Stoen? Telling Jim Jones to "don't be alarmed if I act like I'm on the other side?" That she has to do this because... she's the only one who can offer *really* damning information on the church?

And not to chase after her because it might endanger *her* life? What of how she could endanger *us*? After all, she had the numbers of the Swiss bank accounts, and indeed, gave them right over. Even if the church had survived the Ryan visit, how to make a transition overseas, or anywhere at all? A thousand people left stranded now? With no funds? Stranded with ongoing threats of mercenaries?

This is what was left for Jim Jones when Teri left barely three weeks before the end. Probably the old saying, "Just because you're paranoid, doesn't mean they're not out to get you" was *written* for times like these. When people say "paranoid," what they often mean is *delusional.* Here, **would it not be virtually irresponsible not to be "paranoid"?** Like "What kind of a leader *are* you if you are not worried sick that you may *all* wind up dead?" Not just the terminally ill leader, but *everyone!* How could any leader in his right mind <u>not</u> be "paranoid"?

Paranoid plus. What if it was all moving one step *past* the unthinkable? What if, for all her frenetic proposals and justifications, hand-wringing and side-changing, Ms. Teri Buford was, in fact, planning to do....<u>no such thing</u>??? Simply go into hiding without a trace? Go into hiding clandestinely with your new attorney. The one you think is going to crack the case. Wait in the wings to be the attack dog on cue "for real." With the guy who was posing as your new best friend.

Why even bother poisoning Jim Jones with a rare exotic fungus, when you can do *this*?

Though remember one thing: whatever histrionics were offered as bait, one thing Teri could not manipulate or slip up on was the *facts* in her parting note to Jim Jones. **If she misstated what he knew to be facts, she would not be believed and could consider herself fodder for happy hunting ground, the last thing she wanted to incur.**

So the facts of this letter should be credited as *true*:

"I have taken the most radical positions of anyone in the group, which some say is the first indicator of an agent-provocateur... Everything the church is presently in trouble for, I organized – did and carried out... ...I heard them talking under the [Conns'] house... ...I heard Dennis Banks first-hand... ...These things others may view as contrived I know as fact because I experienced them first hand... Everyone else [except Carolyn] has less information [about Peoples Temple] than me... ...I signed the last bit of finances out of my name [i.e. they *had been* in her name.]."

So much for having been a mere "glorified relay machine," as she told the press. Of course, next to this Sarah Bernhardt routine, anything else might pale, but for what it's worth, a third candidate for "tainted documents" was her September 4, 1978 letter to the Los Angeles District Attorney, wherein she states "*I was there when the assassin bullets grazed the back of Jim Jones' head*" (the six-day seige of September, 1977); that "*I have evidence of (Stoen) being an agent provocateur*"; and that "*the extent of the conspiracy is mind-boggling.*"

She then volunteers to take "*lie detector tests, voice prints, truth serum, whatever...*" No small offer. Teri was trained to *administer* lie detector tests. The Cleve Backster method. She knew *exactly* what she was volunteering to do.

I already had that letter in my own files, unlike her parting note to Jim, which I was surprised to find in Charles Garry's office. Moreover, Garry insisted that I "xerox, not take," because "Teri had [already] ripped off so much." How her letter to Jim Jones survived was remarkable. Perhaps the "tainted documents" in question were simply so damning when held up against the cover stories that, in abject fascination, someone had xeroxed them to death.

Speaking of death, *unbelievably* Lane went to the Memphis police claiming that "someone" had put Kool-Aid packets on his doorstep, which he claimed was "a death threat by the hit squad"! Double-unbelievably, Lane admitted that his own credibility with the police was so impaired, that they ridiculed his claim, saying he planted the Kool-Aid himself!! That a supermarket owner down the street had volunteered that Lane had purchased the packets a day or two before.

It almost made me discount that Lane himself might be an agent, in that no one could be trained this poorly! Though I would never underestimate this effort's inherent viciousness. These two could take etiquette lessons from tigers in the zoo.

Or perhaps from Joseph Mazor - a player so critical in understanding not only the mindset, but the *reality* of what the residents of Jonestown were up against. While some saw fit to play cloak-and-dagger games for self-aggrandizement, others had obviously been about the real business of destroying innocent human lives:

What *of* Joseph Mazor, "man of a million hats" - Interpol agent, convicted felon, P.R. front man, private investigator, leader of the six-day seige, then, perhaps most insidious, both our attorneys' new "best friend"? He gets far more attention than the Mertle/Conn team, but amazement of amazements, it is all *positive!* Why is Lane so solicitous of the creepiest card in the deck? Back to "tainted documents":

A transcript was prepared of a taped meeting between Mark Lane, Donald Freed, and Joseph Mazor on September 5, 1978 in San Francisco. This "transcript" was sort of like "the evil twin" of the mysterious "manuscript" in James Redfield's "The Celestine Prophecy" - the latter glistening into Light, the former strictly a scourge to be buried. Lane and

346/SNAKE DANCE

Buford neither produce the dreaded document, quote it directly, nor confirm that any copies may have survived, yet they refer to it continually in the negative tense - it didn't say this, it didn't imply that.

Lane actually goes to lengths in "*The Strongest Poison*" to *deny many questions no one even posed*, one of them regarding possible "off the record" contacts with Joseph Mazor. "There were none," he said. Though this is obviously impossible. The transcript *begins* with, *"Freed: The principle investors in this ... [need] ... insurance policy..." "Mazor: I carry it, yeah..." "Lane: For films?" "Freed: ..a very strong ... dramatic script... gunfire in the jungles of Jonestown..."* (See DOCUMENTS, p. 25.)

You don't start a transcript talking about an action movie of Mazor's raid on Jonestown without having discussed the raid itself *prior* to that ongoing discussion! That's like starting the tape rolling on *"La Boheme"* with Mimi gasping her last breath!

But the real thorn, even here, was Tim Stoen - specifically, what Mazor said of him, who relayed that information to Jim Jones, who was responsible for bringing Mazor, ostensibly "an enemy," right into Jonestown just weeks prior to the tragedy... and *why*. Or did you imagine that Jim Jones invited the likes of Joseph Mazor to Jonestown for a picnic? Not likely.

There was, in fact, *considerable* discussion of whether Stoen was C.I.A. *This was the "trump card" for getting Mazor into Jonestown* - the claim that Stoen was C.I.A., as extracted by none other than Mark Lane. Indeed, an overwrought Jim Jones addressing the community October 16, 1978, credits news of Stoen being C.I.A. "breaking through someone Lane and Freed knew."

Lane makes a huge point of denying that the claim that Stoen was C.I.A. had been transmitted to Jim Jones through *him*. Rather, defying all logic, the source was said to have been Jean Brown, Scapegoat No. 2, who was *not present at all* during the taping of the transcript, much less the author of: *"Freed: I want to type up the idea of Joe going to Jonestown."* (See DOCUMENTS, p. 25.)

Indeed, as if to make the point entirely moot, **Lane himself had told the press in March of 1979, that the claims about the C.I.A. [i.e. Stoen]** *"came from Joe Mazor"!!* (See DOCUMENTS, p. 24.)

Naturally, the transcript which was the subject of so many denials, is *never even produced!!* Nor is the October 3 press conference even mentioned, wherein Lane implicated Mazor in the mercenary attack, and

Stoen as the international financial mastermind who "laundered money through neutral countries."

Indeed, they are amazed, so they claim, that Jim Jones believed any of Mazor's claims at all, claims that he, Lane, had personally extracted. Much less that Jim believed that "fat, out-of-condition" Mazor could have possibly led the infamous raid of September, 1977.

Lane protests he had never even met Mazor before Jim Jones materialized this guy before their eyes! They hadn't the slightest idea why Mazor had been invited to Jonestown. At Lane and Freed's personal request? Perish the thought!

Much less why he, Lane, had been invited: "While I had been invited to discuss the assassination of Dr. King... *I now believe that I had been asked to Jonestown for other reasons as well.*" "Now" meaning a year and a half after the tragedy? Like the September 5 interview, which *preceded* his visit, never happened? Like his bringing Mazor to Jonestown never happened? Like the taping of Mazor's confession, with Lane winding up with the tape, never happened? Like Lane's October 3 revelations to the press never happened?

Yet before we slip too far off this slippery slope, an equally interesting question was surfacing as Lane having wallpapered the past. When the past (i.e. Lane befriending Mazor) was still the present, what was intended for the then-*future* – which turned out to be the Jonestown Tragedy? Lane was no passive bystander – he brought us Mazor. Had this *ever* been done with honest intent, to "save Jonestown," as Lane passionately proclaimed his exposé and lawsuit would do? Or was it a mere lethal dose of "*The Strongest Poison*"?

Why *did* Lane bring us Mazor, anyway? To see where tractor-trailers and airstrips are located? To "case the joint," so to speak? Nothing could dwarf the danger that Mazor and his various cohorts posed to the peaceful utopia the residents of Jonestown were so proud to build.

But we can now begin to capsulize why all the murky, devious ploys involving Mazor were so critical – their timing, their context, their repercussions. We may even be able to enter the most hidden sanctum of them all: ***"What really happened at Jonestown?"***

XLVIII. Did The C.I.A. Have A Contract Out On Jonestown?

We have to go back to the mercenary raid on Jonestown in September, 1977. Even Teri Buford was there, claiming in her letter to the Los Angeles District Attorney, that *"I was there when a bullet grazed the back of Jim Jones' head,"* then offering to take a lie detector test about it. She was indeed there, and she did indeed know that it happened – **that Jim Jones had nearly been assassinated and the community terrorized.**

Up until then, we had been in the early stages of a smear campaign. Bad, but perhaps still redeemable. Jim had still wanted to return to San Francisco, and speak on his own behalf in person.

But now, he (and by extension, us) was not even safe in a remote jungle! Moreover, the attack having come on the heels of the Stoens' attorney travelling to Jonestown to serve papers, sounded an early death knell: If you do not release the child (Jim's own child, but by extension, any child), violence will ensue. Suddenly *no one* was safe.

This is critical for the public to understand. We hear so much of seige *mentality*, but that is still *mental*. What happened at Jonestown was more like an actual *state* of seige. The dangers were physical. They were real. **An attack had already happened.**

What ensued, so called "white nights," were, by descriptions of survivors, rarely "suicide rehearsals" (I believe that was tried once and the children got frightened, so it was not pursued), but more in the nature of civil defense drills, like people lining up to defend the community against attack, or to protect its most vulnerable members.

And who would not do such a thing? Would it not be irresponsible not to do *something*? Undoubtedly, heated, even at times hysterical-sounding rhetoric, may have ensued, and people can resent such pressure. But the *reality* was that the community had been *attacked*, and if there were not *some* preparations made (mental and emotional, if not concrete physical contingency plans), then someone in leadership was not doing their job. Even the Israelis provided gas masks for their citizens to protect against the Scud missiles of Saddam Hussein.

It was undoubtedly difficult for people inside the community (and virtually impossible for people *outside* the community) to make requisite adjustments, even mentally. This was not a military camp. This was a community that was a paradise for *children*.

The person to ask was not Jim Jones, but the men aiming guns at a peaceful community, why such a threat was perpetrated in the first place. What abysmal cruelty motivates such actions? Because you don't like people's *political* beliefs? Because you don't like *racial integration*? All anyone ever heard about was "the terrible cult leader." What about "the terrible mercenaries"?

Yet the outside world appeared impervious. The conspirators controlled the press, and obviously would not expose their own maneuvers, however in violation they were, or especially *because* they were in violation of the very sanctity of human life. They would not even concede that the mercenary attack had happened. In fact, in all the avalanche of publicity dominating the post-tragedy press, *it was never even mentioned.*

Jonestown was also a special case, in that it was remote and isolated, both geographically and vis-a-vis communications with the outside world. There were not even phones, only the ham radio. Moreover, the surrounding jungle was menacing. Escape routes to Venezuela were investigated and deemed too dangerous. Were there the necessity of evacuation, the older folk (and perhaps many others) would not make it. Indeed, there would not even be any *warning* for an evacuation. Once they attack, they attack. The whole idea is *surprise*. Once it already happens, you are trapped.

The attack in September, 1977 was apparently perpetrated by just a few men. What if the next time, there were many more? What do you do? Call 911? Not in the remote Guyanese jungle you don't!

This is part of why the whole dilemma was excruciating. A normal response to attack (physical attack, even verbal or emotional attack) is "fight or flight." But here, *both* options were rendered null and void. "Fight"? The residents of Jonestown were pathetically underarmed, nor was there the expertise, personnel, or capacity for military training. Moreover, there was no way to "call in help." *Anything* could be done clandestinely, and the world might never learn the truth. So much for the "fight" part of the equation.

As for "flight," to where? The jungle full of snakes and insects, and not even a clear road through?

So what if there were ever a full-scale military attack? Because, remember, there <u>already had been</u> a military attack. "Small- scale," yes, but life-threatening, and extremely frightening. What if they came back?

The people of Jonestown did not even know for sure who "they" were. Or what they might face the next time around. But they would have clear reason to suspect a direct connection with Stoen. Because it was the attorney handling the custody suit for the Stoens who had been there just before the shooting started!

And then, finally, the Congressman, who writes Peoples Temple just weeks in advance of his visit, "<u>Timothy Stoen does have my support in regaining his son</u>." Well, "regaining Timothy Stoen's (alleged) son" meant *gunfire before!* And now the weight of the whole Federal government has been brought into the deadly deception! And Tim Stoen himself goes and threatens to the American Embassy in Georgetown on October 3, 1978, that if the courts will not award him John, he will send in mercenaries!

And no one even seems to notice. If they care at all, it is to *support Stoen*. The same one who (acccording to Tim Carter, who infiltrated Stoen's group in search of Teri Buford towards the last) **"vowed to destroy Jonestown"** and was **"counting on Jim [Jones] to overreact."** ("Overreact" to the mere visit of the Congressman? Or to.... his <u>assassination</u>?)

Then the Congressman comes. Then he gets assassinated by "parties unknown," and *whoever* did it, it will surely be blamed on Jim Jones and Jonestown. The world doesn't care anyway. What do *they* know? Torrents of bad press about some hellhole. "A concentration camp," says Mr. Stoen. Poor little kids. John. "His son," whom every single conspirator knew was not his. Let him go. Let them *all* go.

Now I have a question. For anyone. How safe would *you* feel, and what might you be likely to do?

But now, in addition, let's factor in Mazor:

He shows up, ostensibly to "switch sides" just before the Congressman's trip. He "claims credit for" the mercenary attack. We already have him pinned as an Interpol agent. He claims he knows that Stoen is C.I.A. He says that the mercenaries' orders had been to **"first kidnap the children and then kill all the adults,"** but that since they found the community a peaceful one, they left it at sniping for a few days, then departing. And Jim Jones *believes* it. He believes that their intent had been, and may yet again be, mass extermination.

Was not someone very skillful, diabolical, indeed evil, if they *falsely* conveyed that the mercenaries had, and may still yet have, a plan for mass extermination?

Even if this were *not* true and you did not know that, would you still not be scared to..... *death?*

Did the C.I.A. Have a Contract/351

And conversely, if it *were* true, what contingency plans would *you* devise? *No* contingency plans? Just sit there with the threat of slaughter? And not just slaughter of you personally, but of helpless children?

Note that Mazor claimed that this had been the plan even *without* a Congressman being assassinated! In September, 1977, people were just going about their daily business.

It was, in its own deadly way, plausible. We were already under attack by presumed agents from the F.B.I. (the Mertles) and C.I.A. (Stoen). This was bouncing off J. Edgar Hoover's 60's and the C.I.A's Cold War. We were interracial. We were socialist. Our leader had a powerful, influential voice, and was gaining ground in the *mainstream*. He wanted to transform the face of the inner cities. He wanted to equalize America's wealth. He preached about it passionately, continually, without cease. He had the will, the motivation, the faith, to *do* it, had he been given the opportunity. We had already established the most incredible role model for what disempowered people could achieve. Everyone who came to Jonestown raved about its beauty and accomplishments.

Yet we had been smeared, harassed, and every kind of foul dirty trick pulled, then blamed on Peoples Temple. After the mercenary attack, we knew we were not physically safe. Moreover, we were actively planning to re-relocate to the dreaded then-Soviet Union during the Cold War.

The Soviet Union may have, in fact, been the only way out. It was being negotiated. Just one more month and there was a scouting party scheduled to go at the invitation of the Soviet government. But they were cut off at the pass by the events that transpired on November 18, 1978. Surely *that* kind of exodus could not be allowed!!

Now. Do *you* think the C.I.A. was just some malignant figment of Jim Jones' imagination? Why do you think that? *Reason* dictates that it was not.

Now. The next level. Did the C.I.A. actually *have* a contingency plan to exterminate the community? Or was this "merely" a brutal, inhumane scare tactic that Mazor threw our way?

Well, assume for a moment (you may not have it all thought through, but assume it for a moment) that it was *not* Peoples Temple members who assassinated the Congressman, but rather a *frame-up*. That case was laid out in previous chapters: Dum-dum bullets; sophisticated military formations; calm, silent, methodical killers; no credible eyewitness i.d.'s; a second vehicle; no "orders" from Jim Jones (to the contrary!); no forensics; and an apparently confiscated film.

How safe was the community *then*? In the wake of the assassination of a United States Congressman? An assassination that would surely be framed on Peoples Temple?

What would you do if *you* were there waiting for what might happen next? Well you, like most, would probably *not* consider suicide, but rather "take your chances" with some sort of "rescue." Or maybe you would just run into the jungle and take your chances there. A few did.

But what if you were someone who had virtually no chance at a good life, if not for this incredible, unparalleled opportunity that had come your way? What if you thought that the only alternative to fresh air, homegrown food, the empowerment of building one's own homes, creating and managing one's own community, was being forced back to an environment rife with drugs, crime, filth and urban neglect? What if you knew that forcing seniors back to the States would kill them? Or that little children could see their parents murdered before their eyes, or vice versa? Or that you had just "come too far," and you could never turn back? Or that even if *you* "escaped," you would be leaving others littler, or too young, too old, too vulnerable, to face their doom? Would *nothing* ever force your hand? Do you *know* that? Do you know that *for sure*?

And what of the disinformation trail? Why go to such extreme continuing lengths to cover up something that was not an extremely sinister *clandestine* operation? Even the Garry Scharff mess. The Mertles tried to drop out and got themselves killed. So *right on the heels of that*, suddenly materializes Garry Scharff with the Cult Awareness Network, as an "ex-Temple member," although no one had ever met this guy or recognized him. Said he knew the Mertles real well. Except he never surfaces at all until they are murdered. Now *he* will be the anti-Temple spokesman. <u>For at least nine years</u>. And you say "No one is covering up"? Or "Prove it"?

Or what of the botched autopsies? All of SEVEN bodies, not a single one tested for poisoning, and then they get shipped back to the United States *already embalmed*? Then there's the Guyanese coroner, Leslie Mootoo, shouting, "not suicide ~ murder!," claiming that "at least 187" people were skillfully injected from behind, all in the exact same place. Yet the American doctors could not even find any needle marks!

My friends, if *that* happened at all, it was surely at the hands of skilled medical personnel, and moreover, *after* the deaths ~ not by a rapidly diminishing population of civilians, hastening for fear of an imminent attack. It boggles the minds what they may even have been *thinking*. Was it thought that perhaps suicide, however gruesome, can engender *sympathy*? But murder at the hands of a "psychopath" – *never*. Once it is chalked up to "derangement," no one will even look for a logical scenario.

Or the Holsinger disinformation, that "Jim Jones was C.I.A." and responsible for "recruiting mercenaries for the C.I.A. in Angola in 1975" and it just so happens that that scenario was *Congressman Ryan's* big exposé of the C.I.A.! So you feed that lie to *the Ryan family*, the most incendiary thing you could tell them! Even though it is 100% false. Never mind. They'll be so enraged they will never look anywhere else. And it will spread the disinformation, even give it *credibility*. Look, the most aggrieved people, relatives of the prestigious Congressman, believe it. Why not you? It will ensure (or so they hoped) that **no one would ever learn what really happened at Jonestown.**

Nor would I minimize Ryan's aggressive anti-C.I.A. stance (The Hughes-Ryan Act of 1974), however diabolically Ryan personally was manipulated by pro-C.I.A. Stoen. How much the better to set *him* up for death? Leo Ryan and Jim Jones at one fell swoop. Like "killing two birds with one Stoen." Someone high up may have thought this plan "brilliant." Of course, Ted Bundy and Jeffrey Dahmer were "brilliant" in their own way, too. But they only got so far. They didn't get away with it forever.

Please understand, I do not expect this to suddenly not be controversial. Some people would not condone mass suicide under *any* circumstances. But look at *this* circumstance. You don't have to condone. But you do need to *comprehend*. If those people had lived, how long do you suppose they would have lived, and under what conditions?

What did the community of Jonestown believe? And what did Jim Jones believe? We know: **When Jim Jones said on the final tape, "We have no choice now. Either we do it or they do it." he believed, in anguish, desperation and panic, that the plan was to exterminate the entire community. He believed that there was a C.I.A. contract out on the entire community, even shy of the assassination of a United States Congressman! He believed it because he had cause.**

Do you think such a person was a "monster"? Deranged? At the last, he was not even *violent*:

"They are not taking our lives. We are not taking their lives. We are laying down our lives in protest against conditions of an inhumane world. We're a thousand people who said we don't like the way the world is."

Me? I do not ask anyone to accept anything. I do ask people to _think_. You may never personally have any calling to "lay down your (own) life in protest against conditions of an inhumane world." All I am asking is that you honor those who _did_.

And please understand about Mazor. Mazor, who was right in the thick of the conspiracy. Mazor, who got on t.v. mere days following the tragedy and announced that *"It was thought that Jim Jones would become a major political force in the Caribbean within five years."* Mazor, who was, by late date (September, 1978), "claiming credit for" having led the raid against Jonestown. Offering up information. Maybe even changing sides. Befriending _both_ our attorneys ~ Garry and Lane. Then in the damning "transcript," he makes a huge show of (allegedly) _disliking_ Stoen, of _distrusting_ Stoen. Would rather hire a dog to be his attorney than that man.

Mazor would never have been let into that community without that stance. **Nor would he have been let in <u>unless the mercenary raid that he was "claiming credit for" had really happened</u>.** If it had not happened, then his "claiming credit for it" would not be credible.

Moreover:

a) We believed him to be an employee of Interpol. It was published in our newspaper, the Peoples Forum, and Teri Buford told me personally that "we have his Interpol i.d. number";

b) He said that he personally knew of Stoen being C.I.A.; and

c) He said (as per Lane) that the plan had been to *"first kidnap the children and then kill all the adults."*

Admittedly Lane, as has been made clear, is **not** "a credible witness," in that his accounts appear to be a mass of self-serving contradictions. But _I_ am a credible witness. And I heard the taped confession first-hand and I know exactly what I heard. Moreover, Marceline Jones (whom _no one_ has ever implicated in lying, or in "paranoia") was there as well, standing _in assent_. She had just finished telling us how she was there when a bullet whizzed right by Jim's head, when Lane whipped out the Mazor tape.

And I know that Jim Jones believed this personally because he _said_ so. From a message broadcast at Jonestown, October 16, 1978, a single month before the tragedy:

"It's more serious than some people want to see. We have several enemies. **We had enemies that sent that little man who was here ~ the detective [obvious reference to Joseph Mazor] ~ and he told us all. It's all written up in affidavits under penalty of perjury.**

Did the C.I.A. Have a Contract/355

What he was going to do if he had not seen that our faces looked happy. [i.e. the threat to invade and kidnap children, then kill all the adults.] And he saw no guards and he saw no barbed wire. He saw determined people that looked to him like they were voluntarily circling our community. That caused him, and this is a testimony from the mouth of the detective himself, that caused him to withdraw from the situation. ***And then later through our contacts we broke him, he talked through someone that Dr. Lane and Dr. Freed know, he broke and talked and spilled all the beans and there were lots.***

"Stoen had been stealing money at a secret bank account in England. Stoen was also being funded by high level members of the conspiracy. So now he's a class enemy. This man [meaning Mazor] once bitterly despised us for socialism and communism and still does not accept our views politically, but nonetheless he admires our care for one another and he has given us services free." (Mazor did in fact tell the *Los Angeles Times* that he ***"could not help but be impressed"*** by Jonestown.]

And in the very same message, all whilst being so worried about warning people that their very lives were in danger:

"I demand – it's going to be a matter of observation. . . if people do not smile and give encouragement to people as you pass. Friendly greeting and a pat on the shoulder occasionally or warmth. We need to quit cliquing and show love with all people. All of us owe at least friendliness to each other.

"People are not appreciative enough. They have so many things going for them. I want to see you speaking, because if you come up for not speaking or not showing a friendly smile, you will be given a warning. . . . ***So please all of us start showing love to the children, some kindness and love to the children. I've said this before. Give them that kind of love. Hug them every now and then and show them warmth as you pass them. It will help them like flowers grow. Even plants respond to love.***"

So what does this community sound like to you *now*? Robots, psychopaths, brainwashed "cultists"? Or "Why care about them anyway? Except maybe to pity them. They were in a hellhole of a concentration camp. And besides, they were poor, they were black. The 'expendable' ones"?????

How much the more reason *to* care! The people of Jonestown, so many of them, came from environments with *no options*. This was not only a miraculous new beginning for them, but a *role model* for all who were left behind. A shining *hope*. Like Jesse Jackson says: "Keep hope *alive!*"

They killed off a *hope*, those damnable people. Driving innocent people to their deaths was surely enough, but maybe they went even one step worse. They killed off *hope*. They killed off hope.

XLIX. Sticks and Stoens and Set-ups.

We may never know the full extent of Mazor's role in the final horror of Jonestown. Nor Stoen's. Much less the clandestine tapestry that stitched in countless malefactors we had never even met – the phone harassers; the international press smearers; the people who set off false alarms in hotels, or broke into homes, or splattered dum-dum bullets into their unfortunate targets. If you asked me who were these people's "handlers," I would not know their names.

But before we leave the sick, murderous world of what passes for "intelligence," reserved are some choice words about Timothy Stoen. More specifically, from a person who had reason to know: Teri Buford.

No, I would not vouch for her honesty. Yes, what was done to Jean Brown and Mike Prokes bordered on unforgivable. Yes, the Mertles were virtually ignored, though she knew their culpability.

Tim Stoen, however, was another story. Exposing the Mertles might have *endangered* Buford. (Good guess! Took them all of five days to get murdered after trying to jump ship!) But exposing *Stoen*, she apparently thought, could *extricate* her. Thus the book, so "saddened" by Mike Prokes' death, while virtually ignoring the Mertles is, for some evident reasons, vitriolic against Stoen.

Nevertheless, although what was perpetrated against Mike Prokes and Jean Brown was shameful, I would tend to *credit* what was said about Stoen, if only because:

a) Buford wouldn't have come out against someone as dangerous as Stoen unless she had facts to back her up;

b) she had no motive, obviously, to implicate *herself* in shady and/or illegal actions except to expose her former boss, Mr. Stoen;

c) enough documents, copies of notes written in Stoen's own hand, had fallen into my *own* hands, to credit her story as true;

d) he did fit the classic mold for an *agent provocateur*: fanatical loyalist; leading proponent of violence; sophisticated m.o. of "dirty tricks"; evidence he was planning his "defection" years in advance; actual "defection" just before the heat came down; clandestine far-right-wing background; absolute falsity of "cover story"; and a bald *political* agenda of defamation, lobbying and threats; moreover, hugely expensive to maintain and with no visible means of funding; and

e) Buford had come to hate Jones, with no motive to protect him, indeed tried to call him a "murderer"; yet every manner of dirty dealing she lays not at the door of Jones, but of Stoen.

In an emotional vendetta, Teri describes being frantically caught up with the *tiniest* group within the whole of Peoples Temple – "tiny" meaning no more than five or six at the most, in a cast of thousands. So tiny that, **according to her own testimony, much of the time Jim Jones did not even know what was going on.** Jones wasn't the director of this breakaway unit, called the "Diversions Department." Tim Stoen was.

This is where (for those readers who lack the political background), the phenomenon occurred which was better known in the 60's, when such characters often infiltrated left-wing movements: *"agent provocateur."* That's when you infiltrate a group whose politics you oppose, provoke it into acts of violence, then clear out of the way when the heat comes down.

Buford, as source, makes a deadringer case for *Stoen* having been an "agent provocateur." He was the one, she says, who set up the "Diversions Department," she said, to try to steer the Temple towards a "dirty tricks" mode of operation, and preferably, into outright violence – starting with anonymous phone calls to "enemies," and ending with terrorist proposals like poisoning the water supply of Washington, D.C., and building bomb factories. Thank God no one followed through.

She even tells of once approaching Jim Jones and telling him of Stoen's plan for her and a fellow named Tom to live together for the purpose of starting a bomb factory. She reports *Jim Jones said* (no, **not**, go do it, but rather) *"That's crazy. You'll blow your heads off;"* and then (*of Stoen*), "There's something wrong with that man."

That said, in *"The Strongest Poison,"* Buford describes at length, her conscription by Stoen into the so-called "Diversions Department," which began in 1973 with no violent intent, just as a way to manipulate public opinion – like calling *both* candidates before an election, pledging support of Peoples Temple, then claiming credit for the electoral victory for whichever side won. Its character, she avers, shifted as key vindictive members left the group, moving into the "dirty tricks" department, like anonymous threatening phone calls or unsettling letters, disguising voices and wiping fingerprints clean.

Stoen, she said, assumed control of this "department," deliberately concealing his plans from Jones, he told his small cadre, to "protect Jim from liability."

Sticks and Stoens and Set-Ups/359

Stoen had also, clandestinely, on his own (not highlighted in their book), performed "thousands" of improper notarizations, according to defector Neva Sly; though Stoen having himself defected, this was never pursued. Ex-members Marvin and Jackie Swinney, meanwhile, claimed Stoen had threatened them, to bilk them out of their home, even catching his efforts on tape; though Stoen having defected, this was privately settled and dropped in the press. Even the Mertles had pressed an early suit against Stoen for fraud, before they knew he had changed sides. So the Stoen track record for clandestine operations was already clear.

In his role as director of the Diversions Department, Stoen tried (without Jim's prior knowledge, much less approval, Buford admits) to get Buford trained in firing weapons, making bombs, and poisoning city water. Buford was supposed to research how to wreak all this havoc by making trips to out-of-the-way libraries, using odd disguises and fake i.d.'s.

Stoen's other proposals were said to include a "hit list," kidnapping high officials in the event of Jim Jones' arrest, and taking over a National Guard Armory to steal weapons. Stoen, says Buford, also *"prevailed upon a unit within the Temple to accept his leadership rather than Jones' in the area of contingency planning for terrorist activities..."* Needless to say, Stoen also favored "mass suicide" - well, for the rest of us, at least. Those who balked at his extremism were called "afraid to die."

Diversions disbanded after Stoen's defection, but Stoen's typical m.o.'s kept showing up, like Rosalie Wright of *New West*, complaining of anonymous threatening calls at 3 a.m., Kathy Hunter (and Steven Katsaris) the same, *plus* goons coming to her house, breaking in and forcing alcohol down her throat.

"After Stoen left the Temple" Buford states, "the Diversions Department was phased out of existence... *Yet someone familiar with [Stoen's] methods... evidently carried forth those projects. In every such instance, Jones and the Temple were publicly branded as the culprits, and Jones, frustrated and panicked by the unfair and untrue charges, became angry and then increasingly frightened by the invisible trap into which he sensed he was falling.*"

Most flagrant, and the final tip-off that it was **not** Peoples Temple engaging in these tactics, were the three anonymous phone calls reportedly received by the wife of Will Holsinger, a Ryan aide in the San Francisco area, on the very night of the tragedy, "between 8:30 and 10:00 p.m.," telling her that "Your husband's meal ticket just had his head blown off and he [your husband] might be next." (See DOCUMENTS, p. 40.)

We at the San Francisco Temple were still in shock and disbelief. We didn't even know who Holsinger *was*. **NO ONE** from Peoples Temple made those calls. Not in a million years. Never did, never could, never would. It wasn't just morally unconscionable. It was **IMPOSSIBLE.**

The implications of that may have been more chilling still. It suggests that *someone out there was NOT taken by surprise by the assassination, but rather lined up in advance to make the death threats on cue.* No one in Peoples Temple even knew who Holsinger *was*. It was *Tim Stoen,* who had been courting Ryan for over a year, who knew. This vile "dirty trick" was obviously the work of the conspirators. But in trying to (again) wrongly implicate Peoples Temple, they tipped their own hand: ***that they knew in advance that the Congressman was about to be assassinated.***

In any case, this would require *personnel*. Under the surface charade of "media heroes" like the Mertles and Stoen, had to be a much larger cast of supporting characters.

Surely if someone harassed *those* particular people (Wright, the editor of New West; reporter Kathy Hunter; "concerned relative" Steven Katsaris; and Ryan aide Will Holsinger), it sure wasn't us -- it was even *counterproductive to our interests*. And Stoen was the presumed expert in such tactics. This makes it credible that Stoen could have engineered the various nasty and dangerous antics that were blamed on us, and moreover, that "agency support" provided personnel to get it done.

After all, some of this was *internationally-based*, like the elaborate antics against Kathy Hunter (who had been personally coached by Stoen) while in Guyana, and the identically-worded smears in the Canadian and Soviet press. Stoen acting alone could never have gotten all that done, though with his skills in international banking, and the discovery of several hidden "private" funds, he might have been able to *finance* various misdeeds. Moreover, when Stoen left Guyana to begin his anti-Temple campaign in June, 1977, his first stop was not the West Coast, but *Washington, D.C.*, where he set up an office, ostensibly to "lobby" against the church.

As proof of the *agent provocateur* role, even locally, Buford offered the lawsuit which Stoen prepared for Jim Cobb against his own former client, Peoples Temple, possibly a disbarrable offense. Such a suit would daren't have even come to trial, which Stoen surely knew. You would have to "silence" (whatever that might entail) any witness who could reveal that the plaintiff's attorney, Mr. Stoen, was himself the author of the plaintiff's complaints! Such a suit could only be brought for the purposes of harassment – *i.e. to smear Peoples Temple and/or drive its leadership over the edge.*

Stoen's suit for Cobb claimed that the "Diversions Department" had been founded only *much later on*, like "June 23, 1977" (Stoen already being conveniently gone), citing all the various "dirty tricks" that he, Stoen, had himself instituted, Buford says, even citing as "grievances," <u>antics he had pulled against Cobb himself</u>, but at a much earlier time. (See DOCUMENTS, p. 26.)

And *this* (believe it or not, ladies and gentlemen) is why Jim Cobb ("eyewitness extraordinaire," as you may recall) was suing Peoples Temple for millions of dollars by the time of the tragedy at Jonestown!

Was Stoen a classic *"agent provocateur"*? Suspicions were first aroused when papers linking Stoen to a spying trip in East Berlin were discovered upon moving some boxes to Guyana in the Spring of '77. Now the jig was up: A far-right wing ideologue avowed to fight communism, and with such "field experience," could be an *agent provocateur* indeed. Worse still, too knowledgeable and too highly-placed in the community to risk cutting loose, not to even mention the volatile matter of the Stoen/Jones child. It was also during that time that his bank accounts in London and France were reportedly discovered, places where the Temple had done no banking. (Mazor later claimed for him an additional clandestine account in Venezuela.)

Stoen's cover was unravelling. Jim resisted believing it until reality piled on top of reality was too much. Buford revealed there had also been an earlier incident setting the stage:

Jim had a brief, then quashed, arrest record. He had not committed any criminal act, was probably framed, but it looked bad:

One day in Los Angeles, Jim had snuck off to a movie with his son Lew, *telling no one but Stoen where he would be.* Jim had prostate and urinary problems, and apparently had to massage himself to urinate when the problem was acting up. This happened at the movie theatre, exactly when, "by coincidence," an undercover cop was in the next stall. It looked like masturbation, and he was arrested "for trying to proposition an undercover cop." If he was set up, it could only have been by *Stoen*, the only one who knew where he was that day.

Being set up by Stoen didn't occur to Jim at the time. He just wanted the record quashed, and apparently Stoen was sent to Sacramento, the state capital, to get the job done. Done it was – the record was sealed. Yet Buford tells in *"The Strongest Poison,"* that when moving church materials down from Ukiah to San Francisco in late 1974, they came upon "two copies of an official Los Angeles record." It was passed onto Jim with, "This looks like your arrest record" – the very one that Stoen had been sent to quash!

Jim was upset and "asked Stoen why he had made copies of a record they had worked so hard to seal." Stoen assured Jim that no other copies existed. Yet apparently, later that same day, they *discovered six more copies!*

That was undoubtedly the most telling evidence that **Stoen was planning to do Peoples Temple in years before he left.** The only remaining question is, **did he intend to do Peoples Temple in <u>before he even joined</u>, i.e. <u>was he an infiltrator in government employ?</u>** His background, although admittedly not a legal proof, would certainly suggest that he *was.*

Stoen was also more thorough than Peoples Temple was able to ferret out. Later, in the midst of the smear campaign, *"the motion that had been filed [by Stoen] to unseal the record of Jim Jones' arrest, in fact accomplished that very purpose. It had attached to it a record of the arrest."* The reported wry comment by that late date was, "Well, now I don't have to guess. I know now that Stoen kept at least one more copy."

Buford also relates that she was once picked up by Customs where *only Tim Stoen knew she would be.* Worse, Stoen had advised her to *commit suicide* if she were ever caught in such a jam! He thought she would be illegally carrying large sums of money across borders, but fortunately, unbeknownst to Stoen, Jim had nixed such a mission as "too dangerous."

We can begin to see who the "dangerous" ones really were. Yet it is interesting to note (especially for those quick to aver that Jim Jones was "a monster," nay, "a psychopath"), that if Jim Jones wanted to *harm* Tim Stoen, the one person who was poised to harm *us* more than *anyone,* there was ample opportunity to do it and it wasn't even considered. Stoen was in Guyana for long stretches of time with Jim after he had already stated he wanted to leave the group, and all the damning evidence against him had been discovered. Yet he let Stoen go on his way. (So much for "holding people hostage"!) Stoen had promised, Buford avers, after hours of pleading on Jim's part, that he, Stoen, would **never do anything to harm**

Jonestown, and that he would *never move to have Jim's son John removed.* Needless to say, he went on to do both with a vengeance.

Yet even at the point where suspicions had progressed to panic, Buford says, Jim Jones "wasn't talking about killing anyone." He was "rational," she says, and "deeply concerned." Even by the time of the final tape, made at the beginning of the suicides at Jonestown, he expressed, in great anguish, **_an absolute aversion to killing._**

In fact, for all the condemnation of Jim Jones as a "psychopath," and remarkably, even unbelievably, for all her inside knowledge and experience, plus her obvious hatred for the man she once adored, she *fails to implicate him in a single violent act, or even as suggesting any manner of violence.* Only *Stoen.* Even when the decision was apparently made to have some guns at Jonestown, she herself admits Jim Jones' decision was *purely defensive and reactive against blatant military threats against a defenseless community.*

Sometimes, even now, I am aghast. The press, so manipulated by such horrible people, yet in such a mad rush to crucify. Did it ever occur to anyone in that precious fourth estate, that they may have been crucifying the wrong man?

Yet Stoen appeared to have emerged unscathed. Unluckier by far --and in chillingly scant time past the tragedy-- were his cohorts, the infamous Mertles. Shortly after Lane & Buford had taken such pains to resuscitate the mythical "hit squad," another pair had reason indeed to feel threatened, by a "hit squad" of another calling entirely. They failed to heed the call, and it was to cost them their very lives.

XLVIII. They Kill Their Own.

Elmer and Deanna Mertle a/k/a Jeannie and Al Mills were still very much on the scene following the tragedy, taking in referrals from the psychiatrist that the City of San Francisco had assigned to the returning survivors from Jonestown. I suppose he assumed that the Mills were "the good guys." After all, they tried to prevent all this from happening, didn't they? Maybe they could help the returnees adjust to a normal life. Deanna and Mert had somehow prospered, they claimed, by "buying the property of elderly residents of their rest homes" (another can of worms no one presumed to open), and "The Human Freedom Center" in Berkeley came to be a place that some of the younger returnees apparently thought a stopping point between the extremes of trauma and a future of more normalcy.

The San Francisco/Bay Area had an aftermath all its own ~ one I never, to be truthful, felt I either wanted or missed. The disillusioned survivors seeking out the anti-Temple brigade. The "Maybe they were right all along." We know how that goes. Judging right and wrong, black and white, who is the victim, who the perpetrator, without anything resembling a fair trial, or any trial at all, much less discovery. The dead cannot speak for themselves. Only the living carry the day.

So the aftermath of many of my friends was the melting pot that the Bay area became ~ the Deanna Mertles and the Debbie Blakeys who talked, who socialized, who commiserated with the bereaved. Deanna even met with the Jones boys at her ad-hoc Center, expressing empathy for their plight to the media, and that they (and the rest of us?) posed no danger.

Everyone so wanted not just to live, but to live *with* what had happened. Perhaps by clustering together and pooling the chipped pieces of their broken hearts, some could, if not emerge whole, at least find a livable mooring on one of the favored platforms between "Just like Jesus Christ returned to Earth" and "Damn him to hell forever!" "It started out wonderful, but then it went downhill," and the like. Rationales for demoralization perhaps seemed a better alternative than irreconcilable confusion or raw disbelief.

Some, I'm sure, even wanted compassion to flourish between perpetrators and survivors, to know that the sorrow was shared and that all was forgiven. Many seemed to conclude in a soupy, en masse sort of way, that they, the survivors, had been used in the service of some wild rhetoric which like the spray of Patty Hearst's bullets in her ill-begotten "Stockholm syndrome" of a bank robbery, spawned only cold, immovable death, not the hoped-for social change.

The Deanna Mertles and the Debbie Blakeys, presumably, *weren't* used. And was there really any conspiracy? Maybe all they did was try to prevent it all from happening. If there was anyone in contention for heroism, was it not *them?*

It's ironic how people so pressed into a cardboard mold in their mad dash to "face reality," had so little interest in what had actually happened! I tired of offering people copies of the final tape, for takers there were none. Though I know as well as anyone, that much of others' unwillingness to go outside the official view arose from aversion to reopening wounds and pain. Almost like *I* had averred going to Guyana, when I was given the choice. I could have gone, but I didn't. I couldn't bear to re-open wounds and pain.

Thus what appeared to *me* to be horrifying reconciliations with the deadly Mertle crew, may have simply been the best that people who, after all, never wanted to hurt *anyone* and now wanted peace, could manage. At any rate, it was happening. Bizarrely, the cloistered Peoples Temple lot, survivors and anti-Temple agitators alike, were seeming to coalesce into almost a kind of community. Those who had been in the loop, like the Mertles, were not keeping their distance from the survivors. Indeed, they were taking them in.

And why not? Deanna and Mert may not have been told of death plots against the community. They were demonstrably experts in demolishing I.R.S. tax exemptions (the follow up to the original *New West* smear quoted the I.R.S. Tax Code chapter and verse), but had not advocated terrorism, as had Stoen. So far as they were concerned, perhaps they had convinced themselves that they *had* "tried to prevent it from happening."

Whatever the Mertles' motives, however, this could not have been what their *employers* wanted to see. To the contrary. Far from setting their shadowy handlers at rest, more likely it produced a predictable response: Would their tongues at some point slip, and reveal their true role? How they got involved in the first place, and from whence their directives came? They could pose a liability life-long.

Indeed, by anniversary time in November, 1979, "Jeannie Mills" had softened to the version of her presented in The New York Times Magazine:

> "People in the temple were hard workers.. Our experience in the temple made us strong. It made our children independent. We learned to live on very little. We learned to get happiness from watching a bird fly overhead. We learned to accept people confronting us. To stand and face a crowd. There were very, very good things we learned. It was important for me to accept these things... in order to own my own life."

Various things they dutifully did, like their book "Six Years With God," but that got done by the first year. Presumably they could have had long, successful careers as anti-cult deprogrammers, but lo and behold... they didn't want to!

On February 21, 1980, "Jeannie Mills" addressed a group of students at Marin College and told them that "**they no longer feared being killed by a Peoples Temple hit squad... The Millses told the group that they planned to give no more public lectures about the Peoples Temple, and that they were anxious to build a normal life.**" (See DOCUMENTS, p. 27)

Kissing Peoples Temple good-bye seemed to be the kiss of death. Five days later, on February 26, 1980, she, Mert, and a daughter who had accidentally wandered in, were murdered by (the police surmised) "someone they knew," "at point blank range." It seems someone indeed "hit" these two and their daughter Daphene. Dum-dum bullets seared through their heads execution style, and the police surmised that they knew their attackers, for it was early evening and there were no signs of forced entry.

The end of this pair's usefulness was also the end of their lives. Me, I was happy enough to no longer be on site to enquire "who could have done this." The F.B.I., on whatever pretext, entered the investigation. After a relatively short, fruitless hunt for any "Peoples Temple hit squad" (naturally the F.B.I. would have no inclination to investigate... the F.B.I.), the matter was dropped and left unsolved. No one ever pursued any other theories or leads.

As for the Temple survivors, whatever they thought, no one mumbled a word. Many reportedly had gone into hiding. It was something I could empathize with, but not understand. I didn't see how much clearer things could be made.

The press had no inclination to pursue it either. Tacitly, it was probably written off as "an irony." That here this valiant crusader, Mrs. Mills, said she was no longer afraid of a Temple hit squad one week, and was murdered the next. Of course, no one dwelled on her assertion that she would no longer speak out against Peoples Temple, much less *The New York Times* write-up that (for her) was beginning to sound almost conciliatory. Never mind any two plus two theory of the killings. No one even enquired if there was *anyone else* out there who might want to do them in. Who, after all, might that be?

At that, this was probably clever timing on the part of "the unknown murderers." The Mertles wanted to be free of speaking out? They were becoming friendly with the enemy? Their reminisces weren't all of horror? This could become dangerous. So go and do these people in just as the pressure was letting up. It will slam it back down.

And so it did. Temple people were now more fearful than ever. No one would dare even voice it: "Who will be next?"

I folded in the news clippings someone had been thoughtful enough to send me about the murders. Into the write-ups, letters, inclusions, to whomever I approached, however futilely, on the subject of Jonestown. Like everything else, it seemed to matter nought. So three more people died. There was no public context into which to weave this new event, except possibly "the hit squad." There *could* be a hit squad, couldn't there, or why were these people "hit"? No one was about to presuppose that the murderer may have surfaced from their own circle of friends. Who would want to do *them* in? Was this not just one more tragic travesty that no one could understand?

I wondered if anyone, anywhere, even *thought* what I was thinking. That if the Mertles, of all people, were murdered by their own, was Jim Jones' last frantic plea, that the community at Jonestown could be facing an impending slaughter did they not suicide out, really so far-fetched? They murdered their own and they were intent on sparing us?

Even Lane acknowledged the obvious, saying publicly following the murders: "*This [killing] was done very, very professionally, not at all the way Peoples Temple members ever did anything.*" (Oh? And the assassination of Congressman Ryan? That *wasn't* done "very, very professionally"? "Not the way Peoples Temple members ever did anything"???)

Maybe we could even begin to decipher Lane & Buford's book, convolutions of disinformation and all. Proclaim that there is a hit squad. Proclaim it loudly. Pull out all the stops and fire away. Hit squad, hit squad, hit squad. Look. We're saying there's a hit squad, so you'll leave *us* alone, won't you?

But even the insatiable public appetite for horror seemed to be growing weary, finally. I could hardly say that this new confirmation that killers, not heroes, had conspired to destroy Jonestown, gave me a second wind either. It seemed, rather, one more excuse for others to slam the door on the evidence cache. I sent the clippings about the Mertles, citing the obvious, to the Congressional Committee. If it got to anyone, I never knew. No one responded.

I was to make just one last attempt to set the record straight before the long-neglected task of a new life for *me*, like a proverbial bill collector dunning at my door, finally came due.

XLIX. A Last-Ditch Effort Fails.

Somehow I got a meeting lined up with the Director of ABC's "*World News Tonight*," at that time a woman named Pat Lynch. In response to their coverage of the second anniversary on November 18, 1980. The second anniversary had not been as outrageous as the first -- a muted grief, now not as fully-inflamed. Only phantom perpetrators, such as the Holsinger disinformation leads, remained to be pursued; and since that had been designed by dead-end specialists to lead nowhere, the trail was about to run cold.

Of course, there was one piece missing entirely, namely, the film of the assassination; plus the original cast of characters had modified somewhat, since the Mertles were no longer even alive. No one questioned how they had been killed. How omissions speak thousands of words.

I brought Al along for moral support, though we must have seemed an odd pair. Al, a tall dark presence offering low, dire, hyper-punctuated tones on cue, resonated, at best, to his own pulse. His eccentric Uranus in Aquarius sticking up from his chart like the proverbial sore thumb (meaning a *very* odd fellow indeed!), inspired confidence in counterculture milieus, but seemed oddly out of place in this sanitized office setting. He didn't wear a suit and I managed little more than jeans myself.

As for me, I was nervous. I mean, *really* nervous. I might actually shoot my moment's worth of unsolicited cross-fire onto the network screen. But suddenly it seemed intimidating -- not a prize to be coveted at all.

I offered a short history of what I had tried to *do* about Jonestown, it being impossible to convey such an unfamiliar paradigm of what I thought Jonestown *was* in such a condensed time and space. When I got to Berdes & Smeeton, the Washington obstructionists, Ms. Lynch suddenly lit up, weaving into my resumé that "Yes, Steven Katsaris [Maria's father] told us that Smeeton was the C.I.A. plant on the committee." Oh, God (my inward groan). My sinking ship now seemed eye-to-eye with the lapping waves. It was the first time it occurred to me that I may have been inadvertently responsible for provoking the eradication of key evidence -- that film.

I continued on in a disoriented rush of words. I felt caught between what the person I was talking to had already heard, and where, if any place, it enabled them to go. It suddenly seemed I had little to offer that was not totally unfamiliar, and I found no ready mast upon which to stake my right to speak.

I had prepared a booklet, plainly, if defiantly, entitled, *"Jonestown: A Case for Frame-Up?"* In hyper-dramatic fashion, I began by mimicking CBS' grotesque "*Guyana Tragedy*":

"'The mercenaries are coming. The mercenaries are coming.' The loudspeaker was blaring. People were running to and fro in a kind of forced chaos, an oddly-synchronized St. Vitus's Dance of fear, as paranoia was pumped to a fever pitch into the defenseless and demoralized residents of Jonestown, Guyana.

"So portrayed the opening of 'Guyana Tragedy' shown on CBS last April. The film went on to characterize people many of whom I did not recognize at all for all my eight years in Peoples Temple. Into chronologies that never happened; circumstances that never existed; liars rendered into heroes; the wonderful, vibrant people I cherished crushed to a fiber not fit to feed carrion crows."

"When I had quelled my rage to a keen edge, it occurred to me how careful the network had been to *not* portray Jim Jones as ordering anyone to go shoot at the Port Kaituma airstrip... Nor were any of the guntoters at the airstrip shown disembarking from their approach vehicle before firing, in... contrast to the actual film clip taken by one of the slain newsmen, revealing disembarkment by a sophisticated military formation - a slip on the part of CBS so vital, history might pivot on that one fact alone.

"CBS isn't alone in its elision. **Neither Congress nor the Courts know who ordered or executed the assassination of Congressman Ryan.** The 782-report released by the House Foreign Affairs Committee on May 15, 1979, makes *no mention whatever of the accused.* Robert Fabian, Court- appointed Receiver of the Peoples Temple of the Disciples of Christ, acknowledges in his brief... that there is 'no legal basis to award wrongful death claims,' as there is 'insufficient evidence' to indicate that Peoples Temple members were responsible for the death of anyone.'"

"It is time to assert the obvious - that the facts do matter and no one appears to have them."

As for the rest, it was one previously unaired scenario after another. The six-day siege. The attempt to bribe/blackmail Dennis Banks. David

Conn, never a Temple member, yet leading the charge with the Mertle/Mills. Mazor, the licensed P.I. with a 75-page criminal record. Lane's role in exposing Mazor, then covering him up. How the community was both geographically trapped and militarily defenseless. The suspicious backgrounds of both Stoen and the Mertles. The bogus paternity claim used to bring Congressman Ryan to Jonestown. The harassments by Customs, the Postal Service, the Social Security Administration, the I.R.S., the C.I.A., the F.B.I., the F.C.C . The press smears both in the U.S. and abroad. Investigations whipped up, then dropped for lack of evidence. The murder of the Mertles days after they announced they were off the anti-Temple circuit.

The film. The film. Again the film. Why nothing about the film washed. The visit of the Soviet mouthpiece, TASS, to Jonestown. The scouting trip to Russia planned for December, 1978, had not the tragedy intervened. Mazor with his, **"It was considered that Jim Jones would become a major political force in the Caribbean within five years."**

My write-up was 36 pages long, and may have struck ABC as a great script for "General Hospital," but a strange play in the world of hard news. There wasn't a single thing in *"Jonestown: A Case for Frame-Up?"* that had surfaced anywhere else. Maybe taking on something that so was so at odds with the official view seemed too daunting.

I had managed to put the most pressing matter, the film of the assassination, front and center stage. So I suppose I could give this paper an "A," did grades matter. But this wasn't school, it was life, and tangles of papers may have confused, rather than pressed, the point. Could I ever replay this scene again, I might have put *only* that in front of Ms. Lynch, and pleaded the case of locating and analyzing the film as the *only* thing to do.

Years later on, I did confront the producer of *"West 57th Street"* on CBS, after their tenth anniversary program, as to why the film that had been taken of the assassination now only showed *an empty airport*, and he averred, to my dismay, *"NBC said it was all they had."* My heart sank. But maybe no one would have looked into the film without the *motivation*. The outlook. The paradigm. Jim Jones had been branded as a murderer all 'round. Surely anyone who would sacrifice all those lives, many of them children, would not hesitate to kill a mere Congressman, would they? Maybe *anything* I had to say of it was only bound to be ignored.

Could I appear on t.v. and make a case from out of nowhere? My nervous, almost frenetic urges to cram the facts rapid-pace down the nearest receptacle, both spurred me and deterred me. Suddenly the event was again so close, and just the thought of rubbing elbows with Katsaris, or the Stoens, or Blakey, made me want to run the other way and hide. Here a high level newsperson was telling me that the Congressional aide I talked to was a C.I.A. plant? Was it even true? I had been tripped up before; would it happen again now with the whole nation giving a listen?

I left *"Jonestown: A Case for Frame-up?"* without feeling there was much chance they would go with *me*. A callback a few days later proved that the case.

Still, I'm not entirely sure to this day why that became my stopping point. Maybe it was reaching the top, a major network, and being turned back with no place else to go. I had given these people absolutely explosive material, and it was merely... *dismissed*.

Neither was it a side point that no one from Peoples Temple would join me. One or two gave lip service ~ how far does *that* go? My cadence now was between a rock and a hard place, an establishment on the one hand that would not listen, and our own people who would not rise out of their grief to join the forward charge. I had written letter after letter and made trips back West as well. There were no takers.

I wanted to press on, but it was beginning to seem futile. At some point, *someone* has to listen. It couldn't just be *me*. And there was no listening to be had.

So I made a pact with myself. My life was a mess. Except for reawakening my odd interest in astrology, I didn't *have* much of a life. I couldn't make a dent with this now, with pursuing Jonestown, but surely, my own life was painfully overdue to rebuild. So I would give this up... *for now*.

In occasional glimpses ahead, like a brief stint with binoculars onto a distant and still-darkened stage, intangibles calibrated themselves onto the outstretched abacus of time. I turned to Al one day and said, "It takes about twenty years, doesn't it. Maybe in twenty years, enough time will have passed, that people will listen." With a philosophical sideward toss of the head, he agreed. "Yeah. That might do it. Twenty years. That sounds about right."

Certainly I was long past the "I never promised you a rose garden" view of life. But I could promise *life* something. If I were still around in twenty years... Where would I be, and with whom, and doing what? But if it were still there, the looming necessity of "Arise, arise, the last shall fall to thee," then somehow destiny would meet me in the shadows and lift me to the time, the place, the hour, where it all might still happen. If it were still there. If I would be there to meet it. How could I know this? So many questions, so many years ahead. I just felt this must-might-must-might be so.

Truthfully I was relieved. The morass of loosely-collected papers could turn into packing cartons, the catalogs of notes into file boxes. If I could just manage to extricate myself from my mini-noose of paper trails, mementos, imprisoning memories et al, I might finally move on.

V. "ALMOST DONE. NEW JOURNEY BEGINNING."

"There are more things in heaven and earth, Horatio, than are dreamt of in your philosophy."

William Shakespeare.

L. To Be or Not to Be ... Again.

Sometimes, with an eerie clarity, I would remember that all I ever really wanted was to listen to the angels. *"Allegory"* was like that. The angels weeping for Jonestown. The angels weeping for *America*.

How Jim Jones, even for all his passion against inequities, did love America, especially its forgotten ones. And how the force of our collective love, our collective compassion and pain, could have lit the inner cities darkened by squalor and shame. This was the wholesome America: the adopted children, the service programs, the counselling, the drug rehab, the legal aid, the medical aid, education for the kids. Now, it seemed, this America might never be. Surely the angels would weep over that.

And what would be left now of *me*? Of my spirit, my heart, my hope? The long fight had wound down, seemingly hopeless, to no avail.

Ironically, I thought I had faced everything by now. But you know the wisdom of "Look not to cast out the beam in your brother's eye before you cast out the moat in your own." My desire for public contact now spent, I relaxed my guard. That can be dangerous. I was about to discover inner demons that I had not yet exorcised at all.

I had my own apartment now in Washington Heights. My sister-in-law's piano (the infamous trade of Chapter 1) fit handily into the large front room. Unimaginably, my mother had sprung me some money, a payment from some dividend, and I took several months off "work," my motley assortment of temp jobs.

It was 1981 by now. Months earlier my mother had spurned my weeping pleas and sold the family house that my father had built when I was only eight. I spent much of childhood there, and though the family fought, the setting was idyllic and, far more than our rented apartment in the Bronx, it was home. I had now lost my adopted home of adult years and my family home alike.

I had wanted to prevent the sale with a hurt too tortured to release into daylight, so it invaded my sleep with a new crop of repetitive dreams, co-existing uneasily alongside my "second suicide" dreams of Jonestown. The loss of my birth-family inheritance, and the loss of my extended family, intersecting in my sleep, hatched a weird brew of nightmares, like spices too pungent to feed even to the hungry, and worse yet, best not to be mixed together at all.

Something had to resolve. Surely I couldn't lose *everything*.

The suicide dreams had returned with a vengeance. Finally I dreamt that I had to do *something*. I had to express that I was . . . *ambivalent*. I had strings of hanging-on-the-ledge dreams. I had to find some way to express that I wasn't sure. That I wasn't sure it was a good idea.

Still later on, it occurred to me, in a dream which had long since lost its numbered place in such a chaotic nocturnal morass, that I should pass a note up to Jim. Tell him that I didn't want to do this. I looked around for someone to pass up the note. I spotted... *Tim Stoen*. There was Stoen, most surely alive and as always, impassive, observant, cautious, controlled. He just stood there next to Jim, not freaking out like many of the others. Give it to Stoen, Laurie. To good, solid, loyal, impassive Stoen. I gave him the note. That was all. Just the note passed up. That I didn't think this was a good idea.

By now, the muted grey of my ambivalence was oscillating periodically into light and back into shade, looking to surface above the newly-threatening wave of death and reach upwards out of harm's way. I felt more acutely anxious each time I awoke, more frightened at the consequences of saying no directly to Jim Jones. How could I affirm that I wanted to live, that those of us who were left should not have to die?

Then one night, the impulse quickened. Suddenly going through an intermediary was not enough. I had to talk directly to Jim. I had to tell him face-to-face that I did not want to do this. I had my brief moment. "Jim. . . ." I felt a rush of terror, but *no*. I *had* to. It had suddenly welled up in me, an uncontrollable flood of panic, terror, and tears. No more illusion of a choice. I *had* no choice. I had to release the flood or drown: "I won't do this. I want to *live*." I didn't await the answer. I awoke, shocked and startled into a new brimming wakefulness. I had *told* him.

Then came the great shock. I began, sporadically, to erupt into rage. Blind, fierce, unbridled, uncontrollable rage. I screamed and cursed: "You son-of-a-bitch! You goddamn son-of-a-bitch! How could you do this to us? If you were sick, if you were dying, why didn't you have the decency to crawl off into the jungle alone like a wounded animal and let our people live? How could you do this to us? I hate you! I despise you! Damn you! Damn you to hell!"

I cried, screamed, ranted and raved, shook violently and wept. But it wasn't enough. Rage at the recent past would not suffice. This had to register *eternally*. I would choose the future. And it wouldn't include *him*.

Not him ever again. "I never EVER want to see you again EVER. Not in the next life, not in the one after, not **EVER!!!** I *demand* to never meet up with you again. Not this century, not next century, not ever! You are banished from me!" (Ah, do we *really* "banish" people this way? Has hatred really less holding power than love?)

Ah, but he must also pay. In the worst way. Make him helpless and dependent upon others for his fate as he did to us. "All I want is for you to be born helpless, in a wheelchair, unable to move or speak, totally helpless and dependent upon others for your very long, totally helpless, dependent, miserable life! Why didn't you just kill *yourself* and leave all of *us* alone!"

I repeated all this again and again, the mantras of overbrimming rage. My fury was volcanic. It spared nothing in its molten wake. I couldn't believe this was surfacing from me. Nor could I stop it. I screamed and cursed for days. I swore he would get no mercy from anyone ever. That he would be made as helpless as he made everyone else. That he would pay for every last drop of blood lost because he didn't have the raw human decency to just crawl off into the jungle and die. *"Die! Die! Crawl off and die! Leave us alone! Let us live in peace!"*

There was more. I would find his grave. I would find it, tear it up and gouge out his eyes. I would pulverize him. I would rip out his eyes and tear off his limbs. In death he would know the disempowerment he foisted upon *me* in life. The son-of-a-bitch would pay forever.

I looked around the room. There was a picture of Jim I had put into a frame. I had it right there out in the open ever since I got my own apartment in New York. I grabbed the frame. I took the picture out and slammed it face down. Then I looked down startled. *I had stopped biting my nails.* I had bitten my nails my entire life. I had torn *myself* to shreds my entire life. This had now stopped. It seemed like it had stopped *itself.*

It was now going on three years since the tragedy had happened. Finally I could drag myself up out of the mire this much. Tell him to his face that I would *live* -- that no one would pressure me again *ever* to give my life. My life was *mine*. For the first time, I was really, fully, wholly sure that my life must be mine.

It would be a long time before I would reconsider such outbursts or regret them in any way, beyond resenting the resentment of the resentment of the resentment -- those seemingly never-ending, self-perpetuating cycles of rage which clearly detriment *us* more than any possible object of our rage. Yet what a huge surprise that this all came out, finally, with such violence, and .... *what a relief!*

For the time being, I did not even care that it seemed to countermand everything I had tried to do in the wake of the tragedy to turn the tide. It may have well been that it was Jim Jones who would have *gladly* had his limbs cut off or eyes gouged out, were it only to guarantee *us* safety. I honestly never saw him not sacrifice, or take the easy way out. I'm not even sure that he saw that the empowerment he bestowed upon people *collectively*, was extracted, at least in part, from *dis*-empowerment of us *personally*. Even all the times we voluntarily kept our silence. Rather quash oneself than risk opening up dangerous floodgates for us all. *Families* do this, at times even against wisdom, safety, or both.

Nevertheless, I was glad, at long last, to let the floodgates burst. A whole different process could now begin. I had run the gauntlet ~ stepped through (or was forced, or pushed, or shoved, as the case had variously been) the most loaded of psychological minefields. Now, finally, to debrief, to slow down, to recover, to re-discover, or even re-create what was left of me ~ psychologically, creatively, even my life as a woman.

I had been so intent on redeeming our collective carnage, that I had taken scarce moments to redeem my own. My very wardrobe was a panoply of black and blue: black blouses, blue skirts, blue pants, black jackets, blue, black, black, blue. If anyone had imagined that I had not been sufficiently beat up, all they needed to do was to open my clothes closet!

These were the appropriately-muted trappings of despair. Too far in despair to believe I could ever (I would say "ever *again*," but I feared it was simply "*ever*") have a life of any real normalcy. Yet perhaps in echoes more characteristic of my inherent, solitary self, I reached not outwards to embrace any real, human companion, but rather inwards towards my Muse. The glacier had finally broken, flooding into the sea.

In the innumerable, distracted fantasies of yesteryear, I had postulated that some time in life, I would somehow produce *one* of everything: one great work of music, one great poem, one fictional book, one technical book, one book of memoirs, one of every medium I imagined I could handle well. It seemed like latches inside me would click shut when I imagined a life of prolific art. I feared that life would never allow my inner voices dominance. Like I had volunteered for a marathon, but not even against other runners, with ways to pace one's own speed, and supporters lining the way to cheer one on. It was always more like my own personal marathon for God. That I would be given so many tasks of *living*, that all I could manage was samples of what I was most suited to do, not install myself as a permanent fixture in any creative field.

But now was catch-up time. Not surprisingly, it was now, with the pressure-cooker valve of pent-up emotions released, that my creative juices could again begin to flow. There were certain projects I was obsessive about, even years before Jonestown - like, of course, "*Allegory.*" It was my "Comforter" after the tragedy, the Presence with me always, as I read it through again and again, the very words carrying the vibrations of unfailing love. It, He, never failed to comfort or console.

But there was also that earlier obsession - the sublime "*Ode to a Nightingale*" by John Keats. I always knew it was "mine." Mine to bring that epic transcendence of earthly pain to the heights of Spirit, to free its music into the world. I remembered the day I fell down in the street, knowing I would lose so many in death, more than I could possibly bear. That somehow I would produce music that would make its listeners weep with both sorrow and the ecstatic pathos of release.

By the Fall of '81, voices were again whispering their way into my heart - a phrase here, a whole verse there. I envisioned it now as an upliftment, the memorial my friends were never to know. I would write it to soothe their souls. I would write it to dignify their plight. I would write it to heal. Now, finally, my muse would take flight. I could go into ecstasies. I could live, breathe, eat, sleep, dream "*Ode.*"

I, like many artists, process much unconsciously. Surely the psychic mind, that which knows both future and past, like mirrored twins, is more subtle still. I first envisioned "*Ode*" in 1963. The deaths I had so feared happened in 1978. I had produced the musical setting of "*Ode*" by 1982. Only by now, 1997, did I realize in the very opening lines of "*Ode*," how eerily my hauntings had hit the mark: "My heart aches, and a drowsy numbness pains my sense, *as though of hemlock I had drunk...*"!! Hemlock. Suicide of choice for the ancient Greeks! They drank poison, like my poor doomed Jonestown friends.

But me. How could *I* know? Why this premonition of the deaths so many years before? And why again... the *Greeks* ? Why even, in defense of Jonestown, had Jim Jones once said, "It was like in ancient Greece, when parents thought their children's minds were being corrupted." How did he know of such history, and why would he even think it relevant? Indeed, his very words at the last were, "We should *take the poison like they did in ancient Greece* and step quietly over to the other side." I had no idea how the deaths would come that day I wept the reveries from "*Ode*" - only that the pull was inexorable. To this work that began with allusions to suicide by poison.

I began in earnest now, the trance-like states again and again, repeated, heightened, listening, listening. The lines came through, the resonant colors, the sweeps upwards and plunges down. Now my dream. My dream, my life, would finally begin to happen. (Ah, foolish me. To have thought that I had not yet lived?) Like *"Ode's"* entrancing end: *"Was it vision or a waking dream? Fled is that music: Do I wake or sleep?" That* realm. I would listen and listen, and be one with Them.

My life was still a wreck by conventional standards. No status certainly. No steady job. No marriage. A mist of twisted directions to pursue. But somehow I reached upwards, where the angels sing. I only had to listen.

I let the melodies, the harmonies come. They coursed through me again and again 'til each cadence resolved, 'til each unfinished phrase dissolved into forays across the keyboard both lush and stark. I went into trance, into deep, enfolding trance as I fell in love with each phrase, each line, all spun out through time again and again.

This was the music I had longed for in those "missing years." The ones mysteriously abducted for the tasks of someone who was both wholly me and seemed not me at all. What heartfelt relief that my Muse had, at long last, not abandoned me. I was indeed Their own. This was ecstasy. The death, death, death, then transcendent Life of the Nightingale's sweet cry of the soul in the world beyond.

It took six months to complete. It left me exhilarated and cleansed.

Now, finally, I could prepare the feast. Gorge myself on the smorgasbord of words, ideas, the nourishment I had been hoarding so furtively unto a brighter day. I tackled it with a passion, mowing down three book projects in as many years: an "astrological biography" of Bach called *"A Magic Moment" Bach and Beyond"*; one for the United States, called *"Common Sense: America's Roots Revisited"*; and *"How to Rectify a Birth Chart: An Introduction to the Mathematics of Life,"* teaching how to adjust astrological charts for uncertain times of birth. It seemed a special bonus to have the latter translated into three languages – Spanish, Italian and Dutch. I gathered one or more of each for my newly-adorned bookshelf. This was a very delicious feast indeed.

It might have even seemed that I was priming up to go out into the world. It would emerge that I had only just begun to tip open the doors to a renewed life. The most powerful of healings would still await.

LI. "Go Back to California and Forgive."

I would always remember that night because it was so *international.* "We are the world. We are the children... " *Live Aid,* July, 1985. The internationally simulcast concert for Ethiopian famine relief. This picket line child marched on picket lines no more, nor demonstrations, nor any large public gatherings at all. Not after Jonestown. I tried, but I could never join in. I could only stand by the sidelines and cry.

But this was, thankfully, one step removed, on t.v. I was flooded with more than song that summer night, but the outpouring of people from every corner of the Earth uniting to help a hungry world. By evening, I thought I would make a rare pilgrimage to the movies, even though a subway ride away. It was *"Cocoon,"* about magical powers to rejuvenate life. If there were any songs that day at the *"Live Aid"* not belted away at my speed, the beneficent aliens of *"Cocoon"* aimed a mellifluous microphone right at my heart. I was all ready to hop the next spaceship to the stars.

I waited at the Times Square station at midnight for a train ride home. Not too wholesome a place, many would say. And it was hot that night, very hot; hot and steamy on the dark subway ledge. Just waiting, high on my new-found space-world friends, awaiting some mundane chugaloo to zip down the tracks and journey me home.

Then "Someone" began speaking to me. No, not the local unsavory wildlife, just "Someone." *"Go to California,"* He gently intoned. *"Go back to California and forgive."*

I felt... almost a *warmth.* I felt enfolded, almost caressed, by a Presence. I could feel Him and no... yes, I could *see* Him! He was a tall, no, an *exceptionally* tall Presence, with a long white robe and deep, serene eyes. He looked somewhat Indian, but not quite. I was startled, of course! Not just at the Presence, not just at His appearance in *the* most unlikely location, but at the *message.* There were no more messages that night, but He... He... *stayed* with me. Whatever I felt, whatever I thought, at home, at work, on the street, on the... *subway,* He was right there with me. With each passing day, His Presence grew more palpable, audible, intense.

And I began to *feel.* It was a tugging, no, an *opening* in the heart area. It wasn't like an upset, though I *got* quite upset at times, even out on the street. It was more like an outpouring, a welling-up of my capacity to feel. I began to feel like I could open to *anyone,* that I could *love* anyone, that I could *forgive* anyone. I loved so much, I cared so much, it hurt. *He* cared so much, it hurt me not to care even more. He was so wholly there. He was *with* me, He was *above* me, He was *me*.

I called for airline tickets West. I remember Beethoven's glorious "Grosse Fugue" (which does, after all, mean "great flight"!) rippling through my brainwaves as I dialed United to check on the fare.

I had recently written a letter to John Grinder, one of the inventors of neuro-linguistic programming. It was a complaint letter, actually. I said I had enjoyed his books, but I had gone to a practitioner that I thought substandard ~ well, whatever "standards" for alternative practitioners may be. I didn't realize it was all de-centralized and that John didn't even *know* most of the people out there practicing NLP by then. I was surprised to find a message on my answering machine from him personally. Perhaps my long, overwrought letter had intrigued him. Maybe like "a case," or such.

I called back, told him I was going to California and could I stop by and visit and he said fine. I was elated. I had the most wonderful feeling this would lead me to exactly where I needed to go.

Oh, I wasn't quite myself those many weeks of time. All through that summer, I was hardly myself at all. Yet, I was *wholly* myself, more myself than I had ever been before. Sometimes it was upsetting or tearful, as my heart widened and thumped to a new, more expansive beat, but it was a beautiful, an *incredible* heart opening. So much like being in love, but better. He knew you and understood you without your ever saying a word. He lived in your heart, lifted your thoughts, and cleansed your eyes so you could see. I was so much in love with *this* Spirit. My teacher, my beloved, my Self. He felt my burdens and carried their weight ever so gently upon his own Soul; then subtly, from day to day, you discovered, that they had just *lifted*. Finally, it seemed, One had come to me who could both be so above me, and yet so with me, that I wanted this One to be with me *forever*. I would follow *this* One anywhere. California? Easy. Piece o' cake.

I arrived at the San Francisco airport, that place of a million tons' engrained baggage and weight.... *light*. Light and free. I managed to settle in Oakland, with an old friend from the church. I would visit John, then we would see what was up.

I slept peacefully the night before I headed down the coast, even blissfully ~ dreamworld of day, dreamworld of night. Sleep was like an awakening, and I awoke... into my own funeral! It was fascinating. I could see the casket and the mourners, and felt no stress or strain ~ just free, floaty and light. I was led into an antechamber where I was told, here is your new chart, Laurie. Here is your new life. Hugely calligraphed into the parchment beneath my feet were the treasured symbols: Jupiter, Neptune, the Moon. I was excited and happy, like a kid with brightly-wrapped presents under the tree. I awoke into a sweet gentle breeze and sunshine glimmering off the morning dew.

I remember taking a bus down the coast, me and my great angel of a new (no, perhaps very *ancient*) Friend. I lighted off the bus and, having arrived early, clombered blissfully through a woodsy area like a hovering sprite, talking with my sweet angel as I rambled along. Everything seemed perfect. Nothing could make me afraid anymore.

John's house, or be it headquarters, was rather a happy, sloppy, friendly kind of place. He took me to a small side room with scattered papers and books, casually tossing out that this was his "office," but that he had actually never used it thus far to meet with anyone. I liked this man. He was cool, a little flipped, yet so completely down-to-earth one and the same. He couldn't care less (well, judgmentally, that is) that I was with the angels ~ like talking with one on an ongoing basis in the same room! Or about my terribly tragic life. Or how absurdly incongruous seemed the terrible tragedy with the light-hearted angel. It was o.k. to laugh, or cry, or talk lucidly with my angel friend of no yet-known name.

I said I thought there must be *something* in NLP that would work with me. What would he recommend? He made a recomendation of a practitioner. Well, actually maybe the *angel* made the recommendation. John, ergo the angel, recommended ....*Los Angeles*. City of Angels. He even recommended a practitioner named *Angela!* ("Nice going, John!") Of course. But of course, too, so much more. How could my heart open to forgive in any place *but* Los Angeles? What *do* "forgiveness" and "Los Angeles" have in common? (Ah, and how could anyone but my angel know that so well? Or so the song went . . .)

"Angela" met me at the bus stop. We incorporated a relic of an older Indian man, hobbling on one leg, but cheerful enough. Claimed to be a psychiatrist. No, a mystic. Well, one or two of those, or maybe all three. I was spaced. I vaguely remember us bouncing back and forth whether Jesus was really crucified unto death, or survived to live out a long, prosperous life in... *India!* It took us long into the night over tea. I didn't even feel I was in any particular city, or a newly-arrived guest, or engrossed in strange repartee. Everything would be fine.

Sometime the next day about noon, we drifted into a "session." I think the Angela person had the illusion of hypnotizing me. Far as I could see, the only distinction was that she was working at it, and I wasn't. I drifted here, drifted there, followed this directive, that directive, and finally she did... well, I don't know *what* she did. It was like a vertigo. I had no sense of being anywhere. Like my electrical wires had gotten cross-circuited while approaching a cliff.

"This isn't working," I calmly nudged my host. She seemed perplexed. Like it *should have* worked. (Yeah, the "should have" thing.) Then she ventured cautiously, "Do you talk to... *Spirits?*" "Who do you think I *have* been talking to?" Hmm, a chance to seize authority. She reeled off briskly, "Well, o.k. Talk to *him*." (I was *already* talking to Him. Hmm... O.k.)

It was totally impossible to tell whether Angela was inspired or merely exasperated. "He" took over the session from then on in ~ and quite nicely, thank you. Suddenly the way ahead look most promising and bright. I could describe what happened, but I don't know what actually *happened*. I was airborne, that was for sure. Airborne and headed towards a barrier or a border, like the first time into an exotic new land on a spaceship. It was like a divider between *my* territory and *His* territory. The soggy, trodden earth versus an angelic place of place. I felt the barrier pass beneath my feet as I drifted across the great divide.

What awaited me next was *extraordinary*. I looked down and where I was was *green*. I mean totally and completely, lushly, thoroughly, gorgeously, richly green. Never had I ever seen a place as green as this. I was home. And there was everything there I ever wanted ~ a perfect mate, a new life, the most intense, beautifully haunting music. My angel guided and directed my steps, so gently, so patiently, as though He were teaching a small child how to walk. Then He balanced my energies. Left, right, sentient, pulsing. I walked tentatively across the carpet, barely skimming its surface, in my new-found balance ~ happy, excited, free.

I could barely break the entrancement of my new-found Shangri-La on this stranger's living room floor. It was the strangest sensation to now be preparing to go "home" ~ which wasn't even home, just back up to the Bay Area. No one could have ever possibly known what happened in that meadow of magical green ~ I was only totally, absolutely sure it was where I needed to be. I knew, finally, that I had a home. I didn't think it was probably on Earth at all. But it was my "true" home. *I knew there was a place in the Universe that would welcome me always.* No one knows what that means. It's something one has or one doesn't have, knows one has or doesn't know it. And finally, I *knew* it. There was no one ever again who could tell me I didn't belong.

I jumped back onto the Greyhound. The bus was crowded, but my angel was right there by my side. For a moment I wavered, as if leaving Los Angeles might mean leaving *Him*. "Whenever you want to call Me," He told me gently, hear Me say, *'Listen to Me. I am your Heart.'"* Suddenly, like a small child who had finally pushed open the cupboard door, I became curious. Tentative, gentle, yet I really wanted to know: "Who *are* You? Tell me who You are. What is Your name?" The answer was clear, calm and sure: **"Kut-humi."** Did I know this name?

Had I not heard that name somewhere before? As soon as I landed back in New York, I trotted up to the Quest bookshop, the Theosophists' haunt, and tracked it down. Sure enough, there was a passing reference to *Kut-humi*. But wait. What were all these books, anyway? I poured through one after another. Suddenly it seemed that Kut-humi was everywhere! Very famous fellow (thought Alice Bailey, at least), could one only locate his Tibetan address. Well, or if *He* could locate *you*. I looked 'til I was very sure. There it finally was. Kut-humi, it seemed, had been reported to be tall. *Exceptionally* tall. I was so happy. It is disconcerting to meet the love of one's universe and not even know His name. It was amazing he had told me his Name, direct in my ear -- His treasured, special, protected child.

He had even left a calling card. A beautiful Baroque piece was playing on a cassette during the session in L.A.. It would show up on the radio or in a public place every now and then. I finally pinned it down. The second movement of Bach's Orchestral Suite in D, also known as "Air on the G String." Its beautiful, andante strains would intermittently filter through the air. Every time it showed up, I knew something wonderful was about to happen.

LII. What Goes Around Comes Around.

Many years passed. Like a sharp-lensed cameo of today would fade into dusky images of yesteryear, the edge had softened. But the mission, never fully in retreat, still waited in the wings. When it was "time," I could handle it full force, full spectrum on the public stage. This was no part-time, underpowered pursuit, this fairly major overhaul of American history. There had to be a *clearing* for it. I had to be ready to speak, as an empowered, re-energized voice. The world had to be ready to listen. Not just to the politics, but to the paradigms. Even the spiritual ones. If 75% of America already believed in angels, as is now said, no one yet knew.

I could wait. No. I *had* to.

The public may understand a bit better through the recent travails of the family of Martin Luther King, Jr., over the near-death episodes (then passing) of James Earl Ray. Ray had secrets, perhaps even accomplices, in the assassination of Martin those many years ago. He even claimed he was innocent and framed. Yet the King family waited nearly thirty years to press for a new trial, a bungled confession having served as surrogate years ago. They told *The New York Times* in February, 1997, that it had been too painful to do it earlier. Even though the whole world would have sympathized with them, in contrast with the whole world being *against* us.

Only now had *circumstances* demanded it, the door finally pushed against long-held griefs. So the appeals were filed, however belated, however unlikely it was to happen, however out of time and place.

"60 *Minutes*" ran a special once about the victims of Dr. Mengele during the Nazi era, and his perverse, evil fascination with medical experimentation on twins. One set of twins were so traumatized that it was forty years before they could talk about it *to each other*.

The Jones brothers, Stephen, Tim, and Jimmy, finally talked about Jonestown with *The New Yorker* in 1993. Fifteen years after the tragedy. And there was so much they *didn't* say. Just the top off the lid, thick with traumatic haze.

The Rosenberg children went on a belated crusade in adulthood to prove their parents' innocence. People who always believed them innocent, believed it still. Those who didn't still didn't. Did anyone else care? Everyone is quick to scream "McCarthyism" when the tide turns against *them*, even the far right wing. Who even thought how it affected the children?

Time passes and maybe people speak and maybe they don't. It's not even just whether people will speak the truth or lie, offer revelations or rehash the old. Sometimes it is whether they will speak at all. I spoke quickly. But my forays were abrasive, surreal, not to mention battling surveillance, harassment, and grief. I was mission-driven then, and when any possible sounding board seemed to collapse, I had to cease and desist. Getting into a re-start mode was out of the question until I was re-grounded. Into a *life*.

What would, what could, reawaken the mission without being punched out anew by the trauma and its deadening effects upon all it had touched? My vow to pursue it in twenty years, yes. But one does not just awaken one morning and do this. Such a slumbering beast can re-awaken but slowly.

What could re-open the door on Jonestown, the world's prototype of "an open-and-shut case"? Right after the tragedy, you have all that reactive upset, so you speak out *then*. And you get pounded by surveillance and harassment and no one's listening anyway. So you're demoralized and you cease and desist and go rebuild your life. Take years to cleanse out the trauma and become whole and new. But then, how do you get back in? And when? By what means? You have to have the right window of time. You have to locate the right vehicle.

And what happens inside *you* when you re-open your wellspring of pain? Where might you step and falter? Where might your voice fail to speak? What might you need to review, revise, even reverse in your assessments of years passed? Now you can look and *see*. Pieces coalesce and gel and there are dozens of "aha's."

Like the three most drastic precursors of that terrible night: the trial balloon of "How would you all feel about jumping off the Golden Gate Bridge?"; "the grape juice incident" in P.C.; and a so-called "white night" suicide drill in Jonestown? If it was all unprovoked madness, why did it always happen on the heels of something which indeed drove the hammer in deeper towards the heart? The first the departure of "The Eight"; the second the departure of the infamous Mertles; the third the ominous six-day siege. What *does* one do when finally, fully trapped, laden with lives of the very old and the very young, the death knell strikes?

And that final irony: One would have thought Jim Jones the most prepared of all, but even he slipped into a ghastly trap at the last. He who authored to the entire Congressional melange: **"...and they [the people of Jonestown] think that the press has already done its job [with smears], so** *no one will care about the frame-ups."* Surely it was the granddaddy of frame-ups, framing innocents for an assassination of a Congressman. And he, the most "paranoid" one? Where the uncanny feel for treachery now? Life twisted in even him. Ujara, his own, was "guilty as charged." Larry, his own, was "guilty as charged." So who killed the Congressman? Did it not *seem* like it was us?

Yet would our innocence of the assassination have *protected* us from the ax falling upon our heads? Not at all. Probably *less*. If we did it, we get destroyed. If we *didn't* do it, all the more certain we get destroyed, because the world must never know the truth.

Yes. What if Evil *did* reside at Jonestown that ghastly night, and startled, upturned, a glare fell upon its face, and it *wasn't* Jim Jones?

Was it this, the *finality* of this weight, that hung so heavily upon Jim Jones all those years leading up to the tragedy? It may sound fantastical to you, for Jonestown was not even *conceived* when "The Eight" first left, but it cannot sound fantastical to *me*. I lived through "*Allegory.*" It haunted me even years earlier, when the visions of death were so real, I fell, crushed by their weight, in the street.

So I may want to judge a million things about Jim Jones, but I cannot judge *that*. I know too much to judge.

I also know, have always known, too much to not *speak*. I just had to await my wake-up call.

It came in January, 1992, with the release of Oliver Stone's "*JFK.*" It was always a no-brainer that there was something wrong (no ~ *very* wrong) with the Warren Commission report, but that most traumatic day in American history was still as unresolved as the circumstances surrounding Jonestown. But how very many more people cared! And it was all right here, on your local t.v., including the infamous shooting of Oswald by Jack Ruby for "reasons unknown." This was no murky shadow drifting in hazily from a South American jungle. It was clear as day, black and white, step right up and see it for yourself.

Yet still no consensus that there was anything phony or false, trumped-up or covered over. After all those years, it was still wildly controversial to countermand the official view. America's newspeople, bulwarks like Dan Rather. Nope. Nothing wrong with that official report. Looks o.k. to me. Walter Cronkite. "Well," he said, "if there had been anything, surely it would have come out after all these years." *(Hello????)*

James Earl Ray. Not clear-cut, but no one seemed to doubt they got, if not *the* right guy, then at least *one* of the right guys. At least he apparently had wielded a gun. Why, I thought, if the King family wanted to pry more information loose, had no one held the hand of Coretta Scott King and "my four little [now big] children" whom their father wanted judged by the content of their character rather than the color of their skin? Surely someone would care about *them*.

But we awaken when we awaken. The sun rises every day and then one day, suddenly it's "Wow! The sunrise!" "JFK" was more than an exposé. It was a roadmap of how an unresolved trauma, here nationwide, can poison a future ~ the roadmap, the integrity, the soul of a nation and its leaders.

I thought, well, Jonestown is worth another try, at that. Because it was never just the deaths of the people. It was the death of a hope. There's no interracial harmony in our land. There's no economic equality. There's no self-sufficiency of the underclasses in the United States. There are huger disparities and more despair. And the stench of cover-up has never even been opened up the wee-est bit to give America a good whiff. No one was told why those brave pioneers died, who had wanted to do them in, or why. Anyone who knows can't or won't speak. I didn't ask to be "Ismael," but there I was and here I am.

Besides, much had turned, to fuel my personal journey anew. Unbelievably, the man who was to be my darling husband had arrived. I had given up looking and suddenly, true to form, there he was. No ~ *very* true to form. I don't know why that particular past life re-run was so glove-like, so akin to a fingerprint match. But I ran through the Europeans true to form. After the Dutch minister and the suicidal Persian, fate indeed brought me a poet named Rainer, fresh from Germany, when I was exactly the same age as Lou Andreas-Salome had been when she first met her poet love, German's great Rainer Maria Rilke. Yes, I was wildly in love, and yes, he was tragically lost. I mean not just then, but *now*. All the loves gained and lost, echoed like a bad, sad song, a refrain a century old.

Who or what was left? The strange Russian creature, whose life uneasily mirrored through my own, had one more great love to go. The Dutchman, the Persian, the German, and then finally... the *Austrian*. An Austrian Jewish physician named Pineles. Her "unofficial husband" tiding her through her own bizarrely unconsummated marriage.

Finding this would be like... No. I can't even think it. I hadn't a clue where to find such an oddly skewed arrangement of foreigners across a wholly American life. I wasn't even looking. Really, I just wanted someone... *nice*.

Friedrich Pineles had departed Lou's life after she became pregnant and aborted his child for fear of her "real" husband's jealous rage. Pineles couldn't bear it, and finally exiled her from his life. I was just the age now myself when this non-amicable parting of the ways had happened before. But now, instead of a willful termination of a pregnancy, I had finally (at the exact age of Lou's abortion) *wanted* a child, tried strenuously to make it happen, and was left with a system damaged from unsuccessful procedures and drugs. I had done *the opposite* – made every effort to have a child, to no avail. And now indeed, it was when my "Pineles" would not depart, but rather *arrive*.

It wasn't Pineles now, of course. It was *Kahalas*. Dan Kahalas. (Pineles? Kahalas? Yes, God is an incredibly inventive novelist!) Do you remember sweet Amy crying in the street when Al Morrison had unthinkably labelled her "an agent"? Well, she had introduced me to her music teacher to review some of my scores. Then years later, he introduced me to his new love, who introduced me to a friend of hers, who introduced me to... this *Kahalas*.

Oh, it was completely unrecognizable at first. I mean as a re-run. Any possible future marriage, of course, was not just hidden, but patently ruled out! This man *had* no future. It looked like he may even be dying. "Hi. I'm Dan Kahalas. I may only have a few months to live." (Whew!) "All that's important," he continued on calmly, "is that whether I live just a few more months, or several years, that I'm in a high spiritual state when I go." (Double whew!)

The rest was abstruse discourse on a recondite branch of yoga called "advaita" and an odd character from India named "U.G.," who, so far as I could tell, did not believe in much of anything.

It didn't much matter. We talked for hours, even about stuff I could not possibly understand. I thought that at least the link to India would give him some inkling about reincarnation, so I casually jostled him into, "Who do you think you were before?" "Oh,' came the off-hand reply. "I was Nietsche." (Triple whew! My best friend there for a while so long ago.)

I don't know who Danny "was," and perhaps neither does he. But his father was a first-generation Russian Jewish physician and his mother a native-born Austrian Jew! How much closer one could get to an Austrian Jewish physician married to a Russian woman, I'm not sure, but I would not want to run any statistics on that. You would lose the bet.

The rest, as they say, was history. Personal life history. We rushed to compare notes. We were both Jewish, born in the same year on the East Coast, our fathers were born in the same year, both Russian background. We both dropped out of graduate school, dropped in on the hippies, and drop-lifted onto California at virtually the same time. He met his sadguru ("true guru"), Muktananda, just a month-and-a-half shy of his 26th birthday, the exact same age as when I first met Jim Jones. Our broken romances fell out exactly in tandem, dates, ages, years. Our medical setbacks the same. Same, same, same.

How had we met? Or maybe that was the wrong question. How could we *not* meet? His body had been flattened, my spirit. Danny and me. Two "flower children" with their petals badly crushed. Together we would mend, and the world would again bloom.

I didn't stay away from Jonestown, of course. (It was always there anyway, was it not? My lingering shadow.) But what astounded me was that just months earlier, a friend had come along and laid on Danny the final tape! I couldn't believe it. It had been released just for a very short while in 1979. No one I had ever met had that tape but me. *He* had the tape? And was given it just *recently*? The world was not just "small.' It was ours!

So I never had to explain the past. We just went day by day with my new friend's dramatic and unique medical profile. One day it was, "I may only have a few months to live," the next it was "Where shall we travel? The Caribbean, Alaska, Hawaii?" and the next was (oh, so sweet), "Would you like to take a honeymoon cruise next Valentine's Day?" Now who could refuse a proposal like that?! It gave me faith, courage, hope. Now I could again tackle... *Jonestown*. First showed up Danny. Then *"JFK"* was like an omen to me. **It can be done**.

I thought I should contact survivors, and assess the lay of the land. I got all the names and addresses I could. I sent the letters off in a burst of gusto, but this crew was slow, ever so slow... *very* slow to respond. The world had forgotten. Now an unsolicited wake-up call comes from one of their own? Why intrude on such a slumber as this? Let sleeping dogs lie.

No, no one actually *said* that. The responses were just so slow. And everyone had "something." Some cynical about society as a whole, or wanting to simply preserve their memories without further intrusion. Grief still gnawed at the edges. Flickers of guilt, numbness, inner conflicts, despair. One of the oddest was a book by a woman whose relatives had died at Jonestown, who had undoubtedly loved them, and was now publishing people's second-hand, after-the-fact write-ups as "a search for the truth." Some of the participants were petty snipers who had undoubtedly been disappointed not to get in on the limelight, like "the courageous 10 who stepped forward" in *New West*. Plus people who "knew of us." And people who "wrote about people who knew of us." Plus some survivors who had undoubtedly suffered, but answers were few.

Though undoubtedly, it was only paradigmatic of the clueless horizon of Peoples Temple. "Water, water, everywhere, and not a drop to drink." Who out there has stepped forth with "The real story of what happened at Jonestown"? *In twenty years, no one even thought to ask if there were any forensics done on the Congressman!*

But that one entry which struck a special chord. The fellow that claimed to have known Mike Prokes: "Garry Scharff." The bizarre tales -- beatings, druggings, lurid sexual escapades -- all fictional. I was appalled.

Here I had put out a line to reel in real-life survivors, and found this very stinky fish at the end of the line. And *he* was the one who was "willing to talk" -- not the dear, precious people who had suffered and lost so much? Here, by the time of that book, 1989, "Garry" was still working out of the Cult Awareness Network as their prime time star, a "real life Peoples Temple survivor," a complete fraud with a horror load of tales. Who was paying this man? Why would anyone do this? And *someone who didn't even know us?* Eleven years later?

One survivor wrote back and (bless her) said she would tell first-hand what a beautiful place Jonestown was, pressures, problems and all. Only one. But I am glad I wrote around. I learned a few things. Even me, veteran of the wars.

The slumbering recordkeepers within me began to awake, as though an invisible timer had been set to this hour and time. Countdown to twenty years. So very much work to do.

I had never wanted to do a dry documentary. Too much feeling, too many memories were woven into those dry facts. The truth always has more juice.

All one can give is one's life. At one point, I *was* willing to give it -- rightly, wrongly, in blindness or in faith. Now all I could give was my life story -- facts, feelings, memories, and all. To let America finally know all that had happened. This is how it came to me that I had to write *"Snake Dance."*

LIII. Blind Men And Elephants.

We both underestimate and overestimate the power of one voice. If it is one voice only, we underestimate its ring of truth or power to persuade. If it is one voice in tandem with a supporting chorus, especially if spouting the beliefs of the day, we give it a power sometimes entirely undeserved.

We are, in any case, too much like blind men and elephants. Do you know that tale? What is the elephant like? The blind men cluster 'round. One touches the tail. The elephant is stringy and long. One touches the tusk. The elephant is thick, hard, and knifelike. Another touches the skin. The elephant is an endless wall and leathery tough. Another touches the trunk. The elephant squirms like a snake. Another touches the leg. Surely the elephant is like the trunk of a tree.

What is the elephant like?

What happened at Jonestown? Was the whole world blind and me alone gifted with powers of sight? No. Nowhere near as simple and pat as that. But the parade of outsiders, the blind men who happened along at some pre-prescribed angle, set up a deafening roar, while those inside the elephant's skin, who walked his walk and breathed his breath, were denied any voice at all.

Why did not even the insiders who were left speak? Surely they knew how the public view was orchestrated, fabricated, and most foul. A whole group of them walked out, every last one, on a preview showing of CBS' *"Guyana Tragedy,"* which is, to date, the only view America ever was given of .... Jonestown? Peoples Temple? Jim Jones? I don't think so. But where was its replacement?

Admittedly, the whole world was against us, our accomplishments obliterated, our people dead. Surely that was not conducive to speaking out, nor would anyone listen. The magnitude of the grief itself put a lid on people's tongues.

Moreover, for all the massive media blitz, there was little inkling of *the truth*, beyond the notorious body count. Jim Jones was painted, at the most charitable, as "a fanatic," and at that, a fanatic for *ill*, not *good*. Everyone was blaming Jim Jones. Were you *entirely* sure he was innocent"? Would *you* stand by him, whatever you knew, whatever you felt, however much you *loved* Peoples Temple, and with cause? What pressures would you be inviting onto yourself if you did?

Did you even have the means to make a case? The great majority of the people at Jonestown were building their home-grown community, not rummaging through news reports or collecting an incriminating paper trail about a "conspiracy." The people who survived Jonestown were left with little more than the clothes on their backs. And whatever they knew of a "conspiracy" was largely second-hand, through increasingly frenetic harangues of a man everyone knew was prone to "overreact." Many undoubtledly **did** believe there was a conspiracy, foul play, and cover-ups. But believing that, and having the tools to challenge the official view, moreover alone, was too daunting to even contemplate.

Yet for some, it was more. Sometimes the greatest block is simply *conflict*. Like with the Jonestown survivors, who worked so hard to build their paradise, only to have it destroyed, and with ***Jim Jones*** saying. "Take the poison": Jonestown yes. Jim Jones no. Racial and economic equality yes. Jim Jones no. Stand to the death for your principles, yes. Actually die, no. They loved their beautiful community, their beloved, home-grown Jonestown. They were so proud, so happy, so free. ....So *silenced*.

They weren't silent because Jonestown wasn't a beautiful place. It was. *And even though they never could have done it without Jim Jones...* They couldn't live with what they saw Jim Jones become – a failing, dying human being, who, in his desperation to save others, became a protector/smotherer of sorts. The conflict itself was untenable, unbearable, irreconcilable. And they thought the price they paid was because of that, was because of *him*.

They heard the rallying, the exhortations, the desperate cries, but never believed that *it really could come to that*: a utopia, a paradise, turned into a death trap. And not necessarily *because* of Jim Jones, but maybe, at that, *despite* him.

So a vanguard community, who loved and cherished their new lives, witnessed the man who inspired and elevated them to such heights, deteriorate before their eyes both physically and mentally, in health, stability, and strength. The dynamo for whom no replacement could ever be found or devised. They did the best they could. Ultimately, they gave their lives. So feel for them. Feel at least a little.

And the horror. Not just of the physical deaths, but the austere horror that the one who vowed to protect you unto death seemed the very one who overreacted all of you *into* death. Death is too final. The dead no longer stand and speak. How could they have "taken a stand"? They are dead and no one in the world thought they were taking a stand at all.

They thought their own leader, a deranged madman, did them in on his own.

And how many, nay, most, never saw the paper trail at all? Not just because it was paper, written, black-and-white, but because when you can see it, then it goes through your own hands and is patterned through your own brain. Some may have never believed that the forces conspiring against us really considered us expendable. Civil rights casualties. Cold War casualties. Black people casualties. Poor people casualties. That such casualties don't really matter ~ they may even be *justified*. Like "the cost of doing business."

And if you don't see, can't see, what the other side is seeing, or failing to see, in its mad rush to destroy "the enemy," then for whatever reason you cannot see, you are left with conflicts that cannot be resolved, and you can never speak what is in your heart to say.

Even some who believed foul play, could not bring themselves to publicly defend Jonestown, because they could not defend what happened at the end. They couldn't bear to question the sequence of events, or how those events wove their web into the dance of death. Or how things didn't compute, because whether they computed or not, they could not live with what had happened.

And that pervasive need to protect oneself, to shut the door. Does not one just want peace? Yes, one does, we all do. But we also want and need the truth.

I wrote one survivor months after the tragedy. An honest person. As shocked and horrified as anyone. But he wouldn't believe *frame-up*. He believed Jim Jones sent the assassins' squad. Because he saw Jim's deterioration first-hand ("The Jim Jones in Guyana was not the Jim Jones you knew in the States"), where his Achilles' heels were stressed past breaking point. And he undoubtedly never heard the final tape.

He said our own people identified the killers, themselves dead in Jim's cottage. (Dead? I thought you identify killers while they are killing others, not dead themselves and now offered up by the authorities as "Exhibit "A.") Even were this true, our survivors did their i.d.'s several days past the tragedy. And the men who were accused were never inner circle. Men who were likely never in Jim's cottage even in life. Had Jim Jones railed against what they had allegedly done, repeatedly, in anguish, panic and pain, on the final tape, only to invite them into his own home to die, as his "beloved assassins"?

Who, besides an ignorant and pounded public, would believe this? Aye. The grief-stricken, the disempowered, the disillusioned, the broken. Us. Moreover, if those men were indeed found dead in Jim's cottage, rather than in the Pavilion with the others, they would have to have been *placed* there. So *who put them there and why?*

My shocked correspondent undoubtedly never learned that it was Jim Cobb who had collaborated to produce the "eyewitness" account, while at the time of the so-called positive identifications, he was busy running for his own life! He certainly didn't know that Chris Kice saw the film on t.v., scrutinized them all and said, "None of those men are Tom."

He even hastened to add that "My beliefs are the same as always." Yes, Jim Jones gave me the foundation of believing in a more humane life. But now, as sane, humane, even magnificent as it all was, now *he* is discredited, so *I* will not speak. Because of what happened to *him*. And because of what the bitterest disillusionment did to *me*.

Into what traps does the psyche fall. And how very human.

And me? Yes, I did have a catbird seat others did not have. I even preserved the paper trail. But did I not have *emotional* disincentives to speak? Indeed, there were things I put up with for seven years, that I would not put up with for seven *minutes* now.

Yet even I could never forget that I never went to sleep without a clear conscience – that I was living, breathing, believing, acting for a better society, a more just society, an equal society, a loving society, a better world. Why I came and stayed in the first place. *It never would have happened without that.*

And my own story was never all that was – I haven't the narcissism to claim it was. My story is my story, yes. It is whole, valid, mine. But it was still a grace note in the enormity of the good done by Peoples Temple and the evil done *against* it.

My personal story is also, admittedly, a maverick's tale. How my own perspective on life and death was altered forever with "*Allegory.*" How I could never fully be a part, yet had to be *more* of a part, death's reprieve not denying me, indeed giving me, ongoing tasks in *life*.

Even the all-too-human traumas. Like L.A. It was also *protective* for me. Like rushing in to push a child out of the path of an oncoming car. The child gets injured from the push yes, but her life is spared. It meant I could never wind up in Guyana.

Nor could I let factors of trauma stop me from telling the tale. Indeed, it gave a prod. That I would be strong enough to tell the tale whatever the obstacles, the opposition. Even opposition from the demons within.

Not that this has been ever been easy. It took me year after torturous year to see how such assaults could have been launched against me at all. (Much less the destruction of the one person who would later defend *him*. God must hand out some kind of certificate for such a feat!) All those years before I could grasp what was, however irrationally, *intended* against me. To even have some *basis* upon which to forgive. Like many emotion-drenched turns in life, it was veiled.

Even the veil of my own idealism, rendering me slow (and traumatized people are slow indeed) to stare down what was surely a tyrannical debacle. I could not bear to see Jim Jones as tyrannical, but rather tragic. Even now, I cannot forget that he did what no one else in America could. And to have the faith and hope (that someday *America* will have the charity), that however he did it wrong, some future benevolent power (or God's empowerment within *us*) will do it right.... but *do it!* Not for the sake of socialism or any other "ism," but for the dignity, even the very survival of the human race.

I suppose, at the last, what I most want the public to comprehend, anyway, is not my own personal pain, but that these were all *internal* problems; and that the people out to destroy us didn't *care* about our internal problems except to exploit them. They thought it *good* if we had internal problems. The easier to bring us down. They made the world think that "the story" was "concerned parents" and "relatives held against their will" and "fraud," when really, the real story was.... **politics.**

Even those who turned against us were *exploited*. Like Cobb, for example. He lost his mother, three sisters and a brother at Jonestown. Grace Stoen was *exploited*. Her son was used as a pawn to ensnare the king, and if only the king would die, who cared about the pawn, the child? People like Jim Cobb and Grace Stoen expended huge amounts of hatred on the wrong people. They worked with people who honestly cared little who died. Who in fact, most of them, ***did not even know us personally***.

Who even protected the Mertles? They tried to take in a few scared, traumatized kids, and backpedal on their own hatred, and it got them killed.

Look at this, then ***think who cared and who didn't and why.*** Who cared that the people of Jonestown lived, and who would rather have they die if that is what it took to stop them? Who gave them homes and jobs and new lives? Who *didn't* care if poor people died, if black people died, if whole generations of youth had no future? The people of Jonestown killed? Fine. Offed *themselves?* Even better. Just so long as they didn't build a model community of ex-patriated Black Americans in the third world. Just do long as they didn't move to the Soviet Union. Just so long as they didn't prove integration works. Just so long as they didn't give economic power to the poor. Death? Who *were* these people, anyway? The expendable ones. You didn't care about them being snuffed out. You cared about the liability of them living on.

If you see one thing, only one thing clearly, then see **THAT**. ***LOOK AT THE INTENT. Who wanted those people dead???***

Jim Jones made costly mistakes. But when he told a reporter that last day, "I hate money. I hate power. If this does not stop, if we cannot make peace, I don't know what will happen to the lives of a thousand people here," that was an anguished heart that **wanted his people to live**. Yes, he was driven over the edge, with pressures, paranoias, and most certainly with illness. Yes, overreactive in the extreme. **But that doesn't exonerate the persecutors. To the contrary. It compounds their wrongs.**

No one should have been using little children (or *anyone,* for that matter) as pawns in secret political wars. The people of Jonestown, substantially poor and black, were considered expendable to ideology, to racism, to the economic order. And that's just *wrong.* These were brave, wonderful pioneers who would have been thrilled to just be left to build their lives in peace.

So see that one side is the persecutors, the other the hunted. If you want to take sides, at least see what sides there *are*, and how clearly they are defined. It is all too easy to target people for destruction. If you have the money, the power, the influence, the press on your side. It is easy to destroy people. Very easy.

In any case, there is something perverted in making Jim Jones "the villain." For if you begin with the same scenario and could simply remove one side, what would you remove?: Jim Jones, the man who made the miracle of Jonestown possible; or... the persecution which not only destroyed Jim Jones personally but endangered all those lives?

Were things ever that simple, *I* would have opted to eliminate the persecution and let people build their new lives in peace. Let them be a model for those who had no hope. Let them be the model for generations to come. ***Just let them be.*** Don't send in the F.B.I. and C.I.A. and Interpol agents, and threaten to kidnap their kids or smear their good works or try to paint gentle, hard-working people as robots or psychopaths. Nothing right could ever emerge from something so wrong.

But that's how you do it, the destruction of the good. You look at the person you want to destroy and locate their weak spots. If it's womanizing, throw them a hundred gorgeous blondes. If it's drugs, provide a personal drug procurer. If it's money, then bribes will do. If it's none of the above, then why do that? Do something else. Something that will catch. Destabilize by deadly drugs. Because he took pharmaceuticals to function through anything. And play on the desperate protectiveness. Especially of the children. John.

With Jim Jones, it was overreactions, paranoia, fanatical protectiveness that did him in. It was the inability to detach from "family." It was the ideals of strength that most will not put themselves on the line for. Like *death*, for example. The willingness to die for one's beliefs and one's role as a wayshower. So *force* these people to the brink of death. Drive the leader insane with paranoia. Threaten to kidnap his son. Poison him to weaken the body and demoralize the flock. Threaten violence. Have the press smear them to infamy before anyone from the American establishment ever even sets foot on their soil.

They will begin to believe they *cannot* survive. Even take the most tragic personal case – Sharon Amos, who, along with her three children in Georgetown, "did not have to die." They weren't in Jonestown. They were in Georgetown. But even she had her elephant's eye. She believed her children would be dragged away and "as good as dead" if she did not do this. She thought she was Diana Lubarsky.

Do you know about Diana Lubarsky? She was highlighted in a segment of of the t.v. series, "Sightings." She recovered a past life in the Holocaust in recurring dreams. In it, she killed her own small daughter and son, then herself, rather than let them be dragged away by the Nazis. She said, "If my children die, it will be by my hand, not theirs." Then, she said, she remembered having promised a Rabbi before their deaths, that she would *"always remember."* Even, apparently, across lives. So she came back now, in modern- day America, with a mysteriously complete, albeit untrained, talent as a sculptress, with the most moving renditions of Holocaust victims.

I didn't hate Sharon Amos. I *knew* her. I knew how she thought. She wasn't an evil person, indeed very giving in some ways. But she thought she was Diana Lubarsky. That's who she believed she was, and what she believed she was doing when she terrorized Christa, her own screaming little girl.

Do I like telling you this? No. But no one else will *ever* say it for her. She loved her children. There was just this tragic... *blindness*. And that horrendous push towards destruction, the assassination which provoked the suicides, that seemed to confirm for her that her blindness was in fact, *sight*.

But do *you* think that "mere blindness" has never cost human life? It costs it many times over every day! And with people far more ill-intentioned than Sharon Amos ever was. Just look around.

Indeed, sometimes blindness is the sanctioned way. Just look at the media. What of *their* elephant eye? Yes, the media. Everyone's favorite culprit. And did it ever occur to anyone, that all they are doing is reflecting our own myopias, our own oversights, our willingness to be led around like sheep?

It's Orwellian. The special CBS ran as late as January, 1997, about Walter Cronkite. They went way back, and of course included his coverage of the Kennedy assassination. So now, virtually yesterday, he looks America in the eye and says he doesn't believe there was any conspiracy because "after all this time, *something* would have come out."

"*Something*"? Jack Ruby kills Lee Harvey Oswald on national television mere days after Kennedy was killed, and Ruby was... *also* "one lone assassin"? Who would believe this? Who would trust anything about a *denial* of conspiracy... *ever*?

So "the most trusted man in America" looks America square in the eye three decades later on and... *assures* us? How appalling. How shocking. How *unnoticed*. How *accepted*. How *sanctioned*.

So who, after all, would believe *me* about the assassination of the Congressman at Jonestown? I saw that film right on t.v. I saw what I saw and I know what I know **_forever_**. But what does that... *mean*? America saw what it saw and knows what it knows forever about a public, televised killing in plain view that stank like a pack of rotten fish, and there was still no way to turn the tide.

Future generations may look back and think we were crocked. Programmed. Brainwashed. That it wasn't "1984" at all. It was 1963. Double-speak became the officially sanctioned way. We could no longer think. We were *told* how to think. We were told that the Blind Men weren't really blind, and that their vision of the elephant was all that was real.

I remember the tenth anniversary, of the tragedy, in 1988. "*West 57th Street*" on CBS, ran a special with the Stoens. The Stoens and their lies about a little boy. Tim wiping away a tear talking about "my son John." The truth, as usual submerged, was jamming its jagged head back into the glacier field in some remote, hidden land no one would ever see.

I wrote the station what had *really* happened, complete with dismay at no film of the assassination. I couldn't believe they showed a scene of *an empty airport*. I went to Steven Reiner, the producer. He said, slightly startled, "*NBC said that was all they had.*" (Like the fate of John F. Kennedy's brain?) Then I thought, oh my God, straighten this out with a film of an empty airport?

Shock revisited, yes? But I could never understand why that squelches questions rather than raises them. Why is it not *less* reason to believe the cover stories, rather than more? We think newscasters get paid a lot and live glamorous lives. Maybe they are well-paid, glamorized puppets. Some good and decent people, some not, but puppets one and all.

We are trained to all think the same. "Us." The same group, the same club, the same church, the same economic interests, the same race, the same nation, the same gender. Us. It's not wrong per se, but we are outgrowing it as a globe. And its falseness rancors too terribly when something like Jonestown comes along.

And have we exhausted the many ways to touch the elephant? Hardly! A whole *culture* can be "blind"; and like a massive sculpture –unwiedly, resistant and hard–, it can take decades for the culture to rotate. Nor will one come from the same angle as another. Some care only about cults. Others trauma. Others the spiritual journey through life. Others the psychology of death. Other politics. The infiltration by intelligence agencies, like Hoover's infamous COINTELPRO. The many sinister shadows that have haunted the landscape of our hidden political terrain.

And yes, of course, the tragic realities of how people get pushed over the edge. For me it was *Star Trek*: Matter meets anti-matter. The one desperate to save, against the one who had to survive and chronicle that it had *already happened*.

For others, it will be about overcoming racism. The chance to get out of the ghetto, to live a whole, free, new life. I understand that, support it, applaud it. The elephant hasn't only tusks. It has a trunk, it has leathery skin, tree-trunk legs and massive weight. All are equally, pressingly real.

Plus even more original, refreshing views. One most elegant, unexpected, from a new friend: "Do you want to know what really happened at Jonestown?" He cut in with, "Yeah, I know *exactly* what happened. Your group was infiltrated and it was like a virus in a computer. They sent out a signal that provoked the destruction of the community." (Bingo!)

If one can ultimately land down anywhere (and perhaps we can only land down at all when we die), perhaps it is as in the finale of my haunting "Allegory": ***"No. It is worse you've made travesty of my SPIRIT!!!"*** We cannot approach massive violations of action, consciousness, liberty, and life itself, without a willingness to relinquish and release our blind spots, our myopias, our distortions, our illusions, even our myths about how the world does, should, can, or cannot, work.

We should honor one another's experience. There are reasons why we, each one of us, live our lives as we do. Only when we honor that, give it validity, can we learn. The cynicisms, the myopias, are our demise.

We are trained in daily sound bytes how to be blind men and elephants. And I have never wished to speak to a public that is blind and deaf. Or even one that must have one issue only. To see that one issue like it is all, and then have the temerity to claim to be driven by high-mindedness or an immutable morality. Maybe at another time, God will put them in another pair of shoes and they will walk a different walk.

I say this even as I stumble over myopias and limitations of my own vision, experience, knowledge. Everything within me desires to be humble, even knowing how the humble can get trampled and smashed. It is not an easy line to tread.

It is easier to be cynical. But how our cynicism paralyzes us. How it robs us, defeats us, cheats us, paralyzes us. Where is the new world – whole, fresh and pure? It is... at least, it *could* be, God's most beloved child. The world we long for in our dreams. What life might, could, be, if we had the devotion, the purity, the consecration, to bring it forth.

I wanted all this to touch people. To know that you can kill the bodies but you can never kill the soul. That where most only saw dead bodies, we could look again and see valiant hearts and devastated dreams. I imagined that when the whole, multi-dimensional story was finally told, that there would be people here and there, some people psychologically astute, some psychically astute, some politically astute, some philosophically astute, some just plain humanly astute, some "merely" ...*sensitive*. Not necessarily people with lots of degrees. Just real, whole, sentient, living people.

That I wouldn't have to pander to the lowest common denominator with one-dimensional sound bytes. Sure, there would be those who only wanted titillation and sensation. (God knows good works don't seem to be a spicy enough story!) But that somewhere out there, like panning for gold in a muddy stream, there would be people here and there, who could listen, who could distill, who could discern, for whom the diverse pieces of this rich, enigmatic puzzle of a story could resonate with understanding, with comprehension, with the capacity to rise above the fray and ...*see*.

We could have a societal "Field of Dreams": "Build it and they will come." Hold out something ridiculous (like Spock once got rescued by sending up a tiny flare to the already-departing Enterprise) like an oxymoronic "hopeful condemnation of society." Hoping that maybe there are people out there who don't want to be hypnotized into oblivion. And then a few, or a few thousand, or maybe, *hope*-fully, a few million or so, would rise up and say, "Yeah, I hopefully condemn society, too." Because you have to see what's there before you are in a position to alter it.

Even Jim Jones said that Jonestown at the last was *"a thousand people who don't like the way the world is."* I don't much like it either, though not quite in the same way nor, certainly, with the same remedy. And that's o.k. I just want to talk to those who, here and there, do, or want to, *see*.

And even for the whole world's hatred of Jim Jones, how he *cared*. I heard a great teacher say that we, humanity, will condemn someone if they do one wrong thing, but that God will accept you if you do one right thing. This man did thousands of right things for decades, with the steadiest, most loving hand, and no one even *sees* enough to know what a criteria of forgiveness for that man might be.

I am as horrified knowing that everyone thought that Jim Jones wanted his own people to die as I am at how *he* thought *I* wanted *him* to die. I learned this lesson the hard way first hand, crushed and drained through a sieve of tears. No one can speak of this more than me. I earned it. It's *mine*. Perhaps the weirdest twist of all in that enigmatic, "No one will ever understand you. No one ever understands me."

No one cried harder or longer, especially over the children, than me ~ except, perhaps, for those parents outside Jonestown when their children died. I would never compare my grief to another's, for no one can know the measure of another's grief. But even those parents... They were valiant people. People who stood for what they believed, and worked to build a better world. And did they receive any honor for it? They were still looked upon as robots, psychopaths, or deluded fools. And that isn't right.

If there is to be a final peace in all of this, let it be for the blind men who, nevertheless, walked right in the elephant's shoes. Give these heroic people their due. Give them honor. They were, they *are*, "the elephant."

We both underestimate and overestimate the power of one voice. The dead, too, can speak. See the radiant reports of new-found happiness in the lovingly-prepared booklet "A Feeling of Freedom." (See DOCUMENTS, pp. 28-36.) Read the simplest, most moving words from their own mouths. At least do that much before you decide that they did not choose to be where they were or do what they did. Let the final word be theirs.

LIV. Placido Domingo Means "Peaceful Day of Rest."

And be *I* given calling to speak, let it be now. As I clombered towards the final swirl of the ubiquitous snake, a voice whispered gently into my ear, **"Almost done. New journey beginning."** It may be only a personal journey, yes; but the threads of my own journey so intertwined with the souls who perished at Jonestown, that I welcomed with relief for them, too, this subtle cue from a universe which sometimes, perchance, coincides with my own beating heart. It beats on and on, yet also, from time to time, circles 'round.

As am I full circle now. My treasured friend Al Morrison has passed on. And my mother, the star of Chapter 1, she, too. The death of one frail, elderly woman may not seem of sufficient import to close this long multi-storied chapter of my life, but an unexpectedly serene passing it was. I began by telling you of her own wish to pass on in reconciliation with those she loved, and the universe gave her that greatly (and me!) when, by coincidence, she passed right into the closing chapter of this book. So surely it is *most* important. Even an omen, perhaps, that peaceful passings of even tumultuous lives are possible, and that very long chapters can indeed be drawn to an end.

My mother was already in a nursing home, weakened by the infirmities of age, which had somehow rendered her mellow and sweet. Her stroke came early on Monday, October 28, 1996. I went to see her that Monday eve. But it took a few days to realize that this was serious. At first, they said she was able to swallow and eat, then that they had to insert a tube. She was "responsive," then "unable to speak." She was "weak on the right side but felt sensations," then "paralyzed." Still, they said, they would hope for the best. I felt no anxiety. She seemed so calm, even when I could not rouse her from what seemed like an overly lumbering sleep.

We had grand opera Thursday night, October 31st, All Hallows Eve, at The Met. Bizet's glorious "Carmen," with the incomparable Placido Domingo. In our last scurried rush through an otherwise leisurely meal, we realized that the opera was scheduled for 7:00 p.m., not the usual eight o'clock. We were barely seated in time. Domingo did not enter on stage til approximately 7:15. We got home to a phone call from the nursing home. I called. To my surprise, they related that my mother had expired... *"at about 7:15."*

Where do souls go and what do they do? My mother had wondered that, all the way back in Chapter 1, in the wayward musings of an erstwhile atheist pondering if, indeed, there was a spiritual side to life. Now, at 7:15, she would have known. They say that people at first "visit" their loved ones when they pass on. Was mother at the opera with us? I aver that she *was*. I know she must have been. She died at the exact moment of the grand entrance of the Placido Domingo, Spanish for "Peaceful Sunday," or "Peaceful Day of Rest."

I felt nothing but gratitude that I was spared the grieving relative routine. It was so peaceful and calm. I was happy for her, that her long, sometimes stormy, but also quite interesting and giving life, had finally draw to a close... *auspiciously*. Most of those she had loved the most had preceded her to the "Peaceful Day of Rest." Bless her that this could come so clearly, elegantly, as a blessing and a gift.

There were other things, too, about that day. We had pre-arranged to sell the piano, the infamous trade of Chapter 1. (My heart for a piano?) It had been rented out for years now, like an adopted child placed, unthinkably, into an orphanage. There was just no space for it. I could never bring myself to sell it, and the rental agreement dragged on. Then in the summer of '96, a surprise offer. To buy it, restore it, sell it as new. I could hardly refuse. The contract was drawn up. The money was to come due "by the end of October." October 31st, All Hallows Eve. Thus did the family karma virtually liquidate into dollars and cents upon my mother's passing!

Now, mother having passed, there were a few scarce things to attend to in its wake. She had wanted creation, and cremation we did. Then I phoned a beloved grandchild, now grown. I suggested she plant a rose bush in memory of her grandma and scatter the ashes at its base. She loved the idea, but then said, "The other idea I had" (since mother was a "culture vulture") "was to scatter the ashes at Lincoln Center." Lincoln Center? The same place where "Placido Domingo" serenaded my mom into the higher planes? Oh, dear grandchild... they're already there, they're already there.

We still had to figure out bequests. We had salvaged whatever of her money she had safely set aside at an earlier date, but by the time she died, she was destitute. She had wanted bequests for the grandchildren, so Danny and I had decided we would honor that on her behalf. We added up the loose financial ends and still fell short.

Placido Domingo Means "Peaceful Day of Rest"/407

The following week, I got a call from the banker who had been entrusted with her money. They said this was very strange. They just discovered a check made out on that account all the way back in November, 1994, two full years ago. It had never cleared and now they wanted to credit it back into her account and reissue the money to *me*. "How much is it for?" The exact amount we needed!

Imagine the universe taking care of this family after all!

The week following that, I got an unexpected phone call from a cheery lady from the community where the family home had been. She found out about my mom from the obit in the New York Times. She told me that the community would be having its 50th anniversary next summer. I was invited. I honestly hadn't known about returning to that out-of-the-way locale. But now I could do it, honor the wish. Scatter my mother's ashes on the lawn of my father's house.

Even the angels, silent overseers, had gently tread upon my sleep months before to ease the passageways home. Not just for her, but for me:

I was in an apartment. It was a room I had seen only once before in my dreams when, in the recent past, my mother was approaching her end. It was a large, open room high above the ground, with sunlight streaming in from picture windows beaming expansively across their interface with the sky. My mother, a timid, elderly wisp of a soul, had wandered in, tentative but entranced by the spaciousness and light. Large artist's light tables were laid out with photographs of her life lit from behind. She went from one table to another in amazement, thrilled that anyone had taken so much interest in her. I realize she has passed on, but that the passing has been [i.e. *will be*] easy and smooth, like a float into clear space.

In this new dream, it was me in the blissful, airy antechamber between life and the spaces beyond. I dreamed that an aged man, from the family in the apartment next door, had just died. Then comes a knock on our door. Somehow, because the man from the family next door had died, "the people from upstairs" showed up at our door with flowers. It seemed a small delegation, headed by a man with glasses and dark hair named "Jeffrey." "Oh," I thought upon awakening. "Jeff Goldblum." [I had just seen "Independence Day."] "*Gold-Bloom.*" Flowers from a higher plane!

From our angelic visitors came perfect flowers: bright fuchsia roses, and from out of their rich profusion shot up one single, perfect, orange lily. I rarely dream in color, but these colors were magical. The roses were *so* rose, that richest shade of fuchsia that is not garish but soft, yet so very rich, it ekes both velvet and honey at a glance. The orange of the lily was so bright, light, radiant and clear, it shimmered as if glistening in sunlight. The stem of the lily was a soft forest green, but with no leaves – just smooth, soft and bare, like the skin of a tiny child.

I was astonished but perplexed. I asked my visitor at the door, why bring the flowers to us, why not to the family who lost the soul. "No," he told me with gentle surety. *"They are for you."*

I awoke into the day we would make our yearly stop for darshan (blessing) with a visiting Indian saint named Ammachi. Danny and I approached her together, as we had always done before. Even this ecstatic soul had ofttimes seemed muted in receiving us, but this day, something subtle opened. It was different. She beamed and smiled at us again and again, as if sparkling with a treasured secret, then took our hands and repeatedly kissed them! What did she know that we didn't? Then I thought, oh, that orange lily in the dream. That must be *a swami soul*, for the Indian swamis wear orange robes.

We had indeed, just laid plans to set sail for India the following year. I had arranged a boat trip from Singapore to Bombay. We got suitably jetlagged from the plane trip East, and woke up for days at 3 a.m., like an alarm clock stuck at a frozen hour. I would go up on the quiet, pre-dawn deck, and work on my book. One morning my watch stopped. It was 3:30 a.m. I learned the next day that that was the exact time when the boat had shifted course West, to sail for India. It was also the night when, shy of this final touch, I completed **"Snake Dance."** I could greet India, my very first time in this life, relieved and free.

We stopped in exotic Sri Lanka, where I picked up a few stones, barely reflecting on their clear bright fuchsia shade, *the exact same unusually vivid shade as the roses in my dream the year before.*

We arrived in India on March 23rd. We were headed for the North, to spend several days with a beloved saint. Our plane was unexpectedly delayed when we changed at Delhi. We waited and waited, then suddenly, like a fiery, compelling magnet, we felt an energy force sweep past us as we sat. We looked up, and now several feet ahead was a man in the traditional orange robes of an Indian swami. But unlike any swami's robes we saw in India that whole trip. This was an unusually bright, light, clear, radiant orange. *Just like the lily in my dream.*

We edged slowly across the room, like autumn leaves naturally, timely wafted by the wind from their native tree. We arrived in front of a man whose eyes beamed sunshine, so very like his crisp orange robe. The man asked where we were going. Then we asked where was *he* going? *Benares*, he said. He was en route to Benares. Benares, for those who do not know, is a very special place in India. It is where people go to cremate the dead and scatter their ashes in the sacred River Ganges. *Someone had just died.* The thought lingered like an aftertaste of the rich orange sunset of that gleaming robe, so *exactly* like the lily in my dream. Someone had just died, like in my dream, and suddenly there was this swami soul, his orange robe swashed in sunshine, who smiled right into my eyes.

Benares. (*"...to take the ashes of the dead and consecrate them instead of trampling them mindlessly beneath our feet."*) And *whose* ashes? Who had died? My eyes glanced for an instant downwards. Then I saw that this swami had a deformity, a somewhat unusual one: *a withered left hand.* The hand was very small, like a *child's*, but *lifeless and limp.* The *left* hand? What was it telling me? The opening of "Allegory." Yes. "*On my left hand stands a child...*" Yes, of course. The children. *The future.* Re-empower the future that was so brutally ripped apart when those children died!

The Indians believe that scattering the ashes of the dead in the River Ganges will bring the deceased an auspicious new birth. Perhaps our new un-named friend was there to renew the promise, the hope, that children, especially ones as beautiful as those in Jonestown, children of every color and race, will survive and flourish unto a new day.

I may never know who was the perfect swami with (like snowflakes pure and white marred by the soil) the imperfect hand of a lifeless child. He moved me in a way I cannot voice. Some people move your heart. Others can move the earth beneath your feet.

I thought nothing further of it as we moved on. I did not even remember my dream until many days had passed.

It was March 23, 1997, the Jewish holiday Purim, celebrating the ancient liberation of the Persian Jews. Subtly, ever so subtly, I too was free. The book complete, course plotted anew, the signs, the colors, the glimpse of worlds beyond.

It is possible, isn't it, I thought. It is possible to overcome *anything.*

We completed our pilgrimage north, to our treasured saint, then on to Agra. We thought we were headed for the Taj Mahal, but the local cabbie had other ideas. "Where are we going? Not to the Taj?" "No. The marble factory." I thought, well, surely we will buy nothing here. So I simply, casually looked. Then suddenly I spotted a plaque in pure black marble, and etched into its grain were roses in the most rarefied shades of green. I had not seen such radiant, subtle greens since that Los Angeles day with my visiting Angel who had called me back to California to forgive. "Wait," I said. "Let me count the roses." I circled 'round, and circled 'round, and circled 'round, to its shiny star-like core. Ah, ah, ah... 32. The Kaballistic number of the Heart. (*"Listen to Me. I am your Heart."*)

What was this? My "Congratulations!" plaque? "We'll take it," gently slid from my lips. "It will bring good fortune to our home. Lots of love."

Thus did Agra dissolve into the Indian mist. The precarious shuttle between Benares and Agra, our parable about Fate, veering uneasily from life into death, now, as if by miracle or decree, had reversed its course, emerging from death into life. The snake, loosed into a maze of roses half a globe away, could now dance on home. No precipitous step. Never in my life had I been so blissfully certain that a task was *complete*.

I sleep, I dream, I wake, I wonder what it all means. Am I still at long last Neptune's child? Are there more personas yet to unfold? Is this a new poem, to emerge muddied or, perchance, *un*-muddied, in an impure world; or a way to play the poet's Muse in worlds beyond this shadowy vale of tears, sorrow and strife? I wonder as the days pass ~ spring, summer, autumn, passing easefully into a cool and blissful calm.

Did the Angels ever come for my friends at Jonestown? Was their sacrifice recorded and known? Those who in their hearts died for a better world? I believe their sacrifice is honored and known. I believe it because I am human. I believe it as a child of God. Because I heard the Angels weeping for Jonestown, and I am haunted by Their song.

Let the living offer fragrant flowers to the dead. They should never have been pulverized, nay, bulldozed into the dust. I've had to stand at the graves of people long since gone and defend what was their right to live a free life. May God bless them now, even if the world has not.

So gather all these at long last, into that glimmering antechamber, high above the din, flooded with space and light. Gather finally one's own, and strew their pathway with lilies and roses. Be comforted. Be loved. May your hearts be known and souls cleansed. Move on, now, all of you, my friends, move on. I shall do this, too. We can move on together.

"Almost done. New journey beginning." Rest in peace, my friends. Rest in peace.

UPCOMING SEQUELS

ON THE RECORD: THE BOOK OF DOCUMENTS
The Legacy of Jonestown - Part 1

A treasure trove of never-before-published materials about both the known course of events and the hidden course of events, including: news clippings, public records, letters, affidavits, transcripts, press releases, organizational files, tapes, photographs, booklets, petitions, lawsuits, materials from Jonestown, insider common knowledge, etc. Materials presented by both chronology and topic, to enable any researcher, historian, journalist, or the general readership to decipher and piece together both the overall scope and hundreds of exact details leading up to and surrounding the Jonestown Tragedy. Also included are many specialized materials only available in the aftermath.

AND THE ANGELS WEPT: THE STORY OF "ALLEGORY"
The Legacy of Jonestown - Part 2

    I. "AND THE ANGELS WEPT": The text of the author's precognitive work, "Allegory," written about the Jonestown Tragedy four years before it happened. A comprehensive, line-by-line deciphering and matching-up with the context, timing, and circumstances surrounding the suicides. The story of how "Allegory" came to be written, and other groundbreaking psychic discoveries. Of special interest to "New Agers," psychic/spiritual researchers, and of course, a general readership.

    II. "HAIL THE CONQUERING. . . . VILLAIN": "Once upon a parallel universe. . ." The uncanny parallels of personalities, events, timing, circumstances, scenarios, between the life of Jim Jones and the life of a world-renown conqueror from ancient times. The patterns of repeat, reverse, recompense, rectify, which permeate this fascinating "replay" on the world stage. A study in the science of karma. Documented with historical references.

ABOUT THE AUTHOR

LAURIE EFREIN KAHALAS is a native New Yorker, a child of the McCarthy era and the civil rights struggle. She emigrated to California in the 60's as a "flower child," caught up in a budding spirituality and the intense political climate of the day. She joined Peoples Temple long before there was a "Jonestown," and remained for eight-and-a-half years until the end. Entranced with the interracial harmony and humanitarian outreach of the church, she watched on in horror as the Jonestown community, an egalitarian utopia praised as a "paradise," was targeted by right-wing zealots, and destroyed *in absentia* through a smear campaign, mercenary attack, and finally, the suicides following the brutal assassination of a United States Congressman by "parties unknown."

As a veteran of both the magic and the mayhem of a committed, but sometimes fanatical group under siege, she vowed to some day reveal the shocking, suppressed truths about what happened at Jonestown that fateful day. Now, as both a dedicated custodian of a secret archives, and avid researcher of the public domain, she has pieced together anew the high-powered campaign of smears, harassments and violence which destabilized and destroyed the people she loved.

She brings to this saga an especial poignancy, with a breathtaking tale of Angelic guidance through the storm, and her conviction that of all who survived, she is uniquely positioned to tell the world the truth.

Upon completion of her trilogy of **"SNAKE DANCE," "ON THE RECORD,"** and **"AND THE ANGELS WEPT"** (see previous page), she plans on returning to her earliest love, composing, to complete the setting of her precognitive artwork, **"Allegory,"** for chorus and orchestra.

For additional information, or to make a personal query, you may contact the author's website at **www.jonestown.com**.